Blown by the Spirit

Blown by the Spirit

Puritanism and the Emergence of an Antinomian Underground in Pre–Civil-War England

David R. Como

Stanford University Press
Stanford, California
2004

Stanford University Press
Stanford, California

Printed in the United States of America
on acid-free, archival-quality paper.

Library of Congress Cataloging-in-Publication Data
Como, David R., 1970-
Blown by the Spirit : Puritanism and the emergence of an antinomian underground in pre-Civil-War England / David R. Como.
p. cm.
Includes bibliographical references and index.
ISBN 0-8047-4443-2
1. Antinomianism--England--History--17th century. 2. Puritans--England--History--17th century. 3. England--Church history--17th century. I. Title.
BR757 .C68 2004
273'.6'0942--dc22
2003021847

Original printing 2004

Last figure below indicates year of this printing:
03 02 01 00 09 08 07 06 05 04

Typeset in 9.5 / 12.5 Sabon

That which is born of the flesh is flesh; and that which is born of the Spirit is spirit: Marvel not that I said unto thee, Ye must be born again. The wind bloweth where it listeth, and thou hearest the sound thereof, but canst not tell whence it cometh, and whither it goeth: so is every one that is born of the Spirit.

John 3: 6-8

For such are false apostles, deceitful workers, transforming themselves into the apostles of Christ. And no marvel; for Satan himself is transformed into an angel of light. Therefore it is no great thing if his ministers also be transformed as the ministers of righteousness; whose end shall be according to their works.

2 Cor. 11: 13-15

Acknowledgments

Scholarship often seems the most solitary of pursuits. Shut up in our offices, toiling away over books, computers, and index cards (or tattered shreds of paper, as the case may be), there is a great temptation to imagine ourselves as independent and autonomous creatures, locked in quiet isolation with our sources and our grand thoughts. This self-image, gratifying though it may be at times, does nothing but obscure the truth of the matter: we are all utterly dependent on the labors of others—countless scholars, colleagues, librarians, bibliographers, supporters and friends, faces seen and unseen. I cannot begin to name them all; but it is pure pleasure to try.

This book emerged out of a dissertation written at Princeton University, where I accumulated many obligations to friends, teachers, and fellow students. Sandeep Kaushik and Cliff Doerksen provided endless intellectual debate and a steady stream of good humor to lighten even the bleakest of Princeton days. They have graced me with a decade of unbroken friendship, despite less-than-ideal circumstances. Johannes Wolfart, ever a source of warmth-amidst-chaos, helped me through some of my more trying times as a graduate student, a feat for which I am most grateful. Elspeth Carruthers has been a pillar of friendship and advice. Andrew Shankman has taught me much about the Anglo-American world and over the years has offered a brand of camaraderie not often found in this walk of life. Other fellow students who gave me encouragement along the way include Paul Cohen, Brian Cowan, Ignacio Gallup-Diaz, Evan Haefeli, Adam Sabra, and Nat Sheidley. Eugenio Biagini, Bill Jordan, and the late Gerry Geison taught me much; John Murrin and Ted Rabb examined the dissertation and provided many useful comments, which have influenced the final shape of the book.

In the years that followed, many colleagues have shared their time, insight, and knowledge with me. This would not be the book it is without the support, friendship, and advice provided by Michael Winship, who kindly shared with me the fruits of his research on New England's free grace controversy as his own book took shape. He made a number of critical suggestions about where to take the project (and where not to take it), and offered many helpful references along the way. Dwight Bozeman read portions of the dissertation in its infancy, and gave very useful suggestions; although I have not had the pleasure to meet him face-to-face, his work and input have been important to this project. The thesis took its cue from important and provocative papers by Stephen Foster (on antinomianism) and David Wootton (on Familism), both of whom deserve due praise. In the meantime, I have been the very fortunate beneficiary of the generosity and advice of Alastair Bellany, Burke Griggs, Nigel Smith, Tom Cogswell, Joe Ward, and Rachel Weil. Barbara Donagan, Richard Strier, and Ethan Shagan offered helpful comments, while Ethan provided an important reference at an early stage of research. At Chicago, Ben Stone, Rachel Fulton, Tamar Herzog, Dave Van Mill, Sue Stokes, and Erik Grimmer-Solem were exemplary colleagues and good friends. I am deeply grateful to the corps of South Asia specialists—Riaz Khan, Spencer Leonard, Rochona Majumdar, Nikhil Rao, Andrew Sartori—who welcomed me into their circle and showed me the survival skills necessary to make it through Chicago winters (i.e., they guided me toward Jimmy's). Alicia Czaplewski bailed me out more than once. There is no way anyone can go near the early modern program at the University of Chicago without learning a great deal from Steve Pincus, whose help and friendship over the past five years have been very important to me. During my time at Maryland, Marvin Breslow, Jim Gilbert, Richard Price, David Sicilia, and Madeline Zilfi provided ample collegiality and support. David Norbrook and Sharon Achinstein were wonderfully open and giving colleagues. Sumaiya Hamdani of GMU allowed me to rant at her at great length, for which I am particularly thankful. Especially deserving of thanks are Margaret Sena and Bob Crews (to say nothing of Cliff), all of whom went above and beyond the call of friendship in more ways than one—it will not be forgotten.

In England, I have received help, advice and friendship from many scholars, most particularly Ken Fincham, Susan Hardman-Moore, Michael Questier, and Nicholas Tyacke. I would also like to thank Arnold Hunt and Alan Cromartie, each of whom pointed me toward important sources; my work has benefited from discussions with Ian Atherton, John Coffey, Richard Cust, Tom Freeman, Ann Hughes, Sean Kelsey, and Brett Usher. Margaret Bryant, who donated MS. 3461 to the Lambeth Palace Library, cheerfully answered my correspondence concerning the provenance of this priceless document. Karen Britland was extremely kind and forbearant during my final, rain-soaked foray into Grindletonian country, while the Newsome family offered much-needed hospitality when the skies opened up on me. David Purdy and Geoffrey Booth, vicar and churchwarden of Kirkbymoorside, greeted me with open arms and kindly allowed me to consult the records of the parish. As always, librarians, archivists, and staff at various repositories played an indispensable role. Melanie Barber, Thomas Knoles, Amanda Savile, and Chris Webb all went out of their way to help me at one point or another. I am especially indebted to Jane Foster of Chetham's Library and Esther Ormerod of the Borthwick Institute.

I would also like to thank the many friends and coconspirators in California who contributed in their own way to the final outcome of this book: Tommy Adams, Derik Broekhoff, Jesse Castro, Oscar Carillo, Joe Chang, Frankie Clogston, Chris Deason, Lewis Eichele, Paul Glauthier, Carl Gold, Dave Hecht, Jeff Hashfield, Laura Hernandez, Dave Horne, Gabrielle Hull, Chris Hudacko, Ted Hudacko, Dave Lambert, Johnny Lee, Bobbi Sanchez, Pablo Valdez, and John Zimmerman. John and James Reichmuth provided their own bizarre but irresistible forms of inspiration. I am especially grateful to Jonathan Hudacko and Charlene Son for all their friendship and emotional support over these many years.

My greatest debts are to the two scholars and teachers who have shepherded me along this sometimes rocky path. Paul Seaver first introduced me to the study of British history, and has remained a constant source of support, friendship, and counsel over the years. He has been a role model for me, both as scholar and human being. My greatest intellectual debt, however, is to Peter Lake. Long before I had ever met him, his work had begun to shape the way I looked at early modern English history. He was a superb dissertation supervisor, and has continued to offer unflagging support as the book has grown and evolved. He is a great historian, a great teacher, and a great friend. My debt to him is incalculable.

As always, my family is the center of my existence, even when it seems otherwise. Many thanks are due to Pat Brett, Mary and Jack Langton, Angela and Matthew Drozdoff, Leo and Donna Como and their respective families. Above all, I would like to thank my parents, Jean and Joseph Como, whose unstinting support has carried me through these many years. For better or for worse, the present work is without doubt a product of the ways they taught me to think and live. I am forever grateful. This book, dedicated to them, stands as a small and decidedly inadequate token of that gratitude.

Contents

List of Abbreviations

Alumni Cantabrigienses	John Venn and J. A. Venn, eds., *Alumni Cantabrigienses. A Biographical List of All Known Students, Graduates and Holders of Office at the University of Cambridge, From the Earliest Times to 1900. Part I. From the Earliest Times to 1751*, 4 vols. (Cambridge: Cambridge University Press, 1922).
Alumni Oxonienses	J. Foster, ed., *Alumni Oxonienses. The Members of the University of Oxford, 1500-1714: Their Parentage, Birthplace, and Year of Birth, with a Record of their Degrees*, 4 vols. (Oxford and London: James Parker, 1891).
CSPD	Various editors, *Calendar of State Papers, Domestic Series*. Reigns of James I, Charles I, Charles II, and Interregnum.
CUL	Cambridge University Library
DNB	L. Stephen and Sidney Lee, eds., *The Dictionary of National Biography* (New York: Macmillan, 1885-1900).
HMC	Historical Manuscripts Commission
PRO	Public Record Office, London
SPD	State Papers, Domestic Series

Blown by the Spirit

Prologue

Of the thousands of pamphlets, books, and broadsides that flooded from London presses during the revolutionary convulsions of the 1640 and 1650s, few can claim to have exerted a direct and palpable influence on the generations that followed. One work that rather improbably did so was an obscure theological tract called *The Marrow of Modern Divinity*, originally published in 1645 by an anonymous author identified only by his initials "E. F." In its day, *The Marrow* had been a minor bestseller. It passed through seven editions by 1650, finally disappearing from view shortly after the Restoration. Seventy-three years after its initial publication, a Scotsman named Hog dusted off *The Marrow* and reissued it, occasioning a heated controversy that threatened to tear the Scottish Church in two. Defenders of the volume—so-called "Marrow Men"—claimed that the book represented a powerful practical exposition of the doctrine of free grace. Its detractors saw it as a deceptive threat to the orthodoxy of the Church, a work of disguised antinomianism—the heretical notion that believers were free from the Moral Law. The ensuing storm, in which the opposing sides vehemently denounced one another as "legalists" and "antinomians," raged in press, pulpit, and church court for several years, ultimately contributing to the founding of the Secession Church in 1730.[1] By this unlikely path, *The Marrow of Modern Divinity* assumed a place beside the likes of *Areopagitica* and *Leviathan* as a lasting and historically relevant artifact of the English Revolution.

---

[1] See D. C. Lachman, *The Marrow Controversy* (Edinburgh: Rutherford House, 1988) for the definitive account of the conflict.

This story is all the more extraordinary because the author of *The Marrow* was neither a Milton nor a Hobbes. Modern research has conclusively identified "E.F." as Edward Fisher, a London barber-surgeon, amateur theologian, and sometime religious pamphleteer.[2] Viewed from one perspective, Fisher's career has the aspect of a Royalist cautionary tale. His double-life, split as it was between the incongruous activities of setting bones and setting pen to paper, appears as a perfect synecdoche for the anarchy, misrule, and social inversion wrought by the puritan ascendancy. Yet Fisher's story is more remarkable than even this would suggest. For both *The Marrow* and the controversy it sparked in Scotland had an intricate and hidden prehistory extending back into the early seventeenth century, a prehistory that shall occupy the remainder of this study.

The terms "antinomian" and "legalist" were nothing new to the British theological lexicon. As Fisher's own preface reveals, they had been brandished with alarming frequency in England both before and during the civil wars. A "legalist," as Fisher defined the word, was a person who had grounded his or her piety in moral reformation, "a zealous professour of Religion, performing all Christian exercises both publike and private." Such "legal professours" might soldier on in their erroneous ways throughout their lives, dying "sure of Heaven and eternall happiness . . . and yet it maybe all this while is ignorant of Christ and his Righteousnes, and therefore establisheth his own."[3] At the other end of the spectrum were those who recognized their sinfulness, and "hearing of justification freely by grace through the redemption which is in Jesus Christ, do applaud and magnifie that doctrine, following them that doe most preach and presse the same, seeming to be (as it were) ravished with the hearing thereof, out of a conceit that they are by Christ freely justified." Yet they remained sinful: "these are they that can talke like believers, and yet do not walke like believers; these are they that have language like Saints, and yet have conversations like Devils: these are they that are not obedient to the Law of Christ, and therefore are justly called Antinomians."[4] Fisher claimed that *The Marrow* was intended to blaze a middle way between these two errors, which, as he explained, had been the cause of no little consternation among the godly: "not onely a matter of 18 or 20 years agoe, but also within these three or foure years, there hath been much a doe, both by preaching, writing, and disputing, both to reduce men out of them, and to keep them from them, and hot contentions have been on both sides, and all, I fear me, to little pur-

---

[2] D. M. McIntyre, "First Strictures on the 'The Marrow of Modern Divinity,'" *The Evangelical Quarterly*, 10 (1938), 61-70.

[3] E[dward] F[isher], *The Marrow of Modern Divinity: Touching both the Covenant of Works, and the Covenant of Grace*, 2d ed. (1646), sigs. *7v-*8v.

[4] Ibid., sigs. *8v-Ar.

pose," for each group had merely succeeded in driving the other further into error.[5] Here Fisher was of course referring in part to the intractable civil-war disputes between puritan radicals—Crispe, Dell, Saltmarsh, and Erbury, to name a few—and their equally committed godly opponents—men such as Thomas Edwards and John Vicars.

Yet Fisher intimated that the conflicts of the 1640s were hardly unprecedented; he explicitly dated the first rumblings of controversy over the contested issues of grace and the Moral Law to "18 or 20 years ago"—that is, to the period between 1625 and 1627. In alluding to the "hot contentions" of the 1620s, then, Fisher was in fact recalling a series of divisive theological disputes that had shaken the godly community during the later 1620s. These bitter conflicts had been sparked by the growth of a small, vocal protest group that had crystallized in opposition to prevailing styles of puritan practical divinity in the first decades of the seventeenth century. Such godly dissidents—variously and indiscriminately belittled by opponents as "antinomians," "Familists" or "libertines"—vociferously objected to what they saw as legalistic and literal-minded tendencies inherent in mainstream puritanism. By 1629-30, there were at least nine such preachers active in London alone, dragging behind them an increasingly visible penumbra of lay disciples, admirers, and fellow-travelers. Indeed, as Fisher hinted, by late 1629, their persistent and often strident attacks on their fellow puritans had precipitated a crisis that threatened the integrity of the godly community. It is this crisis—a crisis that may justly be called "England's antinomian controversy"—that serves as the subject of this book.

An Underground?

Fisher was in a privileged position to comment on this controversy. He claimed that he had himself been in the thrall of legalism in his early days: "I was a professour of Religion, at least a dozen yeeres, before I knew any other way to eternall life, then to be sorry for my sins, and aske forgivenesse, and strive and endeavour to fulfill the Law, and keepe the Commandements, according as Master Dod and other godly men had expounded them." He claimed that only conference with the famed puritan pastor Thomas Hooker had taught him "that I was yet but a proud Pharisee, and to shew mee the way of faith and salvation by Christ alone."[6] While we have no reason to suppose that he had fabricated this tale about the eminently respectable Hooker, there was another side to Fisher's spiritual progress about which he had good reason to be less forthcoming.

---

[5] Ibid., sig. Av.

[6] Ibid., sigs. *8r-v.

Despite his claims to be piously threshing out a pathway between extremes of antinomianism and legalism, Fisher's critics in both seventeenth-century England and eighteenth-century Scotland argued that his treatment of the subject was far from impartial, and that in fact his irenic pose served merely to camouflage his antinomian sympathies.[7] As if to confirm their worst fears, whether antinomian or not, Edward Fisher did carry with him a deeply suspicious past. In order to reconstruct that past, we must backtrack to the last years of Charles I's Personal Rule, to a moment in which the noose of Laudian ecclesiastical pressure was slowly tightening around London's puritans.

In 1638, fearing a pending High Commission case against him, a young cutler named Giles Creech had approached the authorities with a whopping tale of a seething sectarian underworld hidden just beneath the surface of London society. Creech claimed that in his youth he had made "the acquaintance of Familists, Antinomians, Anabaptists and the like." He further admitted that he had been a "disciple of Dr [John] Everard sometimes lecturer at St Martins in the feilds whereby he became infected with those pernitious doctrines." Only a well-timed sermon by Archbishop Laud had saved him from Everarde's clutches, but now, he claimed, his vindictive coreligionists were seeking to have him prosecuted for the very errors he had repudiated, forcing him to turn informant.[8]

Creech painted a lurid picture of competing antinomian splinter groups, providing detailed lists of the members of four separate London sects, which he labeled respectively "the familists of the mount," "the familists of the Valley," "the Essentualists," and the "Antinomians," each of which adhered to a subtly different set of beliefs. At the core of this sectarian subculture, Creech identified a pair of illegal manuscript peddlers who appear to have served as a nerve-center for the London scene: "They have severall Books teaching . . . their malevolent Doctrines, whereof one is intituled H.N. his Booke. A second is called, the Rule of perfection, but especially that cursed Booke named Theologica Germanica [sic], . . . the most pestilent of all others, whereof some are in Latine, Manuscripts, written by one Fisher a Barber in the old Bayley, and one Woolstone a Scrivener in Chancery Lane."[9]

---

[7] J. A., *A Manifest and Breife Discovery of some of the Errours contained in a Dialogue called the Marrow of Moderne Divinity* (1646), esp. 20; see also McIntyre, "First Strictures," 66-69, for other contemporary suspicions that the Marrowist was, as the presbyterian John Trapp put it in 1647, a "sly antinomian." Other attacks came from Thomas Blake (1653) and Richard Baxter.

[8] PRO, SPD 16/378/241. Creech initially petitioned Archbishop Laud on 17 January 1637/8. Laud referred the matter to Sir John Lambe for investigation.

[9] Bodleian Library, Tanner MS. 70, fols. 181r-v. This represents one of three surviving copies of Creech's deposition. The other two, which vary very slightly, may be found in PRO, SPD 16/520/85 and 16/520/86, the former of which includes Sir

Even if we remain skeptical as to the extraordinary details of this story, there can be no question that the barber-surgeon and illicit manuscript dealer here named was anything but a figment of Giles Creech's imagination: he was none other than Edward Fisher, future author of *The Marrow of Modern Divinity*, who tellingly conceded in his preface that although he had drawn liberally on the publications of "known and approved" authors in constructing his book, "some part of it my manuscripts have afforded me."[10] If Creech is to be trusted, it is clear that Fisher's library was stocked with works by authors who were anything but "approved": Hendrik Niclaes, alias HN, was the infamous, messianic founder of the Dutch sect, the Family of Love. Familism, an offshoot of earlier forms of continental anabaptism, had emerged in Holland during the middle decades of the sixteenth century. From here, it quickly spread to England, provoking a series of panic-stricken pamphlets by puritan moralists, before coming under intense pressure in the Elizabethan church courts. Yet Creech's testimony reveals that those he described as "Familists" were not (like earlier devotees) committed to the words of HN as the only source of continuing revelation. They also treasured a rare and obscure tract known as *The Rule of Perfection*. Originally published in 1609, *The Rule* was in fact the handiwork of the English Capuchin friar, William Fitch, also known as Benet of Canfield. A work of intense mystical piety, the book continued to be venerated in radical circles into the civil war years, when additional parts of it would be published for the first time by the antinomian extremist Giles Randall. Most "pestilent" of all, however, was that most notorious primer of mystical, perfectionist piety—the *Theologia Germanica*. This medieval devotional work had first been published by Luther on the eve of the Reformation, only to be recycled by a long line of radicals and spiritualists throughout the sixteenth century. In England, as on the Continent, it had apparently continued to exert its influence well into the seventeenth century.

In his investigation of Creech's allegations, Sir John Lambe received further information about the barber-surgeon and manuscript dealer Fisher. It was claimed that he "selles old bookes and got Theolog[ia] Germanica translated into English by a minister at Grendleton: called Brierly or Tenant." The men named here were Roger Brearley and Richard Tennant, the ringleaders of the notorious "Grindletonian" movement that had sprung up along the Lancashire-Yorkshire border during the first decades of the seventeenth century.

John Lambe's interlinear notes. Both State Papers copies read "H.N. his bookes," suggesting that more than one of the founder's works were in circulation. Creech's deposition was to my knowledge first analyzed by Stephen Foster.

[10] Fisher, *Marrow*, sig. A2r. For definitive evidence that the man described by Creech was the barber-surgeon, Edward Fisher, see Chapter Three. See also John Davis's note in his *Obituary* of 1650, of the death of "Mr. Fisher, bookseller and barber in the Old Bailey," as cited in McIntyre, "First Strictures," 62.

Having imported this text from rural Yorkshire, Fisher seems to have sold the manuscript to the scrivener Woolstone, from whence it found its way to Everarde "who was in translating it and did two of them, one for the E[arl] of Holland and another for the E[arl] Mulgrave."[11]

This should not be taken as proof that Fisher was a Familist-in-disguise.[12] But as this study progresses, we shall uncover a series of connections which, when held together, corroborate Creech's claim that the Marrowist had a checkered, indeed sectarian, history. This, in turn, allows us to glimpse a rather different vision of Fisher's passage out of pharisaical legalism. Although he almost certainly had conferred with Hooker[13], he had apparently also spent a good deal of time consorting with sectaries, copying out their treasured texts, and breathing in the atmosphere of London's antinomian subculture. Here we see Fisher acting as a sort of clearinghouse for proscribed manuscripts, a focal point for a community of like-minded people that stretched from the hinterlands of Yorkshire to John Everarde's aristocratic enclave in Kensington and beyond. What follows is an attempt to reconstruct that underground and to evaluate its historical impact.

---

[11] PRO, SPD 16/520/85, fol. 126r. Whether or not the details of this story are true, Creech was correct about the fact that John Everarde had executed a translation of the *Theologia Germanica* in the 1630s. Two contemporary manuscript copies of his translation have survived: Folger Shakespeare Library MS. V. a. 222; CUL MS. Dd. xii. 68.

[12] It is worth noting that Creech did not include Fisher in his lists of Familists and antinomians. The question of whether Fisher was an "antinomian" depends on how the term is defined. To be sure, there are certain points where his descriptions of the believer's freedom from the Law ("you are now set free, both from the commanding and condemning power of the covenant of works," Fisher, *Marrow*, 2d ed., 148 and more generally, 147-52) are similar to those of earlier antinomians. See also ibid., 176-77, where once again he replicated certain antinomian arguments and referred to Robert Towne as an "evangelical man." Yet at other points (158-61), Fisher argued that all the commandments are required of believers, although differently expressed, and not as part of the covenant of works. In this and other crucial ways, he parted company with the thoroughgoing antinomians described further on in this study. For a more complete account of Fisher's views on the role of the Law under the Christian dispensation, see *The Marrow of Moderne Divinity. The Second Part. Touching the Most Plaine, Pithy and Spirituall Exposition of the Ten Commandments* (1648), passim.

[13] See Fisher, *Marrow*, 2d ed., 133, 192, where he refers to Hooker as "evangelical Hooker," and "godly Hooker," suggesting that his affections (and probably his story) were genuine. Yet it should be noted that the only other divine who earns the title "evangelical" in the course of *The Marrow* is the altogether less respectable Robert Towne, the notorious antinomian. Ibid., 177.

The notion of an "antinomian underground" is bound to be greeted with skepticism, particularly since many of the sources utilized in the following study were generated by hostile witnesses whose motives and reliability are often open to doubt.[14] This is preeminently the case for Giles Creech, whose detailed and byzantine portrait of the London sectarian scene has been justly questioned by scholars.[15] It is therefore essential that we establish at the outset the trustworthiness of Creech's testimony, both to assess his claims and to provide us with a clearer vision of the community he was describing. In addition to the case of Fisher, we can identify at least two instances in which Creech named individuals whose antinomian associations can be verified, independently and beyond all doubt, through separate, nonhostile sources. Among the so-called "familists of the mount," Creech fingered one "Hareford a Bookebinder in Paternoster Row," to whose name Sir John Lambe appended the comment that "he binds Dr Everard his bookes and knowes all his waies." The man described here was surely Rapha Harford, the sometime bookseller who would indeed publish John Everarde's collected sermons in 1653, together with a reverent, personalized biography of his spiritual mentor.[16]

But we possess a second, extraordinary piece of evidence, which vindicates beyond all question Creech's claim to possess intimate knowledge of the London antinomian scene. Another member of the "family of the mount" was, Creech claimed, one "Stephen Proudlove," who "doth sell small wares with in Bishopsgate streete, in an Alley," and who, according to Lambe, "travaile[d] up and down to faires," peddling his goods. Meanwhile, among the "antinomians," Creech listed another bookbinder identified only by his surname "Howse." This man was quite possibly a relative of Edward Howes, a Londoner whose diary for the years 1643-49 survives among the Sloane Manuscripts, providing us with irrefutable confirmation of the existence of a Familist current flowing quietly beneath waters of London puritanism. Howes's diary contains, among other things, an epistle after the style of HN, exhorting

[14] For a more extensive discussion of the methodological difficulties that accompany the use of such hostile sources, see below, Appendix C.

[15] See, for instance, the discussion in S. Foster, "New England and the Challenge of Heresy, 1630 to 1660: the Puritan Crisis in Transatlantic Perspective," *William and Mary Quarterly*, 38 (1981), 636-38, where Creech's deposition is dismissed as "tainted evidence"; C. Marsh, *The Family of Love in English Society, 1550-1630* (Cambridge: Cambridge University Press, 1994), 237, devotes only four sentences to the deposition, citing it (without even naming or mentioning Creech) as evidence that "The terms 'Familist' and 'Family of Love' were . . . applied with increasing regularity to groups or individuals suspected of holding crudely perfectionist or libertine beliefs."

[16] John Everard, *Some Gospel-Treasures Opened: Or, The Holiest of all Unvailing* (1653).

believers to continue along in the true doctrine of earthly perfection; it records two songs celebrating the "livers in love," both of which were drawn from HN's *Cantica*, a Familist hymnbook that had been published for the first and only time in English in the 1570s; it includes striking examples of Familist iconography; it contains notes on sermons by Robert Gell, one of civil-war London's more notorious perfectionist preachers; and most impressively, it describes several of Howes's "visions" (that is, dreams) together with his own manifestly allegorical readings of those immediate revelations.[17] Remarkably, in one of these dreams, Howes reported seeing a vision of "Proudlove the pedler," obviously one and the same Stephen Proudlove identified by Giles Creech as a member of the Family of the Mount in 1638.[18] Here, then, is a bona fide Familist source, proving that Creech possessed intimate and reliable knowledge of London antinomianism, and confirming his picture of a small, tightly knit, and anything but imaginary community of ideological fellow travelers, stretching from the prewar period into the 1640s.

Although this community was evidently a small and cliquish one, in which insiders knew one another by name and reputation—even inhabiting one anothers' dreams—we should be careful not to dismiss it as an irrelevant band of true believers, isolated from mainstream puritanism. Indeed, it will be argued throughout this study that the disputes between antinomians and their orthodox puritan antagonists were so bitter precisely because no such segregating boundary existed. The tension between them was conditioned by what John Gager has called "a fundamental law of religious dynamics: the closer the parties, the greater the potential for conflict."[19] Antinomians were considered so dangerous because in many important ways they remained members of the godly community, sharing large portions of the cultural and intellectual heritage that defined puritans as a group within the world. This was the case even for self-identifying "Familists" such as Howes, who, as it turns out, had been a close friend of John Winthrop, Jr., the son of Massachusetts' first governor, prior to Winthrop's departure for New England in 1631. An extraordinary series of letters from Howes to Winthrop—straddling the period between 1628 and 1644—survives among the collections of the Massachusetts Historical Society, allowing us to chart the course whereby Edward Howes moved from the conventional, if eccentric, godliness of his youth, to the manifestly heretical blend of puritanism, alchemy, and Familism revealed in his diary of the 1640s;

---

[17] British Library, Sloane MS. 979, fols. 7r-16v, 11r, 15v, 18v-21v, 22r-23v, 30r-34v. See also K. Thomas, *Religion and the Decline of Magic* (New York: Charles Scribner's Sons, 1971), 377n5.

[18] British Library, Sloane MS. 979, fol. 16v.

[19] J. Gager, *The Origins of Anti-Semitism: Attitudes Toward Judaism in Pagan and Christian Antiquity* (New York and Oxford: Oxford University Press, 1983), 143.

together, these sources, which shall be discussed in greater detail below, allow us to peer momentarily into a world—the world of Creech, Brearley, Everarde, Fisher, Howes, and their fellow antinomians—that has been lost to posterity.[20]

[20] The surviving letters have been published in the *Collections of the Massachusetts Historical Society*, 3rd series, 9 (1846), 240-58; 4th ser., 6 (1863), 467-513.

CHAPTER 1

Introduction

Through the centuries, puritans have been made to wear many historical masks. The godly have sometimes been cast as self-righteous and hypocritical busybodies—intolerant, small-minded and repressive; at other points, they have appeared as champions of liberty, the heroic founding figures of a triumphant Whig-liberal narrative of progress and human freedom; in this century, they have not infrequently graced the scholarly stage as the insurgents of a new bourgeois order, the standard-bearers of a proto-capitalistic ethic destined to cut the shackles of feudal bondage. In part because of this seemingly boundless malleability, a number of modern commentators have come to regard the admittedly amorphous categories of "puritan" and "puritanism" with a certain suspicion, some even going so far as to reject them as vague and misleading vestiges of seventeenth-century polemical battles. Yet in spite of such well-intentioned skepticism, the godly have continued to exercise a powerful hold over scholars of early modern England, who remain plagued by a nagging intuition that without "puritanism" (or some synonymous category), we cannot begin to explain the tumultuous political and cultural world of Tudor-Stuart England.

The staying power of puritanism is in part a product of historiographical fashion. The drive to destabilize, or even to banish, the category was pushed forward by the first wave of "revisionism" that swept through the field of early modern English history beginning in the late 1960s. One of the central features of the revisionist assault on Whig orthodoxy was an attempt to downplay the existence of ideological conflict in the century or so before the English civil war. Where Gardiner, Notestein, Neale, and others had posited an escalating conflict over constitutional principles progressing hand-in-hand with a battle between a puritan "opposition" and an establishment Anglicanism, revisionists sought to lay down a picture of relative ideological homogeneity, stability and consensus. Crucial to this revisionist picture was the research of Nicholas Tyacke, whose seminal work on Arminianism suggested that the Church of England prior to the reign of Charles I—far from representing an ideological *via media* between Roman Catholicism and Protestantism—had in fact been dominated by a strain of evangelical Calvinism, a state of affairs that was disrupted only by the rise of an aggressive anti-Calvinist movement in the 1620s.[1] His work had a double effect: it simultaneously undermined the notion of a freestanding Anglican tradition, while likewise implying that "puritanism," if it existed at all, was merely the most fastidious or aggressive manifestation of a broader, consensual Calvinism that was shared by the vast majority of early Stuart churchmen. Tyacke's conclusions were rapidly assimilated into the revisionist synthesis, most notably by Conrad Russell, who used Tyacke's arguments to downplay the existence of ideological conflict prior to the late 1620s, when Arminianism and fiscal breakdown were taken to have produced ruptures that had not previously existed.[2] So, too, in the wake of Tyacke's work, a number of scholars—including Michael Finlayson, Paul Christianson, J. C. Davis and, at certain moments, Patrick Collinson—teased out the implications of his thesis, arguing that the category of "puritanism" was at best overused, and at worst entirely incoherent, a fiction created by a combination of seventeenth-century polemicists and later historians.[3] In recent years, however, "puritanism" as a concept has experienced something of a historiographical renaissance, owing in no small part to what might be termed the "second generation" of revisionist scholarship. Having overturned the conflictual model of the Whigs, revisionist scholars found

---

[1] For the fullest statement of his views, see N. Tyacke, *Anti-Calvinists: the Rise of English Arminianism, c. 1590-1640* (Oxford: Oxford University Press, 1987; Revised paperback edition, Oxford: Oxford University Press, 1990).

[2] See C. Russell, *Parliaments and English Politics, 1621-29* (Oxford: Oxford University Press, 1979).

[3] M. G. Finlayson, *Historians, Puritanism, and the English Revolution: the Religious Factor in English Politics before and after the Interregnum* (Toronto: University of Toronto Press, 1983); P. Christianson, "Reformers and the Church of England under Elizabeth I and the Early Stuarts," *Journal of Ecclesiastical History*, 31 (1980), which, while not rejecting the category "puritan" entirely, seeks greatly to limit its application by reclassifying as "Anglicans" many of those who have traditionally been defined as puritans; J. C. Davis, "Puritanism and Revolution: Themes, Categories, Methods and Conclusions," *Historical Journal*, 33 (1990); idem., "Cromwell's Religion," in J. Morrill, ed., *Oliver Cromwell and the English Revolution* (London: Longman, 1990). For Collinson, see the comments and notes that follow in this chapter.

themselves at length forced to provide a positive explanation for the extraordinary events of the mid-century, leading many of them, including Kevin Sharpe, John Morrill, Peter White, and even Russell himself to seize upon religion, and more specifically upon a godly or puritanical movement to reform the church, as perhaps the central ideological precipitant of the English civil wars.[4] In this, revisionists appear to be joining hands with their "post-revisionist" critics, most of whom have never doubted the existence of significant religious friction in the early modern period. Thus, although large differences remain over details of interpretation, scholars appear to be converging upon a major re-evaluation of the early Stuart period, one in which religious factors, and above all puritanism, will play a very substantial role.

Yet if this felicitous convergence can be explained partly by examining the fortunes of revisionism as a historiographical trend, it also owes much to the seemingly undeniable and inordinate role assumed by militant Protestants in the cataclysmic events of the 1640s and 1650s. Beginning with Clarendon and Hobbes in the seventeenth century, historians who have sought to come to grips with the massive upheaval of the English Revolution have returned again and again to puritans for insight and explanation. This is hardly mysterious. From the apocalyptic fast sermons of the Long Parliament, to the Root and Branch attack on episcopacy, to the iconoclasm of grassroots parliamentary supporters, to the famed psalm-singing roundheads of the New Model Army, the upswell of resistance that led to the civil war had from the outset borne the hallmarks of a rigorous and unyielding form of Protestantism. So, too, the Revolution is rightly linked in our minds with the strange and dizzying proliferation of sectarian groupings that emerged from the wreckage of episcopacy. Presbyterians, Independents, Baptists, Fifth Monarchists, Levellers, and Quakers all appear at least to have evolved out of what might be termed the left-wing of English Protestantism—the world of conventicles, scrupulous nonconformity, and committed, logocentric religiosity that contemporaries often branded with the label "puritan." Indeed, it is in large measure because these sectarian movements are so close to the center of the English Revolution—so crucial to what made the events of mid-century politically, religiously, and intellectually radical and unique—that the concept of puritanism has proved so difficult to bury.

---

[4] J. Morrill, "The Religious Context of the English Civil War," *Transactions of the Royal Historical Society*, 34 (1984); C. Russell, *The Causes of the English Civil War* (Oxford: Clarendon Press, 1990); Peter White, *Predestination, Policy and Polemic: Conflict and Consensus in the English Church from the Reformation to the Civil War* (Cambridge: Cambridge University Press, 1992); K. Sharpe, *The Personal Rule of Charles I* (New Haven and London: Yale University Press, 1992).

For all this, however, there has been surprisingly little substantive scholarship devoted to the process whereby these striking forms of social and religious radicalism emerged from the bosom of pre–civil war puritanism. To put it another way, although scholars now seem to agree as to the centrality of the godly for our understanding of the civil war and revolution, we remain quite ignorant as to how, why, and under what circumstances the English puritan community splintered into numerous competing factions, many of them bearing ideas of seemingly unprecedented social, political, or theological radicalism.[5] The following book represents a first attempt to map out this complex and obscure process.

Two Puritanisms?

To more fully understand how and why such a gaping historiographical void exists, we must turn to the work of the two greatest postwar scholars of puritanism, Christopher Hill and Patrick Collinson. Working from very different perspectives, these two historians in many ways set the tone for the study of English puritanism in the second half of the twentieth century. At the same time, however, an examination of their scholarship helps to illustrate many of the puzzles and contradictions that have beset the field in recent years.

Hill, of course, is perhaps best known for the interpretation of puritanism elaborated in his seminal collection of essays, *Society and Puritanism in Pre-Revolutionary England* (1964). Building on the insights of R. H. Tawney and other socioeconomic historians, but offering his own decidedly Marxian gloss on the matter, Hill argued that puritanism represented the ideology of a newly emergent bourgeois class. This ideology of "the industrious sort of people" stressed the virtues of work, excoriated the wickedness of the idle and able-bodied poor, and waged war on the irrational and festive habits of the English countryside. It was thus very much a vehicle through which the "middling sort" sought to discipline a recalcitrant, increasingly impoverished, and reluctant lower class, so as to create both a pliable workforce and an orderly society at a time of great economic stress. Even as it worked to control the unruly

[5] In certain respects, this gap in our knowledge may again be attributed to the methodological and historical priorities of revisionists, who dominated the research agenda through the 1970s and 1980s. To use Peter Lake's apt phrase "one of the crucial interpretational and rhetorical ploys of revisionism was to decouple the events after the outbreak of the war from events preceding it." Thus, the excessive radicalism of the period after 1642 could be explained away by recourse to the short-term, rapid sweep of events, thus preserving the revisionist view of the prewar period as relatively stable, consensual and free of deep-seated ideological division. Lake, "Introduction" to G. F. Nuttall, *The Holy Spirit in Puritan Faith and Experience* (Oxford: Blackwell, 1946; 2d ed., Oxford: Blackwell, 1947; Paperback reprint, Chicago: University of Chicago Press, 1992), xvi.

and disenfranchised poor, however, puritanism also looked "upward" in that it sought to disassemble the increasingly precarious feudal structures that still dominated the English church and state. Hence, puritanism was simultaneously a force of repression (of the lower orders) and of revolution (against feudal landowners, monarchy and church). Armed with this multilayered schema, Hill went on to interpret the mid-century upheavals as a bourgeois revolution, carried forward by a vanguard of musket-wielding puritans.

This picture, however, presented certain logical problems, for as Hill was always aware, the violent events of the revolutionary decades saw the emergence not merely of a repressive, "bourgeois" puritanism, but also of a phenomenon that might be termed "plebeian" puritanism. Neither the radical demands of the Levellers (whose ranks were swollen with sectaries of many different persuasions), nor the profoundly disturbing and transgressive egalitarianism of the Ranters, nor the Christian communism of the Diggers could easily be explained away as manifestations of an ascendant bourgeois ideology. And in fact, far from seeking to explain away such figures, Hill embraced and celebrated them, holding them up as founders of an ongoing, continuous tradition of British radicalism stretching from the seventeenth century to the nineteenth.[6] This project reached its high point in his famed study, *The World Turned Upside Down: Radical Ideas During the English Revolution* (1972). Here, Hill sought to provide a comprehensive survey of mid-century sectarianism, in all its colorful and outrageous splendor. In the same pages, however, he tacitly revealed that he was himself aware of the potential contradiction implicit in his own work. For if the disciplinary rigor of puritanism embodied the revolutionary aspirations of the "middling sort," how had the same puritanism produced the equally revolutionary, but scarcely bourgeois, ideology of the lower orders?

Even in his early work, Hill appears to have been cognizant of this tension, leading him to suggest at times that during the course of the revolution, the disenfranchised and the poor had seized upon certain aspects of puritan thought and deployed them for their own, counter-bourgeois ideological purposes.[7] By the time of the publication of *The World Turned Upside Down*, however, Hill appears to have adopted a rather different approach to the problem. While still clinging to the notion that the lower orders had appropriated and molded certain aspects of the puritan heritage, he now hinted that

---

[6] See especially his essay "The Norman Yoke," in C. Hill, *Puritanism and Revolution: Studies in Interpretation of the English Revolution of the 17th Century* (London: Secker and Warburg, 1958), 46-111.

[7] See, for example, Hill's discussion of radical appropriations of bourgeois-puritan Sabbatarianism, in C. Hill, *Society and Puritanism in Pre-Revolutionary England*, 2d ed. (New York: Schocken Books, 1967), 210-13.

the radicalism of the 1640s and 1650s had grown in large part out of ongoing traditions of sectarian religiosity that had subsisted at the edges of English society since the Reformation (or earlier), surviving especially among the masterless and poor men of the highlands, the forests, the fens, and other culturally and economically marginal regions of the country.[8] This argument, muted in the book, would be elaborated more explicitly and forcefully in his 1978 article "From Lollards to Levellers." Drawing upon the apparent persistence of various forms of rural dissent in these specific regions, Hill now hypothesized that there might have been a genealogy of plebeian heresy and rebelliousness that began with pre-Reformation Lollardy, mutated into much persecuted forms of heterodox Protestantism—the Marian Free-willers, Familists, Grindletonians, and various flavors of separatist—only to flower again during the Revolution.[9] Such an account preserved Hill's "bourgeois puritanism" while explaining the existence of an apparently separate and distinctive "radical puritanism," which represented the interests of the lower orders of society. Despite its bold scope, Hill's sweeping hypothesis found no champions and few critics, primarily because such claims are profoundly difficult to test against the historical record. The consequence, perversely, was that the most illustrious scholar of English radical religion had provided a daring but speculative account of the origins of that radicalism that was not obviously verifiable.[10]

Understandably, then, both Hill and his would-be interlocutors were reluctant to pursue the matter much further, helping to ensure that the question of the origins of radical puritanism has remained largely unexplored over the past three decades.[11] At a more subtle level, since Hill's account tended to accentuate the chasm between the repressive puritanism of the "middling sort" and the liberatory puritanism of the lower orders, neither he nor subsequent

---

[8] For a more explicit recognition of the tension in his own work, see Hill, *World Turned Upside Down*, 324-43; for hints as to ongoing traditions of religious radicalism in economically marginal areas, see ibid., 35, 39-56.

[9] C. Hill, "From Lollards to Levellers," in M. Cornforth, ed., *Rebels and Their Causes: Essays in Honour of A. L. Morton* (London: Lawrence and Wishart, 1978), 49-68.

[10] Yet see the ambitious and suggestive attempt to trace precisely such genealogies of dissent in M. Spufford, ed., *The World of the Rural Dissenters, 1520-1725* (Cambridge: Cambridge University Press, 1995).

[11] One notable and significant exception to this generalization is to be found in M. Tolmie, *The Triumph of the Saints* (Cambridge: Cambridge University Press, 1977), which traces the links between prewar separatist communities and the Independent congregations of civil-war London.

scholars have been inclined to investigate the connections between the two.[12] The putative radicalism of the sectaries has been, as it were, sealed off from the main body of puritanism, thus leaving the precise relationship between the two largely unexamined. As a consequence, although a handful of scholars have followed Hill in devoting time and energy to the study of the civil-war sects, his work has in certain respects had the paradoxical effect of closing down some of the most intriguing questions surrounding the very radicalism he sought to elucidate.[13] This stands in stark contrast to his work on the bourgeois "industrious sort of people," which gave rise, directly or indirectly, to many of the most important and creative works of Tudor-Stuart social history written over the past four decades.[14]

If Hill's research has thus left enormous unanswered questions about the nature of "puritanism," Collinson's work has probably done more than anyone else's to problematize the concept itself. A historian of a very different methodological temperament, one might say that Collinson has played fox to Hill's hedgehog, combining the skills of a political historian and social historian of religion with a keen anthropological eye to provide a vision of the godly that is at once more multifaceted and less amenable to straightforward description than that of Hill. Where Hill consistently privileged the social underpinnings of puritan religion, Collinson has been rather more inclined to

---

[12] It is not quite fair to say that Hill paid no attention to the relationship. For him, the liberatory nature of the one was very much a response to the repressive nature of the other. Thus, the radical puritanism of the sects denied the rigid mainstream puritan values of work, discipline, utter human sinfulness, and predestination. Their radicalism was thus a sort of socially motivated negative image of the dominant, bourgeois form of puritanism.

[13] For an important collection of essays that owes much to the inspiration of Hill, see J. F. McGregor and B. Reay, eds., *Radical Religion in the English Revolution* (Oxford: Oxford University Press, 1984).

[14] Among the more important works influenced directly by Hill are K. Wrightson and D. Levine, *Poverty and Piety in an English Village: Terling, 1525-1700* (New York: Academic Press, 1979); W. Hunt, *The Puritan Moment: The Coming of Revolution in an English County* (Cambridge, MA: Harvard University Press, 1983); D. Underdown, *Revel, Riot and Rebellion: Popular Politics and Culture in England, 1603-1660* (Oxford: Oxford University Press, 1985); the work of Hill and his followers has in turn spawned a diverse and lively literature devoted to testing, refuting, or modifying their conclusions. Crucial works include M. Ingram, *Church Courts, Sex and Marriage in England, 1570-1640* (Cambridge: Cambridge University Press, 1987); M. Todd, *Christian Humanism and the Puritan Social Order* (Cambridge: Cambridge University Press, 1987); M. McIntosh, *Controlling Misbehavior in England, 1370-1600* (Cambridge: Cambridge University Press, 1998); D. Beaver, *Parish Communities and Religious Conflict in the Vale of Gloucester, 1590-1690* (Cambridge, MA: Harvard University Press, 1998).

take puritans at their own word, accentuating the autonomous power of theological or religious concerns in shaping the behavior of the godly. Where Hill used his puritans to construct a totalizing theoretical model that explained the entire period, Collinson's puritans have come to life in a piecemeal, almost fragmented, fashion, through a series of narratives, detailed case studies and thematic essays that have incrementally, and not always straightforwardly, painted a rich, textured portrait of the godly community as it changed over time. For Hill, class was always the preeminent analytical tool; Collinson, by contrast, tended to ground his puritans in the ebb and flow of politics, as is most evident in his masterpiece *The Elizabethan Puritan Movement* (1967). This unparalleled piece of narrative history traced the origins and development of an impulse within English Protestantism for the further reform of the church, culminating with the story of the rise and demise of a full-blown presbyterian movement. Although not easily reduced to a potted summary, it could be said that *The Elizabethan Puritan Movement* tended, in general, to emphasize the distinctive and disruptive aspects of puritanism as a political and social force. In this respect, it dovetailed with the then-regnant Whig interpretation of Elizabethan and Stuart political history (and perhaps, somewhat more obliquely, with Hill's newly promulgated Marxist interpretation).

Yet from another perspective, Collinson's meticulous researches tended quietly to undermine those interpretations. As Peter Lake has put it, a close reading of *The Elizabethan Puritan Movement* "revealed the myriad ways in which the Elizabethan establishment was shot through with Puritan attitudes and personnel."[15] As Collinson demonstrated, even troublesome nonconformists and presbyterians could count on patrons and protectors in the highest echelons of Elizabethan government, including but not limited to luminaries such as Leicester, Warwick, Walsingham, Mildmay, Knollys, Beale, and on many occasions, Burghley himself. Similarly, and perhaps more surprisingly, Collinson found that many of Elizabeth's earliest bishops and churchmen—Parkhurst of Norwich and Grindal of Canterbury to name two of the more interesting cases—were themselves in sympathy with many of the basic aims of the so-called puritans. This suggested that the relationship between puritanism and the political and ecclesiastical establishments was in fact far more complex than previous expositors had supposed.

His subsequent research on both episcopacy and the godly in the localities reinforced these initial insights, and—perhaps pushed along by Tyacke's emerging conclusions regarding the Calvinist temper of the pre-Caroline church—Collinson eventually arrived at a major reinterpretation of the nature of religion in Elizabethan and early Stuart England, which he elaborated most

---

[15] Lake, "Introduction" to Nuttall, *Holy Spirit*, xiii.

forcefully in his Ford Lectures, *The Religion of Protestants* (1982). This reinterpretation, which ran in step with the broader revisionist trend sweeping the field in the 1970s, suggested that the Elizabethan-Jacobean church was in fact an evangelical protestant church, far more in tune with the reformed communions of the continent than with the High Church Anglicanism of a later era. On this view, the godly were taken to be merely the most zealous and uncompromising members of an otherwise thoroughly protestant establishment. Yet Collinson's work had still another dimension; focusing especially on godly gentlemen and their ministerial counterparts, he argued that even many of the most "puritanically" disposed individuals were neither disaffected from the broader political establishment, nor bent on opposing the government. Rather, theirs was an ideology energized by a passion for moral control, and infused with a resolute commitment to existing social hierarchies. In place of a conflictual view of puritanism, Collinson seemed to hint at times that by James's reign, the Church of England had come in many ways to resemble a puritan church, in which zealous magistrates and ministers piously joined hands in a war on sin. Only the disastrous appearance of Archbishop Laud signaled the end of this orderly state of affairs.

On the surface, this account might appear to have certain affinities with that proposed by Hill in his *Society and Puritanism*. Like Hill, Collinson was arguing that from one standpoint, the gentlemen, magistrates, and ministers who provided the backbone of the puritan movement were obsessed with order, and determined to impose a disciplined regime of holiness on those beneath them. For Hill, however, the puritanism of the "middling sort" had always possessed a revolutionary as well as repressive edge, poised as it was against the waning feudalism of the existing hierarchy. Collinson's account manifestly denied any such revolutionary impulse. In his words, "Wherever we look in the world of late Elizabethan and Jacobean magistracy and ministry we are likely to find a . . . spectacle of Calvinist paternalism, on its own terms and within its own perspectives as factious and subversive as the Homily of Obedience."[16] For Collinson, "A tradition of radical dissent and nonconformity was the most unintended of consequences" of godly rule.[17] In his most exuberant moments, Collinson has not only downplayed the revolutionary potential of puritanism, but has come close indeed to denying puritanism itself: as he phrased it on one occasion, "Jacobean Puritanism had no real ex-

---

[16] P. Collinson, *The Religion of Protestants: The Church in English Society, 1559-1625* (Oxford: Clarendon Press, 1982), 177 and passim. See also idem, "Lectures by Combination: Structures and Characteristics of Church Life in 17th Century England," in P. Collinson, *Godly People* (London: Hambledon Press, 1983).

[17] P. Collinson, "Magistracy and Ministry: A Suffolk Miniature," in Collinson, *Godly People*, 448.

istence, belonging in the eye of the beholder."[18] Instead, Collinson would argue, it was largely a polemical invention, designed by enemies to describe what was merely the most robustly protestant wing of an already deeply protestant religious establishment. Sapped of its putative revolutionary character, and firmly integrated into a broader protestant polity, puritanism seemed in Collinson's hands to be on the verge of vanishing into the dissipating vapors of a dying Whig synthesis.

Collinson has not been entirely consistent in pressing this interpretation. He has always been careful to hedge and qualify his claims, and on occasion, he has even shown signs of backing away from such arguments entirely.[19] Nevertheless, the interpretation laid out in *The Religion of Protestants* has exerted a subtle, and in some ways decisive influence over the tenor of puritan studies as they have taken shape over the past two decades.[20] One of the most visible casualties has been the concept of radical puritanism. Collinson's order-obsessed puritanism left very little room for the teeming, sectarian milieu of Hill's *World Turned Upside Down*.[21] Indeed, in laying out his portrait of a godly community devoted to the maintenance of hierarchy and order, and

---

[18] P. Collinson, *The Puritan Character: Polemics and Polarities in Early Seventeenth-Century English Culture* (Los Angeles: William Andrews Clark Memorial Library, 1989), 12. It should be noted that in this essay, as elsewhere, Collinson vacillates back and forth between this view and one in which he recognizes the reality, uniqueness, and even the revolutionary potential of puritanism. In general, however, he tends to present these qualifications as a foil for his larger, overarching vision of "puritanism" as the voluntary and extra-parochial manifestation of what was in essence an evangelical Calvinist establishment. See also P. Collinson, "A Comment: Concerning the Name Puritan," *Journal of Ecclesiastical History*, 31 (1980).

[19] Most especially in his seminal articles on Protestantism and the Elizabethan polity: P. Collinson, "Puritans, Men of Business and Elizabethan Parliaments," *Parliamentary History*, 7 (1988) and "The Monarchical Republic of Queen Elizabeth I," *Bulletin of the John Rylands Library*, 69 (1987). See also the excellent discussion in P. Collinson, "Elizabethan and Jacobean Puritanism as Forms of Popular Religious Culture," in C. Durston and J. Eales, eds., *The Culture of English Puritanism, 1560-1700* (New York: St. Martin's Press, 1996).

[20] Much of the most significant work on English religion published over the past twenty years has been explicitly "Collinsonian" in style and assumption. See, for instance, the various books and articles of Peter Lake, all of which have been informed by Collinson's work, even as they depart from his conclusions on certain key issues. See also K. Fincham, *Prelate as Pastor: The Episcopate of James I* (Oxford, 1990); T. Webster, *Godly Clergy in Early Stuart England: The Caroline Puritan Movement, c. 1620-1643* (Cambridge, 1997).

[21] In fact it might plausibly be argued that Collinson's later arguments were pointedly, albeit tacitly, directed against Christopher Hill.

fully entrenched within the Elizabethan-Jacobean establishments, Collinson has very nearly banished civil-war radicalism from the history of the period. By and large, the sects simply do not figure into his story; when they do appear, they tend to be presented as enigmatic aberrations, unexplained corruptions of the dominant, and in most respects, utterly conservative "religion of Protestants." If Hill's work paradoxically stifled the further study of radical religion, Collinson's work dealt it an unambiguous death blow, leaving the roiling, sectarian enthusiasms of the 1640s mysterious and virtually unintelligible.[22]

Untangling the Knot: Approaching the Problem of Radical Puritanism

Having arrived at this impasse, how are we to begin to piece together a coherent history of puritanism? How, in short, did Collinson's *Religion of Protestants* revert into modes of worship that were anything but orderly, deferential, and conservative? How, likewise, did a seemingly staid community, committed to the preservation of hierarchy and social harmony, erupt into the chaotic world of name-calling, recrimination, and hysterical polemic that included not only sectaries, but their more conservative puritan enemies of the revolutionary decades? These questions are hardly peripheral to the field of early modern English history. In many ways, they hold the key to understanding the development and direction of events in the 1640s and 1650s. For it is only once we have reconstructed the process whereby the godly community shattered into an array of competing politico-religious factions that we will be able to make sense of the broader fragmentation of the Parliamentary cause during the 1640s and 1650s. Arguably, then, to understand the disintegration of the puritan cause is to understand the course of the English Revolution.

It should be stated at the outset that the point of this study is not to reject Collinson's insights. He has awakened historians to a facet of godly religion that has too often been ignored by scholars bent on attributing to puritans a neatly revolutionary pedigree. His research has established beyond question

[22] It is perhaps a tribute to the thoroughness with which the subject has lain fallow that the most important intellectual history of the origins of radical puritanism, G. F. Nuttall's *The Holy Spirit in Puritan Faith and Experience* (Oxford: Blackwell, 1946) was published more than a half-century ago. Charting godly presentations of the doctrine of the holy spirit, Nuttall emphasized continuities of style and interest bridging the gap between radicals and their mainstream predecessors, arguing that the emergence of civil-war radicalism represented a natural evolution of tendencies that had always been strongly present in godly piety. The following study incorporates aspects of Nuttall's argument.

the extent to which godly personnel and ideals seeped into (indeed, in some ways, constituted) the post-Elizabethan sociopolitical order. It would be a great blunder to reject his crucial insights in favor of a return to a vision of puritanism as an unrelentingly revolutionary force, locked in a death struggle against an implacable Anglican establishment. It is possible, however, to discern two notable weaknesses in Collinson's argument, taken on its own terms. First, he has perhaps understated the extent to which even the most conservative and order-obsessed godly magistrates carried with them, as a consequence of their beliefs, a potential for disruptive, even rebellious behaviors. Impulses that were, under certain circumstances, directed against the sins of the unruly and ungodly masses could, under other circumstances, be directed against bishops, magistrates, other puritans, and even the Crown. Secondly, and more importantly for the purposes of the present study, there are considerable difficulties in attempting to define puritanism as a single, monolithic entity, with a unified ideology. Collinson's paternalistic, orderly, and hierarchical "religion of Protestants" may well have existed, but it was part of a spectrum of belief and practice that included rather less amiably conservative ideals and individuals.

To suggest that the godly community was more heterogeneous than is normally assumed is not to argue that it was pluralistic or "tolerant" in the modern senses of those words. Indeed, throughout the early seventeenth century the puritan community was wracked by a series of contentious internal disputes over the nature of true religion. These controversies were generally conducted informally and semiprivately, within the cloistered confines of a world built and inhabited by godly insiders. Here, in the dimly lit corridors of what Peter Lake and I have termed the "puritan underground," manuscripts and polemical position papers passed from hand to hand, as disagreeing individuals and factions vied to establish the validity of their respective arguments; irascible preachers denounced one another from their pulpits in contests of ministerial charisma and authority; laymen and clerics alike gathered for informal conferences to hammer out disputed issues; rumors and stories burned like wildfire along the tightly knit webs of association that bound together the godly community. All of these mechanisms were in theory designed to allow the spiritually well-endowed to defuse conflict and settle doctrinal disputes quietly and without resort to the distasteful process of official intervention or open, public recrimination. Only occasionally—when disputes grew particularly acrimonious and informal mechanisms of arbitration had broken down—did these events come to the attention of the broader public, either because of the involvement of the authorities, or because one or more of the offended parties opted to advertise the dispute in print. Since the godly were eager to keep these sometimes embarrassing disputes to themselves, modern scholars, like those in the ecclesiastical hierarchy, have remained only vaguely aware of them.[23]

Lake and I have, however, tried to reconstruct this hidden underworld of debate, using it to stake out a preliminary approach to the problem of puritan fragmentation and the related issue of radical puritan origins. We have argued that this subterranean world of intra-puritan debate—with its circulating manuscripts, its informal colloquies, its clerical rivalries, its welcoming attitude toward lay activism, its chaotic circles of gossip and rumor, and its (theoretically) self-regulating mechanisms of dispute settlement—contained within it the seeds of the much more dramatic theological infighting of the 1640s. This might be termed a "structural" approach to the question of the origins of radical puritanism: on this account, the culture of the godly community in itself contained a structural tendency toward faction, division, and theological fragmentation. This tendency, which prior to the wars remained subdued and hidden, became more pronounced as the external pressures of Caroline rule began to place new stresses on the integrity of the godly community. After 1641, the lid was ripped off entirely. Once censorship collapsed, and once the unifying enemy of the Laudian episcopal hierarchy had been removed, this underground world of theological dispute and ministerial in-fighting rose to the surface; accelerated by the intense, high-stakes political environment of the 1640s, the process of fragmentation and division that had expressed itself sporadically and quietly in the years prior to the Long Parliament now evolved rapidly into an open and hostile circus of bitter printed polemic and desperate political maneuver. From this perspective, social mechanisms, impulses, and conventions that were at the heart of the culture of English puritanism (and that were in many ways indicative of a Collinsonian impulse towards order, orthodoxy, and consensus) thus led, albeit unintentionally, to the ultimate disintegration of the puritan community itself.[24]

Although Lake and I opted to emphasize these "structural" features, choosing to gloss over the substantive matters of doctrinal content at issue in these acrimonious contests, we also made it clear that such substantive issues did exist. In the early years of the century, significant and sometimes hostile debate had erupted within the godly community over a broad range of theological flashpoints, including justification by faith, predestination, the continuing validity of infants' baptism, the nature of the coming apocalypse, the legitimacy of the government of the Church of England, and even the divinity of

---

[23] P. Lake and D. Como, "'Orthodoxy' and Its Discontents: Dispute Settlement and the Production of 'Consensus' in the London (Puritan) 'Underground,'" *Journal of British Studies*, 39 (2000).
[24] Ibid.

Christ.[25] Some of these debates carried over into the 1640s, giving shape to later, more celebrated disputes. Of these, the most serious was surely the debate over what would come to be called antinomianism. This fierce struggle engendered deep fissures, animating controversy and leading to ever more divisive polemical battles. The result was the emergence of a self-conscious, and in many respects coherent ideological challenge to mainstream puritanism, one that was nurtured within an emergent underground community, and which would come to have a direct and palpable influence on the dramatic process of fragmentation that took place in the 1640s. Like Edward Fisher, numerous veterans of what I here term the "antinomian underground" would go on to play crucial roles in the religious ferment of the revolutionary years. So too, many of the more distinctive and peculiar strains of radical religion that emerged during the civil wars evolved directly out of the antinomian counter-ideology here described. In short, the antinomian community of pre–civil war England served as a spawning ground for later forms of sectarian religiosity, both in terms of ideological content and personnel. What follows, then, may be seen as a detailed inquiry into the origins of radical puritanism, one that takes into account not only the broad structural features of puritanism that conditioned the process of sectarian fragmentation, but which also traces, in a

[25] Many of these examples of intra-puritan conflict have not been properly explored in the existing literature, and it is my hope to elucidate them in the future. The disputes over imputation involved the celebrated minister Anthony Wotton and his followers; for the disputes over predestination see D. Como, "Puritans, Predestination and the Construction of 'Orthodoxy' in Early Seventeenth Century England," in P. Lake and M. Questier, eds., *Conformity and Orthodoxy in the English Church, c. 1560-1642* (Woodbridge: Boydell and Brewer, 2000); conflicts over infant baptism famously began with the self-baptism of John Smith and continued to excite controversy down to the 1630s, when Anabaptism emerged as a more serious problem within the London godly community; tensions over Millenarianism first emerged with the well-known writings of Thomas Brightman, increasing in scope during the 1620s. For a preliminary discussion of the matter, see D. Como, "Women, Prophecy and Authority in Early Stuart Puritanism," *Huntington Library Quarterly*, 61 (1998); earlier struggles over the Trinity had taken place during confrontations with the so-called "Legatine-Arians" in the first decade of the seventeenth century. Other, more localized, permutations of puritanism (including the piety of the religious renegade Thomas Leamer) appeared sporadically throughout the early seventeenth century. In addition, there were more minor, but nonetheless significant, distinctions in the precise contours of puritan practical divinity, especially after 1620. While this book focuses on discussions surrounding the Moral Law, readers should by no means assume that this was the only intellectual tension or fault line afflicting the early Stuart puritan community.

direct and exhaustive manner, the single most important ideological progenitor of later forms of sectarian religion.[26]

Puritans, Antinomians, and the Fragmentation of the Godly Community

The present study is by no means the first to argue for the importance of antinomianism. Its significance as a radical permutation of puritanism has long been recognized. On both sides of the Atlantic, it exerted a powerful, if poorly understood, influence over the seventeenth-century English-speaking world. One need only peruse the pages of Thomas Edwards's heresiographical masterpiece, *Gangraena*, to get a sense of the significance, real or imagined, that contemporaries attached to the phenomenon in civil-war England. Side by side with the horrors of anabaptism, antinomianism seemed in the public imagination to be a ghastly symbol of the fragmentation and social anomie unleashed by the catastrophic events of the 1640s. More recently, scholars such as Hill and A. L. Morton have seconded this seventeenth-century thesis, according antinomianism a central place in the profound, indeed revolutionary, social transformations that gripped mid-century England.[27] It is no less important to the history of colonial America, for as is well known, the Massachusetts Bay Colony had itself been convulsed by its own "Antinomian Controversy" less than a decade before the outbreak of the English civil wars. Scholars have generally viewed this bitter conflict as the decisive and formative event in the history of first-generation New England, and not without just cause: had the forces of Anne Hutchinson, John Wheelwright, and (most especially) Henry Vane "won" the Antinomian Controversy, it seems certain that English colonists would have carved out a very different pattern of settlement in the forbidding soils of Massachusetts and Connecticut.

Nonetheless, owing in large part to the historiographical trends analyzed above, the early history of this phenomenon has remained obscure. We possess no overarching account of how and why English antinomianism came into being. The only monographic treatment of the subject, Gertrude Huehns's 1951 *Antinomianism in English History: With Special Reference to the Period*

[26] To put it somewhat differently, where Lake and I analyzed "structure," the following account emphasizes "content." Only with both forms of analysis—running in parallel and overlapping—can we fully understand the remarkable events and movements of the 1640s.

[27] C. Hill, *The World Turned Upside Down: Radical Ideas During the English Revolution* (New York, Viking Press, 1972; Penguin Paperback Reprint, 1991); idem, "Antinomianism," in C. Hill, *Liberty Against the Law: Some Seventeenth-Century Controversies* (London: Allen Lane, The Penguin Press, 1996); A. L. Morton, *The World of the Ranters: Religious Radicalism in the English Revolution* (London: Lawrence and Wishart, 1970).

1640-1660, contained a bare fifteen pages on the period prior to 1640.[28] Like Hill and Morton after her, Huehns began in midstream, concerning herself primarily with what she perceived to be the social and political effects of antinomianism during the years of civil war and Protectorate. And like them, she relied almost entirely on the inexhaustibly rich fountain of print material generated by the unfettered presses of the revolutionary decades. Such an approach, however, was almost guaranteed to overlook the origins of the phenomenon she was examining, for antinomianism had in fact taken shape, furtively and outside the printed domain, during the years of early Stuart ecclesiastical censorship. Thus, many of the most crucial sources for the study of England's first antinomians are to be found not in the printed literature of the day, but buried in scattered manuscript collections. As a consequence, despite the considerable efforts of these scholars, the origins and exact ideological nature of the movement have remained more or less unintelligible, even up to the present day. In this vein, a recent and influential collection of essays exploring radical religion during the English civil wars devoted chapters to the Anabaptists, Quakers, Fifth Monarchists, even the elusive Seekers and Ranters, while discreetly passing over the subject of antinomianism.[29] Reflecting this historiographical lacuna, one of the foremost authorities on civil-war religion recently felt at ease remarking that "The rise of antinomianism is as spectral as the rise of the middle class."[30] Indeed, it would not be going too far to say that in spite of the considerable scholarly weight that has been attached to the phenomenon, not only is there no coherent historiography of antinomianism, but we possess no coherent definition of antinomianism.

The following study seeks to fill this void. As we shall see, this is not a simple task, for early Stuart antinomianism was a complex and multivalent movement. It does not lend itself to easy or monochromatic description. To arrive at a satisfying account, we must therefore move through successive layers of definition, which incrementally complement one another to form a unified portrait of the movement as a whole, all the while supplementing printed sources with hitherto unknown or underutilized manuscript materials. Thus, the second chapter of this study provides an overview of the history and nature of early Stuart antinomianism. It first offers a brief, thumbnail description of the theological characteristics of antinomianism; second, it provides an examination of the movement's origins, followed by an attempt to elucidate the

---

[28] Gertrude Huehns, *Antinomianism in English History: With Special Reference to the Period 1640-1660* (London: The Cresset Press, 1951), 55-70; the same is true of T. Cooper, *Fear and Polemic in Seventeenth-Century England: Richard Baxter and Antinomianism* (Aldershot: Ashgate, 2001), 15-26.

[29] McGregor and Reay, eds., *Radical Religion*, passim.

[30] J. C. Davis, "Against Formality: One Aspect of the English Revolution," in *Transactions of the Royal Historical Society*, 6th ser., 3 (1993), 287n102.

cultural mechanisms whereby antinomianism spread and perpetuated itself; third, it lays out the complex network of personal associations that, at a most basic level, defined an increasingly self-conscious antinomian community. Chapter Three provides an extensive description of the conflicts mentioned by Edward Fisher—London's antinomian controversy of 1628 to 1631. The arguments made in Chapters Two and Three are, however, worthless apart from the subsequent chapters, each of which attempts to clarify the ideological or intellectual content of antinomianism. The narrative, prosopographical, and cultural history provided in the second and third chapters thus erects the framework within which the subsequent chapters must be understood, while the intellectual-theological materials analyzed in Chapters Four through Ten validate and flesh out the claims made in Chapter Two and Three. Indeed, it is only through such a process of layered, incremental definition that we can even see what qualified antinomianism as a "movement" unto itself. From one perspective, then, this book may be considered as an extended exercise in definition.

The resulting account serves to transform our understanding of a range of critical events and phenomena that have thus far remained poorly understood. As this book progresses, it shall become clear, for instance, that the present study serves in important ways to elucidate New England's Antinomian Controversy. New England's troubles have hardly been ignored by modern scholars; indeed, the most important recent insights on the subject of English antinomianism have flowed not from students of British history, but from colonial Americanists—James Maclear, William Stoever, Stephen Foster, Janice Knight, Dwight Bozeman, and Michael Winship—all of whom have turned attention to England in order to decipher the monumentally contorted theological debates that beset the Bay Colony between 1636 and 1638.[31] This study incorporates their insights, and seeks to extend their project farther, providing what

---

[31] See J. Maclear, "'The Heart of New England Rent': The Mystical Element in Early Puritan History," *Mississippi Valley Historical Review*, 42 (1956); idem, "Anne Hutchinson and the Mortalist Heresy," *New England Quarterly*, 54 (1981); S. Foster, "New England and the Challenge of Heresy, 1630 to 1660: The Puritan Crisis in Transatlantic Perspective," *William and Mary Quarterly*, 38 (1981); William Stoever, *"A Faire and Easie Way to Heaven": Covenant Theology and Antinomianism in Early Massachusetts* (Middletown, Connecticut: Wesleyan University Press, 1978); Janice Knight, *Orthodoxies in Massachusetts: Rereading American Puritanism* (Cambridge, MA: Harvard University Press, 1994); M. Winship, "'The Most Glorious Church in the World': The Unity of the Godly in Boston, Massachusetts, in the 1630s," *Journal of British Studies*, 39 (2000); T. D. Bozeman, "The Glory of the 'Third Time': John Eaton as Contra-Puritan," *Journal of Ecclesiastical History*, 47 (1996). Bozeman alone among these historians concerns himself entirely with antinomianism considered in its English dimensions.

might be viewed as a prolegomenon to the study of New England's Antinomian Controversy. The following book suggests that Massachusetts's Controversy was, in many crucial ways, a reprise of earlier battles that had been fought in London. The exact manner in which this was the case will be more fully laid out in the conclusion. It shall be contended that the disputes considered below worked to condition and shape the terms of debate and categories of interpretation with which the contestants in Massachusetts understood their own conflict. While the details of New England's Antinomian Controversy lie beyond the purview of this book, it is hoped that this study and the preliminary comments offered here shall provide fertile material for future historians seeking to unravel the troubles in Massachusetts Bay.[32]

In a more direct manner, the research presented here serves to transform our understanding of the emergence of radical puritanism. The present author is at one with scholars such as Hill, Morton, and Nigel Smith, who have seen antinomianism as crucial to the anarchic and fecund religious scene of the English civil wars.[33] So, too, it is in my opinion beyond doubt that sectarian puritanism was disproportionately implicated in many of the most earth-shaking political and intellectual changes of the seventeenth century. The cacophonous milieu of extreme puritanism—a world inhabited by Baptists, Levellers, Diggers, Ranters, Fifth Monarchists, and Quakers, not to mention myriad groupings forgotten by posterity—bequeathed to Anglo-American culture some of its most distinctive and peculiar politico-religious traits, including religious toleration, denominational pluralism, and a political egalitarianism that would resonate down to the present. By tracing the history of antinomianism, the following study thus begins to piece together the story of how these strikingly original, transformative, and, in many cases, disruptive ideas emerged from the unlikely seedbed of early seventeenth-century English culture, never fully to disappear.

The picture that emerges does not fit neatly into existing historiographical accounts. For a start, it calls into question Hill's thesis concerning a distinctive and largely autonomous tradition of sectarianism flowing parallel to a dominant, bourgeois puritanism of the "middling sort." Hill was correct in that there were most certainly crucial heterodox influences at work in the development of antinomianism; nevertheless, even these influences had their effect within the context of the broader puritan community. Antinomianism was from the very beginning a direct response to predominant modes of puritan

---

[32] For a recent and outstanding revisionist account of the New England controversies, see M. Winship, *Making Heretics: Militant Protestantism and Free Grace in Massachusetts, 1636-1641* (Princeton: Princeton University Press, 2002).

[33] See Nigel Smith, *Perfection Proclaimed: Language and Literature in English Radical Religion* (Oxford: Clarendon Press, 1989).

piety (a rough and informal synthesis described throughout this book as "mainstream" puritan divinity). It represented an evolutionary trend within puritanism, rather than a separate and discrete stream flowing from a distinct source. Even as it departed from this broader synthesis, then, many of the central cultural features of antinomianism were in fact direct outgrowths or amplifications upon important aspects of mainstream puritanism.

Moreover, where Hill saw class as the underlying factor shaping the development of radical religion, the following study locates the crux of the matter first and foremost in theology and practical divinity—what divided antinomians from their mainstream puritan counterparts was not class, but rather differing conceptions of the godly life and differing conceptions of how a believer arrived at salvation. This is not to argue that the disputes between antinomians and their mainstream godly counterparts were purely theological; in many cases, the theological conflicts at stake had undeniable social overtones or resonances. Thus, the theological wranglings between antinomians and their enemies were hopelessly intertwined with tensions surrounding the relationship between the godly clergy and their lay followers; with questions about the precise status of believers with regard to the external and coercive framework of ecclesiastical and political authority; and, as Lake and I have noted, with structural idiosyncrasies inherent in the patterns of sociability, discourse, and communal worship that at a most basic level defined the godly community. Nevertheless, all of these undeniably social components of the dispute were sidebars, or appendages, to what was at base an intellectual or theological debate.

Nor is this to exclude "class" from our account. As Hill rightly intuited, by the 1640s, antinomianism had become deeply interwoven with emerging ideas of political and social egalitarianism, and as we shall see below, in at least one case, an early, antinomianizing version of religion did indeed become intimately tied to a radical, perhaps even subversive, social vision as early as 1615.[34] Even this single instance is complicated and ambiguous, however, and it appears that despite certain egalitarian tendencies, pre–civil war antinomianism was not distinguished by an explicit or aggressive social radicalism. Nor, to judge from such scant evidence as survives, was it a religiosity of the lower orders. The emergence of socially radicalized brands of antinomianism would come only later, apparently as certain tendencies and features of prewar antinomianism were liberated and accentuated in the crucible of civil war and political conflict. This rather more complicated story lies beyond the scope of this book. Nonetheless, when that story comes to be told, it will necessarily begin with the framework provided in this study.

---

[34] See below, Chapter Five, for the early career of John Traske.

Finally, and perhaps most importantly, the present work serves to alter the way we look at early Stuart puritanism, considered more broadly. For, as the preceding discussion suggests, what follows is not merely a study of antinomianism, construed as an isolated intellectual or theological movement. Antinomianism cannot be understood apart from the puritan community as a whole. Given that it took shape in opposition to reigning modes of puritan divinity, this study is intimately concerned with mainstream puritanism, understood as the negative referent out of which and against which antinomian modes of religiosity developed. Along these lines, in his incisive recent study of the antinomian heresiarch John Eaton, T .D. Bozeman has suggested that antinomianism "is not well conceived as a type of radical Puritanism. It was less a radicalisation of historic Puritan doctrine and more an oblique or tangential development whose conscious effort was to obliterate that doctrine and replace it with an entirely new point of view. Since a non-disciplinary Puritanism—that is, a Puritanism without passion for moral control and purity—is a patent contradiction in terms, that synthesis is best designated *contra-* and *post-*Puritan."[35]

This study follows Bozeman in his contention that antinomianism represented a rejection of many of the most hallowed priorities of puritan religiosity. Nevertheless, it will likewise be contended that for all their rancor against prevailing styles of godly divinity, even the most enthusiastic first-generation antinomians remained inextricably embedded in what might be called the cultural landscape of early Stuart puritanism.[36] So far as we can tell, all of the

---

[35] Bozeman, "Glory of the 'Third Time,'" 654.

[36] The following study defines puritanism as a cultural, rather than political, doctrinal or ecclesiological, phenomenon. On this view, the godly community is seen as constituted by a set of shared cultural traits—devotion to word-centered religion, shared modes of speech and behavior, an affection for Calvinist or reformed divinity, deep suspicion of Popery in all its forms, to name a few of the most important—rather than by commitment to a specific doctrinal or disciplinary platform. In this schema, the demands of the godly for liturgical or ecclesiastical reform may be viewed as part and parcel of a broader set of cultural characteristics, facets of a more general mode of piety or religiosity, which continued to survive and evolve within a puritan subculture long after the assumed death of presbyterianism at Hampton Court in 1604. At its most concrete level, this puritan subculture was defined by distinctive modes of language, behavior, and social interaction. These included peculiar forms of devotion, such as sermon-gadding, public and private fasting and, above all, informal meetings for prayer and discussion, which were known amongst puritans as "conferences" or "communion," and to outsiders as "conventicles." Although less amenable to historical investigation, there is good reason to believe that in their behavior, dress, and speech—aspects of life that fell under the contemporary rubric of "conversation"—the godly shared particular styles that set them apart from other members of early modern English

major proponents of antinomian or anti-legal religion had been raised in the milieu of (often radical) English puritanism.[37] Like mainstream puritans, antinomians were utterly devoted to logocentric styles of piety, in which the word preached remained the focus of all true worship. Like mainstream puritans, antinomians gadded to sermons, met in "conventicles," and remained at best indifferent, and at worst, overtly hostile, toward the increasingly elaborate liturgy of the English church. They drew on linguistic and theological motifs that were common currency throughout the godly community: as Edward Fisher put it, even the most licentious antinomians "talke like believers, and . . . have language like Saints." They spread and nurtured their message using the very same cultural mechanisms—manuscript exchange, pastoral letters, private meetings—that were central to the culture of English puritanism. And even as they attacked mainstream puritan ministers, and began to forge their own, self-conscious communities of believers, antinomians remained entangled within the webs of social and personal association—networks of kinship, shared knowledge, and personal acquaintance—that at the most basic level defined the godly community. They traveled in the same circles as their opponents, and (most significantly) competed for the loyalties of the very same people, the godly laity, from whom they seem to have drawn most, if not all, of their followers. From the beginning, then, antinomianism was a subculture within the larger English godly community, an underground within an underground. This study is designed to explain how this could be so, to chart both

---

society; these styles both defined the community, and defined individuals as members of the community. Finally, as in all subcultures, puritans were bound together first and foremost by bonds of personal association. They married one another, sent their children to study under godly tutors, and ate and drank with other puritans. It is the contention of this book that even as they negated and rejected certain aspects of mainstream puritan culture, antinomians accepted or modified others, remaining in many ways inextricably embedded within the wider culture of puritan religiosity. It should be noted that this view of puritanism owes much to the discussion in Collinson, "Elizabethan and Jacobean Puritanism."

[37] The various protagonists of this book will be introduced as we progress. For now, it is simply worth noting that all of our surviving evidence suggests that leading antinomians emerged from the mainstream puritan community. Thus, Peter Shaw was almost certainly the son of the Lancashire puritan minister Leonard Shaw, for which see Chapter Eight, below; John Eaton had been a student of the moderate puritan Ephraim Pagitt, as Pagitt confessed in his *Heresiography, or A Description of the Hereticks and Sectaries of these Latter Times*, Sixth ed. (1662), 121; John Traske tellingly referred to his parents as "godly" in the prefatory epistle of his *A Treatise of Libertie From Judaisme* (1620); the spiritual diary of Ellis Crispe, father of Tobias Crispe, survives, and shows a classically godly temperament and worldview (Congregational Church Library MS. I. f. 2); for Roger Brearley's early puritanism, see Chapter Eight, below.

the differences and similarities between mainstream puritans and their antinomian opponents. Put another way, it is the burden of this study to explain how a man like Edward Fisher could carry behind him a past that admitted both a conversion experience at the hands of Thomas Hooker, and a seemingly irreconcilable set of associations to Giles Creech's "Familists, Antinomians, Anabaptists, and the like."

What follows is therefore the story of a dialogue—a sometimes acrimonious conversation—that took place within puritanism itself. The contest between mainstream puritans and their antinomian critics was, at bottom, a contest to define and delimit the nature and shape of true "godliness." It was a war for the souls of the men and women one antinomian called "God's People," a struggle to control the contours and future of the godly community. If the resulting view of puritanism departs from that promulgated by Hill, so too it tends to run against the grain of the Collinsonian interpretation, with its emphasis on order and hierarchy, and its insistence on the close ties between godly elites and the early Stuart political and ecclesiastical establishments.[38] The following account by no means denies that such ties existed; it does, however, seek to break down the notion that the godly community may be characterized as a single, seamless entity. Rather, this study envisions puritanism not as a homogeneous ideology, but as a fractured landscape, a community in which distinctive and in some senses, competing, visions of right religion vied for the attentions of a laity whose imaginative universe was shaped and sustained through incessant engagement with the Christian scriptures.

This view is elaborated most extensively in Chapter Five, "The Kingdom of Traske: The Early Career of John Traske and the Origins of Antinomianism," but in fact it permeates this entire study: the puritan community, I would like to argue, was a heterogeneous and, in some senses, conflicted one, and this was the case many years before the fractious events of the 1640s. As noted above, the conflicts over the Law represent just one of several, intersecting intellectual fissures that opened up within the godly community during the dec-

---

[38] See Collinson, *The Religion of Protestants*, passim; other studies which have in certain respects tended to support the Collinsonian picture include P. Lake, *Moderate Puritans and the Elizabethan Church* (Cambridge: Cambridge University Press, 1982); Fincham, *Prelate as Pastor*; all of these accounts owe much to the work of Nicholas Tyacke. It should be emphasized that although Lake, Fincham, and Tyacke have at times stressed the extent to which the godly were integrated into the English establishment, none has effaced the distinctiveness or existence of a freestanding puritan movement or culture. See N. Tyacke, *The Fortunes of English Puritanism, 1603-1640* (London: Dr. Williams Trust, 1990); P. Lake, "Defining Puritanism—again?" in F. J. Bremer, *Puritanism: Transatlantic Perspectives on a Seventeenth-Century Anglo-American Faith* (Boston: Massachusetts Historical Society, 1993).

ades prior to the English civil wars. Nevertheless, the debates over the Moral Law were without question the most widespread and disruptive of these intra-puritan conflicts. By telling the story of antinomianism, and by reconstructing the manner in which mainstream puritans mobilized the cultural media available to them to identify, silence, and undermine their antinomian critics, we unveil a puritanism—factious, diverse, and, to some extent, divided against itself— that has for the most part been forgotten or ignored by recent scholars. It was a puritanism that was capable—by virtue of its own peculiar cultural characteristics and its own internal dynamics—of giving birth both to zealous Calvinist magistrates, and to the anarchic and revolutionary sects of the civil war and Interregnum. In retelling this tale, then, we begin to piece together the complex process through which the Parliamentarian front imploded and disintegrated during the 1640s and 1650s, an implosion that would have a dramatic and lasting impact upon the ultimate course of seventeenth-century English history.

CHAPTER 2

The Sinews of the Antinomian Underground

The Nature of Antinomianism

The precise ideological contours of antinomianism shall be laid out in detail in succeeding chapters. Nonetheless, we must at the outset make an effort to determine what we mean when we use the word. What follows is a brief and compressed overview of the conclusions that are worked out at greater length below. Much like the term "puritan," the word "antinomian" (together with siblings such as "antinomist," "libertine," or "Familist") was primarily a hostile term of abuse, often used imprecisely, sloppily or maliciously for polemical purposes. Those accused of antinomianism rarely, if ever, accepted the appellation. Nevertheless, as with the terms "puritan" and "puritanism," "antinomian" and "antinomianism" referred to a recognizable and real phenomenon, a series of shared intellectual, theological, and behavioral characteristics that set certain individuals apart from their "non-antinomian" counterparts. The word was used to describe individuals who said and did very specific things. Moreover, those who found themselves stigmatized as antinomians may not have liked the moniker, but they were fully aware that there existed very real differences between them and their opponents. That the word was used polemically and often imprecisely should not therefore blind us to the fact that those accused of antinomianism evinced a set of very particular traits and characteristics that bound them together with one another, set them apart from others, and provoked the animus of their critics. These characteristics are best described as a set of tendencies. For as we shall see below, there were in some respects significant intellectual differences between figures who can be usefully described as "antinomian." Nevertheless, in spite of differences in emphasis or details of argumentation, all of these figures exhibited, to a greater or lesser degree, each of the following tendencies.

Chief among these characteristics was, of course, a propensity to argue that the Mosaic Law, including the Decalogue, was in some sense abolished, abrogated, or superseded for Christians. This tendency in many ways defined and distinguished them from their contemporaries, serving as a rallying point for their evangelical efforts and a focal point for the polemic of opponents (hence, the epithet "antinomian," meaning one who opposes the law). Yet denial of the Law was only one aspect of a more complicated mode of religiosity. For in proclaiming themselves free from the Mosaic code, antinomians were, as noted above, negating a particular version of pastoral divinity that had come to dominate the puritan community in the late sixteenth and early seventeenth centuries.

This mode of practical divinity will be the subject of Chapter Four, but its basic shape may be described here. For all their attachment to the doctrines of predestination, unmerited grace, and justification by faith, English puritans had from a very early stage stressed the importance, indeed the preeminence, of moral, social, and personal reformation. The life of faith as envisioned by godly preachers involved a strenuous and unremitting struggle to do God's will in the world—that is, to extirpate sin and to exalt and glorify God by promoting and performing his Law. In practical terms, this translated into a rigorous and disciplined mode of piety, which included Sabbatarianism, fasting, and careful self-examination, as well as intense hostility to perceived sins such as sexual immorality, drunkenness, and ceremonial idolatry. Sanctification (the lifelong process of purging sin and striving towards holiness), zealous application of the "means of grace," and continuing repentance for transgression were taken to be the marrow of the godly life, the chief tokens and signs of a true, lively, and justifying faith. It was this rigid and preponderant obsession with divine precept and sanctification that was rejected, and rejected totally, by antinomian teachers. Those who earned the epithet "antinomian" all saw mainstream godly divinity as a new form of works-righteousness, an outward, literal, and "legalistic" religiosity that nurtured a slavish devotion to the Law. Hence, godly preachers were routinely likened to "Jews," "rabbis," or "papists," while antinomian prophets often claimed to be promoting the true Christian messages of free grace and justification by faith, entirely apart from any works, legal or otherwise. This aggressive polemical posture—which throughout this study shall be termed *anti-legalism*—was shared by all antinomians, serving as our second identifying tendency.

Thus, at a practical level, the claim that the Mosaic Law no longer applied to Christians was less a rejection of all morality than a repudiation of the practices and demands of puritan pastoral divinity. In this vein, the most robust antinomians dismissed Sabbatarianism and fasting as Judaic, or "monkish" practices. Christians who consoled themselves by supplicating or praying to God, hearing sermons—indeed with the performance of any "duties"—were said to be trapped in a legal or literal servitude to external elements. Most of all, the tendency of the godly to see sanctification, outward holiness, and moral reformation as evidence for divine love or grace, was denounced by antinomians as a pharisaical error. Nevertheless, in constructing this critique of mainstream puritan divinity, antinomians paradoxically borrowed rhetorical and theological resources from the reformed/puritan tradition, revealing a third identifying tendency of antinomianism—the propensity to use images and motifs common to puritanism to attack mainstream puritanism itself.

In this way, for instance, antinomians often portrayed themselves (in piously protestant fashion) as heirs of a long-standing legacy of anti-pharisaism that had passed from Christ to Paul to Augustine to Luther to themselves. Against the strenuous, active faith of mainstream puritanism, they stressed the total passivity of the believer, providing us with a fourth indicator of the antinomian impulse. Each of the antinomian thinkers examined in this study maintained that no act of human effort or will could do anything to earn salvation or assurance, both of which were to come solely from the overwhelming power of Christ's life and death (or, in certain formulations, through the inhabitation of Christ's spirit in the believer's soul). One and all, the figures examined below showed a marked tendency to emphasize the utter sinfulness and inability of naked human effort, while celebrating and emphasizing the raw and irresistible power of the divine will.

Curiously, however, even as they cried down the human will, arguing for the thoroughly abased, impotent, and empty nature of human selfhood, all antinomians likewise showed a paradoxical tendency to claim that believers in their post-conversion state were transformed into exalted (and on some accounts, supernatural) beings. While this exalted status was always assumed to flow from God, this fifth tendency nevertheless belied, or at least complicated, antinomian claims to be celebrating the sovereignty of God alone, as against neo-pharisaical mainstream puritans, who championed the power of man. So, too, it undermined their occasional claims to be merely promoting an unvarnished Protestantism, for their arguments concerning the status of regenerate believers were more extreme than anything seen among mainline reformed authorities.

Freedom from the Law was, of course, the most obvious aspect of the believer's newly exalted status. So powerful was Christ's sacrifice that it fulfilled and abolished, once and for all, the Law of Moses, at least for those who came to possess a true faith. Those who participated in the benefits of Christ's righteousness and death were thus free from the Law and consequently from sin itself, at least in the sight of God. This tendency to pronounce believers in some sense free from sin may be seen as a sixth shared characteristic.[1] Once again, it must be emphasized that the claim that believers were free from sin was intimately related to an attack on mainstream puritan piety: where godly preachers continually exhorted their listeners to scrutinize themselves for sin and to prostrate themselves in humble, sorrowful repentance for their lapses, antinomians argued that such tortured self-examination and continued hand-wringing betrayed a dead, legal professor, who had not yet experienced the glorious transformation and deliverance from sin that followed on God's grace in Christ. Against this "joylesse mourning"—this "pernitious carking care, that cuts the throate of all true Religion"—anti-legalists emphasized the exultant, liberatory, and joyful effects of divine grace, which was said to free the believer from fear and wrath.[2] Here, then, was a seventh, crucial characteristic of antinomian religiosity—the propensity to offer believers a sense of assurance and joy that was more total, more satisfying, and more final than anything to be found in mainstream puritanism.

It must be made absolutely clear at the outset, however, that freedom from sin did not equal freedom to sin. Despite the persistent charges of libertinism hurled at them by their opponents, all surviving early Stuart antinomian texts maintained that true believers would, in reality, obey God's will, despite the fact that they were free from the Law. Each and every figure examined in the course of this book argued that the faithful would do good works. Their good works, however, would be done not out of external compulsion, but by virtue of a new, internalized principle that flowed from true belief. It is this argument—pressed with special vehemence by each of the major antinomian propagandists—which, perhaps more than any other, set antinomians apart from their opponents, and defined them as a distinctive group in the world. Indeed, it may be said to have provided the underlying, emotional foundation for the more celebrated antinomian claim that believers were free from the Law: where pharisaical puritans obeyed out of fear and terror, carefully molding their lives to conform to the external rule of the Moral Law, true believers would obey God freely and joyfully without any extrinsic prompting at all. They needed no extrinsic, legal whip, for they possessed something within them that enabled them to do the things of God without fear of punishment or hope of reward. This intangible "something" was often taken to be Love, which was juxtaposed over and against the Law by a number of antinomian propagandists.

---

[1] Again, however, the reader should bear in mind that different antinomian spokesmen formulated this message in different ways.

[2] The quotation is drawn from John Traske, *The True Gospel Vindicated, From the Reproach of a New Gospel* (n.p., 1636), 38.

In its most extreme manifestations, however, this argument slipped easily into dangerously heterodox territory. For while some antinomian spokesmen contended that the internal principle guiding believers was simply a new disposition of love and thanksgiving, others pushed further, arguing that believers were enabled to obey without the Law because they were somehow inhabited by the Holy Spirit or by Christ himself. Such believers were often said to possess "the mind of Christ," a crucial antinomian catchphrase. This represented the most radical expression of the antinomian tendency to exalt converted Christians, for on this view, true believers were rendered in some sense divine, even as they walked on earth. While this perspective was not universally accepted among those categorized in this book as antinomians, it was an argument canvassed often enough in antinomian circles that it merits comment at the outset.

Antinomianism thus set forth a message calculated to exploit the deepest fears, doubts and insecurities of godly lay people, to tap into dissatisfaction with the strenuous, unforgiving nature of mainstream puritan piety. Although this mainstream mode of piety seems to have proved sufficient for the large majority of godly people, there can be little question that for some men and women, the disciplines, demands, and general tenor of normative puritanism proved to be a passageway into despair and insecurity. For such people, as for those who may have resented the authoritarian claims of the traditional puritan ministry, antinomianism provided a ray of hope, a profoundly attractive alternative religiosity equally rooted in scripture, but—with its exalted claims about the effects of divine grace and the transcendent status of those who embraced the faith—eminently more assuring than its mainstream counterpart. It should be evident, moreover, that the antinomian critique achieved much of its polemical and rhetorical resonance by mobilizing some of the most emotionally powerful motifs of the protestant tradition—such as free grace and justification by faith alone—against the godly themselves. In their battle for the affections of the puritan laity, anti-legalists were thus able to promote themselves as the true heirs of Luther at a time when sensitivities over questions of works, grace, freewill, and predestination were growing steadily as a result of the prevalence of Arminianism in the church. Indeed, antinomianism emerged as a threatening trend within the godly community at the exact moment (1625-1630) that the controversies sparked by Richard Montagu reached their peak in press and parliament, and there are hints that antinomians themselves exploited the growing godly paranoia over Arminianism to undermine their mainstream puritan opponents.[3] So, too, as we shall see be-

---

3 For Montagu and Arminianism, see N. Tyacke, *Anti-Calvinists: the Rise of English Arminianism, c. 1590-1640* (Oxford: Oxford University Press, 1987; Revised paperback edition, Oxford: Oxford University Press, 1990), passim. For hints that

low, mainstream puritans and Laudians would likewise attempt to exploit the emergence of antinomianism for their own short-term political gain. Thus, while the conflict over the Law was largely an intra-puritan battle to define the nature of godly life, this battle was conducted against the increasingly adversarial backdrop of the Caroline politico-ecclesiastical milieu.

Origins

Although joined together by a common aversion to the legalistic ways of conventional puritanism, different anti-legal teachers peddled subtly different varieties of antinomianism. These differences stemmed in part from the fact that some anti-legalists were more deeply imbued with heterodox (and particularly Familist) traditions than others. As a consequence, we can identify two basic but distinct types of antinomianism in early Stuart England. The first category, which has recently received insightful analysis at the hands of the literary scholar Nigel Smith, can be described as "perfectionist," or "inherentist."[4] On this view, believers were held to be free from the Law and sin in that they had achieved an inherent perfection that rendered them actually pure in this life. Their freedom from the Law was a result of the fact that the Law was fulfilled within them. This perfection was assumed to flow from a believer's participation in, or identity with, Jesus Christ.

This mode of antinomian thought owed much to the teachings of Hendrik Niclaes (alias HN), the messianic founder of the Family of Love. Thanks to Smith, Alastair Hamilton, Joan Dietz Moss, M. T. Pearse, and Christopher Marsh, our knowledge of Familist piety is now fairly extensive, requiring no systematic elaboration here.[5] The basic components of this piety included a deeply allegorical mode of biblical interpretation, in which the literal narratives of scripture were taken to be figures for events and transformations that took place in the believer's soul; a tendency to claim that believers had already been resurrected in this life (a tenet that was often taken by opponents to imply that Familists denied the literal resurrection of the body); and most emphatically, the belief that true believers had somehow merged with God him-

---

the antinomians themselves exploited the emergence of Arminianism against their mainstream puritan opponents, see below, Chapter Eleven.

[4] Nigel Smith, *Perfection Proclaimed: Language and Literature in English Radical Religion* (Oxford: Clarendon Press, 1989), 107-43, and passim.

[5] Smith, *Perfection Proclaimed*, 144-84; Alastair Hamilton, *The Family of Love* (Cambridge: James Clarke & Co. Ltd., 1981); J. Dietz Moss, *"Godded with God": Hendrik Niclaes and his Family of Love*, Transactions of the American Philosophical Society, 71, Part 8 (Philadelphia: American Philosophical Society, 1981); M. T. Pearse, *Between Known Men and Visible Saints: A Study in Sixteenth-Century English Dissent* (Madison and Teaneck, NJ: Fairleigh Dickinson University Press, 1994).

self—a belief captured most succinctly by the notorious formula that the faithful had been "Christed with Christ and Godded with God." By virtue of their union with Christ, believers were returned to a state of prelapsarian perfection, and were thus, from one perspective, free from the Law and sin. Familism may thus be regarded as a species of antinomianism, generically considered.

Christopher Marsh has recently provided us with a brilliant and eye-opening study of the fortunes of HN's "service of Love" in England.[6] He suggests that despite promising Elizabethan beginnings, the English branch of the sect petered out in the early seventeenth century. While it is true that Familism in its original incarnation appears to have died quickly, the evidence of Creech, Howes, and other witnesses, such as the godly minister Thomas Shepard, demonstrates beyond question that HN's writings, as well as other "neo-Familist" texts, continued to circulate among small groups of devotees.[7] These sources were often complemented by other mystical or perfectionist works, the most important of which was the *Theologia Germanica*. This fourteenth century mystical treatise, first edited and published by Luther on the eve of the Reformation, had been central to the development of radical Protestantism, influencing figures such as Denck, Franck, Castellio, and very possibly, Hendrik Niclaes. As such, it had come to be regarded as a dangerous and poisonous work of heresy by later reformers, notwithstanding Luther's warm affection for the work.[8] Other crucial sources included *The Rule of Perfection*, a work of Catholic perfectionist mysticism mentioned by Creech and later published by Giles Randall, and the alchemical tradition, which to judge from surviving evidence, often went hand in hand with Familist forms of religiosity.[9] Nevertheless, it is important to understand that the influence of these sources was often indirect. Even those rare men and women who continued to identify themselves as Familists maintained only a slender connection to the original sect, which had centered inordinately on the person of Hendrik Nic-

---

[6] C. Marsh, *The Family of Love in English Society, 1550-1630* (Cambridge: Cambridge University Press, 1994), passim.

[7] For Shepard, see below, Chapters Eight and Ten.

[8] Steven E. Ozment, *Mysticism and Dissent: Religious Ideology and Social Protest in the Sixteenth Century* (New Haven and London: Yale University Press, 1973), 14-60. It is possible that Luther's known enthusiasm for the book contributed to its acceptance amongst radical English Protestants, for as we shall see, Luther himself was venerated in antinomian circles.

[9] For speculation on the connection between Familism and Rosicrucianism, see Hamilton, *Family*, 142-43. It may be surmised that Familism and alchemy traveled together for two reasons: first of all, they shared a deeply allegorical mode of expression and hermeneutics; secondly, both held out the hope of "Begoddedness" or human divinization.

laes. In most cases, Familist, perfectionist, or sectarian writings appear to have been read through the lenses of mainstream puritanism. This process will be examined in greater detail below; for now, it serves our turn to note that perfectionist mysticism was generally blended with more conventional godly influences to produce styles of divinity that were neither strictly Familist (in the sense outlined by Marsh) nor entirely removed from the puritan tradition. In this manner, sectarian ideas continued to exert a limited, but nonetheless tangible, influence throughout the early Stuart period. The resulting "perfectionist" strain of antinomianism shall be examined more fully in Chapters Seven and Eight, which focus respectively on John Everarde and Roger Brearley.

The second, distinct form of antinomianism can be roughly described as "imputative." Imputative antinomians tended to argue that although humans remained sinful throughout their earthly lives, by virtue of Christ's sacrifice, the faithful appeared before God as perfect, just and sinless. Proponents of this view held that believers were not inherently pure, but rather rendered "imputatively" perfect via the exogenous holiness of Christ. True Christians were "clothed in the garment of Christ's perfect righteousness," and as a consequence, God viewed them as perfectly holy, despite their sins. Such an argument came dangerously close to the standard reformed doctrine of Justification, in which the faithful were reckoned just before God by virtue of the imputation of Christ's righteousness. And in fact, this form of antinomianism appears to have developed as an outgrowth from, or an elaboration upon, orthodox protestant divinity, as filtered through an English puritan context. As suggested above, imputative antinomians sometimes asserted their protestant roots, larding their texts with citations from respectable reformed authorities in an effort to prove that they were teaching nothing other than untainted Christianity. Unlike "perfectionist" varieties of antinomianism, this mode of thought was generated from within the heart of early Stuart puritanism, and because it was quite independent of the teachings of Niclaes, it did not necessarily bring with it the allegorical exuberances or "mortalist" consequences that tended to go hand in hand with Familism. This explicitly "puritan" mode of antinomianism, which receives detailed treatment in Chapter Six, was in fact the more influential of the two strains.

These two basic categories can serve as a rough map to the intellectual poles of the antinomian underground. At one end stood genuine, self-identifying Familists, who carried with them many of the oddities of that tradition, including the doctrine of earthly perfection; at the other end, stood purely imputative antinomians, who are at times exceedingly difficult to differentiate from their mainstream puritan counterparts. Yet the reality of the situation was somewhat murkier, for most antinomians in fact fell somewhere between these two poles. Even "imputative" antinomians tended at times to discuss believers as if they were in themselves utterly perfect and free from sin.

Moreover, from the beginning, those interested in "imputative" antinomianism seem to have gravitated toward "perfectionist" ideas, and vice versa; the result was significant cross-fertilization of ideas and personnel, making it impossible to draw a hard-and-fast dichotomy between two distinct and unrelated subgroups. Chapter Nine examines some of the resulting "hybrid" forms of antinomianism, illuminating the process whereby the "imputative" and "perfectionist" strains crossed to produce new and in some cases, strikingly radical, permutations of anti-legal thought. Nevertheless, different anti-legal teachers emphasized one style or the other, ensuring that there were different flavors of antinomianism in England on the eve of the English civil wars.

This situation flowed from the fact that various antinomian sect-masters had come to their positions from one pole or the other. The following pages provide brief sketches of the careers of several of the central antinomian heresiarchs, in order both to orient the reader and to offer a sense of the tangled origins of the antinomian movement. Perhaps the most important of these figures was John Eaton, sometime vicar of Wickham Market, Suffolk. A Kentishman by birth, Eaton was educated at Trinity College, Oxford, where he took his B.A. in 1595 and his M.A. in 1603. Around 1604, he was presented to the living at Wickham Market, after which he appears to have developed his curious opinions. In 1614, Eaton came under attack for making the claim that God did not see sin in those who had been justified by faith.[10] Eaton, the most famous and influential of prewar antinomians, seems to have arrived at his opinions through meditation on the reformed doctrine of justification. His theology, while virulently anti-legal, remained duly "imputative" throughout his stormy career—there are no hints of perfectionist or Familist influence in his thought. And it was Eaton's theology, which he propagated through a series of letters and manuscripts, as well as through sermons and private meetings, that came in time to be recognized as the epitome of antinomianism. For this reason, Chapter Six focuses primarily on Eaton. After his initial brush with authority, Eaton managed to continue on at Wickham Market until 1619, when he was finally deprived by the High Commission.[11] Following this, he appears to have taken up residence in London, where he gathered a

---

[10] See P. Gunter, *A Sermon Preached in the Countie of Suffolk, before the Clergie and Laytie, for the Discoverie and Confutation of Certaine Strange, Pernicious, and Hereticall Positions, Publickely Delivered, Held, and Maintayned, Touching Justification, by a Certaine Factious Preacher of Wickam Market* (1615), 14-15 and passim; Gunter's sermon may have been a response to a sermon preached by Eaton at a clerical synod in Norwich in 1614, for which Eaton had been censured in the church courts (for this last piece of information, I am indebted to a personal correspondence from Kenneth Fincham).

[11] PRO, SPD 14/108/84.

notoriously large following during the 1620s, despite continued ecclesiastical surveillance.[12]

John Traske, meanwhile, appears to have approached an antinomian position quite independently, but almost simultaneously, possibly by merging or assimilating Familist doctrines with those of extreme puritanism.[13] By 1615, he was publicly defending the notion that the elect were free from the commanding power of the Law, and from sin itself, although unlike Eaton, Traske appears to have argued that this freedom was a result of the fact that believers somehow possessed Christ's perfection. Between 1613 and 1615, Traske took up the mantle of an itinerant prophet, evangelizing in Devonshire, Somerset, the Isle of Ely, the London area, and possibly in Dorset. He and several of his followers finally fell afoul of the authorities in late 1617 because their perfectionism had led them into a peculiar Mosaic legalism, in which they pressed strict obedience to the Old Testament ceremonies, including Jewish dietary restrictions and observance of the Saturday Sabbath. Condemned for scandalizing the King and his subjects, Traske was tortured and imprisoned, only to renounce his "Judaizing" errors, and return as a full-blown antinomian—retaining his perfectionism, while rejecting his exacting legalism—in London in the 1620s. Here, perhaps unsurprisingly, he made contact with the circle surrounding Eaton, in a step that can only be regarded as critical in the transformation of antinomianism from a doctrinal curiosity maintained by a number of isolated individuals, to a self-conscious and ideologically unified movement. Chapter Five examines the early career and theology of John Traske and his followers, while Chapter Nine surveys the process whereby this theology mutated into a full-fledged antinomianism.

Meanwhile, at nearly the same time, a third important center of antinomianism opened up in the North, apparently independent of Eaton and Traske. In October 1616, Roger Brearley, the "minister at Grindleton" mentioned by Creech, was brought before the York High Commission to answer a set of articles, as well as a list of fifty erroneous propositions allegedly held by him and his followers along the Yorkshire-Lancashire border.[14] These articles included charges of radical nonconformity, a profound tendency to rely on the

---

[12] For hints of Eaton's later troubles with the authorities, see the comments of Archbishop Abbot at the High Commission trial of John Eachard, transcribed in S. R. Gardiner, ed., *Reports of Cases in the Courts of Star Chamber and High Commission*, Camden Society, N.S., 39 (1886), 320-21.

[13] The possibility of Familist influence is considered below, Chapter Five, and in Appendix A.

[14] The articles, which survive in two separate copies in the Bodleian Library, were first transcribed in Theodor Sippell, *Zur Vorgeschichte des Quaekertüms* (Giessen, Ger.: Alfred Töpelmann, 1920), 50-52. An amended transcription may be found in Appendix D, below.

motions of the spirit, as well as hints that believers were delivered from all doubt and insecurity as to their salvation. In the event, Brearley appears to have evaded punishment by renouncing his opinions and promising full future conformity, maneuvers that can only be described as disingenuous, for the so-called "Grindletonian" movement hardly dispersed in the wake of the trial. Chapter Eight chronicles the rise and growth of this movement, which appears to have gained a substantial following in both Lancashire and Yorkshire between 1615 and 1640. Swept up in the Grindletonian enthusiasm were a number of clergymen—Richard Tennant, William Boyes, William Aiglin, John Webster, Richard Coore, Peter Shaw, and two brothers, Robert and John Towne—whose efforts complemented Brearley's and facilitated the spread of antinomian ideas in the North. From its epicenter in the remote moors of the Pennines, the Grindletonian community appears to have served as a kind of womb, nurturing figures crucial to the further spread of antinomianism throughout England, and serving as a kind of refuge for those who found themselves in trouble elsewhere. Thus, in 1629, when controversy exploded in London over antinomianism, at least two of the young ministers who found themselves at the eye of the storm, Peter Shaw and Robert Towne, appear to have hailed from the Grindletonian conventicles of the North; when each was chased from London, they returned to Lancashire, where Towne at least reestablished contact with the Grindletonian network, now centering on Brearley's new parish of Burnley, Lancashire.

The intellectual origins of Grindletonianism are obscure. Hostile observers often accused the Grindletonians of Familism, but as suggested above, this was a term of abuse that was applied indiscriminately to refer to emerging anti-legal theological opinions. The account offered here suggests that Brearley and his followers very probably did read the works of HN, incorporating key Familist tropes into their message. Yet this by no means does justice to Brearley's divinity. For perhaps even more important to his thought was that great fountainhead of early modern mysticism, the *Theologia Germanica*. It must be emphasized, however, that Brearley and his followers were much more than mystical spiritualists in the tradition of the sixteenth-century radical Reformation. Instead, they read their mystical sources through the spectacles of militant puritanism in order to produce their own distinct and prophetic message. Defiantly protestant, the Grindletonians claimed the legacy of the Reformation even as they advanced perfectionist ideas that were anathema to the mainstream reformed tradition.

Brearley and his followers probably harbored Familist texts and ideas alongside those drawn from the *Theologia*; others most certainly did. One such figure was the London layman John Etherington, who was convicted in late 1626 of being a Familist sect-master. Although he vehemently denied the charges, Etherington's own published statements demonstrate that in the first decade of the seventeenth century, he had indeed flirted with the ideas of HN, providing us with one of our few pieces of evidence regarding the survival of a self-conscious Familist community into the seventeenth century.[15] By the 1620s, however, he had rejected the Family of Love, settling into a more complex doctrinal position that retained some vestiges of his early mysticism within a broader synthesis that (at least on Etherington's account) conformed entirely to the formularies of the Church of England.[16] This synthesis included the tendency to spiritualize and allegorize the sacraments and the Sabbath, and to argue that the mainstream godly ministry generally propagated an overly legalistic and simplistic understanding of such spiritual mysteries. Although it is not clear whether his mature position included the claim that believers were free from the Moral Law, Etherington's criticism of puritan legalism places him close to thoroughgoing antinomians such as Eaton and Traske, and it was this anti-legal tendency that brought him into conflict with the godly ministers Stephen Denison and Henry Roborough, resulting in his prosecution before High Commission.

After 1640, Etherington published several pamphlets defending himself from Denison's accusations. In his efforts to prove his innocence, he pointed the finger at "others . . . that have taught the doctrine of H. N."[17] One was the Lancashireman Peter Shaw, alluded to above. The other was Creech's alleged mentor, the arch-heretic Dr. John Everarde, who represents our final example of the independent development of antinomian ideas in early seventeenth-century England. As we shall see below, Everarde was a voracious consumer of all things esoteric and heterodox, absorbing hermetic, alchemical, and mystical sources into a syncretic and eccentric whole. Unlike Eaton,

---

[15] See John Etherington, *A Brief Discovery of the Blasphemous Doctrine of Familisme* (1645), 10-11; Marsh, *Family of Love*, 239-41. An extensive treatment of Etherington's career and intellectual trajectory is found in P. Lake, *The Boxmaker's Revenge: 'Orthodoxy,' 'Heterodoxy,' and the Politics of the Parish in Early Stuart London* (Stanford: Stanford University Press, 2001). Given Lake's thorough exploration, this study examines Etherington's career only insofar as it elucidates the wider ideological and cultural context of antinomianism. I would like to thank Peter Lake for sharing with me his many insights and discoveries concerning Etherington and Denison (as well as the elusive T.L.), and for allowing me to read his book at several stages of its development.

[16] For an example of the manner in which Etherington adapted HN's ideas, long after he had ceased to consider himself in any way a member of the Family of Love, see below, Appendix A.

[17] Etherington, *Brief Discovery*, 10. Etherington likewise named Dr. Robert Gell and Dr. John Pordage. As noted above, Edward Howes did indeed attend and copy out the sermons of Robert Gell in London during the 1640s. As demonstratd in this chapter, Pordage was dispensing unusual messages in London by 1633-34.

Traske, Brearley, and Etherington, Everarde was also graced with a powerful patron and protector, Henry Rich, the Earl of Holland, who as we have seen, was the recipient of one of Everarde's precious translations of the *Theologia Germanica*. In the 1630s, contemporaries described Everarde as Holland's "chaplain."[18] It was almost certainly Holland's influence that secured for Everarde successive lectureships at the well-heeled West End parishes of St. Martin's-in-the-Fields and Kensington, in addition to at least one rich benefice in Essex. Although repeatedly in trouble with the authorities, both for his incessant sermonizing against the Spanish Match and for his unusual doctrinal positions, Everarde managed to survive and preach throughout the 1620s and 1630s, probably as a result of the protection of the earl, as well as other influential friends, such as Edmund Sheffield, the Earl of Mulgrave.[19] Only in 1639-40, less than two years before his death, did the authorities catch up with Everarde. Convicted in the court of High Commission, he was ordered to appear on his knees before the commissioners, and to confess and retract numerous errors, including the denial of the literal resurrection of the body.[20] Although modern scholars have expressed doubts as to whether Everarde actually read HN, his theology seems to have been suffused with hints of mortalism, a genuine and thoroughgoing perfectionism, and more generally with the Familist tendency to treat scriptural stories, events and characters as allegories for qualities or changes within the believer's soul. Whatever the source of his opinions, by 1626 Everarde was openly and brazenly dispensing perfectionist doctrine from his pulpit.

We thus see that "antinomianism" was a diverse phenomenon without a single point of origin. The fact that at least five distinct nodes of anti-legal opinion could develop concurrently in early Stuart England should probably not be taken to mean that the Family of Love had survived intact, spreading secretly but inexorably beneath the surface of English society. What it does suggest is that orthodox puritanism as it had emerged by the early seventeenth century was deeply susceptible to an antinomian critique, so susceptible in fact

---

[18] Sheffield University Library, Hartlib Papers, MS. 29/2/12B, as cited from *The Hartlib Papers: A Complete Text and Image Database of the Papers of Samuel Hartlib (c.1600-1662) Held in Sheffield University Library*, 2d ed. (Sheffield: Humanities Research Online, 2002), where Everarde is described by Sir Francis Varnam as "Chaplain to my Lord of Holland at Fulham"; see also William Prynne, *Hidden Works of Darknes brought to Publike Light* (1645), 207 (mispaginated as 211).

[19] For a detailed account of Everarde's career, including his many encounters with the authorities, see Paul R. Hunt, "John Everard: A Study of His Life, Thought, and Preaching" (Ph.D. diss., UCLA, 1977).

[20] For details on Everarde's troubles in the 1630s, see below, Chapters Three and Seven.

that such a critique evolved not once but several times, under distinct contingent circumstances. In some cases, these anti-legal critics may have started down their theological paths through exposure to members of the Family of Love, which survived in vestigial pockets here and there. Such was not necessarily the case, however. As Laudian and Catholic polemicists frequently noted, orthodox puritanism, with its emphases on unmerited grace and absolute predestination, and its enthusiastic tendency to rely on the motions of the spirit, contained within it at least the germ of antinomianism; paradoxically, however, the rigors and preciseness of godly piety left puritans wide open to charges of legalism and works righteousness, a charge echoed by each of the antinomian thinkers described above. Having arrived at a position of anti-legalism, a determined religious seeker might imbibe a variety of mystical, perfectionist, or Familist sources, which were secretively passed within small pockets of people who were united above all by a suspicion that orthodox puritanism, with its exacting disciplines and taskmasterly deity, had somehow missed the point of the Gospel. And by the late 1620s, they were united increasingly by geography, as an alarming number of antinomians gravitated toward London. Here, galvanized both by their mutual hostility toward mainstream puritanism, and by an inchoate, common anti-legal impulse, these various thinkers appear to have sought one another out to form what can only be termed a movement. Where previously there had been only disconnected cells of like-minded men and women, there now emerged an increasingly unified subculture.

A Sect?

It is important to understand that this underground was never a "party" in a fixed or rigid sense; not only was there was no antinomian "creed" to which all members subscribed, but as we have just seen, there were sometimes significant variations in the precise formulations propagated by different anti-legal teachers. Nor does it appear to have centered on a single leader or patriarch. Rather, particularly in London, the antinomian community seems to have crystallized around several central prophets, each of whom had a host of devoted followers and listeners, who (like Creech) would have presented their own pet preacher as the center point of the movement.

This appears to have been particularly true for those who, in one way or another, identified themselves as Familists. In his Paul's Cross denunciation of Etherington in 1627, Stephen Denison provided a description of no less than seven "Familist" splinter groups, among which he included "Gringletonian Familists" (Brearley's followers), "Familists of the Castalian Order" (perhaps admirers of Sebastian Castellio), as well as five more obscure groups, the "Familists of Caps Order," the "Familists of the scattered flocke," the "Familists in the Mountaines," the "Familists in the Valleyes," and, of course, the

"Hetheringtonian Familists," who had been founded by Etherington's alleged mentor, a prophetic religious pamphleteer known only as "T.L." Denison likewise denounced what he called "Rosey-crosse-Wolves," certainly a reference to members of the mysterious Rosicrucian Fraternity, who on Denison's account shared with Familists a penchant for heretically allegorical interpretations of scripture.[21] Here, he may have been thinking specifically of Everarde, for in 1640 the antinomian insider Edward Howes, who personally knew Everarde, would refer to the doctor, along with a second, obscure teacher known only as "Dr. Lyon," as "Rosicrucians."[22]

All of Denison's categories, of course, have the feel of fiction, and were it not for corroborative documentation from independent sources, his account would be useless as historical evidence. But in certain instances, his claims were clearly based (however loosely) on fact: as noted above, Giles Creech separately confirmed the split between the "The Familists of the Mount" and the "Familists of the Valley," and although there is a (very) remote possibility that he had derived this unmistakable distinction from hearing or reading Denison's sermon, his intimate knowledge of other aspects of the antinomian underground renders it much more likely that the peculiar Mount/Valley rift had a basis in reality. Meanwhile, an anonymous anti-Familist tract released by English Anabaptists in Holland in 1622 had attacked "divers others (who will not be called Famililists) that are deeply tainted with divers of these things; some, called the scattered flocke," as well as others affiliated with Etherington's alleged spiritual forbear, T.L. The same pamphlet referred repeatedly to another prophet, one "M.P.," who, together with his followers, had published a number of books lauding their leader as "the mighty Prince of the Hebrewes," and proclaiming "God to be the very same in M.P. and servant of M.P. that he was in H.N."[23] Although the books of M.P. and his "servant" survive now only in the fragments published by the outraged Anabaptists, they provide further confirmation of the picture sketched by Denison and Creech, in which distinct groups vied for the spiritual legacy of HN.

---

[21] Denison, *The White Wolfe, or A Sermon Preached at Pauls Crosse* (1627), 38-40.

[22] See the Epilogue, below.

[23] For the "scattered flock," see Anon., *A Discovery of the Abominable Delusions of those, who call themselves the Family of Love* (1622), sig. *3r; for the quoted passage, which was drawn directly from a book by "servant of M.P.," entitled "A true certif.[icate?], see ibid., sig. *2v; in addition the authors cite two books of M.P., called respectively "The Last Trumpe[t?]" (sig. A3v) and "Burning Light" (79-80). None of these works appear to have survived. The context of the ongoing Familist-Anabaptist debate here described was almost certainly the Low Countries, perhaps explaining why neither M.P. nor his books seem to have left any trace in England.

It may well have been the case, as Denison gloated, that there were rivalries, even hostilities, between some of these teachers and their followers.[24] Yet while Denison's account is useful in underscoring the subtle variations within the antinomian community, it is probably equally misleading in suggesting an artificial, sectarian quality to what were in essence loose congeries of ideological fellow travelers. As we shall see, there is every reason to believe that the members of these various groups knew of one another, and indeed recognized one another as struggling in a common cause. It is likely (although inherently unprovable) that antinomian laypeople moved fluidly from one evangelist or cell to the other, listening in on the sermons of different preachers and acquainting themselves with others of similar ideological persuasions.

This is certainly the picture painted by Giles Creech, who claimed to have been affiliated, at one time or another, with all four of the antinomian cells that he exposed; moreover, his detailed list of the members of these cells indirectly suggests that these groupings were open-ended, accommodating significant contact between their adherents; thus, for instance, the St. Sepulchre shoemaker Edward Webster was allegedly associated with the Family of the Mount, although his wife was very explicitly described not as a Familist, but as belonging to the separate "antinomian" grouping. At the same time, an unnamed widow in Dukes place was described as an "antinomian," but she was also said to have hosted conventicles of the so-called "essensualists." Meanwhile, Creech claimed that Everarde possessed friends and followers in both Familist encampments, suggesting fluidity, rather than fixed, formal sectarian boundaries.[25] The permeability and open-endedness of these groupings is equally evident in the spiritual wanderings of Edward Howes, who consorted with several different mystics in the 1630s, testing the waters with a number of figures, including Everarde, before apparently settling into one particular grouping which he cryptically styled "the people that have theire learninge from heaven, from God, from the Sonn of his Love."[26] His experience was probably typical, for even amidst rivalries and disagreements, London's antinomians, Familists and sundry mystics appear to have known one another and to have engaged in frequent dialogue. This impression is confirmed by John Etherington, who despite his protestations of orthodoxy and conformity, clearly remained one of what might be termed London's antinomian cognoscenti throughout the early Stuart period; thus, in 1645, he claimed not just to have heard, but to have conversed with Peter Shaw, John Everarde, Robert Gell and John Pordage.[27] What emerges is a picture of a small and densely in-

---

[24] *The White Wolfe*, 46.

[25] PRO, SPD 16/520/85, fols. 126-7.

[26] See the Epilogue, below.

[27] John Etherington, *Brief Discovery*, 10, in which he claimed to "have both heard and spoken with" all four men.

terwoven subculture, in which leading figures and seasoned veterans knew one another at least by reputation, but more often by direct personal acquaintance.

Social Composition

In his passing efforts to distance himself from the disreputable specter of HN, Etherington has bequeathed to us one of the more striking anecdotal glimpses of this scene. He recalled that in his youth, he had "several times" engaged in personal disputation with an unnamed nobleman who had stubbornly defended HN's doctrines. This nobleman had "plainly professed the doctrine of H.N. and stood to maintain by argument, that every creature is God, and that there was not a resurrection of the body after the common death therof to be expected, whereupon I hearing him, and speaking with him, said, My Lord, out of all doubt, the whole doctrine of H.N. is a very blasphemous deceit, and requested him to beware of it, and did what I could to inform him in the truth which I knew."[28] While Etherington's account may have suffered from a distorting braggadocio, there is no reason to suspect that he had wholly invented either the encounters or the peer; as Marsh has shown, from its beginnings, the Family of Love had attracted supporters from the highest levels of English society, and we have already seen that John Everarde's inner circle included two powerful Earls.[29] More extraordinary than the notion of an openly Familist lord are the setting and the circumstances implicit in Etherington's account: here we see a subculture of conventicles or private meetings between Familist insiders in which a lowly boxmaker felt at ease to joust with a peer of the realm over the merits of HN's ideas. If Etherington's tale is to be trusted in even its vague outlines, we emerge with a vision in which the ties of personal association and ideological affinity holding this secretive community together were strong enough to obliterate with remarkable thoroughness the normal institutional and cultural barriers between the social classes.

This naturally brings us to the question of the social composition of the antinomian community. Christopher Hill, for instance, argued that civil-war antinomianism was unequivocally a heresy of the lower orders, a theological expression of the impulses of the oppressed and the marginal. In Hill's words, "As lower-class sectaries became convinced that they were elect, antinomianism, Calvin's lower-class alter ego, raised its head."[30] This interpretation owes much to Hill's Marxian perspective. Yet in many ways, it simply reproduces

---

[28] For the anecdote, see ibid., 10.

[29] See especially Marsh, *Family*, 116-24.

[30] See C. Hill, *The World Turned Upside Down: Radical Ideas During the English Revolution* (New York: Viking, 1972; Penguin Paperback Reprint, 1991), 162.

the nervous propaganda of seventeenth-century critics of anti-legal religion. Unsurprisingly, such opponents—particularly puritan opponents—habitually implied that antinomianism was possessed of a markedly plebeian character.[31] As Etherington's anecdote implies, this argument, which was self-servingly deployed by the godly to discredit antinomian rivals, appears to have been deeply deceptive. Most of the clerical leaders of the antinomian movement were educated, university-trained divines.[32] And although Familist peers were surely rare birds, the few relevant documents that survive provide little evidence that the social composition of the antinomian subculture differed significantly from that of the wider godly community. Even the early, prophetic ministry of John Traske—the most socially radical and politically threatening manifestation of antinomian or crypto-antinomian ideas here examined—was not without sympathizers drawn from more substantial strata of English society; Traske's critics portrayed his following as a rabble of servants, tailors, and women, conveniently omitting the fact that his itinerant mission had attracted (to name a few) a major Devonshire landowner, a pair of Ely's most prominent citizens, a law student at the Inner Temple, and a minor Sussex gentleman, the last of whom (Returne Hebdon) became a member of Traske's inner circle of proselytes and received ordination at Traske's hands.[33]

Perhaps the most persuasive evidence for the social heterogeneity of the antinomian underground comes from the so-called Grindletonian community of the North. Upon Roger Brearley's death, his convert and disciple, the minister

---

[31] See below, Chapter Eleven, for this tendency.

[32] The exceptions are John Traske, Roger Brearley, and the tailor-preacher Greene; John Eaton took his M.A. from Trinity College, Oxford; John Eachard took his M.A. from Trinity, Cambridge, in 1614; Robert Towne took his B.A. from Oriel College, Oxford, in the same year; Peter Shaw took his B.A. from Trinity, Cambridge, in 1620-21, his M.A. from Magdalene in 1624; Samuel Prettie took his B.A. from Sidney Sussex in 1622; Thomas Hodges took his B.A. from Jesus College, Cambridge in 1623-24, followed by his M.A. in 1627; John Everarde was, of course, a doctor of divinity; there is no record of John Emersone's degree at either Oxford or Cambridge, but in 1634, it was claimed that he was a Master of Arts, for which, see Chapter Three, below; Richard Tennant received his B.A. (1613) and M.A. (1616) from Gonville and Caius; it was said that John Webster had likewise studied at Cambridge, although no record survives (R. A. Marchant, *The Puritans and the Church Courts in the Diocese of York, 1560-1642* [London: Longmans, 1960], 290).

[33] See Chapter Five. Returne was the son of Goddard Hebdon or Hepton of Holmshurst, Sussex, a prosperous yeoman who began to refer to himself as a gentleman during his own lifetime. See N. Tyacke, "Popular Puritan Mentality in Late Elizabethan England," in P. Clark, A. G. R. Smith and N. Tyacke, eds., *The English Commonwealth, 1547-1640: Essays in Politics and Society* (Totowa, N J: Barnes and Noble Books, 1979), 84.

William Aiglin, claimed that at least initially, the great charismatic prophet of Grindleton drew followers "from every quarter . . . both rich and poore."[34] Investigation in local archives confirms this picture. As argued in Chapter Eight, from its very beginnings, Brearley's movement appears to have survived because it enjoyed the forbearance, and sometimes the patronage, of local gentlemen and yeomen. This is not to say that the Grindletonians did not count among their followers men and women of very humble backgrounds, but it does warn that any attempt to portray the movement as intrinsically plebeian, or defined by a particular class interest, cannot be sustained on the basis of the evidence.

Although we possess less information concerning the followers of other antinomian leaders, a close examination of Creech's deposition suggests that there was no obvious class bias within the London antinomian community. The fifty or so men and women named by the cutler and erstwhile Familist were engaged in trades across the spectrum of London life, including (at the more plebeian end) a half-dozen tailors, a carpenter, a weaver, and a maid, and (at the opposite pole) "a rich man within Cripplegate," three linen drapers, two perfumers, a merchant, an ironmonger and a confectioner.[35] Judging from Creech's evidence, if any sector of the London economy was disproportionately represented, it was perhaps the trades associated with print and book distribution. Creech named two bookbinders and a bookseller, as well as Woolstone, the Familist scrivener and manuscript dealer, and Fisher, the barber-surgeon and part-time book peddler. In short, there is little evidence that this was a movement of the poor or ill-educated. Nor, as enemies likewise charged, was antinomianism an intrinsically female phenomenon. While we shall see that a number of women did play active roles in the community, there is nothing to suggest that their numbers were disproportionate to those

[34] Lambeth Palace Library MS. 3461, 235.

[35] PRO, SPD 16/520/85, fols. 126-27. The breakdown by profession is as follows: 5 tailors, 1 tailor/cloak-maker, 1 wine cooper, 1 ironmonger, 1 confectioner, 3 linen drapers, 1 peddler, 2 chandlers, 1 heel-maker, 1 shoemaker, 1 "rich man," 2 bookbinders, 1 perfumer, 1 scrivener, 1 weaver, 1 customs-waiter / tidesman, 1 bookseller, 2 mealmen, 1 maid / starcher, 1 widow, 1 merchant, 2 leather-sellers, 1 carpenter, 1 smith, 1 victualler's wife, 1 perfumer, 1 "good-wife," 1 miller, 1 glover, 1 widow / make-up lady, 1 shoemaker's wife and 3 unknown. To the list, we should add Fisher the barber-surgeon, who was not named as affiliated with any of the four sects identified by Creech, as well as the earls Mulgrave and Holland, who (judging from Sir John Lambe's marginal annotations) appear also to have been named by Creech.

of men, nor (as hostile observers insinuated) that the charismatic pretensions of leading antinomian teachers appealed inordinately to gullible females.[36]

It may have been the case, however, that both antinomian women and plebeian men tended to be more assertive, aggressive, and challenging than was considered appropriate by their social betters. A fine example may be seen in Richard Lane, a young London tailor's apprentice who was tried for antinomianism in late 1631. After a hearing before the Lord Mayor and Court of Aldermen, in which he had openly defended his perfectionist beliefs, Lane was delivered into the hands of the High Commission, where he not only continued to maintain his positions, but engaged in a point-for-point scriptural debate with the predictably irritated bishops. This sort of impudence (which no doubt helped earn Lane a flogging and a sentence of hard labor) certainly contributed to the widespread impression that antinomianism was a dangerously destabilizing lower-class phenomenon.[37] Individuals convinced that the spirit was speaking in and through them could (as many would learn in the 1640s) express themselves with a formidable self-confidence, and it may be that the antinomian tendency to exalt, magnify, and stress the power of the spirit had a leveling effect, which did indeed encourage and foster an unusual assertiveness among humble women and men alike.

Cultural Ligatures

It may also have been the case that the cultural media upon which the antinomian underground relied for its existence helped indirectly to cultivate individuals with an unusually strong grasp of scripture and an usually forthright manner of expression. Since even the most anodyne and carefully contrived theological formulations of the anti-legalists were of questionable orthodoxy, antinomian piety necessarily relied upon vehicles that circumvented the regular parochial and institutional structures of the English church. Even more than mainstream godly religiosity, then, antinomianism was propagated and sustained through mechanisms of the type that Patrick Collinson has associated with "voluntary religion"—most notably, the exchange of pastoral letters and manuscripts, as well as extraparochial meetings, sermons, and conventi-

---

[36] For the claim that antinomianism appealed disproportionately to women, see H. Church, *Divine and Christian Letters* (1636), 27-28; see also Gardiner, *High Commission*, 321, in which Archbishop Abbot claimed that John Eaton had been sustained by women who stole from their husbands to maintain him; William Sclater had made identical claims about John Traske in 1619.

[37] For a fuller analysis of this event, see below, Chapter Nine; Lane was sentenced to be whipped in 1632 after it was discovered that he had impregnated his wife Joan before they were married (CUL MS. Dd. ii. 21, fol. 107v).

cles.[38] Such activities, which were at the heart of the culture of English puritanism, demanded a great deal of attention and effort from practitioners, and were of course likely to produce individuals of remarkable scriptural or spiritual fluency. This was all the more true for antinomians, whose quasi-illegal religiosity depended almost entirely upon such extraparochial forms. Lane, for instance, admitted to the High Commissioners that he had attended regular conventicles at the house of another tailor named Westbrooke.[39] It was this environment of intensely voluntary religion that produced barber-theologians such as Fisher and tailor-exegetes such as Lane.

These cultural media or forms provided the ligatures of the antinomian underground. Yet their informal, ephemeral, and even secretive nature has likewise ensured that little documentary evidence remains concerning the thought and activities of anti-legalists prior to 1640. Skeptics might take this as proof that antinomianism was more the imaginative bogeyman of polemicists than a real phenomenon. This view will not withstand serious scrutiny. In fact, antinomian propagandists appear to have proselytized aggressively and extensively, although generally with a healthy dose of circumspection. To take an example, in the 1630s, two very different witnesses, Laud's Vicar-general Nathaniel Brent, and the nonconformist minister Edward Norice, independently described John Traske's evangelical modus operandi in virtually identical terms: As Brent put it in his 1635 visitation report, "Thraske hath been lately hereabouts [in Gloucestershire], and laboureth much to dispense his antinomaian doctrine; but doth it more in private conference than in the pulpit, where he preacheth only for faith." Three years later, Traske's Gloucestershire enemy Norice described "the way and course [Traske] took in venting" his antinomian opinions, claiming that "first hee would in publicke (wheresoever hee was admitted to preach) deliver ordinary truths in a plaine way, but with extraordinary shew of zeale and affection, thus to gaine him credit, and a good esteeme of all; then, if any were taken with him, he would in private proceed further, and doctrinate them in his mysteries." In his public sermons, then, Traske spoke in noncommittal generalities, only revealing the true marrow of his teachings after he had lured initiates into private conference.[40] Norice further argued that if challenged or accused of heterodoxy, Traske

---

[38] P. Collinson, *The Religion of Protestants: The Church in English Society, 1559-1625* (Oxford: Clarendon Press, 1982), 242-83. Collinson stresses the fact that such meetings did not necessarily lead to individualism or radicalism. While true, in the case of antinomianism, voluntary religion and religious extremism appear to have been inseparably linked.

[39] See Chapter Nine.

[40] Brent to Laud, June 13, 1635, reporting on his visitation of Cirencester, as transcribed in *CSPD, 1635*, xli. Edward Norice, *The New Gospel, Not the True Gospel* (1638), 3.

would deny and unsay all, and to prove his point he published a manuscript paper of markedly extreme perfectionist views that had allegedly circulated among Traske's inner circle of devotees.[41]

Antinomianism spread and flourished in large part through precisely this sort of subterranean manuscript circulation. We have already seen that Edward Fisher had acted as a manuscript broker to London's Familists. Giles Creech hinted that the most coveted of Fisher's texts was the English translation of the *Theologia Germanica*, which had passed circuitously from rural Yorkshire, through Fisher's hands, and finally into Everarde's circle. In the 1640s, when the notorious antinomian Giles Randall finally published the *Theologia* (probably from the Brearley translation), he claimed that during the dark days of episcopal censorship, it had "walked up and down the city in MSS. at deer rates from hand to hand of some well-wishers to the truth, in clandestine and private manner."[42] The rather less enthusiastic Samuel Hartlib corroborated this story from a very different perspective in 1634, recording in his diary that "A MS. goes up and downe in the City called the German Religion which is full of blasphemies."[43] At least three such copies of the dreaded *Theologia* are still extant today: one, preserved among the Sloane MSS. of the British Library, is very likely the Brearley/Tennant translation, while two others, now housed at the Folger Shakespeare Library and Cambridge University Library, identify themselves as the work of John Everarde.[44] In both cases, the *Theologia* was complemented by other short pieces of medieval or reformation mystical thought, translated and included by the copyists in question. Hartlib's angry comments, taken together with the chance survival of these manuscripts, provides the reader with a clear sense both of the wide circulation enjoyed by this valued manuscript, as well as its crucial significance within the developing antinomian community.

---

[41] The paper is examined in extensive detail below, in Chapter Nine.

[42] Giles Randall, ed., *Theologia Germanica. Or, Mysticall Divinitie* (1648), sig. A2v. Smith, *Perfection Proclaimed*, 117, has isolated the key piece of evidence linking Randall's edition to Brearley: a verse fragment attached to Randall's book bears an uncanny resemblance to poems appended to Brearley's collected sermons in the 1670s (Randall, *Theologia*, 146). Smith's surmise is further supported by the survival of a manuscript version of the *Theologia*, written in an early seventeenth-century hand, in British Library, Sloane MS. 2538. This piece varies only very slightly from Randall's version, and contains several of the same fragments appended by Randall, including the suspicious poem (fol. 90r). I would like to thank Burke Griggs, who first noticed this document among the Sloane MSS.

[43] See Sheffield University Library, Hartlib Papers, MS. 29/2/22A, as cited from *The Hartlib Papers: A Complete Text and Image Database*.

[44] British Library, Sloane MS. 2538; Folger Shakespeare Library MS. V. a. 222; CUL MS. Dd. xii. 68.

Yet the preservation of old and treasured texts represented only one facet of this manuscript underground, for the various antinomian teachers eagerly and promiscuously disseminated letters and manuscripts of their own making. Traske himself has left a vivid description of this process. He claimed in 1636 that one of his papers, the "Gospel Grounds," was first written on the occasion of "many and dayly reiterated and vehement intreaties of an English Minister . . . as Rules of direction, for his owne preaching the Gospel." Upon seeing the manuscript "others that observed what was done (as eye and eare witnesses of his request) desired also copies of the same things . . . which were in love sent them as they desired."[45] Typically, not a single copy of this manuscript seems to have survived, although one iteration of the paper was in fact published some eight years after Traske's death.[46] Likewise, John Eaton was a prolific theologian and polemicist, although we would know nothing of his writings were it not for the fact that his admirers carefully preserved them for more than ten years after his death, publishing them in 1642. The same is true for Everarde and Brearley, whose works languished in manuscript for decades after their deaths.

To our good fortune, however, at least three collections of "Grindletonian" manuscripts have survived the test of time, giving us a clear picture of the way in which antinomian ideas floated beneath the surface of English society, quietly perpetuating themselves in the face of ecclesiastical proscription. The two most important collections were apparently pasted together by Josiah Collier of Guiseley, a follower of Brearley and an antinomian lay preacher, who appears to have tried to consolidate scattered Grindletonian writings in the 1650s and 1660s. Using these manuscripts, Collier ultimately published his mentor's sermons and religious poetry (together with some of his own verse) in the 1670s.

One of these manuscript collections, now housed at the Lambeth Palace Library, contains an inscription identifying it "as Madam Baildon[s] Booke." This eclectic compilation contains a brief notice to the reader concerning Brearley's life (written by "J.C."), along with the full complement of sermons eventually published by Collier (presumably reconstructed from "heads of sermons" taken down by one or more of Brearley's listeners in 1631 and 1632); it also includes a considerable number of sermons that did not make it into the published collection; it contains a letter from Brearley to a Newcastle woman named Anne Pethye, further underscoring the important function of pastoral epistles within the antinomian community; this is followed by a long commemorative poem penned by Brearley's convert, the Grindletonian minis-

[45] Traske, *True Gospel*, 8-9.

[46] See *Gospel Grounds; or, Christ Declared to be the onely Treasury of all Good* (1644).

ter William Aiglin on the occasion of Brearley's death; to these, Collier appended a number of his own poems and religious discourses, all of which provide further insight into the nature of the "Grindletonian" variant of antinomian thought.[47] A second manuscript, copied in the same hand, and described on its inside cover as "Josiah Collier his booke," now survives in Chetham's Library. This contains a long poem written by Brearley, "Of Christian Liberty and Libertinisme"—which Collier would publish as an appendix to his mentor's collected sermons—together with some sixty-five folios of Collier's own poetic and theological works, many of which would likewise appear in the printed volume of Brearley's sermons and verse.[48] A third manuscript, also in Chetham's Library, likewise bears witness to the process through which antinomian manuscripts were protected and preserved. Apparently culled from the papers of a Lancashire squire and probable antinomian sympathizer, Robert Heywood, in the second half of the seventeenth century, this manuscript recorded without attribution two religious poems, both, it seems, the work of Brearley.[49] Taken together, these manuscript collections offer us our most striking example of the way in which early Stuart antinomians circulated, sustained, and spread their message in the teeth of official hostility. In each case, the final versions now in our hands were preserved after the fact, in the 1660s. Yet in each case, they were the result of attempts to copy down and consolidate scattered and ephemeral manuscripts that had circulated among Brearley's admirers before and immediately after the great prophet's death in 1637.

As in the case of the *Theologia*, the Brearley manuscripts were plainly preserved and intended for the benefit of partisan devotees. They were to serve as instructional or pietistic works for those already friendly to the cause. In other cases, however, manuscripts were clearly designed for broad public consumption, specifically engaging the arguments of puritan opponents. For instance, the Ipswich laymen Henry Mudd, Henry Firmin, and Francis Bridges, who apparently began their excursion into antinomianism around 1625, stood accused of having scattered about position papers containing their ideas, presumably both to challenge their opponents and to win over followers.[50] In certain cases, works that had initially been written for polemical purposes began in time to circulate amongst antinomians themselves, taking on a secondary function as pastoral texts. Such appears to have been the case with the works of John Eaton, whose vitriolic screeds against mainstream puritanism were apparently collected, read, and preserved by avid disciples. In this way, the process that Harold Love has recently dubbed "scribal publication"—

[47] Lambeth Palace Library MS. 3461.
[48] Chetham's Library MS. A. 2. 24.
[49] Chetham's Library MS. A. 2. 132.
[50] CUL MS. Dd. ii. 21, fols. 77v-78r (High Commission Act Book).

whether in the form of pastoral letter, polemical tract, or secretive catechism—became an essential vehicle through which the antinomian underground sustained and propagated itself.[51] In 1631, when conflict between London's orthodox puritans and their anti-legal critics finally broke into the public realm of print, Thomas Taylor hinted that his account of antinomian error was pieced together from the papers of at least four separate teachers.[52] Here, then, was a lively underground of clandestine tracts, expressing a developing counter-orthodoxy, accessible to us now only in fleeting glances and fragments.

But as suggested above, these manuscripts represented only one of the media through which antinomians perpetuated their ideas. As with orthodox puritan devotion, antinomian piety relied above all on small discussion groups, prayer meetings, and private sermons—what might be termed the culture of the conventicle. We have already seen that Traske allegedly broached his most controversial opinions only in private discussion; the same accusation was made against another (unnamed) London antinomian in 1631.[53] Although we cannot be certain that these hostile charges were true, we are on firmer ground

---

[51] See Harold Love, *Scribal Publication in Seventeenth-Century England* (Oxford: Clarendon Press, 1993).

[52] Thomas Taylor, *Regula Vitae, The Rule of the Law under the Gospel* (1631), sig. A5r. Taylor wrote of his enemies that "*One preacheth, that* the whole Law since Christs death is wholly abrogated, and abolished. *Another, that* the whole Law was fulfilled by Christ 1600 years agoe, and we have nothing to doe with that. *Another, that to* teach obedience to the Law of God, is to teach popery, and to leade men into a dead faith. *Another, that* to doe any thing because God commands us, or to forbeare any thing because God forbids us, is a signe of a morall man, and of a dead and unsound Christian." He was clearly referring here to specific individuals, each of whom carried his own particular slant on the antinomian message. It is likely that these brief summaries of their opinions were drawn from manuscript papers. Taylor was surely in possession of Eaton's papers, for which see ibid., 144, and compare against John Eaton, *Discovery of the Most Dangerous Dead Faith* (1642), 33.

[53] See Taylor, *Regula Vitae*, 63-64, in which Taylor reported the following extraordinary story: "one of their Masters," had recently "(in the hearing of a Minister, who himselfe related the story unto mee) taught a number of silly women gathered into his house on the saboth day; That the Law was wholly abolished: That God could see no sinne in the justified: That they were as perfectly pure as the Angels; yea as Christ himselfe: with great vehemency and contention both establishing these and the like grounds and principles of his Catechisme, and reviling our legall Preachers, that leade men into a dead faith. But upon the thursday after, meeting the same Minister at the High Commission Court, and fearing some danger towards him; he disclaimed to him with as much earnestnesse, all that hee had then taught in every particular."

with John Everarde. When Everarde's disciple Rapha Harford published his teacher's sermons, he prefaced each with a note informing the reader whether it had been preached in a public or private meeting place, showing that throughout the 1630s, the doctor had delivered regular sermons in secret, beyond the institutional boundaries of the English church.[54] Moreover, although Everarde was never a man of discretion, it is evident that even he showed greater caution in the pulpit than in his private sermons, which offer a more transparent and explicit view of his ideas. Such conventicles, which were little more than an extension of the well-established godly practice of conference and mutual prayer, were the preeminent means through which anti-legal teachers canvassed and maintained their proscribed ideas, a fact that led one London enemy to complain that while the orthodox proclaimed their doctrine openly from the pulpit, the Christ of the antinomians appeared only "in their private meetings, the nurseries of al heresies."[55]

This claim was only half-true, however. In situations of lax ecclesiastical oversight, preachers of even markedly peculiar opinions could sometimes air their views with little danger. In particular, early Stuart London, with its scores of densely packed parishes, its proliferation of unregulated and sometimes casual lectureships, its floating population of unbeneficed ministers, and its poorly overseen peculiar jurisdictions, proved amenable to antinomian evangelists, at least initially. Hidden beneath the chaos of this London lecturing scene, they succeeded in insinuating themselves into various city pulpits, often by way of informal or even illegal arrangements. John Traske confessed in 1627 that he had preached without a curate's license "for the last place he was in," but that "hee was . . . ready to take it out, and onely hindered by the incumbent who retayned him with him not as his curate but as his freind."[56] In 1630, a second London antinomian, Samuel Prettie, apparently installed himself in the pulpit of St. Michael Paternoster Royal entirely without the knowledge or approval of the authorities.[57] Perhaps most spectacular of all was the story of the antinomian tailor-evangelist, known only as "Greene."

---

54 J. Everard, *Some Gospel-Treasures Opened: Or the Holiest of all Unvailing* (1653).

55 Thomas Bakewell, *The Antinomians Christ Confounded and the Lords Christ Exalted* (1644), 27.

56 PRO, SPD 16/72/45, fol. 71r. Unfortunately, Traske's friend is not identified.

57 CUL MS. Dd. ii. 21, fol. 8v (High Commission Act Book), where it was alleged on Oct. 20, 1631, that "in or about the xvth of November last past taking uppon him to preach in the parish Church of St Michaells Pater noster Royal within the City of London . . . being neither Parson, vicar nor Curate, nor soe much as Lecturer there, nor licensed by the Ordinary of the place tooke uppon him to preach there to a great Auditory, and in his said sermon delivered many irreligious, and false points of doctryne contrary to the tenet of the Church of England."

After a spell in Bridewell prison for antinomianism and a short time in Cambridge, Greene apparently returned to London where he managed to pass himself off as a "Cambridge scholar" and minister. In 1631, it was alleged that he had managed through one means or another to wheedle his way into a variety of well-known London pulpits, including St. Stephen Coleman St., Blackfriars, Bridewell, and St. Margaret New Fish Street.[58]

These rather impressive examples bear witness in part to the resourcefulness of the antinomians in finding outlets for their less than orthodox opinions, and in part to the sheer inability of the authorities to regulate the pulsating, labyrinthine religious scene of London. Indeed, between 1629 and 1631, we can conclusively identify at least nine antinomian ministers active in the capital, although it is possible that their numbers were greater still.[59] A succession of young preachers—Samuel Prettie, Robert Towne, John Emersone, Thomas Hodges, Peter Shaw, an obscure minister known only as "Mr. Gray," along with the aforementioned tailor-evangelist Greene—joined Eaton, Everarde, and Traske to create a formidable presence in the city. Yet the antinomians' success in securing preaching venues in London also proved in time to be their undoing. As these evangelists gravitated to the capital, they began to disseminate their message with increasing and sometimes alarming openness, ultimately provoking confrontation with both the puritan establishment and the ecclesiastical authorities.

London's Antinomian Teachers: Webs of Association

This fierce confrontation will be examined in detail in Chapter Three. First, however, we must analyze more exhaustively the ties that bound together the various antinomian leaders in London and beyond. This is a crucial exercise, for only once we have explored the networks of direct personal association that emerged between and among the various anti-legal teachers can we see how and why it makes sense to think about England's antinomians as a community—that is, a group glued together by shared ideological impulses, a sense of solidarity, and direct personal relationships. The most remarkable example of this sense of community may be found in a pastoral letter written by the Suffolk parson John Eachard in 1631, after the onslaught against antino-

---

[58] See Chapter Nine for a more extensive discussion of Greene and the sources on which our knowledge of his activities is based.

[59] Gray's date of arrival cannot be conclusively determined, and he is not therefore included among the nine active preachers. Likewise, this figure does not include Tobias Crispe, who was preaching casually in London in the mid-1630s, and may therefore have been active in the city earlier. For Crispe's emerging antinomianism and his connection to the Eaton circle, see below, 62-63. It is also possible, although by no means certain, that Giles Randall, later to emerge as a notorious city antinomian in the 1640s, was in London in the late 1620s.

mianism was well under way in London (transcribed below, as Appendix E). Eachard, vicar of Darsham, had apparently been converted by the antinomian patriarch John Eaton in the 1610s. In mid-1631, shortly after Eaton's death, Eachard sent a letter to Samuel Prettie, a young London antinomian preacher who was at the time imprisoned and awaiting trial before the High Commission. Intercepted by the authorities, the letter was subsequently used to jail and try Eachard himself, after which it made its way into State Papers.[60]

Eachard began by praising that "faithfull servant of Jesus Christ Mr John Eaton," as an evangelist of apostolic stature, a "planter with Paul," who "to your knowledge . . . begat many in the faith and the L[ord] blessed his labours more than any mans in our time." He then momentarily appropriated Eaton's voice, blending it seamlessly with that of Paul himself, in order to admonish his readers against backsliding and apostasy. Eachard warned Prettie, and indeed all those that "profess free justificacion by the blood and righteousnes of Jesus Christ that hath made the Church without spott or wrinkle in his sight" not "to forsake the Comunion of the Saints which you say you beleeve and know are Saints." This communion of saints was defined, as Eachard made plain, by adherence to antinomian doctrines, as well as personal association with other "faithfull friends," all of whom were bound together by the belief that the elect were utterly free from sin in God's sight. The disputes of the previous years had evidently had the effect of forging an undeniable sense of group, even sectarian, consciousness among antinomians. Eachard closed his epistle with an appropriately pompous, pseudo-Pauline flourish, "hopeing that the Lord shall reveale his will unto my loveing brother Mr Pritty, I desire you my faithfull fellow labourers. Mr Towne. Mr Thrask. Mr Hodges. Mr Emmerson, and all others the faithfull in London to reade this to him with the spirit of meeknes." This roll call of prominent London antinomian ministers, offered as it was by a "fellow-laborer" from rural East Suffolk, leaves us with little doubt that by 1631, antinomianism had crystallized into a self-conscious movement, a network of social and ideological commonality that stretched far beyond London. When examined closely, Eachard's list allows us an unobstructed passageway into England's antinomian underground.

The object of the letter, Samuel Prettie, was a university-trained minister originally from Rutland. He had taken his B.A. from Sidney Sussex College in 1622, shortly after he had received ordination in the diocese of Peterborough. His whereabouts and activities in the years immediately thereafter remain obscure, although it seems probable that he remained in Peterborough, during

---

[60] PRO, SPD 16/520/80, fols. 119-21, transcribed in Appendix E, below. The following paragraph is based on this document (which was, to my knowledge, first noted by Stephen Foster). For Eachard's imprisonment and trial, see below, Chapter Three.

which time he appears to have come into contact with antinomian ideas. This inference is based on a fleeting but revelatory aside made by the Northamptonshire puritan divine Joseph Bentham in 1630. Having launched a withering assault on the antinomian contagion in his 1630 book, *The Societie of Saints*, Bentham passingly referred to his opponents as "equivocating *Pretteians*," a phrase which would appear to demonstrate that Prettie had earned a reputation in Northamptonshire as a notorious anti-legalist by this date.[61] In all likelihood, both his antinomianism and his infamy were well established as early as 1627, for by October of that year, Prettie had been licensed to preach throughout the diocese of London, suggesting that he had abandoned Northamptonshire for the lure of the capital (perhaps in part as a consequence of his quarrels with hostile divines such as Bentham).[62] By 1630, Prettie was lecturing at the parish of St. Michael Paternoster Royal. Here, once again, his open antinomianism brought him into conflict with mainstream ministers, resulting in his imprisonment and trial before the High Commission, and eliciting Eachard's impassioned plea for solidarity.

Yet equally fascinating is the clique of "faithfull fellow labourers" to whom Eachard appealed. "Mr Thrask" was of course the inimitable John Traske, the subject of extensive discussion in Chapter Five, below. Traske's whereabouts during the 1620s are difficult to trace with certainty, but his penchant for trouble has left a trail of archival footprints. In 1621, he was apparently living in London; in October of that year, he and his wife Dorothy baptized a son in the parish of St. Bride's, Fleet Street.[63] Shortly thereafter, he moved on to a position preaching in the parish of Tillingham, in Essex. How long he spent here, and in what capacity, is entirely unclear. He may also have returned at some point to his native West Country, for in the 1630s, it was claimed that Traske had preached in both Dorset and Gloucestershire, although again, he does not appear to have possessed a formal cure. By the middle of the 1620s, however, he was back in London, where he was retained by a now unknown minister as an unlicensed and informal curate. In 1627, Traske was again in trouble, this time for delivering a factious sermon at the execution of one Joshua Purcas, a London puritan who had been convicted of rape. In 1629, Traske wrote a remarkable letter to his diocesan Bishop Laud, in which he complained, in a tone that vacillated between desperate fawning and scornful insolence, about his ongoing suspension from the ministry. Although the details remain vague, our surviving evidence suggests that Traske spent the sec-

---

[61] Joseph Bentham, *The Societie of the Saints: Or, a Treatise of Good-fellows* (1630), 182-83.

[62] Prettie was licensed to preach throughout the diocese of London on 18 October 1627. See London Metropolitan Archives DL/C/343, fol. 25v (vicar-general's book).

[63] Guildhall Library MS. 6536, unfoliated (3 October, 1621).

ond half of the decade of the 1620s based in London, at which point he presumably forged an alliance with the other ministers of the Eaton circle.

The "Mr Towne" named by Eachard was Robert Towne, whose clerical career had begun more than a decade earlier in the North. In 1614, Towne had received his B.A. from Oriel College, Oxford; in 1615, he was ordained priest in the diocese of York and installed as curate of the East Riding parish of Sancton. At some unknown point prior to 1629, Towne made his way to London, although we possess no record that he ever held a regular cure or lectureship in the city. Towne is a figure of central importance. As noted above, it is very likely that his journey into antinomianism began at the hands of Roger Brearley and the Grindletonians. Yet upon arriving in London, Towne clearly made contact with the Eaton circle, such that his mature theology appears most closely to resemble that of John Eaton. This striking fact allows us to draw a direct line connecting Grindleton to London, and from thence to East Suffolk. Figures who had come independently to similar doctrinal conclusions in entirely separate parts of the country had now sought one another out to create a broad, trans-English movement. Unsurprisingly, when the pressure of ecclesiastical justice forced Towne to flee the city, he eventually made his way back to the North, taking up a cure in Accrington, Lancashire, just a few miles from Roger Brearley's parish of Burnley. Here, predictably enough, he reestablished contact with the Grindletonian network that operated along the Lancashire-Yorkshire border; twenty years later, the well-known northern minister John Webster, a confessed Grindletonian and Brearley's successor in the curacy of Kildwick-in-Craven, would write a glowing, personal testimonial for his old friend Towne.[64] Even if Towne had not known Brearley or his followers prior to his arrival in London, he had clearly learned of them during his time in the capital, and by the 1630s, when the courts made him an ecclesiastical refugee, he recognized the Grindletonians as allies to be sought out.

The "Mr Emmerson" identified by Eachard was probably John Emersone, who in 1646 would publish *The Worlds Prospect*, a short tract expressing in muted form a series of classically antinomian claims. On the title page, Emersone identified himself as "sometime pastr" and "Despencer of the word in private"; the skeptical presbyterian stationer George Thomason dismissed him in somewhat less dignified terms as "a privat Sectary."[65] Indeed, the Londoner

---

[64] For Towne's Yorkshire ordination and his cure at Accrington, see Marchant, *Church Courts*, 313; for the Grindletonian community of Yorkshire during the civil wars, see Chapter Eight, below; for Towne's connection to Webster, see below, Conclusion.

[65] John Emersone, *The Worlds Prospect: or, a Commentarie upon the 33 of Isaiah* (1646), British Library, Thomason Tracts, E. 1183(2), title page, for both his self-description and Thomason's written note. He is almost certainly the same "Mr.

Thomason may have based this dismissive judgment on Emersone's reputation in the capital, for it seems that despite his evident presence in the city, Emersone never occupied a formal cure or established lectureship in London. Like Traske and Towne, he appears to have dispensed his opinions in a casual manner, remaining just below the radar of the ecclesiastical authorities. Yet as Eachard's letter makes clear, he was a known fixture within London's antinomian community by mid-1631, which would seem to suggest that he was active in the city by 1629-30, at the very latest.

Emersone would not always exercise his ministry secretly, however, for he is almost certainly the Sussex curate John Emerson, M.A., who would stand as a compurgator for Tobias Crispe in the latter man's High Commission trial of 1634.[66] Crispe, a member of an elite London clan and incumbent of the lucrative living of Brinkworth in Wiltshire, was at the time in trouble over allegations of simony, but he is, of course, more famous for his activities in London in 1642-43, when he emerged as the spokesman and standard-bearer of a newly energized and open antinomian movement in the city.[67] Crispe's passage into antinomianism has hitherto remained mysterious, but his apparent association and friendship with Emersone, an acknowledged member of the "Eaton" circle, provides us with a tantalizing clue. Although Crispe does not appear to have occupied a formal preaching position in London, his family connections probably had him in the city in the late 1620s, where he may have made the acquaintance of Emersone and his coreligionists; in 1634-35, although beneficed at Brinkworth, Crispe was still preaching occasional sermons in the city. That year, a London woman named Sarah Wilson recorded one such sermon, in which Crispe cautiously broached a series of identifiably antinomian sentiments.[68] Given his London connections and his friendship

---

Emmerson" who would be denounced as an antinomian by the Westminster Assembly in the early 1640s (see below, Conclusion).

66 PRO, SPD 16/261, fol. 45v (High Commission Act Book), where he is identified as "John Emerson Clerke Master of Arts Curate of Shoreham."

67 For Crispe, see C. Hill, "Dr. Tobias Crispe, 1600-1643," in J. Prest, ed., *Balliol Studies* (London: Leopard's Head Press, 1982).

68 CUL MS. Dd. vi. 70, fols. 139v-126v contains a sermon by a "Mr. Crispe"; the volume shows a date of 1634 at fol. 126r. CUL MS. Dd. vi. 47, fol. 107v, a volume of notes taken by Wilson in 1635, records a sermon by "Toby Crispe." Although Crispe was careful to moderate his statements, he at several points lapsed into crypto-antinomian rhetoric, arguing for instance that "because God is perfect and therefore we giveing perfect obedience it Can in noe waie be . . . but by giveing god the heart. Lett it not seeme strange that I say A perfecte obedience may be given to god for I say noe more but what god s[ai]th of Jobe Calling him perfecte and Just doutlese it was not in outward actions for he had some fallings. . . thoug[h] A man be Joyles with sin we have St paules warrant for it not his that

with his compurgator Emersone, it is almost certain that he had acquired and nurtured these beliefs in the tightly knit antinomian community that was taking shape in the capital.[69]

Less elusive is "Mr Hodges," surely none other than Thomas Hodges, M.A. of Jesus College, Cambridge. After receiving his degree in 1624, Hodges served as curate of Ilford in the mid-1620s before moving on to a succession of London-area pulpits, including St. Edmund Lombard Street, St. Olave Jewry, Highgate Chapel, and after 1635, St. Bartholomew by the Exchange.[70] In late 1631, just before his departure from London, Robert Towne apparently requested permission to be married in Hodges's cure of Highgate Chapel, further testifying to the close ties of personal association that bound members of London's antinomian community.[71] Four years later, Hodges was

---

doth it yea sainte John tels us plainly that he that is borne of god sineth not that is aproves not of sin but his delight is in the Lawe of the Lord after the Inner man there is a perfection of p[arts] as we use to say A very Instant of Regeneration that is there is A universall abollishment of sin and an infusion of grace." (CUL MS. Dd. vi. 70, fol. 128v-127v).

69 According to his friend Robert Lancaster, however, Crispe "had both learned and preached abundantly this faithful Doctrine of God's Free Grace, which you after your scoffing manner call New Divinity, not onely before any thing of Mr. *Eatons* was extant, but even before he had so much as heard of his Name," suggesting that Crispe had not known Eaton personally. R. Lancaster, *Vindiciae Evangelii: Or, A Vindication of the Gospel with the Establishment of the Law* (1694), 8.

70 He was born around 1603. After taking his B.A. from Jesus College, Cambridge, Hodges assumed the curacy of Ilford in 1625, for which see London Metropolitan Archives DL/C/341, fol. 129r (vicar-general's book). He received his M.A. in 1627. A "Mr Hodges" was lecturing at St. Edmund Lombard Street in 1628-29, for which see Guildhall Library MS. 9537/13, fol. 69r and Lambeth Palace Library MS. 942, item 14, fol. 1v (I am grateful to Paul Seaver for this reference); for his lectureship at St. Olave Jewry between 1631 and 1634, see P. Seaver, *The Puritan Lectureships: The Politics of Religious Dissent, 1560-1662* (Stanford: Stanford University Press, 1970), 142-43; for the fact that he preached at Highgate in the 1630s, see Everarde, *Gospel-Treasures*, 428. Hodges was presumably serving this cure in July 1633, when he referred to himself as "clerk, of Highgate" (G. L. Armitage and J. L. Chester, eds., *Allegations for Marriage Licenses Issued by the Bishop of London, 1611 to 1828*, Publications of the Harleian Society, 26 [1887], 212); for his lectureship at St. Bartholomew, which he held throughout the later 1630s, see E. Freshfield, ed., *The Vestry Minute Books of the Parish of St. Bartholomew Exchange in the City of London: 1567-1676* (London: Rixon and Arnold, 1890), 127.

71 Guildhall Library MS. 10091/13, fol. 189v. Towne applied for a marriage license in Oct. 1631, requesting to be married in the "parish Church or Chapple of Hornsey." It is likely that the "chapple" to which he was referring was Hodges's

purportedly purchasing books for Philip Nye, a figure whose own curious relationship to the emerging antinomian ideology will be considered in greater detail below.[72] In 1638, when John Lambe pursued Creech's allegations, Hodges was still deeply suspected as an antinomian sympathizer: as Lambe scrawled on his copy of the deposition, "Mr Hodges is lecturer just behinde the Exchange, he hath all these bookes Theol Germanic: e the rule of perfection."[73] Indeed, in the same investigation, Lambe appears to have unearthed the existence of a group he cryptically labeled "the Hodgekin," probably a wry allusion to the group of supporters who followed Hodges (much as John Eaton and Peter Shaw had allegedly attracted their own devoted bands of true believers).[74] Yet despite the authorities' evident knowledge of Hodges's activities, it seems that no official proceedings were ever initiated against him. Here, as in the case of Everarde, this good fortune was very likely a result of the protection of the Earl of Holland. Hodges appears to have been a kinsman of the earl or his wife, and he was without question in the peer's good graces in 1641, when Holland, together with Edmund, the Earl of Mulgrave, interceded with Bishop Juxon to secure for Hodges the vicarage of Kensington, allowing him to assume John Everarde's old role as Holland's de facto chaplain.[75] It was probably the earl's potent influence that would allow Hodges, bizarrely enough, to take a seat in the Westminster Assembly in 1643, marking only the first strange twist in a career that would end after the Restoration, with Hodges conforming to gain the deanery of Hereford.[76] Along the winding spiritual path from sectarianism to conformist pluralism, Hodges seems to

---

Highgate Chapel, which was located in Hornsey, and which was used as a chapel-of-ease for St. Mary Hornsey.

[72] For Hodges's role in buying books for Nye in 1635, see Sheffield University Library, Hartlib Papers, 29/3/27A, as cited from *The Hartlib Papers: A Complete Text and Image Database*. For Nye, see Chapter Three.

[73] PRO, SPD 16/520/85, fol. 128v.

[74] Ibid., fol. 126v.

[75] T. Faulkner, *History and Antiquities of Kensington* (London: T. Egerton, 1820), 144, wherein is transcribed a manuscript, then in the possession of the vicar of Kensington, which reveals that "Henry Earl of Holland, Edmund Earl of Mulgrave, and some others of the principal inhabitants of Kensington, did, by their entreaty, prevail with the R. R. Father in God William Juxon, Lord Bishop of London, and Lord High Treasurer of England, to confer it on the Rev. Thomas Hodges, clerk (then Lecturer in the church of Kensington, and a relative of the said Earl of Holland, or his Countess,) who was collated to it by the said Bishop, June 11, 1641, pleno jure, and possessed it, without disturbance" until his death in 1672. Hodges's affiliation with Holland continued until the latter's execution in 1649, when Hodges attended his condemned patron on the scaffold (ibid., 74-75, citing *Perfect Diurnal*, and *Kingdome's Weekly Intelligencer*, March 9, 1649).

[76] For which see *Alumni Cantabrigienses*, s.v. Hodges, Thomas.

have lost his taste for mystical religion— indeed, in the 1640s, he can be found *denouncing* antinomianism and Familism before the Long Parliament— but given the evidence presented here, there can be little question that in his earlier years, he (like Everarde) had acted as an in-house antinomian spiritual minister to the Earl of Holland, a man whose personal religious proclivities appear in this light to take on a distinctly heterodox hue.[77]

Hodges, in fact, serves as a crucial link between the ministers of the Eaton circle named in Eachard's letter and the apparently more rarefied connection surrounding John Everarde. As we shall see, Everarde's idiosyncratic theology in many respects sets him apart from other antinomians considered in this study. Nevertheless, when Everarde's legal difficulties began to intensify during the 1630s, his affinity with other members of London's antinomian underground became apparent. Having been stripped of his London lectureships, Everarde was forced through much of the decade to preach casually either in illicit, private venues or from other men's pulpits. Above all, he apparently relied on the friendship of none other than Thomas Hodges, who shared the pulpits of both Highgate Chapel and St. Olave Old Jewry with Everarde in the early 1630s.[78] Even Everarde, then, whose aristocratic clientele and unique personal theology would seem to distance him from the likes of Traske and Eaton, appears to have been linked in a direct and intimate way to at least one of the men named in Eachard's letter to the antinomian faithful.

Other members of the fraternity of London antinomian ministers cannot be linked directly to the Eachard letter. We have already taken notice of the mysterious tailor-preacher "Mr Greene," about whom we know precious little beyond the bare fact of his existence. Yet it is likely that he, too, was active in London by the late 1620s; in his 1629 survey of London lecturers, Laud noted an otherwise obscure figure called "Mr Green" who was at the time preaching at St. Nicholas Olave, very probably the same man who would be denounced as a nomadic preacher two years later.[79] As noted above, by 1631, he had allegedly infiltrated at least four other London pulpits, although once again he seems to have done so on a casual or occasional basis.

More significant, perhaps, was the notorious antinomian lecturer Peter Shaw, who had probably abandoned London by the time Eachard wrote his

---

[77] For the impressive about-face he experienced between the early 1630s and 1647, see his 1647 sermon *The Growth and Spreading of Haeresie*, which not only attacked the notion of toleration, but included explicit denunciations of antinomianism and Familism.

[78] Everard, *Gospel-Treasures*, 428, 444, 467, in which Rapha Harford noted "two Sermons" "preached for Mr *Hodges* at the publick meeting place at Highgate in the Forenoon" and another "preached for Mr *Hodges* at his Wednesday Lecture in Old Jury."

[79] For St. Nicholas Olave, see Lambeth Palace Library MS. 942, item 16, fol. 5v.

exhortation to Prettie. Shaw had been ordained in Yorkshire in 1625, taking up the cure of Ashton-under-Lyne in Lancashire. Here, he was apparently accused of antinomianism; when the London authorities launched their investigation into his activities in 1629, Shaw "confessed (& there is evidence) that the Ministers of Lancashire made the same oppositions to his sermon's as do the Ministers of this citie."[80] As with Towne, Shaw's antinomianism almost certainly owed something to the influence of the Grindletonians (see Chapters Eight and Nine). Whatever the origin of his opinions, Shaw soon abandoned Lancashire. Perhaps enticed by the promise of a lucrative lectureship, or perhaps fleeing the hostility of his fellow ministers in the North, Shaw made his way to London. By 1628, he had become an established figure on the city lecturing circuit. Preaching from the pulpits of St. Lawrence Old Jewry and St. Michael Crooked Lane, Shaw began to disseminate his opinions with appalling openness, apparently attracting a substantial following of lay disciples in the process. Shaw's case receives more detailed treatment below; for now, we need only note that prior to his show trial before the High Commission in 1629-30, he was a key figure in the London antinomian scene.

Shaw's efforts appear to have been complemented by those of one "Mr Gray," an obscure and youthful preacher whose precise identity remains a mystery. In his manuscript notes on the Creech investigation of 1638, Lambe had observed of the so-called "familists of the Valley" that "Mr Shaw and after Mr Gray a young minister were great on this way."[81] While we possess no independent information to corroborate this claim, the layman Thomas Bakewell likewise named both men in the same breath, remarking that "I should here have told you how [antinomianism] poysoned *Shaw*, so that he is become a profest enemy of Jesus Christ and how young *Gray* was tainted and the Lord in mercy to his Church, smote him that he died."[82] The most likely suspect here is one Enoch Grey, who had settled down in London in 1634 after being suspended by Bishop Corbet of Norwich "for unsound doctrine preached by him."[83] Over the next five years, Enoch would go on to cross swords with the ecclesiastical authorities in London, Essex, and Kent, before

---

80 Como and Lake, "Peter Shaw," 710.

81 PRO, SPD 16/520/85, fol. 126v.

82 [Thomas Bakewell], *A Faithfull Messenger Sent after the Antinomians* (1644), 28.

83 William Laud, *The Works of the Most Reverend Father in God, William Laud, D.D.*, W. Scott and J. Bliss, eds. (Oxford, 1847-1860), 5:328 (from Laud's reports on puritanism for 1634). Grey was admitted as curate of St. Olave Hart Street, London, in Oct. 1634, for which, see Guildhall Library MS. 9539A/1 (subscription book, 1627-42), fol. 47r. I owe this last reference to Paul Seaver.

he was finally chased off to the Netherlands through the persistence of Laud.[84] While Enoch Grey is an interesting figure in his own right—he would return to London to denounce the King and the Bishops after the convention of the Long Parliament—he was very much alive in 1644 when Bakewell wrote his book, suggesting that he may not have been the antinomian in question.[85] At some point prior to Christmas 1629, a man tellingly identified only as "yong Mr Gray"—probably not Enoch, who had only just arrived at Cambridge in 1628—had preached at least two sermons at Blackfriars.[86] It is thus impossible at present to establish with certainty either Gray's identity or the date of his arrival in London. Given the disparate range of sources attesting to his activities, however, there can be little doubt that this aptly named young antinomian did indeed haunt London pulpits during these years. Once again, the Marrowist Edward Fisher has left us with an important clue, providing us with our single tangible shred of evidence about the opinions of this shadowy figure: among the several antinomian sources cited in *The Marrow* was a work—perhaps culled from the barber's private stock of manuscripts—by a "Mr Gray junior," called "Ser[mon] of the Perfection of a Christian."[87] This self-revelatory title tends to confirm Lambe's picture of Gray as a well-known

---

[84] By 1638, he was preaching in Maldon, Essex, where he found himself in deep trouble for provocative political statements against the King and Queen; he then fled to Kent, where his almost comical collision with the authorities can be traced by comparing Laud, *Works*, 5: 362 against Grey's own account, contained in a printed petition to Parliament of 1649. Grey's legal troubles in Maldon, Kent, and London may be traced in the various documents—including his printed petition—contained in Lambeth Palace Library MS. 3391 (Bramston Papers), fols. 39r-41r, 74r, 76r, 80r, 103.

[85] He was rector of Wickham Bishop, Essex, from 1644 to 1650 (*Alumni Cantabrigienses*, s.v. Grey, Enoch), wrote a book entitled *Vox Coeli* in 1649, and petitioned Parliament in the same year. The only other clerical Gray active in London in the 1630s was one Alexander Gray, who was licensed as a schoolteacher for Acton in 1631 (London Metropolitan Archives DL/C/343, fol. 122v) before assuming the London curacy of St. Augustine sometime before 1636 (Guildhall Library MS. 9537/14, fol. 36v).

[86] At some point in the months prior to Christmas 1629, the inveterate sermongadder Robert Saxby reported hearing a "yong Mr Grey" preach twice at Blackfriars. See CUL Additional MS. 3117, fols. 18v, 19r, and for the probable dating, see fol. 20r; for Enoch's admission to Emmanuel in 1628, his eventual degree in 1631/2 and his ordination at Norwich in 1633, see *Alumni Cantabrigienses*, s.v. Grey, Enoch.

[87] E[dward] F[isher], *The Marrow of Modern Divinity: Touching Both the Covenant of Works and the Covenant of Grace* (1645), 68; idem, *Marrow*, 2d ed. (1646), sig. A8r.

city antinomian of perfectionist proclivities, whose name would have been instantly recognizable to London puritan insiders.

There may well have been other antinomian clerics active in London during this period. The minister John Cordwell, alias Cardell, was certainly active in London by the mid-1630s. During the late 1640s and early 1650s, Cordwell appears to have emerged as a well-known antinomian sympathizer. Although he later suggested that he had been a friend and admirer of John Everarde prior to Everarde's death in 1641, there is no hard evidence that Cordwell was openly preaching antinomian doctrines during the early part of his career, so this hypothesis must remain speculative.[88] Similarly, Giles Randall, who would become a much celebrated and much reviled hawker of antinomian ideas in civil-war London, may have been in the city at some point prior to 1640. Randall had inherited a house in the Minories in the early 1620s, and his comments (cited above) concerning the clandestine dissemination of manuscript copies of the *Theologia Germanica* suggest that he may indeed have spent time in the capital. Again, the evidence is suggestive but not certain.[89]

We are on somewhat firmer ground in the case of Rice Boye, a West Country preacher and alleged associate of John Traske. Boye made his way to London in the 1630s, took up residence in the puritan hotbed of St. Stephen Coleman Street, and affiliated himself with a radical splinter group of the "semi-separatist" Jacob church. In the mid-1630s, Boye would exchange a series of

---

[88] Cordwell, also known as Cardell, and Cardwell, was lecturing at Allhallows Lombard Street by 1636. He was apparently suspended briefly in 1638 (I owe this information to the kindness of Paul Seaver, who has examined the Allhallows churchwardens records (Guildhall Library MS. 4051/2)); in 1653, while sharing the pulpit of Allhallows with the radical (and sometime Grindletonian) John Webster, Cordwell and Webster each apparently celebrated the posthumous publication of John Everarde's sermons. Their "testimonies" were then bound into the book as proto-advertisements. Cordwell suggested that he and many of his parishioners "knew [Everarde] in the flesh," further remarking that "I, *for my part*, if I had the *most precious Balme*, or the most *Odoriferous ODOUR* in the *whole* Earth, I could freely *pour it forth* upon the *NAME* and *Memory* of that man, as upon any *English* man I ever *read* or *heard*, or ever were *acquainted* with" (Everarde, *Gospel-Treasures*, sig. B8r-v); see also M. Tolmie, *Triumph of the Saints* (Cambridge: Cambridge University Press, 1977), 83.

[89] For the London house inherited from his uncle, the puritan minister John Randall, see PRO, PROB 11/139, fol. 445v. An unidentified Mr. Randall was serving as curate at Wapping Chapel, London, in 1628, for which see Guildhall Library MS. 9537/13, fol. 60v. In 1636, Giles was serving as curate to the Huntingdonshire parish of Easton, at which point he found himself in deep trouble for having preached that the forced loan and ship money were felonious sins that had brought down the wrath of God on England. PRO, SPD 16/355/8, fols. 10-11; 16/361/64, fols. 123-24.

polemical pamphlets with the Gloucestershire puritan minister and zealous Traske-hater, Edward Norice, airing a standing controversy between them that dated back to the late 1620s. In attacking Boye, Norice hinted that Boye was a follower of John Traske, and although Boye did not articulate antinomian positions explicitly in these pamphlets, he repeatedly smeared Norice as a "justiciary" (allegedly an epithet commonly hurled by antinomians at their "legalistic" opponents in the London controversies during the late 1620s).[90] On Norice's account, Boye was responsible for the illegal publication of John Traske's *The True Gospel Vindicated, from the Reproach of a New Gospel* (1636), the only book of overtly antinomian theology to reach print prior to 1641. Boye's involvement in the illegal book trade eventually brought him into conflict with the authorities. In 1637, he would be among those named in the Star Chamber bill against Burton, Bastwick, and Prynne; according to the future Fifth Monarchist Edmund Chillenden, Boye had approached Chillenden with fifty copies each of Prynne's *Newes from Ipswich* and the *Divine Tragedy*, all of which Chillenden then forwarded to Norwich for sale. Unfortunately, the evidence relating to Boye's activities is gallingly thin, while his writings are so cloudy and labored that no conclusive statement may be made concerning his theological position, despite Norice's insinuations. Indeed, we do not know whether he found a pulpit while in London, nor do we know what happened to him after 1637, when he disappears from the records.[91]

It is tempting to wonder whether Boye rubbed shoulders with an equally obscure antinomian teacher, Robert Lancaster, who likewise lived in the parish of St. Stephen Coleman Street beginning in 1625. Lancaster is even more of an enigma than Boye: a close associate of Tobias Crispe, in 1642 Lancaster would be responsible for the publication of John Eaton's masterwork, *The Honey-Combe of Free Justification*. In 1643, he would write a hagiographic preface to the posthumous collection of his friend Crispe's sermons. Despite his obscurity, Lancaster was apparently a figure of some intellectual distinction—a later admirer would claim that he was an accomplished scholar of "Oriental" languages; in the mid-1640s, apparently still tightly connected to the Crispe clan, he allegedly acted as tutor to Toby's daughter Mary, teaching her Hebrew by the time she was fifteen years old.[92] Only in the late 1640s,

---

[90] For the use of the term "justiciary," see Chapter Three, below. For Boye's opinions, see R. B[oye], *The Importunate Beggar, for Things Necessary* (n.p., 1635); for his use of the term "justiciary," see idem, *A Just Defence of the Importunate Beggars Importunity* (n.p., 1636), passim.

[91] For Boye's residence in Coleman Street, and his involvement in the distribution of Prynne's books, see PRO, SPD 16/349/52, fol. 101r-v; for accusations concerning Traske, see Norice, *New Gospel*, 4.

[92] Lancaster, *Vindiciae*, sig. A2r; Bodleian Library, Rawlinson MS. d. 106 ("Life of Mary Carleton"), fol. 24v: "when scarce come to womans estate her naturall

when he took up the pulpits of Quarley and Amport in Hampshire, does Lancaster appear to have accepted a pastoral charge.[93] It is not known how he made his living prior to this, nor whether he dispensed his antinomian doctrines prior to the civil wars. Yet it appears that he was continually resident in London from 1625 to 1639; given this, it seems likely that as in the case of John Emersone, Lancaster probably exercised his spiritual and intellectual gifts in the privacy of his home in Chimney Alley.[94]

The case of Lancaster should serve to remind us that the ordained, ministerial leaders of the group, while important to the growth and spread of anti-legal ideas, were not absolutely essential to the continued existence of this underground community. In the world of conventicles and private meetings that had initially fostered the development of antinomianism, lay initiative and participation had always been of paramount importance. This ensured that the London antinomian community could sustain itself in the absence of ministerial leadership, a fact that was of crucial importance once the official crackdown against antinomian ministers had driven the chief clerical propagandists from the city. Thus, in 1634, the London gossip-hound Samuel Hartlib reported that "One Pordage broches new-fangled opinions concerning the signes, that No Man can trie himself by them, but was to stay by for an overpowring light." The man named here was surely the physician John Pordage, soon to emerge as a celebrated civil-war radical, and the host of what might be termed a sectarian salon in Berkshire in the 1640s. Although the opinion recorded by Hartlib contained no specific reference to the issue of the Law, Pordage's opposition to using "signs," (that is, sanctification and outward holiness) as evidence for saving grace, as well as his emphasis on the immediate revelation of the spirit, place him firmly within the boundaries of anti-legal religion. It is thus not surprising that London's orthodox puritans subjected Pordage to much the same treatment that had been doled out to earlier antinomians: as Hartlib remarked, "Mr [John] Davenport hase preacht against him et much taken against his tenents."[95]

---

parts were so ready and quicke that she was thought fit to learne the hebrew tongue; which she attayned in a good degree of Mr Lancaster about her age of fifteene." As she had been born around 1629 (see ibid., fol. 6v), her apprenticeship with Lancaster may be dated to 1644.

[93] For Quarley, see Lancaster, *Vindiciae*, title page; for Amport and for additional details on Lancaster's later career, see A. G. Matthews, ed., *Calamy Revised* (Oxford, 1934), 313.

[94] See Guildhall Library MS. 4457/2 (St. Stephens Coleman Street, Churchwardens Accounts), fols. 243v, 342v, 355v, which shows him residing continuously in Chimney Alley from 1625 to at least 1639.

[95] Sheffield University Library, Hartlib Papers, 29/2/40B, as cited from *The Hartlib Papers: A Complete Text and Image Database*. There is a slight possibility that

To judge from the information furnished by Creech in 1638, Pordage appears to have been only one of several lay antinomian teachers who had been active in the 1620s and 1630s. The most obscure of his four groupings, the so-called "Essensualists," allegedly held that "that there is no sinne at all, but what is brought to passe, God doth all of what kinde soever it bee"; according to Creech, they "had their opinion from one Mistris Dunbarre a Scottish-woman." Whether this Dunbarre was active in London in the 1630s is not known, but one of her disciples, a tailor named Lockey, seems to have been keeping her message alive: "he hath many meetinges up and downe; and will spend 20s or 30s at a meeting; his cheife place is in the Dukes place, at a widdow womans howse, who doth Dresse Ope cheekes."[96] Similarly, the "familists of the Mount" appear to have had their own lay prophet, a "James Thomas," according to Creech "the greatest of them all," whose disciples included a rich inhabitant of Cripplegate called Lockerish or Lickerish. James was dead by 1638, but others, including the tailor Edward Hill ("a cheif man of the family of the Mount") and Edward Howes's associate, Stephen Proudlove the peddler, appear to have perpetuated this Familist cell into the late 1630s.[97] Likewise, Howes himself made the passage into antinomianism first by way of contact with John Everarde, and then, in a more intense manner, through the tutelage of a now unknown lay teacher. It was through such a process of furtive and underground survivalism, maintained by networks of extra-parochial and often lay sociability, that antinomianism survived into the 1640s and beyond. Such underground lay networks were crucial particularly after 1633, when the hostility of mainstream puritans, combined with official pressure from the ecclesiastical authorities, had made London unsafe for the open expression of antinomian ideas. It is to this story—the story of London's antinomian controversy—that we now turn.

Hartlib was reporting on events that had taken place in the Low Countries, since Pordage had attended medical school in Leiden, and since Davenport had fled England in December 1633. However, Hartlib tended to record mainly English and especially London puritan news in his diaries, rarely commenting on Dutch events or the Dutch puritan community. Pordage was very certainly in London by 1637, when the Royal College of Physicians denied him a license to practice medicine on the grounds that he was also a minister, and in a later case it was suggested that he had been practicing in London as early as 1634. See G. Clark, *A History of the Royal College of Physicians of London* (Oxford: Clarendon Press, 1964), 1:247-48.

[96] PRO, SPD 16/520/85, fol. 126v. A Buckinghamshire youth named John Lockey had been apprenticed to the London merchant tailor John Newporte on 5 April, 1630, for which see Guildhall Library, Microfilm 316, Merchant Taylors' Company Apprentice Binding Book, 10, 89.

[97] PRO, SPD 16/520/85, fol. 126r.

CHAPTER 3

London's Antinomian Controversy

As Edward Fisher had claimed in *The Marrow of Modern Divinity*, the "hot contentions" over the issue of the Moral Law started to intensify in the mid-1620s. Beginning in 1625, London witnessed a series of acrimonious disputes between mainstream puritans and their antinomian opponents. These disputes, which reached a crescendo between 1629 and 1631, eventually spilled over into the church courts, ultimately resulting in the full-scale suppression of antinomian ideas. The following chapter seeks to chronicle this little known chapter of English history. That historians have largely overlooked this chain of events is not entirely accidental, for much of the debate and disputation that took place during these years was conducted not in what might be termed the "public sphere" of legal court and printed pamphlet, but in the far less accessible world of rumor, pulpit dispute, and informal conference inhabited by puritan ministers and their lay admirers. Indeed, there are signs that London's puritans at certain points actively attempted to smother the conflict in an effort to keep what was in essence an embarrassing in-house dispute out of the prying eye of the ecclesiastical authorities and the broader public. For this reason, many of the duels between antinomians and their opponents have left their mark on the historical record in a frustratingly indirect manner—through offhand comments, passing remarks in scattered sources, occasional fragments of information processed through the church courts, and most importantly, in works published long after the fact, when the breakdown of episcopal licensing allowed people such as Fisher to dredge up past quarrels. At the outset, then, it is important to realize that much of our evidence concerning London's antinomian controversy is maddeningly vague, particularly on the issue of exact chronology. Often, for instance, we know that an event took place, but we cannot pinpoint when or under what circumstances. Often, too, commentators neglected to name names, opting instead to leave the precise identities of participants unclear. In certain cases, we can make reasoned inferences regarding these details; but too frequently, we must content ourselves with an image that remains only half rendered. Nevertheless, fragmentary and unsatisfactory as it may be, the surviving evidence reveals quite clearly an escalating conflict, one that by 1633 had effectively driven London's antinomians underground.

It is important to understand that these disputes actually helped play a role in defining antinomianism as a distinctive mode of piety, and in creating an antinomian community. To be sure, even before the quarrels in London, there were substantive differences separating mainstream puritans from those who would come to be labeled "antinomians." At the outset, however, it seems likely that many of the issues under dispute may not have been clearly defined. As we shall see, there are signs, for instance, that at least initially, some godly people did not consider antinomianism to be a serious threat. Many seem to have regarded the anti-legalists as erring brethren—eccentric perhaps, but not worthy of condemnation, and certainly not dangerous enough to merit denunciation before the ecclesiastical authorities. Only through a process of continual engagement (made inevitable through the assiduous activities of extremists on either side) were hard-and-fast boundaries drawn. In the process, differences that might once have been seen as vague and negotiable began to harden and sharpen, until at length the dispute widened, and differences grew irreconcilable. Only at this point were large numbers of participants willing to carry the debate into the public eye, in the first instance by denouncing their opponents before the church courts, and then at length by assailing their opponents in print.

Yet it is also crucial to understand that these disputes were not carried out in a vacuum. Rather, they were played out against the increasingly fraught background of Caroline ecclesiastical politics. For this reason, it is not accurate to think of England's antinomian tumults as a purely intra-puritan affair. They were in fact deeply interwoven with the shifting circumstances of English politics. In the previous chapter, it was suggested that the root cause of the conflict in London was the drift of a number of antinomian ministers to the capital, and the gradual development of a web of association between these figures. Yet it might just as easily be argued that the conflict between mainstream puritans and their antinomian opponents would not have happened—or at least would not have happened the way that it did—without the external pressure of political and ecclesiastical circumstances that transcended the broils over the Law.

The Politics of Controversy

The context for the controversy was, in short, the rise of Laudianism. Historians have in recent years expended much energy attempting to work out the precise ideological character of the early Stuart church. Stimulated by the groundbreaking work of Nicholas Tyacke, scholars have engaged in intense and sometimes acrid debate over the doctrinal makeup of the early Church of England. The focus of these disputes has been the much contested question of the extent to which the pre-Caroline church was or was not Calvinist in its orientation, and the equally contentious issue of whether the reign of Charles witnessed the growth and triumph of a genuinely Arminian faction in opposition to this previously dominant Calvinism. As I have tried to argue elsewhere, the balance of the evidence suggests that in fact there was a shift away from a pre-Caroline Calvinist consensus, although the question remains in dispute.[1] Whether "Arminian" in a strict theological sense, however, there seems little doubt that the late 1620s saw the ascendance of a new and in many ways distinctive ideological grouping to power within the church.

This faction—which may loosely, if not entirely accurately, be dubbed "Laudian"—was committed to a sweeping agenda, only part of which involved the promotion of an anti-Calvinist doctrine of predestination. Other central aspects of the Laudian program included a drive to shift the focus of the church away from a sermon- and word-centered style of piety and toward a more sacramental and "liturgical" mode of worship; to beautify and resacralize churches as loci of public worship; to free the church from lay influence and to restore it to a position of wealth and autonomy; to promote a broad and strictly enforced uniformity of practice centered on the prayer book and canons; and this last goal was intimately related to what was perhaps the most crucial aspect of Laudianism—its hostility to the cultural forms and distinctive practices of English puritanism. The Laudian drive for order and uniformity was specifically directed against what were perceived to be the wild, chaotic, and disruptive ways of the godly, all of which were taken to be corrosive of stability in church and state. Thus, unsurprisingly, Laud and his allies waged war against long-standing practices of puritan nonconformity, such as refusal to receive communion kneeling or to use the cross in baptism. Yet Laudians went further, effectively attempting to stamp out puritan Sabbatarianism, to limit and control the provision of unbeneficed lectures, and to create or apply for the first time "tests" of conformity, such as bowing at the name

---

[1] See D. R. Como, "Puritans, Predestination and the Construction of 'Orthodoxy' in Early Seventeenth Century England," in P. Lake and M. Questier, eds., *Conformity and Orthodoxy in the English Church, c. 1560-1642* (Woodbridge: Boydell and Brewer, 2000); and D. R. Como, "Predestination and Political Conflict in Laud's London," *Historical Journal*, 46 (2003).

of Jesus or toward the altar.[2] This had the effect not only of driving longtime nonconformists deeper into opposition, but also of radicalizing many moderate puritan clergymen, who had previously conformed but who now became convinced that new definitions of conformity and "puritanism" were being enforced by an inquisitorial, perhaps even crypto-Papist, regime. The results would become all too clear after 1640.

This summary, brief as it is, should serve to show, however, that Laudianism was much more than simply an internal movement to impose order on the church. It also had undeniable political overtones. From the outset, the spokesmen of this emergent ideological position explicitly set themselves against what they perceived to be the subversive political tendencies of puritanism, tending to champion the royal prerogative, and taking a hard line on those who called into question royal policies. Indeed, this would appear to be a large part of the reason that James I, despite his own evangelical protestant proclivities, deigned to patronize and promote the progenitors of the Laudian program throughout the first two decades of the seventeenth century. Churchmen such as Richard Neile, John Howson, Lancelot Andrewes, and John Buckeridge continually received royal favor—and bishoprics—throughout James's reign, despite the fact that their doctrinal views and pietistic style stood in contrast not only to the king's own, but to the broader currents within the English church. James allowed these men to prosper, it seems, precisely because he saw them as bulwarks against the potentially dangerous consequences of puritan political activity, and as ardent supporters of his own high-flown opinions concerning the power and prerogatives of kings.

In fact, it was precisely this calculus that helps to explain the rise of the Laudians to dominance in the 1620s. As Kenneth Fincham and Peter Lake have persuasively argued, James I began to move ever closer to this nascent "Laudian" circle of churchmen beginning in the late 1610s, largely as a result of the king's ill-starred (and much decried) plans to secure a Spanish bride for Prince Charles. The virulent opposition that greeted the negotiations for a Spanish Match erupted not only along the radical puritan fringe, but at the very center of the Jacobean Calvinist establishment, a fact that led James increasingly to turn toward anti-Calvinists such as Neile and Andrewes for advice and counsel. This process continued when Charles I came to the throne in 1625. Successive battles with Parliament over money, war policy, the Forced Loan, and Arminianism provoked in Charles a suspicion that he was up against a popular puritan conspiracy bent on nothing less than the gradual usurpation of monarchical authority. The solution, needless to say, was to

[2] For the best succinct study of Laudianism, see P. Lake, "The Laudian Style: Order, Uniformity and the Pursuit of the Beauty of Holiness in the 1630s," in K. Fincham, ed., *The Early Stuart Church, 1603-1642* (Basingstoke: Macmillan, 1993).

turn to churchmen who were committed both to radical anti-puritanism and to very exalted, not to say authoritarian, notions of royal political power.

This transformation was complete by 1629, when the disastrous collapse of Parliament in early March prompted Charles to place the reins of the church once and for all into the hands of Laud, Neile, and their associates. Yet throughout the 1620s, as Laudians gradually increased their strength at the center, godly ministers had found themselves under sporadic but mounting pressure prompted by the success of anti-Calvinist prelates in winning the trust of successive Stuart kings. Two examples will suffice to illustrate the point. In 1621, for instance, the renowned godly minister William Gouge was summarily imprisoned for having engineered the publication of Henry Finch's book, *The Calling of the Jewes*, a work of eschatological speculation in which Finch had predicted the imminent conversion of the Jews and the coming of a new, world monarch who would usher in the thousand-year reign of Christ. Gouge was a man of great stature within the godly community, a renowned preacher whose personal ties and reputation made him almost a byword for London puritanism; yet despite the fact that he may have harbored some doubts about ceremonies, there is no sign that Gouge was a hardened nonconformist, and in fact throughout his career he showed a surprising willingness to work together with the ecclesiastical authorities. But Gouge now found himself the victim of a power play at court; as his son later explained it, when the tract came to James's attention, the king became convinced that Finch "had in that book declared, that the *Jewes* should have a Regiment above all other kingdomes, thereupon was beyond all patience impatient. And *B. Neal* and others putting him on especially against the Publisher of the Book, made him so fierce as he would admit no Apology." Gouge's indiscretion thus earned him a nine-week spell in prison, undoubtedly a rude surprise given the fact that the unlucky minister was merely publishing a book that had been duly licensed for the press by Archbishop Abbot's chaplain, Daniel Featley, in 1619. In the end, Gouge was rescued by Abbot himself, whose own evangelical Calvinist sympathies and political position at court left him with little love for churchmen such as Neile and Laud. The skirmish was not quite over, however; shortly thereafter, Laud preached a sermon before the king denouncing Finch's ideas as at once subversive and ludicrous, thus trying to squeeze maximum political capital out of the affair before it faded from the king's memory.[3]

---

[3] W. Gouge, *A Learned and Very Useful Commentary on the Whole Epistle to the Hebrewes* (1655), sigs. bv-b2r. On Finch and his book, see W. Prest, "The Art of Law and the Law of God: Sir Henry Finch (1558-1625)," in D. Pennington and K. Thomas, eds., *Puritans and Revolutionaries: Essays in Seventeenth-Century History Presented to Christopher Hill* (Oxford: Clarendon Press, 1978), 94-117;

Four years later, a similar fate would befall Thomas Gataker, the moderate puritan minister of Rotherhithe in Surrey. Like Gouge, Gataker was well on his way to assuming a role as a scion of London's godly community, although perhaps even more than Gouge, Gataker appears to have been a thoroughgoing conformist, who despite his godly connections was entirely reconciled to the ceremonies and government of the Church of England (at least in its Jacobean incarnation). Much like Gouge before him, Gataker found himself imprisoned, suspended, and then placed under house arrest for having written an ostensibly uncontentious prefatory epistle to a book by the recently deceased London puritan minister Edward Elton. Once again, a seemingly uncontroversial book had become the center of a maelstrom of court intrigue. Apparently prompted by the behind-the-scenes lobbying of Laud, Neile, and their confederate John Cosin, the king once again took umbrage at the contents of Elton's works, together with another published by a puritan named William Crompton. Having detected in these books hints of immoderate puritan radicalism on the issues of the Sabbath, relations with Catholics, and infant baptism, James ordered Elton's books to be publicly burned, together with a third book by the godly London lecturer Stephen Denison, who had allegedly taken it upon himself to defend Elton's opinions from the pulpit, a move for which the conformist Denison had been suspended. Again, these maneuvers appear to have been closely related to an ecclesiastical power struggle in the highest circles of court, for the books of Elton and Crompton had, like Finch's book, been licensed by Abbot's chaplain, Featley; in both cases, the Laudian churchmen were thus in effect smearing their Calvinist court opponents by seeking to associate them in the king's mind with a subversive puritan threat to orthodoxy. Yet court politics aside, the message was a very real one for London's godly ministers—Gataker was imprisoned, Denison suspended, and Elton's posthumous reputation wrecked in a spectacular ritual display of official anti-puritanism.[4]

Taken together, these two incidents may be viewed as symbolic of the shifting circumstances in which godly ministers found themselves in the 1620s. Although the Laudian stranglehold on the church was by no means secure until the end of the decade, there can be little question that the godly, particularly in London, were increasingly at risk of legal or extra-legal harassment from on high. This was true not just of unabashed nonconformists but of figures such as Gataker and Denison, who had every reason to believe them-

---

D. R. Como, "Women, Prophecy and Authority in Early Stuart Puritanism," *Huntington Library Quarterly*, 61 (1998).

[4] See P. Lake, *The Boxmaker's Revenge: 'Orthodoxy,' 'Heterodoxy,' and the Politics of the Parish in Early Stuart London* (Stanford: Stanford University Press, 2001), 86-90.

selves to be solid and respected members of the early Stuart ecclesiastical establishment. To borrow Professor Collinson's phrase, these men were in many respects perfect exemplars of the Jacobean "religion of Protestants"—learned, conformable, socially respectable, and deeply committed to the maintenance of what they perceived to be order and orthodoxy, such figures were to all appearances anything but regicides-in-waiting. They now found themselves, however, in new and unfamiliar territory: under the constant threat of scrutiny from above, such men now had to tread very carefully for fear of getting swept up in the net of ecclesiastical justice. Yet the result was not, in the first instance, a retreat into hostility and opposition to the Stuart regime. On the contrary, for many Calvinist and moderate puritan members of the early Stuart church, the primary instinct was not opposition, but an impulse to prove both their loyalty and their commitment to notions of orthodoxy and political obedience.

This, then, was the context within which London's antinomians and their mainstream puritan opponents waged their battle. Certainly, the arrival of a phalanx of antinomian ministers in the capital would probably have caused a stir under any circumstances. Their tendency to harp incessantly on the legalistic failings of their mainstream puritan counterparts was a sure invitation to conflict. But the particular situation in which the godly found themselves in the 1620s ratcheted up tensions in London, such that an explosive eruption became almost inevitable. Antinomianism, in short, became a means through which mainstream puritans could prove to the authorities that they were not in fact the subversive radicals of Laudian slander. By attacking antinomians as the purveyors of poisonous error, godly ministers could reclaim their credibility and establish their firm and heartfelt commitment to theological orthodoxy, thus undermining the polemical claims of their increasingly powerful opponents at court and in the church hierarchy.

This was all the more crucial in the light of the nature of that polemic. The Laudian claim that puritanism was by nature subversive of political order had always had a theological subtext: Laudians hinted that the doctrine of predestination, maintained with special vigor and intensity by the godly (although not merely by the godly), was in itself antinomian, taking that word in the largest and most imprecise sense (that is, predestinarian thinking encouraged moral license and disobedience to authority). By convincing people of their own election, the Laudians reasoned, puritan ministers created in their followers a sense of sanctimonious presumption and dangerous security, which not only liberated the godly from the burden of working out their salvation in fear and trembling, but freed them from the duty to obey God's ethical dictates, thus leaving puritans all too ready to chastise their neighbors and challenge their divinely ordained superiors. From the Laudian perspective, then, there was a natural equation between puritanism, predestination, and a subversive moral presumption, which led almost necessarily to political sedition.

This helps to explain why Laud and his allies were so keen to suppress predestinarian discourse. It also ensured, however, that the emergence of a genuine theological antinomianism, peddled by the likes of Eaton, Shaw, and Traske, represented a potential public-relations bonanza for the Laudians (and an equally grave potential threat to the godly). Antinomians were in many ways the fulfillment of all the most jaundiced Laudian prophecies about puritanism. With their spectacular claims of freedom from the Law and sin, antinomian ministers and laypeople could be made to appear as the logical and inevitable product of the Calvinism preached by mainstream puritans (and indeed by conformist churchmen such as Abbot and Featley). Predictably, then, Laud and his allies proved more than willing to chase down, imprison, and publicly censure antinomians in the church courts. The existence of such antinomians could then be mobilized in pulpit and print to chastise and humiliate the godly more generally. These themes are all explored in much greater detail in Chapter Eleven, below. For the moment, we need note only that given the thrust of Laudian polemic, it was absolutely essential that mainstream puritan ministers distance themselves from their antinomian counterparts; to fail to do so was to leave themselves open to very serious polemical damage which they could ill afford given the precarious politico-ecclesiastical situation of the later 1620s. This led to a most curious set of circumstances in which London puritans—including some open nonconformists—joined together in uneasy and short-lived alliance with the Laudian authorities so as to silence their antinomian critics.

For mainstream puritan ministers, then, antinomianism represented both a serious threat and a potential opportunity. Yet the rise to power of the Laudians served to escalate the situation in one other crucial respect. The publication of Richard Montagu's *New Gagg* and *Appello Caesarem*, together with the subsequent favor lavished upon Montagu and his friends at court, created a widespread fear amongst many committed Protestants that a small circle of Arminian churchmen, devoted to a quasi-Pelagian doctrine of free will, were on the brink of seizing hold of the Church of England. Moreover, the furious theological discussion triggered by Montagu—which quickly bled into tense political debates at Westminster—had the effect of pushing to center stage questions surrounding the conditionality of God's grace, the role of works in the process of salvation, and the nature of divine predestination. Public controversy, together with the looming threat of Arminian success at court, thus had the effect of sensitizing many English Protestants to these nettlesome issues. And it was on these vexed questions that antinomians staked much of their polemical claim to the affections of the godly. By consistently portraying themselves as the most aggressive defenders of the idea that salvation came through the mere, unconditional, free grace of God, antinomians were in effect taking advantage of the paranoia and defensiveness engendered by Montagu and the threat of Arminianism. Anti-legalists were able to market their own version of Christianity as the only logical, coherent, and courageous antidote to the virus of Arminianism. Even more threatening, however, was the fact that in denouncing their mainstream puritan opponents as prophets of a species of deadly works righteousness, antinomians implicitly or explicitly suggested that most godly preachers were in fact no better than the Arminians. Committed to their own version of salvation by works, mainstream puritans were in the eyes of their antinomian opponents at best dangerously deluded; at worst, they were engaged in a cowardly, collaborationist sellout that served only to aid and abet the slow reintroduction of Popery to English soils. Such claims were all too likely to strike a resonant chord in the tense atmosphere of the late 1620s and early 1630s, and they grew more plausible and convincing each time the godly colluded openly with the authorities to bring down an antinomian critic.

London's mainstream puritans thus found themselves in an exceedingly difficult position. On the one hand, as the 1620s wore on, they came increasingly under pressure from an aggressively anti-puritan ecclesiastical establishment, for which puritanism was virtually synonymous with antinomianism (taking that word in its broadest and nontechnical sense, that is, as an amoral and subversive spiritual presumptuousness). At the same time, however, the godly were faced with a new and threatening protest movement within their own ranks—a thoroughgoing theological antinomianism, in which it was claimed that traditional puritan divinity was little more than a disguised Arminianism. Confronted by official harassment from without and an attack on their spiritual authority from within, mainstream puritan ministers fought back as best they could, trying simultaneously to prove their orthodoxy in the eyes of the king, to ward off the continual polemical and judicial pressure of their Laudian opponents, and to protect their flocks from antinomian predation. The result was England's antinomian controversy.

Eager Bickering, Bitter Invectives

Due to gaps in the surviving ecclesiastical records, the first rumblings of the controversy remain obscure. Fisher's attempt to date the initial stirs to 1625-27 seems plausible, but owing to the destruction of the records of the court of High Commission for the period before autumn 1631, it is impossible to know when and under what circumstances antinomianism first began to raise eyebrows in London. It may be that John Eaton and his followers started to attract significant attention at this time, although in the absence of further information regarding the so-called "Eatonists," such a conclusion must remain entirely speculative. Our first definitive indication of escalating activity, however, can be traced to 1624-26, when the godly minister Stephen Denison became convinced that the sometime boxmaker and pipe fitter John Etherington had been seducing his parishioners into conventicles, where they were then indoctrinated into the mysteries of Familism and Anabaptism. The dispute between Etherington and Denison has been subjected to extensive analysis elsewhere[5]; nevertheless, because it reveals certain patterns that would characterize the controversy as a whole, it serves as a crucial starting point for our narrative.

Although he vehemently denied the accusations of heresy lodged against him, there is no doubt that Etherington possessed eccentric, perhaps even heterodox, views, which did in fact owe something to the influence of HN. Whether or not he was the lay preacher and sect-master of Denison's imaginings, it does seem clear that the erstwhile boxmaker was not shy about airing his opinions in private, extra-parochial meetings of godly lay people. Having been alerted to this by some of his parishioners, Denison began a concerted campaign against Etherington from his two London pulpits of St. Katherine Cree and Allhallows the Great. Etherington alleged that he initially tried to arrange a meeting with Denison in order to sort out the matter, but that his overtures were rebuffed. This led Etherington to complain to the diocesan authorities, a move that merely exacerbated the conflict, for an angry Denison at that point cited the boxmaker before the High Commission for his putative errors. Etherington's case, which began at some point before King James's death in March 1625, would not be officially concluded until the last months of 1626.[6]

Yet this was merely the outward face of a dispute that was conducted with considerable intensity in the much murkier world of what Peter Lake and I have termed the London "puritan underground." Thus, for instance, Henry Roborough, minister of St. Leonard's Eastcheap (a younger preacher whom Etherington repeatedly dismissed as Denison's "curate") reported to the High Commission that he had met with the boxmaker "and his company to dispute in matters of Religion." In addition, Roborough testified that he had exchanged "writings" with Etherington, presumably as a prelude to or continuation of their face-to-face meeting.[7] Such manuscript exchanges were in fact a frequent means used by the godly to hammer out in-house theological debates, and to this extent, the Etherington affair initially proceeded according to established norms of intra-puritan dispute settlement. Similarly, the godly often

---

[5] See Lake, *Boxmaker's Revenge*, passim.

[6] For the dating of the dispute, see John Etherington, *The Defence of John Etherington against Stephen Denison* (1641), 16, 47.

[7] Ibid., 5. Etherington here reproduced a number of the depositions against him (including Roborough's), to which the boxmaker apparently secured access.

relied on private meetings, conducted semi-formally before witnesses, as a means of defusing conflict without recourse to the authorities. Indeed, Etherington reported numerous meetings with both Roborough and a succession of Stephen Denison's lay followers—most notably the joiners Rowland Tompson and Thomas Rogers—both before and after Denison initiated legal proceedings against Etherington. These meetings, conducted in the houses of interested laypeople, were offered ostensibly as a means to reconcile Denison and Etherington and to bring the affray to a happy conclusion. Yet on Etherington's account, this turned out to be a mere pretense, designed to gather information against him, information which was then offered up to the High Commission as evidence of the boxmaker's heretical ways. Tompson, Rogers, Roborough, a porter's wife named Susan Price, as well as two ministers named Stephens and Cleaver (who had also met with the boxmaker) proceeded to testify against him, ensuring his conviction on the last day of November 1626.

On 11 February 1627, Etherington appeared in chains at the foot of Paul's Cross, where he was forced to endure a three-hour denunciatory sermon by Denison. The sermon, subsequently published in 1627 under the title *The White Wolfe*, allowed Denison to parade his own commitment to orthodoxy, order, and clerical authority, thus undoing some of the damage that had been inflicted when his book had been burned at the Cross in 1625. Viewed from this perspective, Etherington's prosecution, which had been engineered almost entirely through the efforts of Denison, Roborough, and godly laymen such as Tompson and Rogers, represented a defiant vindication of puritan claims to oppose heresy, lay enthusiasm, and the allegedly antinomian consequences of Familism.

Yet not all members of the godly community were pleased with the result. Indeed, Denison complained in his sermon that "howsoever there were many which disliked the Hetheringtonian faction, abhorred their opinions, complained of them to ministers in secret and murmured against them . . . yet for any that would lend their helping hand to set forward this matter of so great importance for the common safety of the Church, I found none." In fact, many godly people were uncomfortable with Denison's relentless campaign against Etherington: "Some in their ignorance would be ready to say that, though this faction held some absurd points, yet that they held nothing against the foundation."[8] In other words, few members of the godly community were willing openly to support the attack on Etherington. With the exception of a handful of Denison's friends and admirers, London puritans seem at this stage to have been willing to offer the ex-Familist Etherington a high degree of latitude, despite his eccentricity and his scarcely submerged sectarian past. In late

[8] Denison, *The White Wolfe*, sig. A7r.

1626, the perceived threat of anti-legalism was not yet great enough to break the bonds of godly solidarity, bonds that were constituted as much by shared habits of thought, language and behavior as by strict doctrinal unity.[9]

Yet there are indications that anti-legal preachers were coming in these months to express themselves with disconcerting assertiveness. In November 1626, just days before Etherington was sentenced by the High Commission, Bishop Mountaigne questioned John Everarde concerning an offensive sermon preached at St. Martin's-in-the-Fields, in which the doctor had allegedly denied that Christians should pray for temporal blessings. Everarde submitted a certificate defending himself, and promised to answer his critics in a satisfactory sermon.[10] On December 10, he did so (albeit in a manner that was not likely to have satisfied anyone) before an audience that included an ecclesiastical informant, who submitted detailed notes to the authorities.[11] The doctor claimed that his original sermon had been misunderstood, arguing "That Temporall blessings might be taken 2 wayes: as opposed to Eternall, and so he denyed them not to be prayed for. And as opposd to spirituall in which sense he held." Yet he then went on to defend his position in revealing terms, expostulating "That howsoever it might be lawfull for them that were children and Infants in Christ and such as were not yet perfect to pray for temporall blessing, as health, and wealth etc. . . . Yet that it was not necessary, no nor convenient for them so to doe, as being an allaying and an Embasement of their Prayers. For which case they that are perfect and sublime us'd it not." That the doctor was willing to express these perfectionist sentiments so openly—incredibly enough, in a sermon that was intended as an apology before the watchful eye of his enemies—gives us an idea of just how audaciously he was willing to ventilate his opinions. When it was objected that "by this doctrine he opposed the Liturgie of our Church in which there be many prayers for temporall things," Everarde snidely answered "That the Church had wisely provided for all sorts of men, spirituall things for the perfect men, and temporall thinges for the weake. If men be in love with Gew-Gawes, and trifles and

---

9 See P. Lake and D. R. Como, "'Orthodoxy' and Its Discontents: Dispute Settlement and the Production of 'Consensus' in the London (Puritan) 'Underground,'" *Journal of British Studies*, 39 (2000); and for a more exhaustive discussion of the social and theological implications of the dispute, see Lake, *Boxmaker's Revenge*, passim.

10 For Mountaigne's letter to Laud, dated November 18, see PRO, SPD, 16/40/1, fol. 1r. For Everarde's brief certificate in defense of himself, see ibid., fol. 2r.

11 The sermon notes are preserved in PRO, SPD 16/41/73 (fols. 109-10). The following paragraph is based upon this document. For an extensive discussion the reliability of this document, see Appendix C, below.

bawbles there they are for them."[12] This outrageous performance was no doubt offered as a challenge to those in authority, a challenge that the ecclesiastical governors were only too happy to meet. Shortly after the sermon was preached, Everarde appears to have been banned from the pulpit of St. Martin's, and Bishop Mountaigne, acting on King Charles's command, installed a royal chaplain to the vacant lectureship.[13] But Everarde, with his powerful backers, was not to be silenced. He slid immediately into a lectureship at Kensington, the home parish of his friend, Holland, where he continued to dispense his controversial opinions unabated.[14]

Everarde's difficulties appear in this instance to have been created mainly by the hostility of the authorities, who had long suspected him as a political provocateur and a man of "unconstant disposition."[15] As in the case of Etherington, there are few signs of widespread godly support for the campaign against him. However, in the months immediately following these incidents, the emergence of several other antinomian preachers in London would disrupt the godly community, dissolving the sense of solidarity that had obstructed Denison's crusade against Etherington. In 1625, Thomas Hodges arrived in the London area; he was followed by Samuel Prettie in 1627; Shaw and Towne likewise seem to have migrated south in this period, and they were certainly in London by 1628. The tailor-evangelist Greene, the private preacher Emersone, and possibly the notorious "young Mr Gray" also appear to have been active in the city by 1629. Some of these figures brought fully formed anti-legal opinions with them from the provinces—as noted above, Shaw had

---

12 While it is possible that the note-taker distorted or exaggerated the details of this performance, Everarde's surviving sermons, as published by his disciple Harford, show that Everarde did in fact hold precisely these opinions concerning prayer for temporal blessings. See J. Everard, *Some Gospel-Treasures Opened: Or, The Holiest of all Unvailing* (1653), 238-43, 572-78 (the latter of which duplicates almost exactly the style of argument he had allegedly used in his recantation at St. Martin's).

13 For Humphrey Peake's somewhat arbitrary installation, see P. Seaver, *The Puritan Lectureships: The Politics of Religious Dissent, 1560-1662* (Stanford: Stanford University Press, 1970), 141. In fact, it is not entirely clear what Everarde's status was at the time he preached these sermons at St. Martin's, for it seems that John Andrewes had already assumed the formal lectureship in his place (Paul R. Hunt, "John Everard: A Study of His Life, Thought, and Preaching" [Ph.D. diss., UCLA, 1977], 68). It would thus be inaccurate to say that Everarde was removed from the lectureship, although it seems that he was never allowed to return to preach at St. Martin's.

14 Guildhall Library MS. 9537/13, fol. 56r shows that Everarde was lecturing at Kensington by September 1628.

15 The phrase is Bishop Mountaigne's (PRO, SPD 16/40/1).

already been accused of antinomianism in Lancashire, while Prettie appears to have earned a similarly notorious reputation in Northamptonshire prior to his arrival in London in 1627.[16] Others may have acquired newfound theological allegiances upon arrival in the capital. Nevertheless, it is clear that by 1629, a sizable antinomian bloc had formed in London. Other clerics, such as the future Independent leader Philip Nye, and the St. Antholin lecturer John Archer, while not overtly antinomian, appear to have championed certain aspects of the anti-legal critique, earning the suspicion of fellow ministers.[17] London's godly clergy thus found their status and authority increasingly challenged by a corps of divines who argued that traditional puritan devotion was shot through with a pharisaical works righteousness. The result was a heated contest that ultimately saw many city puritans cooperating with the Laudian authorities in an effort to marginalize and silence the primary advocates of anti-legal religion.

To all appearances, late 1628 appears to have represented a pivotal moment in this struggle, one in which measured disagreement escalated into vicious backbiting. At the center of the storm was the outspoken Peter Shaw, perhaps the most inflammatory member of London's antinomian fraternity. By 1628, Shaw was openly and confrontationally dispensing his ideas from various city pulpits, including St. Magnus the Martyr, St. Lawrence Old Jewry (where he appears to have preached with some frequency), and St. Michael Crooked Lane, where he delivered a regular Wednesday evening lecture.[18] His brash style and unusual opinions appear to have made him something of a celebrity in London. It was alleged that he had "begot such a faction, that if he preach not, his followers, have refused upon the Sondayes to heare either sermons, or divine prayer, but rest at home." Shaw's opinions receive further attention in Chapter Nine; for present purposes, we need only note that he was preaching a particularly strident brand of anti-legalism, one so extreme in its identification of believers with Christ that many of his accusers, rightly or wrongly, took him to be a Familist, a claim that would later be repeated by

---

[16] For Prettie, see the comments of the Northamptonshire godly minister Joseph Bentham, discussed in Chapter Eleven, below. There is no evidence as to how Prettie might have come upon such opinions in Northamptonshire.

[17] For contemporary accusations of antinomianism against Archer, see Robert Baillie, *A Dissuasive From the Errours of the Times* (1646), 80.

[18] The following paragraphs are based upon the documents and commentary in D. R. Como and P. Lake, "Puritans, Antinomians and Laudians in Caroline London: The Strange Case of Peter Shaw in its Contexts," *Journal of Ecclesiastical History,* 50 (1999), which reproduces the various pieces of evidence gathered for Shaw's trial, as contained in PRO, SPD 16/139/91, fols. 174r-177r.

the antinomian insiders Etherington and Creech (who placed him among the "familists of the Valley").[19]

Whether or not these accusations of Familism are to be trusted, Shaw's unflinching criticism of his fellow ministers, together with the alarmingly large band of devotees who clustered at the foot of his pulpit, quickly attracted hostile attention from Laudians and puritans alike. At some point (probably in or shortly after March 1629) the authorities launched an investigation into his activities and opinions. This remarkable inquiry brought together over two dozen witnesses, ultimately generating an extensive dossier of evidence, which has been transcribed and discussed in greater detail elsewhere.[20] Although by no means as comprehensive as we might hope, this dossier sheds considerable light on the events leading up to his prosecution. What is remarkable about the case is not simply the unusual number of witnesses who gathered to bear witness against Shaw, but also the composition of the coalition against him. Perhaps predictably, a number of Shaw's accusers were fierce anti-puritans. At the center the prosecution case against him were ministers such as Brian Walton, William Brough, Samuel Baker, William Watts, and Christopher Dow, all of whom were to emerge during the 1630s as staunch supporters of the Laudian program. Walton and Watts, in particular, turned over copious evidence against Shaw, including many of the most damning accusations of libertine excess. Indeed, to judge merely from the weight and quality of the evidence provided, it seems likely that these Laudian extremists were Shaw's most enthusiastic pursuers. Yet they were not his only enemies. Somewhat more surprisingly, the roster of witnesses assembled by the authorities included many men who had no love for Laudian sacramentalism. Indeed, a number of the articles were signed by figures of unquestionably puritan proclivities. Among the witnesses who gave evidence against Shaw were Stephen Denison, still fresh from his victory over the unfortunate Etherington, Cornelius Burges, parson of St. Magnus the Martyr and one of London's most illustrious moderate puritan divines, as well as the nonconformist clerics James Nalton, Elias Crabtree, and Abraham Grame. Other ministers, such as Richard Culverwell, Andrew Castleton, and Nathaniel Waker, appear to have had godly connections as well. Shaw's opinionated and adversarial style had thus galvanized a broad, not to say incongruous, coalition of London divines, all united against the alleged threat of Shaw's overt antinomianism.

---

19 For Creech's claim about Shaw, see PRO, SPD 16/520/85, fol. 126v.

20 See Como and Lake, "Peter Shaw." The date of the investigation remains speculative, and is based on the fact that all of the dated evidence against Shaw derives from March 1629 or earlier. Yet the High Commission case against him appears to have dragged on until at least the end of 1630, for which see the comments of the Oxford diarist Thomas Crosfield (Queens College MS. 390, fol. 54r).

It would be a mistake to suppose, however, that these strange bedfellows came together for precisely the same purposes. Indeed, it seems likely that in pursuing Shaw, the Laudians were in fact attempting to expose and silence a man whom they believed to represent the epitome of puritan presumption and libertinism. Thus, the most scandalous charges against Shaw—for instance, the claim that "what sin soever a believer commits as adultery, murder etc. and how oft soever iterated, yet he is no further from God, but hath as much interest in God and right to heaven as the most sanctified man in the world"—were lodged not by the godly, but by accusers such as Brian Walton and Christopher Dow. To such observers, Shaw's antinomianism was but puritanism writ large. For them, as for Shaw's diocesan Laud, the prosecution of Peter Shaw provided a golden opportunity to underscore and undermine what they perceived to be the most characteristic (and most subversive) tendencies of godly divinity. The wonderful polemical possibilities of the situation would be exploited a few years later by Christopher Dow; writing against the rogue puritan Henry Burton, Dow would cite Shaw's alleged opinions concerning baptism—"That the outward washing of water in Baptisme, is no more then the washing or dipping of a doggs foote in water"—as representative of a general puritan disrespect for God's holy sacraments.[21]

What such tactics ignored, however, was the fact that mainstream puritans viewed the style of divinity promoted by Shaw with equal suspicion and hostility. When Dow wrote his treatise, for instance, Burton had long since established himself as one of London's most ferocious opponents of antinomian error. This should not come as a surprise, for the main thrust of antinomian propaganda was directed not against Laudian innovators, but against the godly themselves. This helps to explain why men such as Denison, Crabtree, and Burges felt the need to cooperate with the authorities in bringing Shaw to his knees. Yet it is also the case that Shaw's puritan opponents appear in the documents as somewhat less enthusiastic than their Laudian counterparts. Where men such as Walton and Watts handed over extensive and detailed evidence, designed to trumpet Shaw's heretical excess, the godly participants proved more reticent. They signed fewer articles, and lodged less spectacular charges of heterodoxy. Indeed, Denison, Crabtree, and Castleton signed no articles against the minister, instead crafting a more general complaint that Shaw was "a very unprofitable preacher (besides the errors where of he is accused)" who "affecteth uncouth and strange phrases which the people do not understand." While we should not want to infer too much from such subtle differences in tone, this hesitant and measured participation is perhaps a sign of the tortuous situation in which the godly found themselves. On the one

---

21 Christopher Dow, *Innovations Unjustly Charged upon the Present Church and State* (1637), 197.

hand, they felt compelled to silence Shaw, perhaps the most vocal and critical of London's newly emboldened anti-legal preachers, in order to shut down the threat such ministers posed to their authority; at the same time, they undoubtedly saw the need to preempt an event that might easily, without their participation, have turned into something like a grand exercise in anti-puritan propaganda. Only by helping to topple Shaw could the godly undercut the polemical intentions of their Laudian opponents. Yet at the same time (as Denison had learned in the case of Etherington) they needed to tread warily. For such cooperation with the authorities—particularly in the tense moments immediately following the collapse of the 1629 Parliament—was not likely to sit well with many godly laypeople. This was particularly the case when the object of their wrath was a man who, despite his strange opinions, undoubtedly appeared in the eyes of many puritans to be a member of the godly community by virtue of his affect, his language, and his associations. From this perspective, the muted and halting nature of their participation may be seen as a sort of compromise, an attempt to reconcile a set of mutually incompatible priorities that were pulling them in different directions.

This surmise is perhaps rendered somewhat more likely given the fact that the formal legal proceedings against Shaw represented only the culmination of a protracted process of backroom negotiation and dispute. As in the case of Etherington, Shaw's prosecution had been preceded by significant debate within the puritan underground.[22] It was here, in the dimly lit world of semipublic debate, pulpit feud, rumor, and maneuver—the social universe of the godly—that the battle between antinomians and their opponents was waged in earnest. Thus, the nonconformist lecturer Abraham Grame appears to have conducted an extended polemical campaign against Shaw, repeatedly and personally denouncing the man and his opinions from the pulpit of St. Helens Bishopsgate. Meanwhile, the godly engaged in agitated private conference with Shaw and his followers, seeking first to assess, and then to contain his errors. As a result, much of the evidence used to convict him appears to have been gathered in informal meetings between Shaw and his supporters, on the one side, and various lay puritan opponents, on the other. Thus, for instance, Nathaniel Waker reported an exchange with one Joseph Smith, a chandler of Bishopsgate Street and a notorious follower of Shaw. Similarly, many of the articles against Shaw were offered up by one "John Wilson gathered from his mouth at home," and countersigned by a "Mr. John Palmer of Paternoster Row." Even more tellingly, several articles were signed by the indefatigable joiners Rowland Tompson and Thomas Rogers, Denison's associates who had in fact engaged in similar private disputes with John Etherington three years

[22] See Lake and Como, "'Orthodoxy' and Its Discontents"; Como and Lake, "Peter Shaw."

earlier, providing evidence central to the High Commission case against the boxmaker. As in the case of Etherington, it is likely that these meetings may have been semi-formal disputations, held at least ostensibly with the intention of coming to a shared consensus. The involvement of Tompson and Rogers suggests first of all that Denison's role in the affair was rather more extensive than his limited participation in the prosecution might lead one to believe. Secondly, it would appear to suggest a high degree of continuity between the two cases. Certain members of the godly community were now beginning to see themselves as engaged in an ongoing battle against a unified, pernicious opponent, an antinomian "other" that needed to be stopped at all costs.

This sense of increasing polarization appears to have worked both ways, a fact reflected most clearly in an anonymous letter that had been sent to the godly lecturer Abraham Grame in the weeks preceding the trial. Grame had apparently played an active part in recent events, taking it upon himself to denounce Shaw from his pulpit. When he received the letter, he evidently turned it over to the authorities, ensuring its survival amongst the State Papers. Although the writer of the letter identified himself only as "HP," the surviving copy of the letter notes that "Mr. Joseph Smith in Bishop's gate street is conjectured to be the author or factur in this letter because his wife proferred 20s. to one to steale it out of my study." Whether Smith or not, the writer presented himself as an impartial and disinterested party—"I professe my selfe to be none of his disciples"—whose only motive was to defuse the "great quarrell . . . most cunningly contrived and fomented between you and one Shaw." Yet the author went on to warn Grame that if he continued in his plan to draw court articles against Shaw, "be sure ont, you wilbe called to an account not only for breach of a canon, which for bids pulpitts opposition but also for far greater things, laide to your charge, which if they should be proved would crush you to pieces." The writer suggested a further meeting with Grame "in some private place, where neither of us are knowen," presumably so that he could reveal the details of the sinister conspiracy brewing against Shaw in high places: "Therefore, let me tell you, the plott is laid for you. You shall have all faire audience, till you have done your utmost against Shaw, and so soone as that is done, you shalbe the next man that shall tast of the severitie of justice, as some in great place have already discovered and professed." Smith's letter thus sought to invoke a language of godly solidarity in an effort to persuade Grame to desist: "Tis that Arminians and Papists gape for, to see the Puritans, as they terme you, to dash them selves in peices one against another." Yet despite its claims to be offering disinterested counsel to a godly friend, the letter was brimming with malice, bearing between its lines a clear threat of retribution. Thus, Grame was advised to "leave towne for a while" in order to allow the squall to blow over.

The sense of solidarity and godly insiderhood that had hindered Denison's campaign against Etherington was now on the verge of disintegration. Although Smith was still able to pay lip service to the bonds of saintly communion, it seems clear that by early 1629, there could be no easy resolution of the conflict between London's mainstream puritans and their anti-legal critics. Where Denison, Roborough, and their lay associates appear to have stood virtually alone in their campaign against Etherington three years earlier, a broad range of godly ministers and laypeople now willingly stepped forward to participate in a formal, judicial action against a popular godly lecturer. So, likewise, proponents of anti-legal ideas seem to have increased the pitch of their attack on their mainstream opponents. Quiet, behind-the-scenes negotiation and debate seemed ever less likely to yield peaceful resolution to what was in fact an escalating crisis.

Without question, the pressure exerted by the Laudian regime had helped to escalate the crisis. There is good reason to believe that the action against Shaw, which apparently followed immediately on the heels of the dissolution of the 1629 Parliament, was the first salvo in a concerted campaign by Laud to purge his diocese of the disruptive and anarchic influence of puritanism run amok. In the following months, the bishop would begin to exert increasing pressure on the godly, calling many godly ministers to answer for a whole range of offenses, most of which would have escaped the attentions of previous episcopal regimes. Indeed, in the two years following the Shaw case, at least four of the puritan ministers involved in the attack on Shaw would be hauled before the church courts for disciplinary breaches. Nalton, Burges, Crabtree, and the unfortunate Abraham Grame would all find themselves called to answer to the Laudian authorities by 1631, with Denison following a few months later on a charge of attempting to seduce several of his female parishioners. Joseph Smith's dire prophecy thus received stark fulfillment: godly participation in the crusade against Shaw ultimately did nothing to allay the suspicions or to mitigate the hostilities of the newly ascendant Laudian regime.

When Shaw's case began in early 1629, however, the rigorous anti-puritan policies of the Personal Rule were still in their infancy, and the godly proved willing to maintain their uneasy coalition with the ecclesiastical authorities. What is clear is that the case of Peter Shaw did not put an end to debate over the contested questions of Law and free grace. By June 1629, John Traske likewise appears to have been inhibited from preaching. Although neither the reason for nor the timing of Traske's suspension is now clear, a surviving letter from Traske to Laud—in which the inveterate puritan characteristically labeled his diocesan "implacably cruel" before begging him for mercy—seemed to blame Laud for the suspension, suggesting that Traske had been inhibited after Laud became bishop of London in August 1628.[23] Whether Traske's suspension had anything to do with his antinomian proclivities must remain an open question. But on June 25, Robert Towne was likewise suspended by the High Commission.[24] Here, there is no doubt about the nature of his offenses. Towne was accused of doctrinal heterodoxy. This we know because in the 1640s and 1650s, Towne published two polemical works, in which he chronicled some of his troubles in London. The first of these works, *The Assertion of Grace*, had originally been written in the early 1630s as an answer to the published attack of the puritan cleric Thomas Taylor, one of Towne's ministerial opponents in the capital; although not published until 1644, Towne claimed on its title page that the work had been sent to Taylor in manuscript prior to the latter's death in 1633. This piece, together with Towne's later self-defense, *A Re-Assertion of Grace*, provides brief but revealing glimpses of what appears to have been a widespread and escalating conflict, involving not just Shaw and Towne but a whole series of anti-legalists and an increasingly hostile set of godly critics.

Once again, the exact details of Towne's account remain murky: he offered neither exact names nor exact dates in describing his conflicts with his godly opponents. Yet his descriptions are quite vivid. He claimed that at some point (presumably in early 1629) he tried to arrange meetings with certain ministers who had been criticizing him. As in the case of Etherington, these olive branches were allegedly refused. Yet on Towne's account, some lay puritans were willing to meet with him for purposes of disputation. As he explained it,

> certain of their noted disciples . . . with oily words . . . urged me, as the Jews did Christ, to speak many things . . . saying they intended me no harm, I must not have such a thought of them: and at our parting gave me the hand never to open their mouth more against me. And yet the next news was, (can you credit me?) that out of our Conference, misconstruing and perverting what was said, they had compiled and exhibited to the Bishop eighteen Propositions or Articles. By this kinde of Ministers and Professors (who can set a fair gloss on all their doings, pretending much of God, and for the Law) I have been brought into divers Courts, and into High Commission, where I

---

[23] PRO, SPD 16/144/75, letter of June 13. In 1627, Traske had been questioned, and very possibly imprisoned, by Bishop Mountaigne for his involvement in an incident involving a sermon preached at the execution of one Joshua Purchas, a puritan convicted of rape. It is possible that his inhibition may have dated from this period.

[24] For Towne's suspension, see PRO, SPD 16/145/55.

was twice imprisoned, my ministry restrained, and I compelled to attend the Court two yeers together.[25]

Like Etherington and Shaw before him, then, Towne's prosecution before the High Commission appears to have relied in large part on the testimony of godly lay people, accumulated in private conference. It is clear, however, that these debates did not cease with his suspension, for Towne (who consistently claimed to be preaching nothing more or less than orthodox protestant doctrine) managed to gain his freedom in the following months, probably by offering the authorities assurances of his orthodoxy and conformity. At some point, possibly in the winter of 1629-30, he preached a sermon at St. Bartholomew by the Exchange in which he argued that "the Gospel, and not the Law was the seed and doctrine of our new birth, yea that the Law did not sanctifie, &c. which divers Ministers and others excepted against; and many affirmed that the Law was made effectuall by Christ for that end and use."[26] At another point, Towne claimed that an adversary had crept secretly into the shadows of a church to take notes on one of his sermons.[27] The picture that emerges from Towne's recollections is quite remarkable. By 1629-30, London's puritans appear to have been embroiled in a very public dispute over the role and status of the Moral Law, a dispute that was now being conducted openly from the pulpits of London, and in which ministers eagerly and suspiciously listened in on one another's sermons.

These sermon battles, which were not limited to Towne and his critics, apparently reached their highest pitch in February 1630. In that month, the godly minister Thomas Gataker reported to his Cambridge correspondent Samuel Ward that "about some . . . points concerning the use of the moral law, whither infidelity be a sinne, faith commaunded in the law, and the estate of a Christian et. hath ben eager bickering among some of our London divines, and bitter invectives either against other in pulpit."[28] There can be no doubt that Gataker was here referring to the disputes between antinomians and their godly opponents. One of Peter Shaw's alleged errors had been "That infidelitie or want of justifieing faith in Christ is no sinne," while Thomas Taylor, in his 1631 denunciation of antinomianism would claim that one of

[25] R. Towne, *A Re-Assertion of Grace. Or Vindiciae Evangelii* (1654), preface, sigs. A2v-A3r. Although Towne does not explicitly date this conference, it may be inferred that he was referring to his 1629 High Commission case, since he claims that these events took place prior to his removal to Lancashire c. 1635. The conference may therefore be dated, with a fair degree of safety, to early 1629.

[26] R. Towne, *Assertion of Grace* (1645), 163. The sermon at St. Bartholomew was preached before 1631.

[27] Ibid., 51.

[28] Bodleian Library, Tanner MS. 71, fol. 35r. 11 February 1629/30.

the characteristic mistakes of his London opponents had been "their elevating the sin of infidelity, (which strongly savors also of liberty) as that it is no sinne; or at least of the morall law . . . though I am sure the Scripture maketh it a sinne."[29] Indeed, Towne's own sermon at St. Bartholomew by the Exchange, which had earned the hostility of his ministerial listeners, may have been one installment in the noisy public disputes that Gataker here described. Such "bitter invectives" represented a grievous violation of the unwritten codes of godly decorum, attesting to the breakdown of attempts to ameliorate conflict between antinomians and their critics. Yet it should not be assumed that even at this point, all godly people, or even all godly ministers, had been won over to the view that anti-legalists were pernicious heretics. In fact, Gataker's matter-of-fact description may be revealing in this respect. His account contains no overheated denunciations of "antinomians" or "libertines." Not yet having consigned proponents of anti-legalism to the scrap heap of sectarian error, he described the antagonists in more neutral terms as "our London divines," perhaps even suggesting that he thought of men such as Towne as legitimate members of the godly community (a scruple that would dissolve in the 1640s, when Gataker himself became a very public critic of civil-war antinomianism). This might well suggest that the more aggressive puritan opponents of anti-legal ideas had not yet convinced all members of the London godly community that their opposites were beyond the pale of true religion. Even in early 1630, the situation and the theological issues at stake appear to have remained fluid and open to contestation.

Yet throughout the months that followed, tendentious doctrinal questions of Law and grace continued to be canvassed in London pulpits, escalating tempers and perhaps further sharpening and hardening the battle lines of the debate. In October 1630, for instance, Obadiah Sedgwick, one of London's most popular and charismatic godly lecturers, carefully refuted that paradigmatic "Eatonist" shibboleth, the claim that God could see no sin in the elect.[30] At the same time in Kensington, John Everarde was busily delivering weekly diatribes against the soul-killing literalism of mainstream puritanism, while dispensing his own extravagant and brash perfectionist alternative. In the heightened tension of the moment, however, such incendiary rhetoric was growing ever more difficult to sustain, and Everarde soon found himself once again beneath the magnifying glass of official scrutiny, resulting in his removal

---

[29] Como and Lake, "Peter Shaw," 708; Thomas Taylor, *Regula Vitae, The Rule of Law under the Gospel* (1631), 124-25. See below, Chapter Nine, for a discussion of the way that this question intercut the broader theological debate over the Law.
[30] British Library, Harleian MS. 1198, fol. 8v-9r.

from the Kensington lectureship.[31] By December 1630, the atmosphere had grown so tense that even mildly anti-legal statements concerning the Law and the Gospel were automatically interpreted as countenancing, or even promoting, antinomianism. In that month, the young Philip Nye, lecturer at St. Michael Cornhill, delivered a sermon, which, while not explicitly antinomian, recalled and even replicated some of the claims made by more extreme figures. His indiscreet statements were duly recorded by a hostile listener, who submitted notes to the authorities. It was further reported that "These things and such lyke delyvered by Mr Nye were so fowle and so much dislyked that Mr doctor Dennyson," the scourge of London antinomians, "did preach diverse sermons against them."[32]

It was probably as a result of these ongoing "eager bickerings" that Towne, apparently together with other accused antinomians, met with their ministerial opponents in a succession of private conferences. Unfortunately, Towne did not name any of the participants in these debates, although it seems likely that Towne's sparring partner, Thomas Taylor, was present. At one of these meetings, Towne had argued—in obvious opposition to what Traske called the "joyless sorrow" of mainstream puritan divinity—that a believer "ought exceedingly to rejoyce, in that he was so freely justified and saved." One of Towne's opposites (probably not Taylor, this time) objected, claiming that justification and salvation were two distinct states: although a believer was justified in this life, salvation was a thing only achieved in death. Towne's opposite further threatened to "bring his opponent in before Authoritie, unlesse he would recant what he had said." A second meeting was decided upon, and "a Moderator" chosen, so that "Authors might be consulted with," and the question resolved, "yet nothing could be effected." In the meantime, "the said

---

[31] Everard, *Gospel-Treasures*, 264, in which the editor, Rapha Harford, noted that Everarde had been "taken off his publicke preaching at *Kensington*" before he had finished a sermon cycle called "Of Suffering and Reigning with Christ." Although the completed sermons in the cycle are undated, several internal clues allow us with reasonable certainty to place them, and hence Everarde's removal, to 1630-32. See, for instance, ibid., 211, 214, where Everarde made light of his duty to catechize his audience, undoubtedly a reference to the King's Instructions on Preaching (1629), which held that afternoon lectureships should be converted into catechizing sessions, strongly suggesting that the cycle was preached after early 1630, when the instructions went into effect. Yet we also know from both his sermons and the articles against him that he held the Kensington lectureship no later than 1631-1632 (compare Guildhall Library MS. 9537/13, fol. 56r; Everard, *Gospel-Treasures*, 168; Bodleian Library, Tanner MS. 67, fol. 144v). This allows us to pinpoint 1630 or 1631 as the most likely year of his removal.

[32] PRO, SPD 16/177/68. For a transcription of the sermon notes, and a discussion in the context of Shaw's case, see Como and Lake, "Peter Shaw."

Minister published it to all, and so it was reported that wee held perfection in the flesh," an accusation that Towne (a classically "imputative" antinomian) denied. In December 1630, Towne wrote a long letter to this unnamed critic, defending his initial position and denying that he maintained that believers were actually perfect in this life (a letter he later appended to the *Assertion of Grace*).[33]

The sort of semi-formal disputation described by Towne appears to have occurred with increasing regularity in this period. Hence Henry Burton, the famed godly divine, complained in 1631 of John Eaton "comming sometimes to contest with mee, and to charge mee for preaching the dead faith."[34] In fact, it would be precisely such a verbal duel that would lead to the next major antinomian prosecution. Late in 1630, William Cooper, rector of St. Thomas Apostle and a friend of Stephen Denison, visited St. Michael Paternoster Royal to eavesdrop on the afternoon sermon of Samuel Prettie. As Cooper described it, he "understood the said Samuel Pretty was appointed to preach at the church articulate . . . and having heard say that he was a schismaticall preacher this deponent having donne his sermon at his owne church he went to hear the said Samuel, and having some ability to write shorthand he, this deponent, applyed himselfe to take notes of the said Samuel's sermon as diligently as he could." According to Cooper, Prettie delivered a number of erroneous opinions, including the claim "That all effects of sinne are taken away from believers," and that "God cannot be angry with a believer for his sinne." After the sermon, Cooper privately challenged Prettie's doctrine, and the two "divers tymes" engaged in debate over contested theological issues, including the question of whether "justification and salvation are all one." Given that this was precisely the point at issue between Towne and his nemesis, it might be speculated that the arguments between Prettie and Cooper were related to, or at least sparked by, the more formal disputations described by Towne. In any event, Cooper shortly thereafter decided to inform the authorities of the debates; in October 1631, Cooper's testimony would secure the conviction of Prettie before the court of High Commission, marking the third of London's major antinomian trials.[35]

---

[33] For Traske's comment, see Traske, *The True Gospel Vindicated, From the Reproach of a New Gospel* (n.p., 1636), 27. For Towne's conferences, see *Assertion*, 156-57. It is not possible to establish the exact date of these conferences, although 1630 is the most reasonable surmise. They certainly took place before December 1630, when Towne wrote his letter. The letter is printed in ibid., 157-61.

[34] H. Burton, *The Law and the Gospell reconciled. Or, The Evangelicall Fayth, and the Morall Law how they stand together in the state of grace* (1631), 21-22.

[35] S. R. Gardiner, ed., *Reports of Cases in the Courts of Star Chamber and High Commission*, Camden Society, N. S., 39 (1886), 182-84. Cooper would stand as a

While Prettie was imprisoned and awaiting trial, John Eachard, vicar of Darsham in Suffolk, penned his crucial pastoral letter to his "faithfull friends" in London. As we have seen, this letter exhorted Prettie to cling to the truth in spite of the threat of persecution, pointing to the patience and courage with which the recently deceased John Eaton had undergone his own tribulations. Perhaps somewhat unwisely, Eachard then went on to call on other members of the London antinomian community—Towne, Traske, Emersone, and Hodges—to read the letter to Prettie and to encourage him to remain steadfast. Unfortunately for Eachard, the authorities intercepted the letter. How, precisely, they managed to do this is not clear. Possibly Prettie lost his nerve and turned it over himself; alternatively, it might have been confiscated from his cell against his will; a final possibility might be that the authorities possessed an informant within the antinomian community, although very little evidence survives to suggest that this was so. In any case, Eachard's misfortune represents our gain, for it has ensured that the letter, together with some brief marginal annotations, has survived among the State Papers (see Appendix E, below). Unsurprisingly, when Eachard was summoned before the High Commissioners on 20 June 1632, the prosecution produced the letter as the chief article of evidence against him, and large portions of it were read aloud before he was sentenced. Eachard was recommitted to prison and ordered to renounce his antinomian opinions or face deprivation. Initially Eachard heeded his own counsel to Prettie; he steadfastly refused to recant. Eight months in the Gatehouse appear to have eroded his resolve, however. In February of 1633, Eachard offered up a retraction and was released by the authorities.[36] This represented the fourth and final major High Commission trial of the period, effectively completing the official onslaught against the antinomian ministerial leadership.

The Laity

Yet the heated activity and maneuvering that lay behind these high-profile trials was by no means limited to the clergy. The vehemence of these continuing disputes flowed from the fact that London antinomians were mounting a challenge to the doctrinal and spiritual hegemony of mainstream godly ministers. This was very much a contest for the affection and support of the puritan laity, and it is therefore no surprise that we see signs of lay interest and involvement in these issues. We have already observed that Shaw and Towne had both been convicted partly through evidence gathered in conference with

---

compurgator for Denison in the latter's High Commission trial in the mid-1630s. See PRO, SPD 16/414/23 I., fol. 40.

[36] See Gardiner, *High Commission*, 316-21; CUL MS. Dd. ii. 21, fols. 76v-77r, 86r, 88r, 101r, 113r, 141v; PRO, SPD 16/520/80, fols. 119-21.

godly laypeople. Nathaniel Waker, a London lecturer, had meanwhile locked horns with Joseph Smith, a chandler and notorious disciple of Shaw.[37] The same Smith was, as noted above, thought to have written a threatening letter to the godly preacher Abraham Grame, a letter that Smith's wife allegedly sought to steal back from Grame's study to keep it from the authorities.[38] But to judge from such fragments of evidence as remain, these disputes and divisions were not limited to feuding ministers and their closest lay disciples; rather, arguments and anxieties over these contested issues appear to have quickly diffused into the wider consciousness of the godly laity, provoking sometimes sharp debate and initiative independent of the pulpit sparring of the clergy. Thomas Bakewell, a London layman, reported extensive disputes, both in conference and writing, between himself and certain unnamed antinomians, which he dated to 1630.[39] Similarly, in early 1631, Henry Church, a haberdasher of St. Martin Vintry, received a letter from an unidentified correspondent maintaining that the elect were not guilty of sin after justification; Church, who like his future brother-in-law Nehemiah Wallington spent much of his spare time acting as a spiritual counselor to his godly brethren, immediately denounced this position as tending toward that of the "Eatonists," noting that "these although their Heresie hath bin confuted in Pulpits, and convinced by Scripture, yet with fury goe on."[40]

Obviously, then, these were hardly rarefied theological debates conducted in cloistered, clerical secrecy; they were noisy public affairs in which the laity were being asked increasingly to take sides. Unsurprisingly, a succession of laypeople who cast their lot with the antinomians ended up before the authorities. In 1631, following on information provided by the renowned puritan Samuel Ward, the Ipswich laymen Francis Bridges, Henry Mudd, and Henry Firmin were called before the High Commission.[41] They were followed

---

[37] He was identified as Joseph Smith of Bishopsgate, probably the chandler of the same name of St. Helens Bishopsgate, for whom see W. B. Bannerman, ed., *The Registers of St. Helen's, Bishopsgate, London,* Publications of the Harleian Society, 31 (1904), 21-22.

[38] See Como and Lake, "Peter Shaw."

[39] [Thomas Bakewell], *A Faithfull Messenger Sent after the Antinomians* (1644), 1, 23, 25, 28. See Chapter Six for a discussion of one point at issue between him and his opponents.

[40] H. Church, *Divine and Christian Letters* (1636), 20-29. Church's response is dated April 11, 1631. For Church's marriage to Wallington's half sister, c. 1632, see P. Seaver, *Wallington's World: A Puritan Artisan in Seventeenth-Century New England* (Stanford: Stanford University Press, 1985), 70.

[41] CUL MS. Dd. ii. 21, fols. 77v-78r, 86v, 90r (High Commission Act Book); for an eyewitness account of one of their appearances before the court, see Gardiner,

by the Londoners Richard and Joan Lane, allegedly admirers of the antinomian tailor-evangelist Greene.[42] In 1632, John Eaton's widow, Susan, sought in the aftermath of her husband's death secretly to publish his magnum opus, "The Honey-Combe of Free Justification." Somehow the authorities got wind of the plan, and she too was dragged before the High Commission, where it was demanded that she surrender any and all copies of the manuscript, which "she absolutely refused and denyed to produce." For her trouble, she received a four-month stint in Newgate.[43] In the next year, a stationer named John Bartlet, together with our now-familiar friend, the Marrowist Edward Fisher, were likewise summoned before the Court. As the records at one point referred to Fisher as a "stationer," and at another point as a "barber," it is safe to assume that the charges against them related in some way to Fisher's activities as a clandestine manuscript and book dealer. Whatever the nature of his offenses, it was claimed in November 1633 that Fisher "had trifled and dallyed with the Court in not giving his personall Answers to the Articles objected against him all this Tearme" and consequently "he was ordered to be attached and comitted" to jail until he cooperated.[44]

In 1631, the godly broke their self-imposed silence, finally commenting in print on the "hot contentions" and "eager bickerings" that had been afflicting their ranks. Two books, one by Henry Burton and the other by Thomas Taylor, appeared to confute the errors of the antinomians.[45] As we have seen, both Taylor and Burton had been involved in face-to-face disputes with anti-legalists in the preceding years. What is significant, then, is not so much their decision to attack their opponents in the press, but the fact that it took members of the godly community so long to actually permit these disputes to enter the public domain of print. No longer could the explosive questions of free grace be soft-peddled, glossed into insignificance, or contained through the processes of debate and conference normally preferred by the godly in cases of internecine theological dispute. Accordingly, a spate of puritan divines, in-

---

High Commission, 270-71. For further comments on their religiosity, see below, Chapter Nine.

[42] Gardiner, *High Commission*, 188-94; and Chapter Nine, below.

[43] CUL MS. Dd. ii. 21, fols. 89v, 148r.

[44] Ibid., fols. 223v, 231v, 253r. This surmise is rendered even more likely by the fact that in 1634, Samuel Hartlib mentioned a "Mr. Bartlet" as a London manuscript dealer who had laid out a large sum of money to copy various works of Richard Sibbes. Sheffield University Library, Hartlib Papers, 29/2/20B, from *The Hartlib Papers: A Complete Text and Image Database of the Papers of Samuel Hartlib (c.1600-1662) Held in Sheffield University Library*, 2d ed. (Sheffield: Humanities Research Online, 2002).

[45] Burton, *The Law and the Gospell Reconciled* (1631); Taylor, *Regula Vitae, The Rule of Law under the Gospel* (1631).

cluding Edward Reynolds, Joseph Bentham and Samuel Torshel (who, like Towne, had preached at St. Bartholomew by the Exchange in 1629) joined Taylor and Burton in publishing books that sought to clarify the contested issues of grace and the Moral Law, thus seeking to close down the theological ruptures that had been opened by anti-legal preachers.[46] These disputes were thus widespread and divisive. Few London puritans would have been oblivious to the conflicts and questions posed, with varying degrees of hostility and forthrightness, by those accused of antinomianism. In 1631, Torshel provided a fitting commentary on this state of affairs: "The Questions of *Free Justification*, of our *Christian Liberty, and of the use of the Law*, are agitated of late, not without much heat, while one side carefull, the other side fearful of good works, doe both strive for Christ, and mistake each others grounds. They are untoward names wherewith Christians brand one the other: while one is called a *Legalist*, another pointed at for an *Antinomist*, and this man repayes the former, with the hateful name of *Justiciary*."[47]

Aftermath

By 1633, the combined efforts of London puritans and the ecclesiastical authorities appear to have effectively muzzled the "Antinomists," ending widespread public debate and driving well-known exponents further underground. Given the succession of unequivocal sentences handed down by the High Commission starting in 1629, it was no longer possible for antinomian preachers to proclaim themselves publicly as defenders of free grace and orthodox protestant doctrine (a dubious claim even at the best of times); there could now be little question that their opinions would be vigorously exposed

---

[46] See E. Reynolds, "Of the Use of the Law" in *Three Treatises of The Vanity of the Creature. The Sinfulnesse of Sinne. The Life of Christ* (1631), 370-92, which was designed to rehabilitate and clarify the saving and evangelical role of the Moral Law, as against the "the ignorance and absurdity of those men who cry downe preaching of the Law, as a course leading to despaire and discontentment" (388-89). Reynolds was at the time lecturing at Lincoln's Inn; J. Bentham, *The Societie of the Saints: Or, a Treatise of Good-fellows* (1630), 180-93; S. Torshel, *The Three Questions of Free Justification. Christian Liberty. The Use of the Law* (1632), passim. This treatise, which was based upon sermons preached by Torshel at St. Bartholomew's, and which was published at the request of some of his erstwhile London auditors, struck an irenic chord, but in fact contained caustic and clearly pointed attacks upon the positions and arguments of the London antinomians.

[47] Torshel, *The Three Questions*, 1-2. The preface is dated 1631. To my knowledge, the only figure to use the term "justiciary" in print prior to 1640 was John Traske's alleged associate Rice Boye, who used it to refer to Traske's enemy Edward Norice (see Chapter Two, above).

by their godly enemies, and vigorously prosecuted by the church. Unsurprisingly, several leading antinomians seem to have abandoned London in this period. Perhaps most damaging to the cause was the death of John Eaton, probably in early 1631.[48] Of the various antinomian ministers who had occupied pulpits in London in the late 1620s and early 1630s, only Thomas Hodges, shielded by his powerful patron Holland, continued to preach freely in the capital throughout the Personal Rule.

For those who lacked the backing of ultrapowerful courtiers, episcopal vigilance appears to have made London a less than hospitable environment by 1632, and many accordingly retired to more amenable jurisdictions. Emersone, for instance, seems to have moved into the curacy of Shoreham, Sussex. At the same time, Traske appears to have been proselytizing vigorously in Gloucestershire, perhaps with the help of his friend Rice Boye. In nearby Somerset, the minister John Crandon reported theological debates with antinomians in the 1630s; here, too, the culprit may have been the Somerset native and notorious itinerant Traske or his associates.[49] Meanwhile, at some point after October 1631, Robert Towne appeared in Nottinghamshire, where he obtained a curacy, and apparently resumed his habit of antagonizing local puritan clergymen.[50] Once again, he found himself under threat of ecclesiastical censure, and he fled to Lancashire, now the home of Roger Brearley.[51] Here, as we have seen, he reestablished contact with the "Grindletonian" network that operated along the Lancashire-Yorkshire border. Like Towne, Peter Shaw also returned to Lancashire, where he had first dabbled in antinomian ideas. In 1632, he obtained a fellowship at the Collegiate Church of Manchester, followed shortly thereafter by a living in nearby Radcliffe (although as in the case of Hodges, the provision of a permanent eccesiastical benefice appears to have taken the edge off his earlier, very strident antinomianism).[52] Samuel Prettie's whereabouts during the 1630s are unknown, although it is clear that he had actively championed anti-legal ideas in Northamptonshire in the

---

[48] A "John Eaton clerk of Donnstone Stockwod" witnessed the will of John Amey (or Ames), an inhabitant of the London parish of St. Giles Cripplegate, in Sept. 1630. PRO, PROB 11/158, fol. 101v. This was probably Eaton the antinomian.

[49] J. Crandon, *Mr. Baxters Aphorisms Exorcized and Anthorized* (1654), 264-66. I am very grateful to Michael Winship for turning my attention to this source.

[50] R. A. Marchant, *Puritans and Church Courts in the Diocese of York* (London: Longmans, 1960), 313; D. D. Hall, ed. *The Antinomian Controversy, 1636-1638: A Documentary History* (Durham and London: Duke University Press, 1990), 32.

[51] Towne, *Re-assertion*, sig. A3r.

[52] See Como and Lake, "Peter Shaw." Shaw had arrived at the Cathedral Church of Manchester by Oct. 1632. See H. Brierley, ed., *The Registers of the Cathedral Church of Manchester, Burials—1616 to 1653*, Lancashire Parish Register Society, 56 (1919), 456.

1620s, and he too may have abandoned London for familiar (and less dangerous) ground. From a certain standpoint then, the efforts of their enemies had succeeded in making London unsafe for outspoken antinomian preachers. Yet this success scattered many of the movement's leading clerical proponents throughout the countryside, perhaps contributing in an unintended way to the wider dispersion of their ideas.

The atmosphere in the city may be gauged by examining John Traske's fate; at some point, probably in 1635, he returned to London, where he appears for a time to have ministered to the Southwark "semi-separatist" congregation that had been founded by Henry Jacob. Despite the fact that this "congregation" consisted of an informal gathering of believers, meeting privately and outside the boundaries of the institutional church, the authorities managed to learn of Traske's whereabouts. In 1636, an agent of the High Commission confronted him at the home of one "Mr Digby"; Traske refused to yield to the warrant, instead insisting on a hearing before the Lord Mayor, who promptly deposited him in jail; only death, which struck later in 1636, freed Traske from his endless legal troubles.[53] Other suspected antinomians, including two perfumers called "Callon" and "Cox," were independently arrested by another ecclesiastical pursuivant and hauled before the High Commissioner Sir Henry Marten, where they were presumably interrogated.[54] At least one other sometime antinomian sympathizer, a victualler's wife called "Farthing Jane" appears to have been questioned by Sir John Lambe.[55]

Yet the laity apparently proved far more difficult to discipline than the ministerial leadership of the movement. It seems clear that the onslaught of 1629-31 had not succeeded in eradicating the movement entirely: it merely drove it beneath the surface, forcing anti-legalists deeper into their private conventicles. In 1672, when looking back penitently on his misspent sectarian youth, the sometime Anabaptist William Allen confessed to Richard Baxter that

> As I have been taken in the Snare of Separation for a time, so I was in that of *Antinomianism*, about 37 or 38 years ago, not long after my first coming to *London*; as not being able to withstand the Insinuations of it, and yet to retain the Opinion of the Imputation of Christ's Righteousness in that Notion

---

[53] From the so-called "Gould manuscript" (Jacob church memorials), transcribed in Champlin Burrage, *The Early English Dissenters in the Light of Recent Research (1550-1641)* (Cambridge: Cambridge University Press, 1912), 2: 300.

[54] PRO, SPD 16/520/85, fols. 126r, 127r. Lambe claimed that they had been caught by "Vesey," a well-known High Commission pursuivant, for whom see Burrage, *Dissenters*, 2: 300.

[55] PRO, SPD 16/520/85, fol. 127r, where it was claimed that "she hath inform against them [the antinomians]."

> of it, in which I had been instructed; and never fully recovered my self till I heard Mr. *John Goodwin.* The Experience of what I suffered my self, and occasioned others to suffer by my running into those Errours, hath put me upon doing more to warn others against them, or recover them out of them, then otherwise I should have thought fit for me to have done.[56]

Assuming his memory is to be trusted, Allen's slide into imputative antinomianism may be dated with some safety to the mid-1630s—that is, the period immediately after the official purges had cleansed London of many of the most important antinomian clerics. It is perhaps no surprise, then, that once the veil of ecclesiastical oversight was lifted in the early 1640s, antinomian ideas experienced an almost immediate recrudescence in the capital. The connections between prewar antinomianism and its civil-war offshoots receive preliminary discussion in the epilogue and conclusion. First, however, we must turn to examine the ideological shape of early Stuart antinomianism. For it is only once we have come to understand the intellectual architecture of the antinomian community that we can see clearly how and why it became a community in the first place.

---

[56] Matthew Sylvester, ed., *Reliquiae Baxertianae: Or, Mr. Richard Baxters Narrative of the most Memorable Passages of his Life and Times* (1696), Appendix, 98. I would like to thank Michael Winship for this reference.

CHAPTER 4

The Intellectual Context of Controversy: Law, Faith, and the Paradoxes of Puritan Pastoral Divinity

The Law and the Gospel; or the Pauline Contradiction

To understand the bitter, early Stuart disputes over the nature of true godliness, we must briefly examine the Judeo-Christian legacy of thought concerning the Law. The theological concept of "law," as used by early modern Christians, had its most remote ancestry in the Jewish concept of *Torah*. In its original incarnation, the Hebrew word *torah* had meant, simply enough, any rule, law, or ordinance. It is used in the Jewish scripture to refer to specific statutes. To transgress against any divinely appointed torah or ordinance was to violate the will of God (otherwise known as sin). But by the second temple period, when Christianity sprouted off from Judaism, the term had taken on a different connotation, and it was this connotation that would be decisive for Christianity. Perhaps as a consequence of Hellenistic influences, in which each distinct religion was seen as a "law" (*nomos*) with its own "lawgiver," the word torah had come to be used more generally to apply to the first five sections of the Jewish scriptures. These five sections (or "books," according to Christian usage) laid out the *nomos*, that is, the rules, traditions, and ordinances governing the Jewish people, as handed down by Judaism's lawgiver, Moses. *Torah* had thus come to connote, in a general sense, the divinely revealed rule that governed the Jews, and in a more specific sense, the first five books of scripture, in which these laws were laid out.[1] Saint Paul and other early Christians used the word in both ways. In time, the dominant Christian understanding of Torah would come to center not so much on the first five books of scripture, but on the specific commandments that had been handed down by God to the Jews through Moses. These injunctions—the Ten Commandments, as well as all of the various rules and ordinances laid out in the five books—taken together would be called the "Jewish Law" or the "Mosaic Law" by Christians. This manner of conceptualizing the Law still held sway in early Stuart England. Before turning to the seventeenth century, however, it is necessary to examine the manner in which the concept of Law was used in the New Testament, for the conflicts under discussion in this book were in part conflicts over what the New Testament meant.

As is clear from even the most cursory glance at the Gospels and Pauline epistles, Christianity was at least in part a heretical rebellion against entrenched, first-century forms of Jewish legal practice. If we are to trust the Gospel narratives, Jesus had apparently mounted a fairly substantive critique of certain interpretations of Jewish law in his own day. He rejected strict interpretations of the Sabbath, condemned the Deuteronomic teaching on divorce, and consistently flouted pharisaical rules governing rigid separation from "unclean" elements.[2] With great fanfare, he openly violated large chunks of what had apparently come to be standard and sacred applications of the Law. These very public and very defiant gestures did much more than pique local curiosity and earn the hostility of the Judeo-Roman authorities; in fact, the sentiments that underlay such acts of calculated, public sacrilege appear to have been very close to the center of Jesus' movement, at least as it was preserved and remembered in the Gospels. Yet it should not immediately be assumed that this represented a rejection of the Law of Moses. For at other times, Jesus apparently made claims suggesting that he believed himself to be establishing, or perhaps reinvigorating, the Commandments of God; in this vein, he allegedly issued forth a whole variety of moral teachings and warn-

[1] For a succinct and informative discussion of the development of the concept of *Torah*, and its various usages in Jewish tradition, see R. J. Zwi Werblowsky and G. Wigoder, eds., *The Oxford Dictionary of the Jewish Religion* (New York and Oxford: Oxford University Press, 1997), 696-97. See also J. Gager, *The Origins of Anti-Semitism: Attitudes Toward Judaism in Pagan and Christian Antiquity* (New York and Oxford: Oxford University Press, 1983), 67-88 for the widespread Greco-Roman tendency to see Judaism as a divinely revealed religious philosophy that had been handed down to its lawgiver, Moses.

[2] For his disregard for strict Sabbath observance, see for instance, Luke 6; for divorce, cf. Mark 10, Deuteronomy 24; for his tendency to ignore pharisaical injunctions against eating with sinners, see Luke 7: 36-50; 15: 1. All scriptural passages in this chapter are drawn from the Revised Standard Version.

ings that, on his account, emanated from heaven. Nonetheless, even if we accept Jesus' claim to be "establishing" the Law, it seems indisputable that in doing so, he was attacking the existing understanding of that Law, and attempting to supplant it, or at least reshape it along new lines.

The individual most responsible for elaborating the early Christian critique of Jewish legal practice was, however, Saint Paul, the lapsed pharisee whose writings examined in sometimes obsessive detail questions surrounding the validity of the Jewish ordinances in the wake of Christ. As the "apostle to the Gentiles," whose evangelical effort had from its beginning been aimed at non-Jews, Paul naturally and almost inevitably confronted questions of the Law from the outset of his ministry; he was, after all, attempting to win Gentile converts to a Jewish messianic movement. Consequently, one of the first puzzles facing both Paul and his potential converts was whether and to what extent Gentile followers of Christ needed to submit to the Torah and its regulations. Were they bound by the welter of statutes and ordinances that sat at the heart of Judaism? To judge from the Epistles and the Acts, hovering behind this problem was the specter of circumcision, for it is clear that Paul recognized the bloody ritual—so central to Jewish identity—as a serious sticking point for Gentile converts. It would not be going too far to suggest that this intellectual conundrum—along with the threat it posed to his ministry—defined Paul's thought and, in the process, defined Christianity in a way that Christ himself never had. Paul, of course, resolved the problem by declaring that true Christians were somehow free from the Law. They were not bound by circumcision, by dietary laws, and indeed, as he famously argued at length in his letter to the Romans, their salvation came not from any work in the Law, but rather through faith, which was the unearned gift of God. These doctrines were explosive and controversial from the moment Paul uttered them. For a start, they appear to have run counter to teachings being proffered in Jerusalem by the surviving disciples of Jesus, immediately creating tension between Paul and more established leaders such as James and Peter.

That such contention could exist even among the very first Christians may be explained partly by the fact that the Jesus of the Gospels never provided an explicit, absolute, or programmatic account of divine law; for all his many criticisms of the pharisees and scribes, he made no overarching statements about the status of the Torah and its many regulations; nor, despite his many moral and behavioral injunctions, did he elaborate any systematic, positive legal regime of his own. His followers were thus left to sift through his ambiguous legacy after his death, creating much room for tension. Thus, while Paul seems to have inherited an unstructured but authentic anti-legal spirit from the early Christ movement, it seems clear enough that his own sweeping statements on the Law were improvisations of his own making.[3] His deep suspicion of the Law followed naturally from principles that Paul would have imbibed among early Christians, but his conclusions were radical and (to judge from the responses that greeted him) not obviously or unambiguously in line with the teachings of Jesus. Hence, other Jewish followers of Christ—in particular James and Peter, who had known Jesus and had been privy to his teachings—recoiled at Paul's wholesale rejection of the Law as an inauthentic corruption of their master's teaching. The point, ultimately, is this: despite Jesus' marked and clear opposition to Jewish practice of his day, even his most enthusiastic first followers could not agree on precisely what it was that he had had to say about the ongoing status of the Law.

Despite his efforts to clarify the subject, Paul likewise left an ambiguous textual legacy. Although his statements on the Law at times have a directness and clarity that is absent in the Gospels, Paul, too, lapsed into an occasional obscurity that had lasting repercussions for those who followed him. For on the one hand, he could argue, in terms that seem entirely unequivocal, that followers of Christ were utterly free from the Law: as he put it in the letter to the Romans, "now we are discharged from the law, dead to that which held us captive, so that we serve not under the old written code but in the new life of the Spirit." In this way, Paul could dismiss many of the demands of the Jewish Law: all foods were lawful for Christians, and all days held equal status; circumcision, as he forcefully argued in the epistle to the Galatians, was now superfluous, as apparently were all other works under the Mosaic Law: "before faith came, we were confined under the law, kept under restraint until faith should be revealed. So that the law was our custodian until Christ came, that we might be justified by faith. But now that faith is come, we are no longer under a custodian." He reminded the Galatians that "Christ has set us free" from the law, and implored them to "stand fast therefore, and . . . not submit again to the yoke of slavery." These statements would certainly seem to suggest, in no uncertain terms, that Paul was pronouncing his Gentile followers entirely free from any and all laws handed down to Moses. Although Paul never explicitly defined what he meant by "law," he certainly appears to

---

[3] In an effort to escape post-Reformation exegetical prejudices, modern biblical scholars have come to question the extent to which Paul's theology represented a rejection of a "legalistic" Judaism. While this revisionist perspective has corrected the protestant view of first-century Palestinian Judaism as a religion of formalism and works righteousness, it has tended to obscure the very real anti-legal elements in Paul's thought. For instructive comments on this point, see T. R. Schreiner, "'Works of Law' in Paul," *Novum Testamentum*, 33 (1991), esp. 241-44.

have placed within its purview all the commands that had been given to Moses, the Decalogue included.[4]

On the other hand, however, Paul often made statements implying that even if believers were somehow free from the Law, they were not free from moral duty to God. His letters are littered with instructions to his followers to avoid works of the "flesh," particularly unseemly sexual acts. In I Thessalonians, generally considered to be Paul's earliest authentic letter, he admonished his readers that "this is the will of God, your sanctification: that you abstain from unchastity. . . . For God has not called us for uncleanness, but in holiness. Therefore whoever disregards this, disregards not man but God, who gives his Holy Spirit to you."[5] Paul thus seemed to be saying that although free from the Law, believers were still bound to perform certain holy, pure actions in conformity with the will of God. To the Colossians, in one breath he declared "let no one pass judgment on you in questions of food and drink or with regard to a festival or a new moon or a sabbath," denouncing those false teachers who taught Christians that one food was more pure than another, one day more holy than the next; in the next breath, Paul exhorted his readers to "Put to death therefore what is earthly in you: fornication, impurity, passion, evil desire, and covetousness, which is idolatry."[6] Paul's most morally didactic statements were handed down to the community at Corinth, where certain renegade teachers (very probably Paul's own proselytes) appear to have deployed his arguments about freedom from the Law to claim that Christians were free from all moral standards.[7] To counter this threat, Paul vigorously rehearsed his arguments about freedom from the Law while at the same time handing down what he called "command[s] of the Lord," some of which were based on the Torah. In this spirit, he warned them that "neither the immoral, nor idolaters, nor adulterers, nor sexual perverts, nor thieves, nor the greedy, nor drunkards, nor revilers, nor robbers will inherit the Kingdom of God."[8]

---

[4] See E. P. Sanders, *Paul, the Law, and the Jewish People* (Philadelphia: The Fortress Press, 1983), 83.

[5] I Thess. 4: 3-8.

[6] Colossians 2: 16-23 and 3: 5. This presumes that Colossians is an authentic Pauline letter.

[7] For a recent, if controversial, account of Paul's ministry, which views his opponents at Corinth as "over-converted followers of Paul," and which suggests that gnosticism grew directly out of this tradition, see G. Lüdemann, *Heretics: The Other Side of Early Christianity*, John Bowden, trans. (Louisville: Westminster John Knox Press, 1996), 91-93, 120-69.

[8] See I Cor. 5-11. At I Cor. 7: 25, after issuing a series of moral orders, Paul observed that "concerning the unmarried, I have no command of the Lord, but I give

It should be clear that there was a tension, if not an outright contradiction, implicit in these passages. Paul was saying that the Law, which was God's revelation to his people, and which contained the many regulations and statutes that expressed God's will, did not bind believers. This seemed—at least on the face of it—to do away with the entire thicket of scriptural regulations governing human interaction, behavior and worship, to free believers from their obligation to obey the Torah. Yet for Paul, this obviously did not obliterate the need for some sort of obedience: humans were still bound to submit to God's will, as shown by the several passages cited above. Nowhere, though, did Paul explain how, if free from the dictates of the Torah, one could even know God's will, since God's will was known only through scripture—that is, through the Law. Whence came Paul's various enjoinders to shun immorality and sexual perversion if not from the Law of God? If believers were free from Moses' Law, what law bound them, and what law underlay Paul's frequent and vehement moral axioms? What was the divine standard against which Christians were to measure and order their own lives?

The controversies explored in this study revolved around these critical questions. For although many have proposed answers, the fact remains that Paul himself did no such thing.[9] He left no definitive resolution to this apparent contradiction in his own writings. His words avail themselves of a multiplicity of plausible interpretations. Of these interpretative possibilities, one in particular demands our attention, if only because it would play a central role in the story told here. On a handful of occasions, Paul suggested that he believed Christians to be under another, new law, distinct from the Mosaic Law. Thus, he told the Romans, "the law of the Spirit of life in Christ Jesus has set me free from the law of sin and death [that is, the Law of Moses]."[10] To the Corinthians, meanwhile, he similarly argued that "To the Jews I became as a Jew, in order to win Jews; to those under the law I became as one under the law—though not myself under the law—that I might win those under the law. To those outside the law I became as one outside the law—not being without law toward God but under the law of Christ—that I might win those outside the law."[11] In both of these passages, Paul seems to contrast the Law of Moses to a different law—described here as the "law of Christ" or the "the law of the

---

my opinion as one who by the Lord's mercy is trustworthy." This implied that his previous orders were "commands of the Lord," but that this one was not.

[9] See Sanders, *Law*, passim, which reveals quite clearly that despite increasingly sophisticated methodologies and hermeneutics, modern Biblical scholars have been thoroughly unable to arrive at a satisfactory account of Paul's thought regarding the Law, a fact that underscores the cryptic and inconclusive nature of the Apostle's own statements on the matter.

[10] Rom. 8:2.

[11] I Cor. 9:20-21.

Spirit of life in Christ Jesus"—and suggests that both he and other followers of Christ are bound by this new and distinctive "law toward God." On this basis it might be speculated that Paul thought that his various moral commands and injunctions were part of this new law—that he was handing down this new law of Christ as a vessel of the Holy Spirit. But he does not say as much in a clear manner. Nor does he explain in any detail whether this new "law of Christ" retained any components of the old law. Rather, Paul chose to hint, in rather vague terms, that those who were under this law of the spirit would know what was right simply because they were possessed by the Holy Spirit.

This tendency—together with Paul's fundamental schizophrenia on the matter of Law—is best captured in the letter to the Galatians, the text at the heart of the controversies discussed in this book. Because of the importance of this epistle, it deserves to be quoted at length:

> For you were called to freedom brethren; only do not use your freedom as an opportunity for the flesh, but through love be servants to one another. For the whole law is fulfilled in one word, 'You shall love your neighbor as yourself.' But if you bite and devour one another take heed that you are not consumed by one another.
>
> But I say, walk by the Spirit, and do not gratify the desires of the flesh. For the desires of the flesh are against the Spirit, and the desires of the Spirit are against the flesh for these are opposed to each other, to prevent you from doing what you would. But if you are led by the Spirit, you are not under the law. Now the works of the flesh are plain: fornication, impurity, licentiousness, idolatry, sorcery, enmity, strife, jealousy, anger, selfishness, dissension, party spirit, envy, drunkenness, carousing, and the like. I warn you, as I warned you before, that those who do such things shall not inherit the kingdom of God. But the fruit of the Spirit is love, joy, peace, patience, kindness, goodness, faithfulness, gentleness, self-control; against such there is no law. And those who belong to Christ Jesus have crucified this flesh with its passions and desire.

Here, Paul once again pronounced Christians free from the Law; yet at the same time, because they were led by the spirit, and their flesh had been crucified, they were also bound to avoid works of the flesh—hence the admonishment against fornication, impurity, and the like—and were bound to produce fruits of the spirit—love, peace, patience, and so on. Yet the contradiction remains unresolved: what Paul does not explain is how, without a "law" of some sort, works of the "flesh" can even be discriminated from works of the "spirit." Paul simply and without explanation claims that "the works of the flesh are plain." Yet without some sort of law—that is, a standard—the works of the flesh are not quite as "plain" or self-evident as Paul suggests. So once again, the implication is that believers are free from the old law, but bound by some new law, or perhaps by some fraction of the old law. However, nowhere is this new law systematically explicated—apart from some vague and cryptic statements about love fulfilling the law—nor is its relationship to the Law of Moses laid out in explicit terms.[12] From one perspective, it might be said that there are two apostles present in the epistles: crudely, "Paul the antinomian" and "Paul the moralist." These two Pauls sit in an uneasy and sometimes logically problematic relationship with one another. This ambiguity and lack of clarity thus left much room for uncertainty. It was in the murky, ill-defined interstices of Paul's rhetoric that later battles over the Law would be fought.

The Orthodox Solution

The tensions that emerged between Paul and the Jerusalem Christians by no means passed with the first generation of Christians. Indeed, just as Paul's own struggle with the problem of the Law worked to define the intellectual contours of the new faith, much of the early history of Christianity would be shaped by the battle over precisely what Paul meant when he declared himself free from the Law. Successive conflicts with groups now known as Ebionites, Gnostics, and Pelagians all flowed out of this fundamental and original conflict, in many ways defining what would become the orthodoxy of the Catholic Church. So too, from an intellectual standpoint, the Reformation, as well as the disputes under consideration in this book, can be seen as the afterbirth of these first disputes among the early followers of Jesus.

This is not to say that no Christian solution to the Pauline puzzle of the Law emerged; indeed, by the fourth century, successive heresies ensured that there was a very well elaborated normative or orthodox position that attempted to resolve the most problematic ambiguities of Paul's rhetoric: Christ's coming had abrogated *part* of the Mosaic Law. In a shrewd but somewhat arbitrary manner, Christian theologians managed to divide the Law of Moses into two distinct compartments—moral and ceremonial. The "Moral Law" included the Decalogue; the "ceremonial" included the rites, regulations, and restrictions governing Jewish religious life (further exegesis resulted in the subdivision of the "nonmoral" portion into "ceremonial" and "judicial" components, categories that had become standard by the early modern period).[13] Extrapolating outward from statements in the New Testa-

---

[12] For interesting comments about the possible Jewish origins of this formula concerning "love" and the fulfillment of the Law, see E. P. Sanders, *Paul and Palestinian Judaism: A Comparison of Patterns of Religion* (Philadelphia: The Fortress Press, 1977), 112-14. But here, the caveat of Schreiner, "'Works of Law,'" should perhaps be given special emphasis.

[13] See M. F. Wiles, *The Divine Apostle: The Interpretation of St. Paul's Epistles in the Early Church* (Cambridge: Cambridge University Press, 1967), pp. 66-69.

ment, Christians determined that only the Moral Law—that which bound all humans in all times—remained in force after the coming of Christ; the ceremonial and judicial components of the Law—which had reference only to the Jewish people of ancient Palestine—were context-specific, and were abrogated by the coming of Christ. This move allowed Christians to follow Paul in doing away with circumcision, dietary laws, and the sprawling array of rites, penalties, and prohibitions scattered through the Torah, without sacrificing the basic moral prescriptions that had been handed down to Moses at Sinai. This left a bedrock of ethics intact; the lawless consequences that seemed to flow from some of Paul's more exuberant attacks on the Law could be avoided without rejecting the words of the Apostle entirely. This exegetical trick thus had the simultaneous effect of preserving moral order, jettisoning the baroque and demanding regime of Jewish ritual, and reconciling some of the more troubling and contradictory passages of the New Testament.

It was a clever solution, and one that still dominates Christianity to the present day. Nevertheless, the ambiguity mentioned above did not disappear. For the fact remained that this tripartite distinction was entirely unscriptural—nowhere did Paul give even the least hint that he compartmentalized the Law in this way. When he claimed that Christians were free from the Law, he made no distinctions between different "subsections" of the Mosaic code. In fact, the contrary is true: he appeared to use the word "law" to describe everything that God had given Moses, and on at least one occasion, to describe everything in the Old Testament, including not only the Torah, but the prophetic books.[14] Thus, although the tripartite division of the Law provided a plausible reading of Paul's letters, which resolved the aforementioned logical problems, it was open to very serious challenges. Pauline ambiguity remained forever embedded in the scriptures, a persistent artifact of tensions that had existed within Christianity from its first generation, and a continual threat to the integrity of the Christian community.

The Reformation represented the latest incarnation of this dispute. Although it would be absurd and ahistorical to claim that Luther's quarrel with the Roman church simply replayed controversies that had beset the early church, there is no question that, at a doctrinal level, the storm unleashed in Wittenberg swirled around the very same scriptural ambiguities and tensions that had animated earlier struggles over the Law. Just as Luther was very much a product of a "humanistic" rekindling of biblical knowledge and awareness, so too the intellectual revolution he sparked at one level represented the rebirth of the great Pauline contradiction. Luther and his followers conducted their polemical war on the Roman Catholic church in explicitly

---

[14] I Cor. 14.21, in which he refers to a passage from Isaiah as being part of the Law.

Pauline terms. He castigated Catholics as works-mongers, new pharisees who failed to heed the fundamental Pauline message that true Christians were free from the Law. Christian salvation came through faith, not works of any sort. In its most extreme form, Luther's polemic replicated the more strenuously antinomian elements of Paul's rhetoric. Thus, at times he could imply that believers were entirely free from the Mosaic Law: "the Ten Commandments did bind me. But against that law, I have another law, even the law of grace; which notwithstanding is to me no law, neither does it bind me, but setteth me at liberty. And this is a law against that accusing and condemning law." The Law indeed had a spiritual use, but that use was entirely negative: "the law, when it is in [God's] true sense, doth nothing else but reveal sin, engender wrath, accuse and terrify men, so that it bringeth them to the very brink of desperation. This is the proper use of the law, and here it hath an end, and it ought to go no further." At other times, however, Luther left absolutely no doubt that the Ten Commandments, the Moral Law, continued to be the rule according to which Christians should walk. They were the "first part of Christian doctrine," and he thus told his listeners to "exhort your household to learn them word for word, that they should then obey God and you as their masters, and that you too should obey God."[15]

This conceptual vagueness engendered serious confusion even in Luther's own lifetime; by the early 1530s, the Wittenberg reformers found themselves dogged by a set of radical Protestants (led by Luther's friend and erstwhile disciple Johannes Agricola) who seized upon the most extreme anti-legal facets of Luther's teaching to deny the role of the Law in working repentance and salvation. Embarrassingly (but not entirely without justification) these readers actually appropriated Luther's own writings in their efforts to promote their position. Appalled, Luther struck back, denouncing Agricola and his followers as "softly singing Antinomians," thus coining the epithet that would later be applied to English anti-legalists. Luther confessed that some of his early writings had indeed stressed the notion that believers were free from the Law, but claimed that such excessive rhetoric had been necessary to deliver men from the bondage of papal works righteousness. "Now, however, when the times are very dissimilar from those under the pope," such rhetoric was no longer necessary, and if misunderstood, could lead men to an amoral, fleshy security that threatened the very fabric of the moral and social order. Agricola and his followers were accordingly assimilated to a long line of "false brethren" that included Müntzer, the Anabaptists, and Carlstadt.[16] Given the finality of these

[15] John Dillenberger, ed., *Martin Luther: Selections from his Writings* (New York: Anchor, 1961), 125, 144, 208.

[16] For a brief discussion of Luther's quarrel with Agricola, together with a translation of his polemical treatise "Against the Antinomians," see *Luther's Works*, F.

pronouncements, it might be thought that Luther's assault on the "antinomians" would have shut down, once and for all, any possibility for debate over the subject of the Law within Protestantism. Yet at another level, the controversy merely underscores the deeply complicated, and in some senses, self-conflicted, nature of the protestant message, for even in his most intemperate attacks on Agricola, Luther never quite managed to provide a coherent, logical explanation of how his own ultra-antinomian rhetoric concerning the Law and faith could be made square with his equally exuberant defenses of the ongoing role of the Ten Commandments.[17] Luther, like Paul, left behind him an ambiguous legacy.

Agricola was not, however, the only reformation thinker to raise serious questions about the role of the Law in human salvation. The religious turmoil of the 1520s produced all manner of radical religious speculation, leading most famously to the Anabaptist Peasants' Rebellion of 1525 and culminating in the establishment of the notorious and ill-fated Anabaptist "kingdom" at Münster in 1534. These movements were brutally suppressed, but many varieties of radical religious thought lived on, surviving the disastrous collapse of "revolutionary" Anabaptism. One of the strains that emerged out of the fecund soil of reformation anabaptism was a loosely defined impulse often labeled "spiritualist" by historians of religion. Partly in rejection of the revolutionary excesses of the early Anabaptists, such "spiritual" thinkers tended to shy away from schemes to reform the world, to establish God's kingdom on earth, or to build purified, Apostolic congregations. Instead, they focused attention on inner religious experience. Often under the influence of late medieval mysticism (most importantly the *Theologia Germanica*), thinkers such as Sebastian Franck, Loy Pruystinck, David Joris, and Hendrik Niclaes turned toward "internal" forms of religion, which stressed the immediacy of the spirit in the faithful, and which often envisioned the Christian life as one in which the believer became "deified" by imitating Christ's life and sufferings. Such ideas clearly had antinomian overtones, since "deified" believers were taken to be in some sense perfect and above the Law. So, too, "spiritualist" beliefs tended to undermine ecclesiastical authority: since such people were united with God, they had little or no need for the childish external ordinances of the Church, including the sacraments. In the cases of Joris and his friend Niclaes, this indifference to ecclesiastical forms was given a novel spin: Jorists and Fa-

---

Sherman, ed. (Philadelphia: The Fortress Press, 1971), 47: 101-19. For a more detailed examination of the conflict, see M. U. Edwards, *Luther and the False Brethren* (Stanford: Stanford University Press, 1975), 156-79.

[17] For a revealing collection of some of Luther's more ultra-antinomian rhetorical flourishes, see A. H. Newman's note on the German antinomian controversies in *The New Schaff-Herzog Religious Encyclopedia* (New York and London: Funk and Wagnalls, 1908), 1: 198n1.

milists adhered to the principle of "Nicodemism" as a matter of faith. Followers were instructed to conform to the customs and regulations of the reigning ecclesiastical power. If necessary, proselytes were to blend into local Catholic or protestant congregations, practicing their faith secretly and beyond the institutional boundaries of the visible church. If detected for heresy, dissimulation was not merely permitted but encouraged.[18]

Needless to say, magisterial reformers, whether Lutheran or reformed, were disturbed by the existence of such secret, underground sectarian movements. Although the history of their influence is for obvious reasons somewhat shadowy, it seems clear that "spiritualizing" movements had achieved considerable success by the early 1540s, spreading out of the Netherlands and into French-speaking lands. Thus, in 1545, Calvin felt compelled to take up his pen against a group he labeled as "libertines" (thus popularizing a word that would frequently be used to describe "spiritualists," as well as seventeenth century English antinomians). The Genevan reformer denounced these so-called libertines for their habit of allegorizing scripture, their overt antinomianism, their claims to human divinization, and their Nicodemism.[19] While the public opposition of Calvin and his allies no doubt helped slow the spread of such ideas, spiritualist tendencies proved difficult to eradicate entirely.

In particular, Niclaes's Family of Love grew and prospered into the late sixteenth century, giving birth to various offshoots that would continue to irritate magisterial reformers in the decades that followed. We have already noted that Familism had made inroads in England by the 1560s. In the Netherlands, spiritualist doctrines, often inspired by HN, seem to have persisted in various guises for many years. Perhaps the most interesting case has been uncovered in Utrecht, where in the late 1570s, the ex-Familist Hubert Duifhuis found his way into the pastorate of the Jacobskerk. Here, he set up shop as an evangelical spiritualist, denouncing his local Calvinist opponents for their external, legalistic brand of Christianity, and creating a fissure that would continue to plague the presbyterian authorities for many years to come. Indeed, the conflict between Duifhuis, with his strident Familist-inflected mysticism, and Utrecht's Calvinists bore a remarkable structural and rhetorical similarity to

---

[18] On Dutch Familism, see especially Alastair Hamilton, *The Family of Love* (Cambridge: James Clarke & Co. Ltd., 1981); for spiritualism more generally, see G. H. Williams, *The Radical Reformation* (Philadelphia: The Westminster Press, 1962), passim.

[19] John Calvin, *Contre la secte phantastique et furieuse des Libertins qui se nomment Spirituels* (1545), translated in *Treatises Against the Anabaptists and Against the Libertines*, B. W. Farley, ed. and trans. (Grand Rapids: Baker Book House, 1982).

the controversies that are the subject of this book.[20] In part, this is attributable to the fact that Duifhuis, like many English antinomians, took inspiration from a common spiritualist tradition, which included the wisdom of HN as well as the ever-important *Theologia Germanica*. At a broader level, however, it should be emphasized that the similarity was not simply one of common origin; in each case, the antagonists were in many ways struggling over tensions at the heart of the Reformation itself, seeking to impose unity on a movement that from its beginnings had given expression to a variety of distinct and in some sense contradictory impulses.

This is not to argue, however, that early modern European protestantism was consistently torn by internal conflicts over the questions of Law, grace, and spirit. In England, as in other parts of the reformed world, sixteenth century Protestants by and large discreetly ignored the more troublesome aspects of the Pauline conundrum. Sidestepping the overtly antinomian passages of Luther's works, and decrying even the slightest hints of "spiritualist" mysticism, the vast majority of English protestants simply accepted the notion of justification by faith alone and muddled along with the contradictions unspoken but intact. As was traditional, they claimed that Christ's coming had abrogated only the ceremonial and judicial components of the Law, and that Christians thus remained bound to obey the dictates of the Decalogue. To use the generally accepted formula, believers were free from the curse and condemning power of the Moral Law, but not from its commandments. Yet at the same time, they argued—following Paul and Luther—that salvation had nothing to do with legal obedience. No man, no matter how holy, could earn salvation by following the dictates of the Ten Commandments. Salvation came by faith alone, and faith was the unmerited gift of God. In fact, as Luther's comments reveal, according to standard protestant readings, not only were people incapable of obeying the Law perfectly (thereby meriting salvation), but their very inability to keep the Law was central to the true path to salvation. Only by learning the Law, by trying to keep it, and failing utterly—as all fallen humans inevitably would—could the believer come to see his or her own fallen state, along with the need for Christ. For most Protestants—and in particular for English puritans—the Moral Law remained a central and binding part of the religious life, even as they declared in no uncertain terms that salvation had nothing to do with it, and that Christians were in some important sense entirely free from the Law.

---

[20] B. J. Kaplan, *Calvinists and Libertines: Confession and Community in Utrecht, 1578-1620* (Oxford: Clarendon Press, 1995), esp. 85-104.

English Puritan Practical Divinity

This study does not attempt to define English puritanism; nor do the following pages provide an exhaustive account of puritan practical divinity. Nevertheless, if we are to understand how and why antinomianism emerged as a potent intellectual force in the seventeenth century, we must provide a brief overview of puritan pastoral divinity. As stated at the outset, antinomianism was a rebellion against the mode of piety that had come to dominate puritanism by the early seventeenth century, and any attempt to trace its origins must reckon with the nature of the thing that it sought to alter or negate, here designated "mainstream puritanism." I am of course aware that the following account is partial and incomplete. Nevertheless, it captures aspects of puritan practice that until now have remained ill-explored in the existing literature on the subject. So, likewise, readers should not presume that all puritans from the Elizabethan settlement to the 1640s subscribed to a precise and uniform "orthodoxy" or dogmatic platform, for as noted in the Introduction, there were multiple ideological fissures crisscrossing the godly community in the early years of the seventeenth century. Most of these disputes tended, however, to be conducted within and in spite of an overarching consensus as to what constituted proper pastoral divinity. Thus, for instance, even those who disagreed about the exact nature of the millennium, or about the precise architecture of God's decrees of predestination, tended to share in and accept the pastoral assumptions synthesized and laid out below. Some may have tended to highlight one facet of the synthesis more than others, but virtually all early Stuart puritans embraced and propagated the rhetorical and theological tropes outlined in the following pages.

Peter Lake has written that "Protestant religion had two sides to it: firstly the objective realm of doctrinal truth, and secondly the subjective religious experience undergone by the godly in their internalisation of those truths."[21] Practical divinity may be seen as the point of intersection between these two faces of Protestantism. It was the body of ideas, pastoral strategies, and rhetorical tropes used by the puritan minister to bring the formal truths of reformed doctrine home to his listeners or readers. It was one thing, for instance, to tell a woman that she was "justified by the imputation of Christ's active and passive righteousness," but quite another to engage her in the subjective experience that this abstract doctrinal statement represented. Practical divinity was the means used by the godly teacher to translate such complex doctrinal truths into a language that the ordinary layperson could understand; and more importantly, to translate them in such a way that they would have a

[21] P. Lake, *Moderate Puritans and the Elizabethan Church* (Cambridge: Cambridge University Press, 1982), 155. The following account of puritan practical divinity owes much to Lake's analysis in ibid., 116-68.

powerful effect on the listener, making those truths meaningful to flesh and blood. Although grounded in the realms of scripture and doctrine, practical divinity was to some extent independent of both the Bible and the formal theological truths on which it was based. For in the process of translating reformed doctrine to the level of subjective experience, these doctrinal truths needed to be manipulated and even reinterpreted. Certain aspects of scripture and doctrine came into sharp relief, taking on increased significance, while others faded into the background. Both pastoral experience and pastoral expediency worked to shape and reshape the way that biblical truths were disseminated to popular audiences. The result, over time, was a distinctive system of practical divinity that can be usefully called "puritan."[22] This system included such novelties as the motif of the covenant, Sabbatarianism, and the culture of the fast. Although recognizably based on the Bible and reformed doctrinal truths, the ways of English puritan practical divinity were thus in some respects highly particular and unique. It was, moreover, an ideological system that week in and week out was broadcast relentlessly from hundreds (or even thousands) of pulpits throughout England.

Puritan practical divinity began with the preaching of the Law. Following Saint Paul, godly ministers held that the beginning of the religious life was a profound and disturbing awareness of sin. This awareness could come only through the Moral Law, Paul's "ministry of death." For it was in and through the preaching of the commandments that human beings became aware of their own inability to obey God's statutes, and of the dreadful curse that hung over those who violated his Law. The Law, then, was the instrument through which human beings were brought to a deep and life-altering sense of their own sinful, miserable, and hopeless condition. Yet at the same time, it was the instrument that first awakened in them a sense of the need for something greater, for an external savior. It instilled in people a "holy despaire of any remedie from our selves, or any other creature."[23] For godly ministers, the Law was thus the first step on the road to Christ. Contaminated by sin, in constant violation of the divine will, and plagued by the fearful expectation of eternal damnation, the sinner (at least in theory) had only one choice—to turn

---

[22] This is not to say that "puritan" practical divinity was utterly divorced from that promoted by non-puritan, evangelical Calvinists. Many of the pastoral commonplaces described here were shared by English Protestants who cannot in any meaningful sense be called "puritans" (although such figures, including for instance bishops such as Davenant and Hall, might usefully be classed as "godly"). Nevertheless, it is the system of practical divinity described here—which included distinctive characteristics such as strict Sabbatarianism and frequent fasting—which in many ways defined puritanism.

[23] Richard Rogers et al., *A Garden of Spirituall Flowers* (1609), sig. A4r.

to Jesus Christ, whose sacrifice on the cross represented the only hope for salvation.[24]

In unison with the protestant tradition, the godly held that the benefits of Christ's death came through one and only one means—belief in the all-powerful and all-sufficient sacrifice of Jesus Christ, which alone paid the penalty for human sinfulness. Puritans remained utterly attached to the notion that only faith, awakened by the unmerited grace of God, allowed humans to escape the just punishment they so richly deserved. In tune with all reformed expositors, the godly clung to the idea that this faith could not be earned; it could not be extorted from God; it could not come through human will or exertion. It was solely the gift of God, who according to his goodwill and pleasure granted saving faith to those whom he had predestined to salvation from the beginning of time. Against what the godly took to be Popish works righteousness, puritans (like the vast majority of English Protestants) clung to the notion that believers were justified solely through the extrinsic righteousness of Christ, apprehended passively by faith. In this, they did justice to the most virulently anti-legal statements of the Apostle Paul.

This, however, leaves certain questions unanswered. What did it mean to be justified by faith? What was faith and how did one get it? And what were the consequences for the believer's life? It was one thing to proclaim that believers were justified by faith alone, but quite another to bring this doctrine to life in the minds and experience of ordinary churchgoers. For as Roman Catholics habitually argued, on the face of it, this doctrine would seem to lead to either passivity or flat libertinism. On the one hand, if salvation were entirely in the hands of God, and no works of the human will could influence the dispensation of God's grace, what incentive could be laid before people to serve God or pursue the religious life? On the other hand, if faith saved without works, what was to stop believers from doing precisely as they pleased, since after all, it was faith and not works that justified people before God? The godly heartily denied both of these consequences, arguing firstly that men and women should strenuously prosecute their own salvation, and secondly that true believers would necessarily obey God's will, doing good works and abstaining from sin. Indeed, despite their ostensible commitment to the idea of justification by faith alone, mainstream puritans found numerous ways of reinserting human will and action into the process of salvation.

---

24 For a summary of this initial process of legal humiliation, which required knowledge of both the Law and knowledge of the saving remedy of the Gospel, see W. Perkins, *A Treatise Tending unto a Declaration Whether a Man be in the Estate of Damnation or in the Estate of Grace* (1590?), 33-46. This doctrine would later become more formalized into a system that has been called "preparationism" by modern historians. It had been present, at least in its basic outlines, a generation before Perkins.

Faith and Doubt: The First Tension

Late Elizabethan and early Stuart puritans defined "faith" as a full persuasion that Christ had died for your sins. This persuasion was, they argued, entirely assuring, at least in theory. Those who had faith were certain that they would be saved. As Arthur Dent put it, "he, that hath the spirit of God, knoweth certainely he hath it; and he, that hath faith, knoweth that he hath faith: and he, that shall be saved, knoweth he shall be saved."[25] In typical protestant fashion, they held that the "grounde of this perswasion is not laid in our selves . . . but onely in the righteousnesse of Christ, and the mercifull promises of God."[26] Yet in the same breath, and in a manner characteristic of puritan divinity in general, Dent likewise informed his readers that those who "beleeveth in truth, feeleth sometimes doubtings and waverings." Even those "which are grown to the greatest perswasion" of their salvation, would sometimes question their own spiritual estate.[27] How could these two claims stand? For if faith was fully assuring, how could a believer experience doubts? Faith and doubt would seem to be antithetical, implying a patent contradiction in the very foundation of puritan practical divinity. For Dent, however, there was no contradiction at all: "although the children of God feele some doubtings, at sometimes; yet the same doe no whit impeach the certaintie of their salvation: but rather argue a perfect soundnesse, and health of their soules."[28] In other words, doubt itself became an argument for a true faith. A true faith would necessarily question itself, and would thus at times lapse into uncertainty. Nonetheless, eventually, the awareness that Christ had died for the believer would return to overcome these doubts and to restore an even stronger persuasion of one's spiritual safety. In this manner, puritan divines imagined

---

[25] Arthur Dent, *The Plaine Mans Path-Way to Heaven* (1603), 239.

[26] Ibid., 244-45.

[27] Ibid., 242. Dent was here almost certainly plagiarizing William Perkins, whose manuscript dialogue, "Consolations for all troubled Consciences," had argued that "he that never doubted of his salvation, never beleeved; and . . . he which beleeveth in trueth, feeleth many doubtinges and waverings, even as the sounde man feeles many grudginges of diseases, which if that he had not health, he could not feele." From Rogers et al., *Garden*, sigs. Cv-C2r. This piece had been circulating in manuscript under the initials "W.P." before its publication in 1609, for which see British Library, Egerton MS. 2877, fol. 93v.

[28] Dent, *Path-Way*, 242. This ambiguity within puritanism was first noted by Perry Miller in his *New England Mind: The Seventeenth Century* (Cambridge, MA: Harvard University Press, 1939; Reissue, Cambridge, MA: Harvard University, 1967), 370-71, who correctly surmised that it was crucial to the development of antinomianism.

doubt and faith working together to produce an ever-growing assurance in the heart of the believer.[29]

In time, this claim that faith was imperfect, and subject to sporadic doubts and waverings, would become almost an article of faith within mainstream puritanism.[30] This was in many ways an example of pastoral divinity responding to pastoral reality: ministers quickly realized that even their most spiritually mature parishioners sometimes doubted and questioned their own faith. Nevertheless, it is also the case that in placing this caveat on the fully assuring nature of faith, mainstream puritan ministers created for themselves a number of potential difficulties. Most significantly, by implying that doubt was a necessary part of faith, they had created a mechanism that could, under certain conditions, actually foster doubt and insecurity in believers. The godly were told not only that doubt went hand in hand with faith, but that doubt was a necessary concomitant to faith. Although pastors like Dent, George Gifford, and William Perkins assured their listeners that these doubts would ultimately pass, for many, doubt and insecurity—fear of hell and damnation—became a constant companion, a persistent side effect of the godly life.

Accordingly, mainstream puritan divinity was open to the charge that it undermined its own claims that faith—the simple belief in the extrinsic merits of Christ—was fully assuring, providing all that was necessary for salvation. Thus, for instance, in 1625, the young puritan Simonds D'ewes wrote to his friend, the Suffolk minister Edmund Cartwright, complaining about Cartwright's suggestion that it was impossible to attain an absolute certainty of salvation in this world. In opposition, D'ewes asserted that "Where there is true beleevinge there wilbe Joye and peace; howe cann there be Joye and peace, where there is noe certaintye? This indeede is the heighte and Comforte and fruict of Relligion in this world to those that canne obtayne it, it maye trulye be called arcana Imperii of the Kingdome of grace heere in this life."[31] D'ewes was here merely expressing in muted terms a sentiment that would be more fully developed and exploited by antinomians in the same decade. Antinomians in essence charged that the "mixed" faith of puritanism (a faith that

---

[29] Or, as Dent argued, "when wee looke downewarde to our selves, wee have doubts and fears: but when we looke upward to Christ, and the trueth of his promises, wee feele our selves cock-sure, and cease to doubt any more" (Dent, *Path-way*, 243).

[30] For an excellent exposition of this position, see Obadiah Sedgwick's sermon of 1630 in British Library, Harleian MS. 1198, fols. 20v-30v. It should be noted, however, that Sedgwick makes it clear that there were some in the godly community who clung (erroneously) to the opinion that faith had to be absolute and unwavering to be true.

[31] British Library, Harleian MS. 374., fol. 63v. Simonds D'ewes to Edmund Cartwright, pastor of Norton, Suffolk, 1625.

incorporated doubt) was nothing but a subtle trap whereby mainstream puritan ministers snared unsuspecting listeners, delivering them into a state of bondage, insecurity, and fear.

There was more than a whiff of truth to this charge. For although no puritan minister ever openly commanded his auditors to leave divine service in a state of despair or doubt, there can be no question that they often did press listeners to examine themselves and their hearts for evidence of the true faith. Tacitly, godly ministers thus invited people to call into question the authenticity of their own faith. Believers were persistently warned of spiritual maladies that were termed "carnal profession," "counterfeit repentance," or the "dead faith." As we shall see momentarily, the "dead faith" resembled the true, lively and justifying faith, mimicking many of the traits often associated with true belief. By creating such archetypes of false profession, godly ministers subtly but persistently warned their listeners that not all faith was true. A man could believe in Christ—even believe that Christ had died for him—but be deceived. It was therefore imperative that the godly constantly try their own faith against these dangerous and spurious imposters.

Although no one admitted so, doubt was therefore the mechanism that godly pastors utilized to ensure that their auditors diligently and unswervingly pursued the life of faith.[32] Faith was not a thunderclap that came upon believers in an instant, suddenly assuring them that Christ had died for them, and ending all obligations of religious life.[33] As Charles Hambrick-Stowe has put it, "Salvation was the culmination of a life process rather than a state achieved at first conversion; the soul was in transit from sin to salvation through life, and the goal could not finally be reached until death."[34] Faith—like love, holiness, and all other graces of God—was a quality that grew over time, increasing subtly, and by degrees.[35] In its first stages, true faith was often not

---

[32] A point brought out well in Lake, *Moderate Puritans*, 158-59.

[33] In theory, of course, it was always assumed that there was a single, notional moment of conversion, in which God's grace entered the believer's heart for the first time, justifying him or her and bringing true faith. It was likewise assumed, however, that this moment was not clear-cut in the believer's consciousness; justification and its fruits were made known to the believer only over time, and by degrees.

[34] C. E. Hambrick-Stowe, *The Practice of Piety: Puritan Devotional Disciplines in Seventeenth-Century New England* (Chapel Hill: University of North Carolina Press, 1982), 21-22.

[35] See Perkins, *Estate of Grace* , 48: "There are divers degrees and measures of this unfained faith, according as there be divers degrees of Christians: some are yet in the wombe, and have *their mother* the church *traveling of them*: some are *new borne babes feeding on the milk* of the word: some are *perfect men in Christ, come to the measure of the age of the fulnes of Christ.*"

even recognizable to those who possessed it. An immature faith manifested itself as pain and longing, a sense of remorse for sin and a heartfelt desire to turn to God. Only after a measured process of spiritual growth would this infant faith blossom, emerging to provide true comfort and assurance. So too, all the other spiritual graces that followed as a consequence of faith—repentance, holiness, hope, and love, to name a few of the more significant—would increase, sometimes imperceptibly, over time, until at last these imperfections were wiped away in death. The goal of pastoral divinity, then, was to ensure that this process of slow, incremental growth proceeded apace, never faltering. One of the most salient characteristics of the "dead faith" was that it was static and ungrowing: as Richard Rogers explained, "if we grow not, we began but counterfaitely."[36] Like a fragile vine, the true faith needed perpetually to extend itself, to thicken, to mature. And the special weapon for maintaining this process was doubt, or rather, self-examination, which alone could force believers to pursue diligently the "means of grace" whereby faith in Christ was nurtured.

Faith and Works: The Second Tension

For as George Gifford warned his Essex parishioners, "there is no man almost but will acknowledge that a strong faith is a most rich jewell: but when it commeth to the matter they deprive themselves for the most part, either deeming that they have it or can have it in their owne power resting in a vaine shadowe, not knowing at all the nature of the true, lively and powerfull faith: or if they do acknowledge it to be the gift of God; yet they never seeke it by those meanes which he hath ordained to worke it in men, and to nourish it up in them. When wee are therefore willed to resist the Devill stedfast in the faith, it is as much as to saye, give all diligence, and use all the wayes and meanes that may be to increase and strengthen your faith."[37] In other words, God had implanted specific, earthly means into creation, means whereby he imparted his grace in time. What were these means? As William Perkins assured the immature believer, "feare you not, only use the means which God hath appoynted to attaine Faith by, as earnest prayer, reverent hearing of Gods word, and receiving of the Sacraments; and then you shall see these things verified in your selfe."[38] These, then, were the public means of godly piety, often classified simply as God's "ordinances." Yet as Hambrick-Stowe has demonstrated, the godly likewise counted amongst the "means of grace" not just these formal, church-centered activities, but also all manner of private devotions, in-

---

[36] Rogers et al., *Garden*, sig. A7r.

[37] George Gifford, *Certaine Sermons, Upon Divers Textes of Holie Scripture* (1597), 50.

[38] Rogers et al., *Garden*, sig. C6r.

cluding household scripture-reading and prayer, private conferences, psalm-singing and fasts, as well as personal meditation over God's word.[39] As godly ministers regularly reminded their listeners, only through strenuous and unremitting application of these means of grace could believers grow up to a full and comforting Christian faith. In effect, this amounted to a conceptual engine whereby human activity—theoretically banished from the realm of right religion by the reformed commitment to faith and predestination—could be re-injected into the soteriological economy. The means of grace were the conduit pipes of God's spirit.

While use of these means did not guarantee salvation (God's grace was still assumed to be free and unmerited) the diligence and pleasure with which a person approached God's ordinances was taken to be a good, rough indicator of his or her spiritual estate; moreover, the means, zealously applied, were the only way that a believer could possibly continue to grow upward and outward in divine grace. Hambrick-Stowe has rightly characterized the theory behind this homiletic commonplace: "The Holy Spirit would come wholly from outside the realm of human activity and ability . . . [it] would nevertheless enter the soul through the means of well-established forms of devotion and worship. It is important to understand that in Puritan spirituality God did not come *because* someone engaged in a certain exercise; but if God was going to come, He would do it through means of that exercise. For Puritans, God provided both the content of the exercise (in Scripture) and the will to undertake it (through grace)."[40] The London turner Nehemiah Wallington had very similarly noted that "I may look to my graces as evidence of my part in Christ and salvation but not as causes; I may make use of duties as means to bring me to Christ and salvation but not to be saved by them."[41] Such declarations were necessary, however, only because there was such a fine line between Wallington's view and one in which the "means" and "duties" were taken to be causes in themselves.

Indeed, in some of the more exuberant pastoral presentations of this doctrine, godly ministers flirted with the idea that good works were themselves legitimate means of grace. Thus, for instance, George Gifford explained a key difference between a true and lively faith and the "dead image" of faith:

---

[39] Hambrick-Stowe, *Practice of Piety*, esp. 93-193; for an extensive contemporary account of the "means," both public and private, see R. Rogers, *Seaven Treatises Containing such Direction as is Gathered Out of the Holie Scriptures* (1604), 222-307; for fasting, see A. Hildersam, *The Doctrine of Fasting and Praier, and Humiliation for Sinne* (1633).

[40] Hambrick-Stowe, *Practice of Piety*, 45.

[41] P. Seaver, *Wallington's World: A Puritan Artisan in Seventeenth-Century London* (Stanford, 1985), 17.

> He that will attaine to the true, lively and justifying faith . . . must first of all know for certainty, that he hath not so much as anie spark thereof of himselfe: we are all of us by nature shut up under unbeleefe, and in miserable blindnesse: which while many doe not know, they rest and content themselves in a certaine dead image of faith, and are utterlie seduced, for that faith hath no power. He that knoweth this indeed, beholding the depth of the calamities which hee is in will look up to God who is the giver of faith. He is desirous to know what the promises of God are which he is to beleeve and what the way is in which hee must walk to performe the duties of a Christian life: for the true faith worketh by charitie . . . and cannot be without good works. He searcheth the Scriptures . . . hee doth bend his ear to hear the holy Gospell of Jesus Christ preached, feeling therein the power of God to work faith. He doth cry and cal unto God day and night for to teach him, to lighten him, to give him understanding, and to increase his faith: He findeth the blessing of God in these meanes and therfore applieth them. But now on the contrary part, he that resteth in this, God giveth faith, and if it be his will, I shall have it, and so despiseth all meanes, not considering how God giveth faith, is utterly awry and out of the right way.[42]

Here, we see what was perhaps the central paradox of puritan practical divinity. On the one hand, Gifford insisted that humans were completely incapable of achieving faith or knowledge on their own. Any good inhering in man came through the free grace of God. In the same breath, however, he told his listeners that God had appointed means for the increase of faith—these means were constant attendance upon the word, heartfelt prayer, and dutiful attendance upon God's commandments (for "faith worketh by charity"). Any person who rested idly in the knowledge that faith was a gift of God, given freely and without regard to man's efforts, was "utterly seduced." Whether these means were viewed as "causes" in themselves, or merely as tools, there was no question that through their vigorous insistence on "means," "duties," and "ordinances," godly divines had readmitted the human will to the drama of salvation, if not in theory, then surely in practice. In this paradox, we see a second region of seismic instability within puritanism. For despite their obsessive insistence on free grace and justification by faith alone, then, puritan ministers had set up a system in which human labor, diligence, and effort were absolutely essential to the life of piety. This in turn opened a space for dissidents to claim that puritan piety had compromised the central reformation truths of free grace and justification by faith alone.

Nor were "means of grace" the only mechanism used to ensure that good works remained a part of true religion. Far from relieving the saints from their duty to act righteously, the true, lively, and justifying faith would, puritan

---

42 See, for instance, Gifford, *Certaine Sermons*, 51-52.

ministers argued, produce a steady stream of holy actions. As Rogers put it, "the beleever being thus sanctified and changed, must give all diligence to keepe his heart in that estate afterward, and endeavour to practise the godly life in his perticular actions; that is, deny ungodlinesse in his behaviour, and worldly lustes in his heart: and contrarily live soberly himselfe, in moderating affections in all lawfull liberties, righteously towards men, in giving every one their due, and holily towardes God, in worshipping and serving him onely. In which things standeth true repentance."[43] Repentance, like faith, was taken to be a lifelong process; with each transgression against the divine will, the believer was to turn to God in true and unfeigned repentance, imploring him for forgiveness, striving zealously to avoid this offense in the future, and reapplying the means of grace with renewed alacrity.[44]

Faith was thus inseparable from repentance, and repentance from good works.[45] To separate them was, as George Gifford explained, the chief sign of a dead, counterfeit faith: "for if a man do assent and beleeve, that all those things are true, which the father, the Son and the holy Spirit have testified of Christ in the scriptures, and yet be voide of the spirite and the power of Christ unto sanctification (as many that are even learned men are) it is a manifest declaration that his faith is but a dead faith." Such carnal Protestants might "heare the word with joy," and "seeme to be stout and excellent professors." Moreover, "if a man talk with them from morning to night, they are able to continue speach in reciting stories and places of Scripture, and will utter matter against the doctrine of the Pope"; indeed, they were almost indistinguishable from true Protestants: "they labour for knowledge, yea, they holde that men may and ought to come to the assurance of their salvation, and professe that they be sure thereof themselves." Yet, for all this, they remained utterly devoid of true faith in Christ, for they had "put asunder . . . those thinges which God hath coupled together," namely "justification in Christ" and "sanctification."[46]

---

43 Rogers et al., *Garden*, sig. A8r.

44 See, for instance William Perkins, *A Commentarie or Exposition, upon the five first Chapters of the Epistle to the Galatians* (1604), 415: "Some man may say, I am vexed and turmoiled with wicked thoughts, and desires, so as I feare I am not Gods child. I answer againe, for all this despaire not. For, if thou hate and detest the lusts, that are in thee: if thou resist them, and wage battell against them: if beeing overtaken at any time, thou recover thy selfe by new repentance, they shall never be laid to thy charge to condemnation."

45 See Rogers, *Seaven Treatises*, 188.

46 George Gifford, *Foure Sermons upon Several Partes of Scripture* (1598), sig. D5v, E2v-E3r; *A Sermon on the Parable of the Sower, Taken out of the 13. of Matthew* (1582), sigs. Bii.v, Biiii.v, Bvi.r.

This style of religiosity hardly died with the presbyterians of the Elizabethan puritan movement. In 1626, the minister Ephraim Huit, later of New England, took it as given that faith and zealous good works were utterly inseparable:

> our Apostle, we see, contents not himselfe with the graces of faith and hope, but proceeds to the practice of externall obedience: Whence arises this observation,
>
> [Doct.] Inward grace is accompanied with outward obedience. Jam. 3, 13. Such as have learned this heavenly wisedome, must expresse it by a holy and blameless conversation.
>
> [Reas. I.] Gods grace is Immortall; this seed once sowen never dies, ever fructifies; so that the plant of grace having the sap and juyce of grace ministred, cannot but abound in the fruits of righteousnesse and holiness.
>
> Besides, Livelinesse is the essentiall difference twixt true and fained grace, there is a faith that is lively & active in good words, purifying the heart, Act. 15. 9. and there is a faith that is dead without fruits of holinesse; now a disposition to worke, is the essentiall difference of these two.[47]

When the godly told their listeners that they needed to examine themselves scrupulously to ensure their faith was not "dead" or "feigned," they were in fact urging them to examine themselves for signs and evidences of true sanctification. As Arthur Dent told his readers, "There be eight infallible notes and tokens of a regenerate mind, which may wel be tearmed the eight signes of salvation." These eight signs were "A love to the children of God," "A delight in his word," "often and fervent praier," "Zeale of God's glory," self-denial, "Patient bearing of the crosse," "Faithfulnesse in our calling," and "Honest, just, and conscionable dealing in al our actions amongst men."[48] The godly were thus to engage in a cycle of constant self-examination, whereby they tried their faith by their own holiness, both outward and inward. A faith that lacked the requisite signs of sanctification was a dead faith, for those who truly believed in Christ were sanctified by him, dying to sin and being reborn in righteousness. Aspiring saints were to inspect their lives, their wills, the innermost recesses of their minds for hidden lusts and sinful tendencies. They were to keep a careful watch over their behavior and the behavior of their families. And above all, they were to seek to glorify God in the world by performing and promoting his holy Law in all aspects of their lives.

---

[47] Ephraim Huit, *The Anatomie of Conscience* (1626), 5-6. I would like to thank Michael Winship for turning my attention to this source.

[48] Dent, *Path-Way*, 30-31.

The Meaning of the Law: The Third Tension

By "Law," however, the godly meant much more than the Ten Commandments, narrowly conceived according to the letter of the Decalogue.[49] Under the rubric of the Moral Law, the godly subsumed all the moral injunctions of the New Testament, including the Gospel commandments to love, which were taken to be identical to, and inseparable from, the moral code handed down to Moses at Sinai.[50] Moreover, puritans extrapolated outward from the Commandments, including under the purview of the Moral Law a whole range of offenses that were nowhere explicitly condemned in the Decalogue. This tendency is illustrated magnificently in a passage copied out by the young Simonds D'ewes, entitled "A briefe meaning of Gods Law":

> Thou shalt permit none to reside with thee in thy family which is noted to ere in his judgment, from the undoubted truth of Gods eternall word or in his manners to desent from the true practice of his divine Law; if any delight in the ignorance of God; or be careless to approve himselfe, as one that altogether dependeth upon his providence, or that doth not love him, nor feareth him, nor endeavoreth to walke in the wayes of godlinesse; as in the sight of so great a majesty; if any be given to idolatry, superstition, or false worship, and regardeth not in every part of life and conversation; to embrace Gods holy will or if in the parts and dutyes prescribed, he semeth cold and negligent; or perverteth his true worship, his titles, attributs, or sacraments of the church; or be given to superstitious monuments, times, customes, or such like vanityes; if any dishonor the name of God, in blaspheming, abusing, or unreverent using the same or not rightly using it; with preparation at the fore, fealing at the present, and fruit after; as is evidently taught in his holy word; or if any profane his holy sabboth; by vaine pastimes, going to playes, or give not themselves to the exercises appointed on that day, according to his divine law, if there be any, that contemn, or neglect speciall dutyes, to their

---

49 The most comprehensive treatment of godly attitudes towards the Law may be found in E. F. Kevan, *The Grace of the Law: A Study in Puritan Theology* (London: The Carey Kingsgate Press Limited, 1964).

50 See Perkins, *Galatians*, 405, for the manner in which godly divines identified the Ten Commandments with the New Testament commandment to love, ultimately subsuming both within the broad purview of the first commandment. To the question "how the whole law should be fulfilled in the love of our neighbour?" Perkins answered "The love of God, and the love of our neighbour are joyned together, as the cause and the effect: and the love of God is practised in the love of our neighbour. For God that is invisible, will be loved in the person of our neighbour whome we see, and with whome we converse. And the first commandement of the law, must be included in all the commandements following: and thus the love of God is presupposed in every commandement of the second table: he therefore that loves his neighbour, loves God also."

> equals, superiors and inferiours; either in yeares, giftes, or authority; namely majestrates, Ministers, Masters, parents, servants, children, or people. if any declare not a conscience to eschew evil and to doe good or doth not represse profane anger, wrath, hot and chiding answers, contention, reveng, malice, backbiting, striking, fighting, deriding, or hurting the person of any, in his soule, or body; or be not carefull to defend the same according to his power or calling, if any be found unchast in body, words, or countenance, untemperate in diet, gesture, or apparel, not endevouring to maintaine the contrary, which is holy conversation in himselfe and others, if any care not for the goods of annother, but by falsehood, usury, flattery subtilyty, or oppression, diminish the same, or be negligent in his owne to encrease the same by lawfull, laudable, and honest meanes, if he mispend his time, in idle sporting, trifling, gaming, and such like; if any care not to maintaine the good name and reputation of others; or be given to unnecessary pratling, blasing, or upbraiding, the infirmityes of men, by scoffing, and using false and frivilous illuding, if any seeme remisse or careles to approve himselfe, or to restraine the motions, allurements, or enticements to sinne and the lust therof, then without partiality or respect of persons, such lawfull meanes shall be used and put in practice, and urged as may represse, and surprise all such wicked manners inclinations and dispositions whatsoever. [51]

Clearly, the Law of D'ewes was not the Law of Moses, which in spite of its many minute and often arcane regulations, contained no proscriptions against indecency in apparel, "idle sporting," "pratling," or "frivilous illuding."[52] Moreover, as D'ewes made clear, obedience to the Law meant not only seeking to purge oneself, but striving to suppress sin wherever it reared its head, thus explaining the godly affection for schemes of ecclesiastical coercion. This vision of the Law was systematically and extensively elaborated at a pastoral level, most famously by John Dod and Robert Cleaver in their best-selling handbook, *A Plaine and Familiar Exposition of the Ten Commaundements.* By the early seventeenth century, mainstream puritans had constructed an enormous machine for moral regulation, which was based only marginally and inferentially upon the bible.

Here, then, was a third and final instability or inconsistency within puritan practical divinity. In many ways, this specifically and idiosyncratically puritan

---

[51] British Library, Harleian MS. 339, fols. 1v-2r. From Simonds D'ewes school notes, endorsed "the summe of the Law."

[52] For an interesting example of this process of stretching the boundaries of the Moral Law, see the notebook of Robert Saxby, which contains a meditation by Saxby on fasting. Here, the quintessentially puritan institution of the fast is accorded status as a commandment of God's Law (indeed, Saxby argued, it was "the first lawe, that God made, in the Commading Adame to abstayne from eting the forbiden frut."). CUL Additional MS. 3117, fols. 62v-63r.

version of the "Law" developed in direct relation to the cultural landscape of early modern England. Godly preachers had from a very early stage waged war upon certain cultural practices and institutions that were at the heart of late medieval English society. This war included campaigns against concrete targets—the alehouse and the theater—as well as attacks on more fluid, but nonetheless pervasive cultural practices, such as the casual use of oaths in everyday speech.[53] In this way, they stretched and reshaped the Ten Commandments to adjust them to the realities of early modern English life. The fact that drunkenness was nowhere forbidden in the Moral Law, for instance, did not for a moment diminish its status as a grievous sin. As the Ipswich preacher Samuel Ward explained, "the reason why Drunkennesse is not specially prohibited in any one of the tenne Commandements [is] because it is not the single breach of any one, but in effect the violation of all and every one, it is no one sinne, but all sinnes, because it is the Inlet and sluce to all other sinnes. The Devill having moystened, and steeped him in his liquor, shapes him like soft clay into what mould hee pleaseth."[54] Like Ward's malleable drunkard, the tables of the Law became in the hands of puritan preachers clay-like and plastic, ready to be reshaped to suit new ends. The godly themselves would of course have rejected this interpretation; from their perspective they were simply teasing out the plain implications of scripture. They would surely (and justifiably) have protested that they were merely following Saint Paul, whose laundry lists of "works of the flesh" had included not only drunkenness, but many other offenses that seemed to go beyond the particular prohibitions of the Torah.

And in this, mainstream puritans were struggling to give life to "Paul the moralist." From one vantage point, it might be argued that puritanism was a movement that attempted to preserve and reconcile the antinomian and the moralizing elements of the Pauline epistles. In their unabashed defense of the doctrines of justification by faith alone, puritans eagerly incorporated the anti-

---

[53] See, for instance, Dent, *Path-Way*, 142, which denounces seemingly harmless everyday oaths such as "By my Faith" or "By my Troth" as dangerous sins. Indeed, it might be argued that these "non-Mosaic" transgressions against the Moral Law became in time the emblematic and archetypal sins against which the godly labored. Thus, for example, on the title page of John Downame's *Guide to Godlynesse, Or a Treatise of a Christian Life*, was affixed an image of a woman who represented "Repentance." Beneath her feet lay the discarded and defeated emblems of sin: playing cards, a theatrical mask, and a mirror. It might be objected that these particular sins lent themselves to iconographic representation, but it is also the case that in foregrounding them, the godly were in subtle ways reshaping and redeploying the Old Testament for seventeenth century ends. The image is discussed and reproduced in Hambrick-Stowe, *Practice of Piety*, 40-41.

[54] Samuel Ward, *Woe to Drunkards* (1622), 14-15.

legal aspects of the Apostle's thought; while in their exaltation of holy duties and legal works, they likewise sought to replicate the strict and uncompromising moral rigorism that wound its way through all of his epistles, adjusting this rigorism to the particular cultural milieu of Elizabethan and Jacobean England. This conclusion may be viewed as an elaboration upon J. S. Coolidge's attempt to portray puritanism as an ideological movement that collectively embodied what Coolidge calls the "antinomies" of Paul's thought.[55] Perhaps inevitably, the tension arising from the particular "antinomy" between Law and Lawlessness would ultimately lead to a deep internal fissure, a fissure from which the first antinomians would emerge.

The word "inevitable" is appropriate in this case if only because mainstream puritanism gave birth to antinomianism not once, nor even twice—but multiple times, under distinct and apparently unrelated local circumstances, in entirely different parts of England. This suggests that whatever else we might say about mainstream puritanism, it most certainly lent itself to what might be termed an "anti-legal" critique, in which the antinomian elements of the New Testament could be privileged over and against the moralizing elements. From this standpoint, antinomianism as it will be laid out in this study appears not as an aberration, but as the product of a deep structural instability within puritanism itself, the unwanted by-product of normative godly divinity.

Let us momentarily reiterate the shape of this divinity. Puritanism began by inculcating in listeners a deep sense of sinfulness, evoked by the preaching of the Law and its curse. Having been reduced to a sense of hopelessness by the word, sinners were thus brought to see that their salvation rested not in themselves but in Christ. This was the beginning of true faith. Such infants in Christ were admonished to follow the first penitent stirrings of grace by diligent application of the means of grace. This meant not only attending on all public and private ordinances, but engaging in what Perkins called "a continuall fight against Sinne," a daily struggle to purify one's self and the world in accordance with God's Law.[56] Insofar as they were thus enabled by God's grace to employ the means zealously, and to die to sin with Christ, God freely granted these penitent sinners further grace, carrying the nascent believer upward in a continuing spiral-ascent of spiritual growth. At every step, however, the godly were reminded to try themselves for a dead faith, to search themselves for the least tokens of uncleanness, and to cry out in repentance for each transgression committed, consistently acknowledging their own abiding sinfulness and their reliance on Christ alone.[57] In this way, by pulling the be-

[55] J. S. Coolidge, *The Pauline Renaissance in England: Puritanism and the Bible* (Oxford: Clarendon, 1970).

[56] Rogers et al., *Garden*, sig. D2r.

[57] It should not be assumed, however, that godly preachers simply pushed their listeners to search themselves incessantly for good works. They also warned against

liever into a dialectic of faith, tempered by doubt, answered with a zealous application of the means, which in turn sowed increased faith, the godly minister slowly but surely nourished the believer up to maturity. Faith, repentance, and outward holiness would, it was hoped, grow and increase continually in a process that ended only in death.

Looked at from one perspective, this system was notable for its ingenuity. Puritan practical divinity managed to hold together difficult, some might say, irreconcilable aspects of the Bible in a tight, if complicated, unity. It likewise took into account the sometimes messy realities of pastoral practice, leaving significant room for the inevitable doubts and imperfections that dogged even the strongest and most devout believers. It managed to promote the reformed centerpiece of justification by faith in Christ alone while asserting the use, indeed the necessity, of diligent human action; in fact, through its rigorous insistence on the performance of duties, mainstream puritanism managed to recapture a moral rigor that was in its own way every bit as stringent as anything in either the Old Testament or the New. Here, one might argue, the intense puritan focus on conformity with the divine will ensured that in the theater of humanity, God would be glorified, and Christ exalted.

Pastoral Breakdown

It should be clear, however, that the system had its weaknesses and fault lines. Perhaps the most significant of these weaknesses, from a purely pastoral standpoint, was its tendency to encourage doubt and insecurity amongst professors of religion. As we have seen, godly divines on the one hand told their followers that faith was a fully assuring persuasion. On the other hand, they persistently engaged their auditors in a process of self-examination and self-questioning that was calculated to produce doubt. In theory, such doubts were to amplify the believer's assurance (since, as we have seen, doubt was seen as a necessary concomitant of a true faith). Indeed, there is good reason to believe that the system proved effective for the vast majority of godly people. Nevertheless, in certain cases, this process could lead, paradoxically and unintentionally, to a breakdown of all assurance. The historical record is littered with cases of aspiring puritans who were emotionally and psychologically

---

hypocrisy, that is, the presumption that one's external good works were a certain sign of election. Even the holiest professor, they warned, could be damned if his righteous works emanated from an unfaithful heart. Thus godly divines tacked back and forth between admonishments concerning "carnal profession" (claims to protestant faith that were not accompanied by works) and warnings concerning "hypocrisy" (great outward holiness that did not flow from a true and lively faith). The result, in both cases, was to foster a salutary sense of self-examination and doubt, which would force the believer back to Christ and the means of grace.

crushed by the insecurities created by godly divinity.[58] Having been split open by the hammer of godly preaching, some believers found themselves not assured and comforted, but plagued by the fear of death and hell. Tortured by their own abiding sinfulness, or unsure whether they possessed the true and lively faith, such professors were unable for their own reasons to find solace in the curatives of puritan practical divinity. Even those who had achieved a substantial outward holiness could find themselves haunted by fear that they were in fact nothing more than pharisaical hypocrites; an unnamed friend of Thomas Gataker complained of precisely such fears in 1631, beseeching the puritan minister for pastoral advice and comfort.[59] In some extreme cases, the resulting despair could be devastating, leading to depressive or even delusional mental states. Paul Seaver's work on the young Nehemiah Wallington has given us a glimpse into the profound, indeed suicidal, depths to which professors could be driven. As Wallington retold his own story

> The Sabbath day before Ester: when I came from church I went my selfe alone into the parlor and I would eat no meate: now my Father and the rest of the household was in the hall at dinner: and after my Father had dined he came into the parlor unto me and asked me how I did. With that I fell out a crying aloud: and said the Divell will not let me alone. Then my Father shut to the parlor doore and bead me hold my peace: and asked me what troubled me: Then said I oh my sinne against my God: which hinders me I cannot be saved and I then being then mellacolly Said the Divell can com in any liknesse he can com in the liknesse of my showes and then I flong away my showes. Then I said the Divell can com in the likenes of an Angel of Light or in the liknes of Master Robroh: Which that Master Robro oppened the parlor doore, then I runn to the other end of the parlor and Master Robro came to me: and helde my armes for I began to be unrulley and I tould him he was a divell then he Said unto me I hope you will not say I am a Divell, yes that I will Said I.[60]

Here, Wallington's doubt about his own spiritual status—his fear of his own sinfulness, his insecurity about his own salvation, and his profound awareness of the diabolical presence—all conspired to translate into not only depressive but dangerously paranoid behavior. Wallington's shoes—not to mention the flesh of his puritan pastor, Henry Roborough—had become in his eyes camouflaged repositories for the spirit of darkness. Nehemiah's doubts

---

[58] For a recent exploration of the subject of puritan religious despair, see John Stachniewski, *The Persecutory Imagination: English Puritanism and the Literature of Religious Despair* (Oxford: Clarendon Press, 1991), esp. 17-84.

[59] CUL MS. Dd. iii. 83 (19).

[60] Guildhall Library MS. 204, fol. 7r, and discussed in P. Seaver, *Wallington's World*, 24.

did eventually depart, but not before his despair had driven him to try to take his own life.

Much like the London turner Wallington, the godly gentlewoman Dionys Fitzherbert of Bristol experienced a bout of despair and fear so incapacitating that it shaded off into psychological states that would now surely be attributed to mental illness. Several years after her malaise began, Dionys came to retell her story with a rare vividness and candor.[61] While living away from home in another gentlewoman's household, she had grown melancholy and taken to bed. On her account, she had at first feigned sickness. This lie soon began to torment her. She became obsessed with hiding her lie, an obsession that apparently drove her to distraction. Fitzherbert began to interpret "every thing to be a Judgment of God against me for my sinns," and became convinced that he was about to punish her with death in just recompense for her transgressions. She likewise began to suspect that her brother—who appears to have tended to her as she descended into her paralyzed despair—was not actually her brother, but a secret enemy. In time, her condition worsened, until at length she concluded that she was already in hell. Although her account grows somewhat hazy at this point, she appears to have believed that she had already died, that she was a devil, and that the minister Edward Chetwind, into whose house she had been transferred, was God. Chetwind and his confederates—Mrs. Chetwind and the brothers Fitzherbert—were, she speculated, plotting to stuff her up the chimney, where she would roast everlastingly as a reward for her sins.

In her more lucid moments, Dionys recalled her former profession of religion, a profession that, on account of her present condition, she now judged to have been false. This only compounded her agony, for it convinced her that she had committed the unpardonable sin of blasphemy against the Holy Ghost. Her fears were likewise exacerbated by the haunting words of an unnamed minister: "that which did most trouble and afflict my sowle, was the words of a Preacher (and as I thinke the same my brother made Choice of to Come to me) who being demaunded If one of Gods elect might not be in my Case? answered, that his opinion was, that God would keepe his from such blasphemies; A Cruell sentence which shutt the dore of all hope from one in my state, who was too ready to pronounce itt upon my selfe, and lay the burthen of ytt on myne owne sowle"[62] Dionys's abject state was therefore inseparably linked to her fear that she was not a justified member of Christ. According to another preacher who visited her in Bristol, she had alleged that the cause of all her woes was the fear that "I want faith." When he asked her why

---

[61] What follows represents a summary of her own narrative, as contained in Bodleian Library, Bodleian MS. 154, fols. 14-27.

[62] Ibid., fol. 13r.

she doubted her own faith, she allegedly replied "I am not assured that I am justified and shall be saved." In other words, she was laboring under the impression that faith, in order to be true, needed to be fully assuring. Her own doubts and insecurities regarding her salvation thus became not (as godly preachers urged) a testimony as to the veracity of her faith, but horrifying evidence that she could expect nothing but an eternity of infernal flame.[63] It would be foolish to ascribe Fitzherbert's woes to her religious scruples alone; her testimony bears all the hallmarks of genuine mental fragmentation. Nevertheless, it seems clear enough that it was puritan practical divinity that shaped and informed the ultimate manifestation of her illness, providing a deeply dangerous context of fantasy and delusion into which she could set her increasingly paranoid musings. In this case, puritan practical divinity had backfired with terrible consequences.

This said, however, it is also true that Dionys Fitzherbert, like Wallington, eventually escaped her spiritual hell. The delusional world of inexpressible, "extreame feare and trembling" that she struggled to articulate seems to have dissolved much as it had come. And just as puritan divinity was implicated in her celebrated slide into despair, so too, puritan divinity helped her to climb out of her pit. She singled out for special praise a now obscure tract by John Freeman entitled *The Comforter*, a book which was designed mainly to help the weak of faith from despairing of salvation. Indeed, it seems clear that this work had a deep impact on Fitzherbert, both in helping her out of her private hell, and in providing her with a new framework in which she could interpret

[63] John Downe, *A Treatise of the Nature and Definition of Justifying Faith; Together with a Defence of the Same, against the Answere of* N. *Baxter* (Oxford, 1635), sig. A2v. In passing through Bristol around the year 1600, Downe, sometime fellow of Emmanuel College, paid a visit to "A certaine grave and godly Matrone of that City having beene a long time sore afflicted with sicknesse both in mind and body." Although he does not name her, it seems clear that this woman, who was suffering from an incapacitating spiritual anguish, was none other than Dionys Fitzherbert. In fact, Downe tried to convince her that her self-assessment was too harsh, and that faith could not be equated with full assurance. After preaching a guest sermon in Bristol to this effect, a city minister named Nathaniel Baxter challenged him, claiming along with William Perkins that faith was nothing other than complete assurance. The two men subsequently engaged in an acrimonious manuscript debate over the nature of justifying faith, a debate that was published posthumously under Downe's name in the volume cited above. The two men appear to have been struggling over the aforementioned ambiguity within the puritan doctrine of faith, with Baxter stressing the aspect of full and infallible assurance, and Downe emphasizing the inescapable doubts that afflicted even the strongest believers. It is interesting to speculate as to whether Baxter may have been the minister whose inopportune words had so discouraged Fitzherbert.

the chaos of her own madness. Following Freeman, she was now able to organize her entire experience as a vast conspiracy of Satan, who had sought to lead her to despair, atheism, and ultimately suicide.[64] In a similar manner, Wallington eventually came to a settled assurance of his own salvation, but only through years of diligent and zealous application of the means of grace, as laid out by mainstream puritan divines.[65] From one standpoint, then, each of these troubled people might be taken as a vindication of the power of puritan divinity to provide lasting spiritual succor.[66]

There is, however, a second, and considerably less charitable, view of the matter. On this interpretation, men and women such as Wallington and Fitzherbert were merely the most visible casualties of what was in essence a system of ideological bondage. By awakening in their listeners a sense of all-consuming sin and hopelessness, mainstream puritan ministers opened up a gaping spiritual void, a void which only they themselves could fill. For on their own account, only they—the ambassadors of God, the mouthpieces of the spirit—could convey the redemptive power of Christ. Yet although they promised an all-sufficient remedy in Christ, in reality their cure was a long, painful, and partial one. Doubt, insecurity, and sin would persist throughout life, ensuring that professors would need constantly to return to the puritan ministry for spiritual sustenance and guidance. From this standpoint, mainstream puritan divinity appears as little more than a deceptive species of spiritual addiction, imposed by a tyrannical ministry bent on perpetuating its own dominance.

This dark assessment of normative godly religiosity was at the core of the antinomian critique of mainstream puritan divinity. Puritanism, antinomians charged, reneged on its lavish promises of assurance. Having held out the tantalizing lure of salvation in and through Christ alone, godly ministers at the last moment snatched this bait away from their hungering disciples, leaving them suspended helplessly between doubt and faith, sin and righteousness, God and the devil. In place of a savior, mainstream puritan divinity offered believers a lifetime of fear and narcissistic self-questioning. Instead of promoting justification by faith, they instilled a deep dependence on legal works of sanctification. Instead of exalting Christ alone, godly preachers exalted

---

[64] See J. Freeman, *The Comforter: Or a Comfortable Treatise, Wherein are Contained Many Reasons Taken Out of the Word, to Assure the Forgiveness of Sinnes to the Conscience that is Troubled with the Feeling Thereof* (1600), esp. 155-88, which when compared against Fitzherbert's account of her own experiences demonstrates that her recollections were carefully related so as to fit into the framework of Satanic temptation laid out by Freeman.

[65] Seaver, *Wallington's World*, 43-44. On Seaver's account, Wallington's own doubts did not fully dissolve until he was in his fifties.

[66] I owe this point in large part to repeated conversations with Peter Lake.

themselves. By bullying and terrifying their charges into a perpetual cycle of means and duties, they created what was, at bottom, an addiction to their own form of divinity, thus ensuring their own social and cultural hegemony. The result was rampant legalism and formalism, a religion that hid behind a mask of Christian piety even as it sold its adherents into a state of perpetual slavery.

Antinomians promised to emancipate believers from this bondage, to reconfigure and redefine the meaning of "godliness." As we have seen, this was much more than just an intellectual exercise; it involved a war of words, in which anti-legalists deployed cultural media common to the puritan community in order to alter the cultural and ideological shape of that community itself. In the process of fighting this war, antinomians would likewise utterly reshape the puritan concept of "Law." Where mainstream puritanism sought to reconcile both the moralizing and the antinomian elements of the New Testament, antinomians clipped away all remnants of moral injunction, until at last they cast away the Law in its entirety. In doing so, they believed they had recaptured the meaning of Christianity, leading their followers out of the slavery imposed by a crypto-Jewish puritan ministry. Having begun as a protest movement that sought to dislodge regnant modes of pastoral divinity, antinomianism in its most robust and mature forms thus utterly negated and replaced many of the most sacrosanct assumptions of puritanism. Throughout the account that follows, however, it must be remembered that antinomianism could not have existed without puritanism. It subsisted in a symbiotic, or perhaps more appropriately, parasitic relationship to mainstream puritanism, feeding off the scattered remains of Fitzherberts and Wallingtons, and offering sustenance to those who had been damaged or estranged by the puritan way of salvation. To their mainstream counterparts, the antinomian solution was facile, a "fair and easy way to heaven." For those who found solace in it, antinomianism was instead a deliverance from the hell that had been prepared for them by the godly ministry.

CHAPTER 5

The Kingdom of Traske: The Early Career of John Traske and the Origins of Antinomianism

The following chapter explores the genesis of this protest movement. In Chapter Two, we saw that it is in fact quite impossible to locate a single fountain or origin point from which all Stuart antinomians trace their ideological roots. Rather, it is best to think of the evolution of antinomianism as a process in which several separate streams, each emanating from a distinct source, came together to form a single, larger river. Later chapters will attempt to demonstrate precisely how this might have happened; for now, I want only to provide the reader with a single, coherent account of how *one* of these several streams came into being, that is, to chart the path whereby one godly man arrived at the brink of an explicitly antinomian position. In fact, we are fortunate to have even one such opportunity, for in only a single case—the case of John Traske—do we now possess historical texts sufficient to recover this process in any detail. For reasons that will become obvious as we proceed, Traske left behind him a meandering trail of incriminating historical evidence. Much of this evidence was generated by Traske himself, while other pieces derive from his friend and accomplice Returne Hebdon, who bequeathed to posterity a detailed theological notebook composed from prison.[1] Still more may be ascertained by comparing and collating these firsthand sources with the ample texts produced by Traske's enemies within and without the ecclesiastical establishment. The resulting story has its gruesome aspects, but it likewise re-

---

[1] Returne Hebdon, *A Guide to the Godly* (1648). This book passed from Hebdon to Traske's wife Dorothy after Hebdon's death in prison around 1625.

veals much about the nature of early Stuart puritanism, as well as the antinomian protest movement it spawned. Fortunately, it also breathes life into the carcass of one of early Stuart England's most eccentric characters, a man whose life precariously straddled the fine line between tragedy and sheer absurdity.

Star Chamber

John Traske entered the annals of English history inauspiciously. On June 19, 1618, the court of Star Chamber sentenced him to be fined, whipped, pilloried, branded, to have his ears nailed to the pillory, and then to be committed to jail at the pleasure of King James. Traske was convicted of bringing "detraction and scandal on the King's most excellent Majesty," of "scandalizing his Ecclesiastical government," and for "a seditious practice and purpose to divert his Majesty's subjects from their obedience."[2] More specifically, he had set himself up as the head of a sect of ultraprecise separatistic puritans who claimed that the Old Testament Law, including the Saturday Sabbath and Mosaic dietary restrictions, remained in force for Christians. Having arrived in London sometime around 1615, Traske had gathered about him a small, but apparently vociferous following in and around the city. At some point in 1617, their unusual activities provoked the suspicions of the authorities, who promptly deposited the sect-master and a handful of his disciples into prison.[3] There Traske languished for months, subsisting on a diet composed wholly of bread, water, and (in mockery of his opinions) swine. In June 1618, perhaps as a consequence of negotiations over the Spanish Match, it was decided to prosecute him in Star Chamber.[4] At his trial, Traske apparently did himself few favors, breaking into a rant about his treatment at the hands of the bish-

---

[2] A copy of the sentence against Traske survives in the Bodleian and has been published, with an incorrect date, as "Trask in the Star-Chamber, 1619," in *Transactions of the Baptist Historical Society*, 5 (1916-17), 8-14. The date was later amended to 1618.

[3] Traske was in prison by November 1617, as is evident from the sentence against him. Ibid., p. 9.

[4] The possibility of connections to the Spanish Match is speculative, but it is worth noting that Traske's trial took place just days before the Spanish ambassador Gondomar was set to return to Spain, and in the wake of a conciliatory offer to allow imprisoned English Catholic priests to leave with Gondomar. This suggests that Traske may have been punished as an example of James's commitment to aggressive anti-puritanism. For more on this rapprochement, see A. J. Loomie, "Bacon and Gondomar: An Unknown Link in 1618," in A. J. Loomie, *Spain and the Early Stuarts* (Aldershot: Variorum, 1996).

ops.[5] With characteristic wit, Lord Chancellor Bacon handed down the brutal sentence, commenting that Traske's branding (with the letter "J," for Jew) would ensure that "he that was schismaticus might likewise be stigmaticus."[6] Within weeks, the punishment had been carried out.[7]

The story of an ultra-legalistic Judaizer might seem a counterintuitive place to begin an investigation into the theology of antinomianism. But as noted above, Traske's career did not end with his punishment. Rather than obligingly dying in the Fleet, Traske renounced his Judaical errors, and returned to the ministry in 1620. He slid back into the London puritan community, only to emerge a few years later as a full-blown antinomian. The following chapter retells the first part of this story, providing an account of Traske's early career and divinity. As we shall see, the seeds of his later antinomianism (which will receive treatment in Chapter Nine) were already present in the theological and social position he and his followers had adopted by 1615. Only through a close examination of the early thought of Traske and his follower Hebdon, then, can we begin to imagine and reconstruct the path whereby puritanism mutated into antinomianism. One might object that it is a mistake to treat Traske's career as representative of anything, let alone the origins of a puritan protest movement. He was, after all, spectacularly idiosyncratic, a perpetual nonconformist among nonconformists. From another perspective, however, it might be argued that Traske's life embodied many of puritanism's most salient features. On this view, his habitual excesses serve to bring into sharp, almost grotesque, relief many of the tendencies and contradictions embedded in the early Stuart godly community. The result not only tells us much about the genesis of later antinomianism, but reveals volumes about the ways in which puritanism could, under certain conditions, produce wildly aberrant, and indeed radical, modes of religiosity.

---

5 H.M.C. *Calendar of the Manuscripts of the Marquis of Bath*, 2: 67-68. James Lorkin to —— [June 23], 1618. Lorkin reported that Traske had been charged with "inveighing against our bishops under the termes of bloudy butchers, which in publique court he offred to make good for that half a yeer together they had kept him in prison with no other allowance then bread and water, whilest in the interim Popists (sic) Priests were there suffred to feast and banquet, and that indeed was his fare, but of swines flesh he might have eaten his fill every day." Traske apparently refused the pork.

6 Henry Bourgchier to James Ussher, 1618, in C. R. Elrington, ed., *The Whole Works of the Most Rev. James Ussher, D.D.* (Dublin: Hodges, Smith and Co., 1864), 16: 359.

7 The sentence was carried out sometime between June 23 and June 30. See the letter of Thomas Lorkin to Sir Thomas Puckering, June 30th, 1618, printed in T. Birch, ed., *The Court and Times of James the First* (London: H. Colburn, 1849; reprint, New York: AMS, 1973), 2: 77.

The Wandering Prophet

If we are to reconstruct Traske's theological peregrinations, we must first step backwards to examine briefly the details of his life prior to his fateful appearance in Star Chamber. For Traske adopted the Saturday Sabbath in 1617, long after he had embarked on his career as a rogue minister and sect-master, and then only at the prompting of one Hamlet Jackson, a follower who claimed to have received a fiery spiritual vision concerning God's Law.[8] Jackson, a London tailor, had been well seasoned for this revelation; he was one of a band of loyal disciples who had come to regard John Traske as a prophet and who had already followed him in resurrecting a number of Jewish ordinances, such as refraining from kindling fires and dressing meats on Sundays.[9] Yet even this progression into Judaic ritual represented only the culmination of a long process in which Traske and his followers had adopted increasingly unusual, even heterodox, opinions and practices, which set them apart from mainstream puritans. Traske's now famous "judaizing" phase was merely the latest and most ostentatious stop on a long spiritual journey that had begun at least a decade earlier in his native county of Somerset.

We know almost nothing of the first twenty-five years of Traske's life. He was in all likelihood born in Somerset, c. 1584-85, possibly in the town of

---

[8] The two indispensable modern studies of Traske's career are B. R. White, "John Traske (1585-1636) and London Puritanism," *Transactions of the Congregational Historical Society*, 20 (1968) and D. S. Katz, *Philo-Semitism and the Re-admission of the Jews to London, 1603-1655* (Oxford: Clarendon Press, 1982). See also B. W. Ball, *The Seventh-Day Men, Sabbatarians and Sabbatarianism in England and Wales, 1600-1800* (Oxford: Clarendon Press, 1994).

[9] Our best contemporary evidence concerning the Traskite movement is provided by the anonymous London puritan, "T.S.," who wrote a letter and an extensive biographical "relation" concerning Traske in the mid-1630s. The former was published in Edward Norice, *The New Gospel, Not the True Gospel* (1638), 6-8, while the latter was included in Ephraim Pagitt, *Heresiography: or A Description of the Hereticks and Sectaries of these Latter Times*, Sixth ed. (1662), 184-97. For proof that this second "relation" was written by T.S., compare his comments on Dorothy Traske (ibid., 197) against those contained in a letter by the same man, which was unpublished until transcribed by B. R. White in his "Samuel Eaton (d. 1639) Particular Baptist Pioneer," *Baptist Quarterly*, 24 (1971), 18-19. T.S.'s claim that Traske was converted to Seventh-Day observance by Jackson (a claim that has been questioned by B. W. Ball) may likewise be confirmed by comparison with a manuscript examination of Traske from 1627, in which he admitted that "he . . . and his wyfe were both drawen into theise Opinions by one Jackson nowe a professed Jewe dwelling at Amsterdam." See PRO, SPD 16/73/64, fol. 96r.

East Coker, to parents he would later describe as "godly."[10] Having received what appears to have been a basic grammar school education, Traske took up as a schoolmaster in an unnamed gentleman's household in Somerset.[11]

It may have been while serving in this capacity in the town of Frome that he had experienced the first of many encounters with the English courts, an incident that in many ways sets the tone for the rest of our discussion. In December 1608, Traske was accused in Star Chamber of libeling a Somerset lawyer named Charles Best. Best claimed that a pair of "lewd" men, described only as laborers, had swindled him in a land deal; among other fraudulent, but rather ingenious tricks, the two had sold him a parcel of land they did not own. A series of legal wrangles and threats appear to have followed, during which time Traske, a companion of the two laborers, had written and circulated a libel "to bringe a scandall and perpetuall blott" on Best's name. The libel ridiculed the lawyer's ineffectual and hapless maneuvers, ending with a series of statements that reflect sentiments rarely articulated in early modern England: "Best optime which for his skill which he had studied for soe many yeares, sought with foolish sotts to worke his will, but now such fooles hath putt him in such feares that he is like to turne by weepinge crosse, doe what he can he shall receive the losse, alas poore foole it greives me now full sore. what? to be cosened and a counsellor, tow[12] search bocrome bagge [a buckram bag was a generic description of a lawyer's tools, or in this case a lawyer's bag of tricks] is there noe knavery in store? well ever hereafter beware the clowted shoe by my consent, bycause thou hast plaid the foole putt on longe coates and goe againe

---

[10] In his 1616/7 allegation for a marriage license, Traske claimed to be about thirty-two years old. Guildhall Library MS. 10091/6, unfoliated, 8 Feb. 1616. He may, as is often assumed, have been John, son of Lionell Traske, born in East Coker in 1585, although a close examination of the published records of this family suggests that this John Traske died in 1634, when the minister was still very much alive. See extracts published in *New England Historical and Genealogical Register*, 54 (1900), 279-81; Traske described his parents as "godly" in the prefatory epistle of his *A Treatise of Libertie From Judaisme* (1620).

[11] For his (lack of) education and his schoolmastership, see John Falconer, *A Briefe Refutation of John Traskes Judaical and Novel Fancyes* (St. Omer, 1618), 8-9, and Norice, *New Gospel*, 7. He may have been the "Mr Traske" suspended from the curacy of Brimpton in 1605 for failure to wear the square cap and for being unlicensed, although he would have been little more than twenty years old at the time. See Somerset Record Office [hereafter SRO], D/D/CA 140, 379.

[12] The word "tow" was used during the period by hunters as a command or exhortation for calling in hawks or urging on greyhounds, and it is in this sense that Traske seems to have used the word.

to scoole."[13] Clouted, meaning patched, was again a generic description for the garb of the poor, and there can be little question that (snide humor aside) Traske's warning—"ever hereafter beware the clowted shoe by my consent"—represents an unusually straightforward invocation of what can only be called class antagonism.[14] This strain of sympathy for the poor, and a parallel suspi-

---

[13] PRO, STAC 8/61/27. Punctuation has been added to the verse for clarity. That this John Traske of Frome Selwood was the John Traske of later fame is inherently unprovable, but extremely likely. Transcripts of the parish registers of Frome (SRO, DD/SOG/1208, 1211, 1214) contain only a single reference to Traske (for 1610, when his son was baptized), demonstrating that he was not a native to the town, and that he moved on shortly thereafter, all of which is consonant with our knowledge of the minister Traske's career and whereabouts.

[14] The image of clouted shoes or "cloutshoes" possessed a long-standing connotation of popular political action, often conjuring up the threat of violence. Thus, in the first year of Henry VII's reign, a group of London tradesmen had been charged in King's Bench with conspiring against the king and of having gathered in arms under various banners, including the plough, the woolsack, and the clouted shoe. In Henry VIII's reign, Elizabeth Wood, a sympathizer with the Norfolk "Walsingham conspirators," had been executed for claiming that "it was pity that these Walsingham men were discovered, for we shall have never good world till we fall together by the ears, and with clubs and clouted shone/shall the deeds be done, for we had never good world since this king reigned." More impressively, it was used as a term of self-description by the Norfolk followers of Robert Kett during the rebellion of 1549. They had drawn inspiration from an alleged fragment of prophecy, which had been widely circulated and repeated in the days prior to their decisive defeat in August of that year. The prophecy read "The country gnoofes [knaves], Hob, Dick, and Hick/With Clubs and clouted shoon/Shall fill up Dussindale/with slaughtered bodies soon." In 1589, the term would again be invoked, this time disparagingly, by Thomas Nashe, who sneered that Martin Marprelate and his presbyterian coconspirators had made headway in England only because they had "closde with clouted Shoes," that is, pandered to the lower orders. Shakespeare likewise borrowed the image, putting it into the mouth of Jack Cade, who warns in *Henry VI Part II* that "We will not leave one lord, one gentleman/ Spare none but such as go in clouted shoon." Half a century later, John Lilburne would likewise deploy the image, appealing to "Hobnayles and clouted Shoes," during the early stages of the Leveller agitation. See D. Loades, *Politics and Nation: England, 1450-1660* (Oxford: Blackwell, fifth edition, 1999), 77; S. L. Jansen, *Dangerous Talk and Strange Behavior* (New York: St. Martin's Press, 1996), 81-82; K. Thomas, *Religion and the Decline of Magic* (New York: Charles Scribner's Sons, 1971), 403; *The Complete Works of Thomas Nashe*, ed. A. Grossart (London and Aylesbury: The Huth Library, 1883-84), 1:126; A. Wood, *Riot, Rebellion and Popular Politics in Early Modern England* (Basingstoke: Palgrave, 2002), 3; I. Roots, *The Great Rebellion, 1642-1660* (London: B. T. Batsford,

cion of wealth and power, would inform Traske's ministry in the years to come, giving shape to a strikingly egalitarian theological synthesis.

This theological synthesis would develop as Traske moved from his position as a schoolmaster, to a curacy within the church, to a role as a wandering evangelist and self-styled prophet. In 1611, two years after Best's defamation suit, Traske was ordained against the objections of the ecclesiastical examiner Samuel Ward, who suspected that Traske, a self-taught preacher who had never been to university, was unfit for the ministry.[15] Within two years, Traske had been suspended from his first Somerset curacy. He appears to have escaped into the diocese of Exeter, where he took up residence in the household of John Drake of Axminster, Devonshire. Here, perhaps while serving as Drake's chaplain, he preached publicly throughout 1613, while operating as a sort of local spiritual adviser out of Drake's home.[16] For reasons that are not entirely clear, however, by early 1614, he had left the southwest, taking up the mantle of itinerant evangelist that would characterize the rest of his career.

In May 1614, he appeared on the other side of England, in the diocese of Ely, where he was accused of unlicensed preaching in the parish church of Littleport, in the town of Chettisham, and in the household of a prominent citizen in Ely itself.[17] How and why Traske undertook the lengthy journey to Ely remains an open question. It should be recalled, however, that Ely had been and would remain an outpost of sectarian religion for some time to come, raising the possibility that Traske's destination was less than accidental. This possibility will be considered further on; for now, it should simply be noted that his appearance in Ely seems to have marked an abandonment of the parochial structures of the English church. Traske had now assumed a peripa-

---

1966), 117. I would like to thank Ethan Shagan and Peter Lake, respectively, for drawing my attention to the second and fourth references.

15 The claim that Ward had initially opposed Traske was first made in Thomas Fuller, *The Church-History of Britain; From the Birth of Jesus Christ, Until the Year M. DC. XLVIII* (1655), 76.

16 Traske likewise preached at Honiton in 1613. See Irene Cassidy, "The Episcopate of William Cotton, Bishop of Exeter, 1598-1621: with special reference to the State of the Clergy and the Administration of the Ecclesiastical Courts," (B. Litt. Thesis, Oxford University, 1964), 87. Traske's friend John Pecke also claimed that Traske had preached at a visitation sermon at Honiton, for which see National Library of Scotland, Advocates MS. 33.1.6, vol. 20 (Denmilne State Papers), fol. 60. I owe these references to Kenneth Fincham and Arnold Hunt, respectively.

17 CUL, Ely Diocesan Records (EDR) B/2/35, fols. 3r, 62r, 76-77, 82r, 113-14, 190r. Most of those brought before the court stood accused of attending a sermon preached by Traske in Littleport. In addition, however, two laymen admitted that they had allowed Traske to pray in their homes in Ely and Chettisham. These records were originally discovered by Dr. Kenneth Fincham.

tetic ministry more akin in style to the secretive missions of Roman Catholic priests than to any existing ecclesiastical office or function.

By November 1614, he had returned to Somerset, where he and several of his lay admirers were called before the church courts. Traske stood accused of preaching doctrine derogatory to the Church of England, and of "running up and downe from parish to parish" as a "wandering minister."[18] In the investigation that ensued, it was revealed that Traske had preached from at least five Somerset pulpits in the previous months, in addition to praying or preaching privately in the homes of sympathetic lay people.[19] Traske himself seems to have gone underground; he failed to appear before the court and was duly excommunicated.[20]

Where he went from here is unclear; there is reason to believe that he may at some point have passed through Lyme Regis in Dorset, near his old haunting grounds in East Devonshire.[21] Our next sighting, however, does not occur until a year later, when in late November 1615, Traske was detained and imprisoned in Middlesex upon warrant from the Archbishop of Canterbury, and the bishops of London, Ely, and Rochester. Once again, it was alleged that he had been "going up and down as a wandering minister."[22]

---

[18] SRO, D/D/CA 189 (Consistory Court Act Book), fol. 150v, 22 Nov. 1614. Traske's Somerset activities were first uncovered by Margaret Stieg.

[19] Ibid., fols. 183-84, 20 Dec. 1614. Traske had shared Richard Bernard's pulpit at Batcombe, in addition to preaching from the parish churches of Mearston Magna, Stratton, Broadmeareton, and Doulting. It was also revealed that Traske had prayed, and possibly preached, in the homes of two laymen of Shepton Mallet.

[20] Ibid., fol. 158v, 29 Nov. 1614.

[21] See HMC, *Report on the Records of the City of Exeter* (1916), 95-96. In early 1616, Bishop Cotton of Exeter had challenged the presentment of a preacher named John Hazard to the Bodley lectureship at Exeter. Hazard's report of his subsequent conference with Cotton, which took place on April 5, 1616, includes these comments, which suggest (although not definitively) that Traske had disseminated his teaching in and about Lyme Regis: "B. You have preached false doctrine [but would not show me wherein, because I knew he could not]. And beside (sayth he) you have been a companion with Trasque.–H.: My lord, ytt is not so, for I can bringe good testimony that I have twise publickly in two severall sermons att Lyme confuted the erroneous fancyes of Trasque, beside my brief notes I have yett to shew and I refere you to Mr Knowles his testimony of the truth of this the whole towne of Lyme can wittnes the same." William Knowles was vicar of both Chilton Cantelo, Somerset, and Axminster, Devon, the sites of Traske's first two cures. His relationship with Traske is unclear, although it might be assumed that he began as Traske's patron.

[22] William Le Hardy, ed., *Calendar to the Sessions Records*, Middlesex Sessions Records, New Series, Volume 3, 1615-1616 (London: Sir Ernest Hart, 1935), 107.

So far as we can tell, this appearance in the London area marked the beginning of the Traskite movement. Having set down roots in the cacophonous religious scene of the capital, Traske began to preach his message with characteristic vehemence, although largely outside the purview of the institutional church. There is no evidence that he ever possessed a living, a lectureship, or even warrant to preach in London; in September of 1616, he would again be imprisoned in Newgate for offenses that appear to have included preaching without a license and holding a conventicle.[23] Despite his lack of a settled benefice and his repeated legal difficulties, Traske managed in his brief but dramatic spell in the capital to capture a noticeably large group of followers. These followers appear to have been attracted both by Traske's charismatic style and his peculiar theological teachings, which he flaunted openly in an effort to set himself apart from other ministers. Having converted an obscure minister identified only as "Mr Gr.," Traske allegedly "marched like Jehu most furiously, making divisions in the Church about London" with his innovative message.[24] Before analyzing these innovative and infamous teachings, I would like to peer momentarily into the Traskite movement itself, for the spiritual environment of the Traskite community sheds considerable light on the origins and trajectory of Traske's theology.

Blown by the Spirit

According to the most perceptive observer of the Traskite movement, the men and women who followed Traske believed him to be nothing less than a divinely ordained prophet, the second Elijah foretold in the book of Malachi.[25] We have no idea how many people shared this belief; there can be no question, however, that Traske attracted an inner circle of impassioned devotees, several of whom would continue to adhere to his teaching long after their prophet had renounced his own "Judaism." Among these disciples were his wife Dorothy Coome, the illegal schoolmistress of St. Sepulchre parish, who wedded Traske in early 1617; an Inner Temple student named John Pecke, who had made Traske's acquaintance in his home county of Devonshire in 1613, and who imprudently agreed to deliver one of Traske's manuscripts to the king; and the men ordained by Traske to carry his message abroad, including the tailor Jackson, and one Returne Hebdon, the son of a minor Sus-

---

[23] National Library of Scotland, Advocates MS. 33.1.6, vol. 20 (Denmilne State Papers), fol. 60.

[24] Norice, *New Gospel*, 7.

[25] Ibid., 7; Pagitt, *Heresiography*, 190.

sex gentleman, who refused to recant with Traske in 1620, ultimately dying in prison for his seventh-day beliefs.[26]

These men and women had apparently been swept up in an exuberant and enthusiastic atmosphere of piety. Observers universally agreed that the Traskite movement was characterized by a spiritual excitement that was excessive even among the ranks of radical puritans. Traske's exhortations to repentance allegedly elicited from some of his listeners responses so emotional "that inhabitants in several places of the City were disquieted many times in the night season by his Converts." Traske "himself gave them an example, for both in City and Fields he prayed so loud, as if he would have peirced the Heavens."[27] Thomas Fuller, an eyewitness to one of Traske's sermons, likewise commented on the unusual robustness of Traske's pulpit mannerism, remarking that "when his Auditors have *forgotten* the matter, they will *remember* the *loudness* of his stentorian voice, which indeed, had more strength, than any thing else he delivered."[28] A Catholic priest named John Falconer, who seems to have spent time with Traske in prison, told a very similar story: "His owne and his disciples prayers are commonly roaringes, and such loud out-cries as may be heard in distant roomes and houses, voluntarily framed."[29] These tales of effusive, even ecstatic, behavior were, of course, recounted by hostile witnesses seeking to portray the Traskites as a perverse and ludicrous band of fanatics. Taken together, however, their comments (which came from a puritan, a Catholic, and the archetypal "Anglican," Fuller) impart to us an undeniable hint as to the flavor and temperature of the early Traskite movement.

It seems clear, for instance, that these meetings, some of which were held, revival-like, in fields adjoining the city, were as much spectacles as sermons. Here, much in the style of modern charismatics, Traske and his followers opened themselves to the movements of the spirit, falling into what from all accounts appear to have been dramatic outpourings of extemporaneous prayer. In doing so, they were merely taking to its logical conclusion a tendency that had been buried in militant puritanism from its beginnings, the

---

[26] T.S. alleged that there were four such ordinands. For hints that their efforts at itinerant evangelism may have met with some success, see D. Beaver, *Parish Communities and Religious Conflict in the Vale of Gloucester, 1590-1690* (Cambridge, MA: Harvard University Press, 1998), 139-40, which demonstrates that three members of the town elite of Tewkesbury (George Shaw, Edward Hill, and Roger Plevy) were prosecuted for seventh-day Sabbatarianism in 1620. It remains possible that their opinions represented an independent and parallel development of seventh-day ideas.

[27] Pagitt, *Heresiography*, 184.

[28] Fuller, *Church-History*, 76.

[29] Falconer, *A Briefe Refutation*, 7-8.

tendency to reject all set forms of prayer in favor of spontaneous spiritual inspiration. This attitude, which had reached its fullest expression in the writings of separatists such as Barrow and Greenwood, cast aside the homilies and prayer book for what Falconer called "voluntarily framed" prayer. Indeed, it seems that both before and after his judaizing phase Traske was notoriously fond of gracing those who invited him into their homes with extended, extempore performances that skirted a thin line between prayer and sermon.[30] To hostile observers, this extreme "spiritism" gave the Traskite movement a carnivalesque and comical appearance; to the faithful, however, these ecstatic performances no doubt created a heightened, almost electric, sense of the God among them. This sense of palpable divine immanence is evident in the words of Traske's disciple and fellow minister Returne Hebdon: "If it be so that many do meete together which have the gift of the same spirit, the more there are, the greater is the presence and power of God, that even the place doth shake at the glory of the one invisible Majesty of God, inspiring and expiring

---

[30] See CUL, EDR B/2/35, fols. 3r, 76v. In December 1614, when the Ely gentleman Nicholas Massey was presented for hosting Traske and several other families at a Sabbath dinner in his house, he admitted that he had permitted the minister to pray there, although the authorities complained that "what prayers he used we cannot learne." In the same month, a Chettisham man likewise confessed that Traske had prayed in his home "not by the book, but as he thought fit or thought good himself"; see also, SRO D/D/CA 189, fols. 183v-184r. As noted above, by the time of the Ely presentations, Traske had returned to Somerset, where two admirers were likewise accused of having attended conventicles at which Traske preached. The accused host, Thomas Millard, denied that "John Thraske did to this respondents knowledge preache or expound anie part of Scripture, or say anie kind of prayers in this respondents howse to his knowledge more then before, and after meales when he hath dyned or supte in his howse." This pattern apparently persisted after Traske's release from prison in 1620, for in 1634 it was alleged before the High Commission that the Dorset gentleman Richard Strode "within these fewe yeares last past did entertaine the said Thraske into his house where he said Thraske did pronounce prayers extempore and expounded a Chapter or Text of scripture to the said Sr Richard Strowd and his family" (PRO, SPD 16/261/ fols. 56r-57r). In 1627, Traske was imprisoned on suspicion of having proclaimed the innocence of a convicted rapist at the scaffold, where he had delivered an extemporaneous prayer for the soul of the condemned man, a prayer that allegedly included an invitation to the earth to open up and swallow those who had come to scoff at the felonious puritan. Traske denied this, providing the authorities with what was undoubtedly a doctored version of the original prayer. Although unquestionably altered from its original form, this account nevertheless provides a good example of Traske's effusive and flowing style of prayer. See PRO, SPD 16/72/45, fol. 71r-v.

the severall effects of the essence of Gods spirit."[31] Hebdon's extraordinary description captures, as no other document, the ambiance and excitement of the early Traskite movement. In his words, we can almost hear the "expirings" of the divine spirit, flowing freely among those who had been caught up in the whirlwind of Traske's ministry.

For our purposes, what is crucial is the fact that extreme spiritism of this sort was likely to lead those in its thrall to new and sometimes startling discoveries concerning God's will. For as Hebdon's words make clear, this sort of performative, ecstatic prayer represented more than just a style of worship in which God's spirit was taken to be intimately present among believers; it also carried with it implicit consequences for how believers imagined their relationship to God, and how they interpreted scripture. If God was spiritually present among the true saints, then saints were obligated to yield to the motions of the spirit, even if the spirit carried them in novel and perhaps heterodox directions. This impulse was particularly strong among separatists, whose clean break from established parochial worship often involved a rejection not only of the institutions of the English church, but a much more dramatic repudiation of the traditions and dogma that were presumed to have been passed down from the early Christians. The point was made most dramatically by John Fokes, a Norfolk separatist who broke with his fellow Brownists in 1620. Offering an account of his spiritual progress to Bishop Harsnett of Norwich, Fokes confessed that under the tutelage of East Anglian separatists, as well as exposure to various radical puritan writings, he had come to believe "that since Sylvester the Pope his time, there was neither true ordinance, nor calling of the ministerie in any place of the Earth, but that all was turned into the bodie of Antichrist: and so, that every private man, that had gods spiritt in him, was a true Church within himselfe, and was to looke for no other instruction, but from Gods spiritt, and the reading of the Bible."[32] In Fokes's case, this assumption did not apparently produce any serious departures from the established doctrine of the Church. Traske and his associates shared Fokes's basic perspective; they appear, moreover, to have had little compunction about submitting to what they perceived as the winds of God's spirit, even when it led them directly away from the safe harbors of orthodoxy.

Thus, according to the unidentified London puritan T.S., when the Traskites took their ill-fated leap into Saturday Sabbatarianism in 1617, they did so not solely as a result of a measured examination of the letter of scripture, but through an immediate revelation vouchsafed to Traske's ordinand, the preacher-tailor Hamlet Jackson. Jackson, unlike Hebdon, was not a man

[31] Hebdon, *Guide*, 19. See Acts 4: 31 for the probable scriptural basis for Hebdon's comments.

[32] National Library of Scotland, Advocates MS. 33.1.6, vol. 20, fol. 59v.

of education; according to T.S., he was a tailor who could not "write true English, nor read it truly, but as he learnt it lately by a habit of reading."[33] Formal education, however, was by no means one of the qualifications for Traske's Kingdom. Believers were first and foremost identified by their outward holiness and their spiritual charisma, traits that Jackson appears to have possessed in abundance, perhaps explaining why his vision was taken seriously by members of the Traskite community, including the leader himself. As T.S. recalled,

> [Jackson] traveling the Country on a Saturday, which he then thought to be the right Sabbath, but did not observe it, as himself said, saw a shining light about him, which struck him into an amazement. . . . And thereupon he concluded that the light of the Law was more fully discovered to him, than to any since the Apostles. And it was thought, that the two witnesses *Rev.* 11. which he interpreted to be the Law and the Prophets, yea in a manner the whole letter of the Scriptures lying dead, from the Apostles daies to our times, were now revived and stood upon their feet.[34]

Although this narrative, which has been likened by one author to a reverse Pauline conversion experience, may be apocryphal, it was recounted by a Londoner who personally knew both John and Dorothy Traske, and who had clearly been a curious witness to many of the excesses of the early Traskite movement.[35] A manuscript statement privately submitted by John Traske a decade later, during a separate ecclesiastical investigation, repeated T.S.'s claim that Traske had been convinced of the Saturday Sabbath by Jackson.[36] We can thus be reasonably sure that even if Jackson never experienced any such vision, some similar process of illumination, followed by a period in which disciple and leader reversed roles, did ultimately take place in the clandestine world of prophecy and spiritual experimentation that was developing among John Traske and his followers, leading into the full-blown judaizing of later fame.

This pattern of immediate revelation was by no means exceptional amongst Traske and his followers. There are clues, for instance, that Traske and his associates considered the interpretation of dreams to be a fundamental and ordinary means whereby God's spirit informed and instructed the minds of the elect. After his punishment, while imprisoned in the Fleet, Traske's warden

---

33 Pagitt, *Heresiography*, 167.

34 Ibid., 188.

35 For the observation that the structure of Jackson's epiphany represented a negative image of Paul's conversion, see R. M. Smith, "Christian Judaizers in Early Stuart England," *Historical Magazine of the Protestant Episcopal Church*, 52 (1983), 125-34.

36 PRO, SPD 16/73/64, fol. 96r.

alleged that the sect-master kept a secret diary, which included among other items a running account of his "dreams and interpretations."[37] The journal itself has not survived, but Hebdon has left us with one critical diary entry of his own, which throws light on Traske's practice: "In my sleepe by night, I was instructed in the righteous judgements of our God, by comparing them with the judgements of men." He proceeded to give a detailed interpretation of his dream which led to the conclusion that even as Kings hunted, tried, and executed "Heretickes, Schismatickes, and Rebells against the present religion or worship of God, consitituted by their Authority," so too would God have his day with those who had violated his holy Law.[38] Such an interpretation, which clearly referred to Hebdon's experience at James I's hands, carried ominous, if latent implications, which shall be explored momentarily. For present purposes, however, what is significant is the fact that this revelation, or instruction, had come to Hebdon in his sleep, and that he appears to have regarded it is as manifestation of the divine spirit. We may assume, given the fact that Traske kept a running commentary on his own dreams, that this mode of visionary dream interpretation was a normal, even commonplace feature of the Traskite movement. Nigel Smith has shown that such practices were common among civil-war radicals, who often used the words "dream" and "vision" synonymously.[39] As the example of Traske, Jackson, and Hebdon shows, this method of visionary spiritism seems to have predated the civil wars, at least at the frontiers of the puritan community.

The point, ultimately, is that the Traskites were immersed in a style of piety that was almost sure to lead them to new and indeed innovative conclusions about the nature of true religion. This ecstatic mode of piety, which relied on spiritual inspiration both to inform their extemporaneous prayers and to "instruct" them in God's ways, may have owed something to an underground sectarian tradition, for as we shall see later in this study, spiritual dream interpretation appears to have been an important component of Familist religiosity. Even if this is true, however, it is equally true that such habits meshed perfectly with practices and tendencies that had always been at or near the heart of puritanism. Extemporaneous, ecstatic prayer and prophetic biblical interpretation were anything but marginal within the puritan community.[40]

---

[37] *The Oeconomy of the Fleet*, Camden Society, N.S., 25 (1879), 48-49.

[38] Hebdon, *Guide*, 100-101.

[39] Nigel Smith, *Perfection Proclaimed: Language and Literature in English Radical Religion* (Oxford: Clarendon Press, 1989), 73-103.

[40] For this sometimes overlooked aspect of puritan religiosity, see D. Como, "Women, Prophecy and Authority in Early Stuart Puritanism," *Huntington Library Quarterly*, 61 (1998). It should also be noted that the ascription of religious or prophetic significance to dreams was not unheard of even among the most self-consciously "orthodox" puritans.

And as the example of the Traskites shows, such practices possessed a potential, even a likelihood, to burst out of the shackles imposed by magisterial arbiters of orthodoxy. In this manner, it was alleged that John Eaton had arrived at his doctrinal innovations partly through what he took to be immediate revelations vouchsafed through prayer.[41] The case of Traske and his followers likewise shows how deeply centrifugal this tendency could be, for no sooner had Traske led his disciples down the road to heterodoxy, than his followers in turn led him in a new, spiritually informed direction. So, too, when the Traskite movement fragmented, each of the major protagonists followed a different theological path, as exemplified by the very different careers of Traske, who turned antinomian, and Jackson, who allowed the spirit to carry him to Amsterdam, where he converted to Judaism.[42]

The Kingdom of Joy

Traske's magnetic hold upon these people seems to have flowed from both his charismatic style and his unusual and novel teachings. These teachings, which progressed hand in hand with Traske's increasing alienation from the established church, set him apart from all other early Stuart divines.[43] When, precisely, these opinions came to fruition is not clear; in early 1616, however, a Devonshire preacher was forced to defend himself from the accusation that he shared "the erroneous fancyes" of Traske, suggesting that at least some of Traske's innovations had developed well before his arrival in London.[44] Fortunately, in 1615 and 1616, Traske managed to publish three tracts, which when carefully compared against the hostile claims of his critics, allow us to reconstruct these "erroneous fancies" with some certainty.

It should be pointed out that the manner in which his ideas were presented was hardly straightforward. In order to get his works through censorship, Traske was forced to couch his arguments in terms that conformed to the

---

[41] See Chapter Six.

[42] For details on Jackson's later conversion, see Smith, "Christian Judaizers." Hebdon, meanwhile, appears to have begun to question the validity of infant baptism. See Hebdon, *Guide*, 26, in which he remarked that "in the baptism of Infants the doctrine of regeneration is quite extinct and abolished under a forme of words." It is not clear whether this represented a wholesale rejection of the immersion of children and a call for adult baptism, or merely an attack on prevailing understandings of the regenerating effects of infant baptism.

[43] It was claimed that Traske's "judaizing" had been preceded by a period of separatism. See PRO, SPD 14/96/15, fol. 35, in which John Chamberlain claimed Traske had been a separatist. See also Pagitt, *Heresiography*, 165-66.

[44] HMC, *Report on the Records of the City of Exeter*, 95-96. From the conference between the Bishop of Exeter [Cotton] and the minister John Hazard, April 5, 1616.

conventions of mainstream Calvinist divinity. The peculiar aspects of Traske's message are therefore carefully submerged beneath a surface that was designed to avail itself of an orthodox reading, often emerging only as passing or opportune asides. Even more striking is the fact that Traske's two 1615 pamphlets were constructed as explicit attacks on various forms of puritan error, which undoubtedly lubricated the licensing process. The first treatise contained a passing refutation of Anabaptism, as well as a critique of puritan pharisaism. The second is framed as an overarching attack on separatism, and more generally, on the godly obsession with the niceties of ecclesiastical government. Entitled *Christs Kingdom Discovered. Or, That the true Church of God is in England, clearely made manifest against all Sectaries whatsoever*, this short piece ostensibly followed a well-worn tactic used by non-separating puritans to refute the claims of separatists, mimicking the classic godly argument that since the English church had nurtured within it true believers, it must necessarily be a true church of God.[45] Yet, as we shall see, Traske deployed this format not to defend the Church of England—which he had to all appearances abandoned by 1615—but to elaborate his own very unorthodox vision of Christ's Kingdom rightly construed. What follows, then, is an attempt to distill from his writings the distinctive or constitutive aspects of that Kingdom.

Let us begin with our most extensive contemporary account of Traske's early ministry. The anonymous puritan gossip T.S. has left us with two separate descriptions of Traske's early theological position. Although these accounts were both written retrospectively, in the 1630s, T.S. had clearly been a close observer of Traske's activities in London, most likely because his own child had been tutored by Traske's wife Dorothy, who ran an unlicensed school at the time.[46] T.S. claimed that prior to his adoption of the Saturday Sabbath, Traske had hit upon an unusual soteriology in which all people could be divided into one of three states: nature, repentance, and grace.

In the first, unregenerate state of nature, humans were unaware of sin and utterly separated from God. To these, Traske preached repentance. In some ways, this resembled closely the standard puritan assumption that the ungodly needed first of all to hear the Law and its curse preached, in order to awaken in them a sense of sin and condemnation, and the attendant need for Christ. But Traske's notion of repentance went beyond a simple awareness of sin. Repentance was for him a state of intense sorrow and rigorous self-mortification, akin to what we might call a state of "penitence." Consequently, he enjoined followers to crucify their flesh, apparently urging them to extremes of physical

---

[45] See P. Lake, *Moderate Puritans and the Elizabethan Church* (Cambridge: Cambridge University Press, 1982), 77-92.

[46] For which, see Pagitt, *Heresiography*, 209-10.

endurance, which included fasting, hard labor, the wearing of sackcloth, sexual abstinence and possibly prolonged periods of sleep deprivation.[47] It was, moreover, a period of waiting, in which the penitent sinner patiently mortified his or her flesh in expectation of the coming of faith.

This advent of faith brought the believer into the third estate, that of grace. Here, the rigors and miseries of the period of repentance were entirely wiped away, and the believer was "passed from death to life, they should have no more sorrow, all joy; sadness and sighing should be fled away."[48] This state of justifying faith brought with it complete assurance of one's election; on the account of T.S., Traske also claimed that those so transformed "might know anothers election, as certainly as his own"; and, perhaps most radically, that "none that were justifyed did commit sinne." These last two claims were corroborated by other, independent witnesses: in 1619, the puritan William Sclater attacked Traske for having violently appropriated Sclater's manuscript notes on I Thessalonians in order to justify his claim that the elect could infallibly recognize one another. Meanwhile, the Catholic priest John Falconer, who may have been imprisoned with Traske in London, confirmed T.S.'s report that Traske was "infallibly assured, that he himselfe hath truly repented, and is made sure of his eternall election in Christ: and that he can in this life neither sinne, nor repent any more."[49]

It should be evident that if T.S.'s claims were accurate, then Traske's message amounted to much more than a particularly rigorous or exaggerated version of mainstream puritan divinity. For several of the arguments ascribed to Traske here—particularly the notion that the elect could infallibly recognize one another, and that believers were free from sin—are opinions typically associated with antinomianism. These are not the sorts of beliefs that we should expect to see from an ultra-legalist, or a judaizer, who insisted that believers should perform every jot and tittle of the Mosaic Law. These are not the sorts of belief that one finds anywhere within mainstream puritanism at the time. Nor was T.S.'s description of Traske's divinity mistaken; indeed, when we look at his early writings, not only is this account of Traske's message verified, but it is considerably amplified, in ways that make him look even more distinctive and out of place.

Traske's first pamphlet, entitled *A Pearl for a Prince*, represented a sort of charter for his ministry, a primer designed as he claimed, for "the little ones,

---

[47] For stories of fasting, hard labor, and the wearing of sackcloth, see ibid., 184-85; for hints of sexual abstinence and sleep deprivation, see *Christs Kingdom Discovered. Or, That the true Church of God is in England, clearely made manifest against all sectaries whatever* (1615), 54-55.

[48] Pagitt, *Heresiography*, 187.

[49] W. Sclater, *An Exposition with Notes upon the first Epistle to the Thessalonians* (1619), 14-31. Falconer, *Briefe Refutation*, 7.

for whose sake I penned it."[50] It was an introductory work, and as such holds out tantalizing prizes rather than revealing the marrow of Traske's teaching. Nevertheless, its broad outlines confirm the picture painted by T.S. Thus, we find Traske explicitly claiming that repentance preceded and ended with faith. In a standard puritan maneuver, he urged his readers to look to themselves in order to try themselves for the signs of a true faith: "The ground wher Faith is sowen, is an humbled soule, a wounded spirit, or rent heart; to such God giveth the grace of Faith, as are so prepared for it. . . . Hast thou felt thy soule sick with sinne? Hast thou beene pressed downe with the burden thereof? Hath thine hart melted within thee, and thine eyes gusht cut with teares for thy sinnes?"[51] The miseries of Repentance, however, were completely effaced by the joy that arrived with the coming of true faith. In this state, believers were, as T.S. reported, transported to a state of unadulterated joy. If only, Traske mused, his readers "did but knowe what *Peace* I feele, what *rest* I have obtained," they would drop everything and take up the cross. He described this passage from repentance to grace as an utterly transformative, almost mystical experience. In his original state, "even in laughing my heart was sorrowfull, and the ende of that mirth was heavinesse. But since I have received the assurance of the Love of God in Christ, I have beene so comforted, for the most part, that I have beene constrained to breake foorth into singing: yea, the high praises of God have bin in my Mouth, and I have sung a loud upon my bed, yea night and day I have had *Melody in my Heart.*"[52]

Here was a gospel of rapture and jubilation, in which the soul was thoroughly, indescribably "ravisht with the *Love of Christ.*"[53] This banished all fear and doubt, so that "whereas before the shaking of a leafe, would put me in feare: and great men would affright me with their high wordes . . . now I feare them not, for I knowe they shall die and fade as grasse: neither can the greatest oppressor touch one hare of my head for hurt."[54] Indeed, Traske claimed that in this estate of grace, "I am so well acquainted with the rich inheritance of the Saints in light, that if *Repentance* were again to bee taken up, though it were a thousand times more difficult then it was, yet could I undergoe it, for the happinesse which I doe already enjoy."[55] Repentance, then, was a stepping-stone, which delivered the believer into a state of ecstatic joy. "Hereby thou maist trie thy selfe. Hast thou beene troubled, and terrified with

---

[50] *A Pearl for a Prince, or a Princely Pearl. As it was delivered in two sermons* (1615), sig. A3v.

[51] Ibid., 10-11.

[52] [John Traske], *Heavens Joy, or Heaven Begun on Earth* (1616), 141-42, and more generally, 139-59.

[53] Ibid., 142.

[54] Ibid., 144.

[55] Ibid., 157.

the sight of thy sinnes? And art thou now at Peace? Hast thou mourned? And dost thou rejoyce? Hast thou hated God in his Word, in his Prophets, or poore children? And dost thou delight in his Law, receive his Prophets, because they are his Prophets; delight in the Saints, because they are children. . . . Hast thou feared death, and trembled at the time of dissolution? . . . And canst thou now wait with Patience for the time of thy dissolution? Then maist thou take comfort to thy soule, that all the promises of God doe belong to thee, be thy nation, estate, sex or age, what it will."[56]

As this passage indicates, not only did Traske hold before his readers a tantalizing and rapturous vision of the effects of true faith, but he did so in explicitly inclusive terms. The gospel was proclaimed to all, and all were invited to believe. There was nothing obviously unorthodox about this proposition, but Traske deduced from it a set of striking conclusions. Traske deliberately and carefully used the notion of the universal promise to appeal to the most powerless members of early modern English society, the poor, women, children, and servants. Hence he claimed, "Here . . . by this, are discovered the darke courses of such as, dare impudently to affirme, that women have no soules: and that servants, are of no esteeme with God; or that children, shall bee damned."[57]

While these claims were by no means novel in the context of early Stuart puritan divinity, there can be little question that in emphasizing the inclusiveness of the promise, Traske was extending an invitation to these most marginal of groups, a conclusion that is confirmed by his subsequent comments on magistracy. God's blindness to the particular state or status of individuals, and his willingness to confer salvation on them regardless of their condition, should be seen as a general pattern for human behavior: "The Magistrate may hence learne, to judge impartially, to execute judgement, without respect of persons, to deale uprightly, betweene the rich, and poore, the bond, and free. Hereby *hee shall draw neere to God* and be most like him: he is no respecter of persons, he not onely offereth, but bestoweth salvation upon all sorts indifferently."[58] Here, magistrates were warned not to allow their wealth or rank to pervert justice. On Traske's account, such lapses made a mockery of God's own egalitarian stance toward the human race. This doctrine, he argued, "reproveth the practise of those Magistrates, that regard mens persons in judgement, favouring some for their riches, and oppressing others that are but of mean estate. Herein they differ from God, and do manifestly discover themselves not yet to be his."[59] These were strong words; from Calvin onward, re-

[56] Traske, *Pearl*, 13-15.
[57] Ibid., 6-7.
[58] Ibid., 4.
[59] Ibid., 5.

formed thought had been very much dominated by the notion that inequalities in wealth and power were not only to be tolerated, but to be seen as an inherent aspect of the fabric of creation. While puritan ministers might employ similar rhetoric to upbraid usurers and engrossers, or to remind magistrates of their duty to mete out justice fairly, they often counterbalanced such statements by emphasizing the fact that inequalities in wealth and power were ordained of God, citing the numerous scriptural passages enjoining obedience to superiors, and portraying the Christian community as a body composed of diverse (unequal) parts. Traske's comments carried with them no such qualifications, and hence tended to undermine, rather than support, the standard corporatist vision from which his rhetoric was drawn.[60]

In a similar manner, but with even greater vehemence, he deployed the doctrine of the universal promise to attack what he perceived as hypocrisy and greed within the clerical establishment: "such Ministers are reproved as flatter the rich, and fawne upon the mightie, but scorne the weake, and despise the poore. These swarme in all parts where the Gospell is preached: Not onely amongst those of Babels side, but also even here amongst us. Yea those that are so conversant about Touch not, Taste not, Handle not, these that would bee reformers of others, are herein most irreformed themselves. Oh, fearefull is the condition of such: surely the Lord never sent them; or if they say he did, they must prove it, by that they have such a commission, as Christ himselfe never had. He professeth himselfe to be sent to the poore."[61] Traske had removed Christ's universal promise from a purely theological domain; he invoked it not only to challenge magistrates who exploited inequalities in wealth to their own advantage, but also to attack the orthodox clergy. His vision of swarming, hypocritical ministers, bowing hungrily before authority, even as they lectured the poor about the virtues of the Moral Law—a most curious claim, given Traske's reputation as an ultra-legalistic judaizer—represented a thinly veiled critique of the puritan ministry, and (one suspects) a bald appeal to those who resented the domination of lay and clerical elites. Moreover, this critique suggested that the proper audience for the Gospel, indeed the true heirs of the Gospel promise, were the poor, for whom Christ himself had exercised his ministry.

Here, then, was a message freighted with social overtones that were not characteristic of contemporary puritanism. Perhaps unsurprisingly, then, we can likewise detect in Traske's words a subtle, but nevertheless discernible discontent with the ways of puritan religiosity. In this vein, he repeatedly chided ostensibly pious people who "flatter themselves with the outward perform-

---

[60] See, for instance, William Sclater, *A Sermon Preached at the Last Generall Assise Holden for the County of Sommerset at Taunton* (1616), passim.
[61] Traske, *Pearl*, 5-6.

ance of duties." Puritan ministers often attacked those they called carnal gospelers or hypocrites, but Traske's criticisms of "outward" Christians took that critique one step further: "If they bee able to beare in mind the Doctrines delivered, and repeate them to their Families, shew much love to Ministers, kindnesse to professors, such as they themselves are . . . here they rest, and doe esteeme themselves the best sort of beleevers *Albeit* a man may doe all this, and be damned."[62] Traske seems here to have been describing ordinary members of the godly community, that is, people who believed the word as preached from their pulpits, who allowed the Bible to suffuse their households, who consorted with and considered themselves to be zealous "professors."

Interestingly, Traske laid the blame for this situation squarely on the shoulders of the puritan ministry. Not only were such "Touch not, Tast not, Handle not" ministers prone to sycophancy and greed, but they were systematically ensnaring their godly followers in a web of false, outward religion:

> *England* doth swarme with *Pharisees*: such as are conversant about Touch not, Tast not, Handle not. Such as having voluntarie humilitie, and pretended sinceritie, doe despise government, and speake evill of dignities. Presumptuous they are, and selfe-willed, and speaking evill of the thing they understand not, they creep into houses, and lead captive silly women laden with sinnes. . . . These are they that take advantage of weake consciences, ceazing on them as their own, by cumbring them with outward things, and by telling them, here is Christ, or there is Christ; when if the truth were knowne, they never yet had Christ themselves. . . . Yea, that open prophane ones are sooner drawne to sinceritie, then these, and apter to receive instruction, So wise are they in their own eyes, and prudent in their own sight, that there is more hope of Fooles then of them; yea, that there is more humanitie and greater love amongst those whom they terme profane, then amongst themselves.[63]

It is here, in Traske's hostile assessment of (at least some) puritan ministers, that we find our first clue as to the origins of later antinomianism. His words contain the germ of the impulse which, throughout this study, is termed "anti-legalism"—the belief that mainstream puritan religiosity was hopelessly mired in external and legalistic modes of worship, by which its adherents were led into a perilous neo-pharisaism. As we shall see momentarily, Traske's critique of puritan pharisaism was attached to a negative estimation of the godly program for ecclesiastical reform; pushing toward the religious orientation that J. C. Davis has dubbed "anti-formalism," Traske and his follower Hebdon in fact believed that such obsession with outward forms stifled the spirit, which

[62] Ibid., 23-24.
[63] Ibid., 26-27.

needed no external discipline to perform the works of God.[64] Such "anti-formalism" might seem odd in a man generally deemed to have been an ultra-legalist, who had taken puritan biblicism and moralism to its ultimate extent. This apparent contradiction will be examined further on. For present purposes, the crucial point is that Traske's vision of true religion, including his resurrection of the Mosaic ceremonies, appears to have progressed hand in hand with an escalating disaffection not only with the Church of England, but with the puritan wing of that church.

This vision emerged more clearly in Traske's second and third pamphlets, published anonymously and in rapid succession in 1615 and 1616.[65] As already noted, his second book, *Christs Kingdom Discovered*, was ostensibly directed against separatists. Traske thus set out to prove that the various scriptural passages referring to Christ's Kingdom, the Kingdom of Heaven, and the Kingdom of the Son of Man all referred to this life. This fact could be turned against those who claimed that the true Church was not in England: "I heare one cry out for want of *Discipline*; others for *Order*; some for *Christs Officers*: one saith, *Here is Christ*; another, *there is Christ*."[66] Such puritanical preachers were false prophets and deceivers, unable to see that the true church was in England, because they themselves had no experience of Christ's kingdom.

Yet this was no ordinary antiseparatist tract. Ecclesiological writers often talked about the Kingdom of Christ as if it were immanent in the world. Yet when they did so, they usually meant simply the church or the discipline of the church. Traske had something very different in mind. Having adduced the immanence of the Kingdom to scold forward puritans and separatists, Traske subtly shifted the terms of the argument to attack a second, entirely distinct opponent. The claim that the Kingdom was in this life, which had ostensibly been broached to attack puritans, was now redeployed to refute those who claimed that the Kingdom of Heaven referred to the afterlife. Traske pointed out that the scriptures explicitly used the present tense to describe the unshakable kingdom of Zion in Hebrews 12: "*We are come to it; not, we shall; but*

---

64 On "anti-formalism," see J. C. Davis, "Cromwell's Religion," in J. Morrill, ed., *Oliver Cromwell and the English Revolution* (London: Longman, 1990); idem, "Against Formality: One Aspect of the English Revolution," in *Transactions of the Royal Historical Society*, 6th ser., 3 (1993).

65 *Christs Kingdom Discovered* was initially published anonymously, but was reissued in 1616 under Traske's name; *Heavens Joy* (1616), was also published anonymously, but an examination of internal evidence has led the editors of the STC to ascribe it tentatively to Traske (see Pollard et al., *Short-Title Catalogue of Books Printed in England . . . 1475-1640* [London: Bibliographical Society, 1976-1991], 1: 569; 3: 313), a judgment with which I wholly concur.

66 Traske, *Christs Kingdom*, 42.

we are: and, *we receiving a Kingdome*: not, *Seeing we* shall *receive a Kingdome*; but, *Seeing wee* doe receive. . . . What shall I say? Arguments of this sort are very many in holy Scriptures: yea, even those places which they most abuse to the contrary, do yeeld many plaine arguments to every impartiall Reader. . . . And let this be observed, that where the *holy Ghost* speaketh any where of the *life to come*, it is alwaies in *very short speeches*, or *briefe sentences*."[67] This, in fact, may be seen as the primary theme of the treatise. Traske argued, carefully but explicitly, that the Kingdom of Christ and the Kingdom of Heaven not only referred to this life, but that they referred to this life *alone*.[68] The claim that the Kingdom of Heaven was a this-worldly estate, having nothing at all to do with the afterlife, is not one found frequently in the writings of pious puritans. In fact it is so unusual, and its implications so peculiar and potentially radical, that one wonders how it escaped the sleepy eye of the censor. For although Traske did not deny the afterlife, he most certainly sought to shift the emphasis away from it, and to transfer many of the privileges and transformations normally associated with heaven, to earth itself.

Predictably, then, Traske's vision of Christ's Kingdom bore no relation to any real geographic or ecclesiastical entity. The kingdom, he claimed, "is not *bounded* within any *Nation*, or *limitted* unto any *one People* or *Kingdom*. So that no man can say it is in this Company, and *no where else*, as divers false Prophets have assumed, and dared to maintaine."[69] Rather, it was a spiritual kingdom, composed of believing saints in all nations and under all ecclesiastical dispensations. Those familiar with the terms used by seventeenth-century people to discuss the church will recognize that Traske seemed to be applying to the visible church terms normally used to describe the invisible church of true believers. But he was arguing, moreover, that this Church, or Kingdom, as he preferred, could only be recognized by those who, having been transformed by the overwhelming experience of grace, now belonged to the Kingdom as subjects. Only true believers, in short, could recognize the kingdom and its subjects, and they did so infallibly and definitively. To use his words:

---

[67] Ibid., 18-19.

[68] Ibid., 6-8, where Traske develops this argument. He argued that there are four New Testament uses of the word "Kingdom": "Kingdom of God," "Kingdom of Heaven," "Sonne of Mans Kingdome," "Kingdome of Christ." Traske carefully avoided denying the afterlife, arguing that "Kingdom of God" "doeth indifferently concerne the estate we do here enjoy, with that hereafter." Yet, having said this, he went on to argue that even the "Kingdom of God" normally referred to this life: "Yea, and the first doeth concerne moste the estate of the Church in this life, and is so alwayes to be understood, where there is no manifest difference in the same Scripture." Meanwhile "the other three [Kingdoms] concerne the Church, heere in this life," and were interchangeable.

[69] Ibid., 28.

"The *onely way* to know that *Wee*, (that is, the *true Ministers of Christ*) are *in Christ*, is, by the *knowledge of your selves* to be *in Christ*: Giving us to understand thereby, that *none* can *truely know* a *Childe* of *God*, but he that is *in truth* the *Childe* of *God* himselfe."[70] This verifies definitively the accusation, lodged by both T.S. and Sclater, that Traske argued that the elect could recognize each other with certainty.

If believers could recognize each other, Traske reasoned, surely they could recognize the government or rules that inhered in the kingdom. Once again, these rules (predictably) had nothing to do with the institutions of church and state. In fact, Traske's kingdom was without governors of any sort; as he put it, "instead of *Officers*, thou shalt have *Peace*: yea, all the *Subjects* of this *Kingdome* are *Peace-makers*."[71] Rejecting any notion of episcopal or presbyterian oversight, Traske argued that true believers were governed by the Holy Spirit, which led them inexorably to obey God's commandments willingly and without any compulsion of ecclesiastical discipline. This represented a major departure from the puritan mainstream, and provides further evidence of a developing anti-formalism within the Traskite community. Believers, on Traske's account, did not *need* the structures of coercion and discipline supplied by an eldership or consistory. Their discipline was entirely internal, flowing ineluctably from faith itself.

This was Traske's rather utopian vision—a kingdom without hierarchy, in which believers obeyed the dictates of God's Law in purity, or near-purity, because the Law was written in their hearts. But was Traske's vision of divine Law the same as that peddled in extreme puritan or separatist circles? Certainly, like most other godly ministers, he endorsed a strict legalism, in which the scriptures were to be searched for eternal rules of conduct. As he argued from the book of Malachi, "*Remember yee the Law of* Moses *my Servant*. . . . These are the Lawes of this Kingdom; to which whosoever shall adde, he is accursed of God. . . . And from which, whosoever shall take away, God shall take away his part out of the Book of Life."[72] This typically puritan attitude, when pressed to the perfectionist extremes suggested by Traske, helps to explain his ultimate passage into Mosaic ceremonialism. Nevertheless, there was one rule in his kingdom that sets him at odds with every other godly minister of his day: as he hinted at the end of his treatise on the Kingdom, the commandment to love one another entailed making goods common, either among true believers, or more generally for distribution among the poor.[73]

---

70 Ibid., 41.
71 Ibid., 15-16.
72 Ibid., 11.
73 Ibid., 64-66.

This strain of Christian communism, which has been overlooked by modern scholars, may be corroborated by holding various pieces of evidence side by side. The most vivid example is provided by the anonymous T.S., who looked back on the enthusiasm of the early Traskites with this passing comment: "Their silver and gold cast into the streets, as *bread upon the waters* given to the poor, (so did Master *Trask*) And some sold lands and goods, and distributed the price of them."[74] In 1619, the Somerset minister Sclater had interpreted the same phenomenon in less flattering terms: "They must therefore that will be his disciples, take up this crosse; to keepe backe none of their temporalities from thier Paraclete; as hee said merrily, upon paine to forfeit their election." The results, Sclater mockingly reported, were plain for the world to see: "What marvaile then if some besotted silly women, and servants, have purloyned from their husbands, and robbed from their masters, to maintayne this Saint-seeing-Saint-making-Saint."[75] To remove all doubt of the fact that (at least some) Traskites practiced a form of communism, we need only turn to the meditations of Returne Hebdon, one of Traske's disciples. Writing from prison in the aftermath of the routing of the Traskites, Hebdon wrote: "Therefore it is the judgement of the holy spirit, that whosoever is false in the common communion of goods, cannot hold the love in the holy communion of the body and blood of the Lord." Hebdon noted that this communion was to be "left free to the will of the possessor, and not in bondage under the feare of carnall compulsion; for this is contrary to the nature and holy spirit of love."[76] Nevertheless, for Hebdon as for Traske, anyone who did not fulfill the law of love, including communion of goods, could not be a true believer.

Here, we are faced with a vision of the true church that is significant mainly in its departure from the orthodoxies of the time. But when Traske discussed the "Kingdom of heaven," and the "Kingdom of Christ," he did not refer solely to the order laid down by Christ for his church in this world. Rather, he veered back and forth between discussing it as an outward kingdom and an inward kingdom, between a description of the ordinances of Christ, and the subjective state of true believers. The tendency to discuss the kingdom of heaven as a subjective state of joy is most evident in his third pamphlet, aptly entitled *Heavens Joy, or Heaven Begun on Earth*.[77]

---

[74] Pagitt, *Heresiography*, 185.

[75] W. Sclater, *An Exposition with Notes upon the first Epistle to the Thessalonians* (1619), 31.

[76] Hebdon, *Guide*, 32-33.

[77] The pamphlet begins with this cryptic statement: "This small Treatise of Hell being fitted for the presse, it was thought fit by the learned examiner, that it should not passe alone, but that as much at least of *Heaven* should be added to it: that as the reader should be driven by *Judgements,* so he might also be drawne by *Mercies*, to turne unto God by true and unfeigned *Repentance*." This comment

Once again, Traske vehemently criticized those who argued that the rapture of heaven was something to be enjoyed in the afterlife: "the Apostle plainly affirmeth, that such as have beleeved *do enter into Rest*, not *shall* hereafter, but *doe*."[78] This resting place was likened to a spiritual mountain: "so are the children of God at *quiet* when they sit down on the top of this *glorious mountain*, which with great difficultie they have climed."[79] As the subtitle of the pamphlet suggested, heaven was hardly a distant, other-worldly dimension, but a concrete experience, to which believers had access while still on earth. At times, he seemed to suggest that those who had been rewrought by grace were actually carried into heaven, where they experienced a privileged vision of God himself.[80] For the lucky recipients of grace, the "*Love* of Christ doth ravish the soule, and makes it to mount on high, yea, to be above in heavenly *Meditations*."[81] This rapturous "love of Christ" not only created in the believer a desire to be constantly above with God, but as we have seen, instilled in them a heartfelt and irresistible desire to obey God's Law.

---

seems bizarre, since there is little or no reference to hell throughout the treatise. One possibility is that there may have been a companion treatise "of hell," which was subsequently suppressed by Traske, or his publisher. It is equally likely, however, that this was a coded message, suggesting that the contents of the treatise had been altered because of difficulties in licensing the original, perhaps less acceptable version of the treatise. This reading is supported by the fact that on the "errata" page, which would have been attached after licensing, this suspicious note has been inserted: "There is a little Booke called Christs Kingdome discovered, which is worth thy reading." *Christs Kingdom* had been more straightforward in its claim that the "Kingdom of Heaven" referred to this life, denying that the term referred in any way to the afterlife. Traske may have been forced by the censor to dilute this message, and may thus have been directing his readers to the earlier, more extreme and authoritative text. *Heavens Joy*, sig. A4r, 1.

78 Ibid., 11.

79 Ibid., 12.

80 For instance, see ibid., 34, in which Traske argued that believers were overcome with a "*Love* wherewith the soules of the children of God are ravished, with a desire to see God face, to face." Although he refrained from claiming that believers already participated in this heavenly vision, the hostile observer John Falconer claimed that Traske went further, defining the church as "a small number of such little ones as have truly repented, and are made sure of their election in Christ, hated and persecuted by men, but beloved by God & guarded by Angells, seeing the face of their Heavenly Father." Traske very certainly claimed that true believers were guarded by angels, but it remains a question as to whether he actually believed that they saw the face of God in this life, a privilege that Moses himself had been denied. For Traske's notion of angelic protection, see ibid., 85-86. For Falconer's comment, see *A Briefe Refutation*, 33.

81 Traske, *Heavens Joy*, 30.

Yet this obedience was not an obedience of bondage, but of liberty. Indeed, Traske's descriptions of obedience tended, as T.S. had charged, to veer off into antinomian excess. Thus, Traske claimed that "believers are no longer under a *Schoolemaster*, or a *Law* commaunding: but they having the Spirit of Christ, have libertie: yea, a glorious *Libertie*, which is not the least tast of *Heaven* upon *Earth*."[82] Here, using a conventional Pauline formula, Traske had carefully insinuated into his pamphlet the notion that believers were free from the commanding power of the Moral Law. Even though they obeyed the Law out of the love of Christ, the faithful were nevertheless free from it as an external compulsory rule. Traske admitted that believers suffered occasional lapses, but argued that these peccadilloes were not *actual sins*: "there is," Traske explained, "great difference betweene *having* sinne, and *sinning*."[83] Thus, although both experience and scripture testified to the fact that the faithful had sin *dwelling* in them, they were no longer to consider those sins as their own: "Yet all this doth not prove that which some would urge out of these, and such like places, that they *commit sinne*, and this is most evident: for if they should *commit*, then were they still the *servants* of *sinne*, as it is written, *Whosoever committeth Sinne, is the servant of sin*."[84] To use Hebdon's phrase, such were "the children of God that cannot count sin."[85]

On Traske's account, then, believers were free from the commanding force of the Law, and delivered into a state of sinlessness. As he put it, the Saints were "*holy Men and Women, pure, cleane, undefiled, and harmless*."[86] All of this was accomplished using ostensibly neutral Pauline phrases, glossed and arranged in a way that was thoroughly unacceptable from an orthodox perspective. Indeed, Traske used such tactics to argue that "the same minde is in [believers] which was also in Christ Jesus, *who being in the forme of God, thought it no robbery to be equall with God*."[87] Here, we see Traske at his most theologically radical, asserting the perfection of believers, indeed their identity with the person of Christ, even as they walked on earth.

Hebdon's meditations are accordingly laced with an idiom of perfection and perfectionism that is quite alien to the mainstream puritan tradition. Thus, in refuting those he cryptically called the "Protestant Christians," Hebdon argued that "the new man must needs have a perfect birth, before it can be a new man, and so before the Resurrection. For after [spiritual, not in-

---

82 Ibid., 37-38.
83 Ibid., 59.
84 Ibid., 60-61.
85 Hebdon, *Guide*, 28-29.
86 Traske, *Christs Kingdom*, 13.
87 Ibid., 22. See also 69-70, which repeats the claim that believers "have the mind of *Christ*," citing 1. Cor. 2 to show "the wonderful *Wisdome* of a Child of God, in whom *Christ dwelleth*."

fant] Baptisme, this new man which is new created in body, is in his account risen from the dead, and living together with Christ." So, too, writing of "those who are gathered unto Christ," he argued that "their spirits are perfected." These true Christians were "gentle, perfect, simple," "perfect in love to the Lord," and "walk perfectly in the Love of Christ." At another point, he alluded to the believer as the "perfect man," while referring to the "excellent thing required in Christ in the state of perfection," to wit, "the perfect love of God."[88] As in the case of Traske, this rhetoric of perfectionism seems for Hebdon to have been linked to a sense of the immediate union of the believer with Christ. Hence, along with Traske, he affirmed the presence of Christ's mind in believers: "being baptized into his death . . . I put on his immortality upon my mortall mind, and in all things have the mind of Christ to guide me in my life."[89]

We have here arrived at a crucial point, both for mapping Traske's theological trajectory, and more generally for understanding the nature of seventeenth-century English antinomianism. Traske argued that believers were free from the Law; indeed, by virtue of the fact that they shared the mind of Christ, they were in some sense without sin. But this sinlessness and freedom did not mean that the faithful could or would sin at will. Where unbelievers were guided by the external whip of the Law, believers were guided by the indwelling of the spirit, which led them inexorably to do God's will. Hebdon articulated this concept with utter clarity when he wrote from prison that:

> Christians . . . have the living God, his word, power and authority within them, and their heart is to him as the Arke to hold his Law, and their body to containe his glorious essence so far as every one is capable of it, and this part or distribution of the spirit of God to every body, doth witnesse and testifie to the Conscience, together, with the invisible and inconceavable Majesty of the spirit of God above, that they are of the seed and Children of the living God of immortality, whereby also they may serve God in truth without any legall forme or visible worship, in place or company.[90]

This remarkable passage is worth bearing in mind, for it shall condition the rest of our study. Hebdon, like Traske, was saying that believers were in-

---

88 See Hebdon, *Guide*, 26-31, 40, 58, 59, 84.

89 See also ibid., 50, wherein Hebdon argues that the sufferings of the believer resulted in the birth of Christ's mind in them: "in this estate the mortall body of a man is as a woman in travell, which cryes out, not to be eased of the payne, but to bring forth the fruit of her wombe, and this in Christ is a travell of a Christian, he hath conceived the mind of Christ, and for this cause is persecuted, and suffers all things, untill from out of the greatest torments of the heart, he is able to deliver or bring forth the spirit of that immortall seede unto Christ, whose it is."

90 Ibid., 18.

wardly moved by the mind or spirit of God. Since this inhabitation was not total—each possessed the spirit in different measure and in spite of the flesh—no believer would perfectly obey the Law in this life. Nevertheless, since "the same spirit of Jesus Christ which is in heaven liveth in them," believers possessed within their bodies the essence of God himself, and were consequently, from a certain standpoint, perfect and sinless.[91] Inhabited by Christ, each believer's body was thus "as the Arke" of the Covenant, a receptacle for God's holy Law. Given this fact, believers could not but carry out the divine will as prescribed in scripture. As Hebdon elsewhere put it, "the Law is within them."[92] Here, then, is the ultimate explanation for the Traskite insistence that true believers would perform every ordinance of the Mosaic Law with the utmost rigor. Yet this obedience was not forced, involuntary, or legalistic; it demanded no external prompting or ecclesiastical discipline. Despite the apparently ultra-legalistic nature of the Traskite movement, Hebdon could thus argue that true believers served God without "legal form or visible worship." They needed nothing but scripture and the spirit within.

This notion—the idea that believers had somehow internalized the Law in a way that made it superfluous as an outward rule—was perhaps the defining element of antinomianism both before and after the civil war. It would characterize all the later permutations of anti-legal thought, as examined throughout the remainder of this book. Freedom from the Law meant obedience to God, explaining how Traske's early theology accommodated both explicitly antinomian and strenuously legalistic elements in a seemingly paradoxical unity. This is not to argue that Traske was by 1617 a full-blown antinomian (as he would be ten years later); it is merely to point out that almost all of the elements of his later antinomianism were already in place, with one crucial exception—his overweening attachment to the Old Testament Law. Although Traske argued that believers were free from the commanding power of the Law, he and his followers maintained that the ordinances and commandments handed down in the Torah remained a summation of the eternal will of God.[93] Later in life, Traske, like the other antinomians examined below, would as-

---

[91] Ibid., 7. Here it was likewise argued that "everyone that in true love of God holdeth community in the flesh and sufferings of Christ, hath from God the participation of the same spirit of Christ to every use. he is chast as he is chast, He is righteous as he is righteous."

[92] Ibid., 88-89.

[93] Interestingly, the Sabbath is almost invisible in Hebdon's writings, although it is absolutely clear that he continued to maintain strict observance of the Saturday Sabbath until his death; his meditations, which are subdivided according to the day of the week upon which they were written, were all penned between Sunday and Friday, suggesting that he refused even to write on Saturdays. For his continued adherence to Mosaic dietary laws, see ibid., 40.

sume a very different view, recoiling from his commitment to the Law while retaining the spiritist elements of his early thought.

Echoes of HN?

All of this raises one substantial question that we have thus far managed to evade: what were the origins of this peculiar and in many ways deeply radical mode of religiosity? Here, we need to turn for a moment to a sermon delivered some twenty years after the crushing of the Traskite movement. The venue was London, and the preacher was Stephen Denison, one of the most intransigent and fierce foes of antinomianism throughout the 1620s and 1630s. On 20 May 1638, treating the text Ephesians 5: 18—"But be ye filled with the Spiritt,"—Denison warned his audience that

> Wee must be filled with the spirit but not with the spirit of Delusion. . . . But it must be with the spirit that is the spirit of god and this must warily be understoode: for it is not meant wee must be filled with the essence of the spirit of god as though the spiritt of god did dwell in us Essentially eyther as the forme of the manner or as the matter of the manner:/ It is Blasphemy in the wicked familists to Dreame of the Spirit of god dwelling in them in that sence: It is sufficient that the Spirit of god doth Dwell in Christ in that Sence. Neyther must you think to be filled with the spirit of god or the holy Ghost as to have it to dwell in us personally farre be it from every Christian to think such greate Blasphemy as to make himselfe in this respect equall with god. But wee must be filled with the spirit by a Metanomia the efficient for the Effect: with the guifts and graces of the Spirit.[94]

According to Denison, then, the claim that the "essence of the spirit of God" dwelled simply and literally in believers was an abomination of the "wicked Familists." Yet as we have seen, this is precisely the claim that Returne Hebdon had made while in prison. Denison's comments even mirrored Hebdon's rhetoric, referring to the indwelling of God's essence. To an old puritan like Denison, these claims were pure blasphemy. The spirit, he argued, dwelt in us by metonymy, or as he put it in another place, by metaphor: we were "vessels" of the spirit only insofar as we were vessels of honor or dishonor.[95] In short, we possessed not the essential spirit of God itself, but the gifts, graces, and virtues wrought by the spirit acting upon us.

Now it is of course possible that Denison was here engaged in a process of polemical labeling, that he was using the convenient epithet "Familist" to

---

[94] American Antiquarian Society, Worcester, Mass., MS. Sermon Notes, Denison (1637-39), fol. 41r-v.

[95] Ibid., fol. 44r, in which he argued that the phrase "be filled with the spirit" was merely "a Metaphor Taken from vessells and indeed all men be vessells for they are vessells of Honour or of Dishonour."

smear a mode of antinomian piety that he had come over the course of the 1620s and 1630s to deem as dangerous and heretical.[96] I would like in closing to propose a rather different argument, namely that for once Denison knew precisely what he was talking about; I would like to suggest, in short, that both Traske and Hebdon may indeed have been influenced by Familism.

We have seen that Traske's so-called "judaizing" represented merely the outward manifestation of a form of divinity that was peculiarly anti-legal, and at times seemed to flirt with antinomianism. Let us consider for a moment the broad outlines of that divinity. First, Traske claimed that repentance was a state of self-mortification and humiliation that preceded, and ended with, the glorious onset of faith. Secondly, it has been argued that Traske's desire to see his followers perfectly obey God's Law flowed from his claim that true believers were, in some sense, perfect *in this life.* By virtue of the indwelling spirit, they were free from sin, and sharing the mind of Christ, could infallibly recognize one another. Thirdly, Traske and Hebdon showed an overt disdain for any notion of Christianity that tied true belief to a particular structure of church government, a particular mode of worship, or a particular land or people. This attitude allowed him, somewhat disingenuously, to present himself as an opponent of puritan excess. Fourth, although he strongly affirmed the expectation of some sort of afterlife, Traske tended to argue that the kingdom of heaven (or Christ) was as much an internal, subjective state of rest, peace, and rapturous joy, experienced by believers while on earth, as a place of eternal future felicity; the thrust of much of his early writing was designed to show that little or nothing could be said about the afterlife, while very much could be said about heaven on earth. Fifth and finally, Traske enjoined his believers to give up their worldly possessions, and to make their goods common, either to the poor, or to other members of the Traskite community.

It should be pointed out that these arguments—repentance preceding faith, perfectionism, indifference to matters of ecclesiology, the tendency to allegorize heaven and hell as subjective states, and community of goods—are virtually identical to those habitually attributed to the Family of Love.[97] These

---

[96] Such an argument might indeed receive some support from the testimony of Anna Trapnel, the antinomian visionary who alleged that prior to a vision in 1646, she had wrongly believed "that God dwelt essentially in his Saints." See Trapnel, *A Legacy for Saints; Being Several Experiences of the dealings of God with Anna Trapnel* (1654), 36. While there is no doubt that she was referring to precisely the opinion denounced here by Denison, we possess no direct evidence that Trapnel was influenced by Familism. See Conclusion, however, for her spiritual mentor John Simpson.

[97] The notion that perfection was to be preceded by a period of penitent, legal mortification is ubiquitous in the works of HN (see Appendix A, below). It was still being actively pursued by English Familists in the 1640s, when Edward

similarities may, of course, have been coincidental. Accusations against Familists were commonly overblown or inaccurate. Likewise, it is possible that such similarities may have resulted from exposure to some now-forgotten variant of anabaptist thought, which may have owed something to Familism, but which was itself distinctive.[98] Nevertheless, in Traske's case, the similarities seem to have run deeper than the surface. In at least one passage of *Heavens Joy*, Traske produced an unusual presentation of the doctrine of baptism that ran parallel to HN's own highly idiosyncratic conception of that sacrament. This evidence, which requires close textual examination, is surveyed in an appendix.[99] While highly suggestive, readers must decide for themselves whether the argument proves persuasive.

What is beyond doubt is that Traske had had ample opportunity to consort with members of the Family of Love. Let us return to one crucial biographical detail, alluded to above—his curious appearance in the Isle of Ely in 1614. It has long been recognized that Ely had been a center of Familist activity in Elizabeth's reign, but only with the publication of Christopher Marsh's painstaking researches have these suspicions been confirmed and documented. Indeed, in 1609, Ely was the site of what appear to have been the last two provincial investigations into Familism, when a pair of laymen were presented for possessing HN's books.[100] Five years later, Traske, a young preacher whose activities had hitherto been confined solely to a fairly circumscribed area in the Southwest, suddenly appeared at the opposite end of the country, preaching without a living or a license, to conventicles in and around Ely. While

---

Howes copied out a circular letter defending the central familist doctrine of perfectionism, for which see Appendix B. Niclaes persistently criticized those who claimed that their own ecclesiastical organization constituted the true church, attacking those who claimed "We have it, we are the Congregation of Christ, we are Israel, lo here it is, lo there it is, this truth, here is Christ, there is Christ" (quoted by William Haller, *The Rise of Puritanism* [New York: Columbia University Press, 1938; paperback edition, New York: Harper Torchbook, 1957], 207); for the claim that (some) Familists held goods in common as late as 1638, see the deposition of the ex-sectary Giles Creech, in PRO, SPD 16/520/85; for the allegorization of heaven and hell, see ibid.

98 Cf., for instance, the confession of John Smith's followers, written in Dutch, probably for the benefit of Dutch Anabaptists, translated and reproduced in B. Evans, *The Early English Baptists* (London: John Heaton & Son, 1862), 1: 257-72, especially articles 47, 65, 66, 92, which likewise reveal some similarity with Traske's teachings. Nevertheless, Traske's explicit denunciation of those who rejected child baptism would seem to tell against such a connection.

99 See Appendix A, below.

100 Christopher Marsh, *The Family of Love in English Society, 1550-1630* (Cambridge: Cambridge University Press, 1994), 214-18.

none of those implicated in Traske's illicit meetings appear in Marsh's investigation of fenland Familism, there can be little question that these people personally knew members of the Family of Love. Indeed, two men who admitted to being present at one of Traske's clandestine "prayer meetings" would sit in 1616 on a four-person committee with one Luke Saunders, almost certainly a member of the Family. Another accused auditor of Traske, William Gunton of Sutton, was in all likelihood a relative of the Guntons of the Isle of Ely, who left behind an extensive trail of Familist connections throughout the region. A third individual, John Thickpenny, also present at the aforementioned prayer meeting, bore the same unusual surname as the obscure Kentish cleric David Thickpenny, whose association with the Family had been exposed in the 1570s. Others who had gadded to hear Traske preach in Littleport hailed from the village of Downham, still another site of Elizabethan Familist activity.[101]

Although these connections are tantalizing, to say the least, it cannot be proved that any of these individuals was a bona fide Familist. It is probably fair to suggest, however, that they were operating in an environment where Familism was a living religious tradition, that they knew people who identified with the Family, and that they possessed more than a passing notion of what it meant to be a Familist, both ideologically and in practice. Traske's inexplicable presence amongst them may well provide a clue to the singularly strange style of divinity he would later promulgate both in print and pulpit. Either he was there because he was already keyed into an underground network of Familism, perhaps preaching his own messages to receptive ears; or, he encountered Ely Familists in his travels, a confrontation that would shape his central teachings in the years to come.

---

[101] CUL, EDR B/2/35, fols. 76v, 190v, 76v, 62r for the respective references to Traske's auditors. The two Ely residents, both described as gentlemen, were Nicholas Massey and J. Orwell. Massy had allowed Traske to pray in his house, with Orwell present. For their participation with Saunders on the committee to audit the churchwardens accounts of St. Mary's, Ely, see ibid., fol. 82r. For evidence of Saunders's affiliation with the Family, the Gunton clan, David Thickpenny, and Downham see Marsh, *Family of Love*, 46, 103-4, 107, 147-48, 194, 214-15, 259, 274, 279, 282. Another accused auditor of Traske, one Sidrach Cave of St. Trinity, Ely (CUL, EDR B/2/35, fols. 113v-114r), would find his name immortalized by John Taylor "the water-poet" twenty-five years later. Taylor's *A Swarme of Sectaries, and Schismatiques* (1641), 5, which lampooned puritan hypocrisy and presumption, included a verse entitled "*Another sweet youth in a Basket.*" It read as follows: "One *Sidrach Cave* made Baskets late in Elie,/A constant brother, rais'd up his maids belly:/But 'twas in Gandermonth, his wife lay in,/His flesh rebell'd, and tempted him to sin;/And *Cave's* wife tooke the wrong most patiently, /For which the Brethren prais'd her sanctity."

This is not to argue that John Traske was a member of the Family of Love, in anything like the sense outlined by Marsh. If we examine Traske's works, apart from the very noticeable similarities outlined above, there are other areas where his teaching, and indeed his entire style, seem to have run counter to the classic Familism of HN. Traske firmly rejected the Familist suggestion that the Resurrection was merely an allegory or metaphor for something that happened within the believer's heart, instead suggesting that the Resurrection of the Dead and Last Judgment were to be expected as all-too-real events in the future.[102] Similarly, although Traske occasionally lapsed into effusive descriptions of the ravishing power of the "love of Christ," there is very little hint of the bizarrely rhapsodic prose style of Hendrik Niclaes, with its continual, almost talismanic, repetition of and resort to the image of Love.[103] More than anything else, we see in Traske a puritan militancy that is entirely alien both to HN's writings, and to the practices of his early followers in England. Traske's rigorous Sabbatarianism, his insistence on searching the Scriptures for eternal and inviolable rules of conduct, and most of all, his frankly volatile evangelical energy, all bear the mark not of Niclaes's Familism, but of the fervent, almost violent, piety that subsisted at the edge of the puritan community, where presbyterianism shaded off into separatism. For example, the insistence of Traske and Hebdon that the perfection of believers entailed perfect obedience to the Law looks like a caricature, or at the very least, a distinctively godly misunderstanding, of HN's perfectionism.[104] It is as if the antinomian

---

[102] See *Heavens Joy*, 152-55. But see also M. T. Pearse, *Between Known Men and Visible Saints: A Study in Sixteenth-Century English Dissent* (Madison and Teaneck, NJ: Fairleigh Dickinson University Press, 1994), 192-94. Pearse correctly notes that Niclaes was himself ambiguous on the subject of a future, literal Resurrection, although in general his mode of rhetoric tended to suggest that the "end," like "heaven," was purely spiritual and internal.

[103] The phrase "the Love of Christ," which appears on several occasions in *Heavens Joy*, seems to have been a favorite catchphrase of H.N. See for instance H[enry] A[insworth], *An Epistle Sent unto two daughters of Warwick from H.N.* (Amsterdam, 1608), 9, 12, 62, 63, 64. Nevertheless, the larger part of Traske's works do not resemble HN's writings in style and rhetoric.

[104] Having said this, it is also the case that HN is to my knowledge the only influential post-Reformation theorist who argued, even in passing, that Christ freed believers from sin so that they could live according to the "Customs and Rites of Israel." See Bodleian Libary, Rawlinson MS. c. 554, a translation of six chapters of HN's "Glass of Righteousness," 2 Glas. 12, para. 14 (unpaginated). We are called out "not that we should then live unto the Sinne or continue in the Slavery of the Sinne, according to the Course of the heathen or uncircumcised ones: but that we should be released from the Sinne and so through Christ, bring forth fruites unto God/whereby to live in the Customs and Rites of Israel, according to the maner of the holy Fathers: and not in the Wayes of the heathen or uncircum-

and anthropotheic teachings of Familism had been glossed with the biblical literalism and moralism of extreme puritanism. I would submit that this is precisely what we are seeing in John Traske: Familist doctrine decoupled from HN's writings, and refracted through the prism of militant puritanism. The result was a deeply radical hybrid, a sort of evangelical Familism (or "familistical" puritanism) in which the most potentially destabilizing aspects of both traditions blended together to complement one another in a subversively heterodox stew.

This conclusion, if correct, suggests a view of the puritan community that diverges in crucial respects from the one normally adopted by scholars—a view that possesses important implications for our understanding of the origins of antinomianism. From this perspective, puritanism was not a single, monolithic entity bearing a unitary ideology. Rather, it was a culture or a community, in which certain shared values and patterns of thought and behavior bound individuals together, both in their own estimation, and in that of their less enthusiastic outside observers. However, this culture was never static, unitary, or impervious to outside influences. In the example of Traske, we see a puritanism with permeable boundaries, a religious subculture in which various heretical or esoteric religious traditions were continually being absorbed into the seething world of religious enthusiasm and devotion that existed at the margins of the godly community. Here, particularly at the separatist fringe, foreign influences, such as Dutch Anabaptism and Familism, as well as homegrown theological innovations—nurtured by the sort of intense spiritism evident in the Traskite movement—seeped into the puritan community, creating ideological diversity within a broader cultural consensus. On this view, puritanism is best understood as a heterogeneous community in which various styles of evangelism and piety competed with one another for the affections of a Bible-addicted laity. This view helps to clarify the emergence of later forms of antinomianism. As we shall see, this pattern of selective sectarian influence repeated itself again and again, helping to remold the structures of puritanism into the phenomenon that contemporaries would come to identify as "antinomianism." Yet these alien sources were consistently fed through the filter of English puritanism—remolded, that is, to fit into the cultural context of the English godly community. The results were hybrid forms of religiosity, which challenged currents of thought and practice that predominated in the English puritan community, even as they appropriated modes of thought and expression that were absolutely central to English puritanism.

---

cised ones." Here, as throughout HN's works, it is not wholly clear whether he intended the "Customs and Rites of Israel" to be understood literally or allegorically.

John Traske and Puritan Radicalism

In the end, the question of whether Traske was exposed to Familism is less important than the deeply peculiar and idiosyncratic mode of religiosity that he came to promulgate from London presses and pulpits. This religiosity may serve as a model for the process whereby early Stuart puritanism, so often characterized by recent scholars as a conservative social phenomenon, might have mutated into the heterodox and politically subversive strains of godly religiosity that would emerge during the English civil wars. Traske's divinity was, after all, as socially radical as it was theologically extravagant. The authorities had ample reason to be worried about Traske's kingdom, for it left no space for the doctrine and discipline of the national church, and its relationship to secular authority was equivocal at best; of Christ's Kingdom, Traske had written that "wheresoever it is, it have the *preheminence*, or is *above* that Kingdome or Nation."[105] There is good reason to believe, moreover, that those in power recognized the communistic, antielite tendencies of the Traskite movement, contributing to the hasty and violent suppression of the sect and its leader. Although Traske does not seem to have challenged the notion of magistracy itself, his kingdom had little room for those in positions of wealth and power. Even as he argued that some of all degrees would enter the kingdom, he threateningly warned that "the Scriptures doe make it plainely to appeare, and plentifully doe confirme it, that fewest great and mighty ones, yea, very fewe of them shall be saved."[106]

Had Traske and his disciples followed in the footsteps of Christopher Marsh's Elizabethan Familists, practicing their faith quietly, setting up shop in secret, ferreting clandestine books in sheds and chimneys, we might conclude that they represented little or no threat to the established order of church and state. But Traske, as we have seen, peddled his message with an almost megalomaniacal zeal. Not content to preach in pulpits, houses, and fields, nor to pitch handfuls of gold to the poor, he quickly decided to troll for the biggest fish of all, James I. In an apparent effort to convert the mightiest of the so-called "great and mighty ones," Traske began in 1616 to send manuscripts and letters to the royal person.[107] Needless to say, James was not amused, particularly since Traske took it upon himself to refer to the king in the familiar "Thee" and "Thou."

When questioned by the authorities, John Pecke, the Inner Temple student who had delivered one of Traske's more galling manuscripts to the king, pro-

---

105 Traske, *Christs Kingdom,* 34.

106 Traske, *Heavens Joy*, 136.

107 Traske would later claim that he had sent the King twelve letters prior to the trial. See John Traske, *The True Gospel Vindicated, From the Reproach of a New Gospel* (n.p., 1636), sigs. A6v-A8r.

vided striking insight into Traske's reasoning on this subject. Pecke claimed that when Traske had first handed him the document for delivery, Pecke had balked "because the author dealeth with the kinge in so familiar a manner, using the words Thee and Thy." On Pecke's account, Traske initially "said hee would alter them," but "thereupon sate in a muse a pretty while, and in the end answered, surely I will not alter them." When further pressed by Pecke, Traske justified his familiar language by claiming "that the kinge would take no offence at it, because it was the manner of speeche, which was used to God himselfe."[108] Once again, we see Traske's strikingly egalitarian vision of God, as well as his tendency to argue that God's stance toward people ought to be normative for human social relations in general.

James and his ministers recognized the threat inherent in Traske's hubristic rhetoric and posturing, and it was precisely this irreverence that led to his prosecution. When they decided, most emphatically, to punish him, they chose not the court of High Commission, the venue reserved for the correction of doctrinal offenses, but the court of Star Chamber, more typically the site of prosecutions for crimes against the state. And it was for crimes against the state that Traske ultimately suffered his grisly punishment. The thinking (and the fear) behind this move was revealed by Lord Chancellor Bacon a week after the trial, when he warned the circuit judges to pay close attention to the proliferation of puritan sectarianism: "New opinions spread very dangerous, the late Traske a dangerous person. Prentices learn the Hebrew tongue."[109] In the background, behind the terse utterances of Francis Bacon, we can hear the faint footfall of Traske's "clowted shoes."

In John Traske's early teaching, one can detect almost every trait that would come to be associated with sectarian puritanism during the English civil wars, from antinomianism and perfectionism, to the notion that the Kingdom of Heaven was somehow immanent in this world, to Saturday Sabbath observance, to itinerant preaching, to communistic and egalitarian impulses. Indeed, the writings of Traske and Hebdon are laced with "anti-formalism," or an opposition to all ecclesiastical or ceremonial forms of worship, recently proposed by J. C. Davis as a crucial unifying characteristic of civil-war radicalism. Again, the roots of this radicalism are to be located in the permeable

---

[108] National Library of Scotland, Advocates MS. 33.1.6, vol. 20 (Denmilne State Papers), fol. 60r. This document, dated 11 September 1616, records an examination of Pecke. I would like to thank Arnold Hunt for alerting me to the existence of this important discovery, and for graciously providing me with a transcript of portions of the document.

[109] From notes taken by Sir Julius Caesar, as transcribed in *The Letters and the Life of Sir Francis Bacon*, ed. J. Spedding (London: Longman, Green, Longman, and Roberts, 1861-74), 6: 315. This document was first noted by D. S. Katz, *Philo-Semitism*, 25-26.

culture of English puritanism, where the intense prophetic spiritualism and uncompromising militancy of classical English puritanism was reworked, sometimes under the influence of alien influences, to produce new permutations. These permutations were not necessarily politically or socially subversive, but under certain conditions, or in the hands of certain individuals, such recombinations of puritan impulses could, as we have just seen, prove deeply radical. We do not know whether John Traske quietly continued to preach an egalitarian, or even quasi-communistic message after his return to the ministry in 1620. What is clear is that he continued to consort with those men and women who stood at the margins of English society, peddling his new, explicitly antinomian message, to those he once called the "off-scouring of the world."

CHAPTER 6

John Eaton, the Eatonists, and the "Imputative" Strain of English Antinomianism

John Eaton has frequently been cited as the father of seventeenth-century English antinomianism.[1] This tradition stretches back to his own day. Ephraim Pagitt, the London minister who had tutored Eaton in his youth, referred to his fallen pupil as "The first Antinomian among us," a sobriquet that was in many respects entirely deserved.[2] Although Eaton was probably not the first Englishman to harbor anti-legal sympathies, he was without question the most famous, the most prolific, and the loudest proponent of such ideas in early Stuart England. Thus, despite the fact that there were as suggested above several distinct and independent sources from which anti-legal ideas initially flowed, Eaton's own particular brand exerted a preponderant (although not completely decisive) influence over the phenomenon that contemporaries would come to know as "antinomianism." This influence was so widely recognized that observers sometimes referred to antinomians simply as "Eatonists," particularly in London, where Eaton appears to have spent the better part of the decade of the 1620s.[3]

---

[1] Most recently in G. Huehns, *Antinomianism in English History: With Special Reference to the Period 1640-1660* (London: The Cresset Press, 1951), 47.

[2] Ephraim Pagitt, *Heresiography, or A Description of the Hereticks and Sectaries of these Latter Times*, Sixth ed. (1662), 121.

[3] For contemporary uses of the term "Eatonist," see PRO, SPD 16/139/91, fol. 174r (from the 1629 articles against Peter Shaw); Henry Church, *Divine and Christian Letters* (1636), 26; Thomas Gataker, *Gods Eye on His Israel* (1645), 2, who noted that advocates of antinomianism, "from one of the first Authors

For obvious reasons, then, any attempt to trace the nature and history of antinomianism must contend with the thought of its grand heresiarch. This task has been rendered considerably less taxing in the wake of the publication of T. D. Bozeman's outstanding recent study of Eaton's theology.[4] The following chapter in fact covers much of the same ground as Bozeman's article, building on his basic conclusions while attempting to locate Eaton more firmly in the constellation of early Stuart religious thought and practice. Readers will recall that Bozeman concludes that Eaton's theology—and by proxy, early Stuart antinomianism—was to use his words a "post-" or "contra-puritan" phenomenon. As we shall see, this conclusion is in many ways entirely appropriate; nevertheless, in other ways it tends to efface the very considerable connections between Eaton's thought and the ideology, practices, and language of the mainstream puritan tradition from which he emerged. Without a careful examination of these connections, we cannot in my estimation thoroughly understand the Eatonists, nor can we fully appreciate the nature and extent of their quarrel with their godly enemies. What follows, then, is a detailed attempt to track both the similarities and the differences between mainstream puritans and the Eatonists, in order to observe the manner in which Eaton's thought evolved out of prior forms of entirely conventional godly divinity. To do this, we shall draw on Eaton's two surviving publications—*The Honey-Combe of Free Justification* and *The Discovery of the Most Dangerous Dead Faith*—as well as a polemical treatise written by Eaton's follower Robert Towne in the early 1630s. These works will be supplemented with other printed and manuscript sources, most notably a pastoral letter written by Eaton's Suffolk disciple John Eachard in 1631.[5]

The insight gained not only helps us to understand the relationship between antinomianism and mainstream puritanism, but serves to prepare us to look at other forms of antinomianism that emerged in early Stuart England. For al-

---

thereof are commonly called *Eatonists*." All of these references derived from London-area residents.

[4] T. D. Bozeman, "The Glory of the 'Third Time': John Eaton as Contra-Puritan," *Journal of Ecclesiastical History*, 47 (1996). Also of use is the account provided by W. Stoever, *"A Faire and Easie Way to Heaven": Covenant Theology and Antinomianism in Early Massachusetts* (Middletown, CT: Wesleyan University Press, 1978), 138-47.

[5] Eaton's two books were written before 1630-31, the likely year of his death. Shortly thereafter, his widow Susan attempted to have *The Honey-Combe* secretly published, an attempt for which she was imprisoned. The books were finally published in 1642 by Eaton's admirers. Robert Towne's *The Assertion of Grace* was written in the wake of the London controversies of 1629-31, and was complete before early 1633. Eachard's pastoral letter (PRO, SPD 16/520/80, transcribed in Appendix E, below) was written in the summer of 1631.

though the "imputative" antinomianism espoused by Eaton, Towne, and Eachard was surely the most widely recognized variant of anti-legal thought, it was not the only one. It represented one pole on the spectrum of antinomian ideas. At the other pole, there had developed a "perfectionist" or "inherentist" strain of antinomianism, which owed less to the traditions of orthodox protestant divinity, and which diverged from the Eatonist position in crucial ways. Only by analyzing Eatonist thought as against mainstream puritanism, then, will we be prepared to grapple with the complexities and permutations of seventeenth-century antinomianism.

A Protestant Son

Although he left behind a massive and rich corpus of theological writings, surprisingly little is known of John Eaton's life. Born in Kent around 1575, Eaton was a scholarship student at Trinity College, Oxford, from which he took his B.A. in 1595 and his M.A. in 1603. At some point during his youth, he had been tutored by the minister and writer Ephraim Pagitt, son of the renowned puritan Eusebius Pagitt, and later the author of that well-known exposé of sectarian error, *Heresiography*. After holding several curacies, including one under Robert Wright at St. Katherine Coleman Street, London, Eaton assumed the vicarage of Wickham Market, Suffolk, around 1604.[6] Wickham Market appears to have been the site of puritan activity during these years; in 1608, the ecclesiastical authorities discovered that a minister named George Hulkes—recently deprived of his living at Kenton for ceremonial nonconformity—was preaching a monthly sermon in the town.[7] In all likelihood, such a lectureship would not have taken root without the connivance of the vicar, suggesting that Eaton may have leaned toward puritan radicalism early in his career. Within a few years, however, Eaton had developed a distinctive and novel theological style that soon attracted the attention of the authorities. In 1614, he was disciplined for having preached at a clerical synod in Norwich that God saw no sin in the elect.[8] This was the fulcrum of Eaton's theological system, the fundamental innovation upon which his doctrinal vision was based; it seems to have been fully developed by the time he first came into

---

[6] Pagitt, *Heresiography*, 121. "The first Antinomian among us (that I can hear of) was one Master *John Eaton*, who had been a Scholar of mine, and afterwards was Curate to Mr. [Robert] *Wright*, Parson of *Katherine Colema[n]* near *Algate*; he was for his errors imprisoned in the Gate-house at *Westminster*."

[7] S. B. Babbage, *Puritanism and Richard Bancroft* (London: SPCK, 1962), 205.

[8] I owe this information to a personal communication from Kenneth Fincham, who cites Norfolk and Norwich Record Office ACT/45B (11 Oct. 1614). I have been unable to confirm this reference, but the information squares perfectly with that provided by Peter Gunter in his published attack on Eaton.

conflict with his neighbor ministers in Suffolk. How he arrived at such a position is not clear. The Suffolk clergyman Peter Gunter, who penned an attack on Eaton shortly after the synod at Norwich, maintained that Eaton had "plainly avouch[ed] this speciall doctrine was revealed to him by prayer."[9] Although it is perhaps not wise to take this account at face value, if Gunter was correct, Eaton was openly claiming that he had come to his conclusions through a process of spiritual revelation much like the ones experienced by Traske and his disciples. Such a trajectory seems entirely plausible, and would situate Eaton's own piety firmly within the general atmosphere of "spiritist" enthusiasm that pervaded the antinomian subculture of the period.

In the years that followed, Eaton appears to have continued to dispense his message with considerable aggression, winning converts in southeastern Suffolk, including the vicar of Darsham, John Eachard, and several citizens of nearby Ipswich. It was no doubt this success as an evangelist that brought him into further conflict with the authorities. In 1619, Eaton was tried before the High Commission and deprived of his living as "an incorrigible divulger of errors and false opinions."[10] Although no account of the trial survives, Archbishop Abbot later remarked that the court had found him "soe ignorant, and . . . soe simple, that we thought fitt to send him to Westminster Schoole and Paule's Schoole to be instructed," an odd and no doubt humiliating punishment to inflict on an Oxford-trained Master of Arts.[11] Following this half-hearted effort at reeducation, Eaton was allowed to return to the ministry as a curate, but on Abbot's account, he soon fell back to his old ways, presumably resulting in another appearance before the courts. Unfortunately, no firm record survives as to his whereabouts during this period, although there is good reason to believe that Eaton spent much of the next decade in London. In 1621, he petitioned for license to marry Anne Crosman, widow of the Ipswich curate Thomas Crosman, at the parish of St. Bennet Paul's Wharf in London, while in 1630, a "John Eaton, clerk" of "Donstone Stockwod" witnessed the will of John Amey, resident of the city parish of St. Giles Cripplegate.[12] In addition, other less direct pieces of evidence, including Eachard's pastoral letter of 1631 and Henry Burton's published attack on Eaton strongly suggest that

---

[9] P. Gunter, *A Sermon Preached in the Countie of Suffolk, before the Clergie and Laytie, for the discoverie and confutation of certaine strange, pernicious, and Hereticall Positions, publickely delivered, held, and maintayned, touching Justification, by a certaine factious Preacher of Wickam Market* (1615), sig. Br.

[10] *CSPD, 1619-1623*, 41.

[11] S. R. Gardiner, ed., *Reports of cases in the courts of Star Chamber and High Commission*. Camden Society, N.S., 39 (1886), 320.

[12] G. L. Armitage and J. L. Chester, eds. *Allegations for Marriage Licenses Issued by the Bishop of London, 1611 to 1828*, Publications of the Harleian Society, 26 (London, 1887), 106. For Amey, see PRO, PROB11/158, fol. 101v.

the antinomian patriarch spent a substantial portion of time in and around London after his deprivation by the High Commission. Here, Eaton appears to have served as an anchor of the antinomian community that was taking shape in the capital. As noted in Chapter Two, he made contact with other ministers such as John Traske and Robert Towne, each of whom was probably already flirting with antinomian or crypto-antinomian theological opinions. At this point, Eaton seems to have become the center of gravity of a movement of anti-legal ministers that included not only Traske and Towne, but also John Emersone, Thomas Hodges, and Samuel Prettie, to name only those who can be linked directly to Eaton's name. By the summer of 1631, Eaton was dead. Yet as Eachard's exhortation to Prettie demonstrates, he was hardly forgotten; die-hard admirers remembered him as a martyr for the sake of the Gospel and a stubborn opponent of the soul-strangling legalism so prevalent within the community of the godly at the time.

What, then, constituted the Gospel according to John Eaton? Just what was it that seemed so poisonous to his enemies and so inspiring to his friends and devotees? From one perspective, John Eaton's theology appears to have been little more than a peculiarly robust restatement of verities at the heart of the reformed heritage. In a seemingly unequivocal manner, he embraced formal theological concepts that were utterly commonplace both to the wider protestant tradition, and more specifically, to English puritanism. Then, having rearranged them and reworked them, he enthusiastically turned them against the godly themselves.

In some cases, the amount of reworking was slight indeed. Thus, in a manner entirely at one with hallowed canons of puritan practical divinity, Eaton argued that the first step on the road to salvation was the preaching of the Law. To unconverted souls, the Moral Law and its curse were to be delivered with relentless ferocity: "we must preach it as nigh (as I said) as possibly we can, with the same majesty that God spake it, *in thundering and lightening, and terrible earth-quake, and flaming fire, reaching up to the midst of heaven;* for which right nature of it, it is called *fiery Law, Deut.* 33.2. that so it may bee to secure ones, and unto them that are under it, the lightening of Gods wrath, the thundering of his anger, the messenger of death, the hammer and ratling of hell to break in pieces the hard stones, that lie secure in the least sin."[13] Knowledge of the Law, together with the knowledge of God's hatred of sin, and the just punishment that awaited Law breakers, would convince the would-be believer of his or her own inability perfectly to obey. Even the holiest person violated the Decalogue daily (particularly the tenth commandment's condemnation of covetousness); since all sin was an abomination in God's sight, the Law thus awakened in the unconverted a sense of their own woeful

[13] John Eaton, *Honey-Combe*, 124-25.

inadequacy and vileness, much as it had in the sanctified pharisee Saul, who came to understand that "in all his good works he brake the tenth Commandement, and so as much as lay in him, did destroy himselfe in all his good works." This realization created a profound spiritual misery: "This is to bee slaine by the Law, this is to understand the Law rightly, especially the tenth Commandement."[14]

For those so immiserated, Eaton prescribed the impeccably reformed remedy of free justification by faith alone. Aware of their own hopelessly sinful state, and tormented by their inability to fulfill the Law, despairing sinners had no choice but to rely solely and completely on Christ, whose holy life and sacrificial death alone could satisfy God's wrath. Christ's perfect obedience was, to use the Pauline phrase, imputed by God to believers by virtue of their faith, thus freeing them from the just punishment that awaited their sinful disobedience. Thus, humans were saved not through any righteousness of their own, but through the purely extrinsic righteousness of Christ. On Alister McGrath's account, this concept—the notion that "man is justified on the basis of an external and alien righteousness"—was *the* central and distinctive innovation of the Protestant Reformation, and the cornerstone of the new doctrine of justification by faith alone. It had first been formulated by Luther, and had passed via Calvin into the broader world of reformed theology, where it had been taken up enthusiastically and with little resistance within the Church of England.[15]

In its broad, formal outlines, then, Eaton's doctrine of justification not only paralleled standard reformed doctrine, but replicated it with frightening precision. Even in many of its most minute theological details, Eaton duplicated reformed formulae. Thus, for example, God was said to impute to believers both the active and passive righteousness of Christ—that is, his active obedience to the Law and his passive submission to torment and death on the cross—a theological formulation that had become virtually unchallenged orthodoxy amongst Calvinist theologians by the early seventeenth century.[16] Likewise borrowing from the corpus of protestant scholastic wisdom, Eaton held that this imputed active and passive righteousness served as "the formal cause" of our justification.[17] Eaton's theological system thus proudly (some

---

[14] *Dead Faith*, 115-16.

[15] See A. McGrath, *Iustitia Dei: A History of the Christian Doctrine of Justification From 1500 to the Present Day* (Cambridge, 1986), 12-14, 25, and more generally 1-53, 98-121. McGrath makes it clear that the doctrine of imputed righteousness was accepted not only by puritans, but even by thorough-going conformists and anti-puritans, notably Richard Hooker.

[16] See ibid., 45-47.

[17] See Eaton, *Honey-Combe*, 262-63: "the perfect holinesse and righteousnes, not of the Godhead, but of the humane nature of Christ wherein he performed perfect

might argue shamelessly) laid claim to that most time-honored of protestant principles—the idea that sinners were justified entirely by imputation of Christ's extrinsic and all-sufficient merits. No human action could play any part in earning salvation.

This is not to say, however, that Eaton was merely following ingenuously in the footsteps of his English protestant forebears. For although he could justly argue that the basic structures of his thought were modeled on the most revered protestant sources, the conclusions and uses he derived from these sources were by no means incontestably traditional. By rearranging and foregrounding certain aspects of this tradition, Eaton managed to construct a system of divinity that in many important ways violated the most deeply embedded assumptions of puritan practical theology. Standing at the center of Eaton's system was the aforesaid doctrine of the imputation of Christ's righteousness, which served as the center of gravity for his thought as a whole. On Eaton's interpretation, this doctrine necessarily implied that those men and women to whom God imputed Christ's righteousness were in fact perfect and free from sin in the sight of God. Such people were, as he habitually put it, clothed with "the Wedding garment of Christs perfect righteousnesse, by which the justified person is made so truely, and so perfectly holy and righteous from all spot of sinne in the sight of God, that God doth, and (by his actuall power) can see no sin in his justified children freely by faith onely, without workes, *Revel.* 3. 18."[18]

Now in some respects, this too was an entirely conventional protestant argument, and Eaton was able to produce a host of solid reformed authorities to back the basic claim that Christ's perfection was imputed to believers.[19] What is crucial, however, is that Eaton insisted, with a special and vehement passion, that this imputation of Christ's righteousness utterly abolished a believer's sins from God's vision. For Eaton, imputation was no mere decision to

---

obedience, both active and passive in fulfilling the whole law of God, is the formal cause of our Justification; which only after the nature of the forme, *dat nomen & esse*, that is, giveth unto us not only the name, but also the true being of righteous men in the sight of God." Like other reformed theologians he held that Christ's righteousness in its active and passive forms satisfied God's perfect justice and pacified his wrath. See Eaton, *Dead Faith*, 129; idem, *Honey-Combe*, 332.

[18] Eaton, *Dead Faith*, 1-2.

[19] For an example in which a puritan authority made a claim that, taken by itself, was virtually identical, see W. Perkins, *A Treatise Tending unto a Declaration Whether a Man be in the Estate of Damnation or in the Estate of Grace* (1590?), 56: "the elect being in themselves rebellious sinners . . . yet by Christ they are accepted of the Lord as perfectlie pure and righteous before him." Note, however, that Perkins uses the word "accepted," rather than "seen," implying a subtly different connotation.

look the other way, or to count one thing for another. It was not as if God merely averted his gaze when he looked upon his children, choosing to substitute Christ's holiness when he caught sight of their fetid sinfulness. Those who wore the "white robe" of Revelations 3:18[20] were rendered utterly and objectively perfect in God's sight by virtue of their faith alone, despite their own rank condition: "so true faith of *free Justification*, being the having on of this wedding-garment . . . alone doth truly abolish all the filthy nakedness of our sins out of Gods sight, and it alone doth make us perfectly holy, and sufficiently righteous in the sight of God freely, without works."[21] In this utterance, we have the crux of Eaton's Christianity. This catchphrase, with very minor variations, repeats itself dozens of times throughout his oeuvre.[22] For Eaton, the very words seem to have possessed an almost magical quality; he pronounced the chorus of free justification with a frequency, a vehemence—even a compulsiveness—that is almost unnerving for the modern reader (as indeed it seems to have been for his browbeaten seventeenth-century opponents). So too, the notion that God saw no sin in the justified believer became a favored slogan of Eaton's followers, the central and cementing concept holding together an emerging ideology. In 1631, in the wake of Eaton's death, John Eachard addressed his pastoral missive to those of the "wedding garment," that is, "all you that profess free justificacion by the blood and righteousnes of Jesus Christ that hath made the Church without spott or wrinkle in his sight."[23]

Although based on the most respectable of reformed sources, this was not a system likely to endear the Eatonists to their English protestant comrades. Although they espoused the doctrine of imputed righteousness without qualification, few if any mainstream puritans would have assented to Eaton's conclusion. Even the most ardent proponents of the doctrine of justification by free grace (and as a group the godly were surely the most ardent in England) could never have accepted the conclusion that justification utterly banished the sins of believers from God's sight. As T. D. Bozeman has argued, puritan practical divinity rested on the notion of an omniscient and all-seeing God, a sort of internal eye that monitored not only the wickedness of reprobates, but the very hearts and lives of believers.[24] As we have seen, this vision of the deity underpinned a system of pastoral theology, which (while it fully embraced the notion of justification by faith) placed an extraordinary emphasis on the process

---

20 For Eaton's use of the "white robe" metaphor see *Dead Faith*, sigs., A12v-Br.

21 Eaton, *Honey-Combe*, sig. B2v.

22 See for instance Eaton, *Dead Faith*, 67-68; *Honey-Combe*, 24, 184, 185, 236, 257, 259, which represent only a few of the dozens of instances in which the formula is repeated, in whole or in part, throughout Eaton's works.

23 See below, Appendix E.

24 Bozeman, "Glory of the 'Third Time,'" 639.

of sanctification—of weeding out sin and setting up the rule of God's holy Law in every facet of life. Through a subtle restatement of the shared reformed doctrine of justification, Eaton had therefore effected a change of potentially enormous consequences, a change that threatened in some ways to reconfigure (perhaps even to invert) the contours of puritan piety.

Yet it is equally important to understand what Eaton was not doing: he was not arguing that the justified were actually rendered perfect in themselves. Much like mainstream puritans, Eaton maintained that far from being objectively and inherently perfect in this life, justified sinners retained the remnants of sin within them. Sin was abolished "not out of our flesh . . . but utterly . . . from before God."[25] The perfection of a Christian was, as he put it, "to God-ward."[26] The faithful were perfect imputatively (that is, in the divine gaze), but not inherently.[27] This distinguished John Eaton and his closest followers from Familists, whose notorious perfectionist faith Eaton freely denounced.[28] Eaton's critics would, of course, argue that there was no difference—that the claims of the Eatonists were for all practical purposes identical to those of Familist perfectionists. In the early 1630s, when faced with precisely this charge, Robert Towne would ask his sometime puritan opponent Thomas Taylor "Did ever we hold of attaining a full perfection of sanctification in this life? you know even the spirit in your bosome, and in your disciples, that it is an untruth, and a base slander."[29] Rather, as Towne explained, "though we hold a perfection in Christ, we are yet against perfection in the flesh; we hold according to the Scriptures and orthodox Divines a perfection of the thing and condition, and yet an imperfection of faith and apprehension."[30] The claim that "the justified is freed from all spot of sinne" was "True, imputatively," but false if understood literally and simply.[31] Towne, like Eaton, denounced what he identified as the Familist principle of inherent perfection, and vigorously resisted the attempts of his godly opponents to pin upon him what he termed "Familisticall words."[32]

---

[25] Eaton, *Dead Faith*, 126.

[26] Ibid., 71.

[27] In this vein, he claimed that we are "in very deed made, although not inherently and actively (as I said in the beginning, the Papist would have it;) yet objectively and passively, perfectly holy and righteous in the sight of God" (*Honey-Combe*, 271).

[28] For denunciations of Familism, see Eaton, ibid., 148-49, as well as the first appendix to *The Honey-Combe* (unpaginated).

[29] Towne, *Assertion*, 121.

[30] Ibid., 133-34.

[31] Ibid., 68.

[32] Ibid., 124. See 40 for an explicit disavowal of Familism, and for his denial of the Familist principle of "perfect puritie in the flesh."

It is of course just possible that Eaton, Towne, and other Eatonists were playing a game of "familistical" subterfuge—that is, couching a secret perfectionism behind a mist of protestant filiopiety. Little evidence to this effect survives, however.[33] Each of our extant sources suggests that the religiosity hawked by Eaton and his most faithful followers was cut (if somewhat unevenly) from the wholesome cloth of orthodox Protestantism. Certainly, they were at pains to convey this impression. Far from hinting that they were proposing a new, extreme, sectarian—or even *unusual*—form of piety, imputative antinomians noisily proclaimed themselves the true heirs of the Protestant Reformation.

To prove their point, both Eaton and Towne larded their works with citations and passages from the most respectable and orthodox of protestant (and in some cases, puritan) authorities, including Calvin, Whitaker, Perkins, Downame, Willet, Polanus, Zanchius, and Ursinus.[34] By his own account, Eaton was nothing more than a faithful disciple of Martin Luther, "that *Hercules* of Gods glory," the greatest expositor of the true doctrine of free justification.[35] As Bozeman has noted, this almost idolatrous veneration of Luther prompted Eaton to cite his hero over a hundred times in the course of his two books, leading him to borrow phrases, ideas, even entire passages from the reformer's works.[36] In time, this claim to Luther's legacy seems to have become almost axiomatic within antinomian circles.[37] Towne, for instance, placed Luther in a rather exalted category of evangelists that included saints Paul and Stephen.[38] Their use of his works was surely selective, however. Eaton, for instance, showed a strong bias for the most anti-legal of all Luther's writings,

---

[33] Towne's connection to the Grindletonians should not, perhaps, be ignored entirely (see Chapter Eight, below).

[34] *Honey-Combe*, 75-76, 253, 266-67, 289, 306-7, 309, 314, 318. For Towne, see *The Assertion*, esp. 115-72, where Luther, Musculus, Beza, Calvin, Piscator, Zanchius, Perkins, Cudworth, and others are approvingly cited as authorities.

[35] *Honey-Combe*, 179.

[36] See Bozeman, "Glory of the 'Third Time,'" 644. R. T. Kendall, *Calvin and English Calvinism to 1649* (Oxford: Oxford University Press, 1979), 186, puts the exact number at 106.

[37] See for instance S. Torshel, *The Three Questions of Free Justification* (1632), 66-67 for comments on Luther. See ibid., 263-73 for Torshel's more extensive refutation of the opinions of the "*Libertines* and *antinomists*"; See also Gataker, *God's Eye*, 25, who claimed in 1645 that the antinomian preacher John Simpson had borrowed Luther's exposition of Galatians "to disswade Christian people from troubling themselves about *confession of their sins*, as being enough for them *to beleeve, that Christ* here *hath confessed them for them already*." For Roger Brearley's affection for Luther, see Chapter Eight, below.

[38] Towne, *Assertion*, 36.

the commentary on Paul's letter to the Galatians. At the same time, he managed quietly to ignore Luther's vocal denunciations of Agricola and his "antinomian" followers. Nevertheless, Eaton's affection for the reformer appears to have been entirely sincere, as was his conviction that he was merely following in the Wittenberger's footsteps. In this vein, his magnum opus, *The Honey-Combe of Free Justification*, ended with twenty pages of verbatim quotations from Luther, all of which plausibly supported Eaton's own controversial version of the doctrine of justification.[39] This is not to accept at face value Eaton's claims to be doing nothing more than innocently restoring protestant truth to its virginal and uncorrupted state. Rather, he was constructing a particular and partial reading of the works of Luther and other protestant reformers, a plausible, but highly tendentious vision of the true core of Protestantism. Eaton was in essence awakening the antinomian Luther, the sleeping beast that had lain dormant deep within the recesses of Protestantism from its very beginnings.

This vision of the true nature of Luther's Christianity supported what might be termed an antinomian mythology of the history and progress of the Protestant Reformation in England. Again and again, Eaton argued that he was seeking merely to reinvigorate the faith that had been established by "the first restorers of the Gospel in this land."[40] On Eaton's account, then, true Protestantism (that is to say, his own doctrine of free justification) had been legally codified in England during the halcyon days of the early and mid-sixteenth century. Over time, this pure protestant teaching had become progressively tarnished and corrupted, until, at long last, the true justifying faith had nearly disappeared from the land. By the 1620s, when Eaton's works were most likely composed, he seems to have believed that he and his followers represented the last reservoir of true protestant religion in the country, a tiny, embattled flock fighting to restore the pure doctrine of the Elizabethan settlement. As if to validate this odd and vaguely Foxeian reading of the English Reformation, Eaton and Towne eagerly cited the official homilies of the church in support of their own views. The Homilies of Mankind's Misery, Good Works, Repentance, Resurrection, and Salvation were all adduced to demonstrate that "*the established doctrine of our Church is lamentably lost*" and that free justification—once the cornerstone of English Protestantism—was being pulverized under the weight of recent innovations.[41]

---

[39] Eaton, *Honey-Combe*, 466-84.

[40] Ibid., 168.

[41] Eaton, *Dead Faith*, 57-59, 87, 157; idem., *Honey-Combe*, 338-39. See also Towne, *Assertion*, 12, 19, who cited the Homily of Repentance, and claimed that his puritan opponents "deny the established doctrine of our Church, which truly teacheth free Grace, Faith alone, and onely in Christ crucified, excluding and denying all workes before and after."

Like other non-separating puritans, then, John Eaton claimed to be nothing more than an orthodox son of the Church of England, seeking to save that church from certain unfortunate developments that were undermining its foundations. In striking such a pose, he was at one level merely following in a time-honored tradition of marginal English Protestantism, whereby the godly articulated their own attempts to reform the religious establishment in terms of unadulterated loyalty to the church and regime. And like other puritans, he seems not to have been discouraged by the unwillingness of the regime to acknowledge this logic. The fact, for instance, that he had been drummed out of his living for doctrinal error by a High Commission court packed with the most exalted officers of the Church of England appears to have made little dent in his conviction that he and his followers were but zealous defenders of the thirty-nine articles. Perhaps in a calculated attempt to prove his point, Eaton even had the temerity to claim the writings of Bishop Robert Abbot in support of his notions of justification.[42] Robert was of course the brother of Archbishop George Abbot of Canterbury, the man who had presided over Eaton's trial and deprivation in 1619.[43]

If Eaton noticed either discrepancy or irony in this situation, he certainly gave no clue; instead he stubbornly insisted that his own doctrine of "*Free Justification was first enjoyned to be diligently taught for the Reformation of the Church, by King* Henry *the eighth, but was by King* Edward *the sixth, and Queene* Elizabeth, *principally established by Parliament; and singled out from all the rest of the established Articles of Religion; and reduced into Sermons and Homilies, to be (after the Peoples sight of their lost estate, and wofull misery by sin,) principally taught, and chiefly knowne, and understood of all the Subjects and Commons of the Land.*"[44] Those who had compromised this doctrine were thus not only enemies to the cause of true religion, but subversives who threatened the English state itself. Citing the Homily of Disobedience, Eaton excoriated "such Subjects, and Commons to whom, through ignorance of Gods Word, this light of righteousnesse, and Sun of understanding doth not shine, although they may bragge, as did sometimes the Jewish Clergy, and people, that they cannot lacke knowledge, yet are such, by the blind, dead faith, Traytors to God, Traytors to their King, Traytors to their owne soules and bodies, and Traytors to the whole Land and Country."[45]

---

[42] Eaton, *Honey-Combe*, 333-34.

[43] For evidence of Archbishop Abbot's less-than-happy encounters with the man he sarcastically dubbed "Wise John Eaton," see S. R. Gardiner, ed., *Reports of Cases in the Courts of Star Chamber and High Commission*, Camden Society, N.S., 39 (1886), 320-21.

[44] From appendix to Eaton, *Honey-Combe* (unpaginated).

[45] Ibid.

Who then were the pernicious fifth columnists whose "blind, dead faith" had so polluted the English church?

To be sure, Eaton loathed Roman Catholicism. Like almost all puritans, he believed that the Pope was Antichrist, and saw the church of Rome as the negative image of the true church of Christ. Yet the blind, dead faith was not Catholicism, nor even the diluted "Popish Arminianism" that Catholicism had in Eaton's view apparently spawned.[46] Rather, as Bozeman has amply demonstrated, the "dead faith" that Eaton obsessively attacked was none other than the faith of mainstream puritanism. Cloaked behind a superficial veneer of reformed religion, puritan piety was in Eaton's view nothing but a new pharisaism, which had betrayed the English Reformation, leaving the entire nation open to the depredations of the great Romish Antichrist: "these are the traytours that under colour of greatest friendship with God, and of lying in his very lap by working out their salvation, in distrust, in free grace, and in trust in their workes and well-doings, doe break our peace with God in this land, doe betray whole Kingdomes and Countries into their enemies hand. Because they truely know not free justification, that only makes our peace with God."[47]

False Bastard Sanctification

At first glance, Eaton's attempt to portray mainstream puritans as the great hobgoblins of English religion strikes the modern reader as deeply perverse. After all, as Richard Montagu learned in the mid-1620s, the godly were without question England's most ferocious champions of the doctrine of free grace. While by no means a puritan monopoly, the pristine reformed commonplaces upon which Eaton's theology was based—justification through a God-given faith in the wholly extrinsic, alien, and all-sufficient merits of Christ—had always been taught and defended with a special affection and vehemence by the

---

[46] For Eaton's claim that the Pope was Antichrist and his denunciation of Arminianism, see the second appendix to *The Honey-Combe*, which is comprised of "*Certaine fundamentall Positions, or Doctrines of Religion, tending to peace, and to the reducing of Popish Arminians, and Anabaptisticall Ministers, and people, to the true saving faith; and to the established Protestant Doctrine of the Church of England, by the Godly authority, and publique consent of Parliament, to be faithfully taught, and diligently observed, and kept of all the subjects, for the quieting of their consciences, in the assurance of their free salvation by Jesus Christ, and for the suppressing of the Romish Antichrist in all Superstitions, Errors, Sects, and Schisms, for the beating down of sin, and all vitiousnesse of life out of the Land (for the maintaining, and keeping of peace and unity in the matters of Religion, by the pure preaching of the Law, and of the Gospel) as followeth in these five Poynts, or Positions.*"

[47] Eaton, *Dead Faith*, 38.

godly. These concepts were at the heart of puritan self-image, serving as a touchstone of true religion, a mental boundary that divided true reformed Protestants from works-righteous papists. Godly divines such as William Perkins, William Ames, and William Twisse earned international acclaim for their polemics in defense of the twin doctrines of free grace and absolute predestination; meanwhile, godly renegades—such as Ezekiel Culverwell and John Cotton—who proposed seemingly modest modifications to these doctrines, found themselves blasted by fellow puritans as treacherous turncoats.[48] Eaton was surely not ignorant of these facts; he had begun his studies at the knee of the moderate puritan Ephraim Pagitt, and he obviously knew his way through the minefield of reformed theology. How, then, had he managed to construct for himself a worldview in which the godly emerged as the great enemies of free grace, traitorous works-mongers set to lead the nation into the hands of the Whore of Babylon?

To be sure, on Eaton's account, papists represented the archetypal peddlers of the diabolical doctrine of justification by works. By trusting in "Repentance, and Sanctification and holy walking, and such like to beautifie, heale, adorne, and approve us to the sight of God,"[49] Roman Catholics ran headlong "into a preposterous cark and care to approve our selves to Godward, under the name of Sanctification and Repentance, by our owne righteousnesse, wrought in us by the spirit." This same, papistical spirit of works righteousness had by no means been eradicated from the English church, despite outward appearances:

> And yet you shall heare in some Protestants Sermons that which I feare by these manifold absurdities, is farre worse; namely, that we are by Justification made as perfectly cleane from all sinne, and as righteous as Christ himselfe in the sight of God; and yet we are sinners also in the sight of God: these are like a shrewd Cow, that gives a good milch, and then kicketh it all downe, when she hath done.[50]

This in a nutshell was Eaton's analysis of English puritan theology: while outwardly paying tribute to the principle of justification by the imputation of Christ's perfect righteousness, English puritans (here identified as the "shrewd cows" of the English religious landscape) in practice maintained the belief that sin remained visible to God after justification. From Eaton's standpoint, this was equivalent to the claim that Christ had not fully satisfied God's wrath,

[48] For intra-puritan debates on predestination, see D. Como, "Puritans, Predestination and the Construction of 'Orthodoxy' in Early Seventeenth Century England," in P. Lake and M. Questier, eds., *Conformity and Orthodoxy in the English Church, c. 1560-1642* (Woodbridge: Boydell and Brewer, 2000).
[49] Eaton, *Honey-Combe*, 379.
[50] Ibid., 380.

and that some legal works therefore remained necessary to purge sin or earn salvation.

As Eaton explained, sin was an utter abomination before God, and all those who committed sin were necessarily subject to his infinite wrath and punishment. To suggest otherwise was to deny God's perfect and unchanging attribute of justice, "For if we have the least sinne in Gods sight, wee doe not continue in all things, and so must needs be accursed of God; or else his righteous nature must needs be changeable in his definitive sentence against sinne, which cannot bee."[51] On Eaton's view, those who maintained the doctrine of the imputation of Christ's righteousness, but denied the corollary that believers were thus free from sin in God's sight, had lapsed into an absurd and confused state of contradiction, one that threatened to make God mutable or (even worse) a liar.

English puritans had, of course, always affirmed the paramount need for believers to abstain from sin and to do good works. There was never any question among puritan divines that the saints remained subject to sin, and hence to divine correction for their transgressions. The faithful remained fully under the obligations of the Moral Law, even as Christ's sacrifice freed them of its curse and condemnation. In the view of mainstream puritans, simply to assent to the proposition that Christ died to save oneself was not enough; one needed to feel the sanctifying power of his death, to see oneself progressively cleansed of sin and nurtured in holiness. Any faith that did not produce good works was, as we have seen, a "dead faith," more dangerous in the eyes of puritans than outright unbelief. Within the framework hammered out in Chapter Four, puritan divinity may be seen as a delicate balancing act that sought to reconcile, or at least to give embodiment to, both the antinomian and moralizing tendencies within the Gospels and, most especially, the Pauline epistles. Hence, the godly juggled a fierce commitment to the notion of justification by faith alone alongside a strenuous—and at times almost backbreaking—emphasis on the importance of religious duties and outward holiness.

To Eaton, this balancing act looked more like a flat contradiction. Borrowing a motif from puritan practical divinity, Eaton claimed that the godly remained trapped in "the meere literall knowledge of *Free Justification*."[52] As he put it

> the literall knowledge so knowes the mysteries of Gods Word, as a man knowes a thing by reading of it, or as a man knowes a thing that is told him of a strange Countrey; but he hath no experimentall certainty of it in himselfe . . . but the spirituall knowledge . . . so knowes the mysteries of Christ,

---

[51] Eaton, *Dead Faith*, 90.

[52] Eaton, *Honey-Combe*, 221.

> as he knowes a thing that sees it with his very eyes, and hath experimentall feeling of it in his owne selfe.[53]

The godly thus spoke the language of free justification—indeed they "daily, like Parrots, doe blindefoldly prattle of" its excellency—but had not in practice experienced its profound effects.[54] They thus possessed what Eaton called "the blind dead faith." Here was a move that straddled the line between the brilliant and the ridiculous: Eaton had stolen from the godly the homiletic commonplace of "the dead faith," turned it inside out, and redeployed it to attack mainstream puritans themselves. Where the godly had traditionally used the notion to refer to a faith that produced no works, Eaton argued that the dead faith was in fact a faith that slid silently backwards into the bog of the good works (which is to say, the morally strenuous faith of mainstream puritanism). Thus, the godly were

> such as being in name Protestants, and professing themselves utter enimies to Papists, in that . . . they will not give the least piece of Justification to works and holy walking, and will seeme both to themselves and others to hold Free Justification perfectly: And yet, because of their being in the dead faith, they do not understand it; and because by conceiving it after a carnall humane witted-fashion, they feele no sweetnesse in it: therefore declining in affection unto the stablishing of their own righteousnesse, they not only nullife Free Justification, and make it as good as nothing . . . they weaken the faith of others, by running into the very objections of the Papists; and shake hands with them in the main points of salvation, with whom they would seem to be at utter variance. And all this (I say againe) because they lie in the dead faith, whereby they understand not the nature and excellency of Free Justification: and yet one such may doe us more harme in weakening our faith than many Papists; not only, because they professe with us one and same profession, in letter; and so are like homebred flattering enimies; but also, because by great literall learning and teaching, they may beare a great name, that they live, when by the dead faith they indeed are *dead, Rev.* 3. 1. Therefore that these objectors do not weaken our faith, wee must learne to discerne these underminers of our faith.[55]

Mainstream puritans were thus even more dangerous to the country than devotees of the Pope, for puritans paid lip service to inerrant protestant truths while subtly and silently killing the souls of those who followed them. Indeed, the godly did more than simply parrot true doctrine. They showed many characteristics that were identical to those associated with the true, lively and justifying faith of which Eaton claimed to be an apostle: they sometimes mani-

---

[53] Ibid., 226.

[54] Quotation from ibid., 218.

[55] Eaton, *Honey-Combe*, 44-45. See also idem, *Dead Faith*, 32-33.

fested "a kinde of great humiliation and earnest repentance . . . they may have a great zeale of Gods glory, and an earnest endevour of holy and righteous walking in all Gods Commandments." Indeed, these acts of earnest contrition and godly conversation were done "not dissemblingly and for vain glory and praise of men, as many grosse Hypocrites and Pharisees did," but rather, "with a good intent, so zealously ayming at Gods glory, in resisting their corruptions and sins; and . . . fervently *following righteousnesse according to the Law of God, Rom.* 9. 31 to the intent to be a holy people unto God by their workes and well-doings."[56] Eaton's remodeled version of "the dead faith" was so perilous precisely because it looked so authentic, so profoundly holy.

Eaton by no means objected to good works in and of themselves. Against the ceaseless charges of libertinism lobbed at him by his enemies, he persistently argued that those with the true, living faith would in fact do good works. His objection to mainstream puritan piety appears to have flowed primarily from what he viewed as a tendency to make outward works of holiness into the marrow of true religion—that is, the godly attempt to make themselves "a holy people unto God by . . . workes and well-doings." We have already examined the value that mainstream puritans placed upon outward holiness—their obsession with the purity and use of the ordinances—their constant resort to the means of grace as the only effectual way of inculcating true faith—their total war against sins that they perceived to be infecting English society. In all of these concerns, Eaton sensed that the godly had somehow lost sight of that quintessentially protestant insight of free justification, becoming entwined instead in a piety that smelled suspiciously like the very works righteousness the reformation had sought to overthrow. The godly, of course, could counter that they had always taught that outward sanctity was merely a sign or manifestation of justifying faith, freely bestowed by God without regard for any inherent human merit. But Eaton and his followers rejected this maneuver as a cheap ventriloquist's trick. They denounced the tendency to infer the presence of inward grace from outward changes or works. Christians were not to "Shew God thy faith by thy works, nor shew thy selfe thy faith by thy works."[57] Hence, when Thomas Taylor set forth a series of "notes and markes" to allow aspiring saints to determine whether they had been set free from the curse of the Law, Towne rebuked him for corrupting the doctrine of free grace: "What is this but to walk and live without Faith in true Justification, which you professe to know and hold, but indeed deny, and to establish and bring in unsanctified works; or at best Popish contrition in case they

[56] Ibid., 8-11.
[57] Ibid., 162.

fail."[58] Any attempt to extract assurance from an outward change that had taken place in the believer's carriage or conversation was to descend into legalism and works righteousness.

In the minds of Eaton and his closest followers, assurance was to flow directly and without mediation from faithful apprehension of Christ and his meritorious, saving works: puritan legalists, Eaton argued, "labour after the supposed works of sanctification, more than after faith, that should give to Christ only, the sole glory of our assurance; therefore they should first have assurance, and then do, that which they doe, in thankfullnesse for their assurance . . . the having of Christ alone, and his righteousnesse, with his other free benefits depending thereupon, must assure me."[59]

Here, again, we see Eaton claiming the protestant high ground in his battle with his godly opponents. Who, after all, could quibble with the eminently reformed notion that assurance was to come wholly from Christ? Likewise, what self-respecting reformed Protestant could gainsay the idea that humans were entirely passive in the process of salvation, which was effected wholly through the external, gracious work of God? As Towne put it, "God by his Gospel requireth nothing of man to Salvation; but abundantly testifieth, and promiseth to doe all himselfe, that so his promise may be every way firme and free."[60] Eaton concurred, adding that "we being no agents and doers in this businesse, but meere patients: because his righteousnesse wherewith he cloathes us, doth as perfectly abolish from before God all our sinnes, as the Sun-beames abolish darkenesse out of a dark house."[61] Once again, the Eatonists had staked out a position of absolute protestant purity. They were borrowing doctrinal weapons that the godly habitually brandished in polemical conflicts with Arminians and Roman Catholics, and then turning these weapons against the godly themselves. And at times, their rancor against mainstream puritans seemed almost boundless. In Eaton's view, "although their . . . holy, and bloody blind zeale of Gods glory seem very beautifull and be highly esteemed before men, and in their own account; yet that it is a most vile, and horrible abomination in the sight of God."[62]

In all of this, it is important that we not lose sight of the fact that what was at stake in the debates between the Eatonists and their puritan ministerial enemies was nothing more or less than the affection and support of the godly laity. Godly preachers were, of course, notorious for assuming the role of

---

58 See Thomas Taylor, *Regula Vitae, The Rule of the Law Under the Gospel* (1631), 11-17; Towne, *Assertion*, 27.

59 Eaton, *Honey-Combe*, 115.

60 Towne, *Assertion*, 16-17.

61 Eaton, *Honey-Combe*, 25.

62 Eaton, *Dead Faith*, 55-56.

charismatic prophets. They surrounded themselves with disciples and admirers, who regularly attended their sermons, supported them with gifts and bequests, and accorded favored preachers near-celebrity status. As Towne and Eaton sneered, godly ministers were "profound rabbies," whose prodigious (but ultimately abominable) holiness served to fool unsuspecting laypeople into believing their lies.[63] Thus, Towne complained that Taylor misled his "hearers, who have too servilely apprentised their judgements to your Tenents, as Oracles from Heaven,"[64] while Eaton decried puritan clerics who "doe but delude the simple blinde devoted people, with a legall zeale of holy walking for feare of punishment, or hope of reward, and speeding well for the same: seeming, yea, and being as hot as a toste against outward vices, and earnestly calling for all active morall duties, which they call holy walking in all Gods Commandements."[65] It was this hold, this bond of discipleship, that the antinomians were seeking to break, or rather, to usurp. In attempting to portray themselves as the only true heirs of the Protestant Reformation, antinomians were pandering to the deepest prejudices and impulses of the godly laity, attempting to tap into and exploit reformed conventions that resonated with the innermost convictions of ordinary puritans. The point, in the end, was to insinuate themselves and their own doctrine into a similar position of cultural hegemony within the godly community (and, if their claims of loyalty are to be trusted, ultimately to rearrange the shape of the church itself).

At the center of the Eatonists' critique of their puritan clerical opponents was a belief that godly preachers were stringing their followers along with, as Eaton put it, "fear of punishment" and "hope of reward." By extorting an involuntary, forced, and fearful obedience to the precepts of scripture, puritan ministers enslaved their listeners and violated the fundamental principles of Protestantism. It is not difficult to see how this critique evolved. There was more than a little justice to the claim that godly ministers routinely terrified their followers with gloomy warnings of the judgments that awaited unrepentant sinners; this same fear of divine displeasure was manipulated with regularity to prod believers towards the duties of obedience commanded by God—everything from Sabbatarianism, to fasting, to sobriety in drink and dress. To the Eatonists, such forced obedience was an affront, savoring of the spirit of Popery. Godly ministers "indirectly by preposterous urging men to a constrained righteousnesse by legall terrors . . . pervert the Gospell, and become Ministers of the Divell."[66] In this, the Eatonists were again replicating a critique that had been developed by Luther and Calvin in their attacks on

---

[63] For the term "profound rabbies," see Towne, *Assertion*, 92.

[64] Ibid., 21.

[65] Eaton, *Honey-Combe*, 223.

[66] Ibid., 86.

Rome: the faithful would obey—but joyfully and freely, not fearfully and under threat of punishment. Now, however, Eaton took this essential protestant argument and used it to attack the entire edifice of puritan practical divinity:

> And hereupon giving but a flourish of praise now and then to faith in generall; they being utterly ignorant and void of true justifying and saving faith, doe dwell in, rest upon, and stay up themselves and their dead faith principally by workes. And hereupon doe in their hearts dignifie, and their words magnifie, extoll, and extort with legal arguments a preposterous sanctification, repentance, mortification, grace, and graces. Popishly and falsly understood; new life, holy and righteous walking, universall obedience to all Gods commandments, sincerity, humiliation, uprightnesse, fastings, regeneration, Popishly also and falsly understood; and such like workes extorted (as I said) with legall arguments, of . . . hope of rewards and speedings well, if wee doe them; and with fear of punishments and speedings ill, if we have them not: which how much the more they are thus preposterously exacted and legally extorted, so much the more under termes and titles of the Gospell, such Preachers teach but the light of nature, the pride of workes, and vain-glory of man; and so do withdraw people from Christ to hang upon their owne workes and doings, by resting upon the Popish rotten pillar, that God accepts the will for the deed, and so doe drown Christs glory, free Justification, doe destroy faith, waste and consume the Church of Christ, teach a false bastard sanctification.[67]

Of course, such a "bastard" doctrine necessarily produced unnatural progeny. As John Eachard explained, those who failed to understand the principle of free justification would end up "mungrell Christians," suspended hopelessly "between Adam and Christ." Such illegitimate Christians "stand before god sometimes in Christ, and sometimes out of Christ, sometime in Adam or half Adam, and half Christ, half darkness, and half light, half a new creature, and half an old, which the scripture will not allow."[68] Mainstream puritans were, in short, the product of miscegenation between Law and Gospel. There was of course no doubt about the fate that awaited such crossbred Christians. In spite of their preponderant fear of judgment, and their equally fearful pursuit of

---

[67] Eaton, *Dead Faith*, 26-28. For a similar critique of mainstream puritan practice, which echoed Calvin's claim that Catholic piety amounted to an attempt to extort favor from God, see Towne, *Assertion*, 20: "Popish conceits stick to mens hearts naturally closer then their skins to their flesh, to wit, If we could but get the heart to rent, tender, and melt into teares, &c. If wee could fast, and powre out our soules in great bitternesse, and afflictions of mind, be enlarged to prayer, and holy duties, we should then hope, that God would heare and respect us: this would much satisfie and ease the Conscience."

[68] Appendix E, below.

holiness, their works would carry them straight to hell. Since they could never fathom the true principle of freedom from sin in the sight of God,

> these *miscillane Christians* never knew what an horrible thing the least motion of sin is in the sight of God, and therefore fear not horrible corrections for them, untill they come for dallying with Gods Justice, and for their unbeliefe, and robbing of Christ of the glory of the *chastisement of our peace, Esay.* 53. 5. to beare it themselves, they come to bee chastised and corrected in hell, where, I dare warrant them, they shall have correction enough, and nothing but just and due correction for their sins.[69]

Those who failed to understand the true doctrine of free justification (that is, the notion that the imputed righteousness of Christ freed the believer from all stain of sin in God's sight) were subject to the very same condemnation that the godly themselves regularly pronounced against Sabbath-breakers, idolaters and "good fellows."

This profound antipathy for the ways of mainstream puritanism had been forged over many years of often hostile dispute. Indeed, Eaton left considerable evidence concerning his treatment at the hands of the godly.

> If the old matter of the pure Gospel be uttered but after a new manner, otherwise than these like blind mill-horses are accustomed to run round in: or if their literall knowledge, dead Faith, and blind legall zeale be any way a little crossed, or but touched (although a faithfull Minister must needs teach *novè*, but not *nova*, that is after a new manner, but not any new matter) yet these humble ones . . . in that new manner of speaking do rise up against Christ, and count the old mysteries of Christ and of his Gospel to be *nova*, novelties, new doctrines. . . . And feeling their dead faith, and corrupt worship of God to be, as I said, but touched; then their blinde zeale calumniating . . . the faith, words, and workes of true beleevers, boyleth forth into out cries of errours, heresies, and blasphemies: and most innocent Christ himself shall

---

[69] Eaton, *Honey-Combe*, 139-40. This passage serves to qualify T. D. Bozeman's claim that Eaton's God was a purely beneficent, loving, and forgiving being ("Glory of the 'Third Time,'" 645-46). Although Bozeman is correct to point out that threats of divine judgment are rare in Eaton's surviving works, there is no question but that Eaton believed that those who remained in the "dead faith" of mainstream puritanism were headed straight for eternal damnation. From this perspective, each and every time he chastised the godly for their legalism, he was implicitly admonishing them in equally vehement terms that unless they repented, they were bound for hell. Put another way, Eaton's God was indeed utterly beneficent and loving, but only if you embraced the Eatonist faith.

among these not escape the black censure of being counted a seducer of the people, and a blasphemer and troubler of the Church.[70]

Few passages better illustrate Eaton's vision of himself and his own followers as a persecuted flock, suffering at the hands of pharisaical puritans. This paranoid self-image was shared by other Eatonists; in his circular letter of 1631, Eachard would explicitly define a newly emergent antinomian community in terms of patience and steadfastness under persecution, citing John Eaton as an exemplar of such long-suffering faith.[71] Curiously, Eaton's vision appears to have contained pharisees but no Pilate; his printed works at no point explicitly attacked the churchmen and prelates who actually presided over his ecclesiastical punishments. Rather, all his animosity appears to have been reserved for the godly themselves, who in Eaton's fondness for the barnyard metaphor, were intermittently denounced as blind horses, scavenging dogs, shrewd cows.[72]

As suggested above, this may well have been because the most fierce and emotional moments of Eaton's career took place not in ecclesiastical courts, but in private disputes with his godly counterparts. It was in this environment of private debate and dispute, conducted largely outside the domain of the institutional church, that John Eaton's faith undoubtedly took shape. Accordingly, this faith was at almost every point informed by a dialectical engagement with mainstream puritanism, which served as the negative referent for his thought. Yet this vision was not without positive content; as we shall see in the following section, Eaton's theology amounted to much more than a reinvigorated Lutheran Protestantism.

The God of the Honey-Combe

What alternative mode of practical divinity were antinomians thus promoting? It is important to understand that the Eatonist quarrel with their godly enemies was not simply a formal theological dispute over the interpretation of scripture; rather, it was a dispute over how certain scriptures were to be applied in the lives of devoted saints. Eatonists objected to modes of worship, and above all, to psychological states, that were encouraged by mainstream puritan preaching. We have already seen, for instance, that Eaton and Towne showed a tendency to derogate from specific devotional activities such as fasting, one of the cornerstones of puritan practical divinity by this stage. More pointedly, however, the Eatonists denounced the psychological effects that godly divinity wrought upon believers. As Towne explained, the puritan

---

[70] Eaton, *Dead Faith*, 48-51. See also ibid., sigs. A10v-11r; idem, *Honey-Combe*, 218.

[71] See Appendix E, below.

[72] Eaton, *Dead Faith*, sigs. A10v-11r.

style of piety "defaceth Christ, derogates from his sacrifice, obscureth the Gospel, leaveth the Conscience always in feare and danger, spoileth it of all peace, joy, and consolation, it mingleth Law and Gospel, it nourisheth and maintaineth the speciall ground of Popery, it engendereth bondage, and is an enemy to all true goodness."[73] This passage makes it clear that although there were significant disagreements between the antinomians and their enemies over how to interpret crucial theological concepts, these formal disagreements were inseparably intertwined with a critique of the emotional and psychic effects that godly divinity engendered in its adherents. In short, mainstream puritanism, with its rigorous disciplines and relentless deity, sapped Christianity of all joy and consolation.

Accordingly, the Eatonists rushed in to fill the gap; the glorious apprehension of Christ's saving righteousness, and the concomitant awareness that one was utterly free from sin in God's sight was, in their view, to relieve the believer of all feelings of guilt regarding his or her inability to fulfill the Law. The justified sinner was to have "no more accusations, terrors, and condemnings of conscience for sin."[74] Where they saw puritan laypeople cowering in fear for the sake of sins both past and future, the Eatonists held out a glorious freedom from the devastating doubts that too often crippled the godly. The justified went about their business in "a fullnesse of faith, nothing fearing at all any thing that goes about to make us afraid, molest, make us sad, or to work any trouble against us."[75] So too, Eaton strenuously denied that God punished his children for sin. The afflictions of the truly faithful were given by God as evangelical crosses, to try and exercise faith, "not to correct and punish them for their sins."[76] Believers, then, were released from the fear that God was standing over them, waiting to smite them for every transgression. Here was a mode of religiosity that was deliberately crafted to exploit the tensions

---

73 Towne, *Assertion*, 18.

74 Eaton, *Honey-Combe*, 91.

75 Ibid., 422.

76 Ibid., 125, and more generally 120-47. This was of course a necessary corollary of the notion that God saw no sin in believers. If he could not see sin, he could hardly punish it. Nevertheless, this idea was not Eaton's alone; it had been defended, in an almost identical form, by no less a theologian than William Perkins in the late 1580s, for which see Perkins, *Estate of Grace*, 58: "afflictions to the faithfull are no punishments for sin, but only fatherly and loving chastisements." Perkins, however, went on to say that although afflictions could not be considered "punishments" for sin (this would have called God's justice into question) they could be considered as "corrections." Once again, Eaton's novelty was not so much in his specific theological arguments, but in the conclusions he teased out of those arguments, and most of all, in his tendency to use the theological weaponry of puritanism against itself.

and fault lines within mainstream puritan divinity, to reach out to those who might feel less than comforted by the not-always soothing tones of normative puritanism.

As Bozeman has shown, this assuring and comforting doctrine was based upon a subtle but profound reevaluation of the nature of God himself.[77] Where mainstream puritans imagined a sometimes severe judge, who looked after and corrected the sins of even his most beloved saints, the Eatonists posited a kinder and more loving Father, a God who reveled in joy rather than doleful suffering: "God loveth not heavinesse and dulnesse of spirit, he hateth uncomfor[t]able doctrine, heavie and sorrowfull cogitations, and loveth cheerfull hearts: for therefore he sent his Sonne, not to opprese us with heaviness and sorrow; but to cheere up our soules in him."[78] Along these lines, during the private debates and conferences of 1628-31, London antinomians had attacked their godly counterparts for "attributing too much to" repentance.[79] This represented a fundamental critique of mainstream puritan divinity, which as we have seen, envisioned repentance as an ongoing process that the truly justified saint underwent throughout his or her life. For each new transgression, the godly were to meditate upon, confess, and repent of their sins in lowly submission to their divine father, which in turn was to provide them with consolation and assurance that God had indeed forgiven them. On the account of the Eatonists this was to nullify the overwhelming power of Christ's sacrifice (which alone could provide genuine consolation), and even worse, to drag people into a morass of misery and hand-wringing that was utterly at odds with the joyful proclamation of the Gospel.

This brings us to the heart of the Eatonist critique of puritan legalism. It is not that Eatonists objected to good works, or even to works of the Law (provided that these works were not done fearfully or slavishly). Rather, they objected to the manner and style with which the godly had so vehemently promoted good works and denounced sin, to the psychological effects that attended puritan obedience, and to the implicit vision of the deity that underlay godly religiosity. Normative puritanism turned God into a petty tyrant who gloried in the agony of his saints. It turned the good news of the Gospel into a sour and soul-curdling message of fear and bondage. As Towne explained, far from driving believers to despair, Christ's sacrifice should liberate them from the mental torments of Law and sin:

---

77 Bozeman, "Glory of the 'Third Time,'" 645-46.

78 Eaton, *Honey-Combe*, 449.

79 Towne, *Assertion*, 116, implied as much when he chastised his opponent Taylor for accusing the antinomians of denying the necessity of repentance. He wrote "I cannot but thinke that because some condemned your mistake of repentance, and attributing too much to it, that therefore you conclude, that they denie the use of true Repentance."

> whosoever receiveth [true Christian liberty] he doth finde experimentally, that he is set free indeed . . . in conscience he is discharged of his debt and burden; rid of his feares, and delivered from the power and condemnation of the Law, from the wrath of God, and out of the hands of all his enemies, in his condition, he is secure and at rest; in his calling free from distrustfull, and distracting, and heart-eating thoughts and cares; in his affections, he is sweetly seasoned and enclined to love God and man, and to testify the same in the joyfull running in the wayes of the Law.[80]

The fundamental change proposed by the Eatonists was not, as Towne's words illustrate, an alteration in the nature of obedience itself, but a change in the feeling, the affect, the general psychological orientation from which that obedience flowed.[81] It was not, by and large, a change in what people would do, but how they would feel, not just about their own works, but about God himself. Here, then, was the sweet honeycomb of free justification.

Christ, Faith and Grace

Towne's words likewise serve to reveal the enormous, even inordinate, weight that Christ's life and death bore within the Eatonist system of divinity. Just as their religiosity implied a novel and rather rosy estimation of God's disposition, so too it came to rely on an unusually robust conception of the all-powerful sacrifice of Christ. Believers could trust so fully, so joyfully, in the efficacy of Christ's work because Christ had already accomplished their salvation, and hence their justification, with his death on the cross. Justification was thus viewed as a past event, which had already taken place, and which needed only to be apprehended by faith. The idea that justification was already complete in Christ's sacrifice had been laid out in an inchoate manner in Eaton's writings. He claimed that Christ's sacrifice blotted out

> all sin, as sins of commission, and sins of omission; actuall sins, and originall sins; all are done away: For, because originall sin is worse and more horrible than any actuall sin; because it is the spring and fountaine of all other sins: therefore hath God so ordained, that no man shall come to salvation, unlesse hee bee pure and cleane from this sinne. . . . The author and cause of all which, is this grace of Justification; by which alone this originall sin is done away, and we made clean and acceptable before God. . . . Which Christ ac-

---

[80] Ibid., 127.

[81] See Bozeman, "Glory of the 'Third Time,'" 646, who correctly argues that Eaton's honeyed religiosity implied a dramatic change in "the affective charge of English religion."

tually fulfilled, when bleeding out his blood and life upon the Crosse, he cryed out, *it is finished, or perfected, John* 19.30.[82]

In a manner not entirely consistent with mainstream puritanism, Eaton likewise suggested that these benefits were conferred upon the elect not when they *believed*, but when they were *baptized.* The actual work of God in clothing our souls and bodies with the wedding garment took place in baptism, "whereby the inward washing and making cleane, which is wrought by the blood of Christ is given, ratified, and sealed to him that is baptized, if afterwards being come to yeeres, his unbeliefe do not seclude him from the benefit."[83] For Eaton, the fact that the grace of justification was given to us as newborns, when we were "utterly helplesse in our selves," was further proof, "that all this blessednesse may be the more freely upon us."[84] These ideas appear to have been quickly adopted and elaborated by Eaton's followers. Thus, Robert Towne suggested more explicitly that justification and salvation were already complete in Christ, and that both baptism and faith were merely the subsequent "sealing" and personal "revelation" of a preexistent fact:

> all the Elect are saved in Christ, and ordinarily have it exhibited and sealed in Baptisme, where they receive the kingdome of Heaven, as little children do their Fathers inheritance passively. For that Ordinance, is a true, spirituall, and reall ingrafting of them into Christ, I *Cor.* 12. 13. So that Faith is but the revelation of what was secret, and hid before, or an evident testimony, and lively and comfortable apprehension and application in the conscience of the person, of what was conferred and made his before. So that Faith works onely a change as touching the conscience, whilest by an actuall and sensible sprinkling of this blood on the posts therof, it purgeth, justifieth, and saveth, it causeth light there in stead of bondage.[85]

In their efforts to transfer all saving merit from human beings to Christ, the antinomians thus from a certain perspective devalued faith itself, emptying it of its instrumentality. Faith, on this view, did not really justify; rather, it recognized or apprehended a prior justification which had already been effected by Christ's death.

---

[82] Eaton, *Honey-Combe*, 27.

[83] Ibid., 30-31. See also ibid., 185-90.

[84] Eaton, *Dead Faith*, 119-21.

[85] Towne, *Assertion*, 11-12. Eaton too, at one point, argued that "God in baptisme gave unto us his Sonne in the likenesse of water, signifying that Jesus is no Jesus unto us, but as he hath first and before all things with his blood washed away out of the sight of God all our sins," strongly suggesting that the work of justification was complete not only when Christ died, but before "all things," or from eternity (Eaton, *Honey-Combe*, 185).

This idea had apparently become common currency among London antinomians by the late 1620s. Thus, in 1629, Peter Shaw would be accused of holding "That faith doth not save nor damne; justifie nor unjustifie," while in the 1630s John Crandon encountered antinomians in Somerset who allegedly "disrelished altogether that phrase of Justification by Faith, as attributing somewhat to man; and would that all shou'd rather say that we are Justified by Grace, or by Christ or by being found in Christ, or by our union unto Christ, that the praise of our Justification might be reserved whole and entire to the Grace of God in Christ alone."[86] So, too, the Ipswich lay antinomians Henry Firmin, Henry Mudd, and Francis Bridges, at least one of whom was very certainly influenced by John Eaton, were accused in 1631 of having disseminated the claim "that all the Elect were justified and made the sonnes of God by the work of Christ, before they have any faith to beleeve it."[87] When confronted with this charge in the High Commission, they equivocated, saying "they are justifyed actually by faith, but that before faith they are loved of God, and that whatsoever is wantinge in the beleiver is supplyed by Christ Jesus." When pressed on the issue, they furnished an answer redolent of both Eaton and Towne: "as Adam made all men corrupt, soe Christ maketh the elect righteous and acceptable: and you [i.e., the High Commissioners] agree with us in baptisme. Infants are regenerate, therefore they are justifyed, and that is by faith. There is grace though not seene."[88] In 1631, reporting on his debates with London antinomians, Thomas Taylor likewise denounced what he called that "mysticall and spirituall (but fantastical union of theirs) with Christ *before* faith."[89]

---

[86] D. Como and P. Lake, "Puritans, Antinomians and Laudians in Caroline London: The Strange Case of Peter Shaw in its Contexts," *Journal of Ecclesiastical History*, 50 (1999). For Crandon's comments, which were written in 1654, but which referred to events that had occurred "About twenty years since," that is c. 1634, see J. Crandon, *Mr. Baxters Aphorisms Exorized and Anthorized* (1654), 264-66 (I would like to thank Michael Winship for generously alerting me to the existence of this crucial document); in his debates with Gloucestershire puritans in the 1630s, John Traske had probably had something similar in mind when he allegedly argued that faith brought believers into the "joyfull condition" of the "Kingdom of Christ," "yet not as faith is a condition of the Covenant, or an instrument of Justification laying hold on Christ, but only as a qualification in themselves" (Edward Norice, *The New Gospel, Not the True Gospel* (1638), 2). See below, Chapter Nine, for a discussion of this aspect of Traske's later theology.

[87] CUL MS. Dd. ii. 21, fols. 77v-78r. See Chapter Nine for Eaton's influence on Firmin.

[88] Gardiner, *High Commission*, 270-71.

[89] Taylor, *Regula vitae*, 124. The italics are Taylor's.

Indeed, in some cases, those influenced by Eaton appear to have taken this argument to its logical conclusion, arguing that the elect were in fact justified *from eternity*. Thus, in 1644, the London lay presbyterian Thomas Bakewell recalled that during London's antinomian conflicts of 1628-31, he had privately debated opponents who defended precisely this proposition, both in conference and manuscript: "But these builders [the antinomians] have been employed in repairing this old heresie these fourteen years [that is, since 1630], to my knowledg, for then some of these held, that a man is actually in the favour of God, reconciled in Christ, justified, sanctified, called and adopted, all this actually in election, such were *Paul* and *Manasses* before conversion, yea they were borne so into the world, and I have had this disputation in writing by me ever since, which I had with them, and now more enlarged."[90] Held side by side, these various pieces of evidence demonstrate that this peculiar notion—the claim that the elect were somehow joined to Christ, and hence justified, before faith—had filtered widely through antinomian circles, providing a curious dividing line between the anti-legalists and their orthodox puritan enemies.

It must be emphasized, however, that even this theological peculiarity had grown and evolved directly out of mainstream puritanism. In arguing that the elect were justified prior to faith, Eaton and his followers were seeking above all to shift complete responsibility for human salvation onto Christ. Faith, like legal holiness, could from a certain perspective be construed as a quality that inhered in humans. And since the antinomians were deeply concerned to banish any hint that intrinsic human qualities might earn salvation, it was entirely natural for them to exclude even faith itself from the process of free justification. Once again, then, this was little more than an embellishment of the utterly respectable and eminently puritan concept of justification through the alien righteousness of Christ.

In fact, the notion that the elect were justified before faith was not exclusively antinomian; it had cropped up repeatedly in the history of puritanism, and always apparently for very much the same reason—in order to eliminate any hint that faith itself might be seen as meriting or deserving salvation. Indeed, such arguments were being canvassed in Kent in the years prior to 1610, when the godly minister Thomas Wilson published an outraged dialogue exposing a group of opponents for maintaining positions that uncannily anticipated those of the Eatonists. Wilson's opponents allegedly denied "that wee should bee said to bee made righteous by faith . . . as if faith were a cause of our righteousnesse." Rather, they argued, "the Elect are imputed righteous,

---

[90] T. Bakewell, *A Faithfull Messenger Sent after the Antinomians* (1644), 1. Eaton may indeed have taught something similar, although he did not say so explicitly in his works.

and so accounted of God even from everlasting"; faith, they claimed, was merely the apprehension of that eternal justification: "Christ is mine and I have benefit of his death before faith, but I know not so much till I beleeve."[91] Nor was the idea confined to a small band of Kentish eccentrics. In 1614, a Somerset man named John Otteyes had been presented to the church courts for haunting alehouses, denigrating the Book of Common Prayer, and holding "that children are justifyed before they are borne."[92] Meanwhile, in 1623, the puritan elder statesman Ezekiel Culverwell complained that "I see some honestly minded, to imagine that a man may be a true member of Christ, and so be justified, before he thus actually beleeve, and thereby apprehend Christ."[93] All signs indicate that the people here discussed were in some sense members of the godly community—Wilson's chief opponent seems to have been a separatist, Otteyes had been in trouble for attacking the Book of Common Prayer, while Culverwell considered such people to be "honest minded" (almost certainly a coded reference to their puritanism). In short, the notion that the elect were justified before faith appears to have spread with some speed and breadth within the puritan community many years before the idea came to be associated with antinomianism proper.

---

[91] T. Wilson, *A Dialogue About Justification by Faith: Wherein the nature and office, the property and power of Faith is Plainely taught, against such as deny the certainety or particularity and powerfulnesse of Faith* (1610), 98, 102, 131, and passim. The circumstances that led to the publication of this dialogue may be gathered from Wilson's prefatory epistle "To the Christian Reader": "this *Dialogue* differeth from others, because the most part of it was (*res gesta)* a thing truely done, namely so much as concernes the nature and office of faith resisted by a deceived spirit, (or rather spirits, for they were sundry) under the person of *Philautus*: whose shifts and evasions to the Arguments brought against him, as also the objections in favour of their execrable unheard of errour, or errors rather, are here truly set downe without any falsification, and orderly without confusion, as neere as such confused stuffe could be reduced to Order."

[92] Somerset Record Office, D/D/CA 189, fol. 175r, 12 Dec. 1614. Otteyes was presented for haunting alehouses and "uppon a comon fame That hee did wishe the common prayer out of his booke, and that he saith that children are justifyed before they are borne, wheare they shalbe saved or damned. And farther hee said, I know aswell as wheare I stand that I shall be saved." He does not appear to have answered the latter charge, claiming in his defence only that "hee having a bible in which booke was also the booke of common prayer, hee wished that the common prayer were out of his bible, that the booke might be lesser, protesting that hee spake it not of anie contempte or dislike thereof."

[93] Ezekiel Culverwell, *A Treatise of Faith: Wherein is declared how a man may live by Faith, and find releefe in all his necessaries. Applied especially unto the use of the weakest Christians* (1623), 16-17.

This digression into the origins and history of a peculiar and seemingly arcane theological concept is not purely academic. The point, ultimately, is that the Eatonists were here borrowing a concept, a theological motif, that had been generated from within puritanism itself. As in so much else, they were not so much inventing a theology *ex nihilo*, nor departing from an English reformed tradition, as they were appropriating pieces of that tradition, rearranging them, and deploying them in a novel and distinctive manner.

To illustrate this point, we need to look at one final piece of evidence. In 1626, the Newcastle puritan Robert Jenison wrote to his old tutor Samuel Ward, asking for his opinions on certain theological positions that had been adopted by one "Mr. Rothwel" of Mansfield in Nottinghamshire. Rothwel had publicly defended the position that

> *The Elect have the spirit of adoption before their conversion*; this is said generally of all the elect, who hee sayth, are justified, sanctified and in the womb./ his cheife ground is god is inscrutable, Jehovah, and all things are done with god from eternity, the elect in Christ from eternity given to christ and received into Covenants with god christ being a lambe slaine from the beginning of the world. Whom god loves once hee loves ever; nowe loving his elect from eternity, they never were truely under his wrath, but onely in their owne apprehension and conceit, or others, but were ever from eternity the children of god . . . seing there is no change with god, and all things were done with god from eternity. when fayth comes, it (being not a condition) doth onely make manifest gods worke from eternity.

This was a position in almost every respect indistinguishable from those described above: the elect were justified from eternity; they had been united with Christ from before the beginning of time; their faith was merely the apprehension of an eternal truth that had hitherto remained hidden from their eyes. Crucially, Rothwel also maintained that faith was not a "condition," that is, that faith was not a condition of the covenant of grace, in return for which God granted grace to sinners.

Nor were these the only peculiar positions defended by Rothwel. He had likewise asserted that "*It cannot properly be said that god doth afflict his children for sinne,* (but onely by occasion of it)." In support of this claim, Rothwel argued that because God was immovable and unchanging, it was wrong to say that he was moved by the sins of his children to punish them; instead, since the elect were loved by God from eternity (and were indeed justified in Christ from eternity) he afflicted them not for sin, but out of his eternal love.[94] The nonconformist Jenison was confused by Rothwel, whose ideas

---

[94] Bodleian Library, Tanner MS. 72, fol. 129r. Jenison abbreviated several words. I have attempted to fill in the gaps in the text where noted. The reasons are as follows:

struck him as puzzling, perhaps even vaguely unorthodox. Nevertheless, Jenison admitted that he was "otherwise a good scholler," that is, a respectable divine, and he accordingly asked his former teacher Ward for a written judgment on the opinions in question. In fact, to identify Rothwel merely as a "good scholar" was something of an understatement. The man in question was Richard Rothwel, an ancient nonconformist and noted godly preacher who had earned the nickname "the Apostle of the North" for his prodigious evangelical accomplishments during the reigns of Elizabeth and James I. Rothwel, who was over sixty years old when Jenison wrote to Ward, was no unlearned upstart. He was an aged scion of the English godly community, whose life would eventually be immortalized alongside William Gouge, William Bradshaw, and other luminaries by the puritan biographer, Samuel Clarke.[95]

Nevertheless, Rothwel was here defending two positions—that the elect were justified from eternity, and that God did not afflict his children for sin—which two or three years later would surely have been denounced as "antinomian." In the years following 1626, the escalating polemical confrontations between antinomians and their godly enemies sculpted a series of stereotyped polemical positions whereby opponents could identify one another as friend or foe. By 1630 or so, anyone publicly broaching either of the opinions defended here by Rothwel would have come under immediate suspicion for antinomianism.[96] In 1626, however, the opinions in question had not yet been labeled or sharply delineated through such a process of continual debate and conflict. They remained theological curiosities. Hence, although Rothwel's conceits

---

"1 because he is Jehovah, in whom all things move &c and therefore hee is not moved of any other being immovable and g[od?] not of sinne

2 it wil not stand with his glory to afflict his children for sinne he doing all to his glory, even in this kind Joh: 9, 1, 2, &c.

3 hee afflicts man in Love, &c. 4 wh[osoever?] he inflicteth for sinne, he doth it in wrath."

[95] For details on Rothwel's life, see S. Clarke, *The Lives of Thirty-two English Divines* (1677), 67-74.

[96] See, for instance, Joseph Bentham, *The Societie of the Saints* (1630), 182-83, who attacked those he called "equivocating Pretteians," and "*Antinomists*" (referring no doubt to the minister Samuel Prettie). Chief among the "points which you deny" Bentham specifically identified the notions "that God doth afflict his Children for their sinnes, that sorrow for sinne is necessary to the regenerate." Meanwhile the Ipswich antinomians Bridges, Firmin, and Mudd would be prosecuted in High Commission not only for maintaining "that all the Elect were justified and made the sonnes of God by the work of Christ, before they have any faith to beleeve it," but also for the opinion "that God doth chastise noe justified person for sinne." See CUL MS. Dd. ii. 21, fols. 77v-78r.

seemed faintly erroneous, Jenison was unsure what to make of them. This, combined with what was almost certainly deference for the elder man's reputation, led him to seek the advice of his teacher Ward. Nor was Jenison the only respectable puritan curious about Rothwel's opinions: upon Rothwel's death in 1627, the controversial Lincolnshire minister John Cotton secured as many of Rothwel's papers as possible with a view toward publishing them (and here, the reader should keep in mind that Cotton's own mature opinions, which in some respects resembled those maintained by the likes of Eaton and Towne, would come under considerable scrutiny during Massachusetts's Antinomian Controversy in 1636).[97]

Indeed, this story may be taken as representative of Eatonist theology as a whole. As with the case of Jenison, there were few statements made by the Eatonists that cannot be found duplicated elsewhere, at some point, and under some other circumstances by impeccably respectable English godly sources. It was not the matter of Eatonist thought which made it so controversial; rather, it was the arrangement of the matter, the subtle shifts in meaning, and most of all, the uses to which the Eatonists put their newly constructed system that separated them from their puritan opponents.

This was true not just of abstract, formal theological concepts. It was also true of less rarefied motifs of practical divinity. In almost every way, the Eatonists adopted ideas that were at or near the heart of puritan practical divinity. Hence, they borrowed the time-honored pastoral tropes of "means of grace," "growth in grace," and "degrees of grace." As argued in Chapter Four, these motifs were closely related aspects of puritan practical divinity. Godly preachers urged the saints assiduously to apply the means in order to engage their listeners in a progressive process of spiritual growth. According to this view, the godly applied the means, God granted them grace through these means, which then in turn led them to apply the means ever more diligently, in an unceasing process of growth in faith, holiness, and assurance. This process was never completed on earth: even in those who had grown to a prodigious spiritual stature, faith, sanctity, and assurance remained imperfect and incomplete until perfected in the next life (leaving room, as we have seen, for the inevitable doubts and failings experienced by the godly in this life). Nevertheless, this process of slow, incremental spiritual growth may be seen as the basic structure of the godly life as laid out by mainstream puritan divines in the late six-

---

[97] This anecdote was retold by Rothwel's disciple, Stanley Gower, who claimed to have furnished Cotton with the desired manuscripts, most of which were in shorthand. Gower believed that the difficulty in deciphering this shorthand was responsible for the fact that Rothwel's works remained unpublished. See Clarke, *The Lives of Thirty-two English Divines*, 69.

teenth and early seventeenth centuries. The Eatonists borrowed this basic paradigm, but altered details in small and ultimately significant ways.

Thus, Eaton accepted the notion that there were multiple degrees of faith. Moreover, he conceded that only through the use of certain means could the godly climb the ladder to higher degrees: "our faith being weake, gives at the first but weake assurance, and is greater or lesser; sometimes (as I said before) hath a full, and sometimes a wane; but by daily fervent prayer, giving to Christ this glory of his wedding garment, it growes stronger and stronger, to a plerophory and full assurance unto joy unspeakable and glorious."[98] Here we see a structure that aped that of normative puritan divinity. In crucial ways, however, Eaton and his followers attached a subtly transformed flesh to the bare skeleton of puritan pastoral divinity. In a manner of expression not normally adopted by the godly, Eaton thus strongly suggested that the saints could reach a "plerophory" of "full assurance" in this life. Here, again, we see the Eatonists promising a joy, a fullness, that mainstream puritanism could not offer, exploiting the potential weaknesses in the edifice of godly divinity. Where the godly held out a painful, scrupulous, and unceasing process of faith, tempered by doubt, and answered with more faith, Eaton seduced the casualties of puritan divinity with a vision of absolute assurance.

He could do so because, as we have seen, the Eatonists argued that everything necessary for salvation had already been accomplished. Accordingly, the primary "means" was to pray and meditate upon the power of free justification, so "that our will and affections may be ravished and carried after the goodness and excellency of the benefit; this being the right true meanes, both of begetting and encreasing true faith, and of going with a right foot to the truth of the Gospel."[99] This, too, violated the traditional puritan understanding of the means of grace. For the godly, all the ordinances of God could serve as means. This included preaching, public worship and the sacraments, as well as more informal, private devotions such as reading, fasting, conference, and mutual communion with other saints. It was precisely a reliance upon such "duties" that Eaton and his followers sought to undermine. Eaton was seeking to turn all attention away from these ordinances, to focus it once again on what he saw as the object of all ordinances—free justification in Christ. The godly charged that this was to ignore the ordinary, quotidian means through which God dispensed his grace, and to fall back upon the "ravished," immediate (and ultimately illusory) revelations of the spirit. Such an illuminism in their view violated the commandment of God to his saints to work out their salvation in fear and trembling.

---

[98] Eaton, *Honey-Combe*, 155.

[99] Ibid., sig. Br.

Against this accusation, Towne responded by claiming that assurance did not come like a searing blue bolt from heaven, laying waste to all doubt in an instant of spiritual revelation. Instead, he reiterated the Eatonist commitment to a particular version of the concepts of "means of grace" and "growth in grace." Faith did indeed grow incrementally in accordance with the use of certain ordinances. As he explained, "Faith be most diligent in the means of Faith, to receive a daily increase, whereby the heart and spirits be inlightened and inlarged to a more cleare discovery and view, and to a more effectuall and full apprehension."[100] Like the godly, then, Towne claimed that he and his comrades affirmed the notion that "we are called upon to work [our salvation] out, which is carefully to attend upon the Ministery of this Reconciliation." Nevertheless, it should be clear that even here, Towne was creating a distinction between himself and his godly opponents. Where the godly tended to speak of "means of grace," Towne and Eaton wrote of "means of faith." And as we have already seen, for the Eatonists, "faith" was nothing more than the revelation of a hidden fact that had already been accomplished. Towne explained this at greater length:

> Salvation is but one, and in essence indivisible: though Christ hath saved his people, yet is this treasure hid, till God reveale his Sonne in us. *Gal.* I. 16. And make knowne the unsearchable treasures of his grace in him by the Gospel, through the Spirit of Illumination and Faith . . . yea because our sight and strength spiritual as well as naturall of the body admitteth of degrees, we are exhorted daily to edifie ourselves in our holy faith, to grow up in the knowledge and grace of our Lord Jesus Christ: yet all this is but diligence in the means of breeding and nourishing faith, which is the only necessarie work to compasse and lay hold of salvation. Yea and whilest both Pastor and people be thus diligent in the meanes what ever good is wrought thereby is onely ascribed to God. he worketh both the will and the deed, we do what is in the power and reach of Nature; but what ever is spirituall, and any whit available to apprehend salvation that God worketh in us.[101]

For Towne as for Eaton, then, the point of all means was to increase faith, faith in the all-sufficient, and all-powerful work of Christ, which had already saved the elect. Faith was but an awakening, a realization of a preestablished fact that had remained unknown. From this perspective, no "growth in grace"—no ascending spiral of grace, holiness, and assurance—was necessary, for God had *already* granted all the "unsearchable treasures of his grace" in Christ's death. Mainstream puritans saw the godly life as a progressive process of maturation, in which God responded to his saints' diligent use of the means by granting them further gifts of grace. From the vantage point of the

---

[100] Towne, *Assertion*, 55.
[101] Ibid., 90-91.

Eatonists, the puritan focus on such "graces" and upon the means that conveyed them debased the *true* grace of God, which had already been given, and which needed merely to be glimpsed by the eye of faith. By this means, puritan ministers became, as Eaton angrily charged, "white Devils that preach a secret Idolatry under the likenesse of the true Ministers of the Gospel; and for darkning and giving a *Judas his kisse* to free justification . . . doe stand *ipso facto* accursed of God, and excommunicated by Saint *Paul*, though in all other gifts (and as they say graces) they bee like *Angels from heaven.*"[102]

So, too, the Eatonists claimed for themselves the imprimatur of predestinarian purity: as Towne's comments suggest, the Eatonists adopted an ultra-predestinarian, ultra-providentialist self-image, which they contrasted unfavorably with the crypto-Pelagianism of the godly. When Towne argued that "this inlightening, or perfection of faith . . . is Gods act," or when he declared that "in the use of the meanes we are agents; but in respect of successe onely patients," he was implicitly suggesting that his godly opponents believed the opposite—that is, that the means were efficacious in themselves, and that humans played a part in working their own faith.[103] Towne and the other Eatonists were thus claiming for themselves a place in a lineage of extreme providentialism that stretched from Augustine, to Bradwardine, to Luther, to Calvin, to Eaton, a providentialism that had always been explicitly informed by anti-Pelagianism. As Towne neatly summed up this worldview, "all action," whether of believers or unbelievers, "hath God for the Author in whom all live and move."[104] It is crucial to recognize that in adopting this pose, the antinomians were once again seeking to present themselves as more purely reformed than their godly enemies. Thus, the Eatonists were able to submit themselves as the true heirs of predestinarian Protestantism at a time when the Arminian Richard Montagu had turned the question of works, grace, freewill and predestination into a cause célèbre within the English church.

All of this more than vindicates Professor Bozeman's claim that John Eaton's antinomianism was at one level rabidly "contra-puritan." Nevertheless, in the preceding pages we have likewise seen the extent to which the Eatonists had borrowed or even hijacked the artillery of puritan practical divinity: beginning with the formal truths of protestant divinity, and proceeding on through ubiquitous godly tropes such as the means of grace, growth in grace, "experimental knowledge," and the "dead faith," Eaton and his followers borrowed rhetorical strategies that were at the heart of mainstream godly divinity. So too, in their emphatic assertion of the all-sufficiency of Christ's sacrifice, the fullness of grace and assurance, and their extreme providentialism,

---

102 Eaton, *Dead Faith*, 33.
103 Towne, *Assertion*, 55.
104 Ibid., 71.

Eatonists presented themselves as more uncompromisingly "puritan" than the puritans themselves.[105] In short, they had systematically stolen the materials of puritan orthodoxy, in the process turning them inside out, and turning them against the godly themselves.

Eatonists and the Law

We should not of course accept the attempts of the Eatonists to portray themselves as honest protestant renovationists, who sought merely to turn the church back to its Reformation roots. They were doing much more than trying piously to refocus attention on Christ, and to deflate the legalistic disciplines of contemporary puritan piety. The remainder of this chapter seeks to establish how and in what sense the Eatonists actually were, as their opponents charged, "antinomians"; and in the process, to penetrate still further the struggle between Eatonists and mainstream puritans.

As noted, the cornerstone of John Eaton's theology was his contention that the imputation of Christ's perfect righteousness freed believers from sin in God's sight. On Eaton's view, it was absurd to claim that believers could be both perfect and imperfect before God. The faithful were thus perfect before God. This meant, in short, that God no longer viewed believers as subject to the Law of Moses. In his pastoral letter of 1631, John Eachard succinctly reminded his coreligionists of the "two grounds," or doctrinal pillars, of their faith: "First that God doth not behold . . . children under the law, but under grace. . . . Secondly that God doth behold men in Adam or in Christ for once darknes, but now light in the Lord, once the children of wrath, now sons and heires risen with Christ, and sit with him in heavenly places." To deny these truths was "to deny the first and second part of free justificacion, and to say namely that Christ hath not loved us, nor washed us from our sins before his heavenly Father . . . that his righteousnes hath not covered us, and made us kings and Priests unto his Father."[106] Eachard here reiterated the persistent Eatonist claim that if one accepted the doctrine of the imputation of Christ's righteousness, one must necessarily accept the corollary that the just were free from the Law and sin in God's sight. Humans were either out of Christ or in Christ, completely sinful or perfectly righteous before God. They were either under the Law, or completely free from the Law.

---

[105] William Stoever similarly concludes that New England's antinomians were able to present themselves as more purely reformed than their mainstream opponents. See *A Faire and Easie Way to Heaven*, passim.
[106] Appendix E.

This bit of logic, with its totalizing, binary character, was not of course self-evident.[107] It was a logic that ignored the messy contradictions of the Gospels and the Pauline epistles, texts that by virtue of their very multivocality on the subject of the Law tended to speak against this sort of absolutist pronouncement. Thus, when opponents charged that Eaton's claims ignored those passages from the New Testament in which Christ chastised his disciples for their sins and unbelief, Eaton responded by conveniently arguing that these statements belonged to a "middle," mixed period between the Law and the Gospel, and that they therefore had nothing to do with believers in the glorious, "third time" of the Gospel, which had commenced only upon Christ's death.[108] So, too, he managed to ignore all of Saint Paul's many behavioral injunctions, thereby exiling "Paul the moralist" from the field of true religion, and privileging all that was anti-legal in the New Testament. It was this intellectual move, this totalizing, binary logic—in which a critique of puritan legalism mutated into a denial of all Law—which more than anything else, defined them as "antinomians." Moreover, where the Eatonists maintained a distinction between sinlessness in fact, and sinlessness in the sight of God, no such distinction could be maintained with respect to the Law. Believers could not be under the Law in their own apprehension, but free from it in God's sight; thus, the fact that God no longer beheld them under the Law meant that they were objectively free from the Law. As Robert Towne suggested, the faithful were liberated "from the whole governement of Moses," both ceremonial and moral.[109]

---

[107] It would have been possible, for instance, to have launched a critique of puritan "legalism," based upon a conventional, protestant formulation of imputation, which nevertheless made no claims whatsoever about the continuing hold of the Moral Law upon believers. This appears to have been what John Cotton, for example, was doing in Boston in the mid-1630s. By that time, however, any attempt at formulating an "anti-legal" critique was greeted as tantamount to antinomianism.

[108] Eaton, *Honey-Combe*, 102-6 and especially 103-4. The invention of this middle phase, the "time of John the Baptist," appears to have served no other purpose in Eaton's system than to explain such passages. In this manner, the many warnings of John the Baptist to repent for sin, as well as Jesus' many behavioral prohibitions and injunctions, could be explained away as commandments that were not actually part of the Law. They laid open sin without threatening punishment, and were thus not, strictly speaking, part of the "First Time" of the Law. By the same token, however, this middle period had not yet reached the fullness of glory that would come with Christ's death, when sin would be utterly wiped away by his sacrifice.

[109] Towne, *Assertion*, 139.

But what did Eaton, Towne and others mean when they pronounced believers free from the Law and sin? Certainly, they did not deny that the Law had its uses. As we have seen, the Law was to be preached universally in order to bring the unconverted to a true sight of their sins, to hold forth the judgment that awaited those who disobeyed God, and to force miserable sinners to turn to Christ. They even admitted that the Law continued to have a use for believers, although that use was primarily negative: as Towne put it, the Law "keeps [believers] close in spirit and conscience through faith unto Christs righteousnesse, and makes them to live in a continuall forsaking of themselves, and in a neglect, base esteeme, and abhorring of their own vertues."[110] It served, in short, to remind them how lucky they were to be free of it. So, too, as Bozeman has pointed out, Eaton never suggested that believers would violate the precepts of the Law; rather, even as they were freed from it, they would—in an almost involuntarily manner—walk cheerfully according to God's commandments.[111]

In the same manner, the Eatonists admitted that believers would "fall sometimes into sinnes."[112] Justification, as we have seen, was to "Godward." Sanctification, the process whereby believers were purged of sin "to manward," was a lifelong process that was not completed until death.[113] Thus, the church of true believers "hath some sin in the imperfections of her Sanctification that the Devill seeth; and every one of us in our consciences doe feele it: but God sees none; for by reason of Christ, with whom shee is cloathed, shee is all faire, without spot or wrinkle."[114] In fact, Eaton held that it was the dissonance between these two contradictory realities that left room for faith. The justified were utterly aware of the sin which remained in them; this meant that the abolishing of their sins in God's sight seemed like a distant, implausible fairy tale; yet it was this very contradiction, this seemingly irrational paradox, that meant that sinners had to trust unconditionally the truth vouchsafed by God's word, a word which told them that they were in fact clothed with the perfect righteousness of Christ: "If wee had no sin in us, and if we did see, and feel no sin in us, what place were there left for faith to beleeve these sayings of God, that wee have no sin in the sight of God? but now because wee have sin in us, and do see it, and feele it; therefore should wee so much the rather upon these sayings of God, beleeve the cleane contrary to our sense and feeling, that wee have no sin in the sight of God."[115]

---

110 Ibid., 37.

111 Bozeman, "'Third Time,'" 647-50.

112 Eaton, *Honey-Combe*, 450.

113 On this point, see ibid., 50-51. See also Eachard's comment that mortification was "to manward," Appendix E, below. See also Towne, *Assertion*, 92.

114 Eaton, *Honey-Combe*, 38-39.

115 Ibid., 50, 25-26.

If the Law retained uses for believers, and if believers continued to sin in this life, wherein rested their freedom? Certainly, this freedom was at one level a matter of emotional or psychological orientation. Believers would experience "sadness and sorrow" for their sins, but the awareness of their perfection in the sight of God would ultimately dissolve this distress, leading them to a sense of "safety" and comfort: "Joy in the Lord ought alwayes to have the first place with us, and farre to overcome the sorrow and sadnesse that commeth by reason of our sinnes."[116] Contrasting their teachings against those of mainstream puritans, the Eatonists thus suggested that believers were not to flagellate themselves for their occasional breaches of the Law; in fact, the sins of believers, like the Law itself, would ultimately remind the faithful of their perfection in God's sight, thus serving to bring them not sorrow but joy.

For these lucky few, it was as if a suffocating weight had been lifted from their souls. They experienced a sense of palpable relief, of liberation, and freedom not so much from good works, but from despair. Nevertheless, the apprehension of free justification did more than simply change a believer's psychological state. It had profound effects on the believer's outward carriage. As Eaton explained

> Now because this free justification, or the having on this wedding garment, cannot be beleeved and enjoyed by this justifying faith, but by looking into the gaping wounds of Christ, bleeding out his blood and life to effect this free justification upon the beleever. Therefore onely this justifying faith smites the heart of the beleever with the true love of Christ and of God in Christ, which reflecteth back from God generally upon all men, as they bear the image of God, yet resteth principally upon the Church and houshold of faith, and maketh the true beleevers to abound in every good work, *doing good unto all men, but especially unto the houshold of faith*, Gal. 6. 10. and that not of constraint, corruptly and hypocritically; but cheerfully, sincerely, and joyfully: because both Christ and *the Kingdome of God*, and the Kingdome of heaven by this true, lively, justifying faith *is within us, Luke* 17. 21. Into which Kingdome of heaven *no uncleane thing can enter, Rev.* 21. 27. Because this Kingdome of heaven *is righteousnesse, and peace, and joy in the holy Ghost,* Rom. 14. 17. And the more this faith of free Justification, and of having on this wedding garment, encreaseth; the more this peace and joy in the holy Ghost encreaseth. For the which it is called *the garment of joy and gladnesse, Esa.* 61. 3. And the more this peace and joy encreaseth, the more the foresaid love encreaseth, and enflameth the heart to walk freely, cheerfully, and zealously in all Gods will and commandements declaratively to manward, and to doe our vocations, and all good workes freely, of meere

[116] Ibid., 450.

love, without hope of reward or fear of punishment, which is true sanctification.[117]

So, then, free justification led believers inexorably to do good works, indeed, to obey God's commandments, although freely and without coercion. Indeed, to judge from the pre-civil war Eatonist writings, it would appear that the life of a "freely justified" person would be virtually identical to the life prescribed by mainstream puritan preachers. He or she would obey God's commandments—including, presumably, the fourth commandment to observe the Sabbath—and engage in all thc activities generally assumed to constitute godliness.[118] What had changed was not the substance of the godly life, but the impulse—the emotional and psychological orientation—that informed such a person's righteous works and obedience. This was not the extorted, slavish obedience of the godly, who acted not out of love for God, but out of fear for their own souls; rather it was the cheerful, unforced obedience of someone who had willingly internalized the Law itself. No longer a whip of external compulsion, God's Law had become a beloved, internal companion.

Here, then, we have returned to the core of the antinomians' quarrel with mainstream puritanism, the principle underlying all the heated charges of legalism. The godly had set up a Law of external compulsion, of forced obedience, which was directly at odds with the true nature of Christianity. As Towne explained, godly ministers "dare not trust a beleever to walke without his Keeper; as if he judged no otherwise of him then of a Malefactor of *Newgate*, who would run away, rob, kill, and play his former prankes, if the Gaoler or his man be not with him when he is abroad. But who cannot see that whilst you thus over-looke and restraine your Disciples by your *Moses*, that they are onely kept within compasse by the Law, but are not true keepers of it."[119]

Paradoxically, the true keepers of the Law were those who had escaped the clutches of Moses, who had, that is, been freed of the Law of Sinai. Mainstream puritans, of course, charged that in pronouncing believers free from the Law, the Eatonists were opening the door to every species of immoral behavior. When his opponent Thomas Taylor slapped him with this charge, Towne

---

117 Eaton, *Dead Faith*, 76-77.

118 Eaton is silent on the subject of the Sabbath, which would suggest that he (unlike other antinomians) continued to envision it as a crucial part of the godly life. See Chapter Nine, below, wherein evidence is adduced to suggest that Henry Firmin continued to observe the Sabbath even after he had devoted himself to Eaton's teachings. Towne, too, refrained from denigrating the Sabbath in his *Assertion*, although by the 1650s, he would follow other antinomians in claiming that the outward, literal Sabbath of mainstream puritanism was a legalistic form.

119 Towne, *Assertion*, 5.

acerbically rifled back a response that encapsulates the heart of the controversy between the two:

> the doctour takes it for granted, that if it be received and yeelded, that God seeth not (in his grosse sence) the sins of the justified, then is a wide gate opened to all *Libertinisme*, and the justified then may and will enjoy securely all licentious courses. May not any man perceive by this what little acquaintance, and experience he hath of the true nature, office, and operation of Free Justification; and that all his best works be but eye-service, like that of the unfaithfull slave, *Ephes.* 6.6. And in a word, as one wittily said, how he loveth and serveth God *wickedly*. For Faith, and Christ in the Gospel have no power with him in the soule freely, sweetly, and willingly to encline, and enlarge it both to love, and to the duties of Love commanded: but the over-looking eye, the terror of the Law of God, do keep him within compasse.[120]

Good works done out of "terror of the Law of God," out of "slavish and servile feare . . . of blowes, punishment and beating," were not good works at all.[121] The only people who could truly offer up good fruit to God were those who, through the joyous apprehension of their free justification, knew themselves to be free from sin in God's sight.

Without a law, however, how would believers know what constituted a good work? Here, the Eatonists were not entirely clear. At times, they seemed to suggest that believers continued to use God's Law as a sort of guidebook, "an eternall and inviolable Rule of Righteousnesse," which nevertheless no longer bound believers by threat of punishment.[122] In Bozeman's words, the Eatonists "would find in Scripture not . . . exacting demands designed to govern unruly old Adam but gentle invitations and admonitions that harmonised with their own abounding inner and holy desire."[123] Yet at other points, Eaton seemed to suggest that the Law of Moses was entirely unnecessary, that believers would simply act in accordance with God's commandments without any help at all from the written Law:

> this faith of free justification, and this walking in the steps of our father Abraham, causeth us infallibly to walke in the steps of the works of our father Abraham, whereby like Abraham, without the Law of the ten Commandements, we walk holily, soberly, and righteously in all Gods Commandments declaratively to manward, being zealous of good workes, Tit. 2.11, 12, 13, etc.[124]

---

120 Ibid., 105.
121 Eaton, *Honey-Combe*, 142-43.
122 Towne, *Assertion*, 6.
123 Bozeman, "Glory of the 'Third Time,'" 649.
124 Eaton, *Dead Faith*, 191-92.

This was a rather different claim, and a good deal more radical. The implication here was that believers somehow possessed God's Law within them in a way that made the external, written Law superfluous. Eaton's puritan opponent Henry Burton recognized this fact, citing this manuscript passage from Eaton's papers as indirect evidence that in Eaton's view, "faith doth by a continued and uninterrupted act inflame the heart with love to doe all workes of sanctification, and so it hath no neede of Gods word as a rule to bee guided by, but the spirit, is instead of the word."[125]

But did Eaton maintain such a position? We have already seen something similar in the writings of Traske and Hebdon, who held that the believer's body had in some sense been transformed into the Ark of the Covenant. In their case, this claim was explicitly tied into the belief that God's spirit inhabited the faithful, moving them directly to do works of the Law. On paper, Eaton tended to avoid such claims. He consistently sought to give the impression that justification was wholly imputative, that it was the consequence of the external covering of Christ, rather than any internal or inherent holiness wrought by the spirit. In keeping with both Pauline and puritan traditions, Eaton did maintain that after justification, the spirit could in some sense be said to dwell in believers.[126] Nevertheless, at no point in his corpus of writings did Eaton ever claim, as Burton charged, that believers would obey the Law without the word, by virtue of the spirit within them, a fact that Burton himself seems to have recognized. Nevertheless, the famous minister of St. Matthew

---

125 Henry Burton, *The Law and the Gospell reconciled. Or, The Evangelicall Fayth, and the Morall Law how they stand together in the state of grace* (1631), 21.

126 The notion that the spirit in some sense "dwelled" in believers was a puritan commonplace. It was based on indisputable Pauline texts. William Perkins could thus argue that "where the spirit of Christ dwelleth there must needs be faith, for Christ dwelleth in the harts of the faithfull by faith. Therefore as Rebecca, when she felt the Twins strive in hir wombe, though it pained hir, yet shee knewe, both that she had conceaved, and that the children were quicke in hir: so they who have these motions, and holy affections in them . . . may assure themselves, that the spirit of God dwelleth in them, and consequently that they have faith" (Perkins, *Estate of Grace*, 50-51). Yet it is important to understand that Perkins elsewhere explained that "*The Spirit is the gift of regeneration . . . it is a gift*: and this gift is termed by the name of the *spirit*." In other words, when he claimed that the spirit dwelled in a believer, he meant that the *gifts* of the spirit dwelled in that believer (William Perkins, *A Commentarie or Exposition, upon the five first Chapters of the Epistle to the Galatians* [1604], 411). The question was not therefore whether the spirit filled believers (Paul had said it did, after all); it was *how* it was envisioned dwelling in the believer, what effects it wrought, both psychologically and in practice. Compare Perkins's comments against those of Returne Hebdon, cited in Chapter Five, above.

Friday Street insisted that in private conversation, Eaton was far less circumspect: "comming sometimes to contest with mee, and to charge mee for preaching the dead fayth, [Eaton] himselfe did utter so much to mee by word of mouth, that after a man is once inlightened by fayth, the spirit guides him, so as he hath no need of the word, or of the Morall law for a rule to direct him."[127]

Ultimately, we cannot know whether Burton's report was accurate. Nevertheless, the crucial insight is that at certain points, Eaton's writings plausibly lent themselves to precisely such an interpretation, even if he himself did not make the implication explicit. Here, as elsewhere, what was important was not so much what Eaton, Towne and other imputative antinomians said, but what they left unsaid, or rather, what they communicated through subtle and implicit cues and hints. Thus, although their claims to perfection were openly constructed using impeccably reformed notions of imputative righteousness, the language and underlying tone of their writings often pushed believers to imagine themselves as actually and inherently perfect, an idea that was quite alien to the reformed tradition. In this vein, for instance, Eaton could write that "God doth so gloriously forgive us, that with his one offering he hath made us so perfect for ever, that he remembers our sins no more," a statement that invoked perfectionist rhetoric even as it pressed the imputative formula that "God remembers our sins no more."[128] So, too, despite their occasional suggestions that believers were to continue to make use of the Law, their deeply negative portrayal of the Decalogue—the rule of "your Moses"—in fact invited listeners to reject the Commandments more decisively. And as Burton reasonably surmised, this naturally suggested (if only implicitly) that believers were guided by some inner principle—whether the spirit, or simply the "love of Christ"—that rendered redundant Moses' draconian code of wrath and punishment. In all of these ways, the half-drawn conclusions of the Eatonists' rhetoric nudged followers in directions that subtly eroded their claims to be innocently retracing the footsteps of the sanctified giants of protestant history. It should come as no surprise, then, that many antinomians would come to articulate more fully the half-formed perfectionist and spiritist implications of Eatonist theology. Pushing this process along, however, were a series of antinomian teachers who were themselves overtly committed to explicitly perfectionist modes of religiosity. This perfectionist strain, which hearkened not so much to Luther and Calvin as to traditions of medieval, Hermetic, or Familist mysticism, shall be the subject of the following chapters.

---

127 Burton, *Law and the Gospell*, 21-22.

128 Eaton, *Honey-Combe*, 155.

CHAPTER 7

The Throne of Solomon: John Everarde and the "Perfectionist" Strain of English Antinomianism

The following chapter deals with one of the most significant of these "perfectionist" teachers, John Everarde, sometime lecturer at St. Martin's-in-the-Fields and Kensington in London. In 1653, Everarde's disciple Rapha Harford published a collection of Everarde's sermons, all of which appear to have been preached between 1625 and 1636.[1] Together, these sermons provide the most coherent surviving statement of this secondary antinomian tradition. As we shall see, Everarde's theology duplicated certain aspects of the imputative strain of antinomianism, even as it decisively departed from it in other ways.

John Everarde was surely one of the most original and unorthodox religious thinkers of the pre-civil-war period. His early career and intellectual development remain cloaked in mystery. Modern historians have been unable to pinpoint any details concerning his family, his social origins, or his early life. He was most likely born in 1584.[2] He probably arrived at Clare Hall, Cambridge, around 1598, for in 1600/01, he took his B.A, followed by his M.A. in 1607. After this point, there are no signs of his whereabouts until 1616. It seems likely that some portion of the intervening time was spent at Cambridge—Everarde's deep learning, wide reading and razor wit hints at a pro-

---

[1] John Everard, *Some Gospel-Treasures Opened: Or, The Holiest of all Unvailing* (1653). For the probable dates of these sermons, see Paul R. Hunt, "John Everard: A Study of His Life, Thought, and Preaching" (Ph.D. diss., UCLA, 1977), 284-85, and Chapter Three, above.

[2] See Guildhall Library MS. 10091/6, fol. 14r, wherein Everarde alleged in 1616 that he was thirty-two years old.

tracted sojourn in the academy. By 1616, however, he had arrived in London. In November of that year, he requested a license to marry a London "spinster" named Elizabeth Mauditt, giving as his place of residence the parish of St. Dunstan-in-the-West.[3] Two months later, he was installed as weekly lecturer at the affluent West End parish of St. Martin's-in-the Fields.[4]

Although there is no evidence to suggest that Everarde was a nonconformist, from the very beginning he showed a chronic appetite for confrontation with the ecclesiastical authorities. In early 1618, while preaching a sermon at Paul's Cross in order to qualify for his B.D., Everarde apparently reproached the Court of Orphans, the elite, aldermanic body that dealt with the dispensation of the persons and goods of the city's orphans. Presumably Everarde accused them either of negligence or corruption; unsurprisingly, this very public attack on the city's most exalted burghers earned him a censure at the hands of Bishop King.[5]

It is also clear that whatever his connections to the godly community, Everarde was deeply committed to the pan-European protestant cause, a commitment that he expressed in print as early as 1618.[6] This commitment would soon get him into trouble. Everarde quickly emerged as London's most vocal clerical opponent of James I's plan to marry the Prince of Wales to the Spanish Infanta. The plan for a Spanish Match had been hatched in the early 1610s, but it assumed new and frightening dimensions following the defenestration of Prague and the decision of James's son-in-law, Frederick, Elector Palatine, to accept the Bohemian throne. As Frederick and the Hapsburgs spiraled towards war, James seized upon the marriage as a potential means of defusing a disastrous confessionalized conflict; for many of his protestant subjects, however, the king's stubborn pursuit of the match looked increasingly like a dangerous abandonment of his son-in-law, and a potential threat to the survival of Protestantism in England and abroad. Everarde proved to be one of the most outspoken critics of the policy.

In December 1620, just weeks after Frederick's disastrous defeat at White Mountain, Everarde (now a doctor of divinity) reportedly preached a sermon in which he prayed for deliverance from the King of Spain. Two months later, he offered up another sermon in which he denounced Spanish atrocities in the West Indies, an indiscretion that landed him in the Gatehouse. Here he appears to have remained until the end of the year. Yet this was far from the conclusion of his saga. In August 1622, Everarde was back in prison for once again slandering Spain and denouncing the still-pending Spanish marriage. No

---

[3] Ibid.

[4] Hunt, "John Everard," 12.

[5] Ibid., 14.

[6] Ibid., 16-30.

sooner had he been released, than he was recommitted in March 1622/23, this time, in the words of John Chamberlain, for "sayeng somwhat more than he shold" about the marriage plans. Indeed, Everarde's relationship with the authorities seems by this time to have taken on an almost ritualistic quality: he would denounce the match from the high-profile pulpit of St. Martin's; the bishops would then move against him; this would be followed by a stay in one of London's jails, which would end when one or more of Everarde's aristocratic friends would beg the king to have him released; free again, Everarde would immediately attack the policy, only to be recommitted once more. In May 1623, St. Martin's was forced to hire a second lecturer, John Andrewes, who presumably served the parish as a substitute during Everarde's frequent and now predictable periods of incarceration.[7] Later, the doctor would tell his friend and disciple Rapha Harford that he had endured no fewer than "six or seven" separate imprisonments for his opposition to the match; as Everarde told it, the bishops came "*so oft* to King *James about him*, he began to take *more* notice of him, asking *What is this Dr.* Ever-out? his name (saith he) *shall be Dr.* Never-out."[8]

Whether or not this tale of royal punning is apocryphal, it seems clear that Everarde's confrontations with the bishops left an indelible imprint on the doctor. Having begun with advanced protestant leanings, Everarde appears during the early 1620s to have developed an increasing disdain for both the established church and its governors. Harford would later report that his teacher had come by the late 1630s to reject episcopacy entirely, even going so far as to predict that the next Parliament would bring "*the utter downfal of Bishops*."[9] Again, we cannot be sure that Everarde actually delivered this knowing prophecy; nevertheless, by the end of 1626, he was apparently willing to make some very unseemly statements about the liturgy of the church.[10]

Indeed, it was probably during the mid-1620s that Everarde first began to flirt with the opinions that would later bring him into the High Commission court on charges of heresy. Even as late as 1622, when he underwent his last recorded imprisonment, he had apparently not yet experienced the profound spiritual transformation that would lead him away from the orthodoxy of his younger days into the heterodoxy of his old age. As Harford reported it, his various imprisonments took place before the doctor had entered "into that *ever blessed* union and communion with God." Even as he fulminated against the marriage, Everarde was "but a bare, *literal, university* Preacher (as he afterward still called himself)," equipped with "but *skin-deep* learning and phi-

---

[7] For Everarde's troubles over the Match, see ibid., 36-81.

[8] Everard, *Gospel-Treasures*, sigs. a2v-a3r.

[9] Ibid., sig. a3v.

[10] See above, Chapter Three, and below, Appendix C.

losophy (as he termed it;)."[11] Only in his "*latter dayes*" did Everarde come to see his own "former ignorance and vanity."[12]

Fortunately, we can date Everarde's "conversion" with some accuracy to the period between 1622 and late 1626. As noted in Chapter Three, in November 1626, Everarde delivered a sermon at St. Martin's which suggested in no uncertain terms that he had embraced a new and audacious brand of religiosity, one with unsettling perfectionist overtones. During these same months, he also wrote a series of letters to Sir Robert Cotton, in which he eagerly, almost desperately, sought to locate and obtain an obscure alchemical manuscript known as *The Way of Blisse*. These letters reveal that Everarde was passing time with the noted alchemical philosopher Robert Fludd.[13] All of this suggests that Everarde was by this time moving decisively toward the mature religious synthesis that would characterize his posthumously published sermons. As was often the case, then, Everarde's own departure from the orthodoxy of the Church of England appears to have progressed in tandem with his increasing disaffection from the established ecclesiastical order, a disaffection that probably owed much to his repeated experiences with the Bishops and the church courts in the early 1620s.

Yet Everarde's difficulties were only at a beginning. After he was removed from the pulpit of St. Martin's, the doctor appears to have taken up the lectureship of aristocratic Kensington (which he certainly held by 1628). This post was undoubtedly secured for him by his patron, Henry Rich, the Earl of Holland, who, along with Edmund Sheffield, the Earl of Mulgrave, had probably become acquainted with Everarde during his first years in London, and who likely intervened on Everarde's behalf to free him from his repeated imprisonments for preaching against the match.[14] Everarde appears to have maintained his close relationship with both of these men up to his death. It was probably through the good offices of Holland or Mulgrave that Everarde assumed the living at Fairstead, Essex, at some point in the late 1620s.

---

[11] Ibid., sig. a2v.

[12] Ibid., sig. ar.

[13] British Library, Cotton MS. Jul. C. iii, fols. 171-73. He asked if Cotton was in possession of the manuscript: "If not, then let me entreate you to certify this bearer my servant, where one Mr Harrison dwelleth who was lately a Schoolemaister in Red-crosse street (for as Dr floyd of the Black-friers assureth me, he hath it)." More than a year later, Everarde was still searching for the book, and he again wrote to Cotton, telling of another meeting with Fludd: "Doctor Floud assured me yesterday of Mr Harrisons being in towne." Everarde ultimately succeeded in obtaining the manuscript, which was published in 1658, together with his marginal notes, by Elias Ashmole, who had obtained Everarde's copy through a friend.

[14] Everard, *Gospel-Treasures*, sig. a2v.

Fairstead was allegedly a particularly rich cure (according to Harford, it was worth £400 per annum), but there is no evidence that Everarde ever officiated there, a fact that perhaps reveals a peculiarly unpuritanical willingness to wink at clerical nonresidency.[15] From the 1620s onward, Everarde had lived in a house in the southwest London suburb of Fulham.[16] His affiliation with the powerful and unruly Holland was widely recognized by Londoners; on at least two occasions, contemporaries referred to the doctor as Holland's "chaplain," perhaps suggesting that Everarde preached or tended to the spiritual needs of Holland's household, no doubt augmenting his income in the process.[17] Throughout the 1630s, Everarde, Holland, and Mulgrave appear to have maintained a private devotional circle, in which precious and exotic manuscripts passed from hand to hand. We have already seen that Everarde reputedly translated and transcribed the *Theologia Germanica* for Holland and Mulgrave, a translation that was probably completed in 1636 (indeed, the two surviving fair copies of Everarde's translation may be the very manuscripts that were prepared for the earls).[18] Mulgrave, meanwhile, allegedly furnished Everarde with papers written by Nicholas Hill, a mysterious Catholic alchemist, mathematician and philosophical atomist.[19] It is no surprise, then, that Holland and Mulgrave tried to protect Everarde from Laudian harassment; as late as 1638, they supposedly sought to intervene with the Bishops to save the doctor from the very serious charges pending against him in the court of High Commission.[20]

These efforts would prove fruitless. Like many other dissident clerics, Everarde found himself under intense pressure following the rise of Laud. Indeed, Laud seems to have singled out Everarde for particular scrutiny, possibly because of lingering suspicions concerning the doctor's oppositional political activities at the end of James I's reign. Yet such suspicions were no doubt compounded by the fact that by the late 1620s, Everarde was dispensing his dubious theological ideas from the pulpit of Kensington with such defiance that the new and always tetchy Bishop of London could only regard the doctor's

---

[15] Ibid., sig. a3r; Hunt, "John Everard," 107-9.

[16] Hunt, "John Everard," 82.

[17] William Prynne, *Hidden Workes of Darknes brought to Publike Light* (1645), 207 (mispaginated as 211); Sheffield University Library, Hartlib Papers, MS. 29/2/12B, as cited from *The Hartlib Papers: A Complete Text and Image Database of the Papers of Samuel Hartlib (c. 1600-1662) Held in Sheffield University Library*, 2d ed. (Sheffield: Humanities Research Online, 2002).

[18] Folger Shakespeare Library MS. V. a. 222; Cambridge University Library, Dd. xii. 68.

[19] See H. Trevor-Roper, *Catholics, Anglicans and Puritans* (Chicago: University of Chicago, 1988), 15, and for Hill more generally, 1-39.

[20] Everard, *Gospel-Treasures*, sig. a3v-a4r.

behavior as a calculated insult to his authority. The first step was to have Everarde removed from the pulpit of Kensington. Yet this did not silence the doctor. Through the connivance of friends such as Holland and the sometime antinomian preacher Thomas Hodges, Everarde managed to continue to preach, both privately, and on occasion from pulpits shared with him by sympathetic ministers. It was probably this which led Laud, now Archbishop of Canterbury, to initiate a High Commission proceeding against the doctor in early 1636. Although no record as to the charge survives, the case resulted in Everarde's deprivation from the lucrative living of Fairstead.[21]

Yet no sooner had the doctor been punished, than he was once again in very serious trouble. In late November, 1637, amidst the panic and paranoia that gripped the government during the early stages of the Scottish Covenanting movement, the Privy Council issued a warrant for an immediate raid on Everarde's house at Fulham. The Clerks of the Council were ordered "to sease into your custodie all his papers and writings, and to bring away with you such of them as may concerne the State."[22] It appears that this search was in fact carried out; as Harford later told it, "These Sermons we had much *ado* to keep *out* of the Bishops fingers; the Pursevant upon search *for any thing of his*, missed them very narrowly."[23]

In January of 1638, the case against Everarde took a new twist when Giles Creech, who claimed to have been a disciple of the doctor, approached Laud with his wild tales concerning the London antinomian community. This in turn provoked a serious investigation by Sir John Lambe, which garnered further evidence against Everarde. The doctor was accordingly haled once again before the High Commission. The charges appear to have centered upon his doctrinal positions; William Prynne would later argue that Everarde had been charged with heresy. If true, this represented a very serious escalation in Laud's campaign against Everarde. The various antinomian preachers who had appeared before the High Commission in preceding years had been charged with doctrinal error; accusations of heresy were far more serious, and could theoretically result in death. It is unlikely that Laud wanted to see Everarde burnt alive; more likely, he wanted to humiliate him, bring him to his knees, and place the doctor in a position of complete impotence, whether through imprisonment or lifelong attendance on the Court of High Commission. Everarde later claimed that in one of his appearances before the court, the Archbishop had exclaimed that "*he would bring him to a morsel of bread*," a statement not out of character for the sometimes choleric Laud.[24]

---

21 See ibid., sig. a3r; Hunt, "John Everard," 143-45.
22 British Library, Stowe MS. 549, fol. 9v.
23 Everard, *Gospel-Treasures*, sig. a5v.
24 Ibid., sig. a3r.

For almost a year, Everarde was forced to make repeated appearances before the High Commission, until at length he was sentenced on July 19, 1639. The most serious allegations against Everarde were his supposed errors concerning the presence of God in all created things, and his denial of a literal, physical resurrection of the body. Everarde gamely attempted to defend himself, qualifying some of the articles against him, while defending others by citing authoritative texts. As one eyewitness put it, "The Dr. was his owne Advocate and indeavord to prove with some distinctions out of auntient authors, these severall opinions, but yet, hee protested openly hee did beleive the orthodox doctrine of the Church of England, and that hee had held these opinions in private discourse, and not publisht them commonly in his sermons." The extent to which the court distorted Everarde's opinions is considered in Appendix C, below. Inevitably, the doctor's efforts to fend off the charges were hopeless. He received a verbal tongue-lashing from the Commissioners, especially Laud and Montagu, before being sentenced to suspension, imprisonment and a fine of £1000; it was further ordered that his "note books, wherein hee had sett downe all his schismaticall blasphemous, and hereticall opinions, with his reason for the mayntayning of them, should bee burnt."[25] The Bishops, however, noted that they were willing to suspend his sentence provided he make a total recantation of his opinions, and submit in full to the authority and doctrinal orthodoxy of the church. A full year of negotiations and delays followed. But on June 18, 1640, Everarde finally appeared before the court, and upon his knees delivered a long and detailed retraction of his "haereticall, pernitious, and Atheisticall opinions."[26] Although now restored to the ministry, Everarde's health was deteriorating by this stage. Sometime between December 1640 and March 1641, the doctor died, but not before he had read over and approved his own sermons, which had been copied out from shorthand notes and carefully preserved by his friends and disciples.[27]

The following chapter examines these remarkable sermons. In them, we see the doctor preaching in both his public and private modes, affording us access to the mind of one of the most unusual thinkers of his day. Everarde was a chronic syncretist, a voracious consumer of all things mystical and esoteric. The result was a deeply idiosyncratic system of divinity, which challenged almost all the assumptions of early Stuart Christian piety. Modern interpreters

---

[25] British Library, Add. MS. 11045, fol. 37r, letter of E[dward?] R[ossingham?] to Viscount Scudamore, which contains a remarkable firsthand account of the trial, first discovered by Kevin Sharpe.

[26] For the probable form of the recantation, see Bodleian Library, Tanner MS. 67, fols. 143-47; for his performance, see PRO, SPD 16/434/207b.

[27] Hunt, "John Everard," 184-86; Everard, *Gospel-Treasures*, sig. a8r.

have variously labeled Everarde as a Familist, a "spiritual alchemist," a Neoplatonist, or more simply, as a mystic, who followed in the perfectionist tradition of the Radical Reformation.[28] The following chapter does not seek to further this attempt to isolate or trace the origins of his thought. His sources of inspiration were wide and varied. We know that he read or translated a slew of strange and sometimes sectarian mystical texts. These included a host of medieval sources, ranging from Moses Maimonides and Nicholas of Cusa, to Tauler and the *Theologia Germanica*; he likewise showed an affinity for radical reformers such as Sebastian Franck and Hans Denck; at the more exotic end of the spectrum, Everarde translated or read not only the Neoplatonic Pseudo-Dionysius, but also a number of alchemical works, up to and including several texts attributed to Hermes Trismegistus.[29] It is also probable that,

---

[28] The claim that Everarde was a Familist was often repeated in the early seventeenth century. It is likewise adopted in T. Wilson Hayes, "John Everard and the Familist Tradition," in M. C. Jacob and J. R. Jacob, eds., *The Origins of Anglo-American Radicalism* (London and Boston: Allen and Unwin, 1984; paperback edition, New Jersey and London: Humanities Press, 1991); for Everarde as "spiritual alchemist," see R. M. Shuler, "Some Spiritual Alchemies of Seventeenth Century England," *Journal of the History of Ideas*, 41 (1980). Perhaps the most lucid brief account of Everarde's theology may be found in Rufus M. Jones's 1914 study, *Spiritual Reformers in the 16th and 17th Centuries* (London: Macmillan and Co., 1914; reprint, Gloucester, MA: Peter Smith, 1971), 239-52, which touches on many of the themes explored more fully in the following chapter. This should be supplemented with the useful discussion contained in Nigel Smith, *Perfection Proclaimed: Language and Literature in English Radical Religion* (Oxford: Clarendon Press, 1989), 107-43. Smith concludes that Everarde was "the centre . . of an enterprise devoted to Anglicizing [and popularizing] the central mystical anthropology of Medieval German spiritualism as it had been interpreted by the sixteenth-century German spiritualist and Anabaptist Movement" (ibid., 136). The following chapter represents an attempt to extract the kernel of Everarde's mature thought; readers interested in his earlier writings, his biography, and a more detailed account of the rhetorical and imagistic devices deployed by Everarde should turn to Hunt, "John Everard."

[29] For Nicholas of Cusa, see T. Wilson Hayes, "A Seventeenth-century Translation of Nicholas of Cusa's *Idiota*," *Notes and Queries*, 28 (1981); idem, "A Seventeenth-century Translation of Nicholas of Cusa's *De Dato Patris Luminem*," *Journal of Medieval and Renaissance Studies*, 11 (1981); for Franck, Denck, Tauler, and the *Theologia*, see Smith, *Perfection Proclaimed*, 112-21; his Hermetic translations included not just the *Divine Pymander of Hermes Mercurius Trismegistus* (1650), but also the "Emerald Table" and a fragment from Basil Valentinius, for which see Shuler, "Some Spiritual Alchemies." As Nigel Smith has pointed out, in 1656 the alchemical aficionado Samuel Boulton likewise claimed to have made use of "some loose papers of an unknown Mr. but . . . supposed to

as many of his critics charged, he had at least been exposed to the works of Hendrik Niclaes, the founder of the Family of Love, whose ideas may well have been in circulation at Clare Hall in the 1590s.[30]

At times, we can hear the voices of each of these various sources in his works, although no one predominates. Thus, in his stress on the *via negativa*—the state of utter unknowing and ignorance necessary for communion with God—he owed much to Pseudo-Dionysius;[31] in his endless calls for utter self-annihilation, together with his emphasis on unity with God, we can hear the echo of the *Theologia Germanica*;[32] in certain areas, including his concept of the Trinity, Everarde drew upon the thought of the fifteenth-century conciliarist and mystic Nicholas of Cusa;[33] elsewhere, as Paul Hunt has shown, he

---

proceed from that late worthy and Reverend Chymist *Dr. Everard*." See Samuel Boulton, *Medicina Magica Tamen Physica: Magical, but Natural Physick* (1656), sig. A4v.

30 This admittedly speculative conclusion is based on the possible presence of the now nameless prophet "T.L." at Clare Hall in the 1580s and 1590s. T.L. was a biblical expositor and (if Stephen Denison is to be trusted) a sect-master, who allegedly schooled John Etherington in the ways of Familist mysticism. Whether he was indeed a sectarian leader, T.L. was almost certainly influenced by HN, as is demonstrated in P. Lake, *The Boxmaker's Revenge: 'Orthodoxy,' 'Heterodoxy,' and the Politics of the Parish in Early Stuart London* (Stanford: Stanford University Press, 2001), which examines the works of all three men side by side. T.L. began publishing in 1589, when *An Exposition of the XI. XII. and XIII chapters of Revelations* was allegedly printed. This was followed by *De Fide* in 1592 and *Babylon is Fallen* in 1595. In the early 1630s, it was alleged by one of Samuel Hartlib's correspondents that "tho they had some blur because they are fathered upon Hederinghton a box-maker" T.L.'s commentaries had in fact "beene made by an excellent Schollar of Claire-Hall." Cited from *The Hartlib Papers: A Complete Text and Image Database*, 29/3/39B-40A. Although T.L.'s identity remains a mystery, it is of course possible that either he or someone else familiar with the works of HN remained at Clare Hall in 1597-98, when Everarde presumably matriculated (see *Alumni Cantabrigienses*, *s.v.* Everard, John, for his 1600-1601 B.A. from Clare College).

31 See especially Everard, *Gospel-Treasures*, 290-300.

32 For an interesting examination of Everarde's translation of the *Theologia Germanica*, and his rendering of specific statements referring to self-death and "begoddedness," see Smith, *Perfection Proclaimed*, 123-24.

33 See ibid., 133, 131. Everarde even went so far as to name Nicholas of Cusa's *De Visione Dei* in a sermon preached before Thomas Hodges's auditory at St. Olave Old Jewry (Everard, *Gospel-Treasures*, 477).

borrowed images from Moses Maimonides;[34] meanwhile, his radical conception of scriptural allegory appears to have been modeled on the very similar ideas of the Reformation radicals Niclaes and Franck. Here and there, his sermons were likewise sprinkled with alchemical references, which in turn bear witness to the looming bulk of Hermes Trismegistus, a presence lurking ponderously behind all of Everarde's words.

Everarde seems to have believed that all of these texts complemented one another, finding reconciliation in his own system of divinity. In 1635, when Edward Howes approached Everarde with John Winthrop, Jr.'s spiritual queries, Everarde responded in a way that clarifies this sentiment. As Howes wrote, "in the maine he was misticall. This he said, that when the will of God is you shall knowe what you desire, it will come with such a light, that it will make a harmonie amonge all your authors, causing them sweetly to agree, and putt you for ever after out of doubt and question."[35] This, indeed, appears to provide a perfect summary of Everarde's own attitude towards his sources. All of them tended toward a single truth of God, a mystical truth which he believed he had discovered, and which he in turn attempted to convey to his listeners and disciples. What follows, then, is not an attempt to locate the precise sources of his thought, but to elaborate the overarching shape of his theology, placing that theology for the first time in its contemporary context. The result is a striking and clear vision of the nature of what, for the purposes of this study, has been termed "inherentist" or "perfectionist" antinomianism.

The Key to Scripture

To understand Everarde, we must attempt to come to terms with Everarde's understanding of scripture. For it was his method of interpreting the Bible, his distinctive hermeneutic principle, which more than any other single factor cemented his thought together, distinguishing him in a subtle but profound way from the vast majority of his contemporaries. Without this hermeneutic principle, which Everarde himself described as the "key" to unlocking the entire book of God, there could be no salvation. This key, once distilled from his sermons, allows us to wander freely through the forbidding landscape of Everarde's mind; more important still, it lends us crucial insight into the nature of the phenomenon that would come to be called antinomianism, for Everarde's hermeneutics were shared by some (although not all) of the most extreme anti-legalists of the century.

---

[34] Hunt, "John Everard," 222-33, 233n30, shows that Everarde borrowed the image of various courtyards of the temple as an allegory for spiritual progression from Maimonides's *The Guide of the Perplexed*.

[35] *Collections of the Massachusetts Historical Society*, 4th ser., 6 (1863), 499. See below, Epilogue, for further details on Winthrop, Howes, and Everarde.

In Everarde's view, the holy scriptures were a vast riddle awaiting solution. Beneath the bare words of the Bible, there was a secret subtext, and it was the preacher's role to lay bare this subtext. Appropriating the words of the evangelist Matthew at a private sermon preached to his conventicle at Kensington, Everarde advised his listeners that "we must labor to see, in all the words of God, that *the truth*, and the *Word of God it self*, is *hid* and *coucht under* mighty parables; for *without a parable spake he nothing unto them*."[36] For Everarde, then, the mere "words" of scripture were not the same thing as the "Word" of God. The "words" of God were a kind of running story, an extended parable not unlike those told by Jesus. The "Word" of God was, on the other hand, the secret and hidden meaning encased beneath and within this extended parable. He explained this idea further in another sermon preached before the same audience: "From the first of *Genesis*, to the last of the Prophets, there runs *an Allegory, a Mysterie, a Secret Woof*, or *Web*, as I may so call it, which if you have not *the skill and Art* to know it, that so *you may eye it* and see it *through the letter*, for it is hid and covered with the letter, I will be bold to say it, *you have not the marrow*, the life of the Scriptures."[37] Here was the crux of Everarde's understanding of the bible, "in the justification of which, *I dare* live and dye."[38] The scriptures contained a hidden, secret meaning. Only a well-trained eye, possessed of the art—indeed the gift—of interpretation could see this pattern beneath the flux of the word. Never one to underestimate his own skill, Everarde claimed to be able to see this pattern, and promised his audience that they, too, could come to see the "secret web" spun invisibly between the black letters of their leather-bound bibles.

Such an understanding of the Bible was not, of course, without precedent. Orthodox Christianity had from its very beginnings accepted the notion of allegorical biblical interpretation. The word of God, it was widely acknowledged, contained hidden meanings that seemed to go beyond or to transcend the apparent, literal meaning of a passage of scripture. This method of exegesis was applied, above all, to the Old Testament, which was traditionally assumed to have both literal and figurative meanings. Thus, for instance, in addition to their overt, literal meanings, various passages of Jewish scripture were assumed to prophesy the coming of Christ; or, as later interpreters put it, to hold forth "types" or prefigured images of Christ. The roots of this method of interpretation were contained in the Gospels themselves, all of which were written to show that Christ fulfilled prophecies foretold in the Hebrew scriptures, in accordance with what was probably a long-standing tradition of

---

[36] Everard, *Gospel-Treasures*, 590.
[37] Ibid., 278.
[38] Ibid.

Jewish messianism. As with so much else in the history of Christian theology, however, this tradition of Christian exegesis is derived mainly from the epistles of Saint Paul. Paul regularly, almost habitually, applied allegorical interpretations to even the most mundane utterances of the Old Testament.[39] Thus, in the epistle to the Galatians, Paul used the story of Abraham's two consorts, Hagar and Sarah, as an allegorical illustration of the freedom of a Christian, comparing the slave Hagar's son Ishmael to the Jews under the Law, while comparing his wife Sarai's son Isaac to Christians, who were free from the Law. Everarde seized upon this allegorical mode of interpretation, taking Paul's reading of Genesis as an example of normative biblical interpretation:

> what are *these histories* to us? what good is it to us, that there was *a mount Sinai,* and a *mount Sion?* and that *Abraham* had two sons, the *one* by the bondwoman, the *other* by the freewoman? but, *he would* shew and teach us, that the son of the bondwoman *in us*, which is the *son of fear*, should be cast out: and the son of the freewoman, that is, the *son of love*, should inherit: so always reserving the *truth of the letter*, yet not losing the sense and the meaning. But if we rest and *dwell* on the Letter, or on the history, and so *only take it as an Historie*, and not see our own selves in it, and by it: then that *Historie*, that Letter *kills*: but it is the *Spirit* only that gives life, *viz.* the *mind and the meaning*; for there is no Scripture but is as a glass to behold our own *faces*, our own *hearts*.[40]

While it might at first glance seem that Everarde was merely accepting Paul's allegorical method of interpreting the Torah, the reader should beware accepting their positions as identical. Everarde was taking the Apostle's position one step further than Paul himself had; Paul reads the story of Hagar and Sarah as a general parable or allegory to represent the position of believers with respect to the Law in the wake of Christ. Nowhere, however, does he suggest with Everarde that not only this passage, but indeed the whole of the Jewish scriptures, should be read as an allegory or parable for something that happened *within* each individual believer. This was not quite a misreading of Paul, but it was very certainly an enthusiastic extrapolation outward from his

---

[39] See D. Boyarin, *A Radical Jew: Paul and the Politics of Identity* (Berkeley: University of California Press, 1994), esp. 13-38, for an interesting discussion of Paul's allegorical mode of interpretation. Boyarin sees this distinctive hermeneutic as absolutely central to Paul's understanding of Christ (indeed, as the starting point for all of his thought). For an outstanding, but speculative, discussion of the Jewish mystical tradition from which Paul may have emerged, see A. Segal, "The Risen Christ and the Angelic Mediator Figures in the Light of Qumran," in J. H. Charlesworth, ed., *Jesus and the Dead Sea Scrolls: The Controversy Resolved* (New York: Doubleday, 1992).

[40] Everard, *Gospel-Treasures*, 279-80.

words. For Everarde, every passage of both the Old and New Testaments could be interpreted as an allegory for an event or events that occurred within the believer's soul. To read the "Word" of God (as opposed to his "words"), one needed not only to see the "secret web" or allegory beneath a given passage, but to feel and observe the unfolding of that allegory in one's own heart and life (as in a "glass" or mirror).

This mode of interpretation is sufficiently similar to those current among mainstream puritans that, for the sake of clarity, it will behoove us to examine several examples in detail. All orthodox puritans held that for the word to be effectual, the stories and letters of scripture needed to have a powerful effect on the listener's heart. This was typically called "experimental" knowledge, and as R. T. Kendall has argued, it was central to puritan practical divinity, a cornerstone of what Thomas Hooker called "heart religion."[41] And although Everarde used this very same language of "experimental knowledge," he was pointing toward a style of interpretation of which neither Thomas Hooker, nor the vast majority of Hooker's fellow puritans would have approved.

Consider, for example, the doctor's exegesis of Genesis 3: 8, "they heard sound of the Lord God walking in the Garden in the cool of the day." Everarde asked his audience, "what do you think *was meant by that*? that God came at *evening*, when *the sun* was going down? do you think that the day *was too hot* for God to walk in? no, no, that cannot be; but tis meant, he came into the soul in the *cool of the day;* that is, when *lust* was *cool*, when the heat of *adams* desire was *over*, when *his own will* was silent and there was a *calm;* then God spake and said, *Adam where art thou?*"[42] Here, Everarde was engaging in what today might be called "figurative," as opposed to "literal," interpretation of the bible. But he was doing more than this still. He was suggesting that Genesis 3: 8 contained an allegory for something that needed to happen in our souls if we were to communicate with God, enlisting this passage in service of the proposition that it was necessary to "put to silence our own *reason*, all our own *affections*, our own *will*, our own *joys*, our own *fears*, our own *hopes;* and then hear what God shall say. There is *no hearing of God* till all these be put to silence."[43] It might have been objected that this was an improbable—even entirely inappropriate—interpretation of the passage. Nevertheless, not only did Everarde insist on this grossly figurative

---

[41] See R. T. Kendall, *Calvin and English Calvinism to 1649* (Oxford: Oxford University Press, 1979), 8-9 and passim; for Hooker's use of the phrase "heart religion," see his letter to John Cotton, as published in G. H. Williams, N. Pettit, W. Herget, and S. Bush Jr., eds., *Thomas Hooker: Writings in England and Holland, 1626-1633*, Harvard Theological Studies, 28 (Cambridge, MA: Harvard University Press, 1975), 297.

[42] Everard, *Gospel-Treasures*, 219-20.

[43] Ibid., 219.

reading, but he strongly hinted that the literal reading—the claim that God strutted through the Garden of Eden in the fading light of late afternoon—was deeply impoverished, if not wholly preposterous. While he did not overtly deny the literal interpretation, he clearly believed that the "marrow" of this passage lay elsewhere, in the spiritual truth embedded within the letter: in order to hear God speak, the will, with all its desires and drives, needed first of all to be put to death. The man or woman who truly understood this passage—who possessed the "mind and meaning" of scripture—was the person who had not only penetrated the allegory, but who had allowed the allegory to penetrate him or her—that is, to let the word of God put his or her own will to death.

As we shall see shortly, this idea of self-death was at the very core of Everarde's notion of true religion. A similar vision of self-abnegation—of profound submission to the divine will—can be seen in Everarde's almost wildly peculiar exegesis of Exodus 3: 1, "Now Moses kept the flock of Jethro his father in Law, the Priest of Midian, and he led the flock to the backside of the desert and came to the mountain of God, even to Horeb." Here, Everarde explained that even this seemingly innocuous passage possessed a deep, mysterious, spiritual meaning that transcended the bare letter: "*all the Patriarchs* are described to be *Sheep-keepers*. . . . what may be *the meaning of* the Holy Ghost in all this? in one word I will tell you what *a Sheepheard* is, A Sheepheard is one that lives *meerly* and most *properly* by the *providence* and blessing of God upon his *trade*; for they fructifie and increase onely upon Gods will, blessing, and providence, he acts not much, but resigns up his will, and all he hath to God *onely*, and depends *altogether* upon that."[44] The secret, allegorical meaning of the scripture, then, was that "a Sheepheards life is preferred *with God* far before *a* Husbandmans, that is, he that hath *given up* all to God."[45] For Everarde, then, even the passing details that made up the meandering narrative of the Old Testament carried a coded message, available only to those select few to whom God vouchsafed the cryptographic key: "You see then, how this mighty truth is hid under a mysterie, and is couched in two or three words; how *Moses* doth but (as it were) by the way, *glance at it* by the by; and if God open your eyes, you may see how this secret web and woof runs secretly along through the whole *Scriptures*."[46]

As Everarde told his listeners again and again, it was this secretive truth that saved; all other knowledge of the Bible was ultimately worthless. He demonstrated this point at length in two private sermons preached in Kensington in the early 1630s. Here he provided his listeners with the allegorical in-

---

[44] Ibid., 595.
[45] Ibid., 596.
[46] Ibid., 597.

terpretation of Joshua 15: 16-17: "And Caleb said, He that smiteth Keriathsepher, and taketh it, to him will I give Achsah my daughter to wife. And Othniel the son of Kenaz the brother of Caleb took it, and he gave him Achsah his daughter to wife." Everarde first explained that the various names in the text were laden with meaning in the original Hebrew. Keriathsepher was Hebrew for "The City of the Book," or "City of the Letter"; Achsah meant "The rending of the veil," while Caleb meant "My heart," "a perfect heart," or a "good hart." Othniel, meanwhile, meant "Gods good time," or "The Lords fit opportunity."[47] He then went on to decode the scripture, to approach the hidden, spiritual meaning of the text: "And my heart said, or a good heart said, That whosoever smiteth and taketh the City of the Letter, to him will I give the tearing or rending of the vail: And *Othniel* took it, as being Gods fit time or opportunity, and he married *Achsah*; that is, enjoyed the rending of the vail, and thereby had the blessing possessed by *Achsah*, by the vail being rent, both the upper springs, and the nether springs. To him that obtains *this rending of the vail*, to him shall be given the mysteries of the Kingdom of God."[48]

Here we see Everard at his most "allegorical," for here was an interpretation in which the actual, literal story conveyed by the passage was little more than a cipher for a hidden, spiritual meaning. This interpretation may be seen as a microcosm of Everarde's hermeneutic principle. The story of Othniel was, in a sense, an allegory that conveyed the key to its own interpretation. It revealed the principle of exegesis that informed Everarde's entire vision of true religion, the fact that "the *Bible*, as it consists of Words, Syllables, and Letters, is not the Word of God: for it is not, nor *cannot* be the Word of God, without the *mind and meaning*, till it be smitten, till the *shell* be crackt: for the *Word* is a Spring shut up, a Fountain sealed."[49] The letter was a mere shell, necessary only insofar as it carried a secret, spiritual meaning: "*the spirit* of a man you cannot have without the body; and you cannot have the oyster without the shel: so neither can you have these *mysteries*, these Allegories, without the flesh, without the shell, without excrements; that is, *without the letter of the word*. . . . We are not able to conceive of the *spiritual meaning*, and Gods minde, without *something* represented and proposed sutable to our *Element*, to our *language*, to our *sphear*, to our *condition*."[50] He who had "smitten,"

---

[47] Ibid., 276-77.

[48] Ibid., 278.

[49] Ibid., 310-11.

[50] Ibid., 316. See also ibid., 46-47. The outward letters of scripture were "*a means* to convey the *True word* to the heart. And therefore if you think you *have Gods Word*, when you have gotten this *knowledge* of the letter, or of *whatsoever* the outside, or the letter bears, without the *mind* and *meaning*, you are deceived. . . . This is Truth (if ye will believe it from our Saviours *own* mouth) *The flesh*

and "cracked" the shell had rent the veil, passing beyond the letter into the realm of the spirit, into God's sanctum sanctorum.[51]

Again, however, it must be emphasized that for Everarde, the endpoint of the interpretation was not the interpretation itself, nor even the understanding that the interpretation conveyed. It was not enough, for instance, to know the hidden meaning beneath Joshua 15: 16-17. The rending of the veil—the passage from letter to spirit—came when the allegorical meaning of the scripture was effected in the heart of the believer. Elaborating on his reading of the previous passage, he argued that

> Understanding the Scriptures thus, *as fulfilled within* us, we make them our own; hereby the word is made a *living word*, and endureth for ever, as *David* saith. Those that *see and feel* the Scriptures thus fulfilled in them, they have found *the pearl of the Scriptures*, for which we ought to sell all: and the *hidden Manna* which shall feed and nourish them to *eternal life*. Nay, let me tell you, these have the *Spirit and the life* of the Word, though they never heard nor read the Scripture before. If thou hast but felt the *hissing Serpent* cursed in *thee*, and overcome in *thee*; if thou hast seen *Lucifer* fallen from his *Heaven* in thy soul, I say to thee, *This day is the Scripture fulfilled in thee.*[52]

First, it was necessary to understand the secret, allegorical meaning of scripture; this hidden allegory then became a means whereby the truth held forth by the allegory was fulfilled in the believer's soul.[53]

For Everarde, then, the word was constantly being reenacted, or made flesh, within all believers in all times: "there is no part of holy Writ but is fulfilled *alwaies*, in all *times*, in every part thereof, and in every member of the Church, or in the enemies of the Church at one time or other: alwayes the

---

profiteth nothing, it is the Spirit (the mystery) the marrow *that giveth life*. It is *the mystery*, the Spirit that is *eternal life*: That which cannot possibly be known in the *superficies*, in the *outside*, in the *flesh*, in the *shell* of the Letter, except we go further."

[51] Ibid., 354. "Those who had smitten the letter, and thus taken hold of *Achsah*, the word of Truth, were thereby granted entrance": "[*Achsah*]she . . . will admit you *into* the *Sanctum Sanctorum* . . . that you shall not onely have *the nether springs,* the letter of the Word, External Ordinances, and outward Duties, *Bodily Worships*; but you shall have the *upper springs*, the life of the letter, *the power*, the quickning spirit."

[52] Ibid., 281.

[53] It should be noted, however, that Everarde may have seen very little distinction between understanding and internal fulfillment; at times, he seemed to suggest that those who had come to understand the true spiritual or allegorical meaning of the word had already (through this act of understanding) seen the scripture fulfilled in them.

same things are in *doing* throughout all ages."[54] To treat the Bible as a mere history, a collection of stories and narratives that related the acts of God and his people, was to remain trapped in the letter, to miss the crucial point that the scriptures were constantly being relived in the experiences and minds of earthly human beings.[55]

Once again, it could be argued that this tendency was merely puritan.[56] As T. D. Bozeman has demonstrated, the godly obsessively sought to restore, even to relive, the primitive purity of the Old and New Testaments.[57] Everarde surely owed much to this primitivist impulse. This said, however, it is also true that the godly never insisted that the stories of scripture were *actually* fulfilled internally in the believer; although puritan preachers might often exhort listeners to imagine themselves in the sandals of Abraham, or Moses, or Christ, they never even hinted that the various protagonists and events mentioned in the Bible narrative were veiled metaphors for experiences, emotions, or forces within the text of the believer's life. Everarde's hermeneutic—his allegorical mode of interpretation, his insistence that the entire Bible needed to be replayed in the soul of the believer—was quite alien to puritanism. And as we

---

[54] Ibid., 280.

[55] Ibid., 588-89: "he that *through the historie*, shall see that the *historie* was not written barely *for a historie*, but *mainly* and *chiefly for us;* he shall see there is *therein* contained an eternal living sense; he that looks *within himself*, shall finde all verified in himself; and not onely *this Scripture*, but the whole *Scripture*, all the five Books of *Moses, Joshua,* the *Kings*, and *all the battels of the Kings*, and so throughout; that whatever part of Scripture he *shall read*, he shall be able to say and feel experimentally, *This day is this Scripture fulfilled in your ears*; this day *is this Scripture* accomplished in me; for the substance of all those histories *throughout*, is verified to this *day*, and shall be *to the worlds end*."

[56] Indeed, in William Haller's view, Everarde's mode of scriptural interpretation was nothing more than an enthusiastic and emphatic version of commonplace godly conventions: "Everarde was in this . . . but following in the tradition of Puritan preaching, which for its emotive effect on the people wove together out of the scriptures a version of the sacred epic as an image of inner life. He, however, urged this conception of scripture with special and conscious emphasis, [and] even took the trouble to translate Sebastian Franck's *Tree of Knowledge*, wherein it was definitely argued that the temptation of Adam and all that followed thereupon was a picture of what happened within the individual soul, that Christ and Satan, Paradise and Hell, were actually present in the breast of man. Everarde protested . . . that he did not at all deny the letter." See William Haller, *The Rise of Puritanism* (New York: Columbia University Press, 1938; Paperback edition, New York: Harper Torchbook, 1957), 212.

[57] T. D. Bozeman. *To Live Ancient Lives: The Primitivist Dimension in Puritanism* (Chapel Hill: University of North Carolina Press, 1988).

shall see below, both Everarde and his puritan contemporaries recognized this fact.

Up to this point, we have concerned ourselves with Everarde's reading of the Old Testament. Yet the very same principles outlined above controlled his reading of the New Testament, although in a somewhat different way. Where the allegorical, mysterious truth of an Old Testament passage was often completely independent of its literal meaning, the spiritual truths of the New Testament were generally far more obvious, corresponding closely to the texts themselves. Everarde held, quite simply, that Christ's life was an allegory or parable for something that was to happen in the believer's soul. As he put it,

> as our Saviour was typified by *others* who went before him; he was the *Substance* of all those *Shadows*, both of persons and things; even so Christ Jesus himself, he is the *resemblance* and type of himself; his *outward, temporal* actions in the flesh, were a type of his *inward* and *internal* actions in the souls of all Believers, he being their *life* and *resurrection*; they being before *but dead men* in *Trespasses* and *sins*, until his actions be their *life* and *regeneration*.[58]

All of the events of the New Testament were true—they had actually occurred as described in the Bible. Yet on Everarde's account, the outward works of Christ were merely a prelude to the true, spiritual works of Christ in each believer. Or, as he put it elsewhere, "External Jesus Christ is but a *shadow*, a symbole, [a figure] of the *Internal:* viz. of him *that is to be born within us,* in our souls."[59]

This, then, was the epitome of Everarde's divinity. It was a principle so powerful that upon revealing it to his private devotees, Everarde assured them that "this day (through Gods blessing) I shall put *such a key* into your hands, that *unlocks* all the Scriptures; even as a *fine* curious *contrived* Cabinet, which we know not which way to open, yet having found the *secret* Lock of all the *Drawers*, then they all fall to pieces, and every one comes to your hand."[60] This extraordinary key was nothing other than the knowledge that each and every act of Christ needed to be replayed internally in the believer. As with the allegories of the Old Testament, Everarde warned that "To see Christ to be *all* in all *in us*, this is to know him experimentally: and if ye know him thus, then you know him *as you ought to know him*, else he is but a *fable* to you: for *so to know him*, is to have all the Scriptures *fulfilled in you*."[61] Knowledge of Christ's works, no matter how complete, could not save; instead, when one

---

[58] Everard, *Gospel-Treasures*, 545.

[59] Ibid., 55. The words "a figure" were inserted into the 1657 edition of the text at the same point.

[60] Ibid., 72.

[61] Ibid., 77.

read of Christ's actions, they could be effectual only if those actions were replayed in the life and consciousness of the reader: "When you read of the Story of the *Conception*, *Birth*, *Life*, *Death*, *Resurrection of Christ;* of his *Whipping*, *Crowning* with *Thorns*, *Buffeting*, *Spitting upon*, you shall be able *experimentally* to say, and cry out, Alas! *this day is this Scripture fulfilled in me.*"[62] In short, salvation consisted in assuming Christ's life, and unless one did so, the scriptures were worthless: "this . . . daily doing all the Scriptures over again . . . this is *saving knowledge* of the Scriptures; all other knowledge of the Letter, is but the flesh of the Scriptures, that which the *carnal man* may comprehend: and although it be never so *great*, never so exact, it is meer *dirt* and *dung* its not worth one *rush*: for thus to know the Scriptures as I have said, is to have the whole Scriptures fulfilled *in us.*"[63]

Once again, it will be apparent that there was a strong superficial connection between Everarde's claims and those often proffered by mainstream puritans. Like the godly, he made use of the language of "experiment" to differentiate a cold, formal knowledge of scripture from a heartfelt, experiential, and effectual knowledge; like the godly, he held that only such "experimental" and effectual knowledge could save. Yet his vision of what precisely this gracious experience should look like was in fact very far removed from the puritan norm. His distinctiveness burns through the page in statements such as this:

> in regard of his *death* and *crucifying*: whatever he suffered *externally* in the flesh, it shews how he is *internally crucified* daily, even to the end of the world, *Heb.* 6.6. *Seeing they crucifie to themselves the Son of God afresh, and put him to an open shame:* so likewise for all his other *actions* and *passages* related of him; as his *Nativity*, it held out *our spiritual* birth, and Christ his being born in *the soul;* as the Apostle expresseth it, *Gal.* 4. 19. *My beloved of whom I travel in birth, till Christ be formed, or brought forth in you.* So also in his Circumcision, is held forth our *Spiritual* Circumcision; as in that of 2 *Col.* 11. *Ye are compleat in him, in whom also ye are circumcised with the circumcision made without hands, in putting off the body of the sins of the flesh, by the circumcision of Christ. &c.* So also for *holiness* of life: Christs holiness shews us, what *holiness* shall be in them that are *his* children and people, *Mat.* 5. 16. *Let your light so shine before men, that they may see your good works, and glorifie your father which is in Heaven.* So also for his outward Teaching, it represents to us, that all his people should *be taught of God*; he himself would be the true Teacher in us, as *Isa.* 54. 13. *All thy children shall be taught of the Lord and great shall be the peace of thy children:* And Jer. 31. 34. *And they shall no more teach every man his neighbour, and every man his brother, saying Know the Lord, for*

[62] Ibid.
[63] Ibid., 77-78.

they shall know me, from the least to the greatest, saith the Lord. And Christ himself *cites* these places, *John* 6. 45. *It is written in the Prophets, And they shall all be taught of God; every man therefore that hath heard and learned of the father, cometh unto me.* So also in Christs Miracles; as in *opening* the eyes of the *blinde*, it shews that Christ himself must open our eyes, or else we remain *stark blind*: yea as those *born blinde:* And never any man but he was known to open the eyes *of any* born blinde: *David* saith, *Psal.* 13.3. *Lighten thou mine eyes, least I sleep the sleep of death;* And Psal. 18. 28. *For thou wilt light my Candle: The Lord my God will enlighten my darkness*: So also in the opening of the *ears* of the deaf: it is he alone can say to our ears *Ephathah*, *Be ye opened*, and it is so: So also for his *restoring* of limbs, causing those that are *Cripples* from their Mothers womb, to *leap like* an Hart, and to run *his wayes* with delight.

The like also for his *raising* the dead, and feeding the *Multitudes*: And what shall I say more? You may apply them more to your selves: *The time would fail me to* undertake to speak of all his actions. So also of his *Resurrection, If ye be risen with Christ, seek those things which are above,* Col. 3. 2. and so of his *Ascension*, and all other his *Actions* and *Miracles*, to see *all these things* held forth and typified in the *Person, Actions* and *Miracles* of our Saviour.[64]

Here, as elsewhere, Everarde was arguing that the elect needed to relive Christ's life, to experience his birth, his sufferings, his death, and even his resurrection *in this life*. Such a view was anathema to the mainstream puritan tradition. The godly generally held that Christ's acts and life had occurred only once, bringing about salvation for all times; his birth, life, and death had together appeased God's wrath and merited salvation for those who believed; by believing in the all-encompassing efficacy of Christ's sacrifice, the faithful were joined to Christ, thereby participating in the holiness, joy, peace, and (in death) glorification promised to God's elect. Although the godly often emphasized the nearness of Jesus and believers, drawing on the imagery of a single body of Christ, or inviting believers to imagine themselves crucified together with their savior, one is hard-pressed to find any puritan arguing that to be saved, the entire life of Christ needed to be lived over again in the believer's experience.[65] Nor, to reiterate, do we find the godly engaging in this sort of

---

[64] Ibid., 545-47; See also ibid., 694-95.

[65] To illustrate the contrast, see C. E. Hambrick-Stowe, *The Practice of Piety: Puritan Devotional Disciplines in Seventeenth-Century New England* (Chapel Hill: University of North Carolina Press, 1982), 33, quoting Lewis Bayly's suggestion that when eating the bread of the Eucharist, the godly communicant should "imagine that thou seest Christ hanging upon the Cross, and by his unspeakable torments, full satisfying Gods justice for thy sins." Here, the godly were exhorted to imagine themselves within the biblical narrative, and were invited to engage in

wholesale allegorizing, in which for instance, Christ's casting out of demons is read as a parable for the internal exorcism that must occur in every believer's heart.

This internal exorcism was necessary because, as Everarde admonished his listeners, Antichrist was present in all men and women. Just as "external Christ" was a type or figure for the "internal Christ" that lived in true believers, scriptural references to "Antichrist" were in fact references to the Antichrist within. The believer could not even begin to approach illumination and true regeneration until he or she had identified and attacked this internal devil—that is, until Christ had come into human flesh to banish the devil. As Everarde explained in a public sermon, the devil was not so much an external spirit or an entity as an internal force, which went under at least twenty scriptural names, all of them ultimately equivalent—"1. *The Old man* 2. *Adam* 3. *the Serpent*. 4. *Lucifer*. 5. *The Red Dragon*. 6. *The Roaring Lion*. 7. *The Devil*. 8. *Antichrist*. 9. *Sin*. 10. *Rebellion*. 11. *False light*. 12. *Darkness*. 13. *The Flesh*. 14. *Selfness*. 15. *Propriety*. 16. *Self-love*. 17. *Our own will*. 18. *Error*. 19. *Satan*. 20. *The evil one*."[66] He elucidated this further:

> The eighth name is *Antichrist*, I *Joh*. 4. 3 *And every spirit that confesseth not that Jesus Christ is come in the flesh, is not of God; but this is the spirit of Antichrist, of whom ye have heard, how that he should come, and now already he is in this world*. Nay now we are sure we are *all free of this*, he is at *Rome:* if there should be an Antichrist among us, he should soon be had up in to the High Commission Court, and there be censured: but we are no Antichrists, for the Apostle sayes, *That whosoever he be that confesses not that Jesus Christ is come in the flesh, the same is Antichrist:* now we all confess this, *he came into the world 1600 years ago, and he was begotten by the Holy Ghost,* (this is part of our Creed) *born of the virgin* Mary, *suffered under* Pontius *Pilate, &c.* but thinkest thou that this confession with the mouth is enough? But is Jesus Christ come in the flesh *with thee?* is he come into thy flesh? that Christ is born in thee, that he is *glorified* in thy members? then thou art no Antichrist: but if he be not, thou needest not *go far* to see Antichrist.[67]

For John Everarde, then, Antichrist was not so much an individual being as a representation of qualities within humans. In making this argument, he

---

a sympathetic communion with Christ suffering on the cross. However, it is clear that for Bayly, as for all the godly, this act remained extraneous and removed from the believer; the godly were to imagine themselves witnessing the one, only, and all-powerful death of Christ, which had taken place centuries before on the fields of Golgotha, and which alone had satisfied God's wrath.

[66] Everard, *Gospel-Treasures*, 146.

[67] Ibid., 173-74.

challenged the cherished reformed commonplace that the Pope was Antichrist: "I know well the general note is, that the Pope is antichrist: well, let it be so, that he is externally and chiefly at *Rome:* and that the Pope shall be destroyed, and then Antichrist is fallen; I will not for my part contend, let most voices carry it: but take heed you do not so long look for Antichrist *abroad* and at *Rome*, so that thou neglect *one at home.*"[68] Indeed, he went so far as to argue that "there are many Antichrists . . . if a man do but put his hand into his bosome, he shall find enough of Antichrist there: and there are *so many* Antichrists in the world, that a man can very hardly find a true Christian . . . for Antichrist is in *every place*, the *houses* are full of Antichrist, the *Pulpits* are full of Antichrist, the Communion table is full of Antichrist, all places are full of Antichrist."[69]

On display was a way of reading the Bible, indeed an entire style of religiosity, that departed subtly but completely from that held forth by mainstream puritanism. It was a vision in which Antichrist infected every human soul, in which only the internal presence of Christ—"Jesus Christ in the flesh *with thee*"—could set things aright. This vision, moreover, held out tantalizing rewards: Everarde offered resurrection in this life, a promise of extraordinary spiritual knowledge, available only to those who had rent the veil of the letter. Only these passed into the sanctum sanctorum, where they would come to possess the "upper springs," that is, the source of the Word.

Godly Stunted Dwarves

Before peering into the sanctum sanctorum with Everarde, however, we need to examine more carefully his statements concerning the corruption of the English church. What, precisely, did he mean when he charged that "the *Pulpits* are full of Antichrist," and "the Communion table is full of Antichrist"? Was this mere rhetorical bombast, or did Everarde have something more specific in mind?

As suggested above, the crucial dichotomy between letter and spirit dominated Everarde's divinity, permeating all his sermons and shaping his understanding of Christian religion. Yet it also served to discriminate false forms of Christianity from the truth. In Everarde's estimation, failure to comprehend the difference between letter and spirit was the great shortcoming of modern divinity: "But indeed and in truth, there is so much *Literalness*, even among great Professors, and most Teachers, that they are always but at the *very beginning* of the Principles of the *Doctrine* of Christ; and if *those* that profess and think themselves able Teachers, do stick here, and go no further, how can they be a means to bring others on toward perfection? . . . this *dwelling* in the

[68] Ibid., 174.
[69] Ibid., 175.

letter, is that which hath been the occasion of so many *Errors, Rents* and *Differences* as hath been in the Church."[70] Before proceeding to investigate the marrow of Everarde's idiosyncratic vision, we must examine what he meant here, for in decrying these "errors, rents and differences" he was hardly complaining about distant, academic disputes; rather, he was referring in large part to arguments in which he himself was deeply implicated. To understand Everarde's divinity, and indeed to understand the controversies to which he was referring, it is necessary to try to abstract from his sermons a picture of his enemies. Only by reconstructing the negative referents against which the doctor defined himself and his own divinity can we come to a full understanding of the positive intellectual content of Everarde's vision. Who, in Everarde's view, was guilty of literalism? Which "great Professors, and . . . Teachers" remained mired in the letter, and where had they gone wrong?

Had Everarde written up a handlist of these sluggish, literal teachers, it would in all likelihood have included the extreme conformists who were coming increasingly to control the ecclesiastical establishment in the 1620s and 1630s. He appears to have shared a typically godly suspicion of ceremonial conformity, and an even more profound distrust of those who enforced it. On the rare occasions in which he alluded to such men in his sermons, he showed nothing but contempt. Thus, preaching at Putney on the sin of covetousness, Everarde offered the following, less than flattering assessment on the state of the early Stuart church: "Is it not lamentable to see, how men for this *lucre* of Covetousness, will *violate* the laws of God, and of their own *conscience?* and for *gain* and *preferment sake* subscribe and submit to any thing, to any change in Religion; so they may keep *in favour*, and *keep their livings* and *benefices*." Such time-serving conformists "*creep* and *cringe*, and *Issacar* like, stoop down to take up every burthen, and every command that men shall lay upon them, even against the pure worship of God: And if any man speak against these practices, presently *up with him* into the High Commission or Star-chamber . . . not for fear the worship of God goes down, but for fear of their *gain* and their *silver* . . . let men set up and change Religion as they please, so they can but have *their gain* from their places, and from their *quarter*, they are well."[71] If, as is likely, this sermon was preached in the 1630s, we

---

[70] Ibid., 553. In another sermon, Everarde suggested that the difference between letter and spirit was itself the subject of intense discussion and controversy: his intent, he claimed at the end of a lecture preached for Thomas Hodges at Highgate, "was to have discovered what God hath revealed to me, concerning these *deep* points, now so *much* controverted, and wherein there have been such *errours* and general mistakes, even among them who have thought themselves very *knowing* in the Scriptures" (ibid., 478).

[71] For the location, see ibid., 479; for the comments, see ibid., 496-97.

may safely interpret it as a rather sweeping criticism of the entire practice of ceremonial conformity.

Yet there was a deeper subtext here, one that no observant listener could have missed. Everarde was suggesting that the English church was being vitiated, that "the pure worship of God" was under attack, and that men were being asked to go against conscience in accepting "change in Religion." Those who refused to submit to these alterations were being persecuted in the prerogative courts for the sake of conscience. What exactly Everarde meant by "change" is not wholly clear, but by the 1630s, there were plenty of sinister-looking examples from which to choose—bowing before the altar or at the name of Jesus, the introduction of stone altars, altarwise communion-table placement, and the transformation of afternoon lectureships into catechetical sessions (a practice at which Everarde had sneered elsewhere), to name a few of the most obvious.[72]

Whichever practices Everarde had in mind, it should be clear that his was precisely the sort of performance that could easily land one before the Laudian High Commission. Never a man of moderation, however, Everarde chose to take his critique of the English establishment one step further, hinting that the scourge of covetousness did not stop with time-serving, tithe-hungry conformists. Later in the same sermon, he remarked that "Some sins are peculiar to the place of Kings, they having gotten so much power in their hands, they would be *Monarchs* without control, whose assertion is, *That they owe account of their actions to none but God alone;* and they want not for *flatterers* and *Sychophants* to preach such Doctrine in their ears, *That no power on earth ought to call them to Account,* for that they are *above the Law.*"[73] Here Everarde had wandered into very dangerous territory. It was one thing obliquely to criticize the drift of the ecclesiastical establishment, but quite another, given the atmosphere of the late 1620s and early 1630s, to complain about kings who believed they were above the law, and to denounce sycophantic, prelatical toadies who encouraged their masters with soothing invocations of the doctrine of divine-right kingship. Nor did Everarde shrink from predicting the dangers that such monarchs presented. Without some check on absolute kings "Covetousness will make them, make their *lusts* their *Law*, and they *will have* what they *will have*, right or wrong." He thankfully noted that, until now, "they have been still curbed and kept off *this absolute power*, by one means or other," but he sounded an ominous warning for the future: using the example of King Ahab, who on the advice of Jezebel had evaded the law in order to confiscate Naboth's vineyard and estate, he told his listeners

[72] For Everarde's hostile comments concerning his duty to catechize, see ibid., 211, 214.
[73] Ibid., 505.

that "Covetousness will cause *even Kings* to do this, and what not, if they have but Power enough?"[74] Although it might be argued that Everarde was here merely giving voice to sentiments that were very widely shared during the decade of personal rule, few preachers dared challenge the Caroline regime in such straightforward terms. This fact could not have been lost on his listeners, and it was most certainly not lost on the authorities. As Harford laconically noted in a postscript, "Some things in this Sermon also very much offended the Bishops, and heightned his Charge in the High Commission."[75]

Yet despite his heated rhetoric on this occasion, cowardly conformists and sycophantic Laudian prelates did not often appear in Everarde's sermons. It is almost as if they were so low in his esteem, so hopelessly beyond redemption, that they barely warranted comment. The main target of Everarde's wrath lay elsewhere. When he complained of professors and teachers caught in the quagmire of the letter of scripture, Everarde was generally not inviting his listeners to imagine lordly bishops or spineless rectors. The following paragraphs seek to use Everarde's own words to build a multidimensional image of whom, precisely, he did have in mind.

As noted above, Everarde's hermeneutic theory led him to the conclusion that the words of scripture, unless understood in their spiritual sense, were not actually the Word of God. Knowledge of the letter, although an important precondition for spiritual enlightenment, was insufficient to bring salvation: "if we could say all the Bible without book, and *understand* it according to the Letter, *it were nothing* to salvation: If they read the whole *Old and New Testament* over every year, as I have known some have made it their *task*, yea, and made it their *boast* . . . yet this were nothing, for the Devil can do as much."[76] Here Everarde seemed to be invoking that classic godly archetype of "historical faith," or the "faith of devils"—that is, a bare knowledge of scripture that wrought none of the powerful effects of justification and sanctification that were supposed to come with a true, living and growing faith. But if we look more closely at Everarde's comments, we can zero in upon the specific, flesh-and-blood target of his complaint:

> Thou saist thou *readest* [scripture] in the Church, and in thy family twice a day, and thou delightest to be exercised therein, and to see that others do so; *thou doest well*, it is good in *its place*: but *what good* doth it convey *to thy soul?* what doest thou find by this thou so *delightest in*, and so boastest of? where is *the power* that the word hath abroad among these kind of men that seem so much *to throng* after Jesus Christ? what *manner of people are these*, that so champ the *Letter* between their teeth, and *roul it on their tongues?*

[74] Ibid., 506.
[75] Ibid., 522.
[76] Ibid., 325.

> what are they in their lives? have they got *any vertue* from Christ by being so *conversant* with him? are they transformed and *made new Creatures?* do they live *the inward and spiritual life* of the Word? . . . do they *feed* upon anything but *husks*, upon the *Letter* of the word, and upon the world, and upon creatures?[77]

Here we see Everarde bemoaning men who seem "to throng" after Jesus Christ; men who bragged that they had repeatedly read through the entire scripture, and that they read passages of the Bible aloud in their households not once but twice daily; men who knew enough of scripture to conjure at will with its bare words. Yet, as Everarde argued, such individuals were often utterly unfamiliar with the spiritual, experimental, and (to use the terminology adopted above) allegorical meaning of the word. As already noted, Everarde insisted that the scriptural terms "Antichrist," "Devil" and "Lucifer" needed to be understood not as an external spirit or force, but as an internal presence in the heart of every man. In delivering this doctrine to his audience at Kensington church, he had anticipated that when confronted with this notion, many of his auditors would find his mode of exegesis to be alien, startling and incompatible with their previous beliefs. "This," his listeners would object, "is *new doctrine indeed*: had you ever such counsel given you *as this*, before this *odde fellow* came? yet I beseech you examine your selves, have ye not these thoughts within you? then this is *the man*, the *old man*, the *Lucifer*, the *Devil* that we go about to discrie. Are you not ready to say when you hear these things, *What new doctrine is this?* what do you tell me of the *red Dragon*, and the *Serpent*, and the *roaring Lyon?* we know *none of these things*, we are *Christians*, and no such things appear now adayes . . . I believe you will tell me you never heard of such a doctrine as this before: you have been a Professor this 20, 30 or 40 years, and you never heard that these things were *in you* before."[78]

Such "professors," some of whom had been born, raised, and grown old gnawing on the dead husk of the word, remained caught in the quicksand of the letter. For until one realized that Antichrist was in oneself—that when the scriptures referred to the Devil or Lucifer, it referred to the reader himself—he or she could not even begin the pilgrimage toward salvation promised in the Bible. Unaware of the first and guiding principle of true religion (the notion that the events and personages of scripture referred to changes and qualities within the believer's soul) such professors slaved away in obedience to the literal precepts of scripture, only to condemn themselves to hell. By seeking to comfort themselves with tokens of their own holiness, they remained caught in

---

[77] Ibid., 329-30.
[78] Ibid., 147-48.

a deadly cycle of self-absorption and self-worship, a cycle from which there was little hope of escape. Again, he affected the voice of such a professor:

> Oh! what excellent graces have I? how have I *excelled* other men? I have made a fair and *long progress* in Religion . . . here is the *misery of all miseries*, and the height of all aggravations, for a man to go to hell *by his Religion* . . . *by hearing of Sermons*, *by receiving the Communion*, by *praying*, *by preaching*, by *abstinence, and by overcoming of vice, by resisting of sin, giving of alms*, &c to bless themselves and say, *I thank God I am not thus and thus,* as the Pharisee said, *I am not as other men, nor as this Publican*; I do not as other men do, I do not *swear* as such a man, I do not *blaspheme* and *lye*, and *be drunk*, as *such* and *such*; I go to *Church twice a Sabbath*, I attend *diligently*, I read and *repeat the word* in my family, I *pray twice a day*: nay not onely so, but I keep *a strict watch over my heart* and *tongue*: I have *overcome* swearing and *filthy speaking*, and *lying*, and *covetousness*: all these have I *killed*, my life is *unspotted*.

Yet for all this, Everarde asked his auditors, "Are not *all* thy *good deeds fallen upon thine own head?* and hath not all thy *labour* and *pains* that thou hast taken, killed thine own soul?"[79]

Everarde's posture here bore more than a superficial resemblance to rhetorical strategies that were at or near the heart of puritan practical divinity. The claim that it was necessary to recognize "the Antichrist within" could easily have been mistaken for the classic claim that the first step on the road to justifying faith was an awareness of sin; so too, Everarde's critique of pharisaism was not utterly divorced from frequent godly warnings against the dangers of complacency, hypocrisy, and "carnal profession." Yet no mistake should be made here: Everarde was putting these classically puritan homiletic terms to subtly different use. He was suggesting that many, if not most of those who considered themselves "professors" of Christ—who believed that they had been touched by a true, lively, and justifying faith—were actually no such thing. These people remained entwined in the literal meaning of the precepts of God, failing utterly to see the spiritual meaning beneath.

Thus, in a discourse on the true, spiritual meaning of the Ten Commandments, Everarde blasted those who understood the fourth commandment in a literal manner. He explained that the creature that was perfectly at rest, perfectly observing the Sabbath, was divine: "I would be so bold as to say *it were God*: that creature were immortal and everlasting: but it is God only that is at rest, it is *he only is* immortal, and therefore no creature can be. God almighty *he is* the true Sabbath, and those that return to be *one with him*, they only keep *a true Sabbath*." This, then, was the spiritual meaning of the commandment, and "all other *keeping Sabbaths* is but *external* and *bodily labour*, and

---

[79] Ibid., 158-59.

bodily labour *profiteth nothing*, sayes the Apostle: yet most men *that not only* profess religion, but also *most Teachers*, they are *gotten into such a form* of religion and *external* holiness, of *outward and bodily* labour in keeping Sabbaths and *other things* in religion, so that true and real godliness is almost lost; and which is most *dangerous of all, herein they rest and bless themselves* and their Disciples."[80] Such men, who mistook the literal for the spiritual, the external for the internal, were all too easy to find, Everarde argued: "*see the folly* of many men in our days; they think by their pains, and *by their Discipline*, to force men into *Religion*, into faith and good works: and when *thereby* they have *onely restrained the outward man*, they pass for *excellent* Christians."[81]

Yet this was not the only vice that Everarde saw everywhere passing for excellent, godly virtue. He complained bitterly that he "is a great Christian now adayes, that is a *great faultfinder*, he *can pick a many holes*, and reprove *the sins of other men*, and this *must go* for great profession, and a *good progress* in Christianity." Everarde went on to explain, with no small note of bitterness, that "the very *summe* and *quintessence* of their Religion, is to speak *bitterly* and *largely* against their neighbours *sins*, against their *brethrens* infirmities; and forsooth, they conceive they do it out of *zeal to Gods Glory*, and consider not what a *hook* the Devil hath put into their *nostrils*, who draws and puls them which way he pleases: and *under pretence* of serving and *glorifying* God, they consider not how they serve *nothing but the Devil* and their own *lusts*." These self-righteous zealots were no better than "*flesh-flies* . . . alwayes *dwelling* upon the soars of horses, or other Beasts." Even worse, Everarde complained that those who dispensed this doctrine of devil-worship exalted themselves as the true and only preachers of Christianity: "they will be Teachers, and they would fain be accounted great *Rabbies*, and they can expound Scriptures as well as any . . . and these people, if people will not hear them, they are ignorant, they are so well instructed they can go *no whether* to learn any thing; as though all wisdom were born with them, when God knows they are *full of ignorance*, of *pride*, of *self-conceitedness*, as any men in the Town . . . And therefore I once again beseech you, *in the bowels* of Jesus Christ, and for your *own souls* sake, leave off this kinde of Religion, although I would have you *to hate even the garments spotted by the flesh*."[82]

As Everarde's closing comments suggest, although he denounced such religiosity, he rejected neither good works, God's Law (in its "spiritual" interpretation), nor divine ordinances such as baptism, provided that they were "rightly used." "Rightly used" meant that they "be but used as *Means*, and

80 Ibid., 298-99.
81 Ibid., 740.
82 Quotations in this paragraph are drawn from ibid., 434-37.

Schoolmasters, and *Tutors* to bring us to Christ: But if they instead of bringing us to him, keep and bar us from him, away with them: If we begin to admire them, and cry up them, and make *our duties* and the *Sacraments themselves*, though appointed by Christ *himself*, to be our Saviours, we are to slight them, and disesteem them in that regard, as *Paul* did the holy Law it self, in that Epistle to the *Galatians*, and elsewhere."[83] Here again, we see a remarkable rhetorical similarity to normative puritan divinity, which emphasized the paramount need to apply diligently "means of grace" in order to ensure a progressive growth in grace, assurance, and holiness. Yet again, however, Everarde had molded godly rhetorical structures to his own ends. The means, he was here suggesting, had too often become ends in themselves, with the consequence that people had whipped themselves into frenzy over issues that remained utterly peripheral to the true nature of godliness: "And truly with some men, herein lies the *top* or *quintessence* of their Religion, making such ado about *Shadows*, and *Figures*, and *Resemblances*, and they let the *Truth*, the *Substance*, and the *Thing* pass, and regard it not; forasmuch as they are so *zealous* and *hot* about *Forms*: but if they are by any *drawn* up to speak of the *Substance*, they are as men *lost*, *cold* and *heartless*."[84] This epidemic disease, this obsession with externals, could only be cured in one way, by learning to see past the letter: "but if ye had once *known Jesus Christ* after the *Spirit*, ye would not make such a stir about *Forms, Disciplines,* and *Externals*, as if that were *the great* and onely *Reformation*."[85]

When these statements were uttered, sometime in the first three years of the 1630s, there can have been little question about what Everarde meant by "Forms, Disciplines, and Externals." He was, of course, speaking of the tightly linked subjects of ecclesiology and ceremonies, issues that were coming increasingly to threaten the integrity of the English church. As noted above, Everarde was himself disturbed by certain "changes" that were creeping into the church; nevertheless, as this statement indicates, he seems to have considered excessive concern over "externals" to be a sign of weakness and residual literalism. His criticism on this occasion could have applied equally to puritanically inclined opponents of ceremonies or enthusiastic Laudian ritualists. The litany of examples offered above, however, should serve to provide more than a hint as to which of these two "types" figured more prominently in Everarde's sermons.

Let us recapitulate the "literal" or "carnal" traits denounced by the doctor in the passages above, allowing us to sketch a profile of the archetypal and omnipresent villain of Everarde's imagination: these literalists claimed great

---

[83] Ibid., 557-58.
[84] Ibid., 560 (misprinted as "260").
[85] Ibid., 343.

scriptural knowledge, informed by frequent, even obsessive Bible-reading; often, they had professed the gospel for years or decades, and could sometimes boast that they had heard upwards of one hundred separate preachers in their years of devoted piety;[86] they delighted in being exercised in the word of scripture; they laid claim to great feats of holiness, not only in abstaining from sin, but in attending church more than once a Sabbath, and in reading the word in their households; they kept a careful watch over the sins of other men, often denouncing or complaining of the iniquitous works of their neighbors, all in the name of glorifying God; they zealously and strictly observed the Sabbath, making it an important touchstone of true belief; they were obsessed with outward forms and disciplines—the external appurtenances of worship—and made these the object of "reformation." There can be little question that the traits denounced by Everarde together offer a vivid (if entirely biased and negative) description of the culture of mainstream English puritanism, c. 1630. Here was Everarde's nemesis, the great seedbed of soul-killing literalism.

The doctor's spiteful attitude toward the ways of mainstream puritanism had not developed in a vacuum. It was in fact a product of years of observation, argument and—if his tone may be taken as a reliable indicator—great personal frustration. We have already seen that beginning in the second half of the 1620s, conflicts between antinomians and their godly critics had escalated precipitously, with much sniping from the pulpit and mutual recrimination. The statements cited above, most of which were probably preached in 1630-32, were in fact *part* of this acrimonious battle. Elsewhere in his sermons, Everarde left striking evidence concerning attacks that had been made on him by other puritan ministers.

His most withering assault on the mainstream godly ministry (and his most vivid allusion to their attacks on him) had been delivered from the pulpit of Kensington in the early 1630s. After citing Matthew 19: 14—"Suffer little children to come unto me, and forbid them not, for of such is the Kingdom of God"—Everarde addressed an apparent contradiction raised by a second passage, Leviticus 21: 20, using it as an opportunity to launch a fierce and memorable broadside against his critics:

> And yet *Levit.* 21. 20. there tis forbid, that any *Dwarfe* of the Tribe of *Levi*, should approach to offer sacrifice to God. How shall we *reconcile* Gods Commandment, and Christ his practice? Truly thus, I suppose Christ in that saying, holds forth by little children, such as are in an *humble, meek, lowly*,

---

[86] Ibid., 238-39, where Everarde predicted that even the "professors" in his audience would respond with skepticism to his doctrine: "You will say, it may be, Here is a doctrine indeed: what will this Babler *bring us* to at last? . . . I have been an Auditor and a Professor this 20, 30, or 40 years, and I *never heard* such a doctrine as this, and I have heard above a 100 preachers."

> and in a *growing* condition, and coming on to perfection: for saith he, *He that receiveth not the Kingdom of God as a little childe, he shall not enter therein*: But for Dwarves, whose growth is *stinted*, they are *at their highest*, and will never grow *taller:* I mean, such who profess themselves tall Christians, but are not little children? nor cannot *endure* to grow taller, nor hear of new light, or that any should know more then they, this is hateful to them; for they think, they have been brought up with the Scriptures, they have been at the University, sat at the feet of *Gamaliel*, *exercised in the holy Scriptures from a childe*, studied all points in Divinity, searched out the judgement of most Authors, have epitomized the quintessence of their judgements; and shall we tell these men of new light? they cry *New lights* are old *Errours*: Do you think that these men are true Disciples, by him to be led into all truth? . . . And indeed we much *wonder* to see a Dwarf, because that if he live to be never so old, yet he is but *of a childes stature*, and will never increase or grow higher: What are such Christians (if they may be so called) but Monsters? like those silly women the Apostle speaks of, *alwayes learning, and never able to come to the knowledge of the truth*: who cannot indure *strong meat*, to make them grow tall men in Christ, but are stil *feeding* themselves and others with nothing but milk, with the Principles and Beginnings of Christ: But those *Plerophoria's* though they talk of them, yet they never reach them, and those that do *speak* of them, give them an offence, and get their hatred, and hard sentence: He must be a *Familist*, or a *Sectarist*, or an *Antinomian*; or some such like: and to say the truth in a few words, they censure others, and applaud themselves: and though they have been *long* Teachers, yet they themselves *had need be taught* the very lowest things in Christianity; and children they finde their Auditors, and children they leave them.[87]

Here we have Everarde at his most unforgiving, denouncing literal ministers as "monsters" and "stinted dwarves." These monsters, who pretended to be disciples of Christ, could not stomach the notion that someone might hold out further revelation—"new light." And although they mouthed the language of Christian transformation, they could not stand to hear of certain "*Plerophorias*" that went beyond their own teaching. Those who dared teach of such revelations and transformations (and here Everarde was clearly referring to himself, as well as several other city ministers) had been denounced as Familists, Sectarists, and Antinomians. Here was vivid first-person testimony concerning the nature and conduct of London's antinomian controversy. Here, too, was John Everarde's own personal controversy with the blind and literalistic ways of mainstream puritanism.

---

[87] Ibid., 555-57.

Solomon's Throne

For all its rancorous humor, Everarde's performance at Kensington left several questions unanswered. For a start, he had not actually informed his audience what he meant when he used the terms "new lights" and "plerophorias." Although he left no doubt that these had been at the heart of his controversies with other ministers, he was less than forthcoming about what, exactly, had proved so unpalatable to his dwarfen antagonists. What mysteries lay behind Everarde's boasts to special spiritual insight? Speaking privately with his disciples and admirers, he proved somewhat less reticent. Here, he offered comments that mirrored those at Kensington, with several crucial differences. He complained that literalists

> are ready to think and believe that they have smitten the City, when tis *nothing less*; they think they know as much *as can be known*, and glory in this, and so look for praise and *honor to themselves*; and if *any go beyond* them, if they cannot *fathom* what you say, presently they *cry out upon it* as an error, and no body *must know more then they*, and they *must have* the honor and praise *of all*: and yet they must keep men within *their compass* and knowledge, always *holding them* in the letter, in the rudiments, and in the *Pedagogies*, and in the *shadows* of Religion, and *cannot indure* nor hear that *men* should be brought up *to perfection*, to possess those *Plerophо[r]ias,* those full enjoyments *prepared* for them, that so they may be delivered *and set at liberty* from under the Law, and from the killing letter, from bondage and thraldom, that they may come to receive *the inheritance of sons and freemen*, that so the glory and praise of all may be to God almighty (none to them) who hath given the power to smite *Kiriathsepher*, the City of the Letter, that *it* may be *unto us Debir, the word of God.*[88]

Where Everarde had been less than forthcoming in the sermon at Kensington, here he left no doubt about what he had in mind—perfection and freedom from the law. These were the "full enjoyments" that awaited those who patiently attended upon Everarde's God. This certainly explains why Everarde found himself branded by his enemies as a Familist and an antinomian. Yet simply to stop here—with Everarde's bare promise of perfection—is to walk away with a partially obscured view of Everarde's thought, and to miss the marrow of his teaching. It was one thing to boast of perfection and freedom from the Law; but what did it mean to *be* perfect and free from the Law? What sort of experiences did Everarde have in mind when he offered his listeners resurrection from the dead, or when he delivered the rather grandiose promise that they would gain entry into God's sanctum sanctorum? The re-

---

[88] Ibid., 363-64.

mainder of this chapter will be devoted to uncovering answers to these questions.

As suggested above, Everarde saw the progress toward perfection as a long and tortured spiritual pilgrimage that mirrored—indeed recapitulated—the life of Jesus Christ. Christ's life and death constituted an extended parable or allegory for something that was to happen in the believer's experience. But an allegory for what? At its most basic, the process of living and dying with Christ was for Everarde a process of unlearning. It entailed stepping outside of one's individual experience and personal knowledge. Thus, Everarde told his listeners "when we think of God, we must go backward from our *first principles*, that were *born* with us, or *instilled* into us by our *Teachers*, or acquired by our *industry*, and *unlearn* what we have been learning so *long*, or rather transcend and forget and forsake all *that* knowledge of him: we must be stript from all carnal apprehensions of God, so as to *measure* him by any thing we can *comprehend*."[89]

The endpoint of this process was the end of selfhood. To approach God, the aspiring pilgrim needed to unlearn everything he or she had been taught, to strip away all pretensions to knowledge and self-significance: "When you have forsaken, in one word, your selves, that is, all that your *eyes* can *see*, or your *ears* can *hear*, or your *heart* can *think*, and *stript your selves* of all *stark naked*, then you may look to find God as he is *naked*, then you may look to find God as he is in himself, and consequently truth, but not before."[90] Only after one had silenced the din of the self, with all its worldly cares, its aimless desires and its cascasding streams of thought, could one approach God and the "full enjoyments" promised above.

Indeed, this process of self-silencing or self-abnegation was precisely what Everarde meant by "suffering and dying with Christ." The external torments of Jesus Christ were figures or types—that is, allegories—for this internal suffering, this process of ego-death: "to be emptied of our selves, to be made nothing, to forsake our own will, &c. *these* are sufferings indeed; all other outward and bodily sufferings are but the shadow; these are the substance, and the true sufferings."[91] Yet the process of unlearning, of stepping outside the self, did not occur overnight. In fact, it was a protracted project. So important was this process to Everarde's view of true religion that he chose it as the subject of an extended sermon cycle preached at Kensington church in the early 1630s. Here, once again, he resorted to allegorical biblical interpretation to convey his point. The process of suffering with Christ—of self-crucifixion—was typified by the six-tiered dais that led to Solomon's throne: "there be six

[89] Ibid., 398.
[90] Ibid., 602.
[91] Ibid., 141.

degrees in these sufferings, or six steps typified by the six steps that led unto *Solomons* Throne. These six steps we must ascend before we can *sit down* in the Throne of rest, peace and perfection; having overcome all our enemies, and having brought all into subjection, and that all things are *put under* Christs feet, and that he rules in the midst of his enemies."[92] These "six steps," which Everarde carefully reiterated in each of the Kensington sermons, deserve to be cited at length:

> The first is, *Condemnation of our selves*, confessing and acknowledging our own *sinfulness* and *wickedness*, condemning and abhorring our selves *really in* the sight of God.
>
> Secondly, *Annihilation* of our selves, accounting our selves *nothing worth*, as it were, *beating* our selves to dust in our own esteem.
>
> Thirdly, *Abdication*, or *forsaking* all things in the world, of what nature or condition soever.
>
> Fourthly, *Indifferency* to all things, to all *conditions*, whether to *riches* or *poverty*, to *honor* or *dishonor*, to *health* or *sickness,* to *ill report* and *good report*, to *liberty* and *imprisonment,* to *praise* or *dispraise*, to *peace* or to *war*, to *fair weather* or *foul.*
>
> Fifthly, *Conformity* to Christ our head, following him *as our patern*, that in what *condition* soever we are in, *whatever* in such a *condition Christ himself would do*, were he *in our case and condition*, the same do we.
>
> Sixthly, *Deiformity*, when indeed we are no longer *men* but *gods*: mistake me not, that is, when we *act* no longer *our selves*, but God acts *in us*; that if we do *any* thing, yet we *see and feel*, and *confess* it is God *that doth it*; that if *we speak*, it is Christ *that speaks*; if we *think*, it is Christ *that thinks*; if we *go*, it is Christ that *goeth*: that it is no longer *I* that act any thing, *it is Christ that dwelleth in you*: and you and the *members* of your body are *given up to him a living Sacrifice*, and as *instruments of Righteousness*, Rom. 6. 13.[93]

Here we have a crucial clue as to what Everarde actually meant when he claimed that believers needed to relive Christ's life. We were not, of course, to undergo Christ's *actual*, physical torments (although analogous tribulations would often befall believers); rather, his life stood as an allegory, or running metaphor, for a process that occurred internally. As we have seen above, this process started when humans acknowledged the "Antichrist within," the devil of "selfhood" and "propriety" that inhabited all people. Only when this internal Antichrist had been identified and confronted could the tortuous proc-

[92] Ibid., 202.

[93] Ibid., 128-31 (129 and 130 were erroneously omitted by the printer), as also 146-47, 165, 202, 216-17, in which the metaphor was repeated, almost verbatim, from week to week.

ess of suffering and dying with Christ truly begin. To suffer with Christ was to allow the self—the principle that underlay all sin—to die.[94]

The process described by Everarde was an extended and presumably difficult one, which terminated with the obliteration of what he neologically dubbed "Iness"—that is, one's sense of existing as a freestanding and independent being. Once liberated from selfhood, however, the believer was transformed into something quite different, and unquestionably more exalted, than a paltry, human self. This terminal point was what Everarde termed "deiformity," "when indeed" as he put it, "we are no longer *men* but *gods*." In the context of the London conflicts of 1629-31, these were deeply provocative words, calculated to extract an extreme and visceral reaction from friend and foe alike. It is no surprise, perhaps, that Everarde was not allowed to finish this sermon cycle. As noted in Chapter Three, he was removed from the Kensington lectureship before he could treat the last, glorious step up the dais, the step that brought humans into divinity.

Everarde's indiscreet statements show that the doctor promised those who followed him not only resurrection, but a species of godhood, even in this life. Yet as his qualifications suggest, to understand Everarde fully, we need to interrogate further his concept of self-death. Most importantly, we need to clarify what Everarde meant when he hinted that men and women could be rendered divine. What, in short, did it mean for a human being to become God? To answer this question, in turn, we must investigate Everarde's conception of God, for in this as in so much else, Everarde stood apart from his contemporaries.

In keeping with his claim that the road to illumination was a process of unlearning, Everarde recalled that: "I remember I was taught when I was a childe, by my nurse, or by my mother, that God was *above* in heaven; but let us now *put away childish things*: I pray God too too many *old men* be not guilty of this childishness; yea, and *many of these litteral Divines* teach no otherwise; they never bring their hearers any *farther* then to be MONSTERS, always children, always feeding them *with milk*, and never learn them to eat *strong meat*: So that if they come amongst strong men to feed with them, their

---

[94] Ibid., 230: "All that thou callest *I*, all that *selfness*, all that *propriety* that thou hast taken to *thy self*, all this must be brought to nothing; whatsoever creates in us *Iness* or *selfness*, this is *pulvis & cinis:* for take away these, and we are glorious creatures, the workmanship of God himself." Everarde likewise explained that in spiritual life, suffering and death (that is ego-death) preceded birth: "Before we can live the life of Jesus Christ, we must of necessity know his death, and find that he is crucified in us. In a natural life a man must first be born and live, before he can be crucified and put to death; but in the spiritual life *in us* its contrary" (ibid., 78).

stomacks are *so squemish*, they turn at all."[95] We need entertain no doubts concerning the identity of these monstrous, literal divines: Everarde was here referring to pharisaical, literal-minded, and largely (although not exclusively) puritan divines, who failed to understand that the biblical "heaven" was not simply the sky above. Nor, he argued, should we be so childish as to presume that God lived above, in some glorious, celestial kingdom: "He is not present *in the glorious Heavens* in his Majestie, more, then he is *in the Earth*." This meant that God was "as *infinitely*, as *magnificently*, as *gloriously*, as *incomprehensibly* present in the *basest* Creature, in the least *mote*, in *sticks* and *stones*, name what ye will, as he is in *Heaven* it self; and in all the world besides."[96] Everarde went so far as to criticize Saint Jerome for denying this truth: "*O Jerome*! it was *thy fault*, it was thy *weakness*, when thou saidst, that it was *an abasing of God*, to say he was *in a Mouse*, in a *Toad*, in the *base* creatures; for it is *no dispraise* at all to him, to say he is as much in a *Flie*, or in a *pil of grass*, as in *an Angel*; as much in the damnedest Devil in hell, as in the gloriousest Saint & Angel in heaven, but *much to his praise and glory:* for *deny* this, and ye deny *his infiniteness*, his filling *all places*, and all creatures."[97]

For Everarde, then, not only was God not confined to heaven; God filled everything that existed, permeating the entire universe, even the most humble creatures. The doctor would later regret having made this argument publicly. When he was brought before the High Commission in 1639, his claims that God inhabited sticks and stones (not to mention infernal devils) would be used to charge him with blasphemy, and to hint that he maintained a crude pantheism.[98] In fact this was a distortion (albeit not an utter misreading) of his teaching. Everarde absolutely denied that God was coextensive with creation: "though he be in the *Creature*, yet he is not the *Creature*."[99] To look upon the creature as God without qualification was to commit idolatry, for all material, visible, or sensible features were but transient accidents that hid God. God was invisible, and utterly beyond sense.[100] He was present in all creatures as a changeless principle of being, but he was not perfectly coequal with creatures.

Nevertheless, as Everarde insistently pointed out, the fact that God filled creatures meant that he necessarily inhabited all human beings. God, as manifested in his son, Jesus Christ "cannot *fill you* more then he hath *filled you al-*

---

95 Ibid., 418.
96 This and the preceding quotation are from ibid., 609.
97 Ibid., 418.
98 See Bodleian Library, Tanner MS. 67, fol. 143v. For a detailed discussion of the way in which the High Commission subtly reinterpreted Everarde's teaching on this point, see below, Appendix C.
99 Everard, *Gospel-Treasures*, 641.
100 Ibid., 290-94.

ready; neither can he be *nearer* you *then he is*; for he is *one intire act of Being, filling all things with his infinity;* he cannot *come*, nor *go*, nor *remove*, nor *be* more in one place, *nor in one man* more then in *another*." Thus, "*the King of glory is within you* already."[101] All humans, regardless of age or spiritual knowledge, were filled with God, although they rarely recognized it. Indeed, he argued that the internal presence of Christ meant that a part of every human had existed prior to birth.[102] In short, Christ preexisted in all human beings (and indeed in all creatures) as a principle of motion and being.

Here was the centerpiece of Everarde's cosmology. This unusual vision of divine immanence quite probably owed much to neoplatonic-Hermetic conceptions of God as a single, unchanging *nous* (or mind) out of which all things emanated and had their being. Whatever its precise origins, however, we can say with certainty that Everarde's vision of God supported a general conception of true religion that defied the categories normally applied to the study of early modern English history. Since he believed that God inhabited all human beings from birth, his theology in some respects resembled an Arminian system, in which God's grace was assumed to be available to all; nevertheless, as Everarde strenuously and consistently argued, only God, acting alone and outside of the realm of human effort, could bring human beings truly to understand and believe that he inhabited them already and eternally; in this respect, he appears to have shared much with the most robust of Calvinists. In short, he was neither Calvinist nor Arminian, and in fact he hinted that the predestinarian disputes that had split the English church in the 1620s were the product of a malnourished, literal understanding of the spiritual mystery of predestination.[103]

---

101 Ibid., 32. See also, ibid., 341, where it is argued that the phrase from John 1, "He came and dwelt among us, and yet the world knew him not, although it was made by him," meant "that God in Jesus Christ dwells in every creature, but *the creature comprehends* it not, *because the light shineth in darkness, and the darkness cannot comprehend the light.*"

102 Ibid., 17: "For there was *something* of me before I was either *high* or *low*, *great* or *little*, *heavy* or *light*, *old* or *young*, and that was Christ, *the beginning of all things.*" Presumably this meant that something likewise continued to exist after death.

103 See ibid., 475-76, in which Everarde argued that "understanding [the word] *according to the Letter*, hath been the ground of *all the errours*, of all the *schisms*, of all the *rents* in this poor *Church* of ours. But to go further and to give you a little *further light*, I know the Scripture in the *Letter* speaks of *election, reprobation*, and *predestination*; but if we take it *according to men*, we are much deceived . . . when he speaks of *any* of these things, of *election*, or *reprobation*, or his *foreknowledge*, there indeed is such a *kind of thing* in God tis true; but it is *true* as God intends it, and no otherwise."

For Everarde, scriptural references to reprobation and election were allegories that described the difference between those who did not understand the mystery of divine inhabitation and those who did: "though God *be in every creature*, and as much in *one* creature as in another, yet *the accidents* in the creatures hide God from us: And those to whom Christ hath manifested the Father, they in whom *Christ dwells*, they know *that Christ is in them*, and in every creature; but *reprobates* know it not, as the Apostle saith, *Know ye not that Jesus Christ is in you, except ye be reprobates?* Those that be *reprobates*, do not know *that Christ is in them:* but if they be *no reprobates,* they know it, and are sensible of it: Christ hath manifested himself *to be in them,* by *revealing to them* that God *filleth* all things."[104] Calvinists and Arminians, in their debates over the nature and procession of divine grace, had overlooked the true spiritual meaning of predestination. The elect were those whose minds had been awakened by Christ, who had come to understand that God was present not only in every creature throughout the universe, but in every human being, themselves included.

Men and woman who had come to a true, experiential understanding of this reality were, of course, deified. Yet it was not enough simply to understand the words "God inhabited all things"; rather, one needed to believe the proposition, to feel it, to hear Christ himself pronounce it within one's soul. And although Christ inhabited every man and woman from birth, because of the impediments of "Iness," of selfhood, most could neither hear nor hearken to the voice of God within. To reiterate once again, it was thus necessary to silence all lusts and wants, all sensory imaginations, and to wait on the voice of God in stillness: "Thou hast such a *Counseller* and *Comforter* within thee, that is able to *darken* and *obscure* all the counsels and comforts of all *Men*, and all *Creatures:* But thou must first strip thy self of all manner of *thoughts* and *fantasies*, and all *imaginations*, and then thou shalt find such an *infinite, bottomless God,* that thou mayst say of all *Creatures*, as *Job* of his friends, *Miserable Comforters are ye all.*"[105]

Nor was it sufficient merely to believe that Christ lived in you; to join the truly deified, one needed to believe and truly understand that all one's actions—indeed all actions throughout the entire universe—were in fact the actions of God. Nothing occurred, nothing moved, nothing changed, and nothing existed that was not moved in a direct and unequivocal way by God. While this might seem a quintessentially protestant or puritan notion of divine providence, Everarde's opinions concerning the totality and omnipresence of the divine will were extreme for the time. Thus, commonly used theological distinctions between God's "permissive" and "operative" will, or between his

---

104 Ibid., 293.
105 Ibid., 619.

"secret" and "revealed" will—often deployed to discuss problems such as predestination or theodicy—were in Everarde's view nothing more than "*Subterfuges* of ignorance." For as Everarde put it, "all *Power*, all *Might*, all *Strength*, all *Dominion* and *Omnipotency*, are all his *absolutely and solely*."[106] So unflinching was he in his claim that God's will was operative in every movement of creation that—in sharp contrast to even the most hardened predestinarian, providentialist puritans—Everarde was willing to flirt with the notion that God authored sin:

> even *the worst*, the *blackest, saddest Devils* must *say, and acknowledge,* that God *is their life*, without whom *they could not live:* God is their *strength*, without whom they *could not* move: God is *their* BEING, without whom *they were nothing*, and could *not be* at all. Beloved these are *truths*, but are ye able to bear them? take away [God] from the *creature*, and the creature *is not:* and therefore tis *worthy* our observation, that there are very *few* or none, evil *actions* (as they are *actions*) that are *in Scripture* attributed to Satan, that are not likewise *ascribed* to God, either for things *external*, or *internal*. Truly friends, I may not *keep back* any part of Gods *counsel*, for fear of the *Jews*, though they be *angry* at the preaching of these things.[107]

Everarde had good reason to be concerned about those he called "the Jews." In 1639, the leading accusation against him in High Commission would be his claim "That God almighty was not only a bare permitting or forsakeing Cause but an actuall and working Cause of all things and consequently of Synne and so was in the fall of Adam."[108] Everarde could not but plead guilty here, for he had obviously made statements to this effect in knowing contravention of the orthodoxy of the day. Yet in his view, the evil of the action came not from God, but from the creature, or rather from the opposition between separate, creaturely wills. Those who had allowed their wills to die, however, were free of evil, for they had come to understand that none of their actions were their own. These had been deified: they had come to see and acknowledge that "when we act, it is God that acts, when we see, think, speak, go, it is not *we*, but God."[109] Although this was true of every human being alive, only those who had died to the self truly believed it. And dying to the self meant acknowledging that there was no true "self" or mind other than God's mind, no will other than God's will.

This was the true, spiritual interpretation of Moses' vision of the burning bush: just as the fire had burned endlessly without consuming its fuel source, so too Christ was perpetually present in all things at all times. Those who had

---

[106] Ibid., 669.
[107] Ibid., 673-74.
[108] Bodleian Library, Tanner MS. 67, fol. 143r-v.
[109] Everard, *Gospel-Treasures*, 147.

been illuminated, and could thus see past "the bare *vision*, in the bare *letter*," understood this, and understood further that all actions were the actions of Christ:

> dost thou see what *Moses* saw? Dost thou see all *acted, altered* and *changed* by [Christ]? Dost thou see *him alone doing all?* That it is he that *un-makes* and *new-makes*? That it is he that makes men *young*, and makes men *old*? That it is he that *bringeth to the grave; and turneth man to destruction,* and saith at his pleasure, *return again ye sons of men*? That it is he that *maketh* and *formeth* man, and all Creatures, and bringeth them *back again* to their first *principles*; and thereof *creates, raiseth* and *re-makes* new Creatures? Dost thou thus *see*, that the whole *Universe* is but a body *acted* and *guided* by one *soul*, by one *spirit?* And that it is nothing but a *Carcase* moved and *led up and down* by one *spirit?*[110]

Here, then, was Everarde's vision in its nakedness. Christ was the soul of the universe, the flame that perpetually burned through the world, bringing life to dead matter and effecting all changes and motions that transpired in time. Humans, of course, shared this soul (at least to some degree), although they remained ignorantly convinced that they possessed their own, discrete and independent selves. Only when they had let go of this fallacy, acknowledging that it was Christ's soul that inhabited and ruled over their bodies, could they truly understand the vision of the burning bush.

This was the fundamental transformation within Everarde's system of divinity, the resurrection that he promised his listeners. Those who came to experience the continual internal presence of God, to understand that God was working in them and through them, were raised from the dead. Since God was in them, and they were in some real sense God, they were immortal. Those so transformed naturally received a powerful inoculation against fear: "tis as if the Lord should say, *Moses*, as thou seest me *externally* burn *this bush*, and consume it not; the *same* am I in *thee*, and in *all things* else: And if I be *so present* in every thing, and *with* every thing, what needest thou to fear? what needest thou *to fear thine own inability?* what needest *thou to fear Pharaohs hard-heartedness?*"[111] For those who had God in them, pain and death were nothing: "To see God *thus really present* with a man, what will he, nay what can he be afraid of? though there were a *thousand* deaths before him, God being so near a man, to see and believe this really, it would make him *not afraid*, though he were to *enter* into a Sea of *molten lead*; who would be afraid."[112] In this, we see the classic antinomian tendency to pronounce an end to all fear, trembling, doubt, and spiritual torment. The rigors and disciplines

110 Ibid., 657-58.
111 Ibid., 651-52.
112 Ibid., 418.

of mainstream puritanism, with its perpetual regimen of self-examination and its heroic feats of sanctification, were all rendered unnecessary in Everarde's view by the sheer weight of this moment of gnosis.

So, too, this gnosis swept away the Law. The un-illuminated might perform many good and godly works, "but it is not . . . to shew forth the *vertues* of him that hath called us, nor *to glorifie* their father which is in heaven, but tis *to glorifie* themselves, and to *set up themselves*, either for praise or esteem, or for fear, or *for hope* of advantage."[113] In short, the vast majority of people acted in response to some external stimulus or compulsion. Works performed in respect of such extrinsic compulsions were useless, and in fact dangerous: "if either *fear*, or *Law*, or *Heaven*, or *Hell*, *reward*, or *fear*, or any hopes, or by ends, *urge the heart to goodness*, these are but *dead works*."[114] Those who had received true understanding of the Christ within were no longer bound by such external constraints. They were free from fear and Law, and (as we shall see momentarily) they dwelled already in the Kingdom of Heaven. On Everarde's account, they certainly would perform good works, but they now did so without the Law: "they need no Law, they are a Law to themselves: Nay I may say, and say truly (as I may say) they are gotten above *Law*, above *Letter* in this regard: for they have the *Gospel* and the life."[115] Instead, they were driven by a new principle, which Everarde laid out most transparently in a private sermon at Kensington:

> he who is ascended; and gotten within the vail, he works freely and naturally, *he cannot do otherwise;* though there were neither fear of hell or punishment, or hope of the reward, yet *he must work:* And this is that I still say, *let the heart* be set to rights, let the man *be regenerate*, and partaker *of the Divine nature*, and then with such a man you need not keep *such a stir* with Laws and Precepts, and Rules and Disciplines; he hath *that within* will not onely inform and teach, but reform and compel *by the power of Love.*
>
> Beloved, *this is the service* God loves; *He loves a chearful giver*; he cannot abide that which comes *forced, and grudgingly*, and as a forced *imposed* task, that *by sinister respect* they must be *held* to it: but I say *this man* needs no such thing, but turn him lose at all turns, he hath an *Informer,* and a *Reformer* in him: *Those that are led by the Spirit, are not under the Law,* Gal. 5. 18. *but under Grace, and under the power of love, and of a free minde;* for the *Law is not made for a righteous man, but for the lawlesse and disobedient.* This man is no *longer* under the Law, but is *dead to the Law,* that he may live *to God,* and not *unto himself*; for *self* is conquered and dead,

---

[113] Ibid., 358.
[114] Ibid., 743-44.
[115] Ibid., 550.

and Christ now *is alive*, and exalted, *and set in his throne* to raign for ever and ever.[116]

Here, we see once again that most basic indicator of English antinomianism, the claim that believers would obey the will of God not out of the external compulsion of the Law, but freely and voluntarily by virtue of the internal guidance of the spirit.[117] In this, despite many differences of style and opinion, Everarde's argument was virtually identical to those of John Eaton and John Traske. Deploying the most unequivocally "antinomian" passage of the Pauline epistles, Everarde here claimed that those who had made the ascent to Solomon's throne, in the process annihilating the self, were now occupied by Christ, who guided them infallibly and naturally by "the power of love." The "I" and its will had been put to death, replaced by the will of God.

Moreover, like Eaton, Traske, and others, Everarde juxtaposed this vision of internal spiritual guidance against a different version of religiosity, one obsessed with "Laws and Precepts, and Rules and Disciplines." Here we have penetrated to the core of his critique of mainstream puritan ministers, who in his view dominated and bullied their followers with fear and a schoolmasterly legal regime. By favoring externals over the internal stuff of true religion, and by remaining lost in the outward letter of the Bible, such preachers "do but hold men to it as a *Bear to the Stake*, by cords of *humane* inventions, by *self-love* and *self-interest*, by *fears, hopes* and *rewards*, and these *poor things*, without the over-ruling and commanding *natural power* of love."[118] In their misguided zeal for external reformation, these ministers not only kept their followers in an unchristian bondage, but held them back from the extraordinary spiritual vision and transformation which, in Everarde's view, constituted the marrow of Christianity. Unaware of even the first principle of scriptural exegesis, such preachers could never even begin to unveil the Christ that pulsed through the universe, inhabiting each and every human being.

This serves to show that for all his reasoned scriptural argument, Everarde's vision of religious illumination was at its core a mystical one. Nowhere, for instance, did he explain how those ruled by the "power of love" would know

---

116 Ibid., 358-59.

117 See also ibid., 566-67, where this principle is once again laid out in describing the "general estate of all Christians": "First, they are *servants, and under the yoke,* before they come to be *Sons;* but when once *the true heir comes* to age, then *cast out the bond woman, and her son:* as the Apostle alledgeth that of *Abraham* for this very purpose; not that they do *cast away obedience* according to the Law, but that they do it upon another *account*, even from *love*: Then tis no longer a *yoke,* but according to that promise *Jer.* 31. 33. *I will write my Law in their heart;* and so they obey out of love, and not for *fear*."

118 Ibid., 344-45.

what precisely constituted God's will; how, without a law (and hence an external compulsion) of some sort, were believers to know what to do? Everarde, like other antinomians—and indeed like Saint Paul himself—provided no concrete answer to this question. Those who were inhabited and ruled by Christ would simply *know*.[119] They were pushed to and fro by the power of love, a principle that guided them naturally and without any external prompting. Those who had not experienced the internal presence of Christ, and who were not consequently driven by the power of love, simply could not understand either the experience or the principle. True Christians had felt and seen something that transcended words.

In fact, Everarde made it clear that this feeling, this mystical vision of God permeating all things, was transitory and fleeting. It waxed and waned, even among those who were certain of Christ's presence in their souls. For this reason, the external means of worship—the preaching of the word, the sacraments, the practices of prayer, meditation on the letter, to name a few—remained necessary. As he told his auditors at Kensington church, "do not think that I speak against *Law*, or *Letter*, or *Ordinances*; use them (as I say) but *rest not in them:* And know this also, that while the soul is *wrapt up* in the glory, sight and beholding of Jesus Christ, he knows this, that he enjoys that which is the *Substance*, and that which is as *far* above the other, as the *Substance* is above the *Shadow*, and the *Life* above the *Letter*, and the *Spirit* above the *Flesh;* yet he will not slight nor cast away these means or Ordinances, because God hath often appeared in them and by them to him."[120] He went on to suggest that these moments of illumination were ephemeral, coming only rarely even to those who were rendered perfect and beyond the Law: "I grant . . . that the most *elevated, triumphing*, and *most raised* soul, lives not always in this condition; these *things* and these *raptures*, and these *embraces* come but seldom; and the soul comes to fall lower, and have *more use* of Ordinances."[121] Yet again, however, Everarde suggested that the traditional godly understanding of the means of grace discouraged this spiritual ascent: "If ye set up *Ordinances, &c.* so as to *build* and *rest* in them, ye do make Idols of them; or at the best, you play the *Babes* and the *Children* with them, by *resting alwayes on such Crutches* and *Go-bies*." True Christians would use these

---

[119] See ibid., 749. Everarde described this transformation and internalization of Christ's "mind" in these terms: "if Christ be *risen and ascended in us*, he will so *display* his own glories and beauties *in us,* that he will *draw* all our *affections* up to him, so that we cannot but *eagerly* and *vehemently* desire to be like him: to *draw* all our love to the love *of him*, and all our *hatred* to hate that which he *hateth;* and all our *love* to love *that* which he loveth; our hate and love, joy and grief, and all our other affections to be like his."

[120] Ibid., 550.

[121] Ibid., 562.

means, but only insofar as the ordinances and externals of religion brought them moments of illumination: "*Paul,* and *Peter* and *John,* they would have always *enjoyed* those *Raptures: Paul* in the third *Heavens,* and *Peter* and *John* in *the Transfiguration.* But the one had a *prick in the flesh,* and the others came *down again from the Mount;* and in these *declinations,* and *lower enjoyments,* I would not for a world forbid, but of *others,* who may (by those) come to have *the same enjoyments,* making them no more but *means*, and not the end."[122] For Everarde, the godly commonplace of "means of grace" had come to possess a special and distinct significance; the ordinances and externals of worship were crucial not in that they contributed to the ceaseless cycle of growth in holiness and assurance promoted by mainstream puritans, but in that they were chariots whereby the believer could be drawn upward into an evanescent but life-altering mystical state of heavenly understanding. Like Paul on the road to Damascus, or Peter and John on the mount of vision, true believers had in Everarde's view been transported to heaven.

Accordingly, in a manner reminiscent of John Traske, Everarde attacked those who claimed that the magnificent glories of heaven would be experienced only after death. Just as God was not literally above in the heavens, so the "kingdom of heaven" mentioned in scripture did not refer to the material and spatial canopy of the sky above. Literalists "*will dwell in the Letter,* and think all these things spoken thereof, are some *visible* and *ocular* glories . . . And such childish apprehensions have many; yea most men, they please their *fancies*, hopes and *imaginations* with these things; *viz.* That the glory of heaven shall be *onely* hereafter; and that glory to consist in *Thrones,* and *Crowns*, and *Scepters*, in Musick, Harps and Vyols, and such like carnal and poor things." Such men, "though they talk and prattle, that *grace is glory begun*, and *glory is grace perfected*," were utterly deluded, trapped in an infantile and soul-killing understanding of the glories of the kingdom.[123]

In what was perhaps his most revealing performance, preached before a private conventicle in Old Street, Everarde admitted that he himself had once been in the thrall of just such a literalism. "I remember I was taught when I was a *Child*, either by my *Nurse*, or my *Mother*, or *Schoolmaster*, that God Almighty was above in Heaven, *viz.* above the *Sun, Moon* and *Stars* . . . I assure you I had more to do to unlearn *this principle*, then ever I had to *learn it;* and I am afraid *too many* of us are gone *no further* then this *childish* principle; whereupon follows many errours."[124] In his old age, however, he had come to the conclusion that the concept of "heaven" needed instead to be treated in one of either two other senses: "it is more safe taking *Heaven* in the

---

[122] Ibid.
[123] This and the preceding quotation from ibid., 552.
[124] Ibid., 736.

largest sense; either as God filling *all places, and all things*, as well above the Sun as below, and below as above; and so *Heaven* to be *where God is*, that is, everywhere: for he cannot be *excluded* from any place; but he is not onely in every place, but in every place alike."[125] Alternatively, he argued, "heaven" could be understood as a purely internal state achieved by illuminated Christians in this life:

> Or else . . . to take *Heaven* to be in our souls. When God *comes into* our souls, and *dwels* there, that is, when he manifests his *presence* in us, and to us, then he is said *to dwell* there: not but that he *dwelt* there in regard of himself as much before; but then he is there as in his *Temple*, as in the glory, to *us-ward:* then we see him there *in the beauty of holiness*; then he is *compassed about* with our praises, as it is exprest in that 68 Psalm, *It is well seen, O God, how thou goest; how thou, my God, goest when thou art in thy Sanctuary: The fingers go before, and the minstrels follow after, in the midst are the damsels with timbrels, &c.* When God is not onely *in us* as he is *in all Creatures*; but when he is *there sensibly* to us, that we feel him, and see him, and *behold his presence* and glory, and so come hereby to *glorifie him* more.
>
> When ever we come to this *sight*, then are we come into a *degree* of *Heaven*, into Gods *Chamber of presence*; there we shall see all Creatures, all Angels and Saints, and the whole Creation *compassing him round about* with *Glories* and *Hallelujahs;* then, *as to us*, is he set upon his Throne; till then he is *as crucified*.[126]

This passage reveals the marrow of Everarde's teaching. The entire scriptures were a parable or allegory designed to bring the believer to "heaven." "Heaven," however, was itself an allegory or metaphor for an existential state in which the believer came to understand that God had always and always would permeate all creation, including one's very own soul. The protracted process of suffering and dying with Christ was the process whereby the would-be believer came to know and understand that he or she was nothing, possessing no will, self, or being independent of God. This had, of course, always been true, but only through long struggle and pain could individuals come to see this truth manifested and revealed in themselves. This recognition of the preexistent, internal Christ was what it meant to have "God come into our souls and dwell there."

Even the most profoundly spiritual individual broke through the gates of "heaven" only rarely. Nevertheless, this vision of the divine truth, however fleeting, profoundly transformed those who had glimpsed it. Those who had been touched by this sensation were like lone drops of water, which although

---

[125] Ibid.

[126] Ibid., 737.

temporarily separated from the ocean of their origin, suddenly became aware of their nature and source. The notion that one's own soul was an isolated fragment of the divine mind—not figuratively or prospectively, but actually and in truth—was a belief that, in Everarde's view, invested the believer with an extraordinary sense of strength, indeed, of immortality. Thus, like all other passages of scripture, Christ's claim that "All power is given to me in Heaven and Earth" could not be truly and completely fulfilled until it had come to pass in the believer's soul: "till we are made *one* with him, till we are made *like* him, and till we can sit *so loose* to the earth, that we are *with him* ready, willingly and freely *to leave the earth*, we can never claim *this power*."[127] Yet those who had died and been risen with Christ—those who had come to recognize Christ within them—could indeed appropriate this claim to themselves. When

> you have *really felt* all these things *actually done* within you, his death, his life, his birth, his resurrection, that as *his enemies* have overcome and crucified *him* in you, so *you have found him* arise gloriously and triumphantly in you. . . .
>
> You being once come to this pass, *really* in experience, then you also may say, *All power is given to me in Heaven and Earth*; for then you are (as I may say) within an *inch* of being *swallowed up* into God; and then *are you ready* to leave the earth, and all things therein; for this man he is become *one spirit with the Lord*: And if we be one spirit . . . if it be so, then Christ *himself* lives *in us*, and all our *words* are the words of Christ; we have *no thoughts* but the thoughts of Christ; we have *no life*, but Christ *lives* in us. . . And you being come to *this*, as you may *claim* a right *to all things*, so you may claim *a power* over all things; for *you are* set down already in heavenly places with Christ *himself* in the glory of God the Father, who is *blessed for ever*, and you with him.[128]

Such believers shared the mind of Christ; and with Christ, the man or woman so transformed "is made *lord* of the earth, and hath then real dominion over all the Creatures."[129]

These were extraordinary claims by any measure. It should be clear at this point that both Everarde's godly enemies and his opponents within the church hierarchy were entirely justified in their suspicions of the doctor. For although his rhetoric and style often closely mimicked the intonations of mainstream puritanism, the underlying messages he promoted were subtly but deeply opposed to those commonly peddled within godly circles. His was a theology at once more unusual and more extreme than anything we have seen thus far,

---

[127] Ibid., 750.
[128] Ibid., 750-52.
[129] Ibid., 753.

promising adherents nothing more or less than godhood and lordship over the earth. In this, as in many other details of his thought, Everarde stood apart from imputative antinomians such as Eaton and Towne.

Nevertheless, despite these differences, in several crucial respects his "inherentist" divinity mirrored the more explicitly imputative antinomianism then current in London. First, and most obviously, like the others, Everarde denied that the letter of the Moral Law bound true believers. With Eaton, Towne, Traske, and others, he held that believers no longer needed the external compulsion of the Law, that they would do good works simply by virtue of the internal guidance of the spirit of God. This notion of the direct internal guidance of the spirit, shared by all antinomians, was in fact the foundation upon which the claim to freedom from the law was based. And as in the case of Eaton, Towne, and others, Everarde's denial of the Law, as well as his claims of direct divine guidance, were propelled forward by a gross aversion to the ways of mainstream puritan practical divinity. Consequently, Everarde, like other antinomians in London, found himself in fierce polemical battle against the puritan "stunted dwarves" who supposedly inhabited the pulpits of London. Likewise, and again in opposition to mainstream puritanism, Everarde shared the classic antinomian tendency to offer believers freedom from fear over their salvation; so too, he transferred many of the glorious transformations normally associated with the afterlife to the earthly domain: in a manner worthy of John Traske, Everarde insisted that believers were in some sense already in heaven. Finally, with the others, Everarde shared a tendency to stress the absolute passivity of the believer in the process of salvation, a tendency which he juxtaposed against the fretting, activist faith of mainstream puritanism. These similarities ensured that Everarde would become a fixture within London's antinomian subculture. For the same reason, it meant that he became a lightning rod for puritan polemic, and a central figure in London's acrimonious controversies over the Law.

Chapter 8

The Grindletonians: Protestant Perfectionism in the North of England

At the northwest foot of Pendle Hill, nestled amidst the moors and dales at the edge of the Craven district, sits a tiny village called Grindleton. Although now amalgamated into the modern county of Lancashire, in the seventeenth century, this small pastoral village was administratively a part of the West Riding of Yorkshire. It sat in a peculiar knob of the diocese of York, an awkward peninsula of territory that wrapped around the north of Pendle Hill, surrounded on three sides by Lancashire, the ecclesiastical oversight of which belonged to the distant Bishop of Chester. Then, as now, the villages of this clumsy jurisdictional appendage—Giggleswick, Gisburn, Grindleton, Waddington, to name a few—appear to have been as close to the economic, geographical and cultural world of Lancashire, which stretched west and south, as to Yorkshire, much of which would have seemed remote and irrelevant, separated as it was by the imposing massif of Pendle Hill and the Pennines to the east.

Up to this point, our study has focused primarily on London. Yet this belies the fact that the earliest and most important hatching-ground for antinomian ideas was not John Eaton's Suffolk, nor Traske's Somerset, nor even the ever-growing capital; that honor falls instead to the tiny and far-flung hamlet of Grindleton, the cradle of one of the more remarkable and mysterious phenomena of the early Stuart period—the emergence of a sectarian spiritual movement known to contemporaries as the "Grindletonians."

As is well known among scholars of the period, the Grindletonians were allegedly followers of an obscure, charismatic Lancashireman named Roger

Brearley, sometime curate of the little chapel of ease at Grindleton in the parish of Waddington. In late 1616, Brearley had been summoned before the York High Commission, where he was forced to answer charges of having disseminated obnoxious, if not frankly heretical, doctrinal opinions among a group of fiercely loyal followers in and around the Pendle Hill district. Brearley's detractors accused him of having set himself up as a demagogic sect-master, whose simpleminded disciples had been gulled by a deeply radical form of antinomian mysticism. Brearley survived this first ordeal before the High Commissioners, but he and his admirers remained deeply suspect for the next two decades. In the years that followed, the village and the movement appear very quickly to have become invested with an almost mythical aura. Curious outsiders told wild and improbable stories about powerful spiritual experiences—alternately described as either supernatural or satanic—on offer amongst Brearley and his followers. As a consequence, the name "Grindleton" quickly became a byword for the creeping spread of Familist or antinomian doctrines in the 1620s and 1630s.[1]

Modern scholars have been less certain about what to make of Brearley and his followers. Without doubt, some have seen in the Grindletonians a deep

---

[1] For instance, as a young Cambridge student in the 1620s, Thomas Shepard fell into a deep spiritual torpor in which he came to question both his own spiritual estate and the truth of protestant doctrine: then "at last I heard of Grindleton, and I did question whether that glorious estate of perfection might not be the truth and whether old Mr. Rogers' *Seven Treatises* and *The Practice of Christianity*, the book which did first work upon my heart, whether these men were not all legal men and their books so, but the Lord delivered me at last from them." M. McGiffert, ed., *God's Plot: Puritan Spirituality in Thomas Shepard's Cambridge*. Rev. ed. (Amherst: University of Massachusetts Press, 1993), 44-45. Shepard's posthumous biographers offered additional information, writing that "*When he was first awakened to look after religion . . . he was utterly at a losse which way to take, being much molested with suggestions of* Atheisme . . . *and moved and tempted to the wayes of Familisme also; for some advised him in the condition to go to* Grindlestone, *and to hear Mr.* Brierley, *and being informed that the people there were wont to finde a mighty possessing, over-powering presence and work of the spirit when they heard him, he resolved upon the journey; but God in mercy diverted him, having reserved him for better things.*" From T. Shepard, *Subjection to Christ in all his Ordinances and Appointments* (1652), sig. A2v. In 1655, Richard Baxter told a more spectacular, but more improbable tale: "I had an old godly Friend that lived near them [the Grindletonians], and went once among them, and they breathed on him, as to give him the holy Ghost, and his Family for three dayes after, perceived him as a man of another spirit, as half in an extasie; but coming to himself, he came near them no more." Thomas Underhill, *Hell Broke Loose: Or an History of the Quakers Both Old and New* (1660), 10-11. I owe the two last references to the kindness of Michael Winship.

significance that belied their presumably small numbers and their backwoods isolation. Owing in large part to the indisputable geographical overlap between areas of "Grindletonian" penetration and sites of later Quaker success, several authors have explored the possibility that Brearley's followers may have served as a sort of seedbed for the heroic evangelical efforts of the earliest Friends.[2] Similarly, scholars as diverse as Christopher Hill and Nigel Smith have sought to locate in the Grindletonian movement an important precursor to later forms of civil-war radicalism.[3] Yet despite this, virtually nothing concrete is known about the size and precise nature of this presumed movement. While Ronald Marchant's careful research on puritanism in the diocese of York turned up indispensable information on Brearley's various collisions with the ecclesiastical authorities, no scholar has followed his lead to attempt a detailed, local study of the Grindletonian phenomenon.[4] In short, the Grindletonians have from the very beginning existed as a sort of early modern phantasm, a chimerical beast that may or may not have existed, and which may or may not have been centrally important to the history of the Stuart era.

One of the primary culprits here is Brearley himself. As noted above, Brearley in fact left behind a substantial corpus of sermons, dating from his first months as pastor of Burnley in the early 1630s. Most of these would be published thirty-three years after his death by his follower, the lay preacher Josiah Collier. Yet these sermons have from the very beginning proved deeply disappointing as a source for the nature of the famous and frightful Grindletonian movement. Although it was widely given out that Brearley was a powerful and charismatic preacher, and although the articles alleged against him in 1616/17 were of a very radical character, the sermons that have come down to us are frustratingly tepid, containing very little to mark them as the work of a fire-breathing heretic. Alexander Gordon, writing in the old *Dictionary of National Biography* argued on the basis of the sermons that while the accusations against him might have been a "caricature of positions advanced by some of Brereley's hearers . . . they bear no resemblance to his own teaching,"

---

[2] See, for instance, R. Jones, *Mysticism and Democracy in the English Commonwealth* (Cambridge, MA: Harvard University Press, 1932; reprint, New York: Octagon, 1965), 79-104; G. F. Nuttall, *The Holy Spirit in Puritan Faith and Experience* (Oxford: Blackwell, 1946; 2d ed., Oxford: Blackwell, 1947; Paperback reprint, Chicago: University of Chicago Press, 1992), 178-80.

[3] C. Hill, *The World Turned Upside Down: Radical Ideas During the English Revolution* (London, Maurice Temple Smith, 1972. Paperback edition, London: Penguin, 1991), 81-85. Nigel Smith, *Perfection Proclaimed: Language and Literature in English Radical Religion*. (Oxford: Clarendon Press, 1989), 1-2.

[4] R. A. Marchant, *The Puritans and the Church Courts in the Diocese of York, 1560-1642* (London: Longmans, 1960).

asserting even more assuredly that "It is certain that Brereley was not conscious of any deflection from Calvinistic orthodoxy." In much the same vein, the accomplished Lancashire antiquary F. R. Raines opined that "Although wire-drawn and too much broken into divisions, [the sermons] contain many smooth and pleasing sentences, and some felicitous observations. Nor is there anything in the doctrine to cause 'John Swinglehurst [an alleged devotee of Brearley] to die distract,' although as might have been expected, it smacks strongly of the Geneva school of divines." William Self Weeks, another Lancashire local historian, likewise claimed that "the sermons . . . seem to me altogether free from anything of a sensational character, and to contain nothing to which any one at all in sympathy with the puritan view of religion could object; and there is an absence of . . . violence and fanaticism."[5] Even Christopher Hill, never one to underplay the subversiveness of those he studied, observed that the articles alleged against Brearley and his followers "seem much more radical than the views which the curate published in his sermons." To explain this, Hill plausibly suggested that Brearley's followers may have been more radical than Brearley himself, accounting for the apparent extremity of the charges.[6] Justine Darling, the most recent student of the Grindletonians, followed Hill, arguing that Brearley, although not entirely in accord with the theological currents of his day, was little more than a preacher of a sort of mystical Calvinism; he was, she argues, "a relatively orthodox preacher of spiritualist doctrine." Like Hill, she submitted that the apparent discrepancy must lie in the beliefs and actions of his followers, who outstripped their leader and amplified upon his ideas, until they pushed into decidedly heterodox territory.[7]

The following chapter seeks to reshape our understanding of Brearley and the movement he spawned. While a full account lies beyond the scope of this study, this chapter presents new archival evidence, which proves not only that such a movement existed, but which allows us to assess both the extent and the nature of Grindletonian activity. Church court, probate, and local records provide important new data, but the crucial evidence lies in the discovery of three hitherto unknown Grindletonian manuscripts, which were apparently saved and circulated by friends and admirers of Brearley. As we saw earlier,

---

[5] William Self Weeks, *Clitheroe in the Seventeenth Century* (Clitheroe: Advertiser & Times Co., 1927), 175.

[6] Hill, *World Turned Upside Down,* 82-83.

[7] J. Darling, "The Grindletonians: Roger Brearley, John Webster, Robert Towne." (Ph.D. Diss., Columbia, 1988), 52-111, 148-49. She further claims that Brearley borrowed his mystical ideas from John Everarde—a claim for which there is no evidence. Here, Darling is following Hill, who suggests that Brearley and Everarde were friends, but offers no documentary evidence. See Hill, *World Turned Upside Down*, 185.

two of these manuscripts derive from Josiah Collier, a devout follower of Brearley and sometime antinomian preacher who carefully preserved Brearley's sermons and poetry alongside Collier's own writings, together with a commemorative poem written by Brearley's convert and fellow minister William Aiglin. These two manuscripts were separated at some point (probably prior to Collier's death in 1684) but each survived independently, one coming into Chetham's Library in the nineteenth century, the other into the possession of the Lambeth Palace Library in 1986. In addition, a third, independent manuscript survives in Chetham's Library, containing two poems, one of which was certainly, and the other very probably, written by Brearley himself. Taken together, the sum total of this evidence reveals the outlines of an extensive and very self-conscious group of devotees, stretching from London to Northumberland, but centering on the rugged terrain of the Lancashire and Yorkshire Pennines and the adjacent Craven basin. The picture that emerges is one of a movement that owed an immense amount to Protestantism, yet which also very straightforwardly laid hold of perfectionist ideas, resulting in a distinctive but very influential version of antinomian thought. The resulting style of piety was, to coin a crude phrase, a "protestant perfectionism," very different in valence from the grand heterodox vision of John Everarde, outlined in the last chapter, but nevertheless anything but anodyne and orthodox.

Moses at Grindleton

Roger Brearley was born in Marland, a hamlet in the parish of Rochdale, Lancashire, on August 4, 1586.[8] His father, Thomas Brearley, was a farmer with extensive interests in the cloth trade, who appears to have achieved a significant measure of prosperity in this own lifetime; although Thomas described himself as a "husbandman," the overseers who took the inventory of his estate apparently decided that he deserved the more regal title "yeoman," for the elder Brearley's goods and chattels added up to a substantial £250, including £30 in unsold "indico cloth" and a tidy stash of £10 in ready money.[9] As perhaps befitted the eldest son of a rising yeoman farmer and cloth merchant, Roger appears to have received a basic education, probably at the recently established Rochdale grammar school, which had been founded by Archbishop Parker early in the reign of Elizabeth. Unlike Eaton and Everarde, Brearley apparently did not attend university. Nevertheless, he apparently received education sufficient to convince a diocesan official that he was fit for

---

[8] H. Fishwick, ed., *The Registers of the Parish Church of Rochdale . . . from October, 1582, to March, 1616* (Rochdale, 1888), 17.
[9] Lancashire Record Office, WCW 1617, "Thomas Brearley" of Marland.

the ministry; at some point prior to 1616, he received ordination, although not, it seems, in the diocese of York.[10]

What we do know is that Brearley seems to have been immersed from his youth in the culture of English puritanism. Looking back on his life from old age, he himself confessed that in his younger years, "I was sometime (as then a stricter man)/By some good fellows, tearm'd a Puritan."[11] This is no surprise; under the stewardship of the nonconformist ministers Joseph and Richard Midgley, Rochdale during the late sixteenth century appears to have been a lonely outpost of puritanism in the often hostile religious landscape of Tudor Lancashire. The Brearleys of Marland seem to have been exemplary pupils. A number of family wills from this period, including those of Roger's parents, bear unabashedly protestant preambles, and refer to select friends and kinsfolk as "welbeloved in Christ," giving us a clue as to the pietistic atmosphere in the village.[12] Like the other puritan dissidents who alighted upon anti-legal positions in the early seventeenth century, Brearley thus appears to have been bred up in an environment of intense godly religiosity.

It is perhaps no surprise, then, that Roger's first appearance in the records of the time came as a result of accusations of clerical nonconformity. At the episcopal visitation in June 1615, Roger Brearley, Richard Tennant, Thomas Armistead, and Nicholas Waddington were jointly presented "for preaching in the said parish church [of Gisburn] and being all or some of them commaunded to shew their license by the Churchwardens refused so to doe." The churchwardens of Gisburn—a town in Craven some five miles east of Grindleton—likewise cited Brearley "for Christning a Child in the absence of Mr Hoyle the vicar there without the sign of the cross contrarye to the book of common prayer."[13] On the same day, Brearley was separately presented by the churchwardens of Waddington (the mother church of Grindleton) "for preaching at Grindleton Chapel without license thereunto from the Lord Archbishop and for not reading common prayer every saboath day and likewise for not receiving the Holy Communion at Waddington since he came to

---

[10] During his High Commission trial, Brearley was commanded to produce valid letters of orders, which he did; this suggests, however, that he was ordained outside the diocese. Borthwick Institute, HC AB 16, fol. 158v.

[11] Roger Brearley, *A Bundle of Soul-convincing, Directing and Comforting Truths* (1677), appended poems, 3.

[12] For the Midgleys, see R.C. Richardson, *Puritanism in North-West England* (Manchester: Manchester University Press, 1972), 19, 20, 32, 40, 51, 53, 57, 65n171, 66n173, 69n184, 75, 118, 124; See Lancashire Record Office [LRO], WCW 1617, "Thomas Brearley"; LRO, WCW 1641, "Richard Brearley," of Castleton in Marland; LRO, WCW 1621, "Alexander Brearley" of Marland; LRO, WCW 1637, "Abell Brearley" of Rochdale; LRO, WCW 1633, "Alice Brearley."

[13] Borthwick Institute, Vis 1615 CB, fols. 69v, 70v.

preach at Grindleton."[14] Brearley himself failed to answer the charges and was initially excommunicated, although he received absolution early in 1616.[15] This sudden eruption into the church courts was probably not accidental; it is likely that Brearley was in trouble not simply because of his nonconformity, but because his unusual sermons had already begun to attract attention in the area. Both at Waddington and at nearby Gisburn, some village leaders seem to have been alarmed by the appearance of this charismatic, twenty-nine-year-old preacher in their midst.

It is crucial to realize, however, that Brearley was not alone. The fact that he was cited with Tennant at Gisburn is of crucial significance. From this point onward, the names of these two men would be tightly linked together, both by friends and enemies. In 1627, they would again be cited together before the High Commission on suspicion of doctrinal heterodoxy. Yet it was not merely hostile outsiders who looked on them as a sort of team. In 1657, for example, when the ex-Grindletonian and newly minted Quaker Thomas Barcroft wrote to his old coreligionists to try to convince them to recognize the inner light, he evoked the "sweet society and union in spirit in the days of that glimmeringe Light under the Ministry of Breerely, Tennant and some few more whose memories I honnor, called then by the Professors of the world Grinletonians."[16] According to the London cutler and erstwhile Familist Giles Creech, the Marrowist Edward Fisher had allegedly acquired a translation of the *Theologia Germanica* "by a minister at Grendleton: called Brierly or Tennant" (indisputably hearsay, but hearsay that nevertheless squares with all other data available concerning the translation and circulation of the famous mystical treatise).[17] Tennant was in some ways an unlikely bedfellow for the farmer's son Brearley. His father, Henry Tennant, was a gentleman of nearby Malham Waterhouses. Just twenty-four years old in 1615, Tennant was recently up from Gonville and Caius College, where he had taken his B.A. in 1613 (he would proceed to take his M.A. three years later). In 1614, he was ordained as a deacon in the diocese of York; he continued on to the priesthood in 1619, when his father preferred him to one mediety of the rectory at Burnsall, a few miles north of Gisburn.

It should be noted that both Brearley and Tennant were presumably occupying the pulpit of Gisburn with the explicit approval of the vicar, Henry Hoyle, himself a curious figure. The son of a Halifax gentleman, Hoyle was both an inveterate nonconformist and a serial pluralist. Although he was twice suspended by the bishop for failure to wear the surplice, Hoyle was also the

---

[14] Ibid., fol. 82v.
[15] See Marchant, *Church Courts*, 233.
[16] Library of the Society of Friends, London, Swarthmore MS. Vol. 351, fol. 174r.
[17] See PRO, SPD 16/520/85, fol. 126r. See Prologue and Chapter Two, above.

incumbent of multiple livings in the North. Yet he was by no means an indifferent, negligent absentee: Tennant, and probably Brearley, had his full support. Indeed, so taken was Hoyle with Tennant that in May 1619, Tennant wedded Mary Hoyle, the vicar's daughter, in the parish church of Gisburn. We are therefore left with a somewhat surprising conclusion: the infant Grindletonian movement was nurtured and given succor by a respected local clergyman, who like Tennant hailed from West Riding gentle stock. Nor did Hoyle disown his troublesome son-in-law when the young man became tainted by his association with Brearley; in 1632, the elder minister presented Tennant to the Yorkshire vicarage of Kettlewell; before his death in 1636, Hoyle loaned Tennant and a kinsman, William Tennant of Scorborough, the prodigious sum of £400.[18] Indeed, there are signs that Tennant had other backers in Gisburn. When he compounded in 1619 to pay his First Fruits to the Crown for his new living of Burnsall, one of the men who stood surety for the young minister was Richard Monkys, a leading gentleman of the town of Gisburn.[19] In short, the Grindletonian movement sprang up at least in part through the connivance of wealthy and influential members of the local community.

That such a movement was already taking shape by 1615 is clear. Brearley, it seems, had become something of a sensation in the region. Looking back after 1637, the minister William Aiglin, who was present with Brearley and Tennant from the very beginning, offered this very vivid eyewitness recollection:

> When I remember that first mightye call
> of that great watchman, and did see them all
> from every quarter come both rich and poore
> blinde, lame, withered; great and mighty store
> of wise and learned multitudes of men
> came hasteing to that place apoynted then
> for cost they cared not, length of the way
> was then noe burden wandering every day
> to those fair courtes unto thy voyce so sweete
> where all that companye in one did meete.[20]

---

[18] For Hoyle, see Marchant, *Church Courts*, 256, 283. For his living at Giggleshorne, see PRO, E334/17, fol. 34r; for the marriage, see J. Charlesworth and S. Simpson, eds., *The Parish Registers of Gisburne . . . 1558-1745*, Yorkshire Parish Register Society, 114 (1943), 180; for his loan to Tennant, see Borthwick Institute, Chancery Wills, "Hoyle, Henry," Gisburn, March 1636.

[19] PRO, E334/16, fol. 31r.

[20] Lambeth Palace Library MS. 3461, 235-36.

Aiglin, who had been converted by Brearley, was no disinterested observer, and this description may suffer from an urge to lend an epic (perhaps even Christlike) quality to the life of his dead hero. Nevertheless, even allowing for rhetorical excess, Aiglin's description offers crucial information. First, it tells us that Brearley did not initially try to hide his prophetic gifts in the hermetic secrecy of Grindleton chapel. Second, as word of his ministerial talents seeped out, his sermons began to attract significant attention in neighboring districts. According to Aiglin, both poor and wealthy auditors gadded to hear Brearley preach, a fact that accords with the support Hoyle and Monkys appear to have lent the movement in its early stages. This should not come as a huge surprise. Puritans tended to fetishize powerful, charismatic preachers, and all indications suggest that Brearley's pulpit presence was widely regarded as extraordinary, even by the discriminating standards of the godly. When combined with the fact that he was preaching a message that was deemed by many to be novel and special, the lure was presumably irresistible.

Where Aiglin may have been guilty of embellishment was in his suggestion that all who came to Grindleton found joyful spiritual community in the sweet sounds of Brearley's voice. Aiglin himself confessed that while "some of that truth [i.e., Brearley's message] did make a working song," others "waxed wearye of that jorney long." For many eager sermon-gadders, then, the novelty quickly wore off. Even more tellingly, however, Aiglin ruefully recalled that other listeners had not come in good faith: "some sought to catch him and for to betray/that Innocent."[21] The crowds that gathered to hear him preach thus included certain snakes in the grass who, having heard rumors of Brearley's doctrinal peculiarities, had apparently come to spy on him and his admiring audience.

Fortunately, other evidence allows us to make plausible inferences concerning the identity of these scribe-like local knaves. When Brearley was called before the High Commission in late 1616, it was alleged that his followers had claimed that "That Mr Shute vickar of Gigleswicke and mr Brooke minister of Garg[r]a[ve] are both either ignorant or malicious persecutors of sincerity."[22] "Mr Shute" was Christopher Shute, one of the leading godly ministers of the West Riding. Probably seventy years of age in 1615, he had been the pastor of Giggleswick for forty years, acting as a sort of patriarch for the local godly community, and playing a central role in the maintenance of a regular clerical exercise in the Craven district.[23] Although accused of ceremonial nonconformity, like so many other puritans in the North, he appears to have been seen by the Elizabethan authorities as a crucial bulwark against Popery. Thus,

---

[21] Ibid., 236.

[22] See below, Appendix D, item 43.

[23] Marchant, *Church Courts*, 278.

despite his scruples about ceremonies, from 1594, Shute sat as a member of the York High Commission. "Mr Brooke" was Thomas Brooke of Gargrave, a much younger minister, and also a reputed nonconformist.[24] This allows us to infer another crucial point about Brearley's early career: from the outset, Brearley's troubles seem to have been the result of conflict with fellow members of the local puritan community, who were alarmed by either his message, his style, or both. Shute, in particular, may have been irked by the fact that Brearley was siphoning members of his congregation to Grindleton; ministerial poaching of this sort could create tensions between godly pastors, resulting in feuds that staked the authority and spiritual power of one minister against another.[25] When combined with the apparent novelty of Roger's opinions, the threat may well have seemed intolerable, leading Shute to use his connections in York to have the matter brought to the attention of the Archbishop and his subordinate officers.

Hence, in October 1616, the York High Commission opened a case against Brearley on the serious charge of doctrinal heterodoxy.[26] According to Josiah Collier, who probably witnessed the events as a young man, the case had been instigated entirely by Brearley's local opponents. His enemies "raised aspersions against [him]; informing the High Commission against him; who sent their commands to bring him to York, where he was kept in prison for a while, during which time; fifty Articles were exhibited by his Adversaries against him before them."[27] This accords with the official records of the case. By January of 1616/17, a "schedule" of alleged errors had been produced against Brearley. Brearley himself was ordered to be held in custody until he made a declaration on the opinions.[28] It seems likely that he was released at some point, for two months later, when official articles were exhibited against him, he was commanded not to preach in the province of York, and he was once again remanded to the custody of a pursuivant.[29] The articles themselves have not survived, but the attached schedule of fifty "erroneous opinions"—the "aspersions" that had been gathered by Brearley's antagonists—survives in

---

24 Ibid., 234-35.

25 See P. Lake and D. Como, "'Orthodoxy' and its Discontents: Dispute Settlement and the Production of 'Consensus' in the London (Puritan) 'Underground,'" *Journal of British Studies*, 39 (2000). For Brearley and the parishioners of Giggleswick, see Borthwick Institute, Vis 1619 CB, fol. 58r.

26 Borthwick Institute, HC AB 16, fol. 138v.

27 J[osiah] C[ollier], "An Epistle to the Reader," in Brearley, *Bundle*, sig. A3r.

28 Borthwick Institute, HC AB 16, fols. 150r, 158v.

29 Ibid., fols. 152r, 156v.

at least two copies, both now held in the Bodleian Library (a transcript of one of these documents follows in Appendix D).[30]

As was typical of High Commission actions, Brearley's case lingered on for almost a year. In the months that followed at least three dozen witnesses were sent compulsory letters demanding that they attend the court and give evidence in the case. This included both Shute of Giggleswick and Brooke of Gargrave, as well as ten other ministers, all of whom came from the area in the immediate vicinity of Grindleton, and most of whom were probably participants in the Craven exercise.[31] In addition, twenty-three laymen were summoned to testify. Although it is impossible to ascertain why these individuals were summoned, it seems likely that at least some were suspected followers of Brearley. Near the head of the list of laymen was none other than "William Eglin," surely the future minister William Aiglin whose funeral verses would later celebrate Brearley as a hero and latter-day apostle of truth. Also cited was one "William Currer," a member of a prominent Craven family, and probably one of Brearley's patrons in later years.[32]

Unfortunately, neither depositions nor testimony have survived for the case. Nevertheless, by examining the fifty "erroneous opinions" ascribed to Brearley and his followers, we can get a sense of what his enemies thought he was saying, and why they were so alarmed. In many respects, the ambience of the early Grindletonian movement, as described by its enemies, seems to have paralleled nothing so much as that of the Traskites, who were frantically lurching from heresy to heresy during these very same months. Thus, it was claimed that the Grindletonians held that "A motion riseing from the spiritt is more to be rested in, then the word it selfe"[33] and that "It is a sinne to beleeve

[30] Collier's account implied that these fifty "opinions" were the official articles against Brearley; in fact, this schedule of fifty erroneous propositions was distinct from the now-lost articles, for which see Borthwick Institute, HC AB 16, fol. 158r.

[31] Borthwick Institute, HC AB 16, fol. 158r. The ministers were as follows: Shute, Brooke, R. Gibson, E. Watkin, J. Foote, William Harrison, G. Wiber, J. Eastwood, A. Emott, F. Peele, T. Jobson, J. Harrison, and Thomas Drake, for whom see Marchant, *Church Courts*, 234-35, 244, 245, 246, 247, 248, 253, 257, 290.

[32] For the complete list of lay witnesses, see Borthwick Institute, HC AB 16, fol. 160r. They were as follows: John Banister, gentleman of Waddington, William Eglin, Thomas Simpson, William Winsor, Thomas Oddie, James Oddie, John Aspinall, Thomas Baxter, Thomas Peele, Reginald Huber, Roger Wigglesworthe, Robert Fawber, William Currer, John Broxupp, Henry Becroft; in addition, a second spate of letters was issued to Laurence Spencer, Abraham Titley, William Fowles, Ellis Nutter, Richard Mitchell, Henry Stawe, Lawrence Jackson, and Nicolson "de Newcastle." It is not clear whether "de Newcastle" referred to Nicolson alone or to all nine of the names included in this second list.

[33] See below, Appendix D, item 1.

the word, as it is the word, without a motion of the spiritt."[34] Both of these accusations hinted that the Grindletonians privileged internal motions of the spirit over the bare letter of the word of scripture. But what did it mean, in terms of subjective experience, to be "moved" by God's spirit? Some inkling of this is conveyed by a crucial article that charged "They say they are soe filled with the spiritt that they cannot reade a chapter trulie, yet can expound it, and in prayer they are soe ravished that they cannot speake a woord."[35] Two points should be noted here: first, the accusations suggested that the Grindletonians practiced a form of spontaneous and unmediated scriptural exegesis, in which the spirit would lead them to "expound" the true sense of a given biblical text. This, it would seem, lay behind the claim "That everie man should pray without meditation," that is, without thought or calculation.[36] Secondly, such moments of inspiration were taken to be powerful, even ravishing, subjective experiences.

We have seen that this sort of reliance on the spirit was not uncommon in radical puritan circles, particularly at the separatist fringe. Yet according to their accusers, Brearley and his followers seem to have taken this "spiritist" impulse to an extreme, leading them to deny or denigrate the value of human learning and knowledge in favor of a reliance on the immediate tutelage of the Holy Ghost. Thus, they supposedly taught that "Grace being wrought in the heart the spiritt abolisheth all former knowledge, and they bidd away all scripture knowledge," that "it a sinne to chatechise the ignorant for knowledge is an hinderance to grace," and that "He is a devill that ever studieth before he preacheth."[37] From this, it followed quite naturally that episcopal ordination, and the scholarly competency ordination entailed, was irrelevant, since "a man haveing the spiritt may read, pray, or preach without any calling whatsoever."[38]

Indeed, the most serious of the allegations hinted that the Grindletonians allowed their overweening trust in their own spiritual illumination to nullify all the ordinances of the church: "That they have received such abundance of grace, that now they canne stand without the use of the meanes."[39] Such claims to spiritual inspiration were apparently accompanied by equally profound claims to spiritual transformation. One article suggested, for instance, "That after a man hath assurance, of the forgivenes of his sinnes, he can never doubte againe."[40] Although perhaps overblown, this accusation closely paral-

34 Appendix D, item 2.

35 Appendix D, item 18.

36 Appendix D, item 30.

37 Appendix D, items 11, 21, 39.

38 Appendix D, item 33.

39 Appendix D, item 41.

40 Appendix D, item 5.

leled the persistent antinomian claim to be offering a brand of assurance more powerful and more total than that hawked by mainstream puritans. Like Traske during the same years, and like many antinomians who would follow, the Grindletonians reportedly claimed that this certain apprehension of divine forgiveness brought an indescribable flush of inner happiness: "they cannot have more joy in heaven, then they have in this life by the spiritt."[41] Again, in a manner that should now be familiar, this feeling of release and joy was apparently contrasted with the gloomy half measures of mainstream piety: "It is an error (say they) to hould that where there is most grace, there is most humiliation."[42] In the view of their enemies, however, this state of total joy and assurance led to a dangerous spiritual insouciance. Grindletonian converts felt themselves above sin and repentance: one article stated flatly that "The christian assured can never committ a grosse sinne," while another suggested a cavalier disregard for divine moral commands: "They care not for falling into a sinne, for god turnes that to the best."[43] Another article suggested a doctrinaire opposition to the notion of repentance for sins committed: "They hould it unlawfull to pray for forgivenes of sinne after conversion."[44]

These accusations were of course designed to tar Brearley and his followers with the brush of crude libertinism; as stated, they were almost certainly false (indeed, in the years that followed, Brearley and his followers would vehemently deny all charges of moral license). Yet it seems beyond doubt that something very unusual was happening amongst Brearley and his followers. Perhaps most distressing to local puritans was the fact that the Grindletonians seem to have been ferocious and entirely dismissive toward their opponents: "If anie one doe not yeald to their opinions, instantlie they say they see the devill in him."[45] Indeed, they had allegedly maintained that "That there is as much difference betwixt Mr Bryerley's preaching and other mens, as betwixt salvation and damnation, and that a wicked man may doe as much as most men preach, nay may obey all the written woordes, and be damned."[46] In other words, at least some Grindletonians appear to have been calling into question the spiritual status and doctrinal probity of all who opposed them, giving us a clue as to the environment of heated backroom conflict and debate that preceded and underlay the court case as it eventually played itself out.

This last article, too, brings us to a final point about the charges lodged in 1617; they emphasized the importance of Brearley's person to the movement. To his admirers, his preaching was as different from that of his contemporar-

---

[41] Appendix D, item 46.
[42] Appendix D, item 25.
[43] Appendix D, item 7 and 24.
[44] Appendix D, item 15; see also items 3, 19.
[45] Appendix D, item 22.
[46] Appendix D, item 50.

ies as heaven from hell. His followers allegedly regarded him as nothing short of a prophet, "whom they terme the Angell of England and the onelie one of a thousand." They reportedly predicted that "If Mr Bryerley may stand but a while longer 3 or 4 of the best christians in every parish of England will be assembled thither." Indeed, Brearley's followers had come to believe their humble village to be the epicenter of an unfolding divine drama, in which "the prophecie of Joell (your young men shall see visions, and your ould men shall dreame dreames, and your daughters shall prophecie) is now fulfilled att Grindleton" and "the Arke of the covenant is shutt up and pinned within the walls of Grindleton chappell."[47]

Given the extremity of these charges, the most astonishing thing about the case is that in the end, it went nowhere. As the trial progressed over the course of the year, it appears to have shifted direction; what began as an investigation into Brearley's heretical opinions became much more closely focused on the issue of obedience to the rites, ceremonies, and doctrinal articles of the Church of England. Thus, in June of 1617, Brearley was given further time to deliberate on the question of "whether he will Conforme himself accordinge to the booke of Comon prayer" and whether he would subscribe to the thirty-sixth Canon of the church, including the three articles of conformity that were appended to that canon (one of which held that the thirty-nine articles were agreeable to the word of God). To facilitate this process, it was ordered that he confer with George Meriton, the dean of York, and Dr. Phineas Hodson, one of Archbishop Matthew's trusted lieutenants. On August 5, he was once again granted additional time for deliberation.[48] This strategy of lenience and negotiated conformity was a common course in dealing with ceremonial dissidents, particularly during James I's reign, when a meek and humble willingness to confer and deliberate with ecclesiastical officers was taken as a sign of good faith and was often enough in itself to escape punishment. Brearley seems to have pursued precisely this path, thereby ingratiating himself to the authorities and undermining the credibility of his rivals. On September 30, 1617, Brearley appeared personally before the court, and Meriton, the dean of York, certified that the preacher of Grindleton had in fact "subscribed accordinge to the Cannons, and Conformed himself."[49] On Collier's account, Brearley was also compelled to preach a sermon at York Cathedral, presumably to reiterate his submission to the orders of the church.[50] Accordingly, his case was dismissed, Brearley's bond was delivered back into his hands, and he was excused payment of court costs. More significantly, Archbishop Matthew,

---

[47] Appendix D, items 36, 41, 44, and 49.

[48] Borthwick Institute, HC AB 16, fols. 167v, 172r.

[49] Ibid., fol. 176r.

[50] J[osiah] C[ollier], "An Epistle to the Reader," in Brearley, *Bundle*, sig. A3r.

apparently convinced that Brearley was not a dangerous, heretical hothead, restored him to his ministry, allowing the young preacher to return to Grindleton without inhibition, a fact that no doubt galled those among his enemies who had hoped to see Brearley brought to his knees.

Given what we know of Matthew, this is not shocking; the archbishop's liberality with respect to nonconformity was legendary, and Brearley's appearance as a powerful preacher of protestant inclinations probably overshadowed any doubts that the crusading anti-Popish prelate might initially have felt. Perhaps somewhat more surprising, given the extraordinary and outrageous nature of the opinions ascribed to him, is the fact that Brearley was willing to submit unconditionally and without apparent reservation to the court. This pattern of compliance would characterize the remainder of his career; he would continue on at Grindleton until the early 1620s, at which point he took up the nearby curacy of Kildwick-in-Craven; in 1631, he moved yet again, this time just across the border to Burnley in Lancashire, where he would serve as minister until his death in 1637. His career path was not entirely smooth: in 1627, he would once again be brought before the High Commissioners to answer for his opinions, yet once again, he managed to survive, apparently through unconditional submission. All of this might be taken to bolster the view of those modern commentators who have argued that Brearley was not the dangerous, radical sect-master of his enemies' imagination. To be certain, his accusers were guilty of distortion and scaremongering; yet, as we will see in the final section of this chapter, Brearley did in fact collect a core of zealous followers, some of whom continued to cleave to his teachings into the civil war and beyond. Moreover, while the errors ascribed to him were undoubtedly exaggerated and misleading, there can be no doubt that Brearley was offering up a message that differed significantly from that of his contemporaries. It is to the substance of this message that we now turn.

Brearley Speaks Back

What, then, was Roger Brearley's message? What was it that so terrified his enemies and electrified his followers? Modern readers have been hard put to furnish an answer. In most of his surviving public statements, Brearley struck a studiously moderate and self-consciously orthodox note, one that would seem to undercut all the claims of his enemies. But this, in many ways, is itself the point: Brearley's entire career, from his first High Commission trial to his death, was conducted under the microscope of outside scrutiny. The Brearley whose sermon notes and poetry have come down to us was a man perpetually seeking to answer, and indeed to confound, his enemies. This informed his every public utterance. To be sure, Brearley was more candid in some venues than others. Preaching before his fellow ministers at the Halifax exercise in the wake of his first trial, for instance, Brearley would offer up a very carefully worded sermon so as to avoid giving his listeners anything that might resemble a target. The rest of Brearley's surviving sermons, which were mostly preached in 1631 and 1632 before his congregation at Burnley, were only slightly less cautious;[51] this is perhaps to be expected given that Brearley had already endured two major prosecutions in High Commission, and that his new and populous parish would have been full of unfamiliar faces. Somewhat more forthcoming is his religious poem, "Of True Christian Liberty," which was written and circulated in manuscript, presumably with no intention of publication. It is in this seventy-three page poem—and in a second poem, "Of Hypocrisy," also probably the handiwork of Brearley—that one begins to get a more frank appreciation for what separated Brearley from his contemporaries.[52] Yet even Brearley's religious verse, despite its ostensibly private character, in many ways represented an extended *apologia pro vita sua*, a meditative answer to the critics who had dogged him throughout his adult life.

In short, there is no uncensored Roger Brearley. Even his most candid private statements were written in the shadow of what appears to have been an internalized heresy hunter. For this reason, the writings of Brearley's followers provide an invaluable supplement to the works of the master. William Aiglin and Josiah Collier were veterans of the first days of Brearley's ministry, and, as we will see in the final section, they appear to have been two of the chief Grindletonian preachers. Their writings offer an interpretation of what Brearley's closest and most dedicated allies took him to be saying. Only by reading these documents beside and against one another can we begin to peel back the layers of caution and obfuscation to reveal Brearley in full regalia. What emerges is a portrait of an intensely complicated figure, a man deeply attached to the psychological lifeline of the English puritan community, but whose own religious journey had led him to a mode of piety that in many respects subverted the intellectual foundations on which that community was built.

Any attempt to make sense of this paradoxical figure must begin with Brearley's own peculiar sense of himself and his own message. Throughout his career, Brearley took pains to present himself as an orthodox preacher of true protestant principles, whose critics had grossly misunderstood his message. In his poetic apology, written and then expanded toward the end of his life, Brearley for example denied that he had ever exhorted Christians to abandon the means of grace in favor of more immediate forms of spiritual enlightenment. He bent over backwards to refute charges of moral license, claiming along with the other figures named in this study that true Christians would

---

[51] For the dating of Brearley's sermons, see Lambeth Palace Library MS. 3461, 5-223.

[52] For a discussion of the provenance, history, and authorship of these poems, see n.183, below.

always aspire to holiness and rigor. There is no reason to doubt his sincerity. Indeed, the few glimpses we have of Brearley's private life suggest that he possessed a moral sensibility indistinguishable from his puritan contemporaries. His pastoral letter to his friend Anne Pethye, for instance, was laden with dire warnings to avoid the evils of "carnal behoulding" and "fleshly lust."[53] So likewise, when death approached, Brearley drafted his will, leaving a portion of his goods to his wife Anne. As was typical, she was to forfeit this portion to her children if she remarried. Less typically, it was also bluntly stipulated that she "not commit fornicacion."[54] Hardly the fond farewell of a wanton libertine, Brearley's words evince characteristically godly obsessions with carnal impulses, sexual misbehavior, and household discipline (which he apparently hoped to exert even after he was dead and buried).

Indeed, Brearley's sermons often give much the same impression. On Christmas 1631, he admonished his audience, warning them that "We celebrate this Feast, in remembrance of this great Savior. . . . But we consecrate it to *Bacchus*, not to Christ, in Rioting, and Drunkennesse, in Chambring and Wantonnesse. . . . O, if Christ should come, as he will come, and find us thus: One swilling and drinking: another carding, and dicing: another whoring: And all under pretence of love to him: Would he take it well? O no!"[55] Again and again, he warned his listeners to flee from the flesh and from "fleshly" things; Brearley evidently could play the role of censorious puritan killjoy with all the earnest enthusiasm of a Ben Jonson caricature.

This penchant for moral exhortation was matched by what appeared to be a scrupulous and unswerving commitment to received truths of reformed doctrine. Man, Brearley often reminded his listeners, was utterly helpless in himself.[56] He frequently lapsed into a stock reformation critique of works righteousness, as when he complained that humans acted as if God "cannot save us without our help, Works, Wisdom, and Righteousnesse and these must be set up to look at, and we behold Christ through these, and Circumcision: and so we stand not as Beggers to receive of his fulnesse, but as Traders in Religion, to bring something unto him, as a thousand Rams."[57] In language that would have passed muster with even the most fastidious defenders of orthodoxy, Brearley trumpeted the idea that man's "righteousnesse, as his own, brings no ground to believe, but only Gods free grace."[58] Unsurprisingly, the alternative "Doctrine of free will destroyes Faith . . . lifts up man in pride and presump-

[53] Ibid., 225-26.
[54] Borthwick Institute, Original Wills, "Brearley, Roger," July 1637, PROG.
[55] Brearley, *Bundle*, 31, 117.
[56] See, for instance, ibid., 122.
[57] Ibid., 148.
[58] Ibid., 257.

tion, and makes him secure in a few faint endeavours of his own."[59] In this spirit, Brearley repeatedly violated the royal prohibition on predestinarian discourse, denouncing "*Arminius*, who will needs set rules and laws to God," presumably a reference to the doctrine of predestination based on faith foreseen, which Brearley likewise dismissed as a dangerous error.[60] Against Arminius, Brearley held up the example of Martin Luther, who "preached free justification by faith, without the righteousnesse of man, and the whole army of *Antichrist* was up in arms against him." Luther, like the children in King Nebuchadnezzar's furnace, had braved ferocious persecution to make the message heard. As Brearley put it, "these stick to God, and the King is furious," a statement that in the early 1630s might plausibly have been taken to refer to someone other than Nebuchadnezzar.[61]

While these statements might have borne a provocative political edge, none would suggest that Brearley was anything other than a sincere and zealous Protestant, upholding central truths of the Reformation. Indeed, this would appear to be how he saw himself: as he explained in his poetic apology, his doctrine was "the same (say I) that hath been taught, / Since God his Gospel, into *England* brought."[62] Like Eaton, then, he presented himself as an embattled defender of sacrosanct protestant truths. Unlike Eaton, however, Brearley carefully refrained from comparing his critics to ruminants and wallowing beasts. His poetic apology may in fact be seen as a sort of extended commentary on what he identified as "the earnestness and strife, / Which in Gods heritage is now so rife, / Between the *Grindletonians*, so men call them," and their detractors.[63]

Rather than castigating his opponents as demons or dogs, Brearley chose to gloss these "strange conflicts," "jarrs," and "variances" as a sort of colossal misunderstanding, or, as he put it, a series of unhappy "misconceits, 'twixt Christians."[64] The disputes were, quite literally, "verball jarrs" and "Word-strivings," that is, semantic disputes about how to express things rather than quarrels over the substance of true religion.[65] Brearley repeatedly suggested that what his opponents had objected to was his tendency to use "new words" to describe the formal truths of protestant doctrine. He complained that fellow ministers had mistaken his good intentions, leading them to denounce his admittedly unfamiliar expressions as "error-breeders," and "fruits of fancie-feeders," which betrayed a spirit of "newfangledness," and created the mis-

---

[59] Ibid., 16.

[60] Ibid., 223, 251.

[61] Ibid., 223, 150.

[62] Ibid., appended poems, 4.

[63] Ibid., appended poems, 62.

[64] Ibid., 3, 33.

[65] Ibid., appended poems, 46.

taken suspicion that Brearley was in fact teaching "New Revelation."[66] This he denied. Brearley conceded that he had used unfamiliar phrases, but defended the practice by arguing that "Some words tearm'd new, oft gives a greater light / Into the Spirits meaning of the Word, / Then otherwise a sentence will afford."[67] Brearley thus suggested that he taught the very same doctrine as his opponents: "I see not where a real difference is / For this I count as none, where men accord / In substance, though some difference be in word." By his own account, then, his message was at its core identical to that of even his most ardent critics. Like them, he taught nothing more or less than "free Justification; True Liberty, glad tydings of Salvation."[68]

Fittingly, Brearley presented himself as a man of peace, whose verses were intended as an olive branch to his sometime critics. His hope was to repair the breach and bring concord to the godly community in his part of the world.[69] He repeatedly claimed that he bore nothing but "love and reverence" to those with whom he had quarreled in past years.[70] Indeed, Brearley's poem is remarkable if only because it reveals the extent to which he retained a deep psychological stake in his continuing identity as a member in the English puritan community. As he put it,

> What wicked ones may think or censure me,
> Is (I confesse) a thing doth little move me;
> But that Gods Children hardly should conceit me,
> Whose precious balmes, I rather wish should beet me,
> Thou God forbid, or that my latter age,
> Should be secluded from thy heritage.
> I mean the fellowship of Saints below,
> Which if I want, I whither shall I go.[71]

This striking passage shows that even in later life, after a career of dispute and sometimes dangerous collision with authority, Brearley continued to think of himself as a member of the broader community of the godly. No matter how much ill will existed between him and his opponents, he still regarded them as part of that amorphous but distinctive club, the "fellowship of Saints"; the poem itself exudes an almost palpable pain at the attempts of some to exclude him from this community by portraying him as a cancerous threat to the body of Christ.

---

66 Ibid., appended poems, 15, 39, 45-46.
67 Ibid., appended poems, 39.
68 Ibid., appended poems, 4, 35.
69 Ibid., appended poems, 33.
70 Ibid., appended poems, 72-73.
71 Ibid., appended poems, 3.

From Barren Soil

Even if we assume that these protestations of orthodoxy and declarations of brotherly love were sincere, we should take note of the fact that Brearley recognized and admitted that at least superficially, his preaching deviated from puritan norms. Although he tried to present these differences as trivial quibbling over words, many of his opponents obstinately refused to accept such a gloss. For them, his "new words" were anything but harmless novelties; they were the medium for a new message, one that presented a very serious threat to the true Gospel. A close reading of Brearley's sermons amply reveals why this was so. Whatever he may have said and believed about his own divinity, Brearley's vision of the true life of faith and the road to salvation were unique and distinctive. An auditor who gadded to hear him preach over the course of weeks and months would have been exposed to a style of religiosity and an underlying message that had no exact parallel elsewhere in England. While redolent of Eaton and Everarde, Brearley's thought had clearly developed on its own, and it was thus informed by a particular set of concerns, impulses, and idiosyncrasies that set it apart from the similar formulations of other antilegalist preachers.

At the core of this vision was an almost obsessive emphasis on what is sometimes called Christian paradox. Building especially on the final three chapters of Paul's second letter to the Corinthians, Brearley embraced as a sort of controlling paradigm the notion that the Christian life was embodied by a set of counterintuitive inversions of traditional notions of strength, power, wisdom, and holiness. In those chapters, Paul had attacked certain unnamed "false apostles" who had sought to undermine his ministry. Possibly responding to accusations that he was weak, unworthy, or foolish, Paul had reveled in his own weakness and folly, in the process suggesting that Christ's truth was always characterized by such weakness: God, he claimed, had announced to him that "My grace is sufficient for thee: for my strength is made perfect in weakness. Most gladly therefore will I rather glory in my infirmities, that the power of Christ may rest upon me. Therefore I take pleasure in infirmities, in reproaches, in necessities, in persecutions, in distresses for Christ's sake: for when I am weak, then I am strong."[72] Brearley appears to have seized upon this image—in which weakness was paradoxically reconfigured as strength—and used it as a kind of guiding metaphor for thinking about the Christian life. In this way, the life of faith became an exercise in accepting and submitting to paradox. As Brearley put it, in a striking and odd simile of his own making, the converted Christian, finding strength in impotence and poverty, was "like mushroom which from barranes of soyle doth sucke his sapp,

[72] 2 Cor. 12: 9-10.

and filthy liquor boile."[73] Fertility was to be found in barrenness; strength was to be found in weakness and submission; knowledge was to be found in ignorance; joy was to be found in suffering; life was to be found in death.[74]

Accordingly, the point of preaching was to lay men low, for as he explained, once again adapting the principle of inversion, "He that humbles himself shall be exalted: the whole Gospel runs on this string."[75] After all, Christ himself had been born in a humble stable.[76] As he persistently reminded his auditors, true salvation was to be found in lowliness, poverty, humility, and misery. As with all the other figures examined in this study, however, Brearley's vision of lowly and humble religion carried with it a negative referent—forms of religiosity that were, on his account, "high," presumptuous, and downright dangerous. As he explained it, some failed to heed Christ's way, instead choosing other, less harrowing paths:

> 1. One by his gaining the world, not losing it: by saving his life, not by giving it up: to that end is wise, diligent, careful to put the evil away.
> 2. Another by the first Covenant, and stablishing a righteousnesse of his own: but that hath nothing but death in it.
> 3. All hiding and covering, and increasing what they have; and tinkling their old rotten hearts, not by forsaking all and Repentance.
> 4. But we see the way of Life and Freedom, is, by death.

Such false and deluded Christians were guilty of "a stiff conceited Righteousnesse, or high and loftie knowledge . . . and hide themselves under vanitie and falsehood." This was "not the way of Christ: no, His way is a low and dying way."[77] Indeed, the two stock villains laid out here by Brearley—identifiable, for convenience sake, as the "righteous man" and the "lofty, wise man"—reappeared in one form or another in almost every one of Brearley's sermons. Indeed, it is impossible to understand what Brearley meant by "a low and dying way" without scrutinizing these stock anti-Christian characters, for it was only in denouncing them that Brearley's theological vision came into sharpest focus.

"The wise man" simply put, was a man beguiled by his own learning; the "righteous man," beguiled by his own holiness and purity of religious prac-

---

[73] Chetham's Library MS. A. 2. 132, 270-71. Brearley was so fond of this peculiar metaphor that he recycled the image in a different context and with a somewhat different resonance when he rewrote the poem. See Brearley, *Bundle*, appended poems, 8.

[74] See, for instance, Brearley, *Bundle*, 19; ibid., 61: "indeed, mans weaknesse is his strength: the Crosse his Freedom, Suffering his victorie, and Death his Life."

[75] Ibid., 30.

[76] Ibid., 34-35.

[77] Ibid., 118.

tice. Brearley frequently rolled these two stock figures into a single package, as when he declared that "the wise and righteous men are alwayes the greatest enemies to Christ."[78] Both came together in a single New Testament character—the dreaded New Testament pharisee. Indeed, it was a rare Brearley sermon that failed at some point or other to denounce the pharisees by name.[79] They were the archetypal villains, reprehensible not only because they had supposedly persecuted Christ, but also in that they epitomized the most seductive and destructive dangers to the soul of a Christian. Addicted to their own wisdom and knowledge of the Law, the wise pharisees and scribes of the New Testament had utterly failed to see that the true path to salvation lay not in arcane learning or olympian feats of holiness, but in weakness, simplicity, even foolishness.

For Brearley, however, the pharisees of the New Testament were much more than long-dead exemplars from the past. Like ancient Palestine, contemporary England had its share of overlearned, worldly-wise men, whose empty devotions and terminal self-righteousness led to a dangerous, destructive presumption. By slipping from first-century Jerusalem to contemporary England, Brearley subtly and without explicit comment wove within his listeners' minds an analogy between the Jews of old and the modern pharisees of his own day. In his view, this pervasive crypto-Jewish undercurrent amounted to perhaps the greatest danger to Christian truth: "the great Idol in the Church, is mans knowledge and righteousness. This is that the false Apostles set up. This he decketh with Devotion, Zeal and Charitie, but yet not much of that; he worships God before this Idol, he acknowledgeth Christ, yet with circumcision joyned, this we make only God, we bow down as unto it."[80] Like the other anti-legal thinkers examined in this study, Brearley seems to have identified the most pernicious threat to true religion as an exacting, self-righteous zeal, which was so dangerous precisely because it appeared so convincing. As he put it, these false apostles committed "the greatest Rebellion in the Church, covered under religion." Rather than serving God in passive humility, such dangerous pharisees, though posing as "devote men," worshipped Christ "on the Altar of our good qualities, which we have hewen to ourselves. . . . We wait not on God, and his Will and Word, that we may know it: but in the dead greves of our devotions."[81] Thus, to look to one's own internal qualities, or one's external holiness, or indeed to any worldly sign, as a ground for faith, was to "feed on Swines Flesh . . . that is, we feed on the Flesh and filthy world."

[78] Ibid., 150.

[79] For examples, see ibid., 11, 30, 38, 56, 57, 61, 78, 98, 101, 105, 128, 140, 180, 184, 189, 207, 221, 224, 229, 234, 243, 253.

[80] Ibid., 143.

[81] Ibid., 179, 46; see also ibid., 55, 77-78, for similar statements.

Brearley singled out for particular scorn those who made a great show of their own holiness and profession of religion: "*Stand by, for I am holier than thou*: So with all these abominations, there went still a poysoned opinion of holinesse and high thoughts, which made all stink in [God's] nostrils. So that when with Religion there goes a high thought in man, and exalting of himself above others because of his Religion: it poysons all and stinks before God."[82] This, then, was the dangerous, spiritual idolatry so rife in England: by placing faith in their own qualities, or placing confidence in external devotions, men and women worshiped themselves and the world. These were the villains who sought salvation "by the first Covenant, and stablishing a righteousnesse of [their] own." The danger was all the greater because such hypocritical pharisees looked and acted like the holiest and most pious men in the land.

Yet it was not merely the legal knowledge and self-righteousness of the new pharisee that made him such a threat; it was also his claim to monopolize spiritual authority through special command of human learning. Thus, Brearley took particular care to denounce the winding towers that man erected through his own subtle reasonings. The high-flown complexities and lofty notions of the proud were plainly contrary to the lowly simplicity of Brearley's gospel. As he put it "What then are those high mystical Speculations and Comprehensions of Christ, making him so high: like speculative Angels? This is but an airy Christ, but our Christ is low and among us, suffering, watching and praying with us and for us. He comes not for these high thoughts, but for pure and contrite spirits." Indeed, in Brearley's view, "All high thoughted Religion is not of Christ, but of the devil."[83] By "mystical" or "high thoughted" religion, Brearley appears to have been referring not to "mysticism" in the sense in which modern scholars usually define it, but rather to any kind of theologizing that made God abstract and distant, and confined him to a realm of rational speculation. This was a wide rubric, one that might easily have included both the alchemical perfectionism of John Everarde or the "metaphysical" preaching style that was fashionable amongst a certain type of university-trained divine, particularly those of Arminian leanings. At its broadest, it seems to have referred to any kind of complicated theological learning that failed to convey the spiritual power of Christ's word, perhaps most especially, scholastic theology; in this vein, he derided those who "will needs comprehend God without Christ in his Essence, Properties, Attributes, Eternity, Omnipotencie, etc. What a foolishnesse is this . . . ?" This sort of complicated academic learning, bereft of the living power of Christ, was worse than worthless. As Brearley put it, "The Knowledge of the Gospel without the power of Christ

---

82 Ibid., 180.
83 Ibid., 136.

and his death, hardens above all; none such enemies to the simplicitie thereof."[84]

High speculation and school learning in fact hindered the process of coming to the truth: "though the wise men of the *Jewes* rejected the Truth, being justly blinded: yet it was [God's] good pleasure for to reveal it to poor and ignorant men, even to *Babes*."[85] Again, this was not merely a historical fact; it was as true in Brearley's day as it had been in biblical times: "He that in conceit of his own wisdom is lifted up above the simplicity of the Gospel, understands the least of the Mystery and Life of the Gospel: but he that lyes low in himself, seeking to be guided by another, shall understand all."[86] Indeed, *reason* itself could be the handmaiden of Satan: "Reason saith, Come to me, and I will guide thee, and let thee see Comfort: Look at thy righteousness and holinesse, thy diligence and knowledge of the Word: thou art so good, and so good above others."[87] As he put it, again indulging his penchant for paradox, "Reason is a foolish counsellor," which "can make nothing of the wayes of Christ."[88] Only by denying one's own thoughts and reason, by lying low in ignorance, could a person come to the truth. Indeed, this was a sporadic but crucial theme throughout Brearley's sermons: reason was habitually portrayed as a threat, a stumbling block to true faith. Indeed, for Brearley, faith was directly contrary to human reason.[89] Faith believed, despite all reason, and despite the apparent hopelessness of man's position.

We do not have far to search to see why Brearley's opponents might have thought he was an enemy to human learning. Although Brearley tried to deny this charge in his poetry—arguing that he had never opposed learning, but had merely sought to ensure that it remained a handmaid to true faith—in fact his sermons tell a somewhat different story.[90] Reason, learning, and academic knowledge appeared in an unyieldingly negative light.[91] While English puritans often adopted a skeptical posture with respect to human reason and book learning, they generally tended to see these things as necessary tools given by God to help in expounding and understanding Christian truth.[92] In upsetting

---

[84] Ibid., 20, 140.

[85] Ibid., 12.

[86] Ibid., 13.

[87] Ibid., 23. In this way, "Satan . . . crosseth by reason the Truth of God"; cf. Chetham's Library MS. A. 2. 132, 241, where it is argued that the devil "can To further his intent / use Reason too, as speciall instrument."

[88] Brearley, *Bundle*, 222.

[89] Ibid., 199, 206.

[90] Ibid, appended poems, 38.

[91] In addition to the examples cited above, see ibid., 184-85, 218, 221.

[92] See J. Morgan, *Godly Learning: Puritan Attitudes towards Reason, Learning and Education* (Cambridge: Cambridge University Press, 1986), passim.

this balance, Brearley appears to have departed quite decisively from the mainstream puritan tradition.

If, however, Brearley had merely been airing unusually caustic statements about the capacities of the human mind, it is unlikely that he would have provoked the deep suspicion and scorn of his fellow ministers. Far more disturbing, no doubt, was the fact that his continual polemic against high-minded and self-righteous pharisees was much more than just an innocent rhetorical device. At all points, he suggested that these new pharisees were a constant, living danger. Somewhere out there, Brearley argued, were ministers who deluded their credulous auditors by teaching them to place faith in their own qualities of holiness and purity, and by urging them to cling with confidence to empty external devotions, thereby plunging them into the pit of self-love and self-worship. Others, he suggested, fooled people by seducing them with complicated and airy shows of humane wisdom, again leading people to worship themselves instead of God. The "wise and righteous" men who led their followers down these unwholesome paths, although outwardly the most devout men in the church, were in fact "false apostles," agents of Antichrist.

Brearley couched all of this at a level of generality that insulated him from potential criticism. Nowhere did he name any particular devotion or practice. Never did he openly claim that any particular minister or ministers in Lancashire, Yorkshire, or elsewhere, were guilty of such false apostleship. Auditors were left to connect the dots themselves. Yet there was arguably little question about where these dots led—directly to the doorstep of Brearley's puritan contemporaries. Surely, this seems to be how many of Brearley's followers interpreted him;[93] just as certainly, Brearley's fellow ministers detected the same, *sotto voce* message, perhaps shedding light on the question of why they proved so reluctant to accept his demure self-presentation as a man of moderation and peace. It is within this context that we must read Brearley's persistent and apparently uncontentious statements of core protestant principles. When he denounced works righteousness and pharisaism, lambasted Arminius, or lionized Martin Luther, Brearley's primary referent appears not to have been the Pope, nor the many English Catholics who huddled together in great numbers in Brearley's Lancashire, nor even the anti-Calvinist clerics who increasingly held sway within the English church (although these were all bad enough). Rather, like John Eaton, Brearley was using core protestant principles to critique England's most enthusiastic Protestants, in effect skewering the godly on their own spit.

---

[93] See, for instance, Collier's shrill warnings to the ministers of his day to abandon the legalism, "wise cunning," and the "formall way of religion" whereby they "bewitch the people." Lambeth Palace Library MS. 3461, 284-86; 295-300.

To Sail by Hell

Against the deceitful, "reasonable religion" of the wise and righteous pharisee, Brearley postulated a religion of stark simplicity, cut off completely from the sinuous labyrinth of man's imagination.[94] Indeed, one of the most striking aspects of Brearley's thought was his habitual evocation of the language and concept of "simplicity." Brearley's pastoral letter to Pethye, for example, warned of the dangers of the "fleshly power seduceing and withdrawing the simple spirit from its simple beeing and rest in god," bemoaned the sad state of those who through "fleshly wisdome forsaketh the simplicitye of faith," and exhorted her "to keepe faith simple" in the face of the temptations of the world.[95] As he never tired of reminding his auditors, the wise men of the world were deceived because the Gospel and true faith were infinitely simple; the contortions of man's contemplative and self-regarding wisdom served merely to compromise or obscure this simplicity.

By "simple," Brearley meant not merely *uncomplicated* by frothy, speculative reason, but also *unmixed* by any extraneous or impure influence. As he explained, "Puritie is a metaphor taken from . . . mettal, etc. Which is not mingled with any filth, but clear from the Fountain: So we say, Pure water like gold, and that is separated from all other things, and is simple."[96] Thus, a "simple" love was a love without regard for any "profitt or approbation," that is, a love that had no "loving of ourselves joined with it." A "simple" faith was a bare trust in God's word and promise, without any regard to one's own good or salvation, a belief that existed in spite of earthly reason, worldly aspirations, and "without respecte of any creature."[97] Such a simple faith was something utterly pure, something that had nothing else joined to it, "for the heart joyned, or mixed with any other thing, mars it." In a critical passage, Brearley explained that "This was *Adams* simplicitie that is joyned to God onlie, which puritie is a mind cleaving to nothing but God only, and simple truth."[98] A true faith in God thus sought to reproduce this primitive purity, this total union with God, free from any outside influence or object. Such a faith was, of course, completely unconditional, and existed without any hope of reward. A true, simple faith meant an absolute focus on God, to the exclusion of anything outside of or extraneous to him: "a beleeveing of god simply

---

94 Brearley, *Bundle*, 221.

95 Lambeth Palace Library MS. 3461, 225, 227.

96 Brearley, *Bundle*, 229.

97 Lambeth Palace Library MS. 3461, 164-65, 166. Elsewhere he compared the simplicity of true religion to mercury, which remained pure and unmixed in the presence of other substances. Brearley, *Bundle*, 210.

98 Ibid., 229.

for himself, not tying god to any condition, but tying man only to god and there to waite."[99]

Accordingly, the way to Christ was not through learning, or study, or strenuous preparation. Rather, the would-be Christian was to humble himself, to strip himself naked of all proud conceit and high-flown knowledge, to repent of his sins, and wait on the promise. Only by doing so would the spirit descend. As he described it, "Wouldest thou know the wonderful Mysterie of Christ? Sit in thy own ignorance, mourning in blindnesse: and wait in the word of Truth, till the light shine, and thou shalt understand, though not the mind of God, yet the mind of Christ."[100] Here, using a turn of phrase now familiar to the reader, Brearley proclaimed that believers could and would come to know "the mind of Christ." Yet to arrive at this point, they needed to divest themselves of all their jealously defended conceits concerning their own knowledge, abilities and spiritual armor: "wait and attend, and he will reveal Christ and the Father: if thou sit under the burden of thine own ignorance, and content for the time to know nothing but thy own vileness."[101] In this way, even as the pharisee was "justly blinded" by his own wisdom, the true Christian would become truly wise through blindness.

As with the language of "simplicity," Brearley's emphasis on patient waiting in faith was not characteristic of early Stuart puritanism. As we have seen, the godly tended to push their acolytes toward lives of strenuous and unremitting activity. Any person who rested idly, waiting for God to give faith, was probably a false professor; true Christians would zealously apply the means of grace and would strive with all of their abilities to grow up in faith and holiness. Brearley's message was clearly at odds with this mainstream puritan tendency, probably consciously so. Brearley's enemies certainly seem to have detected a difference: to judge from both the 1617 articles and from his poetic apology, one of the most persistent accusations against him held that he and his followers believed they were above and beyond using the means of grace.[102] Brearley denied this charge. Once again, however, it is palpably obvious from his sermons why outsiders might have been forgiven for thinking otherwise. Where mainstream puritan ministers consistently pushed their listeners to attend diligently to the word preached, the sacraments, to holy duties, and to the devotions of religion, Brearley's sermons exhorted believers to surrender all, abase themselves, and prostrate themselves before God in abject submission.

[99] Lambeth Palace Library MS. 3461, 166.
[100] Brearley, *Bundle*, 36.
[101] Ibid., 21.
[102] Ibid., appended poems, pp. 11-12, 14-15, 48.

This is not to say that Brearley failed to exhort his listeners to examine themselves; indeed, he pushed them with relentless force to look inside themselves and to strip away all knowledge, all self-confidence, all belief in their own wills. Much more so than the other figures discussed in this study, Brearley constantly warned his listeners and followers—even those who had already tasted the joys of true faith—about the overwhelming and intractable snares of the flesh. Thus, there was surely a spiritual discipline at play in Brearley's practical divinity. But that discipline was focused precisely on reminding readers that there was absolutely nothing they could do to bring themselves to salvation. Such a stance, of course, could be portrayed as mere Protestantism, a powerful expression of the essence of Luther's message, and it is undoubtedly this that allowed both Brearley and later commentators to argue that his message amounted to little more than a faithful recapitulation of reformed truths.

Yet to stop here would be to fail to see how distinctive and uncharacteristic his method and means were. For as Brearley explained, the period of mournful, blind waiting that preceded spiritual enlightenment was part of a broader program of suffering along with Christ. Again and again throughout his sermons, Brearley told his readers that the life of faith meant not merely believing in Christ, but suffering with him: "None loves the Word, or Gods will, but he that is prepared to bear the Cross."[103] This image, of "bearing" or "submitting to" the cross, was ubiquitous in his sermons. Believers needed to "willingly embrace" "Christ's way of suffering," and to become a "partaker with Christ in afflictions."[104] They needed to be "thoroughly whipt, and beat under."[105] There was "No thriving in Religion but under the Crosse."[106] The "sufferings of Christ" needed to be "accomplished in the Saints in earth" in order to bring them to salvation, and indeed, the man "that partakes of Christs death once through Faith to his Redemption by the power of the same death, dyes daily."[107] As we saw in the last chapter, such rhetoric was not characteristic of mainstream puritanism. Mirroring instead the style and language of John Everarde, this insistence on the daily rehearsal of Christ's sufferings appears to have hearkened back not to native godly traditions, but to an older, medieval tradition, that of the *Imitatio Christi*.

And as in the case of Everarde, this tradition was almost certainly mediated through the *Theologia Germanica*. Even in our earliest surviving account of Brearley's divinity—the list of errors from 1617—the influence of the *Theolo-*

---

103 Ibid., 112.
104 Ibid., 171, 192.
105 Ibid., 154.
106 Ibid., 198. For other examples, see ibid., 178, 200, 220, 250, 264.
107 Ibid., 213, 235-36.

gia seems palpable. One of the errors ascribed to Brearley had been that "A soule sanctified must soe aime at gods glorie, as he must never thinke of salvation."[108] This is a peculiar position, one rarely, if ever, found amongst the godly, who made much of the matter of salvation (even as they sought to exalt and glorify God). Such a position had, however, been laid out in no uncertain terms by the fourteenth-century author of the *Theologia*, wherein it was argued that true Christians "are in a state of freedom, because they have lost the fear of pain or hell, and hope of reward or heaven, but are living in pure submission to the divine goodness"; having died to the self, the "true lover of God, loveth Him or the Eternal goodness alike, in having and not having, in sweetness and bitterness, in good or evil report, and the like, for he seeketh alone the honour of God, and not his own, either in spiritual or natural things."[109] Nor was this an opinion ascribed to Brearley through the negligence or cunning of his enemies; a few years later, preaching before the godly ministers of Halifax, Brearley once again defended a very similar point, arguing that for the justified sinner, "Religion is his treasure. psa. 119. 6. not to gayne salvation, but for the fellowship of god . . . while he liveth. and else would rather chuse to be in hell, with [no?] hope to get out."[110] Yet Brearley appropriated much more than this single idea from the *Theologia*; perhaps even more than in the works of John Everarde, Brearley's entire corpus is suffused with language, themes and preoccupations that might have come directly from the pages of the famed mystical tract.

Following the *Theologia*, Everarde had argued that "dying with Christ" meant allowing the self to be crucified and annihilated. Brearley echoed this argument. Along with the anonymous author of the *Theologia*, he claimed that "Self Righteousness, and Self Confidence, and Self Love . . . are the poyson of all religion, *viz.* Self Witt, and Self Will; these *Adam* got, and therein opposed God."[111] This curse of "fleshly" selfness was the kernel of human evil and the repulsive force that kept man from God. And it was only the way of suffering beneath Christ's cross that would "crucifie the World, and our fleshly Lusts and Self-will," thus bringing man back to God.[112] This was a process of intense, almost infernal torment: "The way to Heaven is to Sayle by hell."[113] Only through a "real and actual denyal of himself" could a person be joined to God in a simple, unmixed communion. This was a rare state: "man is seldom so separate from himself in pure love unto God, but

---

108 See below, Appendix D, item 14.

109 *Theologia Germanica*, Susanna Winkworth, trans. (London: Stuart & Watkins, 1966 ed.), 49-50.

110 British Library, Add. MS. 4933B, fol. 164v.

111 Brearley, *Bundle*, 2.

112 Ibid., 45.

113 Chetham's Library MS. A. 2. 132, 216.

some self-love there is, that is to his fleshly will sticking to him."[114] Nevertheless, this pure simplicity was the goal of all true religion; only by following Christ through suffering, loss and total self-abnegation could human beings achieve a simple, "pure love unto God."

Yet this was more than a secondhand imitation of Christ's life; like Everarde, Brearley believed that for the Gospel to be efficacious, Christ had to be born within the believer's soul. Like the doctor, Brearley took issue with those who claimed that Christ's life and death were something external and outside the believer. As he put it

> We hear of Christ born, baptized, persecuted and crucified, etc.
>
> But not to us; nay, we know this Christ after the flesh, we think well of him, and love the thoughts of him, but not born to us.
>
> Nay, we frame a Christ, and seem to worship him, but not given to us; nay, we have a conceit that he hath done all for us, but not born in us: we defend him, and plead for him, we dispute of him, we talk of him, we read of him: but not born to us.
>
> This teacheth, that Christ was promised of God, and sent in fulnesse of time, and then his spirit sent into the hearts of men.
>
> So there is a waiting for the promise under the Law: but in the fulnesse of time he shal be born and given . . .
>
> So, when thou art past hope, and sees no Reason, then shall Christ be born to thee, for that is the fulnesse of time, and till then, the fulnesse of time is not come: And we see that Christ is nothing to man, till he be born in man.[115]

To the faithful soul, who waited patiently in misery and blindness, Christ would come: "we must pay tribute, and be taxed, and feel Repentance and the bitternesse thereof: and wait in Faith, and then he shal be born unto us."[116] It is crucial to see that Brearley was not just using Christ's life as a moral exemplar of patient, humble suffering; he was suggesting, in a much more visceral manner, that the true believer needed to become host to Christ.

The Case of Adam

In his public sermons, however, Brearley was very reluctant to explain what, precisely, it meant to have Christ "born in us," or to possess the "mind of Christ." For insight, we need to turn to Brearley's apologetic poem, for it is here that he was willing to make his most expansive and uncensored comments on the spiritual estate of believers. Much of the poem was designed to refute the allegations that had been lodged against him: thus, Brearley took

---

114 Brearley, *Bundle*, 240.

115 Ibid., 217-18.

116 Ibid., 32.

pains to deny the claim that he offered believers a carnal freedom to sin as they pleased; that believers no longer needed to use means of grace; that human reason and knowledge were inimical to grace; and that believers could be absolutely perfect in this life.[117] Yet in refuting these claims, Brearley often revealed much about his own thinking on these matters, clarifying what he had and had not meant in ways that served merely to underscore the wide chasm separating him from his opponents.

Brearley's poem may be supplemented by collating it with the other extant "private" manuscripts of the Grindletonians, which serve to confirm and flesh out the basic picture delineated by Brearley. The first of these is the Grindletonian poem "Of Hypocrisy," very possibly written by Brearley himself, that survives, along with an early draft of Brearley's apology, in a collection of religious verse associated with the Lancashire gentleman Robert Heywood. Secondly, we have William Aiglin's funeral elegy written upon Brearley's death; finally, we have the many poems and treatises of Josiah Collier, the sometime minister and loyal follower of Brearley to whom we owe the survival of virtually all of the materials relating to Grindletonianism. While it is true that these supplementary materials do not with certainty reflect Brearley's own views, it should be noted that Aiglin and Collier made no secret of their devotion to, or reliance upon, Brearley as their spiritual master. Aiglin had been with Brearley since the very first days of his ministry, claimed that he had been converted by Brearley, and continued to revere Brearley as a prophet after his death. His poem was presumably written shortly after Roger's burial in 1637. Collier's works were likely written somewhat later than Aiglin's poem, probably during the 1640s or 1650s. Nevertheless, Collier like Aiglin retained a fierce devotion to Brearley. Fittingly, his various writings appear to be remarkably faithful to the thought and practice of his mentor, often replicating exactly Roger's favored arguments and themes, while adding details which, while entirely in accord with Brearley's thought, are never made explicit in Brearley's sermons and poetry. In short, these sources together provide us with a rich and detailed, but surprisingly self-consistent, picture of Grindletonian spirituality as it existed in the private domain of manuscript and conventicle. It is a picture that in many respects plainly contradicts Brearley's own claims to be a peaceable and orthodox member of the Church of England.

The first, and perhaps greatest, absence in Brearley's sermons was any systematic statement on the relationship between believers and the Law. To be sure, as we have seen, Brearley habitually denounced those who, by setting up their own righteousness, holiness, and pretended knowledge "confound Law and Gospel," setting "one in the room of the other, and make the Gospel ef-

---

[117] Ibid., appended poems, 5-6, 11-12, 38, 48-49.

fectual by the Law."[118] While certainly unusual in the obsessiveness with which he returned to this theme, there was obviously nothing about such statements that could lead the orthodox to point fingers. What self-respecting Protestant could have disputed the idea that works of the Law were unable to save fallen humans? Yet to suggest that salvation could not be found in the Law did not address or answer the question of what relationship existed between true Christians and the Moral Law after conversion. On this question, Brearley the preacher was virtually silent. There are a handful of cryptic and suggestive references to the Law in his sermons, but none of them amount to anything like a systematic or clear statement on the subject.[119]

This was no accident. Brearley's reticence from the pulpit appears to have been conscious and calculated. Such reticence was necessary precisely because Brearley *did* have a position on the Law, but it was a position that was hardly orthodox. His clearest and most succinct statement on the subject was buried deep within his poetic apology:

> But to end this, like brother with his brother,
> The Law and Gospel, must be each with other:
> With fire and hammer, that to break the rocks:
> And this to quicken dead and withered Stocks:
> Then afterwards, the Law of Liberty,
> Doth follow both these necessarily:
> Which I according to the Scripture hold,
> To be the Law of love (as I have told.
> When as the love of Christ doth men constrain,
> Duty and Love to yield to God again.[120]

Brearley thus repeated the familiar protestant claim that the Law was necessary to break the hardened hearts of sinners; it was only on such broken ground that the living seed of the Gospel could grow and prosper. Less in keeping with orthodox thought, however, was the claim that another law, here identified as "the Law of Liberty" or the "Law of love," would necessarily take hold of believers. Elsewhere in the poem he repeated this formula, celebrating "That precious liberty, they thereby win: / How sweet a thing it is to master sin: / How this new Law doth set Believers free, / How Christ his yoke is perfect libertie. . . . What power with God, this law of love doth give, How in his Members, Christ is said to live."[121] In other words, the Law that bound believers was a distinct and *new* law, a law of love, that was somehow different from the old law that preceded it. Brearley was vague about the con-

---

[118] Ibid., 88, 133.
[119] See, for instance, ibid., 37, 157, 218, 246.
[120] Ibid., appended poems, 60-61.
[121] Ibid., appended poems, 6.

tent of this new law; at one point, for instance, he suggested that the substance or matter of the new Law was the same as that of the old; what was different was a believer's relationship to the Law: "Not that the Law is for its substance chang'd/ But to Gods Saints in other order rang'd. / Its nature now in Christ so qualified, / That its grim face we better may abide."[122] On one reading, then, it could be argued that Brearley was saying that the new Law that bound believers was the same as the Law of Moses; it was merely that believers were free of its curse and enslavement; they thus stood in a different relationship to it.

If this was what he believed, however, one might wonder why he did not simply say so, rejecting the formulation of a new, distinct Law in favor of the standard orthodox claim that believers were free from the curse and condemnation of the old Law, remaining bound by its commandments.[123] The reason Brearley did not do so is because neither he nor his followers believed that Christians *were* bound by the commands of the old Law. The anonymous author of "Of Hypocrisy," for instance, repeated almost exactly Brearley's formula, "Gods Lawe His deare ones doth in bondage bringe / Yet there is found Another Lawe to Free them / Which doth (though most expect another thinge) / In a more strict and cruell bondage tye them."[124] This new bondage—presumably the same as Brearley's "yoke of Christ"—was "strict and cruel" only because it led believers inexorably to do good works. But the peculiar and paradoxical aspect of this strict new Law was that believers obeyed it without any compulsion at all. They did so with the joyful and sublime contentment of men and women who were perfectly free to do what they desired, but who desired only to do God's will:

> O Cheerful Light, Hidd Manna, Heavenly Bliss
> O Blessed Bond, which Perfect Freedom is
> O Glorious Rule, where All constreininge power
> The Law of Love doth Swallow and Devoure.[125]

The "perfect freedom" of the new "Law of Love" devoured and obliterated all constraining or compulsive power. This made it dramatically different from the old Law. The old Law was a law of forced obedience, which ordered humans to obey under threat of catastrophic punishment. Those freed by Christ were liberated from such compulsory and constraining power. The new law under which they found themselves was not a compulsory law at all. In this

---

[122] Ibid., appended poems, 47.

[123] For an instructive comparison, see William Hinde, *The Office and Use of the Morall Law of God in the Dayes of the Gospell*, 2d ed. (1623), 80, who likewise uses the formulation "law of liberty," but only to affirm the continuing hold of the Moral Law on believers.

[124] Chetham's Library MS. A. 2. 132, 233.

[125] Ibid., 246.

sense, it was (to use the Apostle James's paradoxical phrase) a "law of liberty"—not truly a law at all, or rather a law of a completely new and non-coercive nature.

What, then, did Brearley mean when he said that the substance of the Law had not changed for true believers? Although Brearley did not elaborate, Josiah Collier discussed this point at length, offering an answer that seems entirely consonant with Brearley's position. The key here is to be found in Collier's extensive ruminations on the "two Couvenants of the lawe and the gospell." As Collier explained, "That which was in the beginning, was the word and that word was god, and in that word was life, and that life was the lighte of men, and by that word was Adam created in this creation, and in and by that word was the life that Adam should have lived, if he had not fallen from it into the darke principle of this world."[126] This word was in effect God's true, everlasting and eternal Law;[127] if man had continued on in obedience to it, he would have known nothing but God and eternal life. Having foreseen Adam's fall, however, God "gave unto him [Adam] an aditionall lawe, (to witt) thou shalt not eate of the tree of the knowledge of good and evell."[128] This "additional law" remained in effect after the fall of Adam, binding his posterity in the form of the Law of Moses, or the "Covenant of Works." During the period of the Covenant of Works, God's eternal and true word, although still in effect, remained obscure and hidden from the stage: "the word and the life in it, stands puerly retyred into its owne principle, and remaines still in the truth, for it is the truth."[129]

So according to Collier, there were two laws, the first, God's word, will, law, or mind, which held sway from the beginning, but which had "retired" out of man's view as a consequence of the fall. The second, or "additional law" was given to Adam and his posterity to show them their wayward and sinful nature. The first Law (the immutable word) was associated with the Covenant of Grace, for God had decreed and promised before the beginning of time that he would save his chosen ones ("the royal seed" as Collier called them) through and by this word, which took flesh in the form of Christ; the second law was associated with the Covenant of Works and the Law of Moses. No one would be saved through it, "And therfore those that lead and teach beelevers to guide and square their lives and actions according to the

---

126 Lambeth Palace Library MS. 3461, 265.

127 See Chetham's Library MS. A. 2. 24, fols. 64r, 65r, wherein Collier equates the Law and the Word, conflating "the lawe, word, will, or minde of god" under a single rubric. Moreover, this "undefiled will and Lawe [of God] . . . is one with himselfe, and himselfe is love." Christ was this "lawe, word, will, or minde of god" made flesh.

128 Lambeth Palace Library MS. 3461, 265-66.

129 Ibid., 265.

law of god, as the perfect rule thereof and not under this [new] administration lead them into a laborinth, to comprehend the devine will by the power and arme of flesh and so brings them into bondage."[130]

This did not mean that the "lawe or covenant of god given out of mount Sinai" was false. As Collier explained "though it be a just Lawe holy and good and the matter of truth therein perpetuall, yet as it is a covenant of works, which saith on this wise doe this and thou shalt live, and made with him that was too weake to performe it; it is disannulled by the establishing of the new and liveing covenante with him who was only able by himselfe soe to establish it that every Iota should be fullfilled."[131] This statement clarifies the nature of the relationship between the two laws. The true law of the Covenant of Grace ("or Law of Sion" as he called it elsewhere) was perpetual and pure; the "additional law" of Sinai was also holy and good, and insofar as it contained "the matter of truth," it was perpetual and identical to the true Law of Sion.[132] Yet this suggested that it also contained matter that was not perpetual, and which was not identical to God's true will, expressed in its purest form. What was this essential "matter of truth"? As Collier repeatedly noted, "the truth in the Lawe . . . is love both to god and man."[133] All of this echoes exactly Brearley's claims about the Law and explains very plausibly what Brearley meant when he suggested that the "substance" of the Law had not changed. That which was truly good and holy in the Mosaic Law was love to God and man; the law of Moses was true and good insofar as it reflected this core of love.

Yet the coming of Christ and the unveiling of the New Covenant meant that everything extraneous to this core truth of love could be stripped away. Certainly, this included all of the "ceremonial" rules of the Torah. Perhaps the most important characteristic of the old Law to be abolished under the new dispensation was its coercive and domineering character. This commanding, coercive character was directly opposed to the loving and wholly uncoercive spirit of the true and perpetual Law of Love. As Collier put it (in words that might just as easily have come from Brearley):

> For now instead of liveing by the law,
> or rule thereof which did keepe thee in awe
> And bondage strong, of sinne and feare of death.
> thouse live I say by that eternall breath,
> That issues from the father and the sonne,
> who shall reveale what I for thee have donne.

---

130 Chetham's Library MS. A. 2. 24, fol. 65r-v.

131 Lambeth Palace Library MS. 3461, 281.

132 For the "Law of Sion," see ibid.; Chetham's Library MS. A. 2. 24, fol. 65r.

133 Ibid., fol. 66v. See also ibid., fols. 65v, 67v, wherein "the truth in the law" was also identified as "love."

And breath againe in thee who now art dead
the breath of life, that true and liveing bread
who if thoult eate conformed thou shalt stand
to god his will, thou needs no more commaund,
But Jesus Christ the true unvailed face
of god his minde, who gives to thee that grace
wherby he writes the fathers love in thee
that shall abide and be that liveing tree,
Or rule of life, the truest truth in th'Lawe,
wherby thouse walke in love without all awe
Off bindeing rules whereout there never came
true life to change ould adams nature, name.
Come hither then you that have nought to bring
beleeve my word, Ile make the barren sing.
And cause to beare such lively fruite, which shall
breake forth in love among my people all.
whereout, against, the Law hath nought to say
for loves the Law which shall make thee obey.
A stronger rule then that thats writt in stone,
and of more force and liveing power alone.[134]

Believers were thus no longer under the commanding power of the Law; they were impelled by a more powerful, internal force, which was in some sense in opposition to the Law of Sinai—this force was love, the "truest truth of the Law."

Yet as Collier's words reveal, the Grindletonians believed not simply that human wills were remade anew, but that God actively worked through his chosen people. As Brearley put it, teaching the Law was appropriate for those who had not yet been touched by grace, and who thus needed to be reined in by external commands ("Much like the untam'd Colt, the Horse, or Mule"). Yet this lasted only until "the time appointed, / That they are with the Sp'rit of Sons anointed." At this point, "th'spirit, which from the word ne're swarves, / Guides all Gods Children as occasion serves: / And leading them to what's there spoke or meant / In expresse words, or by good consequent / . . . Serving for Life and Actions as a Law."[135] Like Traske and Hebdon, then, Brearley argued that believers were free from the commanding power of the law, but that they nevertheless had a more powerful, internal guide, the Spirit itself. Brearley was careful to emphasize that the conquest of the spirit over the flesh was never total in this life; each child of God received the spirit in measure, and all people contained a remnant of evil, not least Brearley himself, who piously confessed that "many sins I have." Yet Brearley was also clearly willing to ar-

134 Ibid., fol. 43v.
135 Brearley, *Bundle*, appended poems, 44-45.

gue that this spiritual inhabitation meant that true believers could in a certain sense be classified as sinless: "Yea all things to the spiritual men they do, / Are holy, grace doth alter nature so: / I mean as far, as they regenerate been, / In which respect, its said, they cannot sin. / And so far too, as th'act it selfs not ill."[136] Here, Brearley was probably seeking to explain his position, to free it from misconstructions, and to dodge accusations of libertinism; yet the very fact that he was willing to defend the idea that the regenerate "cannot sin" is in itself remarkable.

The argument that true Christians could not sin was possible for Brearley only because he believed that an intimate union existed between believers and God. And it was in describing this state of union that Brearley and his followers were at their most eloquent and most distinctive. Like Collier, Brearley chose the metaphor of a supernatural wind, blowing through the bodies of the faithful:

> as in Organs, one self breath fulfills,
> Proportionally, the great and little quills:
> Causing the lesse, as well as bigger speak;
> And in each time, in order silence break:
> So doth Gods Spirit, which is his very love,
> Whereby he loves himself, and his doth move.
> Towards himself (which too his working power
> And doth before, at Sea and Land devour,
> Laying the mountains and the valleys plain,
> That nothing might Gods Childrens wills restrain)
> Cause man within the living stock to thrive,
> Or move, as do great wheels the lesser drive:
> So that this will is Gods primarilie,
> Yea, even mans too in a next degree;
> As fully as his eating, drinking, sleeping,
> Standing, or walking, health or harbor keeping:
> For who gives power these things to will or do?
> The very same that gives the other too.
> O happie grafts, who thus transformed be,
> Into the Nature of this living Tree;
> Whose leaves are ever flourishing and green,
> And roots fast fixt, the liquid streams between.
> You Demy-gods, who to this Mount can say,
> Pluck up thy self and plant thee in the sea?
> Whose wills from Gods, receiving still their bent,
> May in a sort be call'd Omnipotent:
> At least so far as by his Spirit ye

136 Brearley, *Bundle*, appended poems, 55.

> Are set a Work, his instruments to be.
> Though here in measure, after to fulfill,
> In perfectnesse the pleasure of his will.[137]

These were bold words indeed. Through the inhabitation of the spirit, believers' wills merged with God's, blending seamlessly into a single entity. From this perspective, believers could rightly be called "Demy-gods," rendered divine, even omnipotent, insofar as they possessed the spirit.

Stepping back for a moment, we now see more clearly the mode of religiosity on offer in the Pennine hills and dales. Brearley pushed his listeners and admirers first to surrender all vestiges of fleshly, or self-directed, wisdom or confidence. They were to prostrate themselves in humble and repentant obedience, waiting in their own blindness, suffering along with Christ in faith. This process of suffering was followed, however, by the birth of Christ within. The birth of this internal Christ was only the beginning; as Brearley never tired of reiterating, believers needed constantly to beware backsliding and needed to continue to struggle against self-will throughout their lives. Nevertheless, so far as believers had escaped the self, enabling God to inhabit and guide them, they could consider themselves free from the Law and sin. Indeed, just as in the case of Everarde, such believers could in some sense consider themselves divine. William Aiglin closed his poem with a powerful expression of this doctrine, calling on all true Christian preachers to:

> Teach Christ in us and wee still sinfull men
> till we by god in Christ be borne againe
> borne not of mortall seed but of the life
> and light of truth and that without mans strife
> by force of love devine prest on the harte
> and soule of man even soe for to imparte
> his verye nature to us, and to containe
> him selfe in us. . . .[138]

This sense of total union with the divine was, in fact, heaven itself. Brearley was cautious about this point; he would say only that God, "Whose spirituall nature is without exception,/Most infinite in Goodness and Perfection" was "The very Heaven of a blessed Soul." Understanding that this was a potentially explosive argument, he immediately qualified it, affirming that "Though I a place grant too above the Pool," so as to defuse the obvious criticism that he was turning heaven into a mere allegory.[139] Yet the notion that heaven was an inward, ecstatic state was clearly a stock argument within the Grindleton-

---

137 Ibid., appended poems, 27-28.
138 Lambeth Palace Library MS. 3461, 248-49.
139 Brearley, *Bundle*, appended poems, 22.

ian repertoire, just as it had been for Traske and Everarde. The author of "Of Hypocrisy," was rather more forthcoming about celebrating the rapturous estate of those believers who had entered into union with God. "What better Heaven can thy Creature holde / Then that his soule in thine Thou should'st infolde? / Whereby the inward facultyes are cleared / To See, and Will the best, And that acquired. / Oah, Once Unite Thy Will, and my desire / What other heaven Can I require?"[140] While Collier, like Brearley, affirmed the existence of an immortal state, he too argued that to enter heaven was "to pass out of our earthly sensuall carnall being and mortalty [sic], into the spirituall heavenly beeing of god and Imortality, that where he is one in spirit, there may we be one, in one also, which may be or is heaven and happines, For where the father son and holy ghost stand eternally blessed in one, into that onenes we beeing brought stands our blessednes for ever."[141] Once again, this suggested that insofar as they were able to achieve this union with God, believers already dwelled in heaven.

This sense of being engulfed in the deity was also, in a sense, a return to the utterly "simple" and unmixed communion that Adam had had with God prior to the fall. From one perspective, then, this heavenly state of oneness with God represented a return to an initial, primordial state. This was, of course, a very dangerous argument, for the notion of a return to prelapsarian purity was one of the classic hallmarks of Familism. Yet the author of the poem "Of Hyprocrisy" nevertheless proved willing to flirt with this most inflammatory claim. Writing of those whose own wills had been obliterated, the poet coyly opined that "For God to such as Thus to Him drawe neer/Is all Good thinges, That heart can once desire/the Height of this By some is said to be/the Case of Adam, in His purity."[142] Thanks to the survival of William Aiglin's commemorative poem, we know that "some" people did indeed make precisely this argument. In perhaps the most revelatory passage of the entire Grindletonian corpus, William Aiglin described Roger Brearley's doctrine in the following terms:

> He opened that misterye hye
> of Christ in power of the deitye
> his power in man, mans power brought to nought
> god all in all, this depth he ever sought
> the soule with Christ in unitye to dwell
> the sinfull poyson thereby to expell,
> the first estate of Innocence to finde

---

140 Chetham's Library MS. A. 2. 132, 193. Elsewhere, the poet referred to "the Heaven of Gods Presence" (ibid., 205).

141 Chetham's Library MS. A. 2. 24, fol. 89r.

142 Chetham's Library MS. A. 2. 132, 245.

> by changeing quallytye of soule and minde
> by powerfull actions of the persons three
> the eye of man clearly the sonne to see
> whereby in that great fount the saints weare washt
> their sinfull soules weare with it all bedasht
> till puer and white, and of another dye
> they weare againe conformed perfectly
> into that Image of the light and then
> stood up again perfect and liveing men,
> from death redeemed and from hell set free
> by plaine experience all this taught hee.[143]

Here, at last, is the authentic voice of Grindletonianism, stripped bare of all qualification, caution, and evasion. Through union with God in Christ, believers were returned to a state of prelapsarian innocence and purity, rendering them "perfect and living men." Although drenched in the language and most basic assumptions of Protestantism—believers were nothing in themselves, and needed to rely wholly and completely on God's free grace in Christ—the core of the Grindletonian message was without question mystical and perfectionist, almost certainly owing something to the direct influence of Hendrik Niclaes or some now unseen disciple of HN.[144]

---

143 Lambeth Palace Library MS. 3461, 245-46.

144 There is significant and persuasive indirect evidence to suggest that Brearley and his followers actually read HN. Brearley's consistent use of the language of "simplicity," together with his habitual excoriation of wise and learned pharisees certainly resembled very closely the rhetoric of HN. See, for example, H[endrik] N[iclaes], *Exhortatio. I. The First Exhortation of H.N. to his Children* (n.p., 1574), fols. 32b, 36b, in which Niclaes praised "All Such as forsake themselves/becom-nothing/and renownce or go-without all their owne Counsell/Will/and Wisdom; turne themselves about; with all their heartes to the childish Simplicitie/and submit them under the Love" and denounced the "unregenerated Scripturelearned: which are arrogant and prowde, in their minde of the owne Wisedom." See also Brearley, *Bundle*, 32, 36: "we must pay tribute and be taxed, and feel Repentance and the bitternesse thereof: and wait in Faith, and then he shal be born unto us," and that the would-be believer should "sit in thy own ignorance, mourning in blindnesse: and wait in the word of Truth, till the light shine, and thou shalt understand . . . the mind of Christ," as against HN's very similar argument that the Lord's people should submit to legal mortification "in their Youngnes or Ignoraunce . . . untill that the Beleef; out of the Power of God; became with-childe through the holie Gost/ and bare or brought fourth a new Man." From HN, *Evangelium Regni* (n.p., 1575?), fol. 32v. For a discussion of Josiah Collier's apparent debt to Familism, see Appendix A, below. Finally, John Webster, the only Grindletonian whose library catalogue has come down to us, did indeed possess a copy of the works of HN, for which see Peter Elmer, ed., *The Li-*

How, then, are we to square this with Brearley's apparently heartfelt pleas to godly unity, concord, and orthodoxy? How was it possible for him to claim that he and his opponents were agreed as to the basic principles of Christian truth when it seems so clear that the Grindletonians were making arguments that were plainly beyond the bounds of received English protestant thought? This is a difficult question, one that perhaps goes to the very heart of the paradox of early Stuart antinomianism. For on the one hand, Brearley clearly felt an organic connection to the broader community of the godly, and psychologically, he appears to have been unwilling to break completely from that community. In large part, he may have been able to retain this psychological connection by virtue of his clear commitment to core protestant notions of free and unmerited grace. There is no reason to doubt his stated attachment to Luther, and indeed, Brearley's affection for Christian paradox, his denigration of the Mosaic Law, and his profound aversion to works righteousness all suggest that he had more than a passing familiarity with the reformer's thought (especially in its earliest stages).

Yet if so, it seems clear that the Martin Luther championed by the Grindletonians was the rogue monk and spiritual seeker who had published the *Theologia Germanica*; given what we have seen here, it appears that Brearley and his followers seized upon the reformer's messages of free and unmerited grace and interpreted them through the lens of the *Theologia*, thereby authoring an antinomian and perfectionist Luther.[145] In this way, there was nothing dishonest about their claim to be bearing the true Gospel as it had been rediscovered in Wittenberg; for on this account, Protestantism was itself mystical, perfectionist, and geared toward effecting a state of union with God that brought with it divinization. Such a perfectionist Protestantism could easily accommodate other mystical sources, up to and including the writings of Hendrik Niclaes, whose own writings were themselves deeply indebted to the *Theologia*. At one level, however, the question of Familist influence is moot. Although he and his followers may have appropriated or replicated a slew of core Familist doctrines, Brearley's fertile and seductive re-invention of those doctrines represented a unique, and distinctly protestantized, variant on the perfectionist theme, one that proved immensely appealing in the uplands of Yorkshire and

brary of John Webster: The Making of a Seventeenth-Century Radical in *Medical History*, Supplement No. 6 (London: Wellcome Institute for the History of Medicine, 1986), 186.

145 That such a reading is anything but far-fetched may be gathered from the fact that a recent school of Finnish Lutheran theologians has come to champion an almost identical interpretation of Luther's thought. See C. E. Braaten and R. W. Jenson, eds., *Union with Christ: The New Finnish Interpretation of Luther* (Grand Rapids, MI: Eerdmans, 1998).

Lancashire, and which would ultimately play a decisive role in the rise and growth of a trans-English antinomian community.

Beyond Grindleton

This influence would work itself out over the course of decades, as Brearley's ideas spread through the agency of his friends and devotees. The final section of this chapter traces this process, reconstructing an emerging Grindletonian connection that took shape in the years following 1617. According to Aiglin, after the first flush of excitement surrounding his ministry, many of Roger Brearley's initial followers "fell away and went wandring/till few was left behinde which gave a blowe/his currage almost quite to overthrowe."[146] Yet Aiglin implied that this phase passed, leading to a resurgence. The archival evidence confirms this: during the two decades that followed Brearley's first High Commission trial in 1616-17, the Grindletonian movement slowly and quietly spread its tentacles outward from the Pendle area, penetrating large swathes of Yorkshire and Lancashire, arriving finally in London in the late 1620s. Brearley and Tennant no doubt played key roles in this process, but it is also clear that much of the evangelical energy of the movement came from young proselytes who had been swept up in the early excitement at Grindleton chapel (not least Aiglin himself).

To be sure, some of Brearley's die-hard followers from the Craven district remained loyal to their spiritual teacher, unperturbed by his censure before the ecclesiastical courts. In his diary, for instance, the gentleman Nicholas Assheton of nearby Downham (Lancashire) claimed that on 18 April 1618, a Waddington man named John Swinglehurst was buried; Assheton noted with disapproval that Swinglehurst "dyed distract: he was a great follower of Brierley."[147] At Giggleswick, meanwhile, Christopher Shute continued to experience nagging problems with his parishioners. In the visitation of 1619, the churchwardens Robert Carr, Gregory Twisleton, and John Houghton were presented (presumably by Shute himself) for failure to give an honest parochial report to the diocesan authorities. It was alleged among other things that "many goe to Grindleton and neglect ther owne parish Church, and none of the defects by them presented."[148] Presumably, these presentments represented a lingering split within the Giggleswick congregation, as Shute continued to fight a rearguard battle against those willing to trek ten miles each week down

[146] Lambeth Palace Library MS. 3461, 236.
[147] F. R. Raines, ed., *The Journal of Nicholas Assheton of Downham*, Chetham Society, Old Series, 14 (1848), 89; the April 18 burial of "John Swindlehurst of the Hyll" is recorded in J. Parker, ed., *The Parish Registers of Waddington, Yorkshire (1599-1812)*, Publications of the Yorkshire Parish Register Society, 88 (1930), 9.
[148] Borthwick Institute, Vis 1619 CB, fol. 58r.

the Ribblesdale to hear Brearley preach. Although we cannot identify the Grindletonians of Giggleswick with certainty, there are some very likely candidates. Among the householders of the parish, for instance, were Henry Becroft and William Windsor, very possibly the laymen of the same name who had been cited to testify before the High Commission two years earlier. Also prominent among Giggleswick householders were members of the Eglin family. Although he does not appear in the parish registers for the period, it seems almost certain that William Aiglin was a member of this kinship network; when he came to write his will in 1661, William possessed a single piece of property—a parcel known as "Sandrigges," within the parish of Giggleswick.[149]

It seems that Brearley's lay followers carried the movement forward, taking up the cause with passion and fervor. Aiglin, for instance, soon left the West Riding, intent on spreading the message farther afield. On 12 August 1622, he was ordained to the priesthood at Derry.[150] His appearance in Ireland represents something of a mystery; standards both for education and conformity tended to be more lax in the Irish church, although it is also possible that his earlier entanglement in Brearley's trial meant that ordination at York was out of the question. Nevertheless, by 1632, Aiglin had returned to Yorkshire, where he took up the curacy of Dunnington, just east of York. In 1636, he would be preferred to the nearby vicarage of Huntington, at which point he apparently represented himself as a Master of Arts (a specious claim, to judge by the surviving evidence). He resigned this living at the outbreak of the civil war, but reappeared again during the 1650s as the curate of the important Pennine cloth town of Heptonstall, overlooking the Calder Valley.[151]

A similar pattern may be detected in the case of William Boyes, whose shadowy career represents a frustrating but crucial piece of the Grindletonian puzzle. On 26 April 1620, William Boyes and James Cowper, both laymen of the parish of Kirkby Moorside, appeared before the York High Commission. Although the information against them does not survive, both men were committed to the custody of a pursuivant until their next appearance. They were likewise warned "to reforme their manner and behaviores, and to submitt themselves touchinge their opinions in matters of religion, and touchinge their conventicles and errors or els to appeare here in Court" during the next term. It is not clear how the case was resolved.[152] Like William Aiglin, how-

---

[149] See R. W. Hoyle, ed., *The Parish Register of Giggleswick, vol 1: 1558-1669*, Yorkshire Archaeological Society, Parish Register Section, 147 (1984), 65, 66, 120, 126, 134, 137, 139, 141, 142, 146, 148, 151, 159; Borthwick Institute, Original Wills, "Aiglin, William," Aug. 1663, Pontefract, EXCHQ.

[150] Borthwick Institute, Inst. AB 6, 118.

[151] Marchant, *Church Courts*, 224.

[152] Borthwick Institute, HC AB 16, fol. 253r-v, 255r. Marchant, *Church Courts*, 40, 231-32 (which should read "James Cowper" rather than "John Cowper").

ever, Boyes soon appeared in a most improbable locale: in 1623, he was ordained priest at Llandaff. How he made his way to Cardiff is as mysterious as how Aiglin landed in Derry, but again, it seems probable that South Wales was selected in part because clerical standards were far less demanding here than in Tobie Matthew's York. By 1627, Boyes would be back in his old neighborhood, serving as curate to the moorland village of Goathland, ten miles up the Newtondale from Pickering. That year Boyes, along with Richard Tennant and Roger Brearley, would again be summoned before the court of High Commission to answer charges of doctrinal heterdoxy. As we will see, all three men would survive the ordeal, and Boyes surprisingly enough was able to continue as minister of Goathland until at least 1651, when he would play an important, albeit hazy, role in the birth of the Quaker movement.[153]

Although details remain very murky, it thus appears that gifted Grindletonian laymen, who perhaps had learned to preach within the conventicles of Craven, were now seeking out ecclesiastical sanction so as to take up more permanent pastoral posts elsewhere. The exception to this rule was Josiah Collier, the man to whom we owe so much of our knowledge of the movement. Collier was born in the West Riding parish of Guiseley in 1595.[154] He was, it seems, a member of a godly clan: his brother Jeremiah would go on to become a well-known, respected, and entirely orthodox puritan clergyman in Bradford. Josiah followed a rather different course. He never attended university. Nevertheless, from very early on, he seems to have been a key spiritual teacher, anchoring the fledgling Grindletonian movement. He clearly knew Brearley (whom he referred to as "Roger"), and indeed his relatively detailed account of Brearley's first High Commission trial suggests that Collier may have been an eyewitness to those first heady days at Grindleton.

Like Boyes and perhaps Aiglin, Collier probably preached and taught in private, although unlike them, he never sought out the legitimacy conferred by clerical ordination. He appears to have lived and died a layman (Collier's career would thus seem to provide a good argument that there was some truth to the High Commission charge that Brearley's more gifted lay followers indulged in pursuits that were supposed to remain the sole preserve of the clergy). While sedulously collecting Brearley's sermons and poetry, Collier was himself writing copious and formidable treatises of theological argument, providing the closest thing we have to a systematic statement of Grindletonian theology. In 1670, he edited the first edition of Brearley's sermons, published at Edinburgh. In 1672, he and another well-known antinomian preacher

---

[153] J. L. Nickalls, ed., *The Journal of George Fox* (Cambridge, 1952), 88-89.

[154] West Yorkshire Archives Service, Leeds, BDP/29/1/1, Parish Registers of Guiseley St Oswald, Baptisms, Burials and Marriages, 1585-1653, 14, June 15, 1595.

named James Hartley took advantage of the new Declaration of Indulgence to apply for licenses to preach in separate households in Guiseley, suggesting that Collier had succeeded in creating a significant antinomian constituency in his home parish.[155] By the end of his life, both his opinions and his reputation as an evangelist appear to have been widely recognized in the West Riding. Thus, on a preaching tour of Bingley in 1676, Oliver Heywood fell to "discourse with Josiah Collier (82 years of age) Mr Collier of Bradfords brother, a great antinomian and preacher."[156] The elderly Collier maintained his allegiance to Brearley to the bitter end, for the next year saw the publication of a second edition of his master's sermons, together with Brearley's long apologetic poem and a collection of Collier's own religious verse (published without attribution). On September 26, 1684, Josiah Collier was buried at Guiseley, the parish of his birth.[157] Eighty-nine years old, Collier may well have been the last survivor of the early days of Brearley's ministry, when people flocked from far and near to hear their homespun prophet deliver the word at Grindleton.

Collier and Aiglin were not the only antinomian preachers who survived the Restoration. Oliver Heywood's diary is sprinkled with complaints about a whole series of Yorkshire ministers who, like Collier, Aiglin, and Hartley, continued to disseminate their errors into the 1670s and 1680s. The key culprits, on Heywood's account, were members of the Towne clan—Robert and his brother John, as well as their respective sons, Robert Jr. and Daniel. Heywood claimed that "all of them are accounted antinomians," but reserved pride of place for "old Mr. Robert Town, the famous Antinomian . . . the best scholar and soberest man of that judgment in the country, but something unsound in principles."[158] We have already had occasion to explore Robert's long and tumultuous career, which established a living link between the London antinomianism of the Eaton circle and the northern antinomianism of Brearley and his followers. In Chapter Six, it was suggested that Towne's mature theology appears to have been most similar to that of Eaton; nevertheless, it seems overwhelmingly likely that his first exposure to antinomian ideas took place when he was a young cleric in the North. Probably a native of Lanca-

---

155 For James Hartley's notorious antinomianism, see H. Fishwick, ed., *The Note Book of the Rev. Thomas Jolly, A.D. 1671-1693*, Chetham Society, New Series, 33 (1894), 14-15; *CSPD, 1672-1673*, 93.

156 Oliver Heywood, *The Reverend Oliver Heywood, B.A., 1630-1702; His Autobiography, Diaries, Anecdote and Event Books*, ed. J. Horsfall Turner (Brighouse and Bingley: A. B. Bayes, T. Harrison, 1881-1885), 3: 177.

157 West Yorkshire Archives Service, Leeds, BDP/29/1/4 Parish Registers of Guiseley, St Oswald, Baptisms, Burials and Marriages, 1654-1720, shows that Josias Collyer of Eshold was buried on 26 Sept. 1684, which would have made him just over 89 years of age.

158 Heywood, *Autobiography*, 3: 192; 4: 7.

shire or Yorkshire, Robert took his B.A. from Oriel College, Oxford in 1614. On 25 September of that year, Towne presented himself for ordination as deacon at Cawood in the diocese of York, and less than a year later, he was ordained priest and admitted to the curacy of Sancton, a tiny East Riding parish.[159] How long he ministered at Sancton is not clear; his whereabouts remain unknown until mid-1629, when, as we have seen, he was cited before the London High Commission for his impertinent antinomianizing in and about the capital. After this, he preached briefly in Nottinghamshire, before making his way back to northeast Lancashire, and thence to West Yorkshire, where he would become a fixture of the Pennine antinomian community until his death in 1664.[160] By contrast, Towne's elder brother John appears to have spent his entire clerical career in the North, although details are scarce. He was probably the John Towne, B.A., ordained deacon in the diocese of York on 8 May 1607.[161] On Marchant's account, Towne then took up a cure at Clitheroe, Lancashire, a market town some five miles to the south and west of Grindleton. Suspended from Clitheroe, he reappeared on the other side of the Pennines in 1618, acting as an "assistant" or curate at Sheffield, a position he held at least until 1628.[162]

The timing and the route whereby the Townes descended into antinomianism cannot be reconstructed; although there is no direct and irrefutable proof that they were part of the Grindletonian network during the earliest years of the movement, the circumstantial evidence is indeed persuasive. Thus, at some point between 1619 and 1623, Roger Brearley and a "Mr Towne"—whether John or Robert remains unclear—preached consecutive sermons at the Halifax exercise, a monthly institution held under the auspices of that doyen of Yorkshire puritanism, Dr. John Favour. A classic example of the "lecture by combination," the Halifax exercise brought together godly ministers from throughout Yorkshire. [163] We should not be surprised to find Brearley partici-

[159] Borthwick Institute, Inst. AB 3, fols. 430r, 431r, 444r.

[160] Marchant, *Church Courts*, 313.

[161] Borthwick Institute, Inst. AB 3, fol. 385r.

[162] Marchant, *Church Courts*, 288.

[163] For Favour and the Halifax exercise, see Marchant, *Church Courts*, 30-32, 246. For notes on many of the sermons, taken by the minister Elkanah Wales, see British Library, Add. MS. 4933B, fols. 156r-203v; for Brearley and Towne, see ibid., 163v-165r. It has been impossible to date these sermons with precision, but as Wales listed all of the clergymen involved, and as the notes were almost certainly taken consecutively and chronologically, it has been possible to collate the names given by Wales with Marchant's appendix of Yorkshire puritan ministers in order to triangulate on likely dates. Unquestionably, the sermons were preached before the death of John Favour in 1623 (for sermons by Favour, both before and after the appearance of Brearley and Towne, see ibid., fols. 162v, 188v). It is also

pating in such an event. For all his eccentricity, he fervently believed (or at least wished to believe) that he remained a welcome member of a broader community of saints. His participation in the exercise suggests that his puritan colleagues, despite the conflicts of previous years, were willing to meet him at least halfway.

Yet the invitation to preach at Halifax was hardly an unconditional offer of fellowship and goodwill. It seems beyond doubt that deep skepticism and suspicion remained. For Brearley and Towne chose (or more likely, were assigned) a particularly barbed scriptural passage for exposition, I Timothy 1: 9: "understanding this, that the law is not laid down for the just but for the lawless and disobedient, for the ungodly and sinners, for the unholy and profane, for murderers of mothers, for manslayers." On one reading, this passage could be interpreted as proclaiming that only sinners, and not justified Christians, were bound by the Moral Law, and hence it offered a potential feast for an antinomian minister; yet for this very reason, it was also the perfect litmus test for orthodoxy. It seems very likely that Brearley and Towne were allotted this passage so as to force them to prove their doctrinal sincerity.

If this was the case, both passed admirably. Indeed, Brearley's sermon reads almost like a direct response to the 1617 High Commission accusations against him; rather than taking the bait, and offering an anti-legal interpretation, Brearley carefully suggested that the fundamental doctrine expressed in the passage was the idea that "All living on the face of the earth, are actually now eyther children of god, or wicked," a statement that no self-respecting Calvinist could possibly gainsay. From this premise, he went on to draw a set of conclusions obviously designed to undermine the charges of heterodoxy that had been launched against him in previous years. The use of the doctrine was "to teach us to examine ourselves," an exhortation designed to calm anyone who might have had lingering doubts about alleged Grindletonian claims to spiritual presumption. So likewise, Brearley set out to counter the High Commission charge that the Grindletonians claimed it was "a sinne to chatechise the ignorant for knowledge is an hinderance to grace." As Brearley succinctly put it in his sermon, "Knowledge is a christians guide . . . its the ground of all graces." This proved the "Necessity of catechizing. we must so speake as we may make knowne the voice of god. Masters of familyes, muste instruct particularly." Such soothing restatements of puritan pastoral clichés—so seemingly contrary to the messages propagated in Brearley's surviving ser-

---

almost certain that they were preached after 1619, when William Styles took his B.A., before proceeding to ordination as deacon and priest in 1620 (for Styles's sermon, see ibid., fol. 187r). It should be noted that a remarkable number of the participating ministers had been or would be disciplined for nonconformity at some point in their careers.

mons before his home congregation—were clearly designed to calm nagging rumors that Brearley and his followers were fanatical heretics who scoffed at human learning and authority.[164]

"Mr Towne" pursued a similar strategy. His sermon, which followed immediately on the heels of Brearley's, likewise sought to sidestep all reference to controversial issues. He did so by limiting the scope of his sermon at the outset: the words "but to the Lawles and disobedient," Towne argued, referred "to the lawles that have no law." This enabled him to restrict his treatment of the verse to the ungodly alone: "I speake only of them without the Church." This canny maneuver meant that Towne's discussion completely excluded any reference to those who had been touched by grace, hence allowing him to avoid completely the more prickly question of the status of true believers. No one could deny, for instance, that the "ungodly [were] not acquainted with god," or that "these want sanctification of the sp[irit]." Nor could it be doubted that the "Law is given unto the lawles. 1. as causing wrath 2. as accus[ing] the conscience, 3. as binding over to the curse and death," that is, "to everlasting fire." Like Brearley, then, Towne focused on areas of obvious agreement, steering clear of the most explosive matters at issue, and effectively avoiding any statement at all that might raise the hackles of his auditors. Sadly, without further evidence, we cannot say for sure which of the Towne brothers preached in Halifax with Brearley. The appearance does, however, strongly suggest that the two brothers had already become associated with the Grindletonians by the early 1620s. This would certainly explain how Robert Towne was able effortlessly to slip back into the northern antinomian community when he was chased from London in the early 1630s. He was, it seems, returning home, bringing with him the experiences and insights he had accumulated during his stormy period in the capital.[165]

Around the time of this appearance at the Halifax lecture, the center of gravity of the Grindletonian movement shifted. At some point before 1623, Roger Brearley relocated to the parish of Kildwick-in-Craven, where he assumed duties as curate, although he seems to have continued to preach at least occasionally at Grindleton.[166] He probably owed his new living to the good graces of the leading family of the parish, the Currers, one of whom owned the manor of Kildwick. As noted, a William Currer had been summoned to

---

[164] For Brearley's sermon, see British Library, Add. MS. 4933B, fols. 163v-164v.

[165] Ibid., fol. 165r.

[166] See W. A. Brigg, ed., *The Parish Registers of St. Andrew's, Kildwick-in-Craven . . . April 1623-Aug. 1678*, Yorkshire Parish Register Society, 55 (1916), 3, 10, 15; that he continued to preach at Grindleton may be inferred from the fact that in 1627, the High Commission explicitly forbade him from preaching there (Borthwick Institute, HC AB 17, fol. 80v).

give testimony in Brearley's trial of 1617.[167] When death approached in 1637, Brearley was faced with the vexing question of what to do with his young children, six of whom were still minors. One of the two guardians he named was Hugh Currer of Halifax, a younger son within the extended family.[168] This would seem to imply a high degree of trust and intimacy between Brearley and certain members of the Currer family. Once again, we are faced with a striking conclusion: the Grindletonian movement appears to have survived at least in part because it received support from key members of the local elite.

The theological tendencies of the Currer clan were probably responsible for the subsequent history of Kildwick parish. After Brearley departed, probably in 1631, the curacy would come into the hands of a young minister named John Webster. In 1653, Webster published a treatise in which he referred to his own conversion to Grindletonianism, which he dated to 1635 (or just after

---

[167] Unfortunately, this man cannot be identified with certainty; there were at least four important branches of the Currer family in these parts, all of which remained closely linked in the early seventeenth century (and all of which tended to dub their sons either William, Hugh, or Henry, making exact identification maddeningly difficult). Of these, two branches are particularly important for our purposes: the first, led by the substantial yeoman William Currer of Stainton Northcote (d. 1624), was a dominant family within the parish of Gargrave, home of Thomas Brooke (Brearley's supposed persecutor) and almost certainly a site of early Grindletonian activity. William's younger brother Hugh (d. 1617) had likewise achieved considerable success, purchasing the manor of Kildwick before his death. Hugh's sons (who bore the imaginative names of Henry, William, and Hugh), were leading householders within the parish of Kildwick, the eldest son Henry often being styled "gentleman." All three were also near contemporaries of Brearley, and it seems overwhelmingly likely that one or more of these Currers were responsible for bringing the embattled preacher to Kildwick. It seems reasonable to hypothesize that the William Currer summoned before the High Commission was either William of Gargrave or his nephew, William of Kildwick Grange.

[168] Borthwick Institute, Original Wills, "Brearley, Roger," July 1637, PROG. Unfortunately, I have been unable to identify this Hugh with certainty. A Hugh Currer of Halifax applied for a license to marry Mary Mitchell, spinster of Sowerby Bridge, in 1642. The most likely candidate here is Hugh, the second son of William, of Stainton in Gargrave parish. In the early 1660s, he was living in Bradford: it is plausible that as a younger son, he had left Kildwick for the more bustling commercial towns to the south and east of Kildwick, first settling in Halifax and then in Bradford. It is also possible that the man named was the younger son of William of Kildwick Grange, also a second son whose prospects as a local landowner would have been limited. Both men would have been adults capable of acting as guardian for young children.

his arrival in Kildwick).[169] By the late 1630s, the hostile attentions of the Laudian authorities had driven Webster from the curacy, but this was just the beginning of a long and remarkable intellectual odyssey that included a stint as a parliamentary army chaplain, a period as a notorious radical minister in Interregnum London, and a second career as a physician and apostle of the new "natural philosophy" of the later seventeenth century.[170] Leaving aside the details of his later career, we need only note that Webster dated his conversion to the year *after* his arrival in Kildwick, suggesting that the flock may have been leading the shepherd rather than the other way around. Kildwick's role as an antinomian stronghold continued for decades. In the 1650s, the parish would secure the talents of none other than John Towne.[171] In 1672, Josiah Collier's fellow antinomian preacher James Hartley was living in Kildwick, and he accordingly sought and received a license to hold a meeting in his house there as well as at Guiseley.[172] In short, Brearley's relatively brief stint as minister at Kildwick seems to have marked the beginning of a half century of antinomian activity in the parish, something that apparently owed much to a strong core of support amongst the layfolk of the parish, and probably specifically to the influence of the Currer family.

Up to this point, we have focused exclusively on Yorkshire. It seems clear, however, that Brearley won followers elsewhere in northern England. The survival of Brearley's pastoral letter to the Newcastle woman Anne Pethye shows that Brearley had admirers as far away as Northumberland. The Newcastle connection may have dated back to the earliest days of the movement, as suggested by the seemingly incongruous fact that at least one of the witnesses summoned to give testimony in Brearley's first High Commission trial was a resident of Newcastle.[173] More certain is the fact that Brearley's message quickly began to spread west, into his home county of Lancashire. Sometime prior to 1622, a manuscript had been "directed and sent" to the gentleman John Fox, sometime steward of the Earl of Derby's Lancashire manors of Bury and Pilkington. The manuscript argued flatly that "In the Church of Christ since his death, the whole Law of Moses is wholly abolished," citing a

---

169 J. Webster, *The Saints Guide, or Christ the Rule, and Ruler of Saints* (1653), sig. A2v.

170 Marchant, *Church Courts*, 127-28, 290.

171 W. A. Brigg, ed., *The Parish Registers of St. Andrew's, Kildwick-in-Craven . . . April 1623-Aug. 1678*, Yorkshire Parish Register Society, 55 (1916), 96, 156, shows that Towne was there by 1653 and served until his death in 1659; Heywood, *Autobiography*, 3: 192.

172 G. L. Turner, *Original Records of Early Nonconformity* (London: Unwin, 1911), 1: 225, 237, 240.

173 For Pethye, see Lambeth Palace Library MS. 3461, 223-29; Borthwick Institute, HC AB 16, fol. 160r, for a witness identified only as "Nicolson de Newcastle."

wide range of patristic and reformed theological authorities in support of its thesis. The target of this anonymous letter was almost certainly the eminent puritan John Fox of Manchester, who died in 1622. Undoubtedly alarmed by the extreme content of this letter, Fox seems to have forwarded it to his brother-in-law, William Hinde, the puritan minister of Bunbury in Cheshire. Although Hinde was initially unable to identify the author, he found it so disturbing that he wrote and published a long theological refutation of the letter, which appeared in London in 1622.[174]

We possess no concrete evidence tying this manuscript to the Brearley circle (indeed, as argued in Chapter Ten, it is in certain respects more blunt and extreme than anything Brearley or his clerical allies were willing to commit themselves to in public). Yet, once again, there are good reasons to suspect that this manuscript did not simply emerge out of the ether, and that it was in some way linked to a Lancashire wing of the Grindletonian movement, perhaps in this case centering on the network of kinship and friendship surrounding the Brearley family. Brearley's wife, Anne Hardman, was a native of Bury, where Fox was manorial steward. She and Roger had been married in the parish church there in 1615.[175]

It is clear, moreover, that Brearley retained close family connections with his Lancashire kinfolk long after he removed to Yorkshire (a number of them named Roger in their wills during the period, while Brearley's own will was witnessed by his brother-in-law, Gabriel Garside of Rochdale). The ties binding Brearley to his Lancashire relatives may have been stronger than blood affinity—some, such as Marland native Alexander Brearley, whose 1621 will named "my welbeloved in Christ" Roger Brearley as an overseer, may indeed have embraced Roger's version of Christian truth. In 1634, Richard Brearley, also of Marland, similarly named his "well beloved kinsman" Roger Brearley to be executor of his estate. Like Brearley's father, Richard appears to have been involved in the cloth trade—when he died, he owned a valuable lease on a London property which included various warehouses and shops, all of which appear to have been managed by one of his sons, who apparently lived in London and conducted business for the family. Richard's will bore an unusually strident preamble—it proclaimed his firm trust "only to be saved by the free mercy and grace of God the Father in the alone absolute merritt and mediacion of Jesus Christ," and looked forward to the "great and glorious

---

174 William Hinde, *The Office and Use of the Morall Law of God in the dayes of the Gospell* (1622), 5. The following year, a second edition—with additional prefatory information suggesting that Hinde now knew who had written the letter—was published.

175 W. J. Löwenberg and H. Brierley, eds., *The Registers of the Parish Church of Bury . . . 1590 to 1616*, Lancashire Parish Register Society, 1 (1898), 202.

day of our Lord Jesus"—an exuberance that may well hint at the influence of his infamous but "well beloved kinsman."[176]

Even more telling, however, was the fact that one of witnesses to Richard's will was a man named Francis Medowcrofte. This was very probably the same Francis Medowcrofte, clothier of St. Lawrence Old Jewry, London, who would stand surety for another young Lancashire minister, Peter Shaw, when Shaw entered into composition with the crown to pay First Fruits on his new benefice of Radcliffe, Lancashire, in 1638.[177] Shaw's troubles in London need not be rehearsed; the allegations against him will be subjected to more detailed inquiry in the next chapter. A son of Leonard Shaw, nonconformist rector of Radcliffe, Peter had been baptized at the parish church of Bury on 9 March 1594/95.[178] After taking an unusually late B.A. from Magdalene, he was ordained in Yorkshire in 1625, and installed as curate of Ashton-under-Lyne, between Bury and Manchester.[179] Here he quickly found himself accused of antinomianism, perhaps prompting him to seek his fortune in London, with results initially spectacular, but finally quite disastrous. Having been run out of London by Laud, Shaw returned to Lancashire as a Fellow of the Collegiate Church of Manchester. Here, comically enough, he found himself once again at daggers drawn with his inveterately godly co-fellows, resulting in a particularly exquisite petition to Laud, in which Shaw solemnly protested his own conformity and denounced his opponents as unruly puritans.[180] His enemies,

---

176 Lancashire Record Office, WCW 1641, "Richard Brearley" of Marland. Although Richard did not die until 1641, the will was composed in 1634.

177 PRO, E334/19, fol. 227r. Medowcrofte, a bachelor, moved from St. Lawrence to St. Stephen Coleman Street, where he was buried on Jan. 2, 1639/40. His brother Giles was given administration of his estate. Guildhall Library MS. 4449/2, Registers of St. Stephens Coleman Street, 1636-1689, fol. 122r; M. Fitch, ed., *Index to Administrations in the Prerogative Court of Canterbury . . . Vol. VI, 1631-1648* (London: British Record Society, 1986), 279. An examination of the existing indices for London testamentary records suggests that during the seventy years before 1640, not a single Medowcrofte will was proved in any London probate court; no Medowcroftes appear in the registers of St. Lawrence Jewry and there were none listed in the ambitious 1638 survey of London householders, all of which suggests that Francis was not a native of London, and may indeed have been an occasional resident. "Medowcrofte" was a surname specific to the area around Bury and Rochdale.

178 Löwenberg and Brierley, eds., *Bury*, 10. Bury was at the time the cure of an elder Peter Shaw, presumably Leonard's brother and Peter's uncle. This corrects D. Como and P. Lake, "Puritans, Antinomians and Laudians in Caroline London: The Strange Case of Peter Shaw in its Contexts," *Journal of Ecclesiastical History*, 50 (1999), 685.

179 Borthwick Institute, Inst. AB 5, 130, 130A.

180 PRO, SPD 16/263/40, fol. 87r.

meanwhile, counterpetitioned, trying to use Shaw's unseemly past as a weapon against him.[181] It is not clear whether Shaw relinquished the eccentric opinions of his youth; he definitely did not immediately surrender his London connections. Thus, when Sir Raphe Assheton preferred him to his father's old rectory of Radcliffe, Shaw turned to two London denizens, the clothier and Brearley family confidant, Medowcrofte, and John Dye, a skinner of St. Andrew Hubbard.

Whether Shaw continued to spread antinomian opinions in Lancashire remains an open question (the fact that he, like Richard Tennant, appears to have sided with the royalists during the civil war may perhaps have been a sign of a genuine turn away from the enthusiasms of his youth).[182] Elsewhere, the Grindletonians undoubtedly survived and prospered. On the easternmost edge of the parish of Bury, we find the village of Heywood, home to Robert Heywood (d. 1645), squire, poet, and (to judge by his unpublished verse) an antinomian sympathizer. After Heywood's death, one of his sons-in-law collected and wrote out a volume of Robert's verse along with other poetic works—presumably from Robert's papers—including an early draft of Brearley's verse apology, and a third, anonymous poem called "Of Hypocrisy," also very likely by Brearley or a near associate.[183] Given Heywood's apparent theological preferences, it is perhaps no surprise that Robert Towne was installed as curate of the chapel of Heywood in the late 1630s. Towne presumably held this post until 1640, when he was once again brought before the authorities on suspicion that he held the "opinion of the Priscilianists and An-

---

[181] F. R. Raines and C. W. Sutton, *Life of Humphrey Chetham*, Chetham Society, N. S., 49 (1903), 50-51.

[182] A. G. Matthews, *Walker Revised: Being a Revision of John Walker's Sufferings of the Clergy* (Oxford, 1948), 230, shows that Shaw had been removed from Radcliffe by 1646, presuming that he was sequestered for royalism.

[183] Heywood's poems are transcribed in Robert Heywood, *Observations and Instructions Divine and Morall in Verse*, J. Crossley, ed., Chetham Society, N.S., 76 (1869), from Chetham's Library MS. A. 2. 132. In addition, the manuscript contains various other religious verses, copied out in the same hand (presumably that of Heywood's son-in-law); the penultimate, "Of Hypocrisy," is unascribed but repeats many of Brearley's stock arguments; at ibid., 228, the poem is interrupted by some scribbling, the date December 1678, and the initials "R.B.," which is highly suggestive although not decisive. The final poem, "Of True Christian Liberty and of Libertinisme," is certainly by Brearley, representing a shorter, variant version of the apologetic poem published by Josiah Collier in 1677. Since the verses were probably copied from Heywood's papers, it seems reasonable to speculate that the shorter version in this manuscript represented an early version of the poem, which came into Heywood's hands sometime before his death in 1645. After writing and circulating this early draft, Brearley returned to it and expanded it, and it is this version that was recorded and later published by Collier.

tinomians, and in these parts by some called Grindlestonians," an accusation he "utterly renounce[d] and disclaimed."[184]

The heartland of Lancashire "Grindlestonianism," however, undoubtedly centered on the Pendle region, in particular Burnley, Great Marsden, and Colne, the communities on the southern and eastern flanks of Pendle Hill. This area, although jurisdictionally part of Lancashire, merged seamlessly into Craven, with Colne bordering on the parish of Kildwick, and it is thus not surprising to find, from the very outset, Brearley enthusiasts in the Forest of Pendle and nearby communities. A number of the men called to give evidence before the High Commission in 1617 appear to have hailed from the area.[185] Thomas Barcroft, the Grindletonian-turned-Quaker, was a gentleman cloth merchant from Noyna, in the parish of Colne.[186] Ambrose Walton, who would serve along with Hugh Currer as guardian to Brearley's children after his death, resided in Great Marsden (also in Colne parish) and came from a family that did business in Burnley.[187]

It was undoubtedly such local support that allowed Roger Brearley to assume the ministry of Burnley in 1631. In 1588, the Crown had granted the parishioners of Burnley the right to appoint their own curate, provided he was nominated by three local JPs.[188] Whether three such magistrates nominated Brearley seems questionable, but there seems to be no doubt that Brearley was able to assume the position because he possessed friends and backers within the town itself. In 1631, when Brearley assumed the curacy, James Wilkinson

---

184 W. A. Shaw, ed., *Minutes of the Bury Presbyterian Classis, 1647-1657. Part II.* Chetham Society, New Series, 41 (1898), 263-65.

185 "Elizum Nutter," for instance, was probably the substantial yeoman Ellis Nutter of Filly Close in Pendle Forest for whom see Mary Brigg, "The Forest of Pendle in the Seventeenth Century," in *Transactions of the Historic Society of Lancashire and Cheshire*, 113 (1961), 69, 71, 87, 91, 93; John Aspinall was likely the Pendleton yeoman of the same name, whose 1642 will bore a rich, godly preamble (Borthwick Institute, Original Wills, "Aspinall, John" yeoman of Upstanden (Pendleton) Lancs., July 1642, PROG); "William Fowles" was possibly William Fouldes, one of the more important inhabitants of the parish of Burnley; John Broxupp may have been John Broxupp of Burnley (for whom, see William Farrar, ed., *The Registers of the Parish Church of Burnley . . . 1562 to 1653*, Lancashire Parish Register Society, 2 [1899], 231, 282, 285).

186 J. T. Swain, *Industry Before the Industrial Revolution: North-East Lancashire, c. 1500-1640*, Chetham Society, Third Series, 32 (1986), 125.

187 Borthwick Institute, Original Wills, "Brearley, Roger," July 1637, PROG; Farrar, ed., *Burnley*, 29; Lancashire Record Office, WCW 1625, "Henry Walton" of Great Marsden, which bequeathed "loose timber boards and Flagge Stones at Burneleye," suggesting business or building interests.

188 W. Farrer and J. Brownbill, eds., *The Victoria County History of Lancashire* (London, 1966), 6:450-51.

was sole churchwarden of the parish. Six years later, when Roger died, Wilkinson would witness Brearley's will.[189] The sum total of this evidence would certainly seem to suggest that Brearley was supported and installed by sympathetic local burghers who conspired to bring the great prophet back to the foot of Pendle Hill, where he had begun his tumultuous career.

Brearley's removal to Lancashire was perhaps prompted by an erosion of his sense of security in Yorkshire. In 1627, Brearley, together with Richard Tennant and William Boyes, had once again been called before the High Commission to answer charges of having dispensed certain unnamed "errors." Unlike the first High Commission action against Brearley, his second trial appears to have been promoted by newly aggressive ecclesiastical officials in York, intent on reversing the effects of Matthew's benign neglect of nonconformity. Ronald Marchant has plausibly argued that Brearley's case flowed out of a broader attack by a nascent "Laudian" administration on the network of puritan exercises and ministerial conferences that had flourished in Yorkshire during previous decades.

Although the details remain obscure, it seems that Brearley and his fellow Grindletonian ministers had been participating in these exercises, perhaps debating their opponents (a surmise rendered more likely given Brearley's known participation in the Halifax exercise a few years earlier). When the authorities, led by the new diocesan Chancellor William Easdall, moved against the exercises, the disputes of previous years erupted to the surface. In an interesting turn of events, Tennant appears to have accused one of his fellow participants, Thomas Squire, of doctrinal error. Squire responded by claiming that Tennant was an unreliable and duplicitous witness, who had "bene lately convented in the same for divers erronious and ungodly doctrines by him delivered in publique sermons by him preached and for divers assertions and opinions by him holden and maynteyned tending to the secte called Grindletonions and deeply suspected of familisme." Much as it had in London, then, the Laudian drive for conformity appears to have inflamed and amplified existing intra-puritan debates over the Law. Since 1617, the godly of the West Riding appear to have been able to contain or paper over their disputes through processes of delicate negotiation and compromise, worked out in conferences and clerical meetings. Easdall's aggressive push for conformity forced these debates into the light of day, opening up simmering animosities and communal dirty laundry to public scrutiny. Once again the Grindletonians survived the ordeal. By the middle of 1628, Brearley, Boyes, and Tennant had all submitted to the authorities and returned to their cures.[190] Despite this, however, Brearley may

[189] Farrar, ed., *Burnley*, 282; Borthwick Institute, Original Wills, "Brearley, Roger," July 1637, PROG.

[190] For the cases, see Marchant, *Church Courts*, 44-48, 231-32, 233-34, 280-81, 283. For Squire's assertion, see Borthwick Institute, HC AB 17, fol. 127r.

have sensed that the environment in Yorkshire was no longer safe, prompting him to accept preferment across the border in the diocese of Chester. The move to Burnley would be the last of his career. On June 13, 1637, after six years tending to his new congregation in Lancashire, Roger Brearley, the old prophet of Craven, was buried at Burnley, leaving a widow and six young children.[191]

Shortly afterwards, William Aiglin wrote his long, eulogistic poem, celebrating Brearley's spiritual gifts and bemoaning the loss of a man he unflinchingly compared to Moses. Yet despite Aiglin's concern that the North had lost its great prophet, a coherent, second-generation Grindletonian movement continued into the civil-war period and beyond. Space does not permit a full account of the later history of the movement, but a single brief and instructive example will suffice.

In 1651, the parish of Bingley, just to the east of Kildwick, appears to have instituted its own lecture-by-combination, inviting select ministers from nearby churches to give sermons in exchange for small sums of money. The lecture was undoubtedly engineered by the merchant and gentleman Benjamin Ferrand, a member of one of the leading families of the parish, who served as Bingley's churchwarden in 1651. [192] This remarkable exercise brought together two generations of Yorkshire antinomians. [193] The lineup was anchored by Robert Towne, Sr., whose close connection to Ferrand is confirmed by the fact that Ferrand would witness Towne's will in 1664.[194] Towne's son, also Robert, preached as well, often on the same day as his father.[195] Also appearing was a "Mr Eagland," undoubtedly William Aiglin, now curate of nearby Heptonstall.

Preaching alongside Aiglin was Richard Coore, a younger minister and the prime example of a "second-generation" Grindletonian. Coore, born around 1607, appears to have been a kind of dynastic successor to Brearley; he married Brearley's niece, Susan Doughty, and at some point became a minister, al-

---

[191] Farrar, ed., *Burnley*, 257.

[192] West Yorkshire Archive Service, Bradford, 5D94/4/1, Bingley All Saints, Churchwardens Accounts, 1651-1686, 18-20; in contemporary documents, Ferrand was described as both "merchant" and gentleman. See West Yorkshire Archive Service, Bradford, Busfield-Ferrand MSS. D/203, D/213.

[193] For the exercise and participants, see J. Horsfall Turner, *Ancient Bingley: Or, Bingley, its History and Scenery* (Bingley: Thomas Harrison for the author, 1897), 140-41, whose comments are based on West Yorkshire Archive Service, Bradford, 5D94/4/1, Bingley All Saints, Churchwardens Accounts, 1651-1686, 18-35.

[194] Borthwick Institute, Original Wills, "Towne, Robert," clerk, July 1664, Pontefract, EXCHQ.

[195] For the career of Robert Towne, Jr., see A. G. Matthews, ed., *Calamy Revised* (Oxford, 1934), 490.

though no ordination record survives.[196] During the 1640s and 1650s, Coore would preach at a number of Pennine parishes, including Heptonstall, Croston, and the chapel of St. Anne's, Halifax (alias Chapel-in-le-Brears) before taking up the curacy of Tong, also near Halifax, by 1650. Although he was driven from the curacy at the Restoration, Coore continued to live at Tong, practicing medicine and styling himself a "gentleman." In 1672, when Charles II issued the Declaration of Indulgence, Coore remarkably enough applied for a license to teach, describing himself as "of the true Christian perswasion not against episcopall presbeterian or independant but called an Antinomian" (perhaps even more remarkably, the petition was granted, and he was enrolled as the host to an "antinomian" meeting alongside Independents, Baptists, and Presbyterians).[197] In 1683, he produced a massive tome of anti-legal theology, a remarkable tribute to the survival of the original Grindletonian community.[198] Like Josiah Collier, Coore continued to preach and teach in private; according to Oliver Heywood, when Coore died in 1687, he was still preaching out of a local barn.[199]

Also performing at the Bingley exercise were two other ministers identified by Heywood as antinomians: Edmund Moore, curate of Baildon chapel, just east of Bingley, and Christopher Taylor, curate of the Halifax Chapel-in-le-Brears after Coore. Moore probably occupied the pulpit at Baildon through the good graces of the widow Jane Baildon, lady of the manor of Baildon through much of the later seventeenth century—it should be remembered that

---

[196] Robert Doughty, Brearley's brother-in-law, was a clergyman and schoolmaster, first at Gisburn and then at Wakefield. It is tempting to wonder whether he, too, was not given to Brearley's and Coore's style of divinity. For Doughty's marriage to Brearley's sister Alice, see Lancashire Record Office, WCW 1637, "Brearley, Abel," clerk; for Coore's marriage to their daughter Susan, see Borthwick Institute, Original Wills, "Doughty, Robert," MA of Wakefield, April 1663, Pontefract, EXCHQ.

[197] G. L. Turner, *Original Records of Early Nonconformity* (London: Unwin, 1911), 1:361, 496.

[198] R. Coore, *The Practical Expositor of the Most Difficult Texts throughout the Holy Bible* (1683); the same work was published twice more in 1683 under the title *Christ Set Forth*.

[199] Heywood, *Autobiography*, 2:150. For additional information on Coore, see A.G. Matthews, ed., *Calamy Revised* (Oxford, 1934), 135. Tong may have been an antinomian enclave before Coore's arrival in 1650. From 1636 to at least 1645 (and perhaps later), the cure had been served by Thomas Robinson, described by Heywood in the 1670s as "an old man, inclined to Anti-nomianism, accounted an honest man, turned out upon Non-conformity in 1662." On Robinson and Tong, see Marchant, *Church Courts*, 110, 274; Heywood, *Autobiography*, 4:323; West Yorkshire Archive Service, Wakefield, BDP 94 1/1/1, 19 March 1644/45, unfoliated (parish registers of Tong).

the Grindletonian manuscript now surviving at Lambeth Palace is inscribed "Madam Baildon booke" (the compiler of the manuscript, Josiah Collier, lived in the village of Esholt, just a few miles from Baildon in the parish of Guiseley, which perhaps explains how it might have come into her hands).[200] Given the presence of the antinomian Moore at Baildon, and given Jane Baildon's stewardship of the precious documents of the Grindletonian heritage, it seems reasonable to conclude that she probably served as a patroness to West Riding antinomianism in its second generation.

Christopher Taylor is an even more intriguing figure. Beyond Oliver Heywood's comment on his antinomianism, almost nothing is known of his early life. What we do know is that while Christopher was rubbing shoulders with his fellow antinomians at the Bingley lecture, his brother Thomas was preaching somewhat farther to the north to a group of radical puritans in and around the Westmorland town of Preston Patrick (shortly thereafter removing to Richmond). The Preston group—which included Francis Howgill, John Camm, and John Audland—would shortly welcome George Fox, an itinerant prophet whose arrival led to a chain reaction of conversions, and in many ways signaled the emergence of Quakerism as a mass movement. Howgill, Audland, Camm, and others were won over during Fox's tour of the Preston Patrick area; within months, they had converted their old pastor Taylor; he in turn journeyed south and converted his brother Christopher. Christopher and Thomas Taylor would become two of the leading evangelists of the new movement in the North.[201]

The Bingley exercise presents striking evidence as to both the durability and the ultimate demise of the Grindletonian community. It reveals first of all that the antinomians of the West Riding had managed to establish a significant toehold in the region, particularly the broken, steep countryside to the north and west of Halifax. Supported by powerful local laypeople such as Ferrand, the Currers, and Jane Baildon, the community seems to have survived in some form until the deaths of Josiah Collier and Richard Coore in the 1680s. Yet the defection of Christopher Taylor is also very telling; like the merchant Thomas Barcroft, and that ancient and stout Grindletonian preacher William Boyes, Taylor's antinomianism seems to have allowed for an easy and fluid transition to the perfectionist exuberance of the first Friends. Together, the

---

200 For Moore's career and his alleged antinomianism, see Heywood, *Autobiography*, 1: 184, 4: 15, and Matthews, ed., *Calamy Revised*, 352; for the Baildon inscription, see Lambeth Palace Library MS. 3461, table of contents; for Jane Baildon and Baildon chapel, see W. P. Baildon, *Baildon and the Baildons* (privately printed for the author, no date), 1: 175-78.

201 Heywood, *Autobiography*, 4: 7, for Taylor's antinomianism prior to his convincement; Norman Penney, ed., *The First Publishers of the Truth* (London: Headley Bros., 1907), 291-92.

ravages of time and competition from Quakerism appear to have ensured that there would be no third generation to perpetuate the gospel of Roger Brearley. Yet this masks the fact that even as Quakerism put a nail in the coffin of the Grindletonians, so too Quakerism was almost certainly the unwitting progeny of Grindletonian divinity. This was true partly because Fox and the Friends were able to recruit old Grindletonians; yet even more crucial was the role of Grindletonianism as an ideological precursor to the Quaker movement. As this chapter has demonstrated, Brearley's distinctive message energized a tenacious band of zealous fellow travelers and evangelists, many of whom played important roles in the development of the antinomian community beyond the North. Carried by his admirers to distant parts of the kingdom, and reworked in new ways, Brearley's divinity exerted a powerful influence on the shape of antinomian thought as it emerged in the 1640s, helping to lay the perfectionist foundation on which the first Quakers built their movement.

CHAPTER 9

Two Strains Crossed: Hybrid Forms of English Antinomianism

The preceding chapters have, it is hoped, revealed the rich variety of antinomian thought as it emerged during the prewar period. In many ways, Eaton and Everarde stood at opposite ends of the antinomian underground. At one end, Eaton embodied an "imputative" tradition that hearkened primarily to standard reformed modes of theological discourse; at the other, Everarde's chaotic but elegant vision, carefully crafted from a jumble of esoteric and sectarian materials, may be taken as an ideogram for what I have here termed the "perfectionist" strain of antinomian thought. Brearley, who drew liberally on both protestant and perfectionist sources for inspiration, might be seen as occupying a kind of middle ground between the "imputative" and "perfectionist" poles outlined here, although in the end, his gospel of simplicity, Adamic unity with God, and the new "law of love" placed him far outside traditional canons of protestant thought. Despite their very real differences, however, these three figures shared certain ideological affinities, a set of overlapping arguments, and above all, a profound aversion to the law-mongering ways of mainstream puritanism. These affinities meant that in the end, all three could and did serve as celebrated leaders within the emerging underground antinomian community of the 1620s and 1630s. Precisely because the social network of the antinomian community stretched between these two poles—including preachers such as Eaton, on the one hand, and Everarde on the other—in practice, the two modes of divinity became blurred. Within the crucible of the London antinomian underground, ideas that were characteristic of the protestantizing, imputative style of Eaton quickly became linked together with ideas drawn from the more explicitly mystical, perfectionist tradition—the tradition of the *Theologia Germanica* and Hendrik Niclaes—embodied by Everarde and Brearley. This marriage produced hybrid strains of divinity. The following chapter shall examine three specific antinomian propagandists, Peter Shaw, John Traske, and an anonymous writer known as the "Cambridge Antinomian," in order to illustrate the nature and consequences of this process of hybridization. By 1640, it had become difficult if not impossible to draw a strict dichotomy between "imputative" and "perfectionist" modes of antinomianism, for the two traditions had interpenetrated one another in myriad ways.

The Firmins of Ipswich, the Lanes of London

Before turning to the writings of these propagandists, however, I would like to examine two cases, both based upon eyewitness accounts, which allow us to visualize this process of hybridization in action. Some sixty years after London's "hot contentions" over the Law, the puritan elder statesman Giles Firmin reached back into his memory to recall his own formative experiences with antinomianism. While attending grammar school in the late 1620s, young Giles had lived with his relative Henry Firmin of Ipswich. Henry was no ordinary householder. As Giles explained, he was the paterfamilias of "an antinomian family," a man who shortly after Giles's departure would find himself summoned to Lambeth to answer for his opinions before the High Commission. While the authorities were less than pleased about Henry's religious proclivities, young Giles seems to have found his benefactor's heresies singularly unimpressive. As far as he could remember, "During the three years of my living there, [giving them their Opinions,] it was as well ordered a Family, as any in the Town, strictly observing the Lord's Day." In other words, Henry and his family looked more or less like all the other godly people with whom young Giles was familiar. Giles did recall one peculiarity that struck him as odd, even at the tender age of thirteen:

> One Notion I observed there, which I never heard before, nor since: It was the Interpretation of the Revel. 12. I. It was a Manuscript fastened to a board.
>
> *I saw a Woman Clothed with the Sun* [That is, the Church Clothed with the Righteousness of Christ, to her Justification] *and the Moon,* [that is, Sanctification] *under her Feet.*[1]

If Giles was telling the truth when he claimed that he had never before or since heard another reference to this admittedly odd exposition, then his com-

---

[1] Giles Firmin, *A Brief Review of Mr. Davis's Vindication: Giving no Satisfaction* (1693), "To the Reader."

ment offers us an extraordinary window onto the antinomian community, one that allows us to examine the modes of cultural expression through which an emerging antinomian identity took shape and developed over time. For the interpretation that had imprinted itself so deeply in Giles's memory was not merely bizarre; it was drawn verbatim from the writings of John Eaton, who had repeated this altogether unusual bit of exegesis in both of his major works.[2] Neither of these books was published until 1642. This undeniably Eatonist "Notion," then, must have made its way into the Firmin home either through manuscript exchange, by oral transmission, or by way of public or private preaching. Both Eaton's old parish of Wickham Market and John Eachard's church at Darsham were within ten miles of Ipswich; given this, we should not be surprised to find die-hard followers in Ipswich and its environs.[3] Firmin's testimony suggests the existence of an Eatonist subculture, complete with homemade religious paraphernalia, pet biblical verses, and idiosyncratic scriptural interpretations.

It is significant as well that Giles Firmin recalled nothing particularly striking about his antinomian hosts; they seemed to behave in all the ways godly people were supposed to behave, most notably by keeping a strict Sabbath. This accords well with the observations in Chapter Six, where we saw that de-

---

[2] J. Eaton, *The Honey-Combe of Free Justification* (1642), 348-52. See also idem, *The Discovery of the Most Dangerous Dead Faith* (1642), 136-37, where he more succinctly summed up his interpretation of the passage in this way: "But what of this woman? . . . *cloathed with the sunne* that shineth in the firmament; that is, clothed with the glorious robes of Christs perfect righteousnesse, making her, wheresoever she sitteth or walketh, to shine as glorious in Gods eyes, as the sunne shineth glorious in our eyes, when shee shineth in her brightest hue. Thus hath Christ made his Church to himselfe a glorious Church, *Ephes.* 5. 27. *And hath the moone under her feet*, that is, the righteousnesse of the Law directing the feet of her walking and conversation here before men, and shining by sanctification declaritively to man-ward, *Matth.* 5. 16. as the moone shineth, and giveth light, that is, man walking in the dark night of this world: and yet hath this moone of sanctification under her feet, as of small esteeme, in comparison of the glorious sunne of Christs perfect righteousnesse, with which she is clothed, *Phil.* 3. 8, 9. *And hath a Crowne of twelve stars upon her head;* that is, hath the doctrine of the Gospel taught by the twelve Apostles and all faithfull Ministers (likened to stars, *Rev.* I. 16, 20.) in highest esteem, as her chiefest ornament or crowne."

[3] Eaton in fact seems to have had at least some personal ties to Ipswich. In London in 1621, two years after his deprivation, Eaton married Anne, widow of Thomas Crosman, who had been curate of St. Peter's, Ipswich from 1604 to 1617. G. L. Armitage and J. L. Chester, eds., *Allegations for Marriage Licenses issued by the Bishop of London, 1611 to 1828*, Publications of the Harleian Society, 26 (1887), 106; John Wodderspoon, *Memorials of the Ancient Town of Ipswich, In the County of Suffolk* (Ipswich and London, 1850), 394.

spite Eaton's war on mainstream puritanism, the actual behavior that he expected of true believers was, it appears, very nearly identical to that prescribed by mainstream puritans. The difference lay not, primarily, in the substance of obedience, but in the subjective apprehension that came along with this obedience. The true Eatonist faithful would, like other godly people, walk zealously in all God's commandments, although without any coercion or fear. Firmin's recollections offer reasonably reliable evidence that at least one antinomian took Eaton at his word, keeping even the Sabbath holy.

In 1629, Giles left the Firmin household for Emmanuel College, Cambridge, and three years later, he and his family departed for Massachusetts. He did not see his hosts again until he returned to England in the mid-1630s.[4] By this time, Henry, along with his fellow Ipswich laymen, Francis Bridges and Henry Mudd, had endured the ordeal and costs of a High Commission trial.[5] Not surprisingly, Giles claimed that much had changed in his absence:

> After I went from thence to Cambridge, and from thence to New-England; upon my return hither, I visited the Family: As to their Morals, they held very sober: But as to their Opinions, more corrupt.
>
> The Lords Day, which they did so strictly observe before, and did not now openly profane it, yet the Morality now is denyed; and one of the Company, who did answer his Name, (Mud was his Name, and very Muddy fellow he was) brought them to these Opinions;
>
> 1. *If there were any such thing, as Sin in the World, God was the Author of it*; [as for Sin, being Res, or Ens, they did not understand that.]
>
> 2. *As dyeth the Beast, so dyeth Man, denying a Future State.* I alledged that in *I Cor. 15.19. If in this Life only we have hope in Christ, we are of all Men, the most Miserable*: They told me, that was a Text something hard to answer; but they thought it might be answered: But there I left them, and never saw them more: When we can make nothing of lesser Errors, God may give us up to them, which are gross.[6]

---

[4] For Firmin's matriculation at Emmanuel, and his movements in the 1630s, see *Alumni Cantabrigienses*, *s.v.* Firmin, Giles.

[5] Their case seems to have begun formally on November 4, 1631, when they were sworn in before the High Commission (CUL MS. Dd. ii. 21, fol. 14r). For an eyewitness account of their appearance before the High Commission on June 21, 1632, see S. R. Gardiner, ed., *Reports of Cases in the Courts of Star Chamber and High Commission,* Camden Society, N.S., 39 (1886), 270-71. Mudd and Firmin were still being forced to attend on the court in October 1634, when at last they presented a certificate from the ministers Samuel Ward and Thomas Foster, verifying that they had renounced their errors. From Giles's account, it appears that this recantation was less than sincere (*CSPD, 1635-36* [London, 1865], xxxvii-xxxviii).

[6] Firmin, *Brief Review*, "To the Reader."

If true, this tale likewise has much to tell us about the nature of the antinomian community as it developed in the years before the civil wars. For the infectious opinions that Henry Mudd had allegedly injected into the Firmin household during the time of Giles's absence were by no means characteristic of John Eaton's theology. While the muscular providentialism of an Eaton or a Towne might have accounted for the claim that God was the author of sin, tendencies towards anti-Sabbatarianism and mortalism were apparently alien to Eaton's thought.[7] They were not, however, unknown amongst perfectionists. Indeed, as we have seen, John Everarde had strenuously denied the binding, literal force of the Sabbath, and had come close indeed to defending overtly the proposition that God had authored sin. And although he seems to have affirmed some sort of afterlife, Everarde spent a great deal of time belittling those who claimed that the "heaven" of the scriptures referred to a future celestial paradise of jangling harps and gilded thrones, arguing instead that believers had already come into the true, allegorical heaven on earth by virtue of their identity with Christ; he likewise confessed before the High Commission that he did not believe that there would be a literal, physical resurrection of the body at the time of the Last Judgment.[8] In this, he was merely

---

[7] Mortalism appears to have been anathema to the Eatonists. Like mainstream puritans, Eaton seems to have maintained an entirely traditional conception of resurrection and afterlife. In 1648, his follower John Eachard would denounce those "mysticall Familists" who claimed that "the resurrection of the Body, spoken of in I *Corinth*. 15. and other places, the perfection, the salvation, the glory, and all whatsoever the Scriptures have spoken concerning Christ and his Kingdome and reign with all his Saints, are now at this present time in a secret, mysticall manner fulfilled, turning all Scriptures into allegories, and making Jesus Christ a mysticall thing, and all persons names, matters and things therein spoken of, and written, to have mysticall meanings, which they undertake to declare in a kind of Philosophicall way." See J. Eachard, *The Great Day at the Dore* (1648), title page, 26-27.

[8] See Bodleian Library, Tanner MS. 67, fol. 143v, for the charge "That I did not beleeve that our bodyes nourished of and by beefe mutton and Capon and the like could rise againe and goe to heaven, affirmeing it to be a senceles conceite to suppose otherwise and concluded that there was no resurreccion eiusdem materia signata quae et principium Individuationis to be expected." At his trial, Everarde defended himself by saying that he denied only that the resurrection was physical, that is, that our selfsame, material bodies would be raised up from the grave. Rather, he insisted that the resurrected dead were of "a new substance," although he did not elaborate on this opinion. See British Library, Additional MS. 11045, fols. 37r-38r, 16 July 1639, letter of E[dward?] R[ossingham?] to Viscount Scudamore (eyewitness account of the trial, first discovered by Kevin Sharpe).

echoing, or running alongside, a living Familist tradition, which had always maintained that the Resurrection was something that occurred in this life.[9]

Wherever Mudd had contracted these opinions, we may say at the very least that they mirrored ideas in circulation among "perfectionists" such as Everarde. Moreover, they appear to have represented a marked departure from (or rather, a significant addition to) the strict Eatonist opinions that the Fermins had maintained in the 1620s. In short, we are seeing the process whereby the two, independent traditions of the antinomian subculture flowed together and reacted with one another to produce new, compound forms.

This process was not necessarily direct or neat. The claim here is not that men and women attended the sermons of John Eaton one week, and the sermons of John Everarde the next week, only to come away in a state of ideological suspension between the two. Rather, what we are seeing in the case of Firmin and Mudd is a process of cultural diffusion, whereby certain ideas entered circulation within the antinomian underground, only to be transmitted and reworked in new and sometimes creative ways as they were passed from individual to individual. In this manner, for instance, individual fragments of Familist thought—such as the notion of "goddedness," aspects of the allegorical mode of scriptural interpretation, or even mortalism—could become detached from their origins, enter the circulating stream of antinomian discourse, only to be plucked out and appropriated by non-Familist antinomians.

The foregoing analysis of Henry Firmin's ideological development relies on the childhood memories of a seventy-year-old man. Fortunately, it is not our only eyewitness testimony to this process of ideological admixture. In October 1631, just before Mudd and Firmin received their summons to Lambeth, the tailor Richard Lane and his lover Joan Wilkinson were likewise summoned before the court of High Commission, where an observer carefully recorded their examinations. The precise source of their antinomianism is not clear, but both Lane and Wilkinson admitted that together with other unnamed people they "did often meet at the house of one Westbrooke a Taylor in Shooe Lane" for purposes of religious discussion.[10] So, likewise, Lane apparently claimed that he had been "confirmed" in his opinions by a preacher whose name the eyewitness recorded as "Greenham." Wilkinson, too, admitted that "she heard the said Mr Greenham preach at a Church upon Fish streate hill and

---

[9] For sixteenth- and seventeenth-century attacks on Familist mortalism, see N. Burns, *Christian Mortalism from Tyndale to Milton* (Cambridge, MA: Harvard University Press, 1972), 59-64. It is not clear, however, that Familists were true mortalists or annihilationists. Although HN clearly believed that humans were somehow resurrected in this life, and that the Last Judgment was already taking place, he likewise seems to have maintained a belief in some sort of eternal life.

[10] Gardiner, *High Commission*, 190-91.

that there he dwelleth."[11] As luck would have it, in this case, we possess a second document—a letter sent from an informant to Archbishop Laud eight days earlier—which throws further light on the identity of this elusive preacher. As we have seen in Chapter Two, the informant named the mysterious preacher not as "Greenham," but as "Greene," describing him as a tailor, originally from Reading, who had somehow managed to worm his way into a variety of London pulpits. According to the informant, this Greene had some time ago been thrown into New Prison "for houldinge god could see no sin in his Children." Upon his release, "he went to cambridge—and in shorte time retorned to london and sett upp his bil[l]es with this Inscribed shorte hand taught by a Cambredge scoller but this fellowe by one meanes or other gott in to preach in the most noted pulpits as blackefriers Mr Dampards bridewell and other and preacheth still here and there and this fellowe is about the towne or he was of verie late." The informant further speculated that "this greene is one of [Lane's] tuters," a judgment that seems entirely plausible given the statements of Richard and Joan before the High Commission.

If the informant was correct, Greene had initially been imprisoned for maintaining the quintessential doctrinal principle of Eatonism, the notion that God saw no sin in his children. Whether true or not, Greene's admirers Richard and Joan were apparently indulging in rather more extreme—indeed openly perfectionist—views in 1631. In the words of the informant, who claimed to have debated Lane face-to-face,

> this fellowe saith he is perfet [and proveth it out of these places] Mat. 19.20 Jam: 3.2. Colo: 1:28: with other places more perfet then the patriarkes and profits Heb: 11:49/ a Christian that is borne of god canot sinn because the seede of god remayneth in him Therefore no difference betweene such a one and Christ and for farther proufe of this hee aledged 1 John 4:17: because as he is so are we in this worlde, proved this by other places and sayinges soundinge this way that it was not for the servant to be above his Master but to be as his Master. if ye object that sent Paule sayth o reched man that I am . . . , and if wee saye wee have no sin, his Answere wilbee sent Paule spake there as representinge the Carnall man as in verse before and for the other place if anie man thinke him selfe so Just by nature as to be without sinn and so not need clensing he deseveth him selfe, but beinge Clensed he is cleane in deede, If ye Aske him why he worketh no meracles he Answereth from Heb: 4: they were a parte of Crists workes which he entering into his rest seased from, as god did from his. If ye goe farther and Inqueere what difference was there betwene Crist and a Christian he lett a worde slipe which he woulde willinglie have recanted that before Crist reseved the holie goste and man reseveth the holie gost Criste at his baptisme man when he is regenerate before

[11] Ibid., 193.

> Criste is bare man onlie and without sinn the other sinfull but after Crists baptisme and the Comminge downe of the holie gost and mans regeneratinge then there is no differance and this doctrin doth so fill him with Joye that he canot containe him selfe is . . . almost in wraptures and for him to Aske for pardon of sinn he houldes it verie needles toulde me playne[ly] he did not, hee is nowe a branche in Crist the vine and he prayes to be pruned . . . that he may bringe forth more frute a great deale.[12]

On Lane's account, then, believers shared in Christ's perfection. In themselves, they were sinful, but in their regenerate state, they had become branches in the vine of Christ, and were thus entirely and inherently free from sin. They thus no longer needed to beseech God for pardon. Following the lead of the first epistle of John, he maintained that there was "no difference betweene such a [regenerate] one and Christ." The informant thus ascribed to Lane a series of positions that were clearly "inherentist" and "perfectionist" in their orientation.

All of this could easily be dismissed as the hyperbole of a self-appointed heresy-hunter were it not for one fact: when brought before the court on 20 October, Lane obstinately and defiantly defended precisely these opinions, trading scriptural proofs with the appalled High Commissioners. Laud drew upon the informant's letter, declaring that "I heare you are an high Familist, and you hould it very lawfull to equivocate. Did not you say that you were as Christ was, God and man?"[13] Lane responded, "I did not say soe; but through Jesus Christ I think I am perfect, and I hould that perfection is and may be attained in this life." To this brazen answer, the Archbishop inquired of him whether he used the Lord's Prayer. Again, Lane responded that "The Lord hath wrought in me that I need not to use it . . . I said that Christ dwelling in a believer, and being his guider and disposer, he may say, 'Repentance is hidd from mine eyes.'" In other words, Lane was confirming the charge that because Christ dwelled in him, he was perfect, and did not therefore need to beseech God to forgive trespasses, since he did not have any such trespasses. When Bishop Morton asked him "What say you, then, to this of St. John, 'He that saith he hath noe sinne is a lyar?'" Lane immediately and unrepentantly adduced "the words of the same Apostle, 'He that is borne of God sinneth

---

[12] PRO, SPD 16/224/26, fol. 54r-v.

[13] A close comparison of ibid., as against Gardiner, *High Commission*, 188-89, 190-94, shows that Laud drew on the informant's letter both in initially questioning Lane, and then in drawing up official articles against him. Laud's comments here were clearly derived from the informant's claims that Lane was guilty of "hie familisme" and that "his religion teach[es] him to equivocate."

not.'"[14] This truly impressive piece of audacity hardly endeared him to the Bishops, who dumped Lane and his companion Wilkinson (who had come to present a petition on his behalf) into New Prison and the Clink, respectively.[15]

At his next appearance, having had a week in prison to mull over his fate, Lane opted to tone down his statements. When Lane's comments from this first hearing were used to produce the article "That you Richard and Joane doe hould that a Christian in this world is as absolutely perfect as Christ Jesus himselfe," Joan wisely denied everything, submitting "her judgement to be guided by the higher powers, the Bishops and the Doctors of the Church." Lane, however responded that "he houldeth the beleiver is not soe righteous and perfect in himself, but is soe accepted for perfect by God through Jesus Christ." This was a very different claim from the one he had defended a week before; he had, in essence, gone from a perfectionist to an imputative position. By clinging to this less extreme position, Lane warded off all the articles against him, arguing that believers were perfect not in respect of Christ dwelling in them, but rather by "acceptation through Christ." When asked to explain his more forward appropriations of scripture the week before, Lane admitted that "he did answere then as is articulate but since being better informed he is sory for the same his indiscretion." Lane realized that his extreme and audacious remarks were "indiscreet." He further realized that only by moderating his statements, by reverting to a more palatably protestant position, could he undo the damage he had done in his first appearance. Laud, for one, was having none of it. Twice he reminded Lane of his prior claims to sinlessness and identity with Christ, complaining that "You said you were as righteous and as perfect as Christ but now you say it is by acceptation, you are as Christ was; why was he righteous by acceptation"?[16] Laud, like Lane, recognized that these were two distinct positions, and that Lane had slid carefully (and in Laud's opinion, disingenuously) from one to the other.

Whether Laud was correct in his assumption that Lane's retrenchment was mere equivocation is ultimately beside the point. What is certain is that Lane was slipping between two very different ways of conceptualizing a believer's freedom from sin. The description of the anonymous informant, when combined with Lane's insolent performance on 20 October, demonstrates beyond all doubt that he was fully conversant with an idiom of perfectionism, in which Christ was taken to be somehow immanent in the believer. Nevertheless, he was also willing and able to resort to an "imputative" conception of a

---

[14] Their first appearance before the High Commission, 20 Oct. 1631, is recorded in Gardiner, *High Commission*, 188-89.

[15] See CUL MS. Dd. ii. 21, fol. 6v.

[16] Their second appearance before the High Commission, 27 Oct. 1631, is recorded in Gardiner, *High Commission*, 190-94.

believer's perfection. From the standpoint adopted in this chapter, we need not determine which of these positions Lane actually held (indeed, it might be wrong to say that he held either of them in a strict, exclusive sense). It is crucial only that the reader see the blurring effect at work here, as Lane moved effortlessly between two distinctive modes of argumentation. It is the contention of this chapter that by 1631, when Lane appeared before the High Commissioners, these two modes—which had different origin points and different areas of emphasis—had begun to bleed together in the minds of many antilegalists, helping to forge positions that appropriated aspects of both Eatonism and perfectionism. Indeed, Lane could have absorbed this "mixed" style in any one of several London pulpits by the late 1620s, for as we shall see, several of the city's more notorious antinomians had by this time already begun to meld the distinctive languages of imputation and perfection. The remainder of this chapter examines three figures who in different ways incorporated elements of each of these traditions into their thought.

Peter Shaw

For a brief but spectacular moment, Peter Shaw appears to have served as the epicenter of London antinomianism. Shaw's case has already been discussed in some detail above. Nevertheless, the details are worth repeating. Shaw was the son of a Lancashire puritan minister. Following his training at Cambridge, the younger Shaw returned to the North, taking up the curacy of Ashton-under-Lyne, Lancashire, in 1625. Despite his godly pedigree and his university education, however, the young preacher seems to have quickly gravitated toward antinomian ideas, most likely through contact with Grindletonians. Preaching in Lancashire, he apparently fell under the suspicion of his fellow ministers, who complained of his antinomianism. Perhaps as a result of this negative attention, he emigrated to London, presumably sometime around 1627. By 1628, his peculiar opinions and his outspoken style had made him a controversial celebrity on the London preaching circuit. When his notoriety caught up with him in 1629, it was alleged before the court of High Commission that "he hath begot such a faction, that if he preach not, his followers, have refused upon the Sondayes to hear either sermon's, or divine prayer, but rest at home." Although it is impossible to know exactly how sizable this faction really was, it seems clear that as alleged, Shaw's "followers" were fiercely loyal; one, the chandler Joseph Smith of St. Helen Bishopsgate, tried in vain to derail the High Commission proceedings against Shaw by threatening the godly preacher Abraham Grame, apparently one of the instigators of the case. So, too, Shaw attracted disproportionate attention, as well as heated opposition, from his fellow London ministers. The case against him involved the testimony of no fewer than eighteen London clergymen, some of them committed Laudians, and others inveterate puritans. Indeed, Shaw's case appears to have become something of a cause célèbre among the theologically aware throughout England; when Shaw came to be sentenced in late 1630, for instance, Thomas Crosfield, Fellow of Queens College, Oxford, noted in his diary that he had received "Newes of one Mr Shawe to be tryed in the High Commission for holding strange tenents touching the Trinity, mans salvation etc."[17] Whatever else he may have been, Peter Shaw was a man who evoked strong responses in friend and foe alike.

That Shaw attracted such disproportionate attention was a consequence of his eccentric and extreme opinions, opinions that he vented with an equally remarkable vehemence from a variety of London pulpits. Unfortunately, we possess no friendly or unbiased record of these opinions. Almost all of our information about him derives from the hostile testimony of his enemies. As Peter Lake and I have argued in a commentary on the documents generated during his High Commission case, such sources demand careful and skeptical treatment.[18] In that article, we laid down a series of evidentiary or methodological strictures that must guide any attempt to use the court testimony as prima facie evidence concerning his beliefs. These strictures must be rehearsed once again before analyzing Shaw's opinions.

First, it must be pointed out that it is impossible to determine whether the specific charges against Shaw represent authentic renditions of his words, or whether his accusers were imposing their own stereotypical categories of interpretation upon his utterances, thus providing an accurate index not of Shaw's opinions, but of their own fears and expectations. In this vein, several of the articles were clearly conditioned by the suspicion that Shaw was a Familist. He was accused of mortalism, and of holding that believers could commit the most heinous sins with impunity; meanwhile, in one article, it was claimed that "Answerably there is fastened on him by his followers," the notion "That a Christian is so Christed with Christ, and godded with god, that he is as Christ before god." Mortalism, libertinism, and (above all) the famous belief that the faithful were "Christed with Christ and Godded with God" were heretical fancies habitually attributed to Familists in this period. Even those who had never met a genuine Familist—who had never so much as scanned a single page of HN's tortured prose—would have been able to identify these as characteristically "familistical" opinions.[19] To accuse Shaw of such opinions was,

---

[17] Queens College MS. 390, fol. 54r.

[18] D. Como and P. Lake, "Puritans, Antinomians and Laudians in Caroline London: The Strange Case of Peter Shaw in its Contexts," *Journal of Ecclesiastical History*, 50 (1999). The dossier of evidence against Shaw (PRO, SPD 16/139/91) is transcribed therein. For ease of reference, the following chapter cites the articles against Shaw according to the numeration adopted in our article.

[19] For an example of the reflex tendency to identify Familism and mortalism, see Congregational Church Library MS. I. h. 48 (unpaginated), which contains an

as it were, to hammer him and his ideas into preconceived, familiar, and widely recognized heresiographical categories. Such accusations must therefore be treated with particular caution. It is likewise true that we cannot treat any single article or statement attributed to Shaw as a transparent reflection of his beliefs. Even when an accusation was firmly based on statements that came straight from his mouth, there is a high probability that those words were altered or misheard in sometimes subtle ways that distorted or simply decontextualized the opinions in question.[20]

This does not mean, however, that the articles are useless as guides to Shaw's professed beliefs (nor for that matter that Shaw was completely innocent of charges of Familism). The sheer volume of evidence offered up in this case ensures that, if we proceed with a certain amount of caution, we can deduce with a reasonable degree of accuracy the basic shape of Shaw's message as disseminated from the pulpit. Thus, although no single article can be accepted as a perfect facsimile of Shaw's own words, together clusters of articles can be used to draw a rough, composite road map detailing the basic topography of his beliefs. If and when two or more witnesses or groups of witnesses independently corroborated one another's testimony, we may say that there is an overwhelming likelihood that their testimony is accurate, at least in its broad outlines.[21] The cumulative effect of layer upon layer of corroborative

---

anonymous sermon on Matthew 7: 13-14, preached in Warwickshire in the late 1630s. The preacher adduced the text "to confute and condemne all Athiests, Epicures Libertines, Saduces and the late upstart family of Love raised out of the ashes of the old Saduces who deny the Im[mortality] of the soule and will not beleeve that there is another life after this."

[20] For a more extensive analysis of the manner in which hostile observers sometimes twisted or misinterpreted their enemies' words, together with a preliminary attempt to lay down a methodology for handling such sources, see below, Appendix C.

[21] For example, Christopher Dow and Thomas Fitzwilliam signed off on the charge that "a belever ought not to pray in the name of Christ as a mediator . . . but to come immediately to god," while Palmer and Wilson reported the very similar claim that "A man looseth his person in prayer, if he take Christ as a 3d person, but is to go up immediately to god." Since the two pieces of evidence seem to have been gathered separately, and were reproduced with enough distinctiveness to suggest that each gleaned his evidence on different occasions, it is probably safe to say that Shaw indeed made much of the fact that in their prayers, believers should not pray in the name of Christ, but ought to approach God immediately. This methodology of course assumes that the separate pieces of evidence were, indeed, generated independently, that is, that Dow and Fitzwilliam were not present when Palmer's and Wilson's evidence was given or read. Unfortunately, we do not know enough about the way in which the articles were generated in this case to solve this problem one way or the other.

testimony is striking in this case. This is all the more true given the fact that in many instances, such testimony was proffered by men of radically different ideological persuasions: puritans and Laudians alike agreed as to the overarching nature of Shaw's opinions, and offered very similar accounts of his errors. Despite the few exceptions noted above—instances in which preconceived fears about Familism may have dictated the way in which witnesses interpreted and reported Shaw's statements—the sheer reiterative weight of testimony against Shaw may be used to yield a highly consistent and (in all likelihood) accurate picture of the general shape of his opinions.

In our commentary, Lake and I attempted to provide a preliminary account of those opinions by abstracting a series of basic and underlying tendencies from the allegations against him. This allowed us to draw a rough sketch of his opinions, which nevertheless left considerable room for the possibility that the specific, individual allegations against him may have been misinterpreted, misreported, or simply invented. What follows here seeks to add an additional layer of detail to that initial sketch by examining Shaw's opinions in the context provided by previous chapters. Many of the articles against Shaw, which appear virtually unintelligible on their own, take on new meaning and significance when viewed in the light of the battles between antinomians and their mainstream puritan enemies. In this way, Eaton, Everarde, and Brearley may be used to elucidate Shaw.[22]

To begin with, several articles hint at his Grindletonian origins. A wide range of witnesses, including the famous godly minister Dr. Cornelius Burges, attributed to Shaw variations on the opinion that "Although a man heare, reads, pray and yet if he looke at his owne salvation he is but a base Christian and shall end in hell: but if he looke only at the glory of god, he shall have salvation into the bargaine."[23] The Laudian Brian Walton separately accused him of delivering that "Whosoever makes salvation his utmost end, hath not

---

[22] It could be argued that in doing so, we risk inflicting on Shaw precisely the treatment he received at the hands of his seventeenth-century enemies—that is, pigeonholing his opinions based on preconceived expectations as to what a Familist or antinomian might or should say. This possibility cannot be dismissed without further evidence. Nevertheless, as we shall see, a number of Shaw's more unusual and unintelligible opinions do in fact make sense *only* within the context provided by previous chapters. Unlike accusations of mortalism or brute libertinism—which may well have been simply imagined by overeager heretic-hunters—these detailed theological points were not the sorts of opinions likely to be conjured up and hurled at an enemy for the sake of tarring him as a heretic. They were, however, the sorts of opinions that were being canvassed from London pulpits and debated in the private conferences of the godly.

[23] Como and Lake, "Peter Shaw," article 20.

the least sparke of true grace."[24] These sentiments presumably provide the backdrop to the statement, reported by three other witnesses, "that if god will a Christian must be as willing to goe to hell as to paradise."[25]

All of this echoed very closely the claims of Brearley, laid out in the last chapter, that for the true Christian, "Religion is his treasure . . . not to gayne salvation, but for the fellowship of god," and that such Christians would "chuse to be in hell" rather than pursue any other end. In his first High Commission trial, Brearley's enemies had rendered the opinion somewhat differently: "A soule sanctified must soe aime att gods glorie, as he must never thinke of salvation." In either case, Shaw's arguments appear to mirror uncannily those of Brearley. It is of course possible that Shaw had arrived at this position on his own, perhaps through exposure to the *Theologia Germanica.* He likewise may have encountered such opinions through another source (John Everarde, for instance, made similar arguments in his sermons, perhaps also under the influence of the *Theologia*).[26] Given Shaw's Lancashire history and connections, however, it seems overwhelmingly likely that this peculiar opinion was a result of his apprenticeship among the Grindletonians. Moreover, the argument was evidently a central and distinctive feature of Shaw's divinity. A decade later, the New Englander Martha Collins confessed before her congregation that one of the dead ends on her early spiritual itinerary had been with a London preacher "Mr Shaw" who taught her "that I should look after the Lord for himself," suggesting that she saw this focus on the glory of God as the defining characteristic of his ministry.[27]

Yet if Shaw was indebted to the Grindletonians, it also appears clear that upon his arrival in London, he quickly assimilated his opinions to the environment of debate as it was taking shape in the capital. He thus appears to have joined hands with the Eatonists in an extreme form of anti-legalism, sharing with them a concomitant tendency to deny the traditional puritan emphasis on sanctification. Numerous witnesses, both godly and Laudian, attributed to him statements that downplayed the role of outward, legal works

---

[24] Ibid., article 16.

[25] Ibid., article 27, signed by the puritan preacher James Nalton and the laymen John Palmer and John Wilson. This article was almost identical to article 26, which was likewise signed by Nalton and the puritan joiner Rowland Tompson.

[26] Everarde had argued that "if either *fear*, or *Law*, or *Heaven*, or *Hell*, *reward*, or *fear*, or any hopes, or by ends, *urge the heart to goodness*, these are but *dead works*." On Everarde's account, such works were done merely for the sake of the self, the I; by contrast, only those works that "*glorifie* [our] father which is in heaven" could truly be said to be good. See Chapter Seven, above.

[27] M. McGiffert, ed., *God's Plot: Puritan Spirituality in Thomas Shephard's Cambridge.* Rev. ed. (Amherst: University of Massachusetts Press, 1993), 192, from Collins' confession before Shepard's Cambridge, Massachusetts congregation.

in the soteriological process. Along with Eaton and Towne, Shaw allegedly held that believers were not to look to themselves or to their own holiness for assurance of salvation: "for a Christian to comfort himselfe, because god hath enabled him to reforme his wayes and to walke upwrightly towards god and man, is to deny Christ and to be entangled in the law."[28] By his own confession, Shaw maintained "That Sanctification and obedience to god's commandments is no part of the forme of a Christian,"[29] an argument that squares well with the Eatonist tendency to downplay or denigrate sanctification. And as with Eaton and Towne, this dim view of sanctification was linked to a suspicion that works righteousness and legalism were rife within the English church. In a sermon preached on 28 November 1628, Shaw had allegedly argued that "Not the want of power against sinne, nor want of exercise thereof, can hinder: He that think's his disobedience, or not observeing any of gods commandements, makes him farther from god; or can stand betweene him and life; he puts Christ from him, and is a Legalist, a morallist, no Christian," echoing the habitual Eatonist critique of puritan moral rigor.[30]

Indeed, Shaw's trademark insistence that believers were to abandon concern for their own salvation, and give themselves over wholly to God's glory—although perhaps based initially on Brearley's argument—appears to have developed more fully as part of this furious critique of puritan practical divinity. The intense godly emphasis on self-examination, continuing repentance, and moral rigor were apparently taken to nurture in the would-be believer an extreme, even narcissistic, obsession with personal salvation. Against this formula, Shaw seemed to be suggesting that believers need only submit themselves entirely to the will and glory of God. By doing so, they would (almost accidentally) receive salvation as "an over plus."[31] On the other hand, those who obsessed over their own spiritual status, persistently examining their lives for evidence of the favor or displeasure of God, and fearfully sculpting their lives to conform to the letter of the Law, were doomed to despair and damnation.

Indeed, Shaw's penchant for diminishing the value of legal works appears to have been so extreme that he could argue that "That a wicked man may forsake every knowen sinne and performe every knowne duty and yet be damned. He may doe all this from the truth of the hearte and yet be damned."[32] The fact that these distinct but related layers of testimony came from numerous witnesses of differing ideological persuasions strongly suggests

---

[28] Como and Lake, "Peter Shaw," article 22.

[29] Ibid., article 17.

[30] Ibid., Watts's sermon notes.

[31] Ibid., article 20.

[32] Ibid., article 24.

that whatever the specifics of his arguments, Shaw appears to have seized upon a critique of mainstream puritan legalism very similar in its broad outlines to that formulated by Eaton and his followers. It is worth noting, too, that there are no hints, at least in these statements, of the "anti-literal," allegorizing bent of John Everarde's critique of mainstream puritanism. Shaw's putative statements, like those of Towne and Eaton, seem for the most part to have had a protestantizing flavor, in which it was hinted that the church had become infected with a strain of works righteousness. Thus, the godly lecturer Nathaniel Waker complained before the court that Shaw's "followers vilifie and defame all other Ministers, clamouring, that because Mr Shaw cutt's of the roote of the Arminians, ergo it is that all the Ministers of the citie oppose him, for they are all tainted with Arminianisme."

Unsurprisingly, then, Shaw's alternative view of the nature of true religion seems to have been based in large part on protestant or reformed conventions. Believers were freed from the Law, and indeed from all conditional duties, by virtue of the fact that Christ had already met all the conditions required for salvation: "A beleever is not bound to doe anything, as the way to life, for he is quite freed from all doeing in that respect, because Christ hath fullfilled all the law for him."[33] Unlike Everarde, then, Shaw seems at times to have emphasized a traditional, substitutionary and imputative view of the atonement. Since human beings had failed to fulfill the Law in themselves, the external obedience of Christ was necessary in place of our own obedience. But where mainstream puritans argued that Christ's obedience and sacrifice freed believers from the curse and condemnation (not the commandment) of the Moral Law, Shaw maintained with the Eatonists that Christ's oblation was so overwhelmingly powerful that it obliterated the Law entirely: as the minister Robert Peake charged, Shaw held "That the morall law as it was delivered at mount Sinai, is not only abrogated to a Christian, as a meanes to attaine life, and in respect of the malediction, and curse, but also as it is a rule of life, now to a Christian."[34] So too, Christ's all-powerful sacrifice brought believers into a new relationship with God, one in which God by virtue of his justice was no longer capable of indicting believers for their sins: as the puritan layman Thomas Rogers and the conformist cleric Richard Dell alleged, Shaw had delivered that

---

[33] Ibid., Watts's sermon notes.

[34] Ibid., article 28. Brian Walton, pastor of St. Martin Orgar, likewise alleged that Shaw had maintained that "A beleever is so dead to the law, that as a man cannot command his wife when she is dead, nor a maister command his servant, after he is made free, so cannot the law, command any after he is in Christ." Ibid., article 32.

after a man is in Christ god hath nothing to doe to call him to an account, for the breach of any of his lawes; and ergo if god should at any time call him to an account, for the breach of any of his lawes; a child of god may answere, with a holy boldnes, that he hath nothing to doe to call him to that account: but as a man that is called into a court, knowing that his businesse is not to be tryed there, may say, he would refuse to be tryed and to answere there. If God should bid him abstaine from such a sinne or he shal be damned, doe such a duty and he shall have heaven, he may say he will not upon those tearmes, there is another covenat betweene me.[35]

This sort of thinking appears to have represented an extreme form of the logic used by the Eatonists to prove their claim that God could see no sin in the justified. Since Christ had already obeyed on behalf of the faithful, to suggest that God could now accuse believers for sin would be to cast doubt on God's perfect justice. The penalty for sin had already been paid, and consequently, "the Moral law, is to a belever, as a cancell'd bond, to one whose debt is paid."[36] Again, without accepting verbatim the accusations of Shaw's enemies, it would seem that he did indeed argue that the Moral Law no longer bound believers, doing so on the basis of fairly commonplace substitutionary and covenantal modes of reformed thought.

Broadly considered, Shaw's divinity, which was first forged in Lancashire, thus appears to have converged over time with that of the Eatonists. Even on more tangential and technical issues, he revealed a remarkable similarity of concern and argument. In a manner reminiscent of other London antinomians, he allegedly warned his listeners "That for a Christian in sicknesse or any affliction, to examine his wayes and to mourne and repent of his sinnes, as the cause why god corrects him, is to deny Christ and to be entangled in the law."[37] We have already seen that the argument that God did not afflict his children for sin had been defended by John Eaton and by 1630 was widely considered to be a distinguishing theological characteristic of antinomianism.

Likewise, Shaw also shared with the Eatonists—and indeed with Everarde—a tendency to abolish all doubt and fear for believers (a strand of argument that would appear to set him apart from Brearley, who alone among those examined in this study appears to have continually warned even the most exalted Christians about the dangers of "fleshly" backsliding). In this vein, perhaps with some exaggeration, the puritan ministers Richard Culverwell and Nathaniel Waker charged that Shaw had claimed that "They are Ideots and fooles, that are not assured of there salvation at all times."[38]

---

[35] Ibid., article 30.
[36] Ibid., article 29.
[37] Ibid., article 23.
[38] Ibid., article 15.

Again, while it would be unwise to accept this accusation in its naked form, the general sentiment was certainly consonant with Shaw's other alleged opinions, and indeed fits very well into the pattern of London antinomian thought as laid out earlier in this study.

Even at the level of detailed theological minutiae, there seems to have been considerable overlap between his ideas and those of the Eatonists. Thus, as we have already seen, Shaw allegedly taught "That faith doth not save nor damne; justifie nor unjustifie," an argument that hints at the classic Eatonist tendency to empty even faith itself of any instrumentality in the process of justification.[39] To reiterate, in their efforts to reduce the possibility that any inherent human quality might be seen as meriting salvation, Eaton and other antinomians appropriated a preexisting (but contested) puritan argument that faith itself merely apprehended a justification that had already been accomplished by the sacrifice of Christ. Shaw appears to have been evincing the same sentiment in his claim that faith did not justify.

A similar habit of thought seems to have undergirded Shaw's supposed claim that "infidelitie or the want of justifieing faith in Christ is noe sinne; nor shall any be condemned for it." Eager to empty the process of salvation from any hint of connection to the Moral Law, Shaw seems here to have argued that faith belonged to a domain entirely outside the realm of the Law and sin. Faith was not commanded by the Moral Law; and hence, infidelity was not a sin; in other words, faith had nothing whatsoever to do with the duties commanded by God (and it was presumably for this reason that Shaw had argued that "Faith is not a grace, nor any part of sanctification").[40] Faith, we may presume, was for Shaw an entirely passive process of beholding, a process that had nothing to do with works, Law, human effort, or activity. Although the precise structure of these opinions must remain conjectural, it is worth noting that two independent witnesses likewise reported that other London antinomians had defended the dual notions that infidelity was not a sin, and that faith was not commanded in the Moral Law.[41] The fact that these were tech-

---

[39] Ibid., article 11.

[40] Ibid., article 12.

[41] See above, Chapter Three. The notion that faith was commanded by the Law and that infidelity was a sin was a puritan commonplace. See, for instance, the comments of William Perkins in R. Rogers, et al., *A Garden of Spirituall Flowers* (1609), sig. C3v. This commonplace had first been openly challenged and debated in the controversies surrounding Peter Baro, the Cambridge "proto-Arminian," during the 1590s. In a manner reminiscent of his puritan opponents, Baro had explicitly defended the claim that faith was commanded in the Moral Law. His argument was picked up and attacked by none other than the notorious T.L., the mysterious religious prophet and sometime follower of HN, who allegedly tutored John Etherington in the ways of Familist mysticism. To my knowledge, T.L. was

nical and fairly esoteric theological arguments—not loaded and emotional accusations of "familistical" deification or libertinism—strongly suggests that they were not simply being invented or constructed from generalized preconceptions.

Once again, then, we see Shaw's opinions nested within a wider matrix of antinomian thought and opinion. In many areas, his arguments appear to have been virtually indistinguishable from those of the Eatonists. At other points, however, Shaw appears to have departed quite significantly from Eaton and his followers, promulgating ideas that were either distinctively his own, or which derived from other sources. Some of these opinions were strange enough (or garbled enough) that they defy interpretation. Such, for instance, were his claims that "That the humane nature of Christ was reprobated by the divine, in the time of his Agony, and the personall union then dissolved," and that there was no such thing as a historical faith.[42] Without additional information, these opinions seem both unprecedented and unintelligible.

At other points, however, Shaw appears to have held opinions that had little or nothing to do with John Eaton. The minister William Boswell thus testified that Shaw had denigrated the sacrament of baptism, claiming "That the outward washing of water in Baptisme, is no more then the washing or dipping of a doggs foote in water."[43] We have already seen that Eaton and Towne had in general taken a rather exalted view of baptism; Eaton in particular argued that infant baptism conferred the benefits of justification on be-

---

the first English religious writer to argue the position that infidelity was not a sin, and he did so in terms that reveal the logic behind later, explicitly antinomian arguments to the same effect: "All the errour of *B[aro]* then consists herein, that hee hath not distinguished the law of life, from the Morall lawe: which yet God in his eternal counsell, and prescript words, even from the beginning hath severed, with as great a distance one from another, as *Hagar* differs from *Sara*: bondage from liberty, *Sina* from *Sion* (64)." To say that faith was commanded in the Law was thus to confound two distinct laws (the Law of Moses, and the "Law of Grace"), and to claim that salvation was by the Law. In fact, "the law of the Decalogue, and the righteousnesse of it which is of workes, is not onely another f[or]m, but also opposit to the law of grace and righteousnesse of God, which is manifested by faith (68)" ([T.L.], *The Key of David, That Openeth the Gates to the City of God* [1610], 47-71). Insofar as it argued for a radical dichotomy between the Mosaic Law and the New Testament Law, this position presaged arguments made by Brearley, Traske, and the Cambridge Antinomian thirty years later. For further analysis of T.L. and his possible influence on Etherington, see P. Lake, *The Boxmaker's Revenge: 'Orthodoxy,' 'Heterodoxy,' and the Politics of the Parish in Early Stuart London* (Stanford: Stanford University Press, 2001).

42 Como and Lake, "Peter Shaw," article 2.

43 Ibid., article 33.

lievers. If indeed Shaw had actually delivered this flippant and incendiary opinion (Boswell claimed that he had done so on more than one occasion), this would therefore represent a fairly major departure from the Eatonist line of thought. It would, in fact, place him far closer to the erstwhile Familist fellow traveler John Etherington, who in the late 1620s strenuously argued (and suffered) for the idea that the elemental "Baptism in the flesh" did not confer grace.[44]

There are other reasons to suspect that Shaw may have been indulging in forms of mystical religious experience that were not entirely characteristic of Eaton and his closest disciples. Several witnesses suggested that Shaw in substance denied traditional accounts of Christ's mediatorial office; two testators claimed that he held "That a belever ought not to pray in the name of Christ as a mediator, or 3d person betweene god and him, but to come immediately to god," while another pair attributed to him the opinion that "A man looseth his person in prayer, if he take Christ as a 3d person, but is to goe up immediately to god,—without a mediator." It was further alleged that Shaw taught that Christ's mediatorship was necessary only for human beings in their fallen, unconverted state: "Christ doth not stand betweene god and man, as wee are sonnes, but as wee are sinners." Shaw appears to have been saying that Christ's mediatorship was over and done with after the onset of saving grace. At this point, the believer, now free from the bondage of the Law, was to approach God not through Christ's mediatorship, but directly, as a son and heir: "It is the life of a Christian and a maine principle that when wee goe to god wee must conceive our selves, to be as neare to god as Christ and in as faire a way to goe to god, as Christ himselfe."[45] Here, again, Shaw seems to have been promoting his own unique and idiosyncratic view of true religion (although interestingly, in 1638, Edward Norice would similarly claim that one of John Traske's Gloucester followers had openly wondered "whether God will not accept of our prayers without the mediation of his Sonne").[46] It should be noted that the basic substance of these accusations—that a truly faithful person now experienced a direct and immediate communion with God himself, akin to that between Christ and God—pushed beyond anything seen in the writings of the imputative antinomians. Indeed, such claims began to break down the boundary between the believer and Christ, suggesting that the faithful were to imagine themselves as in some sense equivalent to the Son of God.

---

[44] J. Etherington, *The Defence of John Etherington against Stephen Denison* (1641), 52. This work had been written in the late 1620s.

[45] Como and Lake, "Peter Shaw," articles 3, 4, 5, 7.

[46] Edward Norice, *The New Gospel, Not the True Gospel* (1638), 3.

Indeed, numerous witnesses reported opinions that strongly savored of what has been identified as the "perfectionist" or "inherentist" mode of antinomianism, as embodied by John Everarde. Hence, Shaw had allegedly claimed that "the humane nature of a Christian is not a person, but that his personalitie is in Christ, in whom he subsists, after the same manner, as the humane nature subsists in the divine."[47] To put this in somewhat plainer terms, Shaw apparently argued that believers were united with Christ in the same way that Christ's humanity was united to his divinity. This idea was not unprecedented. As we shall see later in this chapter, a very similar argument was being canvassed in manuscript by another London antinomian at much the same time. And like that unidentified antinomian, Shaw appears to have hinted that this union with Christ brought believers into a state of perfection. In this vein, separate witnesses attributed to Shaw the odd but striking opinions "That god is not perfect, till the creature be perfect: as a father is not perfect, till the child be perfect; and the perfection of a father lies in the perfection of the child," and "That till all the belevers have the same holines with him, Christ is not a perfect Christ."[48] These peculiar opinions may have been garbled by the hostile witnesses who recorded them; nevertheless, there seems to be little question that Shaw was willing—in a manner not entirely characteristic of the Eatonists—to identify believers with Christ.

This tendency came through most clearly in a sermon he had preached at St. Michael Crooked Lane in February 1628/9. According to notes taken by the minister William Watts, Shaw had argued that "a belever hath the same holynes with Christ and that not imputed holiness only, but inherent," and "That there is no speciall difference betwixt the holines of Christ and of a beleever." Again, the reader should take note of the departure from the Eatonists' imputative conception of Christ's righteousness. The faithful were not *covered* by Christ's holiness, they themselves *possessed* Christ's holiness. It might be objected that Watts was mangling Shaw's opinions here, attempting to pin upon him an undeserved "familistical" perfectionism. Yet the rest of sermon as reported by Watts tells against such a conclusion. Shaw allegedly went on to distinguish between material and formal parts of scripture, drawing a distinction between the bare letter of the Bible (the matter) and the living, spiritual word (the form):

> The law he distinguished into the materiall and formall part. the matter of the Decalogue (said he) consisted in those apt expressions used by Christ who was Law giver as a king, and this was the letter or bare words as they are written in our bibles; which he said was not the word of god, nor was it able or powerfull to be the rule of sanctification; no more then the word of

[47] Como and Lake, "Peter Shaw," article 9.

[48] Ibid., article 1, Watts's sermon notes.

> another ordinarie man: but the formall part only was the word of god, and this contained the mind and meaneing of Christ expounded as he was a prophet.

On Shaw's account carnal, or "legal" Christians, no matter how strict their observance of the Law, and no matter how rigorous their devotions, remained captivated by the material, outward shell of the written word; only true believers recognized the kernel within, the hidden spiritual "mind and meaning" beneath the letter. This they did because they shared "the mind of Christ":

> That unlesse a man had the full and perfect understanding of the mind of Christ, the scriptures were not the word of god: this he illustrated thus: as a forme, if you devide it is not the same forme: or as a number, if you take one unite from it is no more the same number; so if Christ mind be not understood, the text is not his word, for Christ hath not a mind, and a mind.
>
> Hereupon he inferred, that the words of scripture pronounced by a divine with out the mind of Christ to them were none of his word, no more then the wordes of a philosopher were.[49]

Here was a conception of scripture that paralleled in almost every way that of Everarde. The outward letter of the scriptures was but a shell, a husk that hid a mysterious "mind and meaning" (the precise words used by Everarde to describe the spirit beneath the letter). Only those who had passed into mystical union with Christ, coming to possess his mind, could actually access the word of God. As in the case of Everarde, for Shaw the words of scripture, understood according to the letter, were not the Word of God. Here, again, we have a set of opinions that fit neatly, almost perfectly, into verifiable patterns of antinomian thought that have been explicated in previous chapters. Moreover, in this case it is extremely unlikely that Watts could have simply pulled these opinions out of the air, foisting them upon an innocent Peter Shaw. This would have required not only a deep and detailed knowledge of the patterns of thought underlying "perfectionist" antinomianism, but also an extraordinarily keen ability for ventriloquizing and reproducing those opinions (the sort of knowledge that could only have come, for example, through repeated visits to John Everarde's private conventicles). In short, we appear to have arrived here at a set of opinions that are very probably Shaw's. It is, of course, not clear how precisely Shaw came to this position (if one bends one's ear, very faint echoes of Grindletonian arguments might be heard lingering deep in the background).[50] But the question of *how* is not essential to demonstrate the

---

[49] Como and Lake, "Peter Shaw," Watts's sermon notes.

[50] See R. Brearley, *A Bundle of Soul-convincing, Directing and Comforting Truths* (1677), 37, for a tantalizing but too-brief discussion of Christ as "law-giver." Note also that in 1617, the Grindletonians had been charged with arguing that "If

basic point: what we are witnessing in Shaw is a process of convergence, in which various strands of antinomian thought appear to have bled together in the maelstrom of London to produce a generic set of antinomian arguments, available to all takers.

Included within this generic pool of ideas were motifs and themes that were clearly derived from mystical and perfectionist sources. The fact that Shaw held such peculiar opinions with respect to the nature of scripture would seem to render it plausible, perhaps even likely, that the accusations of perfectionism and union with Christ were much more than the delusional projection of his enemies' fears, and that Shaw himself was a knowing purveyor of ideas drawn from the sectarian frontier. Whether Shaw actually told his followers that they were "Christed with Christ and Godded with God," we need not look very far to see why Shaw, like Everarde, found himself accused of Familism. As we have seen, however, Shaw's enemies in the High Commission court were not the only people to level this charge against him. Indeed, when they came to renounce the evil ways of HN, both John Etherington and Giles Creech (each of whom had intimate knowledge of what passed for the London Familist community of the early seventeenth century) would accuse Peter Shaw of Familism, Creech suggesting that he (like the elusive "Mr Gray") was associated with the "familists of the Valley."[51] Certainly, the one fragment of information we possess concerning the opinions of young Gray—the title of his "Sermon of the Perfection of a Christian"—lends indirect support to the claim that Shaw and Gray may well have been playing with a form of perfectionist divinity.[52]

In the end, this account of Shaw's divinity and career must remain speculative and inferential. As I have attempted to demonstrate, however, we may

---

they hear a sanctified minister preach, they know when he speakes by the spiritt and when not," and that "A minister unsanctified cannot either convert or confirme," both of which bear a vague resemblance to the position adopted by Shaw; for Josiah Collier's own, much later and less incendiary, rendition of the Grindletonian position, see Chetham's Library MS. A. 2. 24, fols. 69r-70r. None of this can account for Shaw's position, however.

[51] John Etherington, *A Brief Discovery of the Blasphemous Doctrine of Familisme* (1645), 10-11; PRO, SPD 16/520/85, fol. 126v. On Creech's account, familists of the Valley held "that all thinges are done according to the will of God; but they deny the Resurrection of the Bode, and saie, there are no Divells but their owne selves. They denie all praiers and giving of thankes unto God for any thing either in this life, or in the life to come." While not inconsistent with the accusations against Shaw, this description in fact summarizes John Everarde's divinity in a crude but accurate way.

[52] E[dward] F[isher], *The Marrow of Modern Divinity: Touching Both the Covenant of Works, and the Covenant of Grace*, (1645), 68.

draw the following tentative conclusions about him: Peter Shaw's London ministry represented the melding of the Eatonist, anti-legal critique with a more overtly mystical and perfectionist style of antinomianism. While he articulated an assault on the legalism and pharisaism of mainstream puritans that appears to have been virtually indistinguishable from that of an Eaton or a Towne, he seems to have adapted this critique to a less overtly protestant, indeed genuinely perfectionist, form of mysticism that in some respects paralleled the thought of John Everarde. While it is possible that he had come to such a position via the teachings of the Grindletonians, the origins of Shaw's theological style are less important than what he tells us about the development of anti-legal thought in London. The boundaries between different modes of antinomianism had proved permeable; what was emerging was a hybrid antinomianism that borrowed elements both from the reformed tradition and from a mystical, sectarian tradition, fused together by a burning animus against mainstream puritanism.

John Traske

Owing to the nature of the available sources, our conclusions regarding Shaw's divinity must remain provisional, at least until the discovery of new evidence affords greater clarity. No such debility exists in the case of John Traske. As was his wont, Traske has graced posterity with a generous storehouse of information about his own mature opinions. These include his book *The True Gospel Vindicated*, published illegally in 1636, a typically hubristic "Rule of Faith" appended to *The True Gospel*, as well as a short manuscript printed and attacked by his puritan enemy Edward Norice in 1638. In addition, however, our knowledge of Traske's early career and writings facilitates the process of interpreting his later position; as argued above, despite his apparent about-face, many of the structures and imperatives of his early divinity remained intact in his later life, transposed from one pietistic environment to another. The question of whether John Traske had been exposed to Familism in the 1610s remains subject to the reader's judgment; what is surely true is that by 1615, he and his followers had adopted a set of opinions that veered dangerously close to what would later be called antinomianism. Part of the burden of this chapter shall be to demonstrate how these ideas carried over into his later thought, helping to give life to a style of divinity, which (like that of Shaw) hybridized the imputative and perfectionist strains of antinomianism.

We can say with utter certainty that John Traske, unlike Shaw, was associated, both personally and ideologically, with imputative antinomians. As one of the five "faithful" London ministers named by John Eachard in 1631, there can be no question that he consorted with and was influenced by Eatonists. We do not know when or how this love affair began. But given his prior ideological affinities, the message disseminated by Eaton and his associates was well calculated to resonate in Traske's ears. He quickly appropriated certain aspects of their divinity, adopting Eatonist imagery and catchphrases, including the hallowed totem of imputative antinomianism—that the faithful donned the garment of Christ's perfect righteousness. Thus, Traske pointed to the difference between what he called "obedience of Faith, and obedience of Workes; that [which] we can performe by our owne personall obedience to the Law of God, in our most exact walking, according thereunto; and that which we beleeve is performed for us by the Lord *Jesus Christ*, and found onely in him, and his Rich, Royall, Glorious, and everlasting Robe of Righteousnes: This walking by Faith is to walke after the Spirit, and that walking by Workes of the Law was termed a walking after the flesh."[53] Here was the classic Eatonist focus on the exogenous merits of Christ. Justification came wholly through the life and death of Jesus, for through Christ's sacrifice "God is already pacified, his Justice fully satisfied; all mans merit, satisfaction of Gods Justice, all mans performances, in turning away Gods wrath and indignation, fall to the ground"; with a derisively protestant snort, Traske accordingly dismissed all those who, like the Galatians, went on "seeking perfection by the flesh."[54]

In accordance with this imputative orientation—and in a manner reminiscent of Eaton and Towne—Traske at one point explicitly disavowed Familism.[55] So too, he appears to have shared the widespread antinomian opinion, which had its roots with Eaton, to reduce the salvific role of faith: as Traske put it "*The new Covenant hath no condition at all; Faith is not the condition of the Gospels Promises: but onely a qualification in us.*"[56] Faith was not the condition upon which God granted salvation; justification presumably came not by faith, but through Christ, who alone performed God's conditions for the salvation of humanity. Like Shaw, Traske thus seems to have been true to this widespread antinomian doctrinal motif.

Most of all, however, Traske shared with the Eatonists a violent aversion to the shape of mainstream puritan piety. As we have seen, he had shown discomfort with certain aspects of puritanism as early as 1615, in his first pub-

---

[53] John Traske, *The True Gospel Vindicated, from the Reproach of a New Gospel.* (n.p., 1636), 12-13. The image of the "robe of righteousness" was a favorite of Traske. Elsewhere in the same book, he wrote that "the absolute and everlasting perfection of the glorious, rich, royall, and unspotted Robe of that Righteousnes of Jesus Christ, yeelds full, strong, and abounding joy, and delight, when it is known to be the blood of God" (ibid., G4v).

[54] Ibid., sigs. G3v-G4r, 14.

[55] Ibid., 32.

[56] Ibid., 54-55. Traske admitted that this accusation, cited by Norice, had been "produced out of a printed Booke [of Traske's] called *The Path to Peace*" (ibid., 55). Sadly, this book does not appear to have survived.

lished pamphlets. By the mid-1620s, this distaste appears to have blossomed into a fully formed hatred. In his *True Gospel Vindicated* of 1636, Traske offered what was perhaps the most cogent surviving précis of the anti-legal position. When, in characteristic puritan fashion, Edward Norice charged Traske with blasphemously holding that "Beleevers when they fall into any sin, be it of Adultery or Murder, are not to mourne or grieve: (for that savours of the flesh) but still to rejoyce," Traske responded by turning this accusation on its head, jokingly rearranging it to suit what he took to be Norice's own tastes:

> *Beleevers, when they fall into any sinne, bee it of Adultery, or Murder, are to mourne without all Joy, in a hoplesse manner (for that savours of the Spirit) and Joy, is no meanes at all, though it be onely in the Lord, to bring any man out of his sinne.*
>
> Doth this way like the Slanderer [i.e., Norice] better than the other?[57]

On Traske's account, it was precisely this joyless, hopeless mourning that characterized the whole of puritan divinity. For a man who early in his life believed that he had tasted the ecstatic joys of heaven, mainstream puritan religiosity simply would not do. God commanded his saints to indulge in an exultant joy, a holy joy that was ruined by the puritan gospel of misery. As he explained, this "joylesse-sorrow, which it seemes, is maintained by this derision of holy Joy; and that desperate mourning, which is forced by ignorant, and blind guides, is the cause of so many selfe-murders, that abound at this day and amongst whom, if not such as this *Slanderer* is, and his *Likes*, who daily Hang, Drowne, Poyson, Stab, and make away themselves, as being first poysoned by such corrupt legall teaching."[58] But physical suicide was merely the most obvious and dramatic effect of godly divinity; more insidious was the spiritual suicide toward which Norice and his mainstream puritan colleagues led their congregations on a daily basis. They taught an unholy and unchristian brand of legalism, "by which pretended Christian assemblies, are turned into Jewish, and worse then Jewish Synagogues, by the neglect of holding forth the ensigne of the Lord Jesus Christ, and magnifying his infinitely powerfull blood, and Righteousnesse: For in those Jewish assemblies, there were daily sacrifices: but in these meetings, not Christ once named, except in their Prayers in many sermons, but sinne onely cryed downe, and duties inforced on the poore Creature, as if the Creature had power of his owne to doe them."[59]

On Traske's account, the godly were thus ultra-pharisees, worse even than the Jews because they insinuated themselves into the hearts of the people by disguising themselves as sanctified Protestants: "in seeming to be the greatest

---

[57] Ibid., 23, 24-25.
[58] Ibid., 27-28.
[59] Ibid., 28.

enemies of sinne, [they] are the greatest advancers of iniquitie in the world."[60] In contrast to Shaw and other antinomians, who held that infidelity was not actually a sin, Traske argued that "The greatest sinne, and the roote of all others, now under the Gospel, is unbeliefe."[61] Along with the Eatonists, Traske recognized that the godly were formally committed to the notion of justification by faith, but in reality, this commitment was a deceptive sham: "now those men in their throng'd assemblies, doe nourish nothing more, then unbeliefe, Though they doe now and then call for Faith, yet they doe cry it downe with all their might."[62]

With a clarity expressed in no other prewar antinomian writing, Traske explained in detail how, precisely, the contours of godly divinity nourished unbelief. To begin with, he objected to the puritan homiletic standard, examined in Chapter Four, whereby the godly were constantly to examine themselves for a dead faith, that is, a faith that was almost indistinguishable from a true and lively faith, except that it produced no outward works of holiness. It will be remembered that this archetype of "dead faith" was used to pull believers back from the brink of complacency, to keep them constantly striving toward ever greater feats of devotion, charity, and holiness. Traske exposed this trick of pastoral sleight of hand in deeply unfavorable terms: "For they doe tell the people, that faith is not so easily gotten, as they thinke; that it is very hard to attaine unto, and tell them they must strive for it, and presse hard for it, and take heed they be not deceived, for many are deceived with false Faith, for true: and therefore they must looke it be of the right kind; and if it bee, Then they tell them, that these and these signes will follow, as if they have not those signes, as a change of the life, and uprightnesse of heart, and universall obedience to all Gods Commandements, and such like; they have no Faith at all, it is onely a fancy."[63] While Traske's assessment was deeply negative, it was hardly unfair; he was describing a very real aspect of puritan practical divinity, a pastoral maneuver that, as we now see clearly, was at the center of the Eatonist screed against puritan practical divinity.

But this was not the only commonplace of puritan preaching to which Traske objected. Making explicit a charge that had not been fully articulated in other antinomian writings, he denounced the puritan tendency to suggest that a series of preparatory works of humiliation and mortification preceded the onset of faith: "these [teachers] bid men beleeve in Christ, and tell them they must beleeve, but they must first be humbled, and well prepared for Christ, by chang of life, for he will not dwell with men that are ungodly, and

---

[60] Ibid., 29.
[61] Ibid.
[62] Ibid.
[63] Ibid., 29-30.

take up his habitation in such as are sinners, they make them beleeve, that there is a long mourning for Christ, or repentance for sinne, and an absolute turning to God, before Christ may be received, or beleeved on (All which are in none, but in true beleevers)."[64] Here, again, mainstream puritans could only plead guilty. For although the doctrine of "preparationism" was not universally or incontestably accepted within mainstream puritanism, there can be little doubt that many godly preachers did in fact implicitly suggest that faith came only after a season of legal submission.[65] Traske protested that "Christ Jesus came into the world to save sinners: and seekes the lost before they seeke him, and God justifieth the ungodly[,] the ungodly that beleeve in Jesus."[66] As with the tendency to infer grace from sanctification, the godly propensity to stress preparatory, purgative works of humiliation was taken by Traske to be an abandonment of the true principle of justification through Christ's righteousness.

The result of this sort of preaching was not, Traske argued, a general upsurge in religiosity, piety, or sanctity, but an attenuation of the power of true godliness: "these [teachers] do altogether weaken the hands of Gods people, and keepe them so under the bondage of Legall terrours; that the people are forced either to despaire or goe back from all Religion: witnes the many that are glad to slip Collar by Familisme or Antinomisme, or flat Libertinisme; or else doe stand up in defiance of all such Teachers, as hardned in a profane way; rejoycing at their confusion and ruine, under the odious name of riged Puritanes."[67] Like other anti-legalists, Traske thus rejected the label antinomian, for he believed that the only truly holy and morally sanctified people were (to use the term they abhorred) the antinomians themselves; mainstream puritanism bred only hypocrisy and a feigned, legal holiness that drove would-be followers to distraction, libertinism, or anti-puritanism. Anti-puritanism, then, was a natural consequence of godly divinity itself, and Traske hinted the godly

---

[64] Ibid., 30-31.

[65] On this point, see Norman Pettit, *The Heart Prepared: Grace and Conversion in Puritan Spiritual Life* (New Haven: Yale University Press, 1965). There is reason to believe that in response to the challenge of antinomianism, the godly seized upon the concept of "preparationism" with an even greater vehemence, elaborating it more explicitly and formally. Preaching in London in 1638, the antinomians' archenemy Stephen Denison thus reminded his London auditors that "there is in every one of us a stinking Puddell of Corruption This must be emptied before wee can receive the Spirit of grace" and that "wee must first Beginne with this that wee may endeavour to empty ourselves of our Sinnes and Corruptions, and to make ready for to be filled with the fullnesse of the blessed Spirit of god." American Antiquarian Society, MS. Sermon Notes, Denison, fol. 46v.

[66] Traske, *True Gospel*, 31.

[67] Ibid., 32.

had only themselves to blame for their increasingly desperate situation with regard to the Caroline regime: "and thus they doe hale upon themselves, by such meanes, even the powers of men, and doe trouble their owne peace."[68]

But perhaps most significantly, Traske charged that the entire edifice of puritan practical divinity served as a form of servitude—a servitude not just to the Law, but to the ministers who proclaimed that Law. By stringing believers along between doubt and hope, mainstream godly preachers "utterly dishearten all their hearers, keeping them alwayes dependant upon their owne lipps." Traske had here hit upon what was perhaps the least charitable of all possible constructions of puritan piety—that it was a form of spiritual bondage or addiction, created and perpetuated by those who peddled it. As he argued, by the nefarious means of these "Patrons of so much sorrow for sinne, and joylesse mourning . . . such as are not beleevers, are discouraged and hardened; and such as are but weake in the faith, are exceedingly perplexed and insnared." Indeed, through the means of mainstream puritanism, "Gods people were put to a stand in their happy progresse."

Here again, it is important to note that for all his railing against the orthodox puritan ministry, Traske portrayed his struggle as a battle for the collective soul of "Gods people." Again, there can be no doubt about what was going on here: he, like the other Eatonists, was attempting to wean "Gods people"—that is, the godly laity—off their dependency on their legalistic overseers. And in a manner entirely characteristic of Eaton and Towne, he held out a sweet and comforting alternative. In attacking the puritan claim that faith "is very hard to attaine unto," Traske implied that in fact faith was not difficult at all; it was utterly passive and self-authenticating. It required no signs or evidences, no feats of preparatory holiness. It required nothing but the belief, as Traske unflinchingly put it, that God had died for your sins.[69]

And unlike mainstream puritans, who consistently implied that even the strongest faith wavered at times, Traske implied that faith in its mature form was utterly and absolutely assuring: although believers might feel doubts in their infancy, Traske like Eaton held that they arrived ultimately at a "plerophory" of assurance. In this state, Traske suggested, there could be no doubting.[70] Similarly, where mainstream puritans screwed their listeners into fits of

---

[68] Ibid.

[69] Ibid., 65, in which he argued that Norice would never be able to understand the seeming paradox that "God should die" so that man could overcome death.

[70] Ibid., 2: "He that doubteth still of Salvation, beleeveth not yet." For further evidence that this was Traske's teaching, see the comments of his associate, the preacher Rice Boye, who argued against Norice that "where faith is, doubting is not, and where doubting is . . . faith cannot be, for faith admits not of doubting." R[ice] B[oye], *The Importunate Begger, for things Necessary, or Necessity, Without Deniall* (n.p., 1635), 15.

fear and sorrow, Traske promised "holy joy." And in place of the godly emphasis on outward sanctification and mortification, Traske offered freedom from the oversight of the Law.

Here, however, we may begin to chart the differences between Traske and other Eatonists, for where Eaton and Towne argued that the Law had a significant role to play in bringing sinners to Christ, Traske tottered on the verge of dispensing with it entirely. In Traske's view, the Law had nothing to do with working true faith and repentance, which was the effect of the Gospel alone.[71] When Norice charged him with claiming that "The Law, as Law, is not to bee preached to Beleevers," Traske came close indeed to accepting an even more radical proposition:

> And why may it not be affirmed, that seeing there is no Commission to preach the Law at all, now under the Gospel, and seeing the Gospel contains the whole mind and will of God, and that the Apostles did never preach the Law at all, but as subordinate to the Gospel, and doth injoyne *Tymothy*, to charge some that they teach no other doctrine but the Faith; and brandeth such as were desirous to be Law-teachers, to be swarved from the doctrine, and to be vaine janglers, and such as know not what they said: Why shall we not say? That the Gospel onely is to be preached to all, as well to Beleevers; except any can shew a larger Commission then Christ himselfe, or dare leave Apostolicall doctrine, or will deny the Gospel only to be Gods power to save all those that beleeve.[72]

Traske thus came dangerously close to affirming the proposition that the Law had no place at all in English pulpits. It was a relic, an artifact, and as such there was no necessity to preach it, either to believers or unbelievers. As if sensing the extreme implications of this doctrine, Traske quickly retreated, claiming

> Yet, who ever denyed the Lawes use or excellency to discover sinne, convict such as the Gosple shineth not unto, be a ground for all humane Lawes, a notable confirmation of Gospel Precepts, the very rule of Love, and a means to shew the greatnesse of sin, that grace may appeare to be the greater; that it is of use for the Lawlesse and unholy, and for such slanderers as this is; and of very plentifull use for true Beleevers, and against any that oppose the glorious Gospel of *Jesus Christ*. I. Tim. I. 8.9.10.11. Is this to abolish the

---

[71] Traske, *True Gospel*, 52-53. See also, ibid., 14-15.
[72] Ibid., 49-50.

> Law, nay, rather it establisheth it? When men are shewed no life by the Law, but all hope of happinesse onely by Faith in the Lord *Jesus Christ*.[73]

What Traske seemed to be saying, then, was that the Law was useful, but not necessary. It was to be treated as an addendum to the Gospel. In the Christian dispensation, the Law of Moses had dwindled to the status of Apocrypha.

If Traske refrained from making this conclusion explicit, others would be more bold. We shall examine one such figure in our next chapter. At present, I would like to digress for a moment to discuss Traske's later, antinomian divinity in the context of his earlier thought, to examine both the continuities and the divergences that had taken place in the years following Traske's 1620 recantation. To begin with, it is clear that Traske had utterly dispensed with the notion of a preparatory phase of repentance, which preceded and ended with true belief. Gone were all hints that only a period of rigorous legal mortification could catapult believers into the third and glorious estate of faith, with all its joyful consequences. Indeed, by 1636 Traske was sidling away from the Old Testament Law entirely. This, of course, represented a rejection of the strict moralism, indeed the exaggerated legalism, that characterized his early teaching. We might speculate that in the painful mental journey that led from martyrdom to recantation—a journey that lasted from July 1618 until December 1619—Traske had come by virtue of necessity to reject his commitment to the fastidious Old Testament legalism that had permeated the Traskite movement. This retreat was entirely sincere. Traske no longer believed in the Saturday Sabbath. He no longer wanted to organize the Kingdom of Heaven along the pattern established by the Jewish fathers. In order, perhaps, to satisfy his own conscience, he was forced to jettison and reject that piece of his past, to disassociate himself from it as a tyrannical error that had enslaved him.

What he was not compelled to reject, however, were the other aspects of his piety, and these seem to have carried over without modification into his later divinity. His claim that believers no longer committed sin, and that they were somehow free from the commanding power of the Law, reappeared in much the same form. So, too, Traske's effusive, ravishing, and almost mystical vision of the glories of true faith—which brought believers into heaven, even as they walked on earth—was transposed with no difficulty at all into the environment of antinomian piety. It was a perfect fit with the emerging Eatonist faith. With his newborn suspicion of the Law, Traske was no doubt entirely receptive to the ideas of Eaton and his colleagues when he encountered them. Traske's gospel had always been a gospel of rapture, of liberation, of finality.

---

[73] Ibid., 51. To Edward Norice, this looked like a transparent figleaf designed "to hide [the] flat Antinomianism" implied in the previous statement. See *New Gospel*, 15.

The life of mainstream puritanism, with its prosaic and ceaseless war on sin, and its endless bouts of self-examination and humiliation, had never, it seems, been to his liking. Indeed, at the risk of psychologizing, we might argue that Eatonism legitimated his earlier religious experiences. It allowed him to retain the extraordinary, overwhelming, indeed otherworldly, experience of God's grace that he had described in *Heavens Joy*. It fed into an already discernible dislike for mainstream puritans. Finally, Eaton's thought dovetailed perfectly with his newfound and necessary disavowal of the Law in all its forms. This allowed him to dispense with his entire "Judaizing" phase as a (potentially deadly) wrong turn, which had not, nevertheless, negated the authenticity of his powerful visions of divine grace. In this way, we might speculate, an antinomian was born.

Nor were these the only aspects of his earlier divinity that remained. It will be recalled that both Traske and Hebdon tended toward an "inherentist" view of Christ's presence. Believers were in some sense free from the commanding power of the Law. Nevertheless, they would do the things of the Law because they were vessels for God's spirit. As both Traske and Hebdon put it, believers possessed the mind of Christ. As Hebdon had argued, God's essence, his very spirit, inhabited the believer, moving him to obey. By virtue of this indwelling spirit, believers knew themselves to be "the seed and Children of the living God of immortality." We have already seen that although Eaton, too, could advert to the presence of the spirit in believers, he was extremely circumspect about the implications of this inhabitation, at least in his surviving writings. On the whole, he tended to speak of Christ as something external to and beyond the believer. Although Traske borrowed from Eaton the language of "imputative" antinomianism, there can be no question that his earlier inherentism—indeed perfectionism—crept inexorably into his later divinity. In demonstrating this, we gain a keen insight into some of the more radical consequences of antinomian piety.

Traske's inherentism is most apparent in a manuscript paper which he had allegedly circulated privately "to doctrinate his disciples" in Gloucestershire.[74] This paper had come into the hands of Edward Norice, who in turn published it in his answer to Traske's *True Gospel Vindicated*. The paper demands quotation in full:

---

[74] Norice, *New Gospel*, 26. This or another of Traske's manuscripts may have passed through Henry Burton's hands, as well. In his attack on antinomianism, he quoted the position that "*a believer, is as perfect here, as ever hee shall bee hereafter, but onely in regard of manifestation*," an opinion so similar to Traske's in phrasing that it seems almost certain that Burton gleaned the opinion from Traske himself. See Burton, *The Law and the Gospell reconciled* (1631), 69.

> Its a thing to be considered what the new creature is, that new man, that seed of God, which is borne of the spirit: it is not any renovation of the old man, that which is borne of the flesh, the fallen man, for that's from beneath, this from above; that's from the earth, this from heaven; a new creation of nothing; as in the creation of the world: so that the inward or new man, differ as much from the outward or old, as the godly nature of Christ doth differ from his manly nature; and both these natures together, make but one person as in him: this is the reason that he which is borne of God sinneth not, nor can sin, for it is a partaking of the godly nature, and such are as perfect as ever they shallbe, (although not in manifestation,) and yet the old man is as imperfect, as ever it was: for the new creature is not the mutation or change of the understanding from darknesse to light, for then there should no darknesse remaine: nor a change of the will from crooked to streight, for then should no perversenesse remaine; nor any ordering of the same affections, for so all disorder were put away; nor yet a change of the memory, for so were the memory without defect: for, this understanding, will, affections, memory, and rest are gifts from heaven, and must of necessity be perfect, without any defect or superfluity, for our first generation as borne of parents is totally fallen, and cannot be recovered here: but our regeneration is wholly perfect, and can never be corrupted, or sinne againe; for take it in the parts, what is repentance, or faith, or love, or joy, or any of the rest, are they not the gifts of God? and are not Gods gifts all perfect and without blemish? These being distinct in our minds, as the divine, and humane natures of Christ in that one person; we shall not impute our sinnes to our selves, nor yet our good so confusdly, as in times past: the flesh or old man shall have no glory of any good is done, nor the spirit or new man, any shame of the evill or sinne, that the flesh commits; it will not only enable us to know our owne estates, but the holy Scriptures; and we shall see the vanity and folly of the most (if not all) writers, who put all the work upon the change, wrought in this flesh, which can never be changed.[75]

By any measure, this was an extraordinary passage, one which resonated strongly with Traske's earlier writings. Believers were the seed of God, having been utterly reborn in the spirit. This was not a change or a mutation in the believer's pre-existing body or soul, a rehabilitation of previously corrupt faculties; it was, rather, a "new creation" ex nihilo, likened to the creation of the world from nothing, which God overlaid above and against the old, and hopelessly corrupt flesh. But what was this "new creature"? Although Traske used the analogy of creation, it is clear that he believed it had nothing at all to do with the fallen, created universe. It was "new" only insofar as it was utterly distinct from the "old man," for it was in fact a participation in the most ancient of all beings. It was, to be blunt, a "partaking of the godly nature" of

[75] Printed in Norice, *New Gospel*, 26-27.

Christ. Because they were joined to Christ (much as Christ's godly nature was joined to his humanity) they possessed Christ's perfection and sinlessness: "this is the reason that he which is borne of God sinneth not, nor can sin . . . and such are as perfect as ever they shall be." This perfection was not completely manifested in this life, due to the ongoing presence of the "old man," which continued on occasion to break forth and sin. Nevertheless, the new man was perfect, sinless, without stain.

It will be evident that these claims—which echoed and in many ways merely reiterated arguments that Traske and Hebdon had made two decades earlier, and which closely paralleled the arguments on offer among the Grindletonians—went a good deal farther than Eaton or Eachard had been willing to go, at least in print. Believers, on this view, were not accounted or imputed perfect by God. They *were* perfect. Yet as Traske explained, this perfection was not properly their own; it was Christ's. Thus, the holy works of believers were not the actions of the believers themselves:

> Sanctification is by the Spirit only, as we understand it of its operations by mortification, or quickning these our mortall bodies, yet is it not so in us, as mingled with uncleannesse; but as distinct absolutely from the flesh; and being another, or a new nature, yea a participation of the Divine nature, 2. *Pet.* I. 3, 4. which though it make up one person, yet is it none at all of the old man; not of the old creation, but it is that new creation; that new heart, and that Spirit of God which is bestowed upon us. *Ezech.* 11. 19. and 36. 25, 26, 27. which yeeldeth no new habits in the flesh, as if that were changed or renewed, but is so subsisting of it selfe, that it is of power to manifest it selfe, by acts of subduing, and acts of quickning, and reviving, and inabling this mortall flesh, as the life of *Jesus* in it, to doe, though not perfectly, yet to doe that which is good: so that the sanctified person is no further foorth sanctified then he is in union with the Lord *Jesus* Christ: and it is not he that hath any habit of grace in his flesh: but the Lord *Jesus* dwelling in him, doth put foorth the bright beames of his glory, in such vertues as doe best fit the time and place in which he lives. *Rom.* 8. 9. 10. 11. 2 *Cor.* 1. 8. 9.[76]

The good works of believers were thus apparently nothing more than the motions of the spirit of Christ, dwelling in the believer. From one perspective, it was thus true that the "flesh" carried out good works, but only as an engine propelled by Christ. True believers were "alwayes but as Agents, acted by him, and as instruments used in his hand alone."[77] When the flesh of a believer acted on its own, it could do nothing but sin. When it acted righteously,

---

[76] Traske, *True Gospel*, 21-23.

[77] Ibid., sig. G7r.

however, the actor was not the flesh, but Christ dwelling in the flesh, and thus all the righteous acts of believers were perfect.[78]

We are here confronted with a mode of divinity that drew in equal parts upon imputative and perfectionist modes of antinomianism. For although it is clear that Traske had appropriated large pieces of the Eatonist critique, his perfectionism and his insistence on the indwelling activity of Christ in many ways mirror the very different theological styles of John Everarde and Roger Brearley. This was evident in Traske's deceptively simple "Rule of Faith," which as he argued, was intended to serve as a touchstone of true belief, a measuring stick to arbitrate all theological controversies. This one "Short, Plaine, Ancient, Infallible, Universally usefull, Impartiall . . . *perfect rule*" was that "*The Lord Jesus Christ hath already done all that is to bee done, for all true beleevers, to God, and doth all good, in and by them, to themselves and others.*"[79] On its surface, this would appear to be a summation of the imputative position, with all its pretensions to absolute protestant orthodoxy: all spiritual goods came through the extrinsic and alien righteousness of Christ, whose perfect life and death had already accomplished all things necessary for salvation. But if we scratch the surface, it is clear that this is *not* what Traske was saying. Here, the operative words were "in them and by them," for Traske meant not that God's grace in Christ allowed believers to do good, but that Christ literally inhabited the believers, acting in them and through their mortal flesh (an altogether less obviously orthodox proposition). From this perspective, Traske's divinity resembled not that of the Eatonists, but that of Everarde, stripped of Hermetic and Neoplatonic ornament.

Traske's godly opponent Norice recognized this contradiction between "imputative" and "perfectionist" tendencies, remarking that "that which is always perfect can have no bettering: or what need have such of the imputed righteousnes of Christ (of which these men [i.e. the antinomians] talke so

---

[78] Compare this against the subtly, but significantly, different view expressed by William Perkins, *A Commentarie or Exposition, upon the five first Chapters of the Epistle to the Galatians* (1604), 413, 419, who argued that "as the spirit renewes our natures within, so it makes us to change and renew our actions." Because our good actions remained partly our own, the "workes of the regenerate are mixed workes, that is, good workes indeed, yet not perfectly good, but par[t]ly evill." He further explained that "Things proceeding from the spirit of God alone, or from the spirit immediately, are no sinnes: now good workes proceed not only from the spirit, but also from the mind and will of man, as instruments of the spirit. And when an effect proceeds from sundrie causes that are subordinate, it takes unto it the nature of the second cause: hereupon workes are partly spirituall, and partly carnall, as the minde and will of the doer is."

[79] Traske, *True Gospel*, sigs. F7r-F8r, G2v.

much) if they have perfection of all things in themselves."[80] Yet this was not the only place where Traske's argument mimicked that of the Eatonists, departing from it in subtle but crucial ways. Like the Eatonists, Traske argued that those who had been delivered from the Law would in practice do good works. Free from the external coercion of the Law's rule, such believers were now carried forward by a mysterious internal principle that led them inexorably to do God's will without fear or outward compulsion. This impulse had of course always been a part of Traske's divinity; readers will remember that he had always argued that true believers obeyed the Law not because it commanded them, but because they possessed the mind of Christ. Now, however, Traske had completely abandoned the notion that the Old Testament Law, whether ceremonial or moral, represented a summation of God's will. No longer were believers to see themselves as living receptacles for Moses' tables of stone; they were now to view themselves merely as vessels of "the love of God," which was itself the internal principle that moved them, without any external prompting, to carry out God's will: a believer's "direction . . . is not fetcht from without, from the *Lawes Letter*, but flowes from the *Love of God*, shed abroad in the heart: and this kind of obedience doth as far transcend that other, to the Letter, by the flesh, as *Life* doth *Death*."[81] And here, again, Traske was making an argument that veered quietly away from that of Eaton, approaching those of Everarde and Brearley. Whereas Eaton claimed that believers would walk zealously in all God's commandments after they recognized their free justification in Christ, Traske implied that Christian obedience had nothing whatever to do with commandments. Like Everarde or the Grindletonians, he argued that obedience to the will of God was no longer a matter of "laws" and "precepts," but a matter of love, which was wholly disjoined from all law:

> And doth not that obedience which floweth from an inward principle of Love, farre transcend, that which is forced by feare? Is not love of God, and God love? and the Law made onely for the Creature; and not for God himselfe, as no way limited by any Law; and if God doe transcend the Creature in his best estate, so infinitely, as cannot be conceived why may not *Love* be said to transcend *Law*, as *Life* doth transcend *Death*?[82]

Here, it might be argued that Traske had given away his hand. If we look at this passage carefully it becomes evident that he was doing more than simply restating the antinomian distinction between extorted and voluntary works of obedience. Rather, he was arguing that there was simply not an equivalence between the Law as it had been handed down to Moses, and the "law" that

---

[80] Norice, *New Gospel*, 28-29.
[81] Traske, *True Gospel*, 14-15.
[82] Ibid., 15-16.

believers obeyed. Love, the inward principle of obedience in a believer, was something wholly distinct from the Law of Sinai. It was in a different category, and of a different substance. Although they overlapped at many points, they were fundamentally at odds with one another. This marked a radical departure from the puritan tradition, which had always maintained that the moral commandments of the Old Testament, and the New Testament commandments to love were simply different ways of expressing the one, single and eternal rule of God. As Norice put it, "the Scriptures acknowledge" "love and the law . . . to be but one, and the same, love being the very summe and substance of the whole Law, *Matth*. 22. 40. *Gal*. 5. 14."[83] For Traske, as for Everarde, they were utterly distinct. In arguing that they were the same, puritans showed "grosse ignorance . . . in not being able to distinguish between the Law in the letter, and the Law of the Spirit, the Law of Liberty, or of love."[84] To claim that the literal, Mosaic Law and Love were identical was utterly to miss the point of Christ's coming. The Gospel signaled a radical and earth-shaking rupture, a replacement of the Torah with something wholly other.

Traske was not alone in this sentiment: it is almost indistinguishable from the position of Brearley and the Grindletonians. And as we will see in the next section, other radical antinomians in London were likewise struggling during these years to articulate this subtle but irreducible difference between their own position and that of mainstream puritanism. If we scrutinize Traske's statement still further, it likewise becomes clear that Traske believed that the Law and Love were different not just because they held out a different model of behavior—prescribing different things and evoking different subjective states—but because they were of different natures. The Law was creaturely, it was engraved in stone, in matter. Love was spiritual. It was more than spiritual—it was God. Taking the nettlesome claim of I John 4 at face value, Traske here hinted in seemingly unambiguous terms that God was love and that love dwelled in the hearts of true believers, compelling them inexorably and without external compulsion to do not works of the outward, fleshy law, but works of love (that is, the works of God). Here, then, was a mode of divinity that smashed the molds of puritan religion, departing even from the formulations of Eaton and Towne. It suggested not only a new law—a Law of Love—but a different God, a God that dwelled, essentially and personally, within every believer.[85]

---

[83] Norice, *New Gospel*, 18.

[84] Traske, *True Gospel*, 60.

[85] For a remarkable reiteration and adaptation of this basic principle during the English Revolution, see A. Hessayon, "'Gold Tried in the Fire'": The Prophet Theauraujohn Tany and the Puritan Revolution," (Ph.D. Diss., Cambridge, 1996),

The Cambridge Antinomian

Our last and most complete example of the marriage between the imputative and perfectionist styles of antinomianism is an anonymous manuscript now surviving in Cambridge University Library. This one-hundred-page treatise was written, according to its author, to show "the vast difference between God's government of his Church under the Law; and the government of his Church now under the Gospel: and the excellent priviledges of the one beyond the other."[86] Although the manuscript is undated and anonymous, when it is compared against Thomas Taylor's *Regula Vitae*, it becomes apparent that the author of the manuscript was almost certainly one of the antinomian teachers whose ideas were in circulation in London in the late 1620s.[87] For purposes of this book, the manuscript has been designated simply the "Cambridge Manuscript," its composer as the "Cambridge Antinomian."

Although the Cambridge Antinomian was quite probably present in London, his identity is impossible to determine with certainty precisely because he draws upon ideas, images, and language from across the spectrum of antinomian opinion. At times, he expresses himself in terms reminiscent of Eaton, although differences in style, tone, and specific argumentation make it clear that its author was not Eaton himself. In other cases, he produces arguments that are redolent of Robert Towne, while on another occasion, he refers to Christ in terms similar to those allegedly used by Samuel Prettie. Some of his com-

---

84-87, and passim, which reconstructs the thought-world of the London mystic Thomas Totney, alias Tany. Although Hessayon was unable to determine anything certain about Tany's spiritual education, it seems highly probable that Tany was conversant with the modes of antinomian religiosity explored herein.

[86] CUL MS. Dd. xii. 42, "To the Christian Reader."

[87] Compare Taylor, *Regula Vitae, The Rule of the Law Under the Gospel* (1631), 108, which reproduces the specific antinomian argument "That justified persons have no more to doe with repentance; and to repent of every particular sinne is to beleeve that a man is not perfectly justified, or at once but by peecemeale as sinne is committed; yea it is to undervalue the sufferings of Christ, as not having sufficiently satisfied for all sinnes past, present, and to come," with CUL MS. Dd. xii. 42, "To the Christian Reader," which claimed that legalists failed to grasp the central Christian doctrine of "the utter abolishing of Sin...but still are perswaded that sin doth yet remain...As if that justification were not absolute and perfect at once from all sins, past, present and to come; but that we are to be justifyed by piece-meal, from this sin now, and from future sins by Repentance after committed; and so upon every particular guilt, a particular Repentance." These two passages are so uncannily similar, both in argument and in specific phrasing, that it seems almost certain that the writer of the Cambridge Manuscript was one of Taylor's opponents in London, and that Taylor was in fact citing a manuscript written by the same man.

ments regarding self-denial and self-abnegation bring to mind not Eaton or Towne, but the piety of a Roger Brearley or a John Everarde (although again, the author was definitely not Everarde himself). Still other of his more unusual (and less conspicuously Eatonist) opinions resemble some of the more bizarre charges against Peter Shaw. And at several points, he adduces specific arguments and turns of phrase that are uncannily reminiscent of John Traske. In short, without further evidence, any attempt to ascribe authorship would be premature and entirely conjectural. Nevertheless, it is partly this authorial indeterminacy that renders the Cambridge Manuscript so valuable as a source. Its very anonymity—its synthesis of different modes of argument and different styles of antinomianism—is in itself a testimony to the ideological cross-fertilization that took place within the antinomian underground. Here, in the closely knit world of England's emerging antinomian community, ideas were traded and exchanged, debated and reconciled one with another. Distinct strands of argument, drawn from different sources or thinkers, became hopelessly intertwined, until at length they proved impossible to disentangle. From this perspective, the Cambridge Manuscript may be seen as a representative summation of English antinomianism as it had emerged by the 1630s.

The Cambridge Manuscript shares with all other contemporary antinomian writings a profound antipathy toward mainstream puritan piety. As with all the figures thus far examined, it is impossible to understand the Cambridge Antinomian apart from this deeply embedded hostility. Its author decried the works righteousness and pharisaism he saw everywhere triumphant in England, arguing that external works merely served to turn people's eyes from the truth: "the more we stick to the performance of outward holy duties, and expect comfort and enjoyment of God by them, the further off we are from true comfort."[88] At times, his rhetoric duplicated that of the Eatonists, as he denounced those who "run away with a conceit, that the Lord loves them highly because they walk according to his Law."[89] Using one of the pejorative phrases of which Eaton was fond, he argued that such men were filled with a "blind zeal" whereby they sought to get into God's good graces through their own works.[90] Nor was there any question as to who or what the Cambridge Antinomian had in mind when he denounced legalism. In words that could have come as well from Everarde as from Eaton, he declared that

> Now then, to him that shall say, I will conforme my self to the Law of God; I will pray morning and evening; I will hear Sermons, I will instruct and catechize my Family dilligently, I will keep the Sabbath strictly, I will contribute

---

[88] Ibid., 40.

[89] Ibid., 8.

[90] For the phrase "blind zeal," see ibid., 8, 50.

> to the poor liberally, and I will do all duties of piety and charity; for all these things are pleasing to God.
>
> I answer, thou maist do all these things, which for the matter of them are agreeable to the Law, and yet not be accepted with God, nor those actions pleasing to him.[91]

This, then, may be regarded as the fully articulated anti-legal position. When the Cambridge Antinomian decried the Law, he was not merely rejecting the Ten Commandments as a way to salvation (all puritans did as much, at least in theory); nor was he simply rejecting the Ten Commandments as a rule of life (although he did this, too); he was rejecting or at least deflating the most sacrosanct practices of mainstream puritan divinity, and repudiating many of the most important aspects of the culture of English puritanism, which on his view had produced a sort of ritual idolatry in which holy duties were mistaken for true holiness. For mainstream puritans, utterly committed to the value of these external ordinances, the Cambridge Antinomian had in store a scathing warning: "you with all your spirituall signes and tokens of your exteriour cleaness, remain in your filthiness of sin: From the which all your legal performances of Fasting, and Prayer, and Humiliation, etc. nor all the holy duties you do or can performe can ever clense you and bring you into this Church."[92]

Even worse, he lamented, anyone seeking to challenge the assumptions of puritan practical divinity immediately brought down upon themselves opprobrium and hostility. Thus, he complained that the godly "will by noe means receive an ill conceit of the Law and good works. And if you undervalew good works, and go about to perswade them that they stand a man in no stead before God, you shall be accounted no better than a Libertine: And you may as soon perswade them that the Stars will fall from Heaven, as to perswade them that good works do stand a man in no stead before God."[93] Here was a typical Eatonist self-portrait, in which antinomians appeared as zealous, misunderstood Protestants, who had been unjustly denounced and persecuted by cruel and ignorant neo-pharisees.

Unsurprisingly, then, the Cambridge Antinomian also absorbed the characteristic Eatonist tendency to argue that believers were rendered righteous not through any merit in themselves, but through the imputed, extrinsic righteousness of Christ. Believers were perfect in God's sight: "God hath revealed to thee, and thou art to beleeve, that thou art freely justifyed in Christ from all thy sins, past, present, and to come; and that they are now as if they had never been; and that by vertue of Christ's death and merits, God can see no more sin

---

[91] Ibid., 52.
[92] Ibid., 25.
[93] Ibid., 8.

in thee, than he see in Christ."[94] The author here laid out a schema of justification which, like that of the Eatonists, ostensibly followed a trail blazed by the most irreproachable reformed authorities. No works of the human will had anything at all to do with salvation, "Christianity being a thing mearly passive, and consisteth not in doing, but in receiving only; and [the Christian] is that, which he is, in Christ, and not in himself."[95] Salvation was merely and entirely through the unmerited "free grace" of God.[96] And like other Eatonists, he hinted that his puritan opponents had quietly abandoned their commitment to this cornerstone of Protestantism, notwithstanding their professed opposition to all forms of Pelagianism. He alleged that the godly "make the grace of God (which is alwaies free) to depend upon mans action . . . You will take it in great scorn to be called a Papist or Arminian; but tell me how far do you differ from them in this?"[97]

Even though the godly retained an outward commitment to the notion of free grace, then, in practice their undue focus on sanctification and on the diligent use of the means of grace showed that they were as corrupt as any Catholic or Laudian in practice. Like Towne, he confessed that "the Scripture . . . calls upon man to be diligent in the use of means," but he argued that the godly misused the means of grace, treating them as efficacious in themselves:

> we should not look too much unto the means, but unto God in the use of the means, who gives every man his portion freely, what he will, when he will, and how he will; whether by means or with out means: that mans heart might not be carryed out too much after the means, but still to have his confidence in God only. And oh that we could use the means as means! and not as causes! and so make a god of the means; and put I know not what power and vertue unto them; and that if we do but use the means dilligently, we cannot possibly miss of Faith and Salvation.[98]

The godly, then, had made a "god of the means," in the process perverting the true Christian message of free grace in Christ.

So, too, the Cambridge Antinomian replicated other strands of the Eatonist argument. Thus, he asserted that "the afflictions of the Church now under the Gospel, are not punishments for sin, but fatherly chastisements for the tryall of their Faith."[99] Like the others, and in a voice reminiscent not only of Eaton but of Peter Shaw, he argued that to suggest that believers were punished for their sins was to deny the all-powerful sacrifice of Christ and to call God's jus-

---

[94] Ibid., 41.
[95] Ibid., 71.
[96] Ibid., 78.
[97] Ibid., 84.
[98] Ibid., 81, 88.
[99] Ibid., 27.

tice into question. For a believer's debt to God had already been satisfied; Christ had already paid the penalty, and no further satisfaction was necessary

> if you say that God doth afflict and scourge a man (I mean a true Beleever) for that which is sin against him and before his eyes, I say it cannot be; for we say, a satisfyed debt is no debt, neither can it be called any more a debt; but sins are debts, and so called, Gal. 5. 3. for thereby we are indebted to the whole Law, and Gods justice: But by Christ we have both satisfyed the law and the justice of God for all sins past, present and to come; so that sin can not be called any more a debt; For if it be a debt, then it is not paid nor satisfyed for; but if it be satisfyed for, then is it no longer a debt: and therefore God cannot see sin in a Beleever, as sin against him, or before his eyes; for then he should see that which is not: sin being taken away in the bloud of Christ from before God, and he stands perfect as clothed in the righteousness of Christ, and so having neither spot, or wrinkle, or any such thing, but holy and with out blemish, as the Apostle speaks, Ephes. 5. 27.[100]

Believers were "clothed in the righteousness" of Christ. To suggest that they were still under the Law was to call into question both the efficacy of his sacrifice and the justice of God. In this, the Cambridge Antinomian duplicated the totalizing, binary logic of the Eatonists. Here, in fact, was an argument that could have dropped from Eaton's pen, a classic statement of the core concepts underlying imputative antinomianism.

Yet despite his obvious, undeniable debt to Eaton, the Cambridge Antinomian was, like Traske, willing to go farther than either Eaton or Towne in hinting that the Law had no place whatsoever in the Christian era. Early in the treatise, he suggested along with the Eatonists that "it is the property of the Law (now since the Fall) to reveal sin and wrath; and to terrify, and kill men in themselves; that they may look out of themselves for life; which they will not easily be brought unto."[101] This use of the Law was, we should recall, endorsed wholeheartedly by John Eaton. But unlike Eaton, the Cambridge Antinomian went on to qualify (perhaps even contradict) this statement, by calling into serious question the appropriateness of preaching the Law at all. Thus, he remarked that

> I do perswade my self, that if the Law had never been preached to us and that we had never had the knowledg of it otherwise than by the light of nature, as the Gentiles had at first, it would have been as well, if not better, for us, than it is now: For now the Law is not preached in the true use of it as a killing letter, for then it were the better to be borne: but is preached as a bond . . . to keep men in obedience unto it, that men may be[come] holy and

---

[100] Ibid., 95-96.
[101] Ibid., 4.

glorious creatures in themselves, and so have no need of Faith, and of Christ.[102]

Again, although he did not say so explicitly, this antinomian, like Traske, seems to have been flirting with the notion that the Old Testament Law had no place at all among Christians, that it was in fact an impediment or a stumbling block that did little more than ensnare would-be believers in a cycle of self-deception. This statement allows us to observe the process whereby antinomians moved from a moderate position with regard to the Mosaic Law—a position like that of Eaton or Towne, in which the Law retained certain positive uses—to a more extreme stance in which the Law was seen as a vestigial, and even dangerous, artifact of a bygone era. This move was but an extenuation of the anti-legal impulse, the product of increasingly polarized debate between the antinomians and their mainstream puritan enemies. What had begun as a protest movement against the shape of puritan practical divinity had come at last to a position in which the Law itself was virtually argued out of Christianity; where Eaton and Towne had steadfastly claimed that Christians were not to seek salvation through the Law, the Cambridge Antinomian's rhetoric suggested that the Law should simply be dispensed with: "They are much to blame therefore that teach the Law to be observed now under the Gospel: For what doth man more hurt than the Law? Or what keeps man more from Christ than his duty of doing? For hereby he conceivs that his life consisteth in doing."[103]

So, too, there were subtle differences in the tone with which the Cambridge Antinomian expressed his critique of puritan legalism. Eaton, for instance, had claimed that the Law could not save human beings because, as a consequence of our utter sinfulness, we could not perfectly fulfill the Law. Even our finest works were, to use Eaton's favorite phrase, but "menstrous rags" before God; they were thoroughly vitiated and corrupt, and thus appeared as an abomination in God's sight. Only the garment of Christ's perfect righteousness could render them acceptable. The Cambridge Antinomian expressed the same idea, but articulated it in very different terms. On his account, works of the Law were corrupt not just because human beings were hopelessly sinful, but because the Law was itself a rule of corruption, or rather, a rule that encouraged self-love, apart from God. By endeavoring to fulfill the letter of God's commandments, "thou . . . who art so zealous for the Law and works . . . herein thou seekest not God but thy self."[104] Legal holiness was, therefore, a form of preening self-worship. On his account the "sin of self-love is the most dangerous sin of all others," and it was a sin that was inseparable from the Moral

---

[102] Ibid., 21. The word in parentheses is partially blotted out.
[103] Ibid., 6-7.
[104] Ibid., 7.

Law: "what investeth self-love more than the observation of the Law, and works, and doing, wherein man hath something to glory in? For man would fain be some thing in himself: And the more you put him upon the Law and works, the more you increase self-love in him: and the more and further you remove the Law from him, and spoil him of the confidence of his works and doings and make them appear like dung before him; as the Apostle did, the more you drive him from himself; and the closer he will cleave to Christ."[105]

Underlying these claims about the Moral Law was a more general concern with the evils of selfhood. Where Eaton had argued that works were useless because they were hopelessly foul, the Cambridge Antinomian implied that they were useless because they emanated from the self. In this vein, Christ was necessary not just because he perfectly fulfilled the Law (thus making up for what was imperfect in man's works), but also because he was utterly external to man, utterly beyond the self. In order to find salvation, a believer had to "go out of himself . . . having once wholly putt off himself, then shall he wholly enjoy Christ, and not till then. Therefore saith our Saviour, He that will be my Disciple, let him deny himself, take up his Cross and follow me."[106] Indeed, for the Cambridge Antinomian, the pinnacle of religiosity was to escape the self completely, to become one with God: "If thou couldst perfectly beleeve, then thou wouldest live altogether out of thy self, and live in and with God in Christ. Therefore if thou wouldest have nearer communion with God, labour to beleeve more perfectly, and then thou wilt enjoy God more fully."[107] Those who were closest to God were those who possessed no independent selves of their own; those, however, who valued legal works of holiness were the farthest from God, even though they believed otherwise: the legalist, according to the Cambridge Antinomian,

> is perswaded all he doth is well done, and agreeable to the Law: who also performs many righteouse duties, as praying morning and evening and reading the word constantly, and hearing it often, and keeping the Sabbath very strictly, and repeating sermons to his Family, and catechizing his Children and servants. . . . Who will not but acknowledge that this man is a good and godly man, and the child of God? And do you not beleeve he is perswaded of himself? Now do you not think it will be a very hard matter to bring this man to an utter anihilation of himself, to renounce all his good works, and to account of them but as loss and dung? which he must be brought unto, if he is to come to Christ.[108]

---

105 Ibid., 2, 7.
106 Ibid., 3.
107 Ibid., 40-41.
108 Ibid., 21.

Eaton certainly agreed that believers needed to look outside and beyond themselves for salvation—this was, in many ways, the essence of imputative antinomianism. Nevertheless, this rhetoric of "self-annihilation"—of stepping outside of the I and becoming one with God—was not characteristic of his writings. It was, by contrast, absolutely central to the thought of both Everarde and Brearley; like these men, the Cambridge Antinomian had in all probability borrowed it, either directly or indirectly, from the canons of medieval mysticism.[109] Perhaps because of this influence, the Cambridge Antinomian proved singularly reluctant to call upon the resources of reformed theological authorities. Where Eaton and Towne had cluttered their manuscript writings with references to Luther, Calvin, and the church Homilies, the Cambridge Antinomian cited *no* modern authorities, limiting himself to a few scant references to the church fathers.[110]

Were these differences in style and rhetoric his only departure from the Eatonist line, it would still be possible to conclude that the Cambridge Antinomian was providing little more than an enthusiastic restatement of the ideas of Eaton. When we look more closely, however, we discover other areas where the Cambridge Antinomian appears to have owed much more to the "perfectionist" strain than to anything seen in the writings of Eaton. Like Everarde, but unlike Eaton and Towne, he expressed a virulent and explicit hostility to puritan Sabbatarianism. This hostility was articulated in terms almost identical to those used by John Everarde. As he explained, "The whole life of a Christian now is a continuall Rejoycing and praising, and giving of thanks, and magnifying the name of the Lord, for the excellent priviledges and glory which he hath in Christ; his enemies are vanished and gone, his soul is entered into its rest; of which rest the Sabbath or seventh day was a signe."[111] In other words, the external rest of the seventh day was an external prefiguration of the internal, spiritual, and eternal rest that came through true belief: "This rest was a sign of that Rest and perfect sanctification which Beleevers should enjoy by Faith in Christ."[112]

This claim paved the way for an all-out attack on the jewel of mainstream puritan divinity, the Sabbath: "They therefore that observe the Sabbath so as to put Religion and holiness in the observation of it, and so make it a note of

---

109 "Self-annihilation" was one of Everarde's six steps to the throne of Solomon. The notion of self-annihilation was a common theme in certain strains of medieval Catholic mysticism and it was a theme absorbed by the most radical English spiritualists, such as Everarde, Giles Randall, and John Rogers. See N. Smith, *Perfection Proclaimed: Language and Literature in English Radical Religion* (Oxford, 1989), 39.

110 See CUL MS. Dd. xii. 42, 47-48.

111 Ibid., 43.

112 Ibid., 44.

a true Christian, and one that fears God, that makes conscience of keeping the Sabbath day strictly: Let such know, that they keep it very superstitiously and Jewishly."[113] Sabbatarianism was, of course, one of the defining characteristics of puritan divinity, and there can be little question that mainstream puritans *did* in fact make the strict observance of the Lord's day "a note of a true Christian." Here, the Cambridge Antinomian waxed personal, providing us with a glimpse into the emotional progress that led many puritans into antinomianism:

> Do not we now in the times of the Gospel, even they that have beene most forward in religion, and ancient professors (that should have more ancient understanding in these things) observe the Sabbath as fastidiously, as ever did the Jews? Do not we put Religion and holinesse in the very day it self? not only in the observation of the day, but in the day it self? The times have been that I durst not have thought mine own thoughts on that day, nor to speak mine own words, but it hath been a trouble to me, and I thought that I highly offended God in so doing; even those thoughts and words which have been lawfull on an other day. Nay farther, if a Letter had been brought to me from an other, whatsoever earnest business it had concerned; I would not have opened it to read it on that day. Nay if I had met with a friend in the street, I would not have spoken to him, if possibly I could have escaped him, for fear least I should profane the Sabbath in talking to him, and thereby offend God. Nay, I have heard of some that would not give their Cattell meat on that day, nor milk their Beasts, nor have done any business of whatsoever great necessity, least thereby they should break the Sabbath . . . they would not so as dress their own meats which were to eat on that day, but dress it the day before: nor shift their children on that day. Nay what great disputation hath there been among the learned, to know when the Sabbath begins, whether in the morning, or at midnight; that they might know, when to begin to keep it holy, that they might not do any thing on any part of that day: And on Saturday night after the clock had strook twelve, they would have wrought so long, but so soon as the clock had strook, they would have hurled all by, what extraordinary hast soever it had been of. O blind zeal! what superstitious madness was this? to put Religion and holiness and the worship of God in the observation of days.[114]

Sabbath observance, even more than the other "forms" of puritan worship, had in this antinomian's view become a hollow, barren ritual. In their painstaking efforts to sanctify a single day, the godly ministry had built a system of spiritual tyranny, which they then used to enslave unwitting "professors." The Cambridge Antinomian, who had himself endured this Sabbatarian tyranny,

---

[113] Ibid., 46.
[114] Ibid., 49-50.

promised his readers freedom from this ungodly bondage. He argued that mainstream puritans had utterly missed the true significance of the fourth commandment, the notion that "they that do beleeve do enter into Rest. And he that is entred into his rest, he also hath ceased from his own works, as God did from his."[115] Those who entered into rest had, in a sense, ceased to live their own lives.

It might be thought that the attack on the puritan Sabbath was merely a concomitant of the Eatonist claim that believers were free from the Moral Law; in fact, however, it should be remembered that Eaton never explicitly brought into question the sanctity of the Sabbath. He claimed that true believers would in fact walk zealously according to all God's commandments (although without the fear of punishment or hope of reward). This presumably included the observation of the Sabbath, a presumption supported by the case of Henry Firmin of Ipswich. The Cambridge Antinomian was doing more than simply denying that believers were bound to obey the Sabbath as part of the Moral Law—he was claiming that the true meaning of the fourth commandment was not literal, but allegorical. All outward observance of the Sabbath was external and carnal. One who truly kept the Sabbath was one who had "ceased from his own works," that is, who had gotten outside of himself by belief in Christ, thus entering into true, spiritual rest.

This idea, which had been expressed in almost identical terms by Everarde, in all likelihood emanated not from Eaton, but from traditions of perfectionist mysticism. The notion that believers had entered the "rest of God" was ubiquitous in the writings of HN; it was, moreover, adopted by HN's English admirers in the seventeenth century.[116] Let us compare for a moment the comments of the Cambridge Antinomian against those of John Etherington, a man whose debt to Familist sources is undeniable. In the late 1620s, while suffering in prison for his alleged heresies, Etherington defended his own position on the Sabbath in these terms:

> I am sure I never said to any man living, that the Sabbath was of no force, but doe hold that it is in force, and the Commandement also according to the spiritual intent thereof; I meane by Sabbath the true and perfect rest of God, which hee did rest the seventh day, having finished all his workes, therefore called his rest, as he saith, *If they shall enter into my rest.*
>
> And that it is here entred into of us, and kept not through the Law, by doing any kind of worke or works therein contained, but through the promise, even the Gospell of Jesus Christ by beleeving, as Saint *Paul* saith; *For*

---

[115] Ibid., 44.

[116] See, for instance, HN, *Terra Pacis. A True Testification of the Spirituall Lande of Peace: which is the Spiritual Lande of Promyse* (n.p., 1575?), fols. 2v, 8r-v. See below, Epilogue.

wee which have beleeved doe enter into rest, . . . He declareth and saith further, *That they that are so entred have ceased from their owne workes, as God did from his*; that is, from seeking their owne pleasures, and speaking their owne words, from all their corrupt carnall and sinfull pleasures and delights of the world, wherein their soule as well as their bodie and members thereof had walked; (the whole man being corrupted through the fall) and which are therefore called their owne workes and their owne pleasures, and their delight is now in the Lord, and in his holy and heavenly wayes, seeking his face continually and honouring him, etc.[117]

Etherington's explication of the commandment was virtually identical to that of the Cambridge Antinomian. Nor do the similarities stop here; Etherington likewise used this concept to denounce mainstream puritan preachers and their rigorous Sabbatarianism. Such ministers

lay . . . a burthen upon the consciences of Christians touching the day, as Master *Denison* and some others have done, charging the people upon heavy curses and condemnation to doe, and not to doe such, and such kind of things as they prescribe, These things.

Which although you may lawfully leave them undone upon any other day and not sinne, you are bound to doe them in this day in paine of condemnation.

And these and those kind of things or actions, which although you may lawfully doe them on any other day and not sinne, you are bound not to doe any of them in this day on paine of condemnation, and whosoever doth not conscionably, so observe the day cannot be a true Christian, wherewith they have so inthralled the minds of many people, some of tender conciences zealously affected towards God, and have brought them to such distraction and unquietnesse of spirit, by reason they are not nor can be satisfied in every particular action, what they are so bound to doe, and what not to doe upon that day, when to begin and when to end, that there is more talke and questioning among them, and more and more resorting to Ministers for satisfaction about the same, then about any matter of religion whatsoever.[118]

For all intents and purposes, Etherington and the Cambridge Antinomian thus held identical positions on the Sabbath. Here, again, we see a process of crossing-over, in which ideas that had their origins in the perfectionist and mystical anti-legalism of an Everarde or an Etherington were combined with those of imputative antinomians to produce distinctive and novel formulations. In this manner, at least some members of the London antinomian community came to repudiate, explicitly and without qualification, that most puritan of cultural icons, the Sabbath.

---

[117] Etherington, *Defence*, 32-33.
[118] Ibid., 35-36.

It might be objected that in Everarde's case, this notion of the eternal, internal Sabbath was intimately tied to the concept of "deiformity." Believers had entered into "rest" because they had become one with God, who alone was perfect, immovable, and unchanging. Do we find anything similar in the writings of the Cambridge Antinomian? The answer is both yes and no. Although the Cambridge Manuscript contains none of the enthusiastic and forthright proclamations of Godhood that pepper Everarde's sermons, nor the overt statements of "demigodhood" found in Brearley's poetry, its author was in fact given over to particularly strong statements concerning the believer's unity with Christ. So, too, he was prone to rhetoric that was, without question, explicitly perfectionist. Thus, he argued that "Faith doth destroy self-love in man, and all confidence in works and doings, and makes him . . . nothing in himself, but perfectly just and righteous only in Christ; by and through whom he hath neither sin nor spot, nor stain, nor any such thing; but is as perfect as Christ himself."[119] Here, there was no equivocation or qualification. When John Eaton used the language of perfection, he was careful to hedge his statements by explaining that perfection was only in "the sight of God." The Cambridge Antinomian had dispensed with this rider, declaring simply and seemingly without qualification that the believer "is as perfect as Christ himself."

Here, perfection was viewed not as something extrinsic to the believer, but as an internal, and intrinsic presence of Christ (who, nevertheless, was apprehended by faith alone). In terms highly reminiscent of Peter Shaw, the Cambridge Antinomian explained this by referring to the Aristotelian commonplaces of matter and form:

> What is the forme of a Beleever: I answer the forme of a Beleever is Christ himself, so far forth as Christ is receiveable . . . we know, that the humane nature of Christ had no being out of the divine; therefore the divine nature must needs give being to the humane; and whatsoever gives being to a thing, must needs be the forme of that thing to which it gives being; Again the forme and matter must both make up one thing, and so it was in Christ. For though there was a personal union, yet there was not an union of persons, but an union of natures, that is, of two to make up one thing. Whereby you may see, that that must needs be the forme of Christ which gave him a being to be that which he was. And from whence did proceed the operation and action of the worth and excellency of his sacrifice, but from his divinity? and to be a meet and fit saviour but from his forme and matter both? By which you may perceive the excellency of the forme of a Beleever.[120]

---

[119] CUL MS. Dd. xii. 42, 9-10.

[120] Ibid., 56-57.

Just as Christ's human nature was joined to his divine nature, a believer was joined to Christ's nature, such that "Christ and a Beleever are but one, as the forme and the matter make up but one thing."[121] Echoing Traske, the Cambridge Antinomian maintained that by virtue of this union, which was in fact closer than the union between body and soul, believers could indeed say that "Christ God and man is our forme, and so we come to be partakers of the divine nature."[122]

This union was not one of total identity; believers did not, for instance, share in Christ's Kingly, Prophetic, and Priestly Offices, nor presumably, could they perform miracles.[123] Nevertheless, by virtue of his or her merger with Christ, a believer not only osmotically absorbed Christ's divine nature, but he or she possessed Christ's perfect virtues: "And what excellency is in Christ is a Beleevers by vertue of this union; for Christ and a Beleever are but one, as the forme and the matter make up but one thing."[124] In a manner almost identical to Traske's, the Cambridge Antinomian thus argued that a believer's actions were not his or her own, but Christ's. Like a great mind or soul energizing a lifeless body, Christ moved in, through, and by believers. "Again Christ is the Vine, and we are the branches. . . . From hence proceed all actions, and operations, and motions, namely from this stock unto which we are united. And therefore the actions of a Beleever must needs be most excellent actions, which proceed from such a head and fountain; and therefore must needs excell all law whatsoever both of men and Angels."[125] Herein rested "the perfection of a Beleever."[126] This perfection was not a crude perfection in the flesh, but a perfection borne of the fact that believers were moved by Christ, and all their righteous actions were in essence his actions: "look what excellency is in the cause, the same will be in the effect; inasmuch as the effect doth partake of the nature of the cause: But Christ is the cause of our perfection, and therefore our perfection must needs be of the same nature with his."[127]

---

[121] Ibid., 57.

[122] Ibid., 57, 60: "Now the union between the divinity and humanity of Christ is a more near and strong union, than the union between Christ and a Beleever; and the union between Christ and a Beleever than the union between the soul and the body. . . ." It should be noted that the author was here subtly amplifying a standard godly metaphor for the union between Christ and the believer, which on John Preston's account was comparable to "the union that is betwixt the soule and the body." J. Preston, *Foure Godly and Learned Treatises* (1636 ed.), 101.

[123] CUL MS. Dd. xii. 42, 57.

[124] Ibid.

[125] Ibid., 60.

[126] Ibid., 61.

[127] Ibid., 62.

This forthright declaration of perfection allowed the Cambridge Antinomian to make claims that went beyond anything Eaton was willing to commit to paper. In a manner reminiscent of Eaton, he argued that believers sensed this perfection only by faith; they continued to commit offenses which seemed to belie their perfection, and therefore needed to believe, above sense, that Christ had saved them from the Law and sin. But unlike Eaton, who held that true Christians were to believe that they were "perfect in God's sight," the Cambridge Antinomian maintained that they were to believe themselves perfect in fact, by virtue of their union with Christ. They were to trust that they were utterly and perfectly holy, without any sin: "if we be made perfectly holy for ever, then all sin is banished and gone. For as long as there remains any sin, men cannot be said to be perfectly holy."[128] For the Cambridge Antinomian, then, the faithful were to believe not only that their sins were banished from God's sight, but that sin no longer *existed* for them: "Faith beleeves that there is no such thing as sin."[129]

In a series of seemingly small, but ultimately decisive moves, the Cambridge Antinomian had radicalized the Eatonist critique. Everyone, he argued, would be better off without the preaching of the Law; outward, literal Sabbath observance was a legalistic corruption of the true Sabbath, "the rest of God," into which only true believers had entered; believers were joined to Christ as soul to body; as a consequence, they were objectively and ontologically perfect; for the faithful, there was no such thing as sin. These ideas, all of which pushed beyond the messages of John Eaton and his closest followers, were almost certainly crafted with the help of the strain of antinomian thought that has been called "perfectionist" or "inherentist" throughout this study. As with both Shaw and Traske, the result was a crossbreed that was in certain respects more extreme in its rejection of puritan orthodoxy than either of the traditions from which it derived.

And like John Traske, the Cambridge Antinomian attacked that central assumption of puritan practical divinity—the ultimate equivalence of the Law of Sinai and the "law" of the New Testament. The Law of the Old Testament and the new obedience enjoined by Christ were not of the same order. The Cambridge Antinomian tried to demonstrate this by referring to the example of Christ:

> consider the . . . actions of Christ, they will set forth unto us the excellency of this forme. As for example, in the action of Love. The Law saith, Love thy neighbour as thy self, but Christ loved his neighbor better than himself; for he was content to part with his glory and life and all for a time for us and our good. Greater love than this hath no man, that a man lay down his life

---

[128] Ibid., 36.
[129] Ibid., 37.

for his freinds. Joh. 15. 13. But Christ laid down his life for his enemies. Now the Law never required such a love as this.[130]

Here, he was struggling to articulate the concept that the new regime of Christ was qualitatively, undeniably different from the order of the Law. Something more, something different, infused true Christians. For further evidence, he referred the readers to the examples of Saint Paul and Moses himself (who, as a true Christian, had obeyed a higher law even as he promulgated the carnal, earthly Law on tablets of stone):

> But for your further satisfaction, see an example of this in a Beleever, in Rom. 9. 3. What a love the Apostle does express towards his brethren, his kinsmen according to the flesh, that he could wish himself accursed from Christ for their sake. And the like you may see in Moses, Ex. 32. 32 where the Prophet prays for the people thus, O Lord forgive their sin; and if not, blot me, I pray thee out of thy book which thou hast written. What say you to both these Christians? Was not this love above the Law? Doth the Law require that a man should love his brother better than himself, and that a man should willingly part with his own glory and happiness for the good of an other? No certainly, the Law requires a man to love his neighbour but as himself: but these men did express a greater love, for they were willing to part with their own happiness for the good of others; which the Law never required a man to do. Again the Law expresseth no better a perfection than was in mans heart at first; and therefore cannot be a sufficient rule to a Beleever, who hath such an excellent perfection, as the perfection of Christ.[131]

The perfection of believers thus included a kind of heightened, supernatural love that was of a different order from the love commanded in Deuteronomy. The commandments of the Old Testament Law were the expression of Adam's perfection prior to the Fall. It was a compendium of all those duties that Adam would and could faithfully perform in his prelapsarian state of innocence. Yet Adam's creaturely perfection fell short of that which was vouchsafed to believers by faith: "Mans perfection in his first estate was far inferiour to a Beleevers perfection in Christ."[132] This new and greater perfection, brought with it an all-encompassing and perfect love, that superseded anything commanded in the Old Testament. In this vein, he declared that "our Saviour doth give us a new rule to walk by, Love ye one an other, as I have love[d] you. Joh. 13. 34."[133]

---

130 Ibid., 58.
131 Ibid., 62.
132 Ibid., 61.
133 Ibid.

The Cambridge Antinomian was thus attempting to give voice to the notion that Christ brought a "new rule," utterly distinct from the prescriptions and Laws of the Old Testament. Believers, who possessed all of Christ's perfections, possessed also his perfect love, a love that was superior to, and which superseded anything and everything contained in the Law. It was this love, dwelling in them by Christ's spirit, that ensured that they would do good works. Like every other antinomian thus far examined, the Cambridge Antinomian repeated the notion that believers needed no external, legal compulsion; they did all good things voluntarily and freely, by virtue of a new "principle" within them. In answer to the objection "how should I know what duty to performe either to God or man, if it were not for the Law to direct me?" the Cambridge Antinomian answered

> This is as much as to say, I have in me the true art of Logick, and yet I cannot tell how to frame a Syllogisticall argument without a Book by me. Goe learn what these phrases mean, They shall be all taught of God, John. 6. 45. and I. Joh. 2. 27. The anointing which ye have received of him, abideth in you; and ye need not that any man teach you; but as the same anointing teacheth you of all things, etc.[134] If thou canst do nothing but by vertue of the outward teaching of the Law; it argues thy obedience to be but outward like thy teaching; for if thou hadst the principle of life within thee, thou wouldst not need any exteriour thing to help thee, but thou woul[d]st be able to do any thing with out a guide or help. But this argues plainly, that thy obedience ariseth not from any principle within thee, but from the Law commanding, which if it were not, there would be no obedience yielded, just as a child which will obey no longer than the rod is on his back.[135]

Like all other antinomians, this writer thus contrasted the extorted legal obedience of his puritan enemies against the genuine, unforced obedience that flowed spontaneously from a true believer's heart. In a manner perhaps more

---

[134] Cf. Traske, *True Gospel Vindicated*, sigs. Gv-G2v, which used the exact same scriptural passage (1 John 2. 27) and the identical analogy of the Logician to argue that only the "Evangelicall light set up in the soule of true beleevers, that *Law of the mind, Christ in us, that mind of Christ,* that *anointing of the holy One*, by which we *know all things*, and what is *Trueth*, and what is a *Lye* 1 *John* 2. 20. 21. 27" could actually reveal the true meaning of his "Rule of Faith." This he compared to "other Arts and Sciences" in which there "are Rules to be held fast, and not to be parted with; and though none but Artists doe truly understand the Rule, yet may it be evinced to be a Rule for that Art or Science whatsoever it be. . . . So in Logicke, Invention of Arguments, and disposition of them to the thing argued are knowne to the exact Logician, and to none besides."

[135] CUL MS. Dd. xii. 42, 52-53.

extreme than his co-propagandists, he likewise suggested that true believers needed no external input, "guide," or "help" to do God's will.

Like Everarde, Brearley, and Traske, then, the Cambridge Antinomian argued that believers were filled with a spirit of love—distinct from and in some ways opposed to the obedience of the Law—which led them inexorably, and without the need of any external guide or rule, to do good works. Such believers no longer acted out of fear of punishment or in hope of a celestial reward:

> He that hath the spirit of Christ, is now no more a child; he neither learns nor works any more for fear of the rod, or for fear of any thing else, or for the obtaining any thing for himself; but doth all things freely, as the Saviour saith, Joh. 7. 38. . . . All good works, and all gifts of grace shall spring out of him naturally and of their own accord. Thou needest not to wrest good works from him, as a man crusheth water out of a sponge; for they flow naturally from him, as water from a fountain. . . . So if any man aske me (being justifyed by faith) why I work? I answer Love compells me. I do not think my self ever the better, because of my works, nor do I seek Heaven, nor a higher place in heaven for my works sake; but the love of Christ constraineth me, 2. Cor. 5. 14.[136]

Although he did not, like Brearley or Traske, invoke the phrase "law of love" to express this idea, it is clear that the author was articulating the same basic notion—Christians were bound by a rule very different from that of the old Law. What this suggests is that this notion of a separate and distinct "law of love" was coming to be an antinomian commonplace during this period—once again, we appear to be witnessing a process of ideological cross-fertilization, as different figures, who had arrived at anti-legal positions in different places, under different circumstances, began to converge on a core of central, shared arguments. From this standpoint, the process of hybridization taking place in London might likewise be viewed as a process of standardization, as the various strands of argument that had been worked out by figures such as Eaton, Everarde and Traske, were distilled into a more unitary, generic whole.

The Cambridge Antinomian was even more forthcoming than Brearley or Traske about the nature of this new rule of love. When he used the phrase "the love of Christ," the Cambridge Antinomian did not mean "love for Christ" or "love toward Christ." Instead, he meant "Christ's love," for like Traske, he seems to have believed that God's love itself inhabited human beings: "But now a Christian loves the Lord with a new strength even with the same love where with he hath loved him. For he first loves us, and then we love him again. 1 Joh. 4. 19. His love is shed abroad in our hearts, and then we reflect love for love. And is not this a more excellent love than ever was in

[136] Ibid., 73.

the heart of man by nature? and therefore far above the law of nature."[137] Indeed, like Traske, he was willing to follow the lead of the author of 1 John in reducing God himself to love; those who came to experience this love through faith were themselves transformed into love, or rather, into God.

> Thus thou must live by Faith only; and here thou shalt meet with God in Christ, who will present himself to thy soul as a loving father, who is all Love, Mercy and goodnesse, and he will communicate his love, goodness and mercy unto thy poor soul, so that thou wilt be as it wer composed of Love. As the Apostle John speaks, I. Epist. 4. 16. God is love, and he that dwelleth in Love, dwelleth in God, and God in him: and he that so dwelleth or liveth, liveth altogether out of himself; which life is not conspicuous to the eye of sense, for it is only enjoyed by Faith, according as the Apostle speaks, Heb. 10. 38. The just shall live by faith.[138]

Here, I would argue, was the endpoint of antinomianism, a distillation of the impulse that all of the figures examined here had struggled, with more or less success, to put into words. On their reading of the Pauline and Johannine epistles, the crucifixion had opened an insuperable gulf. On one side stood the God of Exodus 34: 14, on the other the indwelling Word of 1 John 4: 16. This, they argued, was a truth that had somehow been lost in the pulpits and conventicles of English puritanism.[139]

It was a truth, moreover, that could only have profound effects on the psychological state of the believer. Those who had come through faith to believe that God dwelled in them, and that they shared his nature could only rejoice:

> Now here is no Law, nor sin, nor sorrow, nor fear, nor death, nor trouble, nor tears: for all sorrow and mourning is fled away; here is nothing but joy and gladness; being according as the Prophet Isaiah speaks, chap. 35. 10.

---

[137] Ibid., 63. Compare this and the next passage against Eaton, who held that God's love was reflected in us, rendering us "the image" of God; he does not claim, as this antinomian does, that God is the love that dwells in us. See J. Eaton, *Discovery of the Most Dangerous Dead Faith* (1642), 76-77.

[138] CUL MS. Dd. xii. 42, 52-53, 39.

[139] Although the nature of civil-war radical religion lies outside the purview of this study, it is worth noting that this very distinctive vision of true religion brought with it certain political and social implications that would be of decisive importance in the 1640s and 1650s. A vision of the Christian polity based on an uncoercive law of love was likely to look very different from a vision of society organized around an attempt to institute a coercive set of divine laws and precepts, and there are signs that this crucial difference played itself out in the competing visions of church and state pursued by different factions within the parliamentary coalition in the 1640s. For a suggestive example, see William Walwyn, *A Word More to Mr Thomas Edwards Minister* (1646), 4-5.

> The ransomed of the Lord shall returne and come to Zion with songs, and everlasting joy shall be upon their heads; they shall obtain joy and gladness, and sorrow and sighing shall flee away. There is no intermission of this joy, to them that live here, for it is an everlasting joy: It is not a little sprinkling of joy only for a time and away; but it is permanent and lasting: nay it is everlasting, if we could live here everlastingly. Oh; that we did but truly know what it is to live by Faith; then we should conclude with the two Apostles at the transfiguration of Christ upon the mount, Matt. 17. 4. It is good for me to be here; for we should then enjoy a very Heaven upon the earth: It is a life worth the seeking for: but this Life thou canst never attain by all the holy performances and dilligent practice of holy duties, nor by all the exteriour cleaness before me; for it is only attained by Faith, and no way else.[140]

At this point, our interpretational wheel has turned full circle; we are back among the Traskites of 1615, who believed that they been carried into the Kingdom of Heaven even as they walked on earth. For the Cambridge Antinomian, however, this was a kingdom not only of joy and exultation, but a kingdom without Law, in which even the most sacrosanct ordinances of puritan practical divinity crumbled into dust in the light of the overwhelming internal presence of the love of God.

---

[140] CUL MS. Dd. xii. 42, 39-40.

CHAPTER 10

Ultra-Antinomianism?

This study would not be complete without a brief attempt to explore the most extreme permutations of antinomianism. It has been argued above that through a process of constant polemical engagement with their godly opponents, many anti-legalists had edged further and further away from the culture of mainstream puritanism. What had begun as a critique of the legalistic bent of mainstream puritan piety had over time mutated into something much more. This process of detachment and radicalization took two main forms.

Firstly, opposition to the fastidious legal observances of the godly had transformed itself into an overt rejection of the Mosaic Law in all its uses. Where Eaton and Towne had stressed certain positive uses for the Law, and where Everarde had suggested that the truly faithful would obey the law in its spiritual (as opposed to literal) form, the most extreme antinomians—prodded along by continual controversies outlined in the first section of this book—came very close to exiling the Law entirely from the field of Christian worship. In this vein, Traske had openly professed that he could find no scriptural "commission" for the ministers of the Gospel to preach the Law, while the Cambridge Antinomian could lament the day that the Law of Moses was first preached to Christian congregations. Both men refused to press this conclusion to its logical extent; this brief chapter demonstrates that there were other prewar antinomians who were less timid in their rejection of the Law.

Secondly, this same war on the puritan obsession with outward obedience and duties prompted a parallel rejection of the many "forms" through which puritan piety manifested itself. The most important of these "forms" or "ordinances" were of course hearing the word, taking communion, and public prayer; they also, however, included the many noninstitutional, casual means of grace that had over time come to characterize puritan devotion—private prayer, Bible-reading, repetition of sermons, fasting, catechizing one's family, and most of all, dutiful observance of the Sabbath. Such forms had always appeared suspect to John Everarde, who believed them to be at the core of a blind, "literal," and soul-killing puritan religiosity; his critique of such "external forms" appears in time to have diffused through the antinomian community, as the Cambridge Manuscript makes clear. Nevertheless, neither Everarde nor the Cambridge Antinomian ever called into question the assumption that means of grace were the ordinary mechanisms through which believers arrived at the coveted state of perfection. They sought merely to shatter what they saw as an overweening puritan tendency to rely on such means. Yet the momentum of this critique of external means pushed ever closer to a position in which all forms disappeared, supplanted by the internal motions of the spirit of God. As J. C. Davis has argued, such anti-formalism lay behind many of the more startling modes of religiosity that cropped up during the 1640s and 1650s. I would like to suggest, at least tentatively, that this position had its roots in the antinomian underground of the pre–civil-war period. It was, in fact, the most extreme permutation of the anti-legal impulse, a child of the internal war that raged within early Stuart puritanism.

Antinomus Anonymus and the Rawlinson Antinomian: The End of the Law

In 1631, when Robert Towne's opponent Dr. Thomas Taylor set out "to prove against [the Antinomians], that true beleevers have a true use of the Morall Law," an indignant Towne demanded of him

> Against whom? I am perswaded that neither you nor any your confederates dare say that ever they heard one of an indifferent judgement, and understanding (and it ill beseemes the gravitie of a Doctor in Divinitie to scrape and receive what ever falleth from the illiterate, and simple, and to bend all his forces, by studie, Pulpit, and Presse, to quell and confute the same) simply to deny the use of the Morall Law to true beleevers.[1]

Towne's comment offers the historian an important scrap of information. On the one hand, in a manner characteristic of Eaton, he forcefully reaffirmed his own belief that the Law continued to possess uses for true believers, even after their conversion. On the other hand, however, he also confirmed, if only indirectly, that he like Taylor was acquainted with certain "illiterate, and simple" people of less than "indifferent" judgment who had in fact defended the position that the Law had ceased to be of use for true believers. As the previous chapter has demonstrated, this should hardly come as a surprise, for major antinomian propagandists could, in unguarded moments, come close in-

[1] Towne, *The Assertion of Grace* (1645), 37.

deed to arguing the Law out of the Christian dispensation. From here, it required only a very small leap to argue that the Law of Moses had no use whatsoever; it was a leap that at least some antinomian enthusiasts proved willing to take.

In 1622, the Cheshire minister William Hinde brought out a treatise called *The Office and Use of the Morall Law*. In it, he reproduced and attacked an anonymous manuscript separate that had been forwarded to the Manchester puritan notable, John Fox, Hinde's brother-in-law.[2] The circular letter had defended the proposition that "In the Church of Christ since his death the whole Law of *Moses* is wholly abolished, or abrogated."[3] In the first edition of the book, Hinde claimed that he had been unable to discover the author's "name or sect," and he accordingly dubbed its unknown author *Antinomus Anonymus*.[4] By the end of 1622, when he came to prepare a second edition for publication, Hinde appears to have uncovered considerably more information about his nameless adversary. He now alleged that *Antinomus Anonymus* "had divulged this his opinion by word and writing in divers parts of this Kingdome, and sent copies of this Pamphlet abroad into the hands of divers people," and "had . . . many followers either in the Country where he was borne or the Citie where he now lives." Hinde likewise suspected, however, that "the Author did plow with another mans heifer in this businesse, and that he had some other Leaders and Abettors of better parts and place than himselfe."[5]

Although this spotty report was apparently pieced together from hearsay, it at least tells us what Hinde believed about his adversary's background: *Antinomus* hailed from provinces, but now lived in a city; he had dispensed his opinion in multiple places throughout England; in the process, he appears to have accumulated a significant number of followers, particularly in his home county; despite his evangelical success, however, *Antinomus* was a man of limited "parts and place" (perhaps indicating that he was a layman, or more likely, a clergyman of modest "place," perhaps a minor stipendiary preacher); Hinde suspected, moreover, that he was not alone in his heresy, and that in fact he was acting as a stalking horse for other, more considerable, figures. Perhaps the most important piece of evidence is the fact that the manuscript had first been sent to Fox, whom Hinde identified as "late steward" of the

---

2 On Fox and his relationship to Hinde, see R. C. Richardson, *Puritanism in North-West England* (Manchester: Manchester University Press, 1972), 95.

3 William Hinde, *The Office and Use of the Morall Law of God in the dayes of the Gospell* (1622), sig. Br-B4v.

4 Ibid., 5.

5 William Hinde, *The Office and Use of the Morall Law of God in the dayes of the Gospell*, 2d ed. (1623), sig. A4r.

Earl of Derby's lordship of Bury and Pilkington.[6] Bury was in Grindletonian country—Roger Brearley had been married in the parish in 1615 and in the 1630s Robert Towne would serve as curate in the chapel of Heywood, on the outskirts of the parish—and it is thus by no means implausible to submit that whoever wrote the manuscript was connected, at least tangentially, to the movement that had recently sprung up around Brearley and Tennant. This may very well have been what Hinde had in mind when he argued that *Antinomus* was following the lead of more substantial (or at least craftier) fellow travelers.

The brief letter Hinde published and refuted is not, unfortunately, particularly enlightening, as it amounts to little more than an attempt to string together arguments of protestant, Catholic, and patristic authorities to support its chief contention. In this, it recalls the polemical style of an Eaton or a Towne, both of whom laboriously rifled through respectable reformed sources to find precedents for their controversial opinions. Yet the proposition defended by *Antinomus* was in fact more radical than anything either Eaton, Towne, or Roger Brearley was willing to condone in public. Indeed, *Antinomus* seemed to be making precisely the argument that Towne contemptuously disavowed in his dispute with Taylor: the notion that the Mosaic Law, including the Ten Commandments, was completely and totally obsolete for true believers.

Fortunately, we possess another piece of evidence that appears to throw additional light on the opinions of this shadowy antinomian. Among the Rawlinson papers in the Bodleian Library there survives a second, eleven-page manuscript separate, written at some point in or after 1623, which defended the nearly identical proposition "That the whole law of Moses is wholy abolished."[7] There is good reason to believe that it too was written by *Antinomus Anonymus*, not only because it proposed a similarly extreme argument with respect to the Law in virtually identical language, but also because it deployed a number of the same relatively obscure theological sources that had been cited by Hinde's adversary.[8]

The Rawlinson manuscript may in fact have represented a direct response to attacks on the *Antinomus Anonymus* circular piece, for the structure and

---

[6] Ibid., Br.

[7] Bodleian Library, Rawlinson MS. d. 1350, fols. 109-14. The manuscript cites a number of theological authorities, the latest of which is Anthony Wotton's *De Reconciliatione* (Basel, 1623), allowing us to set the earliest possible date of composition. This manuscript was, to my knowledge, first noted by David Zaret.

[8] The most unusual sources used in both the letter and the Oxford manuscript were a book by the Catholic theologian de Soto and Augustine's *Of the Spirit and the Letter* (Hinde, *Office and Use* (1623), sigs B2v, B3r; Rawlinson MS. d. 1350, fols. 111r, 111v).

content of the manuscript indicate that it was the product of an ongoing polemical dispute with an opponent who had already refuted the Rawlinson author's basic proposition that the Law was abolished.[9] As such, it is largely technical in nature, quibbling with translations of words, and negating the specific arguments of a now unseen, forgotten opponent. Nevertheless, in the course of this technical discussion—which was hardly the product of an "illiterate" pen—a number of interesting points emerged, all of which tended to support a total and unadulterated abolition of the Law.

In the view of the Rawlinson author, the entire Law of Sinai, including the Decalogue, had been swept away by a new and utterly distinctive Law of Sion. Taking at face value the many Pauline allusions to the abrogation of the Law, he argued that there was no scriptural warrant for his opponent's assumption that what was abrogated was merely the "ceremonial," as opposed to the "moral" part of the Mosaic Law.[10] Using the words "Law," "Testament," and "Covenant" interchangeably, the Rawlinson author claimed that the New Covenant had utterly voided that which came before it: "they are tearmed 2 testaments, whereof one makes the other void: for a testament is a last will and if a testament be not the last will it is noe testament, but ceaseth to be a testament when the last is made." And since the New Testament or Covenant had voided the Old, it had likewise voided the conditions and Laws associated with it. His opponent was therefore "much deceived" in his claim that the "law whereunto obedience is required by both covenants" was "one the same." In fact, the law that came "out of Syon" was in "opposition to that which came out of Sinai."[11] Here, the Rawlinson antinomian was attempting to articulate the now-familiar antinomian concept that the Law of Moses and the Law of the New Testament were qualitatively different, and were in fact at odds with each other. They were of a different spirit, and demanded different things: "Now yt is plaine that by the old covenant obedience to Moses Law formally as it was delivered by Moses in Sinai was required: but by the newe the Lawes prescribed—are of another kind . . . this is his comaundements that wee should beeleeve on the name of his son Jesus and love one another."[12]

---

[9] Ibid., fol. 109r. The opponent does not, however, appear to have been Hinde.

[10] Ibid., fol. 109v. Compare against *Antinomus Anonymus* as cited in Hinde, *Office and Use* (1623), sig. B3r: "*Wheresoever the Holy Ghost handleth the abrogation of the Law, there is never any exception of Morall.*"

[11] Bodleian Library, Rawlinson MS. d. 1350, fol. 110v.

[12] Ibid., fols. 110v-111r. Compare against the claim of *Antinomus Anonymus* who argued in a very similar manner that "*All that any man can say against this doctrine is, that the Morall law or the Decalogue is perpetuall in nature . . . but where the perptuitie of it in divinitie is to be found in Scripture would I faine see: For the holy Ghost in the new Testament doth not exact naturall precepts such as the Decalogue is, for that is fulfilled in one word* Love, Gal. 5. 14. *But the exhortation is*

This, in the Rawlinson antinomian's opinion, represented a total and complete break from the past. Like the Grindletonians, Traske, or the Cambridge Antinomian, this writer suggested that New Testament commandments to faith and love were of a "different kind"—they were indeed new, and any attempt to conflate them with the Laws set down in the Torah was to mistake the nature of Christianity.

On this basis, the Rawlinson author argued that ministers under the New Testament had no "commission," authority, or warrant to preach the Law:

> where was ever any comission given the ministers of the newe testament to preach the lawe I cannot find. The comission given to the Apostles was to teach the Gospell Math. 28. 20 they were appoynted to preach and teach which our Saviour had comaunded them which Mar. 16. 15 is explayned to be the Gospell yea our Saviour himselfe was sent to preach the Gospell Luk: 4. 18. 43. And accordingly he preached the Gospell Mat 4. 23. Mar: 1. 14. Luke 20. 1 and he foretells that the Gospell shalbe preached through the world Mt. 24. 14 and Mar: 13. 10 and Paule plainely sheweth what his comission was Rom: 1: 1 and 15 16. 1. Cor. i. 17 and 9. 17. Gal. 1. 16 and 2. 7 and 4.8 Phil: 2. 4. 2 Tim: 1. 11 And Peters comission was in like manner Act: 15. 7. Gal. 2. 7. And Revel: 14: 6. The Angell had an everlasting gospell to preach to all them that dwell on the earth. And Paul tearmeth himselfe a minister of the Gospell Rom: 1. 9. Eph: 3. 7: Col. 1: 23 25 and not of the lawe—2 Cor. 3. 6. Timothy was allsoe the like 1 The: 3. 2 and soe in other places, Now let my opponent shewe but one place that comission was given to any of the Apostles to teach or preach the lawe or that any of them is anywhere termed a minister of the lawe, and I will yeild him all. If he can doe neither can it be thought that such a comission was given and yet not once mencioned in the booke of God[?][13]

He admitted that there was significant overlap between these two, opposed Laws, but claimed that this fact was almost incidental. They were in some respects of the same matter, but possessed different "forms," distinct essences.[14] The Rawlinson author ended by declaring his judgment that "it seemes very

---

to the workes of the Spirit, none of which are properly commanded in the Decalogue." Hinde, *Office and Use* (1623), sig. B4r-v.

[13] Bodleian Library, Rawlinson MS. d. 1350, fol. 112v.

[14] Ibid., fols. 112v-113r: "it is sufficient if wee doe what the gospell comaundeth without need of the lawe. Besides soe much of the lawe as the gospell teacheth is of the matter of the lawe but not of the forme of the law and soe not of the lawe it selfe. Our common Lawyers administer some things that are the forme that the Civil law comaunds yet doe they not administer the Civil law, they have no comission to doe it neither are we subject to yt, but where the common law gives way to it."

probable, that the Apostle did not preach the decalogue,"[15] a conclusion that naturally absolved all New Testament ministers from any duty to preach the Ten Commandments. New Testament ministers were the preachers of a new Law, a Law whose only commandments were faith and love.

Much of this should, at this point, appear familiar. Particularly striking is the Rawlinson author's use of the dichotomy between the "Law of Sinai" and a separate, distinct "Law of Sion." This, it will be recalled, was the exact formulation used by Roger Brearley's disciple Josiah Collier to describe the difference between the two covenants. This lends circumstantial support to the notion that its author was one and the same man as *Antinomus Anonymus* (and in turn that *Antinomus Anonymus* had Grindletonian connections). Whether or not this proves correct, it seems clear that the Rawlinson antinomian was taking the argument of two distinct laws and pushing into territory that more reputable figures such as Brearley, Eaton, and Towne had clearly wanted to avoid. In the view of the Rawlinson antinomian, the abolishment of the old Law of Sinai, and the coming of the new Law of Sion suggested not just that believers were free from the old Law, but that it had no place in the Christian dispensation. The Apostle Paul had not preached the Law of Moses; no Christian minister had a commission to preach it, either. In this, he was willing to go beyond even the arguments of Traske and the Cambridge Antinomian, who flirted with this argument, but proved unwilling in the end to jettison the Decalogue in its totality. Whatever Towne may have implied, however, this text was hardly the work of an "illiterate and simple" pen; although perhaps somewhat syntactically challenged, the author of the Rawlinson manuscript, like *Antinomus Anonymus*, could read Latin, knew at least some Greek, and was entirely conversant in early modern reformed divinity. He would seem to provide solid evidence that in certain hands, the antinomian critique quickly and decisively radicalized itself, overtaking the more cautious approach of the central clerical leaders of the movement, and pushing into new and dangerous theological territory.

Vision-Seekers

Our evidence concerning the second phenomenon—the tendency to cast off all means—is slim but extremely suggestive. Although we possess no texts written by such ultra-antinomians, there is good reason to believe that there were clusters of people in London who had come to rely mainly upon the indwelling of the spirit for revelation. As we have already seen in 1634, Hartlib noted in his diary that John Pordage, the later civil-war radical, was fomenting differences with London ministers over the use of external signs to measure one's spiritual estate: "One Pordage broches new-fangled opinions con-

---

[15] Ibid., fol. 113v.

cerning the signes, that No Man can trie himself by them, but was to stay by for an over-powring light."[16] While there is nothing here to suggest that Pordage had completely tossed away ordinances, the accusation against him certainly suggests that he was proposing a model of religiosity in which would-be believers were to wait upon the motions of the spirit for illumination. Such a mystical illuminism would in fact have placed him close to Everarde, who as we have seen pushed his followers to use the means as an engine to catapult them into a mystical awareness of their unity with God.

Such illuminism appears to have flourished at the "perfectionist" end of the antinomian underground. As early as 1618, Hebdon and (in all likelihood) Traske were indulging in a form of mystical dream-interpretation, in which dreams were treated as visitations of the divine spirit. As we shall see shortly, Edward Howes, who has bequeathed to us our most precious example of seventeenth-century Familist thought and practice, was addicted to a very similar habit of dream-interpretation. For him, dreams were nothing less than allegorical visions that revealed the divine mind. Such modes of spiritual illuminism need not have excluded "ordinances"; it was entirely possible, for instance, to maintain a theology of mystical rapture that embraced both immediate and mediated forms of spiritual enlightenment. Thomas Shepard, the famous Massachusetts minister, who in his youth had flirted with antinomianism, provided precisely such an account of English Familism. In 1635-36, during the first months of the disputes that would later come to be called the Antinomian Controversy, Shepard wrote a letter to John Cotton, warning him not to be complacent about the threat of HN's pernicious influence:

> on[e] thing more I doe with submission desire you not to [be] mistaken in; as if that the Familists doe not care for woord or ordinances but only the spirits motion; for I have bin with many of them and hence have met with many of there bookes; and I doe know thus much of them, that scarce any people honour woord and ordinances more, for they will professe that there they meet with the Spirit and there superlative raptures; H.N. the author of them cites scripture abundantly, and Jesabell Revelation 2: who hath her depthes, calls her selfe a prophetesse, tis her glory to interpret scripture; and but that I should hold you too long I could send you diverse of there *Theses de Sacra Scriptera*, by which you might soone see what honour they put upon the woord.[17]

[16] Sheffield University Library, Hartlib Papers, MS. 29/2/40B, as cited from *The Hartlib Papers: A Complete Text and Image Database of the Papers of Samuel Hartlib (c.1600-1662) Held in Sheffield University Library*, 2d ed. (Sheffield: Humanities Research Online, 2002).

[17] D. D. Hall, *The Antinomian Controversy, 1636-1638: A Documentary History* (Durham and London: Duke University Press, 1990), 28.

Shepard's words offer a well-informed, if hostile, appraisal of the nature of Familism. Indeed, leaving aside the question of whether John Everarde considered himself a disciple of HN, it is clear that Shepard's account described almost perfectly Everarde's view of spiritual illumination. As we have seen, Everarde maintained that through the ordinances, believers came to experience a mystical vision of God that elevated them above all law and ordinances, if only temporarily. Having descended from these elevated heights, such believers then needed to reapply means and ordinances in order to come to a further sight of their own unity with God.

Yet elsewhere, both Shepard and Everarde told a somewhat different story about practices current at the fringe of perfectionist circles. Thus, in his sermons of the Parable of the Ten Virgins, which were preached during the New England Antinomian Controversy in the late 1630s, Shepard warned against those who taught that the spirit could come without the mediation of the word: "They that would have it [the Spirit] by immediate revelation, by elevations of the Soul to God, a Familistical principle collected from the Apocrypha[,] speculations of devout Monks, received in *Germany* when the Gospel was preached to overthrow it and entertained by the deceitful experiences of some (as in *London*, &c.) she that was converted by dreams, &c. indeed we are to look for the Spirit; but to look for it without the Word is vile."[18] Here Shepard was suggesting that at least some of those steeped in a "familistical" milieu had pressed beyond the word, falling back onto the direct and immediate experiences of the divine spirit. He associated this dangerous error with the influence of German mysticism (probably the *Theologia Germanica*) and with certain Apocrypha (very possibly II Esdras and Wisdom, both of which were much admired by HN, and both of which had substantial mystical overtones). In either case, he was able to produce at least one example—presumably a celebrated example—of a well-known London woman who claimed to have been converted by dreams, that is, through unmediated visionary spiritual experience. Again, Shepard's tale is rendered considerably more plausible given our indisputable evidence as to the existence of such dream-mysticism amongst the likes of Hebdon and Howes.

Shepard's hostile testimony would be open to serious question were it not for a brief passage in one of John Everarde's sermons of the early 1630s. In warding off accusations that he himself subscribed to such a form a visionary illuminism, Everarde reaffirmed his commitment to outward ordinances and means. Although those who had undergone the experience of "deiformity" did at times transcend all earthly means, laws, and ordinances, they did so by and

---

[18] Thomas Shepard, *The Parable of the Ten Virgins Opened & Applied: Being the Substance of Divers Sermons on Math. 25.1,—13* (1660; reprint edition, 1695), Book II, 92-93. I owe this reference to the generosity of Michael Winship.

through the use of means. Partly to defend himself, he admitted, however, that his own doctrine had been abused by others, who were less cautious:

> And so much *more* I will say, to *satisfie* you, that I have great cause to *mistrust* those spirits, whether they come the right way to God, or into such *Raptures*, that leap them on a *sudden*, without use of means or Ordinances, but only of a *Blinde* and *Prophane* condition, come suddenly into these enjoyments: for God doth *usually* make use of these means; yet I may not limit, nor direct, nor circumscribe the Sovereign Almighty: yet usually *faith cometh by hearing, and hearing by the word preached*: But herein lies the *general* abuse of these *truths*, and of these *enjoyments*; that because some may and do come thus to enjoy God, and forsake *Ordinances* at a season, at the *very* time of such *enjoyments*, therefore some having gotten this *in notion*, have presumptuously affirmed that they are above these, and so far abuse themselves, and shew an ill example to others, that they have quite *forsaken the Assemblies*, and the use of any Ordinances. Beloved, all these things *are an offence*, and hereby many a soul by this delusion of Satan, drowns it self in *perdition*: And yet I may say more then all this, and say *properly too*, he that uses them, and rests not in them, *lives above them*: and in this sense, *living above Ordinances* is most properly taken, and is a truth, though much abused; *viz.* That man hath not *his comfort*, his *Life* in them; this man *lives* above Ordinances: I do not say he must *forsake all Ordinances*, as men take it *usually:* But to have our *Life* and *enjoyments* in the *Truth* and *Substance*; and against this Doctrine *the gates of hell shall never prevail*. And this I will say more, those that come into such pretended enjoyments in this *extraordinary* way, that *for the most part* they never hold on in a Christian course, but abusing *this light*, run out into *fleshy* liberty: But the right *enjoyment* of God, is such *a hedge* to a man, that he cannot but love God, and seek to *honor* him with all his *might*. But I conceive *all these things* are but to *lead* us to Jesus Christ; and therefore to put *more* in them, and *depend* more on them then ever was intended, is an high abuse of them.[19]

Here, then, is far more substantial evidence, coming not from an arch-enemy of the antinomians, but from a man himself accused of antinomianism. Like Robert Towne, Everarde was admitting the existence of individuals who had taken his teachings to extreme and unacceptable lengths. When juxtaposed against Shepard's comments, Everarde's words render it difficult to deny that there were men and women in early Stuart London who had shaken off all ordinances, choosing instead to pursue a path of inward and immediate divine revelation. Such individuals presumably believed that they had already transcended the Letter, and could thus dispense with literal "assemblies" and

---

[19] *Some Gospel-Treasures Opened: Or, The Holiest of all Unvailing* (1653), 562-64.

"ordinances" as stepping-stones to be discarded. Despite its brevity, this shred of evidence holds fairly substantial repercussions for the history of civil-war religion. It suggests that the extreme anti-formalism of groupings such as the Seekers and Ranters was not merely the product of civil-war breakdown and confusion; instead, this anti-formalism had evolved out of well-established, if completely marginal, practices that had developed along the fringes of the antinomian community in the years prior to 1640. They were a natural consequence of beliefs and attitudes that had already taken hold in what might be seen as the extreme, Familist wing of the antinomian underground. As Everarde's publisher and disciple Rapha Harford put it in 1653, Everarde had navigated the dangerous waters between the Scylla of the mere rationalist, and the Charybdis of "the *Familist*, who saith he lives above Ordinances, and so hath quite left all Religion, and by degrees hath turned licentious Ranter."[20] In our Conclusion, we shall meet one such Familist-turned-Ranter; so, too, we will speculate further on the fate of the England's antinomian underground in the years of war, regicide, and Interregnum.

[20] From "The Epistle Dedicatory" of ibid.

CHAPTER 11

Forging Heresy: Mainstream Puritans and Laudians on Antinomianism

Few members of the godly community could have remained untouched by the controversies over the Law. Particularly in London, it is clear that disputes were widespread, acrimonious, and in some cases, very public. Many of the city's most famous godly ministers had confronted antinomians directly and personally. Nehemiah Wallington's pastor Henry Roborough engaged in face-to-face debates with John Etherington, as had two lesser known ministers named Stephens and Cleaver.[1] Stephen Denison, of course, had repeatedly and personally denounced the unfortunate boxmaker from the pulpit throughout the mid-1620s, ultimately initiating the High Commission case against him. Meanwhile, Denison, Dr. Cornelius Burges, James Nalton, Elias Crabtree, Richard Culverwell, Nathaniel Waker, and Abraham Grame had all furnished evidence in the case against Peter Shaw in 1629. The puritanically inclined William Cooper, like Roborough a friend of Denison, had jousted with Samuel Prettie in 1630. Thomas Taylor and Henry Burton, two of London's most illustrious godly preachers, engaged in protracted and bitter disputes with a series of antinomian opponents in the years prior to 1631. Samuel Torshel, briefly lecturer at St. Bartholomew by the Exchange, preached a cycle of sermons on the subjects of justification and the Law, in which he denounced antinomian errors. Others, such as Obadiah Sedgwick, Richard Sibbes, and Edward Reynolds felt compelled to attack or refute aspects of the emerging anti-

[1] John Etherington, *The Defence of John Etherington against Stephen Denison* (1641), 5.

legal style of religiosity in the late 1620s and early 1630s. These are only those cases that have left a discernible mark on the documentary record, and therefore represent what is very likely the tip of the historical iceberg. Everarde, for instance, suggested that he had been denounced by godly ministers as a Familist and an antinomian, although no record of such denunciations has survived. Clearly, by the early 1630s, few knowledgeable godly people could have been ignorant of the disputes under discussion here.

The question of why these disputes were so acrimonious has, it is hoped, been put to rest in the preceding chapters. Antinomians were mounting a serious challenge to the hegemony of mainstream puritan ministers. They were seeking to undermine the system of practical divinity upon which the culture of mainstream puritanism subsisted and perpetuated itself, and to replace that system with an alternative mode of religiosity. They were attempting, in short, to redefine the parameters of godliness. The stakes in this ideological battle were the affections, support (and ultimately, the patronage) of the godly laity. It is no surprise, then, that mainstream puritan divines would wage a fierce and determined battle against a polemical onslaught that threatened not only their most cherished beliefs, but their authority and their social standing. As we have seen, this counteroffensive proved successful, at least in the short term. By 1633, most of London's antinomians had been silenced, and mainstream puritan divinity reigned supreme, at least until the chaos of the 1640s brought these conflicts once again to the surface.

The following chapter seeks to provide an account of the content of this polemical counteroffensive. How, precisely, did mainstream puritans defend themselves from the charges of the antinomians? What polemical tactics did they use in their efforts to undermine their opponents? How, in short, did the godly seek to maintain their position of authority amongst the godly laity, to define the antinomians as heterodox and deviant? It is argued here that this polemical campaign was conducted primarily along three lines. First, and most obviously, mainstream puritans sought to undermine the foundations of antinomianism by exploiting scripture to discredit the most crucial premises of the antinomian position, in the process reasserting their own time-honored system of pastoral divinity. Secondly, the godly attempted to assimilate antinomian errors to prior heresies, to place antinomianism, as it were, within a disreputable genealogy of error and heterodoxy. Thirdly, mainstream puritan divines attempted to portray their opponents as a threat to social and moral order. In all of these tactics, they were seeking to appeal not just to the godly laity, whose continued loyalty hung in the balance, but also to an increasingly hostile ecclesiastical establishment. As suggested in Chapter Three, London's antinomian controversies were not conducted in a vacuum; they were in fact intimately tied into the broader polarization of the church under Charles I and Archbishop Laud.

Mining Scripture

The battle to define the contours of godly religiosity was, at its most basic level, conducted as a struggle over the meaning of specific scriptural passages. Precisely because they were in a position of relative cultural hegemony, it was not absolutely imperative that mainstream puritan ministers articulate a grand vision of right religion in contradistinction to that proposed by their antinomian critics. The mode of practical divinity they defended needed no systematic elaboration, for it had already been elaborated piece by piece in university and pulpit over the preceding decades. It permeated the English cultural landscape, and maintained a strong hold over those men and women who had come under its spell. What was necessary, then, was not a systematic explication of their own position, but an opportunistic war of attrition, in which mainstream puritan ministers sought to mine scripture in order to negate the specific premises on which the emerging antinomian ideology staked its claims. Through this means, the godly sought to demonstrate before a broad, lay audience that the antinomian claims to truth—indeed to absolute protestant orthodoxy—were spurious and unscriptural, thereby discrediting their troublesome critics.

The godly set their sights primarily upon two claims—first, the argument that God saw no sin in the justified, and secondly, the assertion that believers were free from the Moral Law. As we have seen, the former argument was the central pillar in the doctrinal monolith of imputative antinomianism. This had been John Eaton's fundamental insight, an insight that he had defended by producing an array of biblical passages which, in his view, supported his claims. It was thus essential that mainstream puritans definitively shut down the scriptural validity of this argument, particularly since Eaton, Towne, and others used it to establish themselves as ultraorthodox, protestantizing reformers.[2]

This was not especially difficult, for the Bible is of course replete with references in which God appears to take offense at the sins of his children. In this vein, for instance, Richard Sibbes adduced Hosea 14: 4, "I will heale their backesliding, I will love them freely, for mine Anger is turned away from him," in order to prove that God loved his saints, freely and in spite of their sins, yet at the same time took notice of those sins. In Sibbes's view, this utterly confounded those "who thinke that God sees no sinne, when he hath once pardoned men in Justification." As he inquired of his audience, "how

---

[2] See, for instance, Peter Gunter, *A Sermon Preached in the Countie of Suffolk, before the Clergie and Laytie, for the discoverie and confutation of certaine strange, pernicious, and Hereticall Positions, publickely delivered, held, and maintayned, touching Justification, by a certaine factious Preacher of Wickam Market* (1615), 5 and passim.

can God heale that he sees not?" He thus concluded that the antinomian position was simply false, judged from a biblical standpoint. On Sibbes's account, the antinomians sought to "Blindfold [God] and cast dust (as it were) in his eyes."[3] Henry Burton agreed that their doctrine made "God like a blinde man, who seeth not those thinges, which he knoweth." He similarly adduced the words of David from Psalm 69: 5, "Thou knowest my foolishnesse, and my sins are not hid from thee," to demonstrate that the sins of a justified saint were visible to God.[4] In much the same way, Thomas Taylor cited examples from the Psalms and from the New Testament epistles to show that both David and Paul confessed their sins after they were justified. He thus asked his antinomian opponents, "Doth he work in us the knowledge of our sinnes, and hee not know them? Nay doth he enjoyne the Saints to set before his eye daily there sinnes in the humble confession of them and prayer for pardon?"[5]

Such scriptural evidence could be bolstered with logical arguments—above all by the claim that Eatonist doctrine contradicted and violated God's omniscience—and through the deployment of select patristic or reformed authorities. Thus Obadiah Sedgwick, one of London's most renowned godly preachers, took a moment to explain to his listeners how, precisely, sin was "covered" before God in the process of imputation:

> How doth God cover it? Doth he soe cover it as that he can not see it in his Children? Noe: I will demand this, whether the thoughts that are in men are not obvious to the discerning power of god: the reason is because the sight of god doth not stand at a distance from the Acts of the Creature, you can not Close up any thing from the omniscience of god, sin may be seene either with the eye of vengeance or with the eye of gods mercy. The sins of gods Children are free from the sight of gods vengeance. Therfore Austen saith god is said not to see sin when he doth not punish it, but yet they are seene by the eye of his mercy.[6]

Taylor rehearsed this argument in almost identical terms, writing that although "God cannot but see with the eye of his simple knowledge," yet "he

---

[3] Richard Sibbes, *The Returning Backslider, or, a Commentary upon the whole XIIII. Chapter of the Prophecy of the Prophet Hosea* (1639), 170. These sermons were preached at some point prior to 1632, when they were licensed for press.

[4] Burton, *The Law and the Gospell reconciled. Or, The Evangelicall Fayth, and the Morall Law How they Stand Together in the State of Grace* (1631), 68.

[5] Thomas Taylor, *Regula Vitae, The Rule of Law under the Gospel* (1631), 94, and more generally 88-96.

[6] British Library, Harleian MS. 1198, fol. 9r. Punctuation has been added to this passage for the sake of clarity.

sees not with his *judiciary* eye: so he sees not the sins of the elect with the eye of severity; hee discernes the sinne, but not with purpose of revenge."[7]

Similar clusters of scriptural evidence were adduced to undercut that second antinomian shibboleth—the claim that the Law was somehow abolished for believers. Not surprisingly, mainstream puritans here invoked the legacy of "Paul the moralist." Thus, against the antinomian tendency to cite the Epistle to the Galatians, Thomas Taylor responded in kind with a citation from Romans: "Christian liberty is not a freedome from the *obedience* of [the Law], but rather from the *disobedience* of it: *Rom.* 6. 18. *Being free from sinne, ye are made the servants of righteousnesse:* We are *called to liberty*, but we must not *use our liberty as an occasion to the flesh*; but to frame to the commandement, *By love to serve one another, Gal:* 5: 13. Where the Apostle plainely proveth, that Christian liberty looseth us not from the observation of the Law, but straitly enjoyneth it."[8] So too, Burton chided his antinomian opponents with Paul's strenuous moral "commandments" from I Thessalonians, in which the Apostle had urged his readers to "abstaine from fornication." Such ethical commandments were proof positive, Burton argued, that Paul had pressed true believers to obey the Moral Law, for "Abstinence from fornication is part of keeping of the Morall Law."[9] Here, once again, godly ministers were reasserting their fundamental belief that the Moral Law and the various ethical injunctions of the New Testament—including the commandments to love—were in essence identical. To prove this point, they had mobilized Saint Paul against himself, exploiting the gnomic, moralizing elements of the Apostle's writings in an effort to undermine the antinomian expropriation of his more overtly anti-legal statements. In this, they were merely reiterating the logic of mainstream puritanism, which, as we have seen, persistently sought to reconcile seemingly contradictory aspects of the New Testament within a tense unity.

All of this suggests that the antinomians and their opponents had elaborated a series of stock scriptural arguments by which they answered one another's claims. Thus, Burton provided a handlist of their "ussual evasions and distinctions," informing the reader of the habitual responses with which antinomians greeted the criticisms of their mainstream opponents.[10] Nor was Burton far from the truth; the Eatonists do indeed appear to have crafted a series of canned answers to the most frequent objections against their opinions. This suggests that by the early 1630s, the contests between antinomians and their opponents had produced what might be called "polemical commonplaces,"

---

[7] Taylor, *Regula Vitae*, 89.
[8] Ibid., 165-66.
[9] Burton, *Law and the Gospell*, 31-32.
[10] Ibid., 68-70.

that is, recurring and standard motifs of argumentation and disputation that could be quickly produced to silence or attack an enemy.[11] These commonplaces readily diffused into the wider godly community. Consequently, when the London haberdasher Henry Church attacked an unnamed correspondent for maintaining the crypto-antinomian position that the elect were not guilty of sin, he was able to proffer a whole series of stock scriptural arguments to the opposite effect, anticipating at least one response that (at least on Burton's account) was routinely deployed by "The Adversaries," that is, "The *Eatonists*."[12] Church's comments strongly suggest that the piecemeal polemical campaign conducted by mainstream puritans had in fact achieved its desired effect: the haberdasher knew what constituted antinomianism, he knew how to counter it from scripture, and he knew, most importantly, that it was flat heresy.

For many members of the godly community, including Church, the notion that anti-legal religion amounted to nothing more than a satanic conspiracy may have come as something of a relief. Men and women who had enjoyed years of comfort and assurance walking the puritan path to salvation would in all probability have seen antinomianism as an unwelcome nuisance. It challenged the truths on which they had grounded their faith, thus calling into question their prior religious experiences. For mainstream ministers, it was therefore essential not just to negate the scriptural premises of antinomianism, but to reassert in a robust manner the fundamental aspects of puritan practical divinity.

Thus, we find Thomas Taylor reasserting the notion that "Faith it selfe in the justified is *sincere*, but not *perfect* . . . yea even in the best faith is imperfect, and mingled with doubting."[13] This doctrine was, as we have seen, at the center of the system of puritan pastoral divinity. For many godly people—that is, those who felt nagging doubts as to their own salvation, but who had nevertheless arrived at a settled assurance concerning their spiritual estate—this commonplace could serve as a comforting validation of their own struggle with doubt and fear. It could thus be mustered to discredit antinomian solutions, which, as we have seen, claimed to give believers full and unadulterated assurance. Similarly, mainstream puritans attempted to recapture the important pastoral motif of "the dead faith," which Eaton had so brazenly pilfered:

---

[11] Cf. Eaton, *The Honey-Combe of Free Justification* (1642), 163-65, and Appendix E, below, in which Eachard duplicated a polemical response that had been dealt with by Eaton, anticipating the scriptural objection from Romans 8 that since the spirit mortified our sins daily, the spirit must consequently *see* our sins. Compare also Eaton, *Honey-Combe*, 92-93, with Burton, 68.

[12] H. Church, *Divine and Christian Letters* (1636), 23-24. Cf. Burton, *Law and the Gospell*, 68.

[13] Taylor, *Regula Vitae*, 75.

"why doe they exclaime against us for preaching and embracing a *dead faith*, while they obtrude on their proselites a faith which must not work by love; which if they will beleeve S. *James*, is a *dead faith*."[14] Here, Taylor unapologetically reclaimed the time-honored puritan assumption that the true and lively faith was a faith that produced good works, thereby rescuing a familiar and deeply ingrained pietistic assumption that would have been instantly recognizable to seasoned professors.

The reader will likewise recall that one of the attributes of this true, living faith was that it was always increasing, always growing. In this vein, Henry Burton told his antinomian opponents that "though the state of grace bee a glorious estate, as being an initiation of glory, being begun here in the soule: yet wee goe from one degree of glory and grace unto another, and never attaine to full perfection, till *this mortall life shall put on immortality, and this corruption shall put on incorruption* . . . the state of grace is in a perpetuall growth here."[15] This was merely to reiterate the long-standing puritan assumption that although believers were wholly justified by faith, their sanctification remained imperfect throughout this life. Sin disappeared slowly over time, as the Christian grew upward in a process of spiritual edification that ended only in death. This was a lifelong, incremental process. It demanded a strenuous, incessant application of the means of grace, together with continuing repentance at every turn. As Taylor reminded his opponents, "never can man be free from repentance, till he be free from sinne to be repented of; which can never be shaken off in this world. The whole life is but one day of repentance, and repentance is the work of that whole day; and who but a profane libertine would not have his Master find him *so doing*?"[16] So likewise, Taylor reiterated the puritan commitment to the external means and ordinances, which were taken to be the vehicle through which God dispensed his grace in time: "Is it a good reason, that because Christ is the principall efficient, and the onely meritorious cause of our salvation; that therefore all the instrumentall and adjuvant causes and means of salvation must be cutt off and cast away? . . . or is it such a peece of popery to say, that the use of the meanes doth further the end?"[17]

At almost every point, then, the primary apologists for mainstream puritanism reasserted with even greater vehemence and clarity the norms of puritan practical divinity. In doing so, they ensured that devoted professors could continue on, confident in the knowledge that the pietistic habits and spiritual comforts they had enjoyed were in fact genuine. This is not to say that puritan

---

[14] Ibid., 69.
[15] Burton, *Law and the Gospell*, 36. See also Taylor, *Regula Vitae*, 131-33.
[16] Ibid., 108-9.
[17] Ibid., 81.

divinity remained utterly unchanged by the antinomian challenge; in fact, as we shall see in the Conclusion, there are hints that the anti-legal critique prompted certain intellectual realignments within the wider godly community. Nevertheless, it remains the case that when engaged in head-to-head polemical debate with antinomian foes, puritans tended to cling to time-honored and well-established modes of divinity. In doing so, they were in essence arguing from past success, or rather, appealing to those members of the godly community who had benefited from the existing regime of pastoral care.

Heretics

Where scriptural proof-texts were deemed to be insufficient, puritan apologists resorted to rather more incendiary polemical devices. First and foremost among these was the tendency to assimilate antinomianism to some prior manifestation of the heretical spirit. This was of course a standard theological ploy, widely used by both protestant and Catholic polemicists in order to discredit opponents. In this manner, new and distasteful opinions could be lumped together with long-dead heresies; in England, for instance, Calvinists tarred Arminians with the brush of Pelagianism, non-separating puritans portrayed separatists as Donatists, and anti-puritans sought to equate Calvinism with Arianism. Here, the antinomians proved to be sitting ducks. Henry Burton charged that "they revive the heresie of the Montanistes, who denied repentance to be needeful."[18] The Northamptonshire preacher Joseph Bentham fulminated at greater length, asking his notional antinomian opponents,

> What intoxicated madness, or giddy vertigiousnesse hath possessed your hearts and heads? What shall I tearme you? *Cerdoniani, Cainitae, Marcionists, Apellitae, Severiani, Manichees, Architae, Patricii? You I meane* who fence, and hedge out the regenerate from without the Old Testament, so farre forth as you may or can: For, prove unto you that God doth afflict his Children for their sinnes, that sorrow for sinne is necessary to the regenerate (points which you deny) the former by *Davids* suffering for his sinne with *Bathsheba*; the latter by his watering his couch with his teares: you reply, they were under the Law, in the time of the Old Testament. *You I meane*, who crie out against the Morall Law, as once the *Babylonians* did against *Jerusalem*, downe with it, downe with it even to the ground: away with the law, it belongs not to the regenerate man. It binds not the conscience of him that is in Christ: You equivocating *Pretteians*, *Antinomists*, I doe not say you are *Marcionists*, *Manichees*, or the like in all particulars; but in this you walke cheeke by joale, hand in hand with those forenamed heretikes. *They* condemned the morall law, so doe you. *They* denied the resurrection of the

---

[18] Burton, *Law and the Gospell*, 35. See also William Hinde, *The Office and Use of the Morall Law of God in the dayes of the Gospell*, 2d ed. (1623), 3-4.

body, and I much suspect that this is one of those other deeper doctrines, you were promised to be indoctrinated in.[19]

Here, Bentham took the liberty of linking Eaton and his kind in an age-old lineage of (mainly Gnostic) error, which dated back to the second century A.D. He further drove the point home by labeling them, according to time-honored heresiographical practice, by the name of their Northamptonshire ringleader, the young minister Samuel Prettie. Bentham echoed Burton in implying that these "equivocating Pretteians" were prone to shifts and evasions. In this vein, he enthusiastically speculated that, although they never said so in public, in truth Prettie and his colleagues maintained a secret and closely guarded mortalism.

In this, Bentham was doing more than simply smearing antinomianism with the taint of Gnostic error; he was invoking the spirit of HN, for as we have seen in examining the articles against Peter Shaw, denial of the resurrection was widely regarded as one of the archetypal errors associated with the Family of Love. Indeed, almost all puritan polemicists echoed Bentham's charge. They repeatedly reminded their readers that this was not the first time antinomianism had infected English soil in recent memory, and they sought to portray their anti-legal critics as nothing more than the impish spawn of HN.[20] Edward Norice, for instance, cited HN's *Evangelium Regni* to show that Traske's cryptic statement on the guiding power of God's love "savours strongly of Familisme, who blasphemously say, that God is manned, and man is Godded, with such like, making no difference betweene the essentiall attributes of the Almighty, and the workes and effects of his Spirit in men."[21] Taylor, too, believed he could detect in the opinions of his antinomian opponents "the ghost of H.N."[22]

Even when Niclaes's name was not mentioned, puritan polemicists tried to force antinomian opinions into a preconceived "perfectionist" mold. Thus, Henry Burton argued that John Eaton's imputative antinomianism was indistinguishable from the argument "that there is such a perfection in this life, as a man may live altogether without sin."[23] This was, of course, an outright manipulation of his opponent's words, for as we have seen, Eaton never denied that believers would sin, claiming that their perfection was merely in God's sight. Even those who recognized that there were significant distinctions be-

---

19 Joseph Bentham, *The Societie of the Saints: Or, a Treatise of Good-fellows* (1630), 182-83.

20 This strategy had been used to counter Eaton from the very beginning. See Gunter, *A Sermon*, 3-4.

21 Norice, *The New Gospel, Not the True Gospel* (1638), 2, 18.

22 Taylor, *Regula Vitae*, 76-77.

23 Burton, *Law and the Gospell*, 16-17.

tween imputative antinomianism and Familism nevertheless tended to elide the two. Thus, in a sermon preached in 1638, Stephen Denison warned that "heresy is a Deceitfull thing. . . . So are many Deceived in these dayes that wee live in Some by . . . popery Some by the way of the familists and of the Antimonians [sic] some in the way of the Anabaptist. Some in the way of the Brownists."[24] Denison knew very well that classic Familism was in many ways distinct from the forms of antinomianism that had emerged in London in the 1620s; nevertheless, he chose to compress them into a single category of error, a single "way" of heresy.

As we have seen, these accusations were not entirely without merit. There were, as demonstrated above, perfectionist elements within antinomianism. Indeed, some of these perfectionist motifs do in fact appear to have entered the antinomian underground through the influence of Familism, which continued to survive in pockets at the very margins of the antinomian community. Nevertheless, to conflate all forms of antinomianism under the rubric of "Familism" was certainly a distortion, albeit a distortion that allowed for considerable polemical advantage. By casting their anti-legal opponents as nothing more than reincarnated Familists, godly spokesmen managed to slur the entire anti-legal critique by associating it with its most extreme, and least representative, manifestation.

There is good reason to believe that such tactics proved effective. By the end of the 1630s, most godly laypeople seem to have been cognizant of the dangers of antinomianism. Many, including Henry Church, felt comfortable in denouncing anti-legalists as rank heretics (rather than pitiable, erring brethren), a shift that attests to the success of ministers such as Denison and Bentham. One final example will serve to illustrate the point. In 1641, the incorrigibly godly Robert Greville, Lord Brooke, published his well-known denunciation of the existing episcopal system of church government. One of the arguments he sought to counter was the idea that bishops were necessary to maintain uniformity and to contain schism and heresy. In answering this objection, Greville evinced a typically puritan conviction that the end was nigh, and he thus came to consider a particularly apocalyptic passage from the Pauline 2 Tim. 3:

> This know also, that in the last days perilous times shall come. For men shall be lovers of their own selves . . . despisers of those that are good, Traitors, heady highminded lovers of pleasures more than lovers of God; Having a form of godliness, but denying the power thereof: from such turn away. For this sort are they which creep into houses, and lead captive silly women

[24] American Antiquarian Society, Worcester, MA, MS. Sermon Notes, Denison (1637-39), fols. 24r-v.

> laden with sins, led away with divers lusts. Ever learning, and never able to come to the knowledge of the truth.

Brooke noted that some might be tempted to apply this prophecy to the Papists, "the corrupter part of the Prelates," or the Arminians. This, he argued was a mistake. For all their faults, Laudian Bishops were not the heretics of the last days. As he argued,

> The maine Thing in which these men (here exprest) pride themselves, is not Learning, or Parts; But (if I bee not much mistaken) somewhat beyond and within all these: That, I suppose, which seemes to them to bee the Spirit. This, I conceive, is the *Basis* of all their vanity, pride, and insolence. They have the Spirit, and so know more than all the Learned, Pious, Godly Men in the world. They have the Spirit, they cannot sinne, they cannot erre; they will not pray, but when the Spirit moves. *Adultery* is but an act of the Flesh, but they are all Spirit, and no flesh. What should these men doe with Naturall affections, they are all Spirit? in this case if they be Traitors, High-minded, Heady, etc. Who will wonder? What may they not be carried up to, by the imagination of the Spirit?

Nor, he argued, did the bishops steal into dark corners, furtively seducing credulous women into error. As he saw it, prelates relied on a frank and brutal "club law" to accomplish their ends. The prophecy, Brooke therefore concluded, must refer to another group:

> It seems very probable to me, that the Holy Ghost in This text points out some such, as the *Family of Love*, the *Antinomians*, and *Grindletonians* are, if (at least) they are not much belyed. And to these, I think, every piece of This Character will most properly belong. Yea and the Close of it also, or the Issue of That Sect. *They shall proceed no farther, for their folly shall be made manifest to all men* . . . Thus you see *Sects*, *Schismes*, and *Heresies* will still come, and must come: And therefore if by keeping such Bishops we think to keep out all Divisions, we are much deceived.[25]

Brooke thus wove together multiple arguments: first, he suggested there was no avoiding heresy and division, for God's plan demanded that such heresies must arise in the last days; secondly, he argued that the bishops with their coercive "club law" had no hope of stopping the spread of such sects and heresies (implicitly, he was adducing as proof of this conclusion the fact that antinomianism had spread, quietly but undeniably, during a period of intense episcopal oversight); finally, it is clear that Brooke, like many other godly layfolk, had come to see antinomianism (here conflated with Familism) as a per-

---

25 Robert Greville, *A Discourse Opening the Nature of that Episcopacie, which is Exercised in England* (1641), 92-93.

nicious and heretical sect, the emergence of which augured the final phase of human history.

Fear of Social Breakdown

In the last resort, puritan polemicists appealed to fear of moral and social breakdown. Antinomianism, they argued, was the first unstable step down a slippery slope that would end in unadulterated libertinism. Without a law to bridle unruly lusts, what other outcome was possible? Here, again, earlier disputes over the Family of Love loomed large, for accusations of libertinism, and in particular, sexual license, had been an intimate part of anti-Familist discourse.[26] Taylor summed up the logic behind this polemical strategy: "for a man to say, that God can no way see the sinnes of beleevers, is to open a wide gate to all libertinisme, epicurisme, atheisme, and whatsoever else is an enemy to the fear of God, and the awefull regard of his all-seeing eye." He further asked, "with what violence must headstrong men be caryed unto unrighteousnesse, when the word as a bridle must not hold them in, nor check or controll sinne in the soule, to lessen either the power or practise of it?"[27] Burton asked the very same question: "For perswade a man once, that being in Christ, and so justified from all his sins, hee hath no more neede of repentance: and what a flood-gate is opened to all impiety, when there is no more conscience of sin?" From his standpoint, the antinomians' doctrines served merely to "nuzzle them in their carnall lusts."[28] Edward Norice went further; he accused some of John Traske's followers of "falling into ingemniated adulteries, to the great scandall of the truth (they seemed to professe) yet not shewing the least remorse for the same themselves . . . but with this come-off in a merry manner, that, if a man be in Christ, no sinne shall hurt him."[29] Indeed, Norice insinuated that Traske's gospel of joy was not quite as harmlessly holy as the antinomian leader had claimed. On Norice's account "as [Traske] professed nothing but mirth and jollity [in religion]; so in his private carriage was he as frollicke, especially with that sexe, in which hee most delighted, towards whom hee used such familiarity, with his embracings and tongue fornications, with such other proffers, as they that were modest, utterly abhorred his private society, and complained thereof secretly to their friends as very foule and shamefull." What Norice meant by "tongue fornications" is not entirely clear,

[26] See, for instance, Henoch Clapham, *Errour on the Right Hand, Through a Preposterous Zeale* (1608), 53-55.
[27] Taylor, *Regula Vitae*, 90-91, 142.
[28] Burton, *Law and the Gospell*, 35.
[29] Norice, *New Gospel*, 3.

but he was if nothing else certain that they were "Agreeable to *Ovids* filthy instructions, and the religion of H.N."[30]

There is, of course, no way to assess such accusations. If the antinomians are to be judged solely on the basis their writings, there would seem to be little question that such charges were nothing more than polemically motivated libel. All of the antinomian spokesmen examined in this study claimed that the truly faithful would, in fact, do good works. Freedom from the Law meant righteousness in the spirit. From the antinomian perspective, the insinuations of Taylor, Burton, and Norice merely served to prove their point; mainstream puritans, as they argued, were driven by a slavish, legal fear of punishment. The fact that they needed a law, and could not imagine righteousness apart from and without fear of punishment, was proof positive that they had no understanding of Christianity. True believers needed no external compulsion, for they had somehow been rewrought by an internal principle.

This, at least, was the theory. In point of fact, it seems that in certain cases, antinomianism did become associated with modes of behavior—above all, sexual behavior—that challenged societal norms. When, for instance, the High Commissioners discovered that Joan and Richard Lane had had "carnall use and knowledge of each others bodyes" prior to their marriage, resulting in pregnancy, they demanded of her an explanation. As the Act Book reported it, "Shee the said Joane being demaunded by the Court why shee suffered the said Richard Lane to have the use of her body before marriage, answered, I could not resist the power of God," a response perfectly crafted to confirm the worst suspicions of her judges.[31] This was certainly an unusual—not to mention ill-advised—answer, which suggested that the Lanes did in fact draw some connection between their perfectionism and sexual freedom. It is also true, however, that it was common practice for early modern English people to engage in sexual relations out of wedlock, marrying only when courtship was consummated in pregnancy.[32] While her excuse thus suggested a genuine, theologically motivated libertinism, the actual practice in which Joan and Richard had indulged was hardly one that threatened to turn the social order on its head. It seems, moreover, that Joan's attempt to link spiritual freedom with sexual freedom was atypical.[33] For instance, the diary of Edward Howes,

---

[30] Ibid., 5-6.

[31] CUL MS. Dd. ii. 21, fol., 107v. For comments on the credibility of the High Commission records in this case, see Appendix C, below.

[32] I would like to thank Michael Mendle for reminding me of this fact.

[33] For the other major example from the period in which antinomian theological beliefs were used to justify sexual promiscuity, see the case of John Underhill of New England (M. Winship, *Making Heretics: Militant Protestantism and Free Grace in Massachusetts, 1636-1641* [Princeton: Princeton University Press, 2002], 154-55).

a man who apparently considered himself a follower of HN, suggests that for at least one individual, Familist perfectionism led not to sexual license, but to an intense struggle against the lusts of the flesh.

Where the fear of moral breakdown was judged inadequate, godly polemicists could play what might be termed "the class card." Thus, Thomas Taylor drew on Calvin to imply "That whereas other heresies were raised, and defended by men of learning, wit, education, and reading: this was set on foot, and maintained by ideots, rude, and illiterate men, that never learned their *frensie* by turning bookes, but in some coblers or artificers shops and places of rude resort."[34] Sibbes, too, alleged from the pulpit that antinomianism was "an error crept in amongst some of the meaner sort of people."[35] Such statements were of course designed in part to discredit the learning and theological credentials of leading antinomians; at bottom, however, they also appealed to upper- and middling- fears of the lower orders, conjuring up the dim but striking image of a Münster-like slaughter. Thus, preaching at St. Bartholomew by the Exchange, Samuel Torshel warned his listeners that "then are the *Anabaptists* mad, who would reject all law, and make the whole world levell; denying obedience to Lawes and lawfull Magistrates, a disease begun in the distempered heads of *John of Leiden*, and the mad men of *Munster*, opposed by the holy zeale of *Luther*, whose doctrine of Reformation was dangerously mistaken by those fanatickes: which I rather note, because some halfe issues of that monstrous Birth, call that blessed Apostle of our latter times, to patronize their conceits and errours about the morall Law."[36]

This inflammatory style of polemic was denounced by John Everarde in a private sermon at Kensington. Here, he invented a stereotypical creature called "Doctor Honour" in order to sum up the accusations of his opponents:

> then comes Doctor *Honour*; and sayes he, what need all this stir about Religion? canst not thou be content to go the *old* way thy fore-fathers went? canst not thou be content to go that way the *State* goes, that way that *Kings* and *Princes*, and *Great* men go? then shalt thou walk safely, and enjoy *thine own*, and be honoured for a *wise* man, *a prudent* man, do not the most go this way? and though thou art not so forward in Religion, thou shalt do as well as they: there is none but a company of poor *beggarly* fellows, *Tinkers* and *Coblers*, and schismatical and conceited fellows that are so hot, and they are every where despised; as it was said in *dirision* the last day, that there

[34] Taylor, *Regula Vitae*, 61-62.

[35] Sibbes, *Returning Backslider*, 170.

[36] S. Torshel, *The Three Questions of Free Justification* (1632), 66-67. This treatise was based on sermons preached in London.

> was none came *running* out of the City to hear me, but a company of *Coblers* and *slight* fellows.[37]

Since it was ludicrous to try to attack Everarde's learning and social status, the doctor's detractors appear to have modified this mode of polemic to discredit his followers.

In all of this, mainstream puritans appear to have been playing fast and loose with the truth. As we have seen, what little evidence we now possess suggests that antinomianism was not, by and large, a heresy of the lower orders. With the exception of Traske, Brearley, and the tailor-preacher Greene, its leading spokesmen were all university-trained divines. The Grindletonians appear to have found support amongst well-heeled country squires as well as poor sheepshearers. Creech's list of Familists and antinomians named men and women from all walks of London life. In short, the composition of the antinomian underground, both in the city and in the Yorkshire dales, appears to have mirrored that of mainstream puritanism, drawing support from every stratum of London society.

Puritans, Laudians, and the Uses of Heresy

Here, we have arrived at the final key to understanding the godly assault on antinomianism. A careful examination of the words he placed in the obsequious mouth of Doctor Honour reveals that the mode of discourse Everarde caricatured was not specifically or exclusively crafted to attack antinomianism; in fact, it was merely a restatement of a certain style of polemic that had always been used by the *enemies* of the godly to stir up fears of puritan subversion. And here we find another clue to the vehemence with which the godly moved to suppress antinomianism: so far as Laudians were concerned, antinomianism was nothing more than puritanism in its most naked and unadulterated form. It was thus absolutely necessary that mainstream puritans stifle this mutiny in their own ranks and disassociate themselves from its authors. To do otherwise was to play into the hands of an increasingly anti-puritan establishment that was only too happy to use antinomianism as a polemical weapon against the godly in general.

In the eyes of anti-Calvinists, the doctrine of unconditional predestination was, ipso facto, antinomian. By inculcating an absolute assurance of eternal election, it led naturally to a profound moral presumptuousness. Thus, the Laudian cleric and poet William Strode served up a scurrilous verse attack on "The Townes new Teacher" who with "Pate Cut shorter then the brow / With little ruffe starch't you know how," drove his auditors to despair with his "doctrine newly brought." Such doctrine led to nothing but hypocritical self-

---

[37] Everard, *Some Gospel-Treasures Opened* (1653), 66-67.

righteousness: "With boldnes in predestination / With threats of absolute damnation / With certainty of somes salvation / Of his owne Tribe not every Nation." Yet the result was not holiness, but moral license: "Good workes for Popery downe banged / All Morrall Lawes from him estranged / Except the Saboth still unchanged."[38] By the late 1620s, this strand of argument had become almost axiomatic among Laudian sympathizers. Thus, even as the godly in London were fighting their battles over the Moral Law, the irascible anti-puritan Giles Widdowes was busily lampooning what he called "*The Presuming Predestinatist* . . . he, whose purenes is an inspired knowledge, that hee shal be saved by Gods absolute election. He is so sure of his salvation, as if he were now in heaven: as if there were no life in him, but Gods essentiall glory. This is to sin without feare or wit."[39] In its basic structure, this style of argumentation mirrored almost perfectly the mainstream puritan line on antinomianism, with one crucial exception: it contended that not only full-blown anti-legalists, but *all* predestinarian puritans were guilty of a de facto antinomianism that would slide inevitably into outright libertinism. In late 1629, preaching from the pulpit of St. Paul's, John Donne had likewise criticized those who

> in an over-valuation of their own purity despise others as men whom nothing can save [and] will abridge and contract the large mercies of God in Christ, and elude and frustrate in a great part the general promises of God. Men that are loth that God should speak so loud as to say 'He would have all men saved,' and loth that Christ should spread his armes or shed his blood in such a compasse as might fall upon all. Men that think no sinne can hurt them because they are elect and that every sin makes every other man a reprobate. But with the Lord there is *copiosa redemptio*, plentifull redemption, and an overflowing cup of mercy.[40]

It is crucial to understand that these words, uttered from the capital's most exalted and public pulpit with the approval of Bishop Laud of London were part of a much larger struggle over the doctrine of predestination. This struggle has been amply documented by Nicholas Tyacke and requires no further elaboration here.[41] By late 1629, it was a battle that the godly were losing, as

---

[38] Bodleian Library, Rawlinson MS. d. 398, fol. 249r. For Strode's fierce loyalty to Laud, see *The Poetical Works of William Strode (1600-1645)*, ed. Bertram Dobell (London: Privately Printed, 1907), xxv-xxviii.

[39] Giles Widdowes, *The Schysmatical Puritan* (1630), sig. C2v.

[40] Donne's sermon cited from N. Tyacke, *Anti-Calvinists: The Rise of English Arminianism, c. 1590-1640* (Oxford: Oxford University Press, 1987; Revised paperback edition, Oxford: Oxford University Press, 1990), 182.

[41] Ibid., passim.

Arminianizing sacramentalists gained an ever stronger foothold within the Caroline church.

Laudian polemicists were in essence claiming that Calvinist predestinarianism lured its adherents into a state of amoral presumption that absolved them of all duties to God and King. Indeed, this argument could be used to explain the escalating political tensions that had left the Parliament of 1628/29 in a confused shambles. As Samuel Brooke, the Arminian master of Trinity College expressed it to Laud in 1630: "I dare say that their doctrine of Predestination is the roote of Puritanisme and Puritanisme the roote of all rebellions and disobedient intractableness in Parliaments etc. and all schisme and sauciness in the Countrey, nay in the church, itself. This hath made so many thousands of our people and so great a part of the gentlemen of the Land Laytons in their hearts."[42] This was, of course, a grossly misshapen argument, one that overlooked the fact that the highest echelons of the Church of England had always been stocked with committed Calvinists, including the sitting Archbishop of Canterbury. Nevertheless, it was an argument that allowed Laudian divines to appeal to the King's already well-formed suspicions about puritan popularity and subversiveness, thus further undermining the already tenuous political position of the godly at court.

Here, the emergence of antinomianism provided the Laudians with further ammunition. Now, anti-puritans could point to men and women such as Richard and Joan Lane as evidence that their claims about godly presumption had always been true. Predestination, puritanism, and flat libertinism could be linked in a tight, polemical chain, which could then be used as a weapon to flog the godly in press and pulpit. In 1637, for instance, while delivering a fierce attack on the godly celebrity Henry Burton, the London Arminian Christopher Dow charged that even as they outwardly professed allegiance to the Church of England, puritans in fact "erected a *new Church* both for *doctrine* and *discipline* far differing from the true and ancient *English Church*." The godly counted "themselves the *wheat* among the *tares*...monopolizing the names of *Christians*, *Gods children*, *Professors*, and the like." This arrogant and self-righteous presumption allowed them to exclude and denigrate all those outside the magic circle of the godly community: "As for all other men they account them no better than *Pagans*, or *heathens, baptized with outward Baptisme*, which, as one of them once expressed it in a Sermon, (though I tremble to relate it) did no more to the making of them *Christians*, than the

---

[42] PRO, SPD 16/177/8, fol. 13r. December 15, 1630. For "Layton" or Alexander Leighton, the radical puritan minister/medical doctor, see S. Foster, *Notes from the Caroline Underground: Alexander Leighton, the Puritan Triumvirate and the Laudian Reaction to Nonconformity* (Hamden, CT: Archon Books, 1978).

washing of a *dogges legge*."[43] Here, in a wonderully ironic bit of polemical bad sportsmanship, Dow had attributed to all puritans the tendentious baptismal errors of none other than Peter Shaw. Dow had been one of the signatories of the articles against Shaw, and it was no doubt during the latter man's investigation and trial that Dow had encountered the allegation that Shaw had preached "That the outward washing of water in Baptisme, is no more then the washing or dipping of a doggs foote in water."[44] Dow thus imputed to all puritans an opinion held by a single antinomian extremist, a polemical move that was all the more audacious given the fact that his ostensible target, Henry Burton, had been one of the most ferocious opponents of London's antinomians during the conflicts of 1628-31. For Dow, however, this seemingly disingenuous maneuver was no doubt justifiable precisely because Shaw seemed little more than an archetypal, unburnished, predestinarian puritan.

In the late 1620s, Richard Burgess, vicar of Witney in Oxfordshire, had taken this line of reasoning one step further, unabashedly conflating puritanism with Familism. As part of what appears to have been a dispute with his more godly parishioners, Burgess allegedly began to deliver biting satirical attacks on puritans when he catechized the youth of the town. In one of his more spectacular outbursts, he defined the godly as

> these black mouthed barkinge byteinge doggs, that barke against the Kinge, against the bishopps and the governors of the Church . . . in everie Citie, in everie towne, yea almost in everie parish, there bee some of these doggs which will shortlie overspread the land, like the froggs of Egipt, and cause it to stincke unles there bee present order taken against them. I have heard some of these Puritanicall Preachers affirme, that everie godlie man is a God, and everie Christian is a Christ; which yf it bee soe, I hope God can see noe sinn in a Puritan knave; but I that am but a weake man can.[45]

Having obtained copies of Burgess's "catechism" and "paraphrase," one of his parishioners denounced him before the Parliament of 1628, and he accordingly found himself under investigation by John Pym's Committee on Religion.[46] It is no surprise that he so incensed godly MPs; Burgess was here

---

[43] Christopher Dow, *Innovations Unjustly Charged upon the Present Church and State* (1637), 197.

[44] D. Como and P. Lake, "Puritans, Antinomians and Laudians in Caroline London: The Strange Case of Peter Shaw in its Contexts," *Journal of Ecclesiastical History*, 50 (1999), article 33.

[45] British Library, Harleian MS. 1219, fol. 305v. This appears to be a transcript of the notes jointly taken by a number of his parishioners, who were subsequently questioned by the House of Commons.

[46] R. C. Johnson, M. Frear Keeler, M. Jansson Cole, W. B. Bidwell, eds., *Commons Debates 1628* (New Haven: Yale U.P., 1977), 3: 131-32, 260, 615, 617-18;

equating puritanism with Familist antinomianism, and suggesting that such religiosity led inexorably to open sedition, a rhetorical move that could hardly meet with the approval of men such as Pym, particularly at a moment of suffocating tension between crown and parliament.

Yet Burgess was in good company. Archbishop Laud himself wholeheartedly embraced this same line of reasoning. In 1641, to answer Lord Saye's parliamentary attack on the church liturgy, Laud set out to refute Saye's charge that separatists agreed with the Church of England in all fundamental points of doctrine. To Laud's eyes, this was patently untrue. To prove his point, he cited "one *Brierly* and his independent Congregation," who held "*That the Child of God, in the Power of Grace, doth perform every Duty so well, that to ask Pardon for failing, either in matter or manner, is a Sin* [and] *That it is unlawfull to pray for Forgiveness of Sins, after their Conversion.*" He likewise noted "*One Spisberrye*" (presumably the cobbler and London Baptist leader John Spilsbury), who allegedly held "*that God works all things in us; and that we are but Organs, Instruments, and meer empty Trunks.* Which is to make God the Author of all the Sins which Men commit: And therefore *Brierley* says expressly, *that if they do at any time fall, they can by the power of Grace, carry their Sin to the Lord, and say, here I had it, and here I leave it.* Will not the Devil one day stop the Mouth of this Blasphemy?" Yet Laud did not stop here. He immediately moved from the genuine antinomianism of the Grindletonians to the firm predestinarianism of William Prynne:

> Mr. *Pryn* himself (who hath been a great stickler in these Troubles of the Church) says expressly; *Let any true Saint of God be taken away in the very act of any known Sin, before it is possible for him to Repent; I make no doubt or Scruple of it, but he shall as surely be saved as if he had lived to have repented of it.* . . . So according to this Divinity, the true Saints of God may commit horrible and crying Sins, dye without Repentance, and yet be sure of Salvation; which teareth up the very Foundations of Religion; induceth all manner of Profaneness into the World; and is expressly contrary to the whole current of scripture.[47]

For Laud, then, there was no essential difference between the antinomian Brearley and the Calvinist Prynne. Both were guilty of deviating from the doctrine of the Church of England, and both maintained an identically subversive tendency to absolve the "saints" from all duty to God and government. For Laud, Calvinist predestinarianism was by its very nature antinomian (in the

---

W. Notestein and F. H. Relf, *Commons Debates for 1629 (Minneapolis: University of Minnesota Press, 1921)*, 63, 202.

[47] W. Laud, *The History of the Troubles and Tryall of . . . William Laud*, ed. Henry Wharton (1695), 502-3. Laud was here drawing on his own manuscript copy of the fifty erroneous propositions of the Grindletonians (1616-17).

crudest colloquial sense of that word). It is almost beyond doubt that Laud was seeking to hammer home precisely this point, when, as Robert Towne alleged, the bishop preached an Ash-Wednesday court sermon in which he "told the King and the rest, what a pestilential sect the Antinomians were; and thus he did labour . . . to make the world believe that there are some abolishers of the law, and that these . . . and all others who go in the same way, are such, and so not to be tolerated in the kingdome."[48]

For this reason, mainstream puritans needed to disassociate themselves with all haste from antinomianism. Having failed to silence their anti-legal opponents through private conference and disputation, the godly found it imperative that they shut down their antinomian critics in the pulpit and press. From this perspective, the printed polemical productions of men like Taylor and Burton were designed not simply to discredit their rivals, but to prove that mainstream puritans were themselves loyal subjects, utterly committed to the values of obedience and moral order. When they elided antinomianism with libertinism, or warned of its socially subversive consequences, they were thus addressing a dual audience—on the one hand, the godly laity; on the other hand, the secular and ecclesiastical authorities, most especially King Charles.

Henry Burton's situation illustrates the point. After starting his career as Clerk of the Closet to Prince Charles, during the 1620s Burton became progressively alienated from the policies of the English church. In 1626, he emerged as one of the primary public defenders of the doctrine of predestination during the disputes sparked by Richard Montagu.[49] Frustrated by the changes he saw gripping the church, he apparently moved farther away from the center, until in 1629, he found himself in trouble with the authorities for a series of deeply incendiary statements made from his pulpit at St. Matthew Friday Street. It was alleged "that in a funerall Sermon there by him preached . . . [he] hath contrary to the Canons of the Church of England and peace and quiet thereof much inveyged against the bowing at and yealding reverence to the name of the holy ghost as at the naming of Jesus. . . . And . . . in another Sermon within two months since he tooke occasion to speake of the times and said that men were growne soe idolatrous and fallen into such Superstition that it was a wonder that those who were zealous in Religion did not . . . drawe their swordes and run them through in the very act of their idolatry."[50]

Here was perfect grist for the Laudian propaganda mill—a presuming predestinatist whose self-righteousness led him not just to criticize royal ecclesiastical policy, but to do so in terms that hinted darkly at the appropriateness of violent resistance. We should not be startled, then, to find Burton trying to

---

[48] Robert Towne, *A Re-assertion of Grace. Or Vindiciae Evangelii* (1654), 67.
[49] See H[enry] B[urton], *A Plea to an Appeale: Traversed Dialogue Wise* (1626).
[50] London Met. Archives, DL/C/343, fols. 80r-v, 81r (Vicar-General's Book).

wriggle out of the trap he had built for himself by denouncing antinomianism in 1631. Unsurprisingly, he dedicated his book, *The Law and the Gospell Reconciled* to his old master Charles I. Burton asserted that "these Antinomians cut off all dutifull and conscionable obedience to Princes, grounded on the fifth commandement," and warned that they would "precipitate inevitable ruine to Princes and Commonweales" unless they were swiftly liquidated by King Charles, who was called upon to trample "this Antinomian Anomian heresie, both syre and sonnes, under your sacred feete."[51] In one swift move, Burton hoped to disassociate himself from all taint of disobedience, to restore Charles's confidence in the loyalty and moral rigor of his godly subjects, and to smash what remained of the antinomian resistance to mainstream puritanism. Much the same hope had probably spurred Taylor forward, for he too had been in trouble with the authorities in 1627.[52] Indeed, as Peter Lake and I have argued, similar expectations undoubtedly explained the unlikely coalition that gathered against Peter Shaw, as a whole series of well-known puritans joined hands with notorious London Laudians to eliminate the obstreperous antinomian lecturer of St. Michael Crooked Lane.[53]

This strategy failed miserably. In his threat-letter of 1629, the chandler Joseph Smith had warned the nonconformist Abraham Grame to desist from his intention to draw High Commission articles against Shaw, pointing out that he was unwittingly playing into the hands of the Laudians: "let me tell you, the plott is laid for you. You shall have all faire audience, till you have done your utmost against Shaw, and so soone as that is done, you shalbe the next man that shall tast of the severitie of justice, as some in great place have already discovered & professed. . . . Tis that Arminians and Papists gape for, to see the Puritans, as they terme you, to dash them selves in peices one against another."[54] In short time, Smith's ominous prophecy would be fulfilled with shocking precision. By 1633, repeated confrontations with Laud and the High Commission had made Grame an ecclesiastical outlaw.

He was not alone; in the months following Shaw's prosecution, Nalton, Burges, Crabtree, and Denison would each find themselves hauled before the church courts for non-conformity. Rowland Tompson, a joiner who had testified against both Shaw and John Etherington, would likewise be called before the Ecclesiastical Commissioners.[55] In 1634, Henry Roborough was cited before the same court for preaching on predestination, for denouncing Sunday

---

[51] Burton, *Law and the Gospell*, sigs. A2-A4.

[52] See *CSPD, 1628-9*, 127.

[53] Como and Lake, "Peter Shaw."

[54] PRO, SPD 16/139/91, Fol. 177r. See Como and Lake, "Peter Shaw" for a transcription of the letter.

[55] For details on the legal problems of Grame, Nalton, Burges, Crabtree, Denison, and Tompson, see Como and Lake, "Peter Shaw."

sports and for "endeavoringe to stirr upp the people . . . to dislike and oppose the present governement of the Church." Among Roborough's putative errors was the claim that "Christs intercession saves us from Condemnation, soe as noe sinnes be they never soe haynous shalbe layed to the charge of the Elect, For that Christ had or hath allready acquitted them from the barr of Gods Justice, Soe then lett every Child of God saye there be tenn thousand sinnes that assault me yett I will never faint or doubt, or once stagger in the matter of Salvation." Here, the Commissioners were in essence claiming that Roborough's forthright predestinarianism amounted to a de facto antinomianism (a charge that must have stunned this erstwhile foe of John Etherington).[56] As the authorities tightened the noose of ecclesiastical justice, the godly discovered that their efforts against the antinomians provided no protection from the severity of Laudian conformism. Far from convincing the Caroline authorities of the harmlessness and fealty of the godly, puritan attempts to expose their antinomian opponents appear to have served merely to harden Laudian suspicions that the end result of puritanism was anarchy and lawlessness. Increasingly, mainstream puritans found themselves simultaneously denounced by antinomians as compromising Arminians, and by Laudians as subversive antinomians. The futility of the godly strategy is borne out most clearly by the unfortunate Henry Burton who, in spite of denouncing antinomianism, was subjected to the rigors of Laudian justice in the late 1630s, thus staking out his position on the scaffold of history alongside John Bastwick and Prynne.

In part, however, Burton had determined his own fate, for even in denouncing the antinomians, he could not resist the opportunity to attack Laudian ecclesiastical policy. While genuflecting before the King in his epistle dedicatory, Burton reminded Charles that as monarch his "chiefe care is for the mayntenance of Gods pure worship without mixture, and for the execution of justice and judgement; these two being the summe of both the Tables."[57] There can be little question that in exhorting Charles to maintain "God's pure worship," Burton was here almost certainly adverting to the "idolatrous" ceremonies and observances that he had earlier denounced from the pulpit of St. Matthew's. But above all, he appears to have been referring to the strict observation of the Sabbath, and he thus devoted nearly half of his tract not to the antinomians themselves, but to the question of the continuing morality of the fourth commandment.[58] The Sabbath was, of course, a deeply volatile political issue. One of the primary strategies of the Laudian program involved demolishing puritan Sabbatarianism, a goal that would be institutionalized

---

[56] For the 1634 High Commission articles against Henry Roborough, together with his personal answers, see Trinity College, Dublin MS. 293, fols. 387-401. For the passages cited, see fols. 386v-387r, 389v-390r.

[57] Burton, *Law and the Gospell*, sig. A4r.

[58] Ibid., 38-67.

with the promulgation of the Book of Sports in 1633. Burton was, therefore, using antinomianism partly as a cudgel to attack the Laudians, and partly to remind the king of his duties as a godly prince.

Within Burton's posture of outward obedience, then, there was an implicit criticism of the drift of royal policy, a barely submerged suggestion that the king had been remiss in his duties as "Vicegerent" of God. In this vein, Burton inserted into his treatise the following passage—couched in generality, but clearly intended as a rap on the knuckles for his old acquaintance, Charles:

> And for Princes Edicts we all reverence, and willingly imbrace and obey them. But without limitation? what if they command against God? what if they shall forbid by public Edict the free preaching of the word of God in any part of it, as such and such points of fayth and salvation not to bee handled, such and such heresies not to bee medled with by way of confutation? . . . What? because *Nebuchadnezzer* erected his Image, and commanded all to worship it, and forbad to pray to any God, but to the King onely, for thirty dayes: must this Edict therefore bee obeyed? Noe surely. And why? Because it was against God; and therefore it ought to have beene of no force to exact obedience of any. But what (will you say?) Must we be rebels, in disobeying our superiours? No it is one thing not obey, and another to bee rebellious; superiours ought not to bee obeyed, if they command against God; Yet this is no rebellion, where men are ready to yeald passive obedience to their unjust cruelty, by not resisting it, though they derect and deny active obedience to their unjust commands.[59]

Burton's conformist opponents might have objected that passive disobedience against a negative command—such as an edict forbidding preaching on predestination—involved nothing other than flat, active defiance. What had begun as a paean of loyalty and deference had thus mutated into a homily of disobedience, a less than subtle warning to the King that he and his ecclesiastical counselors were skating on thin ice. It is not difficult to see why Henry Burton lost his ears in 1637. Yet his case was not isolated; his book may in fact be seen as an emblem of the predicament in which mainstream puritans found themselves by 1630. Under steady and heightening pressure from the external threat of Laudianism, and increasingly compromised from the inside by antinomian critics (to say nothing of resurgent separatist and Anabaptist impulses), the godly community stood ready to implode.[60] This implosion would come in the 1640s, leaving in its wake civil war and sectarian proliferation.

---

[59] Ibid., 62.

[60] The upsurge in separatist and anabaptist activity in the 1630s has yet to be fully explored by historians. For an important start, see M. Tolmie, *Triumph of the Saints* (Cambridge, 1977), passim.

Epilogue: 1640 and Beyond

Our epilogue resumes where our prologue left off, with the story of Edward Howes. Howes's writings allow us to recover the process whereby one puritan layman drifted into antinomianism. Likewise, his diary, which spans the years 1643-1649, affords considerable insight into how antinomian modes of religiosity could themselves mutate and shift shape, producing wholly new, and in some respects, unrecognizable forms of piety. From this perspective, Howes's intellectual trajectory may be taken as a figure for the genesis of civil-war sectarianism, and a bridge allowing us to carry our story into the 1640s.

Howes, Winthrop, and Everarde

In early 1635, John Winthrop, Jr. returned to England as an agent of the Massachusetts Bay Colony. His stay appears to have been hectic. While in the mother country, Winthrop managed not only to find a second wife, but to secure for himself the provisional governorship of a new colony—proposed under the aegis of a set of powerful puritan lords—that was to be established in the increasingly coveted and contested Connecticut River Valley.[1] In addition, however, Winthrop found time to stop in with his old friend, Edward Howes. Together again for the first time in four years, Howes and Winthrop appear to have indulged their shared spiritual interests, interests that had matured a decade earlier when the two men lived together in London. As noted at the outset of Chapter Seven, upon setting sail for Massachusetts, the younger Winthrop even left in his friend's hands a series of spiritual or theological

[1] Robert C. Black, *The Younger John Winthrop* (New York: Columbia University Press, 1966), 77-90.

questions addressed to an unnamed doctor of the soul. On 21 August 1635, just weeks after John Winthrop's departure from England, Howes wrote to Winthrop, informing him of the fate of these spiritual questions:

> I have bin 2 or 3 tymes since with the Dr., and can gett but small satisfaccion about your queries. I doubt he hath some prejudicate conceipt of one of us, or both; yet I must confesse he seemed verie free to me, only in the maine he was misticall. This he said, that when the will of God is you shall knowe what you desire, it will come with such a light, that it will make a harmonie amonge all your authors, causing them sweetly to agree, and putt you for ever after out of doubt & question. To discerne the *fratres scientiae*, I cannot as yet learne of him.[2]

In later letters, this mysterious figure—at one point named by Howes as a "Rosicrucian"—would be referred to as "Dr. E.," and on one crucial occasion, as "Dr. Euer:".[3] Given what we have learned in the course of this study, both about Howes's later immersion in Familism and about the nature of London's antinomian underground, there can be no doubt that the man named here was none other than Dr. John Everarde. By 1635, Everarde had been deprived of his public pulpits in London, and appears to have been preaching solely to a core of devotees at private meetings in Kensington. It was in all probability at one of these ostensibly illegal, but apparently semi-public, conventicles, that Howes approached Everarde with Winthrop's spiritual queries. Given Howes's words—"I have bin 2 or 3 tymes *since* with the Dr."—it also seems probable that Winthrop, too, had attended such a conventicle while in London, perhaps stimulating his interest and curiosity in London's most celebrated mystic. Regardless of the exact circumstances of their exposure to Everarde, Howes's letter provides us with an extraordinary scenario: on the eve of the Massachusetts Bay Colony's infamous Antinomian Controversy, the son of New England's most prominent political figure sought resolution of his own spiritual doubts from London's most notorious antinomian minister, a minister with whom, we must assume, he had at least a passing familiarity.

---

[2] The most faithful transcriptions of Howes's letters to Winthrop are contained in *Collections of the Massachusetts Historical Society*, 3rd series, 9 (1846), 240-58 and ibid., 4th ser., 6 (1863), 467-513 (hereinafter denoted as *Collections, 1846*, and *Collections, 1863*), which are to be preferred over the more recent transcriptions in *The Winthrop Papers*. This passage is contained in *Collections, 1863*, 499.

[3] For references to "the Dr.," see *Collections, 1863*, 499-500; for "Dr. E.," see 502, and for the Rosicrucian "Dr. Euer:" see 507. Comparison of these various passages shows that the same man is being discussed in each case. It should likewise be noted that Howes habitually used "u" in place of "v."

The younger Winthrop's interest in occult religion was nothing new, however. Mystical modes of religiosity had always been at the heart of his relationship with Edward Howes. To judge from their correspondence, Howes was John Winthrop, Jr.'s closest friend prior to his emigration to New England in 1631. It is likely that the two had met in London during Winthrop's none-too-successful tenure as a legal student at the Inner Temple between 1625 and 1627. Howes had been some species of servant—perhaps a secretary or a tutor—in the household of Emmanuel Downing, Winthrop's uncle and sometime host in the city. The two young men seem to have become inseparable companions during this time—Howes on one occasion claimed that had he failed to write to Winthrop, his conscience would have been "lyable to the livinge death of a Turtles solitariness that hath lost her mate."[4] They were, in short, the best of friends. This powerful bond was certainly not grounded in their mutual interest in the law—although both men studied at the Inns of Court, neither seems to have spent so much as a moment at the bar. What they did share, however, was a profound curiosity in alchemy, a fact that led Winthrop's biographer to speculate that Howes was largely "responsible for the curious fact that John Winthrop, Jr. quitted the Inner Temple no barrister . . . but an enthusiastic alchemist."[5] As is well known, the younger Winthrop's devotion to the practice of alchemy would persist throughout his life, shaping his friendships, his interest in medicine, to say nothing of his library, in the years to come.[6]

This mutual fascination with the mysteries of alchemy was evident from the very first of Edward Howes's surviving letters to his friend John, written in 1627/8, before Winthrop's emigration. Like many of Howes's epistles, this one contained a string of peculiar, almost impenetrable statements of vaguely religious connotation. As a postscript, Howes attached two revealing items: a passage from the Apocryphal "wisdom of Solomon," that read "And all such things as are either secret, or manifest: them I knowe," as well as a geometric emblem that included a classic alchemical identification of Christ and "lapis"—that is, the stone, or philosopher's stone. Later letters likewise showed an undimmed enthusiasm for the alchemical arts.[7] In 1632, Howes announced his intention to purchase for Winthrop the recently published folio works of "that famous and farre renouned English man of our tymes, Dr.

[4] *Collections, 1846*, 243.

[5] Black, *Winthrop*, 27.

[6] For a technical account of Winthrop's later practice of alchemy, as well as an attempt to place him in a wider network of alchemists in colonial New England, see W. R. Newman, *Gehennical Fire: The Lives of George Starkey, an American Alchemist in the Scientific Revolution* (Cambridge, MA: Harvard University Press, 1994), 39-50.

[7] *Collections, 1863*, 467-68.

Fludd," that is Robert Fludd, alias Floyd, England's most famous practitioner of the hermetic arts. Howes assumed that Fludd's works would be "well drest for [Winthrop's] palate," and took the liberty to forward at least two volumes to his friend in New England.[8] Like Fludd and other alchemists, both young men also seem to have shown a parallel interest in more practical technical arts, which translated into an affection for medicinal concotions, tales of exploration, and blueprints for improbable engines and machines.[9]

This eclectic hodgepodge of alchemy and applied science points both backward to the world of the sixteenth-century magus, and forward to that of the Restoration virtuoso. Yet for all their youthful eccentricity, their obsession with alchemy seems to have rested side by side, in an unproblematic way, with the puritanism in which both young men had been immersed since youth. Thus, Howes's earliest surviving letters to Winthrop bear all the trappings of a conventional godliness, such as concern with the progress of the Thirty Years War, hope for the conversion of the native American "heathen," and deep interest in the fortunes of the New England plantation; Howes saw the work of Winthrop and his fellow expatriates as the "buylding of [God's] newe Jerusalem," and in 1633, he assured his distant friend that "The Harts of all Gods people here are all bent towards your Syon."[10] Like the good puritan he seems to have been, Howes regularly expressed his own intent to resettle in the Bay, although he never managed to muster the courage to make this move.

Yet having said this, their interest in alchemy seems also to have been the catalyst that led both young men to explore rather more exotic forms of religiosity that subsisted at the margins of the godly community. It was undoubtedly their alchemical curiosity that first led them to the pulpit of John Everarde, who as we have seen, was one of the most outspoken aficionados of Hermetic ideas in early modern London, and himself a personal associate of Robert Fludd.[11] It is likely, although not certain, that they gadded to hear Ev-

---

[8] *Collections, 1863*, 483, 496.

[9] See, for instance, *Collections, 1863*, 476-77, for Howes's recipe for "a wholesome and savorie drinke, for such as are sick, weak, or cannot drink water." See ibid., 491-94, for his discussion of an engine "to boyle in wooden vessells," and 498 for a description of "two devices to kill wolves." Howes also showed a lifelong interest in mathematics. In 1650, he would publish *Short Arithmetick: or The Old and Tedious way of Numbering, Reduced to a New and Briefe Method* (1650). The book is an arithmetical primer, first providing the reader with an account of standard weights and measures, then proceeding through a crash course in the four basic operations, including the addition, subtraction, multiplication, and division of fractions.

[10] *Collections, 1863,* 473, 490.

[11] Everarde may have been publicly renowned as the translator of the *Poimandres* of Hermes Trismegistus, which translation was published in 1650 as *The Divine*

erarde preach during their time together in London in the mid-1620s when he occupied the pulpit of St. Martin's-in-the-Fields, only a few minutes walk from the Downing residence in Peterborough Court. Howes's first letter to Winthrop includes a reference to spiritual perfection that may indicate exposure to Everarde's ideas, and, more revealingly, contains a rather gratuitous and seemingly illogical use of the phrase "plus ultra," meaning "more beyond" (or simply "the beyond"). *Plus Ultra*, interestingly, was a code word used by John Everarde to describe the spirit of Christ, serving as the title of one of his more Hermetically inclined surviving sermons, "The *Plus Ultra* of the creatures."[12]

It is by no means shocking that Howes and Winthrop should have been attracted to Everarde. He was a known student of what might be termed "alchemical" divinity and as such, he represented a likely target for the curiosity of two young men with a taste for the occult.[13] They appear to have viewed Everarde as a great spiritual alchemist, endowed with weighty secrets; in this vein, both Howes and Winthrop seem to have believed that he was a member of the notorious Rosicrucian Fraternity. This perhaps explains Winthrop's desire to learn from the Dr. "To discerne the *fratres scientiae*," or the "wise brothers," which according to no less an authority than Robert Fludd was the alias under which the "invisible college" was traveling in the 1630s.[14] Yet as suggested in Chapter Seven, Everarde was much more than an alchemist in clerical gown; he was in fact an eclectic mystic, whose thought had been influ-

---

Pymander of Hermes Mercurius Trismegistus (1650). For Everarde's friendship with Fludd, see British Library, Cotton MS. Jul. C. iii, fols. 171-73.

[12] For Everarde's sermon, see *Some Gospel-Treasures Opened: Or, The Holiest of all Unvailing* (1653), 523-39; Everarde considered Christ to be the "plus ultra," in that he was the principle or the flame that burned through creation, lying behind or beyond the sensible aspect of each and every creature in existence (ibid., 531). For Howes comment, see *Collections, 1863*, 468: "Come when you will, I shalbe fitted with a *plus ultra*, or something, meane while I meane to make holly daye nowe, and then when I can but finde a holy hower, to praye for our prosperous proceedings, which God graunt to his glorye and our comforts." For an interesting history of the etymology and usage of this phrase, see E. Rosenthal, "*Plus Ultra, Non Plus Ultra*, and the Columnar Device of Emperor Charles V," *Journal of the Warburg and Courtauld Institutes*, 34 (1971).

[13] The phrase "chimical divinity" was used (disparagingly) by the Yorkshire antinomian Roger Brearley, *A Bundle of Soul-convincing, Directing and Comforting Truths* (1677), 4.

[14] Robert Fludd, *Clavis philosophiae et alchymiae* (Frankfurt, 1633), 50: "those who were formerly called Brothers of the Rosy Cross are today called the Wise, the name (of Rose Cross) being so odious to contemporaries that it is already buried away from the memory of man," as cited by Frances A. Yates, *The Rosicrucian Enlightenment* (London and Boston: Routledge and Kegan Paul, 1972; paperback edition, Boulder, CO: Shambhala Publications, 1978), 101-2.

enced by a whole range of sources, including not just Hermetic and Neoplatonic works, but also even less reputable sources of continental mysticism, such as Sebastian Franck, the *Theologia Germanica*, and very possibly the works of that arch-heretic, Hendrik Niclaes, founder of the Family of Love. The end result was not just "chemical divinity"; it was, as we have seen, an extreme form of mystical perfectionism. Howes's and Winthrop's mutual fascination with alchemy had thus led them to a spiritual leader who was not only a reputed alchemist, but one of early Stuart London's most outspoken antinomian heretics.

By 1635, their curiosity had grown deep enough that they were willing to make the trek to Kensington to seek out the spiritual wisdom of the doctor. In so doing, they had entered the antinomian underground. And it was probably within the extra-parochial, subterranean community of antinomian sympathizers—some of whom congealed around Everarde—that Howes encountered the individual or individuals who would lead him into full-blown Familism in later years. This rapid descent into ever more unusual forms of mystical religion may be traced in his subsequent correspondence with Winthrop. Upon receiving Howes's report of his meetings with Everarde, Winthrop appears to have quickly mailed two letters to his friend in London, seeking further elucidation from Everarde. Howes did not respond until 21 June 1636, at which point he informed Winthrop that "The Dr. I have not seene since last Sommer; I doubt all is not gold that glisters like it, and he that would learne to distinguish, may pay too deare for his knowledge. I thinke there is not any thinge that the Dr. hath or knoweth, but a frind of myne neerer home enjoyes as much; I could wish you with him, or he with you, for a moneth or two."[15]

It may, perhaps, have been under the spell of this new spiritual "friend" that Howes began to familiarize himself with more explicitly Familist modes of religiosity. For in August 1636, perhaps fearing that Winthrop had not received his letter of June, Howes again wrote, informing his friend that "I have not seene Dr. E: since last sommer"; this time, however, his letter was couched in ellipses and mysteries, which left no doubt that Howes believed himself on the brink of some sort of spiritual breakthrough:

> I cannot discover into *Terra incognitam*, but I have had a kenn of it shewed unto me. The way to it is (for the most parte) horrible & fearefull, the daingers none worse, to them that are not *destinati filii* ; somtymes I am travelling that way, but the Lord knowes when I shall gett thither, so many flattering foes are still in the way to prevent me, and diverte my course. I thinke I have spoken with some that have bin there. I am informed that the land lyeth where the sunn riseth, and extendeth it selfe southward, the northerne people doe account it noe better then a wilderness; and the spies that they

[15] *Collections, 1863*, 500.

> have sent out to discover & view it, have reported as much: for they knew it was in vaine to reporte better of it. Deare frind, I desire with all my harte that I might write plainer to you, but in discovering the mysterie I may diminish its majestie, & give occasion to the prophane to abuse it, if it should fall into unworthie hands: in many things you have sympathized with me, and whie not in this? After the hint of a thing *facilius est addere*. Let me make a Quere. Was the bodie made for the soule, or the soule for the bodie? Was the house made for man, or man for the house? Doe or did the true lovers of wisdome, studie more for the bodie, then the soule? Did they not know the man? The [bod]ie is but our servant & shall our studies for it take up our endevours as for [torn] Is it not spirituall fornication & adultery to cast the eye of our mind & harte upon sensualitie, or any sensible good, as to lust after it? Must not the five kings be vanquisht & hung up, before Israell can enter into the rest of the Lord? which rest I wish unto you.[16]

Here, again, Howes offered vague clues that the mysterious truths in question belonged to a realm of wisdom unknown to the "northerne peoples," perhaps again suggesting the influence of Hermes Trismegistus, who was usually assumed to have hailed from the Middle East. Nevertheless, Howes's closing statements—in which he denigrated external, physical forms of religion or spiritual practice—more than hint at the fact that whatever else we may say about Howes's *Terra Incognitam*, it belonged to the most extreme realms of the antinomian underground. In particular, his final statement—"Must not the five kings be vanquisht & hung up, before Israell can enter into the rest of the Lord"—strongly savored of Familism. As noted above, "the rest of the Lord" had been a favorite catchphrase of HN, who used it to describe the paradisiacal domain of spiritual perfection in which the illuminated ones dwelled. Equally revealing is Howes's reference to the "five kings," surely a reference to the five enemy kings brutally slain by Joshua and the Israelites in the wake of the battle at Gibeon.[17] These five kings were here taken as representations of internal states, qualities, or events, which needed to be overcome within the soul of each believer before he or she could pass into the land of peace and rest.

Winthrop may well have been confused or confounded by his old friend's mysterious pronouncements. Their correspondence seems to have cooled off for a period. In March 1637/38, Howes again wrote to Winthrop, this time commenting on New England's raging Antinomian Controversy. Here, even in urging a harmonious resolution to the conflict, Howes left no doubt as to where his own religious quest had led him:

---

[16] Ibid., 501-2.

[17] See Joshua 10.

> The relation of your fight with the Indians [the Pequot War] I have read in print, but of the fight amongst yourselves, *Bellum Linguaram*, the strife of tongues, I have heard much, but little to the purpose. I wonder your people that pretend to know soe much, doe not knowe that Love is the fulfillinge of the Lawe, and that against Love there is noe Lawe. But noe marvell: when many have not the beginning of wisdom in them [the feare of the Lord]; and howe can they that feare not God, keepe his commandements or fulfill them? but I hope when I come to find more unitie, peace & love.[18]

Here, Howes was offering Winthrop more or less unadulterated Familist rhetoric: the fear of God was the beginning of true wisdom—love fulfilled the Law—love was an overpowering force that reduced all to harmony. These were all telltale commonplaces that ran through the works of HN.[19]

In his next message, of April 1639, Howes again took the New Englanders to task, chiding them for their disputatious ways even as he himself delivered clues that his own religiosity was veering toward antinomianism. He had received letters from Winthrop concerning the "monstrous births" that had befallen Anne Hutchinson and Mary Dyer, as well as a "generall earthquake," which Howes read less as judgments on the Hutchinsonians than as baleful portents of things to come in New England:

> whoe can tell certainely wherefore God sent them? where is there such an other people then in New England? that labours might and maine to have Christ formed in them, yet they would give or appoynt him his shape, and cloathe him too. It cannot be denyed but we have conceived many monstrous imaginations of Christ Jesus, the one imagination sayes loe, here he is; the other sayes loe, there he is; multiplicitie of conceptions, but is there any one true shape of Him? and if one of many produce a shape, tis not the shape of the sonne of God-Man but an uglie horridd Metamorphosis, neither is it a livinge shape, but a dead one, yet a crow thinkes her owne bird the fairest,

---

18 Ibid., 504-5.

19 Ibid., 504-5. 21 March 1637/38. See HN, *Evangelium Regni* (n.p., 1575?), fols. 18v-19v, where Niclaes argued explicitly that the "fear of God" was the first stage in the progression to perfection, symbolized by the covenant of circumcision. As he put it, this circumcision was a representation of the individual turning away from the flesh, "as also the entraunce into the feare of God/wherout the right Wisdom doth spring: and how wee shall go-forth therin, till unto the Mortifying of all fleashie Mindes/through the Obedience of the Requiring of the godlie Woord and his Service." Likewise, the claim that love was the fulfilling of the law comes directly from Niclaes. See H[endrik] N[iclaes], *Introductio to the Holy Glass of Righteousness* (n.p., 1575?), fol. 9r: "When the Perfection therfore cometh; that we be established in the Love/; then is the Lawe, the Prophecying, and the Knowledge, fulfilled and accomplished: or then is the Obedience shewed in the same Commandement and Doctrine of God. And not before."

> and most preferre their owne wisdome before Gods, Antichrist before Christ; to you I write, with whome I may be bolde; and is't a wonder the Earth should quake at this? O Earth, Earth, Earth, heare the voyce of the Lord, a still silent voyce, yet where it comes it maketh the mountaines to quake, and the hills to tremble.
>
> The bookes you writt for, I have not mett with them as yet at the shopps where I have bin; I could wish you some bookes, but one booke were enough, if you could come by it, its written within and without, its calld by many names, but it is not knowne by the names, but to those that have the nature thereof: to give you the name and nature, its THE BOOKE OF LIFE, where you may read all within you, and all without you; and Him that is all in all; to whose protection I leave you and rest.[20]

Although this intentionally obscure passage eludes exact interpretation, we can see in Howes's words a number of themes that we have already located within the spectrum of perfectionist ideas. Here, he made reference to seeing "Christ formed" within believers;[21] so, too, in a manner reminiscent of Everarde, he identified "self" with Antichrist. Finally, his statements further suggested that religious insight came not from reading books, but from something called the "Book of Life," which was "written within and without," and which could reveal the nature not only of creation, but of "Him that is all in all." This, it would seem, hearkens back to the mystical cosmology of Everarde, which we examined in Chapter Seven. Everarde maintained that Christ, the underlying creative principle of the universe, permeated all things. What was necessary, then, was to silence the self and allow Christ within to speak.

Howes's cosmology, like Everarde's, thus appears to have remained indebted to alchemical or Hermetic sources of inspiration. Nevertheless, it is clear that by early 1640, Howes had moved far beyond Everarde. Winthrop apparently continued to pester Howes for new information concerning the mysterious land in which Howes now resided, but Howes resisted: "what I heare, what I see, what I knowe, would be as tedious for you to read, as for me to write." He went on, however, to answer Winthrop's more mundane questions about his doings in a characteristically evasive and oracular fashion: "to tell you where I am, and what I doe, and when you shall see, is a shorter worke. My bodie is at London, my soule in my bodie, and my mind in my soule, etc. and if you will, in mind I am and canbe every where; while I am writing this lettre, I am with you, and what doe I? Outwardly I am writing,

---

[20] Ibid., 505-6.

[21] In so doing, he echoed one of HN's favorite complaints about his own enemies, that "They cry all (no doubt) loude enough, here, here is Christ, there, there is Christ, the one boasteth him of the belief, the other of works." H[endrik] N[iclaes], *Revelatio Dei*, 2d ed. (1649), 43.

inwardly I am meditating; and still with you, and doe you aske when you shall see me? If you know not I will tell you. When you can see your selfe, or you and I all one."[22] The reader should take note of this peculiar passage, for Howes was not merely playing coy games with Winthrop; he was suggesting that his "mind" (as opposed to his soul) had ceased to be bound within finite space, and that he and Winthrop in fact somehow partook of the same being, despite their separation. At this point, Howes alluded to a letter, no longer extant, in which he had referred to one of his spiritual mentors, a now unidentified teacher known by the name of "Dr. Lyon":

> The Arabian Philos: I writt to you of, he was styled among us Dr. Lyon, the best of all the Rosicrucians[23] that ever I mett with all, farre beyond Dr. Euer: they that are of his straine are knowing men; they tend to live in free light, they honor God and doe good to the people among whom they live, and I conceive you are in the right that they had theire learning from Arabia. But they come much shorte of the people that have theire learninge from heaven, from God, from the Sonn of his Love, such I meane as are livinge men, whose life and conversation characterizeth them, and not theire knowledge; for 'tis written (and we beleive) knowledge puffeth up, and Love buyldeth up; they have knowledge as much as any, but it is not their essence, theire life, theire All.[24]

Everarde, then, was a "knowing man," a man who possessed mysteries and secrets of divine truth (presumably Hermetic truth). In Howes's view, this was not enough; Everarde's prodigious knowledge was not matched by Love, and he and his followers thus fell far short of "the people that have theire learninge from heaven, from God, from the Sonn of his Love." These chosen people, of whom Howes was one, possessed Love as their essence and being.

"The Holy House of God"

Only with his diary of the 1640s, however, can we determine with certainty the identity of this celestial body of true believers. They were, it seems, a vestigial and surviving pocket of self-conscious Familists, who had managed to perpetuate the religion of HN through decades of official hostility. As we should expect given his letters to Winthrop, Howes's Familism was not untouched by other influences. His earlier interest in alchemy continued to shape his thought well into the 1640s. Thus, we find him alluding at one point to Paracelsus; his diary also contains an English translation of the "creation myth" from the third book of Hermes's celebrated *Poimandres*. This

---

22 *Collections, 1863*, 507.

23 For some reason, Howes did not write out the term Rosicrucians, instead drawing a rose, a cross and an "n."

24 Ibid., 507-8.

translation differs radically from Everarde's *Divine Pymander* of 1650, and occasional corrections in the manuscript suggest that Howes may well have executed it himself. In light of this ongoing passion for things Hermetic, it should come as no surprise that—as in his very first letter to Winthrop—Howes continued to identify Christ with the philosopher's stone, suggesting that Christ was the savior of the "lesser world," while the stone was the savior of the "greater world" (presumably an allusion to the alchemical concept of "microcosm" and "macrocosm").[25]

Nevertheless, there can be no question that Howes's interest in alchemy was now wedded to a self-conscious Familism. This is revealed most clearly in a circular letter copied out at length under the title of "A loving Admonition sent from a Lover of the Truth, unto all goodwilling harts to God and his righteousnes: for them to beware of some that are Deceived and would deceive (by seditious Libells and false doctrine) perswading men that it is not possible to attaine unto the perfection, or yet be delivered from the subjection to Sinne, in this life, while men walke on Earth."[26] Although this letter does not appear to derive from HN's extant writings, it clearly appropriated his voice, echoing even the hypnotic and chaotic prose style of the founder, and replicating, with startling precision, the details of classic Familist doctrine. It represented a forthright and unabashed defense of the perfection of believers. As in the case of HN, this state of perfection was to be preceded by a stage of legal mortification and repentance: "Therefore let us first submitt to his holy law, to the mortifieng of our sinfull lusts and desires, wayting for the Coming of the Lord Jesus Christ, whoe (being once fashioned and obtayninge a livinge shape or forme in us in the spirit soe that we may dwell in him and he in us) is at that tyme our PERFECTION, our righteousnes our Ellection, our Redemption; our justification and salvation."[27] Humans were to engage in a process of unfeigned repentance, "resisting and mortifyeng of the sinfull lusts and desires, untill Christ come and dwell in us by faith with out whome there is noe remission of sinnes." Believers thus became temples for the indwelling Christ, who was himself perfection incarnate. Those inhabited by Christ, were, of course, free from the Law, for Christ "taketh away theire sinnes . . . the sinnes of all that beleive, and fastneth all that is against them in the Lawe unto his crosse." They were thus rendered perfect and without sin. This was not a crude perfection, in which believers would perform every act of the Law without failure; indeed, believers would continue to commit transgressions. Nevertheless,

---

[25] British Library, Sloane MS. 979, fols. 2r, 7r, 24-25. Cf. Everarde's more elegant translation in *Divine Pymander*, 18-19.

[26] The following paragraph is based on British Library, Sloane MS. 979, fols. 18v-21v.

[27] Ibid., 19v-20r.

"they have noe pleasure in sinne, and therfore are not theire infirmities (wherewith they are often tymes over taken, accompted any more for sinne unto them, but are cleane put out of remembrance, (and pardoned in Christ) and shall never more be thought upon e[t]c for love covereth them all." As in all other antinomian formulations, freedom from sin did not mean freedom *to* sin. On the contrary, the perfect ones "are alwayes enemies to sinne, [and] strive daylie (in a firme beleife) to the subdueing of sinne."

This neo-Familist circular letter, which is transcribed in full in Appendix B, allows us to decode Howes's earlier comments to his friend Winthrop. Clearly, by the 1640s, Edward Howes was deeply enmeshed in the subculture described in the second chapter of this book, an underground community that relied for its survival in large part on the hand-to-hand transmission of precious texts. Thus, Howes likewise copied into his notebook two songs from HN's *Cantica*, which had presumably been preserved and passed on for decades by way of informal manuscript transmission. Even more remarkably, however, the versions copied by Howes into his notebook were not drawn from the original English edition of the hymnal, which had been published for the only time in the 1570s; rather, they represented an independent translation from the Low German, and must therefore have been transmitted entirely in manuscript, bearing witness to what appears to have been an extraordinary instance of cultural preservation.

But it is in Howes's dreams and interpretations that we gain our most vivid insight into the fruit of his spiritual pilgrimage. In one of these dreams, as we have seen, the sometime Familist peddler, Stephen Proudlove, made an uninvited nocturnal appearance, interrupting a divine messenger in the midst of prophecy.[28] Another vision vouchsafed to Howes a set of coded letters, which he was able to decrypt to reveal a predictable pair of initials—"HN."[29] The most interesting of these dreams, which he saw as unmediated visions from God, are themselves exceedingly difficult to unpack. They bear the familiar haziness of sleep. On one occasion at least, Howes seems to have recorded his comments immediately upon waking, leading to a broken and meandering prose style that at times defies analysis. At other moments, his interpretations

[28] Ibid., 16v. "Thursday Morning 13 Maii 1647. in sleepe a humane shape without beard appeared without dores, and passing through the entry beconed me to follow, I followed it, in the entry it told mee sadd things in Latin, we went out into the streete the hand thereof seemed as the hand of one dead. I speaking English it spake to me in English again. I desired a repetition of the prediction, he told me the same sadd events in English, I was interrupted with Proudlove the Pedler and an other behind following to listen what was said, I reprooved them for want of good manners and they stayed behind."

[29] Ibid., fol. 15v.

themselves demand extensive interpretation and inference. Nonetheless, even when vague or difficult to pin down, they prove remarkably revealing.

The first of these visions came to him just after awakening one night in December 1644. Howes recalled that "the LORD caused me to see a vision upon my bed, and I beheld a Deepe Pitt before me, it was very nigh mee, full of mudd and dirt, such as in the high wayes in winter; and beyond the Pitt was a Drey Man, driving a horse before him with his voyce to that muddy Pitt, and I sawe the beast goe in untill he began as it were to swim, and then the horse staying: the Drey man with his voyce commanded him further, soe that, the horse went untill he began to sinke, then the Drey man cryed out and rann to save his Horse and went into the muddie pitt up to the Chinn and soe further untill he sunke alsoe, and both he and his horse were choaked in the mudd." In this anxious and fretful dream, Howes immediately felt the presence of God, who himself interpreted for Howes the dream's meaning:

> afterward the Lord tooke me and showed me the meaning of this vision and thus he said. The deep Pitt that thou sawest is the bottomlesse unsatiablenes that is in Man, and that it was very nigh thee, is to shew thee, that thou art yet neerer the bottomlesse pitt then me in thy affections and desires, and that it was full of thinn Mudd, sheweth unto thee that Mans unsatiableness is made up all of Earth and standing stinking water, that is the concupiscence of terrestriall things; and the love of the flesh more then of God. And whereas I caused thee to see a Drey Man driving a horse with his voyce towards the pitt which was betweene him and thee, it was to shew thee that thou art that Drey or Car man whoe by the voyce of thy will drivest thy horse thy beast thy bodie to fulfill thy muddie stinking desires; and wheras thou sawest the pitt the drey man and his horse but the drey man saw not thee but only the Pitt and his horse it was to putt thee in mind, that. I the Mind thy God that caused thee to see this vision see allthings, but thou canst see noe more then thou mindest, and that thou mindest soe much thy beast and the Pitt, that thou couldest not see me. ye[a] and how casts [canst] thou have me for thy God, when thou settest any thing before my face, when any thing is betweene me and thee, that is thy mind upon and thy heart runns after it. And whereas thou sawest the Beast goe into the Muddie Pond or Pitt untill he began as it were to swim, and then stayed, the man with his voyce drove him forward soe that the horse went on unto a kind of whirlpool where he sinking, the Man cryed out and ran as it were to save his beast, and was presently up to the Chinn in Mudd. And wheras thou sawes[t] the Man up to the chinn in thick muddy water swime further therein untill he sunke and was overwhelmed.[30]

---

[30] Ibid., fols. 8r-9r.

In the first place, this passage allows us to put to rest, once and for all, the contemporary accusation that English Familism was nothing more than a fig-leaf for a shameless libertinism. Here was a man struggling together with his God to root out sin, and to escape the abiding miasma of the flesh. Yet what is most remarkable about the passage is not the ethical content of the revelation—which was perhaps no more or less strict than one would expect from a man bred in the ways of puritanism—but rather Howes's conception of his God. Howes's God was an internal, ever-present, vocal God: "I the Mind thy God that caused thee to see this vision." Here, "thee" and "I"—the mind of Howes and the God of Mind—bled over and into one another, until they became almost indistinguishable. Although there remained a notional separation, the entire point of the vision was that God, the Mind, was ever-present and omnipresent; God was so close that one could hear him, look upon his face, if only one could avert the eye of the soul from "thy beast, thy bodie."

God was, in short, within the believer. From this perspective, almost anything that presented itself to the believer's experience could be construed as divine revelation. "The Book of Life," as he had told Winthrop, held all of God's secrets. Howes had arrived at a point where scripture and scriptural revelation were no longer deemed to be the ordinary and indispensable vehicle of divine illumination, for he clearly believed that God was speaking in him and through him without the means of the written word. Thus, God informed Howes that a household accident (in which he had sliced off a fingernail) was in fact a sign that "THE CUTTING OFF MY NAILE ON THE LEFT HAND, was to be unto me a Testimonie for ever, not bee worne out with age of the reall and true CIRCUMCISION OF THE HEARTE which the Almightie would himself performe for me in the 8th Day."[31] On this view, not only scripture, but indeed all of human experience, became a dense and complex divine allegory, waiting to be unfolded.

Howes likewise applied this allegorical hermeneutic to his most elaborate vision, which came to him in October 1645. Here, he offered a complicated spiritual analysis of what was in fact a mundane, even worldly, dream. Once again, he recorded both the vision and its interpretation, which is itself so full of pregnant religious symbolism that it seems an allegory in its own right:

> This vision in my sleepe of the night at Radcliff came unto me. And soe in my Fathers howse I looking out at the window above staires before day I beheld a Rainbow in the East and the Skye full of starrs the Pleyades full South, I went downe to open the dore intending to see and contemplate this vision more cleerely out of the howse it being towards morninge. And as I opened the dore a yong theefe did thrust in and rann up the staires. I clapt to the dore and bolted it to prevent others to follow, and called for my ham-

[31] Ibid., fol. 13r.

> mer, which presently I found and going up staires, I called out upon divers maides in the howse . . . to come and help but they coming not, I went into the chamber where my father dyed and there at the dore I mett the yong theefe, and pulld him downe with the hammer, bruised his head his armes and thighes but killed him not. he was all the while speechlesse; then I awaked with the praises of God in my mouth; for vouchsafing me this vision and the interpretation thereof—it being about the second hower towards morning I was bid to remember that my father of heaven was dead in the earthly house I was in and that I behaved my selfe as Mr. of the howse there as at home, and for as much as I was up one paire [?] of staires notes unto me that I was in the midle of the howse the [heart] but not in the roome my father dyed—he dyed next roome towards the west, towards the setting of the Sun of Righteousnes; I was in the Roome towards the East though I was towards the rising of the [sun] of R yet it was night I had noe light to walke by but the starrs of myne owne imagination and that I saw a raynebow in the east by night, notes unto me that God will drowne my world noe more, but that the new heaven and new earth shall appeare in me, and that he wilbe at peace with me, the pleyades being full south in the place of the Sunns exaltation, sheweth that John the Baptist is the forrunner of Christ, the grace of God in the confession of sinns is the highest in my Horizon to prepare the way of the Lord he must decrease that Jesus may increase, it being towards morning and I going downestaires to goe out to contemplate the vision, notes unto me my wandring mind out of Gods house, and from his family among the Elementish things I opning the dore of my heavenly fathers Howse, a yonge theefe thrust in; as I but offer to goe out, evill wil rush in, and if it be but one evill, yet it is daingerous it comes to robb and to kill, and therefore if thou canst not bold [hold?] it out, bolt it in: and seeing the theefe rann up immediately into the Chamber where my father dyed, the evill lett into thy fathers house, will runn to the best Roome the [heart].[32]

Only through very careful scrutiny can we wring coherent meaning from Howes's interpretation, and even then, his ambiguity stymies any definitive reading. The immediate context of this letter appears to be the death of Howes's father, which probably took place after Howes assumed a schoolmastership at Radcliffe (Middlesex) in the 1640s.[33] That the dream unfolded in this house was taken to be evidence that "my father of heaven was dead in the earthly house I was in and that I behaved my selfe as Mr. of the howse there as at home." Barring the literal—and deeply radical—reading of this

---

[32] Ibid., fols. 13v-14r. The words in brackets were represented using a circular and a heart-shaped sign respectively.

[33] Howes's father was still alive in the later 1630s, as may be determined from his letters to Winthrop; he had moved to Radcliffe at some point between 1640 and 1644.

passage, we can only assume that what Howes was saying was that in the earthly, carnal house, God was absent. In the spiritual nighttime, when the sun of righteousness had set, it was as if God were dead, or perhaps crucified, and man alone master of his house. In this state, we were solitary and afraid, waiting for the sun to rise and banish the darkness. Even in the night, however, Howes could make out the presence of John the Baptist, as represented by the Pleiades, who prepared the way for Christ (the sun of righteousness to come).[34] Slowly, Christ would ascend, displacing John the Baptist and filling the earthly house with light, thus transforming it into the "new heaven and the new earth," which were seen as states "in me." All of this, however, was complicated by the presence of the marauding thief, a representation of the creeping evil that was waiting to flood into the heart in moments of weakness or wandering.

Here, Howes's rhetoric implied that his sense of unity with God seems to have waxed and waned over time. Nevertheless, at other points, he left no doubt whatsoever that he believed himself to have experienced an extraordinary communion with God. In this vein, he recorded that

> upon the fast day of the last moneth in the 19 of K[ing] C[harles] in the morninge before it was light, an Angell of God came unto me and said give me thy Heart for God, and I gave it, then the Angell tooke a Carpenters Rule and a paire of Compasses and sett one poynt in the midle and made 3 pricks one at the bottom of the heart and at each side one, each equally distant, then he tooke a Carpenters Ruler and drew a straight line upon the upper parte of the Heart and two lines from each end to the bottom, which made a perfect Triangle, within it he writt or engraved three words namely on the right side PEACE, on the upper side LOVE, and on the left side TRUTH, which three he said was the NAME OF GOD and the name of the Cittie of God, and the Way . . . thither. Then he tooke the Compasses againe and sett one poynt in the Center, and opened them to the ends of the Triangle, and there drew a circle and within the Circle HE writt or engraved these words THE HOWSE OF GOD, and without the Circle he engraved a brightnes as it weare a flame of Fire round about, and writt about it My God is a consuming Fire, then the Angell delivered the Heart to me againe, and Comanded me to make the Patterne thereof, and that I and the Children that God would give me should weare it alwayes about them as a brest plate of Righteousnes

---

[34] For a detailed examination of the role of the preparatory phase of John the Baptist in Familist religiosity, see below, Appendix A. Interestingly, the distinctive phrase "Sun of Righteousness" was commonly used by civil-war mystics and radicals—including Gerrard Winstanley, Thomas Tany, and Anna Trapnel—to describe Christ, for which see A. Hessayon, "'Gold Tried in the Fire'": The Prophet Theauraujohn Tany and the Puritan Revolution" (Ph.D. Diss., Cambridge, 1996), 76, 80.

> and as the Testimonie of the Covenant betweene God and them for ever through out all theire generations.[35]

He then proceeded to draw the emblem as instructed, leaving for posterity a graphic and impressive testament as to the nature of his religiosity. After many years of seeking, Edward Howes believed that he had come to grasp the true name of God, the consuming fire of Hebrews 12: 29. His diary, together with his cryptic letters to Winthrop, allow us to observe not only the path he traveled, but more generally to reconstruct in broad outline the process whereby puritanism, under sectarian and antinomianizing influences, ultimately tore itself apart, giving birth to the revolutionary sects of later fame.

[35] British Library, Sloane MS. 979, fols. 10v-11r.

Conclusion

Puritans and Heretics

In February 1645, some two months after receiving the divine emblem at the hands of God's angel, Howes wrote to Winthrop, declaring once again his intent to settle in New England, where he now expected to establish a school in mathematics.[1] This declaration brings us at last to the question of the precise relation between antinomianism and puritanism. Throughout this study, I have attempted to pay close attention to the threads that connected antinomians to the mainstream puritans they criticized, in order to establish how and in what manner antinomians appropriated, reshaped and transformed the culture of English puritanism to produce new religious forms. The more extreme antinomian formulations, such as the openly perfectionist faith of John Everarde, or the "hybrid" forms of Traske and the Cambridge Antinomian, indeed negated many of the most venerated pietistic forms of puritanism, thereby consuming the tradition out of which they had emerged. In the example of Edward Howes, we see a man whose spiritual pilgrimage from puritanism to alchemy to Familism ultimately led him to a style of worship which departed drastically from the normative habits of mainstream godly piety. From one perspective, Howes may be viewed as confirmation of T. D. Bozeman's conclusion that antinomianism was, ipso facto, "post-" or "contra-puritan."

Nevertheless, if we accept Bozeman's thesis in its totality, we are left wondering what, precisely, Edward Howes had in mind in 1645 when he announced his hope to resettle in that most puritan of polities, the Massachusetts Bay Colony? So, too, we would be forced ask ourselves how John Traske

[1] *Collections of the Massachusetts Historical Society*, 4th ser., 6 (1863), 512-13.

could have aligned himself with the "Jacob" semi-separatist communion of Southwark in the mid-1630s? This informal congregation had been led by the radical puritan button-maker Samuel Eaton and the inveterate nonconformist minister John Lathrop until their arrest in 1631. After Traske's death in 1636, it would go on to become perhaps the single most fertile womb of puritan radicalism in civil-war London, producing Baptists and Independents of all persuasions.[2] Are we then to assume that it ceased to be a "puritan" communion when Traske attached himself to it in the mid-1630s? and in turn that it began to be a puritan communion once again after his death? Similarly, we would be at a loss to explain how Traske's associate and publisher Rice Boye, also accused of antinomianism, and also affiliated with the Jacob church, might have gotten himself involved in the illicit publication, importation, and distribution of the works of that indomitable puritan gadfly, William Prynne.[3] Why did Peter Shaw's disciple Joseph Smith resort to a rhetoric of puritan solidarity to try to coerce Abraham Grame into dropping his High Commission case against Shaw?[4] Alternatively, we might ask how Edward Fisher's *Marrow of Modern Divinity* could have sported enthusiastic laudatory epistles from both famous antinomian sympathizers and from non-antinomian puritans, such as Joseph Caryl and Jeremiah Burroughs.[5] Or, to return to a question raised at the outset, how could Fisher himself have experienced a conversion at the hands of Thomas Hooker, while acting as a scribe for London's Familists and antinomians?

As I have suggested throughout, the answers to these questions lie in the enormous swathes of intellectual, cultural, and even personal terrain shared by mainstream puritans and their antinomian critics. Both modes of religiosity were, at root, radically bibliocentric. They channeled all attention toward the word preached, and showed a distaste for ceremonial or liturgical modes of piety. Each drew heavily on the reformed tradition, and (self-conscious Familists excepted) each claimed to be the true heir to that tradition. Both revealed a tendency toward what Bozeman has elsewhere dubbed biblical primitivism, that is, the habit of attempting to restore, relive, or imaginatively recreate the primitive purity of a pristine scriptural primordium; indeed, John Eachard's pastoral letter of 1631, which assumes the voice of Paul, and draws parallels between Paul's life and the life of John Eaton, might be viewed as an example *par excellence* of the primitivist impulse.[6] And as we have seen, both

[2] M. Tolmie, *Triumph of the Saints* (Cambridge: Cambridge University Press, 1977).

[3] For Boye, PRO, SPD 16/349/52, fol. 101r-v.

[4] See above, Chapter Three and Chapter Eleven.

[5] See E[dward] F[isher], *The Marrow of Modern Divinity: Touching Both the Covenant of Works, and the Covenant of Grace*, 2d ed. (1646).

[6] T. D. Bozeman, *To Live Ancient Lives: The Primitivist Dimension in Puritanism* (Chapel Hill: University of North Carolina Press, 1988); Appendix E, below.

mainstream puritans and their antinomian critics argued that true believers would be utterly sanctified by the experience of divine grace (although they differed in their assessment of how this sanctification would arise, how the believer would perceive it, and what, exactly, constituted a holy life). Even Edward Howes, in his most thoroughgoing "Familist" phase, could not escape the puritanical moral universe of his youth. Given all of this, is it any wonder that Laudians refused to acknowledge the difference between the mainstream puritans and their antinomian counterparts?

But in truth, it was not only Laudians, but also the godly themselves who sometimes failed to draw sharp distinctions between the two. Thus, when the authorities raided the Norwich lodgings of the godly minister John Heydon in October 1628, they found amongst his possessions not only a certificate of recommendation written by Mayor Ignatius Jordan of Exeter, and subscribed by the most famous puritans in London (Taylor, Gouge, Peter, Culverwell), but also "Notes of sermons taken from Mr Taylor, Mr Peters Mr Damporte Mr Foxlie Mr Shawe and divers other ministers of that qualitie."[7] "That qualitie" was, of course, puritanism. What is crucial, however, is the fact that while in London, Heydon gadded to hear not just John Davenport and that zealous defender of the Law, Thomas Taylor, but also the infamous Peter Shaw, whose sermons he took the time to copy out and preserve.[8] So too, in the mid-1630s, Sarah Wilson's tour of the London preaching circuit would bring her to the pulpits of Tobias Crispe, one "Mr. Gray" (very possibly the antinomian of the same name), John Cordwell, alias Cardell (who would later write an enthusiastic epistle in praise of John Everarde), as well as Elias Crabtree, the non-conformist curate of St. Lawrence Pountney, and one of the signatories of the articles against Peter Shaw.[9] The point, here, is that while it might be useful under certain conditions to treat the antinomian underground as something that existed outside and beyond puritanism, such an approach

[7] PRO, SPD 16/119/22, fol. 27r-v. The preachers mentioned are presumably Thomas Taylor, Hugh Peters, John Davenport, Thomas Foxley, and Peter Shaw. I owe my knowledge of this document to Paul Seaver.

[8] It is tempting to wonder whether this man was the "Mr. Heydon" who would later be accused of antinomianism in a petition sent from the Westminster Assembly to the House of Commons in August 1643. If so, his flirtation with Shaw may have signaled the beginning of a drift away from mainstream piety. See *The Whole Works of the Late Rev. John Lightfoot, D.D.*, ed. J. Pitman (London, 1825), 13: 9.

[9] CUL MS. Dd. vi. 47, fols. 20v, 27v, 45v, 60v, 78v, 94v, 107v, 119v. The book is dated 3 Oct. 1635 on its inside cover. Unfortunately, Wilson's hand was so poor that her notes are virtually illegible. For Crabtree, see D. Como and P. Lake, "Puritans, Laudians and Antinomians in Caroline London: The Strange Case of Peter Shaw in its Contexts," *Journal of Ecclesiastical History*, 50 (1999).

by itself fails to explain the complexities of the historical record, leaving us with a partially obstructed view of the nature of early Stuart antinomianism, and an unduly monolithic view of the puritan community as a whole.

To penetrate to the heart of the issue, we need to turn to the powerfully evocative spiritual recollections of Anna Trapnel, the famed godly prophetess. In her *Legacy for Saints* of 1654, Trapnel bestowed upon her readers what is in essence an antinomian "conversion narrative." Reared by godly parents, Trapnel had from her earliest days been weaned on the conventions of mainstream puritanism, although it was not until adolescence that she took up the godly life with special zeal:

> when I was about 14. years of age, I began to be very eager and forward to hear and pray, though in a very formall manner; Thus I went on some years, and then I rose to a higher pitch, to a more spiritual condition, as I thought, and I followed after that Ministry that was most pressed after by the strictest Professors, and I ran with great violence, having a great zeal, though not according to knowledge, and I appeared a very high grown Christian in the thoughts of many, I had great parts, in prayer great inlargements, and in discoursing and repeating of Sermons, I was very forward, and did it with great delight and affection, and much trembling of spirit was upon me, but I was in all this very legall, and yet more legall.

In other words, she had become enveloped in the culture of English puritanism, with its various forms of collective spiritual exercise, its rigorous devotion to the word preached, and its close, almost incestuous, bonds of community. Yet despite her apparent social success within this community, Trapnel's own sense of spiritual worth disintegrated when a sermon by Hugh Peter awakened in her doubt concerning her own share in God's covenant: "without the knowledge of God, to be my God," she concluded, "I am undone; my Spirit is filled with horror, and the terrors of the Law exceedingly oppressed me, and I ran from Minister to Minister, from Sermon to Sermon, but I could find no rest." Indeed, Trapnel's anxiety soon mutated into a sort of spiritual panic. She began to attend sermons every day, and "if I had not shed some tears in a Sermon, I then went home full of horror, concluding my self to be that stony ground Christ spake of in the parable of the sower." Attempting to extract comfort from "marks and signs" of holiness and devotion, she found herself "exceedingly hurried to duty, and to Ordinances, so that I could not sleep in my bed." Even Anna's formidable godly mother began to fret over the scale of her daughter's spiritual and devotional gymnastics, warning that "if thou dost fast so day after day, and run thus up and down, the devill will take advantage against thee." The warnings were to no avail: insomnia was soon coupled with a more profound internal affliction, as Trapnel began incessantly to mull over suicide. Here was a classic puritan crisis of assurance, not unlike those reported by Nehemiah Wallington and Dionys Fitzherbert.

Unlike Wallington and Fitzherbert, however, Trapnel would find succor not in the bosom of mainstream puritan divinity, but in a version of antinomianism. As in the case of Howes, it is not wholly clear how she first came into contact with antinomian enthusiasts, but even as she suffered through her crisis, slaving along under the weight of holy duties and ordinances, she appears to have been rubbing shoulders quite openly with some who had already succumbed to the ways of "free grace": "when I have been among those that have been filled with joy, being Professors of Divine love, and much acquainted with free grace in the power of it, which I was very ignorant of, so that their company was burdensome to me, yet I could not keep from them." Observing her malaise, "many that were inlightened in the doctrine of free grace, took a great deal of pains with me, perswading me to hear those Ministers that taught most upon the doctrine of free grace," but Anna remained stubbornly committed to the more familiar incantations of mainstream godly divinity: "I delighted in the thunderings of the Law, and they pleased me best that preached most upon the Law, and that prest legall qualifications." Indeed, the antinomian solution of "free grace" initially struck her as simplistic and hollow. It was "a cold, lean, poor discovery, I thought." Indeed, to read Trapnel's account, one is struck not by the isolation of these "Professors of Divine love," but by their integration into the godly community; Trapnel saw them not as a clutch of diabolical heretics, but as devotees of a distinctive, pietistic alternative to which some of her acquaintances adhered. Although she initially found this alternative unsatisfying, in time, Trapnel found herself sucked into their world, "and . . . I began to hearken to free grace."

Even once she had come under the spell of the preachers of free grace, however, she continued to lack full assurance. Although she now realized that her own efforts and works were of no avail with God, she had not yet received God's comforting pledge that she was, in fact, one of the recipients of his overwhelming, unearned grace. Such assurance was not long in coming. Trapnel's description of this experience, which she repeatedly dubbed the "sealing of the spirit," came upon her incrementally, but with undeniable directness, in a manner that presaged her subsequent, celebrated activities as a prophetess: "none spake any word that did in the least measure revive me, till that voice sounded that I could not contradict, but I did withstand it, and repulse it as long as I could, and when it spake as a stil small voice, I rejected it a week, before I felt, heard and saw that glorious light and power, sounded into my spirit, which caused an eccho, or answer from my spirit in believing the testimony of the Spirit." Trapnel appears to have been using these images of "sound," "voice" and "hearing" in a disconcertingly literal manner:

> that small voice made such a report in my soul, which made me to listen; it was such a speaking that I had not heard before, therefore it was very strange to me; the word I had was this, *Christ is thine, and thou art his*; and

> no word was spoken to my spirit for six or seven days but this; it followed me where ever I went; sometimes as I have been going along the streets, I have looked behind me, thinking I had heard some locall voice, a voice without me, but sure it was because I was unacquainted with the voice of the Spirit speaking in, or to the soul; I oft-times turned back when I have been going along the streets, to see who it was that spake, taking that for visible which was invisible.

This voice continued to whisper to her until at length it revealed itself. This moment of rupture and transcendence occurred during a sermon preached by the notorious antinomian minister John Simpson on New Year's 1642. Close to the end of Simpson's discourse on Romans 8,

> suddenly my soul was filled with joy unspeakable, and full of glory in believing, the spirit witnessing in that word, Christ is thy wel-beloved and thou art his; my soul was now full of joy as it could hold . . . oh what triumphing and songs of *Hallelujah* were in my spirit, I knew not where I was, nor how to get out of the place where I sat, I apprehended nothing but a clothing of glory of my whole man; I never beheld Saints as I did then, I saw their faces like the face of Angels; Oh what Angelicall creatures did they appear before me, full of shining brightness! oh what a heart inflamed now was mine, filled with the flame of Divine love! there appeared now no smoak, but a clear flame, nothing now before me but christal appearances: oh how my soul was enamoured with Christ! Earth was now gone, and heaven come.

Once she had returned to terra firma, Trapnel found herself exultant and renewed, and for a full year afterwards experienced "exceeding raptures of joy very frequent, little or no intermissions."[10]

Such mystical, firsthand experiences of the divine presence were of course hallmarks of antinomian piety, although Trapnel's case was surely extreme even among the figures examined in the course of this study. Her belief that God's voice was echoing through her skull was one that might have caused a certain amount of discomfort among even the most hardened antinomians. Nevertheless, it fits perfectly into the pattern of her later career. As Phyllis Mack and others have shown, Trapnel would soon become an object of reverence and horror in revolutionary London, when her feverish trances and claims to direct divine communication launched her to contemporary fame.[11] Her spiritual visions, which blended fantastic dreamscapes, biblical imagery, and Trapnel's own well-honed skills of scriptural interpretation, earned her

---

[10] The three preceding paragraphs are based upon A. Trapnel, *A Legacy for Saints; Being Several Experiences of the dealings of God with Anna Trapnel* (1654), 1-10.

[11] P. Mack, *Visionary Women: Ecstatic Prophecy in Seventeenth-Century England* (Berkeley: University of California Press, 1992).

awe in some quarters, while provoking in others the claim that she was "a witch, deluder, [and] Imposter."[12] Here, as with Howes, Trapnel's voyage into antinomianism led her to ever more peculiar and creative modes of mystical religiosity, culminating at length in precisely the sorts of enthusiastic spiritism that bedeviled Presbyterians and Royalists alike during the 1640s and 1650s. Yet despite this, there is little sign that Trapnel's antinomianism ever sequestered her from mainstream puritans. Certainly, some of her acquaintances appear to have bemoaned her initial flirtation with Simpson and his admirers: as Trapnel put it, "many . . . cryed down free grace as a doctrine of liberty to sin," while "some would tell me that I had found an easie way to heaven now, to go to heaven in believing." For her commitment to "this tenent of truth, [i.e. free grace] I passed under the name of Antinomian."[13] These personal jibes, however, suggest not isolation, but continuing discourse with her old acquaintances. Indeed, despite her newfound opinions, she apparently continued to converse with and esteem certain non-antinomian ministers. Among them was the entirely respectable Independent divine, William Greenhill, the "man of God" who prayed with Trapnel at her bedside in 1646, when a mysterious, protracted illness brought forth the first of her notorious visions.[14] For all her eccentricity, neither Trapnel's antinomianism, nor her emerging prophetic pretensions ever cut her off completely from the network of sociability, shared affect and personal connection that held together the godly community.

In the light of such evidence, then, it is probably appropriate to modify Bozeman's conclusion, and to suggest that, at least in its more extreme forms, early Stuart antinomianism stood in a liminal state, suspended between puritanism and something wholly distinct. Nevertheless, even the most extreme permutations retained so many of the cultural and intellectual traits of English puritanism that large numbers of godly contemporaries—people like Heydon, Wilson, the young Giles Firmin, and Trapnel prior to her "conversion"—did not, in fact, see antinomians as anything more than opinionated puritans. Indeed, this was the unacknowledged subtext of the violent diatribes of Burton, Taylor, Bentham, and others: these preachers were seeking to convince the godly laity that antinomians were not quaintly erring brethren, but sinister wolves, cleverly hiding beneath the white woolen garments of a pretended godliness. Such rhetoric was only necessary because most antinomians did, under all but the most careful scrutiny, appear to be godly people; even the wildly heretical Everarde, for instance, led his extra-parochial conventicles in

---

12 Trapnel, *Legacy*, 49.

13 Ibid., 6, 15.

14 Ibid., 29-30.

the time-honored and piously puritan practice of psalm-singing.[15] So long as these profound connections are recognized alongside the very real ideological fissures that separated the two, the question of whether antinomianism was definitively "puritan" becomes largely semantic.

Nevertheless, whether or not we choose to label antinomians as "puritans," we cannot escape the conclusion that the existence of these deeply rooted connections does in fact serve to alter profoundly our understanding of the early Stuart godly community. Where Patrick Collinson has sought to equate puritanism with a deep and unshakably conservative concern for social, political, and intellectual order, the evidence presented in this book suggests that the situation was in fact far more complicated. Indeed, the conclusions reached here suggest that the culture of English puritanism was well suited to produce not only orderly and self-consciously orthodox modes of piety, but permutations of religiosity that can only be described as theologically, socially, and politically deviant. If this complicates the picture presented by Collinson, so too, it raises questions about the origins and nature of radical sectarianism as described by Christopher Hill. For the evidence considered in this study most certainly suggests that this sectarianism emerged not from a separate, marginal tradition of plebeian heterodoxy, but from the very center of the culture of puritanism. It is a point that bears heavily on the arguments of both Collinson and Hill: peculiar cultural practices that were at the heart of puritan religiosity contained within them the seeds of ideological fragmentation and radicalization.

Among these practices were stubbornly voluntaristic forms of extraparochial piety, including compulsive sermon-gadding, collective Bible-reading, sermon repetition, group prayer sessions, exchange of hortatory letters and manuscripts, as well as habitual private "conferences," some of which amounted to little more than friendly social gatherings, others of which resembled nothing so much as formal disputations designed to mediate between disagreeing factions. Indeed, implicit in all of these practices and devotions was the conviction that individual ministers and ordinary laypeople all possessed the ability (perhaps the duty) to attempt to recognize, interpret, and act upon God's truth as manifested in his word. While at one level such behaviors and expectations might be seen as merely protestant, and hence entirely inoffensive, at another level it is quite obvious that their unsupervised, self-validating and improvisational quality rendered them a potential threat not only to the institutional power of the church, but also to the very notion of centralized and centralizing order.

---

[15] J. Everard, *Some Gospel-Treasures Opened: Or, the Holiest of all Unvailing*, 523.

As Collinson has noted, this potential often remained dormant and unrealized. After all, the point of many of these exercises was to bring professors under the yoke of God's truth, which was always taken to be unitary and harmonizing. Nevertheless, the prescriptive goals of order and unity to which all of these practices ostensibly aspired did not fully accord with reality. This was especially true given the fact that the organ or agent that was assumed to lead individuals to truth and to create a sense of holy unity among professors was taken to be the spirit of God. Here, again, the "spirit" was of course assumed to be an instrument that would lead professors to a single, undeniable set of truths. In practice, however, the more individuals tended to trust in the power of the spirit (as opposed to the church, the minister, or even the Bible) to guide them toward the truth, the more likely they were to allow the spirit to convey them away from accepted standards of orthodox belief and practice. There is a logic, a tangible and unbroken thread, connecting Anna Trapnel's youthful sermon gadding, to her "inlargements in prayer," to her tortured flight from the whisperings of the spirit in her head, to her awestruck raptures in John Simpson's congregation, and finally to her dramatic and febrile outpourings of prophecy in the 1640s and 1650s. This thread in fact binds together almost all of the figures examined in this study. Although antinomians embraced such "spiritism" with a special exuberance, they were without question merely borrowing and amplifying tendencies that were evident among even the most conservative and order-obsessed members of the godly community.

Indeed, this tendency to rely on the spirit to reveal divine truth was merely a reflection of the broader godly obsession with the Bible and its interpretation. At the very heart of puritan religiosity was a radical and uncompromising logocentricity, together with a concomitant impulse to bring the truths revealed in God's word to life in the world. This impulse—perhaps best captured by Bozeman's usefully descriptive notion of biblical primitivism—was absolutely central to the culture of English puritanism. Yet like the practices mentioned above, this logocentric/primitivistic impulse contained within it a paradoxical tendency toward discord and conflict. For although the godly always assumed that the scriptures contained within them a single, unitary, and unbending set of truths—one primordial pattern—the ambiguities and multivocality of the bible naturally and inexorably confounded their efforts to discern this pure, unadulterated pattern. In their drive to penetrate to this primal and unitary "core," the godly thus produced varying readings of scripture, leading to heated conflict, conflict which was paradoxically inflamed by the very passion and force with which they clung to the notion that the Bible contained within it the one standard of truth and order. From this perspective, the ideological assumptions that bound the puritan community together as a distinctive entity were almost certain to lead to collisions over the truth, ultimately undermining all unity and order among the godly. The results, as we have seen, were competing and in many cases deeply radical forms of belief and practice. If, as Collinson has rightly argued, late Elizabethan and early Stuart puritanism could sire order-obsessed magistrates such as Edward Lewkenor, Robert Jermyn, and John Higham, it could also give birth to the awesomely idiosyncratic (and diverse) quartet of John Everarde, John Traske, Edward Howes, and Anna Trapnel, none of whom can plausibly be mistaken for pillars of social or ideological stability.

New England's Antinomian Controversy

Given the deep ideological affinities described above, it should come as no surprise that the problem of antinomianism—real or imagined—quickly migrated across the Atlantic to afflict that newfound puritan stronghold of Massachusetts. In the light of the evidence presented in this study, there can be little question that the so-called Antinomian Controversy, which gripped the Bay Colony between 1636 and 1638, had ample and clear precedents. It was, in some ways, a replay of the earlier controversies that had plagued London in 1628-31. Or rather, it might be more accurate to say that the London controversies directly prepared and shaped the perceptions and categories with which New England puritans would interpret the opinions and claims of Anne Hutchinson, John Wheelwright, and their sympathizers. From this perspective, it hardly mattered whether they were or were not genuine antinomians or Familists; the moment they began to denounce their opponents as "legal teachers," enslaved under a Covenant of Works, and beguiled by the mistaken assumption that grace could be inferred from sanctification, their fate was as good as sealed. These were terms with which the godly would have been all too familiar by 1636, and even if they were deployed unwittingly (an unlikely prospect), the response they elicited was predictable, and based upon the expectations and fears that had emerged from the recent English controversies over antinomianism.

As we have seen, in many cases, New England puritans had had direct and demonstrable experience with anti-legal religion. The Firmins, allies of John Winthrop in Boston, were relatives of the convicted antinomian Henry Firmin; others had still more immediate experience. In giving her conversion narrative, Martha Collins of Cambridge confessed that she had engaged in a brief period of spiritual experimentation under the ministry of Peter Shaw in London.[16] Collins's pastor, Thomas Shepard, perhaps the most extreme foe of the Hutchinsonians, famously admitted in his autobiography that he had flirted

---

16 From Collins's church confession, as printed in M. McGiffert, ed., *God's Plot: Puritan Spirituality in Thomas Shephard's Cambridge.* Rev. ed. (Amherst: University of Massachusetts Press, 1993), 192.

with antinomianism in his own troubled youth, fraternizing with Familists and even considering a trip to Grindleton at one stage.[17] Meanwhile, John Davenport—generally viewed as a moderate, mediating figure in the New England controversies—had wittingly or unwittingly shared his London pulpit with the antinomian Greene, and had later clashed with John Pordage, whose alleged opinions bore an uncanny resemblance to some of the claims being canvassed in Boston.[18] Finally, if we consider John Winthrop, Jr.'s evident curiosity in the exotic teachings of Everarde, and his long-standing friendship with Edward Howes, John Winthrop, Sr.'s deep fear and hostility regarding antinomianism may indeed appear to have been more visceral and poignant than has hitherto been recognized. Whether he knew of his son's disreputable interests or not, when Winthrop boarded the *Arbella* for Boston in 1630, the London godly community was fractured by strife over the contested issues of the Moral Law; he and many others like him had been well seasoned for the controversies that would soon erupt in the less restrictive air of the Bay.

This is not to argue that the Colony was shot through with antinomianism, nor even that Wheelwright, Hutchinson, Cotton, and their closest supporters were themselves genuine antinomians, in the sense outlined in this book. Their arguments did, however, tend to replicate in form and tone those that had been made by the likes of Everarde, Eaton, and Traske in the preceding years. Thus, when members of the Boston congregation began to put it about that the elect were justified before and without faith, John Winthrop and other critics had ample reason to be suspicious; as we have seen, the claim that God's children were justified and saved before they actually believed was a characteristic Eatonist argument, which had quickly diffused throughout the antinomian community.[19] Such claims were immediately plotted onto a known map of recognized heretical opinion, identifying their purveyors as hidden antinomians.

The Hutchinsonians themselves appear to have done little to dispel such suspicions. Thus, during his notorious Fast-Day Sermon of January 1637, Wheelwright not only denigrated the practice of fasting—hinting that it was necessary only for those to whom Christ was absent—but suggested that what was required was a spiritual war against those who oppressed God's people with a Covenant of Works. In answering the objection that "This will cause a combustion in the Church and comon wealth," Wheelwright confessed it might be so, but, alluding to the widely held apocalyptic belief that Rome needed to burn to the ground before Christ could reign, he noted that the es-

---

[17] See the sources cited in Chapter Eight and Chapter Ten, above.

[18] See Chapter Two, above.

[19] See the *Winthrop Papers* (Boston: Massachusetts Historical Society, 1943), 3:326-27; see above, Chapter Six, for a discussion of this theological issue.

chatological battle between Christ and Antichrist was one that could only be consummated through flame:

> This battle betweene Micheall and his Angells, the battle betweene Gods people and those that are not, those battles of Christians must be burning, and what is it, but the burning of the word of God accompanied by the Holy Ghost. . . . Brethren, we know that the whore must be burnt, Revelation 18. 8. it is not shaving of her head and paring her nayles and changing her rayment, that will serve the turne, but this whore must be burnt. Many speake of the externall burning of Rome, but I am sure there must be a Spirituall burning, and that burning by the fire of the Gospell; This way must Antichrist be consumed . . . wee know not how soone the conversion of the Jewes may come, and if they come, they must come by the downfall of Antichrist, and if we take him away, we must burne him; therefore never fear combustions and burnings.[20]

Here Wheelwright had essentially identified his enemies with Antichrist, thus fanning the flames of conflict and paving the way for his own banishment from the Bay Colony. As if this were not enough, however, he had done so in terms that were bound to further exacerbate suspicions of Familism and antinomianism. For Wheelwright's words recalled those of John Everarde, who as we have seen, claimed against the grain of puritan thought that Antichrist was not an external entity—the Pope—but was rather an internal presence that infected even the pulpits, communion tables, and members of the Church of England. Everarde, too, had denied the importance of the external burning of Rome, suggesting that the true meaning of the burning of Antichrist was the internal, spiritual bonfire that occurred when Christ came to dwell in the believer: "the more sin, the more fire, the greater burning . . . Christ is this fire; and let me tell you this burning and consuming is for your good; it is that out of the ashes of the old man [i.e. Antichrist] you may have a new life, a new resurrection."[21] The point here is not that Wheelwright was a Familist, nor indeed that his account agreed, in its precise details, with the interpretation offered by Everarde. But in presenting his listeners with this spiritualized eschatology, and in hinting that the external Antichrist of Rome was not the subject of the great apocalyptic conflagration described in Revelations, he was almost begging his no doubt dumbfounded listeners to confirm themselves in their suspicions that he was a dangerous, familistical heretic. Further research will undoubtedly reveal that in large part, New England's Antinomian Controversy progressed and was prosecuted according to just such well-established

---

[20] D. D. Hall, ed. *The Antinomian Controversy, 1636-1638: A Documentary History* (Durham and London: Duke University Press, 1990), 165-66.

[21] Everard, *Gospel-Treasures*, 4-5. For Everarde's belief that the terms "old man" and "Antichrist" were equivalent, see Chapter Seven.

stereotypical categories of interpretation, categories that had been elaborated and disseminated above all in the ten years preceding the conflicts in Boston.[22]

Revolutionary England

All of this was even more true for those who remained in England. When the engines of ecclesiastical censorship and control were disassembled beginning in 1641, the animosities and conflicts of previous years immediately surfaced. Papers that had remained unpublished for fear of episcopal discipline now emerged from London's presses. Ideas that had been effectively outlawed could now be published with impunity. What had been a small, tightly knit underground was now free to take root, mutate, and spread, with dramatic and sometimes spectacular results. Indeed, as noted in the Introduction, antinomianism would be deeply implicated in many of the most radical theological, social, and ideological experiments of the revolutionary years. An examination of the development of these radical ideas and programs lies beyond the purview of the present book, and would in any case involve an exploration not simply of antinomianism but of other important strands of religious thought, including Anabaptism and millenarianism. Nevertheless, even the most cursory glance at the upheavals of the civil wars and Interregnum shall serve to illustrate the basic point.

In some cases, we can trace direct links from the pre-war period into the 1640s. At the "perfectionist" end of the London antinomian community, fascinating continuities immediately emerge. Howes, as we have seen, began his spiritual pilgrimage with an interest in alchemy and John Everarde, progressed into Familism in the late 1630s, only to appear precisely where we should expect to find him in the 1640s—taking notes on the sermons of Robert Gell (at length, Howes would go on to carry his spiritual revelations to the pulpit of Goldhanger, Essex).[23] Similarly, we should not be shocked to learn that in the 1650s, Ludowick Muggleton would encounter one "*Proudlove*, a notable Ranter" in London. This man—presumably the same Stephen Proudlove who had visited the dreams of Edward Howes—had allegedly masterminded a (failed) plot to humiliate Muggleton and his fellow "witness of the spirit" John Reeve, in return for which the eccentric prophets awarded Proudlove the most backhanded and dubious distinction revolutionary London had to offer,

---

[22] See now M. Winship, *Making Heretics: Militant Protestantism and Free Grace in Massachusetts, 1636-1641* (Princeton: Princeton University Press, 2002).

[23] Edward Howes, *Short Arithmetick: or The Old and Tedious way of Numbering, Reduced to a New and Briefe Method* (1650), title page. See also British Library, Sloane MS. 979, fol. 3r. For Gell, see ibid., fols. 30r-34v.

their "Sentence of Condemnation to Eternity."[24] So, too, the mysterious antinomian tailor "Greene," who had managed to obtrude himself into various city pulpits in the late 1620s and early 1630s, may well have been the notorious London felt-maker and tub-evangelist John Green who earned brief celebrity in 1641 for preaching down the Law and legal preparation as paths to Christ.[25] Rapha Harford, the London bookseller who had been identified by Creech as a Familist and disciple of John Everarde in the 1630s, eventually went on to publish Everarde's sermons in 1653. His spiritualist religious radicalism appears to have been matched by a penchant for political radicalism—in 1649, he wrote a bitter denunciation of London's presbyterian clergy, in which he defended the army and justified the execution of the king.[26] Perhaps most spectacular of all was the career of the notorious Dr. John Pordage, also accused of Familism by the insider John Etherington. Whether Etherington was correct or not, we have already seen that as early as 1634, Pordage had earned a reputation as an anti-legal mystic in London; during the 1640s and 1650s, it is no surprise that his home in Berkshire would come to serve as a meeting point for visionaries, religious eccentrics, and extremists of all varieties.[27]

Direct connections can also be traced at the "imputative" end of the London antinomian scene. The towering role that had once been played by John Eaton was now assumed by Tobias Crispe, who arrived in London in 1642, having been driven out of his living in Wiltshire. Crispe quickly won both renown and infamy for his forthright expression of anti-legal ideas, but he was apparently no stranger to the London antinomian scene; as argued in Chapter Two, he had connections to John Emersone of the Eaton circle, and had probably acquired his ideas during extended visits to his native city. Perhaps predictably, in 1642, almost as soon as the bishops had fallen, the group sur-

---

[24] Lodowick Muggleton, *The Acts of the Witnesses of the Spirit, in Five Parts* (1699; reprinted, 1764), 56-58.

[25] For John Green, see *A Curb for Sectaries and Bold Propheciers* (1641); *New Preachers, New* (1641), sigs. Av, A4v, where he is referred to as both a felt-maker and hatmaker, and where he is reproved for attacking legitimate ministers and for instructing them "how to preach the word, not the Law nor legall preparation for the receiving of Christ, that in your opinion is not Gods way." It is also tempting to wonder whether he was not the "Mr. Green" who, together with John Spencer and the antinomian Paul Hobson, apparently gathered what is normally assumed to have been an early Baptist congregation in London in 1639, for which, see Champlin Burrage, *The Early English Dissenters in the Light of Recent Research (1550-1641)* (Cambridge: Cambridge University Press, 1912), 2: 304.

[26] R. Harford, *A Gospel-Engine, or Streams of Love and Pity* (1649).

[27] For Pordage's antics during the Revolution, see C. Hill, *The World Turned Upside Down: Radical Ideas During the English Revolution* (London, 1972).

rounding Crispe rapidly published the posthumous works of the patriarch Eaton. Crispe's friend Robert Lancaster, long a resident of London, set his name to *The Honey-Combe of Free Justification*, while Crispe himself was rumored to be responsible for the release of Eaton's *The Discovery of the Most Dangerous Dead Faith*.[28] Emersone, meanwhile, appears to have continued to propagate his beliefs unabated into the 1640s; in August 1643, the Westminster Assembly complained of his antinomianism in a petition to the Commons, and in October of the next year, he was denied a benefice as a consequence of his notorious opinions.[29] Crispe's impact, both in galvanizing the polemical fury of opponents and in winning new followers, was clearly considerable. Henry Pinnell, the radical army preacher, claimed in a prefatory epistle to Crispe's sermons that he had known the doctor since 1631, strongly suggesting that Pinnell's own path towards religious and political radicalism owed much to Crispe's influence.[30] Similarly, it was at the foot of Crispe's London pulpit that Lawrence Clarkson began the epic and emblematic spiritual pilgrimage that led him through antinomianism, Anabaptism, Ranterism, and finally, Muggletonianism.[31]

Thus, although many first-generation London antinomian leaders had either died or abandoned the city by 1641, their legacy clearly lived on. The community they created and the ideas they planted were eagerly cultivated by the likes of Crispe, John Simpson, and Giles Randall to create a resurgent antinomian movement in the city after the fall of episcopacy. This lineage was taken as given by the godly minister John Sedgwick in 1643, when he sarcastically heralded civil-war London's newly assertive antinomian preachers as "six or seven rare Phoenixes, sprung out of the ashes of one Mr *Trask*, *Eaton*, *Shaw*, and others of that stamp."[32]

Farther afield, the Grindletonian community likewise provided rich fodder for later developments. As we have seen, John Webster, Brearley's successor at Kildwick-in-Craven, would go on to serve as a parliamentary army chaplain before migrating south to London, where he emerged in the early 1650s as a well-known radical preacher. The elderly cleric William Boyes, one of Roger

---

[28] The rumor was reported by Stephen Geree in *The Doctrine of Antinomianisme Confuted* (1644), 41.

[29] *Works of . . . Lightfoot*, 13: 9; S.W. Carruthers, *The Everyday Work of the Westminster Assembly* (Philadelphia, 1943), 160.

[30] T. Crispe, *Christ Alone Exalted in the Perfection and Encouragements of the Saints* (1646), sig. A8v.

[31] See Lawrence Claxton, *The Lost Sheep Found: Or, the Prodigal Returned to his Fathers House* (1660), 9-10.

[32] John Sedgwick, *Antinomianisme Anatomized. Or, A Glasse for the Lawlesse: Who deny the Ruling use of the Morall Law unto Christians under the Gospel* (1643), 1.

Brearley's earliest disciples, would be among the first figures in Yorkshire convinced by George Fox in the early 1650s and for a time accompanied Richard Farnsworth on a whirlwind preaching tour of South Yorkshire. In 1656 the sometime Lancashire Grindletonian, Thomas Barcroft, wrote and circulated an open letter to his former coreligionists in an effort to win them over to Quakerism.[33] Many, however, resisted the blandishments of the inner light. As demonstrated in Chapter Eight, a second-generation Grindletonian connection, centering on the Towne clan, continued to cohere in West Yorkshire into the 1650s. Indeed, stalwarts such as Josiah Collier and Brearley's nephew-by-marriage, Richard Coore, gamely disseminated antinomian doctrines into the 1680s, provoking conflict with more orthodox dissenting ministers such as Oliver Heywood.

Such genealogies are instructive. The critical point, however, is not that all civil-war radical activity can somehow be read as the work of the prewar antinomians or sectaries; rather, it is to suggest that the antinomian underground, as it had developed prior to 1640, served as a kind of womb, nurturing both people and ideas that would have significant impact during the years of civil war and revolution. What had been a small, incestuous, and secretive community grew rapidly after 1640, as antinomian ideas spilled out of the radical underworld and into the cacophonous and free-wheeling public sphere of the civil war, winning over aspiring saints such as Clarkson, Trapnel and Jane Turner.[34] In this environment of relative freedom, antinomian ideas were readily mixed with, or assimilated to, other doctrinal curiosities in order to produce new and sometimes unnervingly heterodox theological permutations. Thus, for instance, many of those who would gain notoriety as Baptists during the 1640s and 1650s—the army radicals Paul Hobson, Henry Denne and John Simpson, for instance—coupled their opinions on church government and believers' baptism with implicit or overt antinomianism. Some likewise began to

---

[33] For William Boyes, see J. L. Nickalls, ed., *The Journal of George Fox* (Cambridge: Cambridge University Press, 1952), 88-89; Library of the Society of Friends, London, Swarthmore MS. 356, fols. 229r-v; for Barcroft, see Library of the Society of Friends, London, Swarthmore MS. 351, fol. 174, dated 24 Oct., 1656, which was written "for the Service of those with whom I have had in tymes longe since past sweet society and union in spirit in the days of that glimmeringe Light under the Ministry of Breerely, Tennant and some few more whose memories I honnor, called then by the Professors of the world Grinletonians, Antinomians, Hereticks, Sectaries." Barcroft dated the beginning of his flirtation with Grindletonianism to 1630-32.

[34] For Turner's story of her own conversion to antinomianism, see Jane Turner, *Choice Experiences of the Kind dealings of God* (1653), 49-52.

blend antinomian ideas with varying shades of universalism.[35] Such spiritual experimentation was perhaps most pronounced in the army, a fact much lamented by Richard Baxter, who, as Tim Cooper has recently shown, was profoundly affected by his confrontation with soldier-antinomians.[36] Moreover, in both the army and in London, there can be no doubt that antinomian ideas often went hand in glove with a deep political radicalism. To take just one enormously significant example, the celebrated Leveller architect William Walwyn testified that he had been won over to antinomianism "long before" 1644, and as J. C. Davis has argued in an influential essay, this theological orientation appears to have been central to the development of Walwyn's political thought.[37]

The significance of antinomianism for the development of civil-war sectarian radicalism cannot be doubted. Yet there is good reason to believe that even beyond the sectarian fringe, the spirit or logic of the anti-legal critique had been absorbed into English religious discourse, with important intellectual ramifications for the fortunes of puritanism in the 1640s; thus, even many of the most respectable of so-called Independents, including Philip Nye, Thomas Goodwin, and John Goodwin, appear to have flirted with anti-legal opinions in the 1630s, borrowing or replicating styles of argument that had been recently deployed by outright antinomian agitators. In 1630, Nye, for one, had made a series of statements so unusual that Stephen Denison felt compelled to denounce him from the pulpit. In a manner reminiscent of anti-legalists, Nye had allegedly maintained that "In generall not onely small but great sinnes . . . against the morall law may stand with our claime in God," an assertion that called to mind the paradigmatic antinomian tendency to suggest that the sins of believers were not apprehended by God. In this vein, he went so far as to argue that "if thy hart be turned against sin, you maist cometh with as much

---

[35] For a classic and well-known example, see *The Power of Love* (1643), often attributed to the Leveller William Walwyn.

[36] T. Cooper, *Fear and Polemic in Seventeenth-Century England: Richard Baxter and Antinomianism* (Aldershot: Ashgate, 2001); Baxter was not mistaken in his assessment of the extent of antinomian penetration. For three interesting examples of antinomian soldier-theologians, see N. Cowling, *The Saints Perfect in this Life, or Never* (1647); R. Wastfield, *Christ Coming in the Clouds; or, The dawning of the Day* (1647); R. Wilkinson, *The Saints Travel to the Land of Canaan* (1648).

[37] W. Walwyn, *Walwyn's Just Defence* (1649), 8: Speaking of his situation between 1643 and 1645, he recalled that "I, through God's goodnesse, had long before been established in that part of doctrine (called then, Antinomian) of free justification by Christ alone"; J. C. Davis, "The Levellers and Christianity," in B. Manning, ed., *Politics, Religion and the English Civil War* (London: Edward Arnold, 1973).

boldnes to the throne of grace as if thou hadst not sinned." Nye likewise manifested a classic anti-legal tendency to denigrate works of the Law and to exalt faith, suggesting that "one act of faith brings more honor to God, then performing of that virtue which is opposite to that sin." So, too, his claim that "A man may call God his God before his sins be pardoned for his sins may be said to be pardoned in respect of Gods Decree," looked suspiciously like the commonplace antinomian argument, discussed above, that justification and salvation were already accomplished before the actual onset of true belief. Perhaps most troublingly, Nye had supposedly preached that believers were to "Looke upon the justice of God as thy justice . . . you being one with christ whatsoever God hath done by Christ thou hath done," an argument that seemed to veer dangerously toward the extreme claims of divine union put forth by certain antinomians.[38] Although Nye nowhere denied that believers were bound by the Law, he appears to have been expressing a general or inchoate anti-legal sentiment, while replicating the structure of certain notoriously antinomian arguments. In the tense atmosphere of 1630, such statements were almost perfectly calculated to raise suspicions, much as the pronouncements of Wheelwright, Hutchinson, and Cotton would six years later in Boston.

Upon his arrival in London in late 1632, John Goodwin likewise appears to have made a name for himself by arguing that "the terrors of the law were not of necessity to be preached to prepare the soul for Christ; but rather, in the nature and tendency of them, did drive the soul farther from Christ."[39] As Goodwin put it in a manuscript position paper, "I conceive it therefore but tyme and labour and opportunity lost at the least, to make any solemne and entire worke of Preaching and urgeing the Lawe upon the Consciences of men, before the Preaching of Jesus Christ, and the Gospell."[40] Here, Goodwin, like Nye, was apparently manifesting a discomfort with the legalistic ways of mainstream puritanism, attempting to turn the spotlight away from the Law, and to focus it once again on God's overflowing benevolence in Christ. Indeed, in appropriating such anti-legal arguments to construct his own modified position, Goodwin may well have undercut the full force of the broader antinomian critique then current in London, for as noted in Chapter Three, the future Baptist William Allen would later confess that only Goodwin's timely preaching had won him over from his own obstinate antinomianism in the mid-1630s. Nevertheless, in the process of working out this modified for-

---

[38] PRO, SPD 16/177/68, fols. 88r-89r. The full document is transcribed in Como and Lake, "Peter Shaw."

[39] William Kiffin, *Remarkable Passages in the Life of William Kiffin*, ed. William Orme (1823), 10-11. Kiffin was much impressed with this argument.

[40] British Library, Harleian MS. 837, fol. 53v, and more generally fols. 49-61.

mulation, Goodwin had duplicated an argument that was being canvassed by full-blown antinomians such as John Traske in the same years. It is, perhaps, no surprise that Goodwin was forced to "answer . . . very many objections, the Scriptures brought by others to the contrary."[41]

Thomas Goodwin likewise expressed certain misgivings about the tenor of dominant forms of puritan pastoral teachings. In 1635, in an unguarded moment, he had admitted to Samuel Hartlib that he desired "Not to set Men to a taske of duties, this is not the day. But those are the worst that fall upon haire, apparel etc., making Men to believe that Religion consists in them." Rather, Goodwin argued, "the gaining of the heart was to bee aimed at."[42] This represented a seemingly blatant critique of a certain style of puritan divinity, which stressed the paramount importance of outward duties (and here one thinks of William Prynne, and his treatise on the "unloveliness of love locks"), revealing a strong kinship with the anti-legal arguments being made by overt antinomians in previous years. At another point, he confessed to Hartlib that he believed that Thomas Hooker, with his stringent, preparationist notions, was "a severe and Cruel Man like John Baptist, [who] urges too much and too farre the Worke of Humiliation." Like Philip Nye and John Goodwin, he appears to have been voicing discomfort with the legal rigorism, indeed the joylessness, that afflicted a certain strain of puritan pastoral divinity. In this he, like the others, seems to have been trying to give voice to a general non-antinomian anti-legalism, which stressed the overwhelming munificence of God, and the joys of divine grace, while downplaying the centrality of legal duties and conditions.[43]

Although none of these figures can meaningfully be described as antinomians, there is a sense in which their uneasiness with the strenuous and duty-based piety of mainstream puritanism may have provided the theological con-

---

41 Kiffin, *Remarkable Passages*, 10-11.

42 Sheffield University Library, Hartlib Papers, MS. 29/2/61B. *The Hartlib Papers: a Complete Text and Image Database of the Papers of Samuel Hartlib (c.1600-1662) held in Sheffield University Library*. 2d ed. (Sheffield: Humanities Research Online, 2002).

43 All of these opinions and comments should be viewed in the light of Janice Knight's recent thesis concerning the theology of those she has dubbed the "spiritual brethren"—Preston, Cotton, Sibbes, and T. Goodwin, being main exponents—who on her account propagated a distinctive practical divinity that stressed the love and benevolence of God, the expansiveness of divine grace, and the unconditional and free nature of the promises. While I disagree with certain aspects of Dr. Knight's formulation, she has detected an important and overlooked rhetorical current that set these figures apart from many of their godly brethren. See J. Knight, *Orthodoxies in Massachusetts: Rereading American Puritanism* (Cambridge, MA.: Harvard University Press, 1994), passim.

text for their rejection of presbyterian church government. Certainly, the controlling nature of presbyterianism, which was designed to impose a single, unitary and undeviating standard of right doctrine on all ministers and congregations, was unlikely to appeal to individuals who may have been questioning certain aspects of the regnant style of godly divinity. At a deeper level, the rigid disciplines of presbyterianism were calculated to impose divine order on society, to allow ministers and their godly lay allies to use various penalties and sanctions to eliminate sin and to fulfill God's will on earth—in short, to enforce precisely the sorts of behavior that both thoroughgoing antinomians and (to a lesser extent) avid spiritists such as Nye and Goodwin saw as legalistic tangents to the stuff of true religion.

Further research may well demonstrate, then, that the battles over church government masked a more fundamental intellectual and emotional bifurcation within puritanism, a split over that most basic of Christian antinomies, the relationship between Law and Gospel. This split may be discerned in a letter, written in 1650 by Nehemiah Wallington to Matthew Barker, who had succeeded Wallington's friend and spiritual shepherd Henry Roborough as pastor of St. Leonard Eastcheap. The presbyterian Roborough had been an active participant in the heated discussions over antinomianism from a very early stage. He had debated John Etherington in conference and on paper in the mid-1620s, had played a central role in the boxmaker's prosecution before High Commission, and had boasted to the High Commissioners in 1634 of his "many opposicions to the noted Heretiques and Schismaticks of theis latter tymes;"[44] Barker, an Independent who three years later would write an enthusiastic preface to the collected sermons of John Everarde, was clearly a man of a different theological and temperamental mold.[45] Wallington complained that although he personally appreciated the pleasing tunes of Barker's sermons, "some may sleep and lie snorting in their sins for many years and scarce be ever awakened by so sweet preaching as yours is." What was necessary was a dose of the Law and fear: "there is a foundation and a humbling the soul in true and sound repentance" that demanded the preaching of the law and its deadly curse, for only "the brokenhearted undone sinner . . . prizes Jesus Christ." As Paul Seaver has argued, "Wallington's quarrel with the Independents was neither doctrinal nor really ecclesiological." Rather, it was a profound matter of a theological tone or tenor, a question of differing visions

---

[44] For Roborough's debates with Etherington, and his role in the High Commission trial, see J. Etherington, *The Defence of John Etherington against Stephen Denison* (1641), 5; his opposition to latter-day heretics was noted in his defense before High Commission in 1634, when he was charged with nonconformity, schism, and predestinarian preaching, for which see Trinity College Dublin MS. 293, fol. 401r.

[45] Everard, *Gospel-Treasures*, "An approbation," signed by Barker.

of true religion; Wallington vehemently expressed this difference in no uncertain terms to a second Independent minister, George Griffith, in the same year: "Oh how pride doth abound . . . and the ministers afraid to tell them of it. Oh the prophaning of the Lord's day, drunkenness, whoredom, the swearing and blasphemies, the errors and schisms, and neither the sword of magistracy nor ministry pulled out against them. What shall I say of the covetousness, the oppression, the cruelty and unmercifullness to the poor. Oh the contempt of the Gospel, the breach of protestations and covenants, and not a minister's mouth opened to reprove any of these sins except a few of despised Presbyterians as they call them." Here, in Wallington's checklist of sins against the divine will, was a perfect expression of the zealous, activist, and coercive vision of right religion that had dominated early Stuart puritanism (and against which the antinomians had launched their fierce critique), now associated explicitly by Wallington with presbyterianism. Here also, in Wallington's bitter complaint that the Independents "make the way to heaven easier than it is," was an equally vehement denunciation of the assuring, passive piety that had received its most forceful elaboration in the pronouncements of thoroughgoing antinomians such as Eaton and Traske. For Wallington, the victory of Independency was tantamount to the failure of puritan reformation, a betrayal of the God on whom he had come to believe.[46]

On the other side, both full-blown antinomians and less extreme Independents such as Goodwin, Nye, and Barker shared a tendency to exalt the Gospel over the Law, and to magnify the independent and creative power of God's spirit on the believer. All were agreed, at a fundamental level, that what was at stake in the battle against presbyterianism was the freedom of the spirit to do its work on believers apart from external compulsion (whether in the form of the Moral Law, ceremonial prescriptions, or the "New Presbyter"). At its most extreme, this "spiritist" tendency, this opposition to outward compulsion to obedience and duty, led its proponents to reject even the less rigid church structures of congregationalism as mere outward "forms," which were taken to bridle and stifle the spirit. Thus, as early as 1642, when Lawrence Clarkson had approached Tobias Crispe for advice concerning the hotly contested subject of church government, Crispe apparently dismissed presbyterianism, congregationalism and Anabaptism alike: "He held forth against all the aforesaid Churches, That let his people be in society or no, though [a man] walked all alone, yet if he believed that Christ Jesus died for him, God beheld no iniquity in him." This belief, which echoed opinions the

---

[46] See P. Seaver, *Wallington's World: A Puritan Artisan in Seventeenth-Century New England* (Stanford: Stanford University Press, 1985), 107. I would like to thank both Paul Seaver and Peter Lake for emphasizing to me the importance of these letters.

Traskites had expressed more than twenty years earlier, essentially rendered the entire subject of church government irrelevant. Antinomians such as Crispe were indeed Independents, but they were Independents by default. As Clarkson explained, the antinomian circle in which he found himself in the early 1640s—a circle that included Randall, Simpson, and Hobson—was really neither a congregation, nor strictly speaking, a sect, "for Church it was none, in that it was but part form, and part none."[47]

And it was this radical conclusion—in which anti-legalism transformed itself into what J. C. Davis has called "anti-formalism," or an opposition to any and all forms of prescribed or preordained worship—that led ultimately to the most celebrated and peculiar styles of civil-war puritan religiosity. At one level, this anti-formalism was but an amplification of anti-ceremonialist and straightforwardly "spiritist" tendencies that had always been integral to puritanism.[48] As we have seen, however, this process of amplification took place not at the center of puritanism, but at the antinomian fringe, where these "spiritist" tendencies were turned against not only the crypto-papist ceremonies of the English Church, but against the most hallowed forms of puritan worship. Where mainstream puritans had focused their wrath on kneeling at communion and using the cross in baptism, antinomians turned the same impulse against the practices of Sabbatarianism and fasting, and finally against the "ordinances" themselves. Trapnel's mentor John Simpson illustrated the logic of this move with great clarity in 1648, when he explained that

> as we are not justified by works before, or after conversion, so we are not justified, and saved, by the submitting to any Ordinance of the Lord Jesus Christ. Salvation is not in these, there is nothing to be found in these availeable to justification. Formes of goverment and Ordinances, doe not make men Christians, but a lively faith in the Lord Jesus . . . So to those that say, men are of the world, until they are under this or that forme of government, and ordinance, I may thus speak; do these things make Christians? Presbytery (all government) is nothing, Independency is nothing, dipping is nothing, but faith which worketh by love.[49]

---

[47] Claxton, *The Lost Sheep Found*, 9, 10. The Eatonist John Eachard would produce a position nearly identical to Crispe's in 1645. See J. Eachard, *Good Newes for all Christian Souldiers* (1645), sigs. A3v-A4r.

[48] For interesting examples of godly concern over the "formality" of the new Laudian ceremonialism of the 1630s, see T. Webster, *Godly Clergy in Early Stuart England: The Caroline Puritan Movement, c. 1620-1643* (Cambridge: Cambridge University Press, 1997), 176-78.

[49] John Simpson, *The Perfection of Justification maintained against the Pharise: The Purity of Sanctification against the Stainers of it: The Unquestionableness of a future glorification against the Sadduce: In several Sermons* (1648), 30-31.

He further advised his readers to beware those who were enthralled by these "ordinances" and the controversies they had produced: "Therefore if any say unto you, you must be baptized, or you cannot be saved, I cannot look on you as a Saint, except you be baptized, you must be members of a Church, or else you cannot be members of Christ, I cannot acknowledge you as my brother, rather pity their ignorance, then yeeled to their exhortations." In Simpson's view, "they that draw Disciples after them by such rigid and Gospel destroying principles" were nothing more than "blinde, and ignorant Formalists, who place Religion rather in conformity to outward formes of Government, and submission to externall Ordinances."[50]

As we have seen, in rare cases, those under the spell of perfectionist sources at times took this process of amplification one step further, suggesting that even the hearing and reading of the Word of God were but empty forms, unless accompanied by an inner and spiritual fulfillment of the truths thus read; this, indeed, was John Everarde's position as early as 1630. Moreover, if Everarde is to be trusted, long before the outbreak of the civil war, certain individuals in London had taken this already radical position to its ultimate conclusion, casting off external ordinances entirely. Here, then, was the ultimate manifestation of the anti-formal tendency, in which all outward religious observances, duties, and means of worship melted away, leaving only the inner voice of the spirit. By 1648, when Simpson wrote, such ideas had grown disturbingly common on the English religious landscape; he accordingly felt the need to attack various ultra-antinomian groupings that in his view had perverted or disgraced the doctrine of free grace, including Familists (now identified, in terms that would soon be taken up to describe the Quakers, as "refined and subtle" Papists), as well as other "abusers and scandalizers" of the doctrine of grace, some of whom were accused of "neglecting all Christian duties, and denying the word of God to be the word of God," presumably a reference to those traditionally known as Seekers and Ranters.[51] Simpson's intemperate outbursts reveal that as in the case of puritanism more generally, the 1640s served to fracture and divide the loose coalition of like-minded individuals who composed England's "antinomian underground." As events pushed antinomian ideas into the open, leading to ever more peculiar and varied permutations of religiosity, cracks and subtle differences that had always existed became both more obvious and more pronounced, until at length

[50] Ibid., 35, 37, 46-47.

[51] Ibid., 41-44, 85-89. Perhaps unsurprisingly, however, Simpson coyly confessed that "I have rune over the bogges of Familisme, but have not beene swallowed up in them," suggesting that like many others who had found spiritual comfort within London's antinomian underground, he had experimented for a time among self-identifying Familists (ibid., sig. A5v).

men such as Simpson and the die-hard Eatonist John Eachard found themselves bleating passionately against the excesses of newly radicalized forms of anti-legal thought.[52] Presbyterians might have been forgiven for arguing that in doing so, they were merely refusing to climb into a bed that they themselves had tidily and exquisitely made. For as Simpson's own words reveal, the dedicated and extreme anti-formalism of Seeking, Ranting, and Quaking was the direct intellectual descendant of the "anti-legalism" of Eaton, Shaw, and Towne. This genealogy was acknowledged in 1654 by the Grindletonian John Webster, who claimed that God had made his old friend Robert Towne "a constant, and zealous instrument to bear forth his testimony against all unrighteousnesse of men, fleshy wisedome, carnall formes, and legall worship."[53]

Webster's letter provides striking evidence regarding the intellectual and personal contiguities between prewar antinomianism and postwar religious radicalism. But it is with another, equally revealing, letter that we shall bring this study to its conclusion. In 1646, the second edition of *The Marrow of Modern Divinity* emerged, printed for Giles Calvert, the radical bookseller and future Quaker who would shortly republish the works of Hendrik Niclaes. In tribute to its success as a work of pacification, a number of London's leading Independent divines (although significantly, no presbyterians) attached enthusiastic laudatory epistles to the book. Jeremiah Burroughs, Joseph Caryl, and the antinomian Joshua Sprigge, all well-known figures on civil-war London's preaching circuit, each testified in turn to the book's spiritual power, commending it as a long-sought-after solution to the deep conflicts over "legalism" and "antinomianism." Far more obscure was the author of the fifth and final prefatory epistle, a provincial minister from distant Weston, Somerset—Samuel Prettie.[54] "E.F." had evidently presented a copy of the first edition to Prettie, who responded to his "loving friend," writing that "I have, according to your desire, read over your Booke, and finde it full of Evangelicall light and life . . . God hath endewed his Fisher with the Net of a trying understanding and discerning judgement and discretion, whereby out of the

[52] See J. Eachard, *The Great Day at the Dore* (1648), 26-27, for his denunciation of those he called "mysticall Familists."

[53] From Webster's "Admonition to the Reader" in Towne, *A Re-Assertion of Grace. Or Vindiciae Evangelii* (1654).

[54] Prettie's reputation as an antinomian was prodigious enough to create serious doubts about his orthodoxy in 1643, when his nomination to the parsonage of Weston was challenged on account of his past heterodoxy. He was repeatedly examined before it was decided to admit him to the benefice. At least one old antinomian thus seems to have found occasional participation in the presbyterian system imposed by Parliament in 1640s to be acceptable. See W. A. Shaw, *A History of the English Church During the Civil Wars and Under the Commonwealth, 1640-1660* (London: Longmans, Green, and Co., 1900), 2: 420.

Christaline streams of the well of life, you have taken a messe of the sweetest and wholsomest fish that the whole world can afford."[55] Here, clearly, was an epistle of recommendation and recognition, designed to evoke immediately the memory of London's antinomian controversies, and to situate Fisher's book with respect to those controversies. Like Edward Fisher, Prettie had been at the center of the "hot contentions" over the issue of the law from the outset, and—again, like Fisher—his associations had earned him imprisonment at the hands of the High Commission in the early 1630s. But this epistle, with its punning play on the Marrowist's concealed identity, and its lavish and warm praise for the author's spiritual gifts, represented much more than a letter of recommendation; it was to all appearances the product of long-standing friendship, a coded message to those in the know, and—even amidst the brewing conflicts alluded to by Simpson—a powerful testimony to the ties of ideological and personal association that constituted London's antinomian underground, both before and after 1641. And it is here, in this subterranean community and in the theological discussions to which it gave rise, that historians must begin to map out the history of early Stuart religious radicalism, and to reconstruct the intimate and complex relationship of that radicalism to the broader tradition of English puritanism.

---

[55] E[dward] F[isher], *The Marrow of Modern Divinity: Touching Both the Covenant of Works, and the Covenant of Grace*, 2d ed. (1646), sig. A7r-v.

APPENDIX A

The Influence of Familism in Seventeenth-Century England

HN's doctrine of baptism provides an important key to verifying the influence of his ideas into the seventeenth century. This influence was oblique; as Christopher Marsh has argued, the Family of Love in its original, Elizabethan form—with its strict and secretive ecclesiastical hierarchy, its careful devotion to the written word of HN, and its closely knit networks of kinship and personal association—began to dissipate by the second decade of the seventeenth century.[1] The markers that Marsh has so adeptly employed to reconstruct these secretive networks—parish registers, wills, court records—tell a story of decline, revealing that by its third generation, the English wing of HN's House of Love appears to have been in serious disrepair. This did not mark the end of HN's influence, however, for it is clear that in certain circles, his works continued their secretive life, passing among small groups of devoted or curious readers in a cycle that continued into the 1640s. One crucial clue as to this survival is provided by John Etherington, sometime boxmaker and pipe-layer of Putney, who was tried by the High Commission in 1624–26 for Familism, Anabaptism, and separatism. Etherington's fascinating career has been subjected to intensive analysis by Peter Lake; for our present purposes we need only focus on a series of important facts about his life and thought.[2] First, although he vehemently denied in 1626 and afterwards that he was a Familist, Etherington's own words make it absolutely clear that he had himself been exposed to, and flirted with, the ideas of the Family of Love in the first decade of the seventeenth century. He claimed that he had abandoned their abominations as soon as he had seen into them, adopting the orthodox doctrine of the Church of England as his own. Yet even in the late 1620s, when Etherington wrote a defense of himself against the charges of which he had been convicted

---

[1] For the elaborate internal hierarchy of HN's rigid ecclesiastical regime, see A. Hamilton, ed., *Cronica. Ordo Sacerdotis. Acta HN: Three Texts on the Family of Love*, Kerkhistorische Bijdragen XV, Documenta Anabaptistica Neerlandica VI (Leiden: Brill, 1988), 206-97. It should be noted that there is no firm evidence that this intensive discipline was ever imported or put into effect by HN's English followers.

[2] P. Lake, *The Boxmaker's Revenge: 'Orthodoxy,' 'Heterodoxy,' and the Politics of the Parish in Early Stuart London* (Stanford: Stanford University Press, 2001).

in High Commission, it is clear that the ambience of Familism had left an indelible mark on his thought, and that there were certain aspects of HN's doctrine that still retained a seductive power over the boxmaker. What I want to do here is compare, very closely, HN's doctrine of baptism, as expressed in his *Evangelium Regni*, with Etherington's doctrine of baptism as expressed in his *Defence*. This in turn will be compared to John Traske's doctrine of baptism, as revealed in the pamphlet *Heavens Joy*, published anonymously by Traske in 1616. Finally, we will survey the doctrine of baptism laid out in the manuscript works of Josiah Collier, Roger Brearley's devout follower and the scribe of the Grindletonian movement.

HN

In HN's *Evangelium Regni*, we find the following description of the sacrament of Baptism:

> when the Time was fulfilled, that God wolde; according to his Promises; accomplish his Woorke/to a good Ending or Fulfilling of all the Services of the Images/figures/and Propheates (which Services have all their Ministration till unto JOHN, the Baptist/which is the true Minister and Foregoer, before the true Light or Face of God/that cometh after JOHN or his Service, with the holie Gost)/So hath John; through the Commaundement of God; had the fore-going, in his Service or Office/to the true Godservice in the Spirit/and; in all the Costes of Jordan; preached and taught the Baptisme of Repentaunce, to the Forgeevenes of Sinnes/[3]

HN argued, in his typical manner, that this "baptism of repentance" (a phrase drawn from Mark 1), was utterly distinct from the outward baptism of infants or adults:

> Consider . . . how JOHN hath ministred the Office of his Baptisme: Not that-men should runne-fourth with an handfull of Water, and so perswade themselves / when they have the elementish Water, that it is there-with enough, for to be a Christian.
>
> 6. O no: The baptisme of JOHN is not in such sort: but hee baptised them that confessed their Sinnes / and where the Water of Repentaunce flowed; inwardlie; in the Heart . . . came the Mercie or Grace of the Lorde: and they were baptised or washed with thesame Water of Repentaunce, in the River of Judgment, to the Knowledge of Salvation and the Forgeeving and Purging of their Sinnes.[4]

So then for HN there was a first, inward Baptism of Repentance (having no obvious connection to the "elementish" outward baptism by water). This bap-

---

[3] HN, *Evangelium Regni* (n.p., 1575?), fol. 45v.

[4] Ibid., fol. 46r.

tism of repentance was equated with what Saint Paul had referred to as "being baptized into the death of Christ."[5] Yet this was not enough; HN argued that this first baptism into Christ's death needed to be followed by what he called "the Baptisme of Christ," or the baptism into Christ's life by the Holy Spirit:

> And evenso after-that, came MESSIAS or CHRISTUS [that is, Annoynted] unto them, to the Safe-making of their Soules: wher-through they were baptised with the living Waters of the holie-gost/to the Reedifyng of the Tabernacle of the living God [namelie/the Generation of Mankinde] wherein God himself; with his Glorie; woulde; to a Light of Men; dwell, live, and walke, as an holie and true God/and everlasting life.
>
> 10. Wherthrough the Man becometh rightlie releassed, from the hande of all his Enemies and the Consummation or Perfection erected by him . . . Beholde/were the Man once baptised in such-wise/so mought hee then verelie, well bost him to be a Christian. but not otherwise. For whosoever is not; in his Minde and Spirit; one Spirit with CHRIST, hee belongeth not unto him.[6]

This pattern of double baptism thus was to be repeated in the experience of every believer, and only those who had experienced both the baptism of repentance, and the baptism of the spirit of Christ could truly call themselves Christians. Moreover, it seems clear enough that these two baptisms were distinct, not just conceptually, but in fact and time. Would-be Christians were first to undergo the baptism of repentance, which was followed by what HN called a "pass-over," in which they confessed their sins and partook of Christ's sufferings and crucifixion. This, in turn, was followed by the second baptism into Christ's life, whereby they were made one with the risen Christ by the baptism of the spirit.[7]

---

[5] See n.7, below.

[6] Ibid., fols. 46r-v.

[7] Ibid., fols. 50v-51r. As Christ had shared his body and blood with believers "Even-thus is Christ; in his Passe-over; gon before his Disciples and Beleevers/tothend that they all should also in such-sort; with his Bodie and Bloud which they had eaten or taken into them; follow-after him, in thesame Passe-over, remember and confesse his Passion/Suffering or Death and becom evenso implanted with like Death into him/ether [Rom 6.A, Gal. 3.C] baptised in his Death/ untill that they with the Bodie and Bloud of Christ; which they had taken into them; were passed or gon thorowe thesame Passe-over/till unto the second Birth of the Making-alive with Christ, in godlie Cleernes according to the Spirit." It is evident that this typology of salvation was not just a convenient or off-hand metaphor, but a repeated and intrinsic aspect of HN's practical theology; see, for instance, Bodleian Library, Rawlinson MS. c. 554, a translation of six chapters of HN's Glass of Righteousness, 2 Glas. 32, para. 6: "so long as the Evill hath the upperhand in you . . . so can yee not confesse Christ according to the heavenly Trueth, even as he is a Light and Life and your Saviour. But in your turning to the Mercy Seate of

Etherington

Now let us turn to John Etherington's description of baptism. In the late 1620s, while in prison, John Etherington had written a pamphlet of self-exoneration, in which he had answered the charges that his puritan accusers (namely Stephen Denison, Henry Roborough and their various lay associates) had leveled against him both in the pulpits and rumor mills of London and in the Court of High Commission. This would be published as *The Defence of John Etherington against Stephen Denison* in 1641. Here, in opposition to the claim that he secretly opposed the sacramental doctrine of the Church of England, Etherington gave a succinct but elaborate account of his beliefs concerning baptism.

He began, like HN, by proclaiming that it was not the outward washing with water that made a true Christian: "Neither Circumcision in the flesh nor Baptisme in the flesh doth give or conferre or worke grace in the heart, to make a Jew or a Christian inwardly; neither are they or either of them any part of the new birth, from above."[8] While this statement was reasonably orthodox, and might in its bare form have earned the assent of just about any puritan preacher, what followed was anything but commonplace, and should appear resoundingly familiar to those who have just finished reading the previous paragraphs on HN's doctrine.

Expounding John 3—"except a man be borne of Water and of the Spirit, he cannot enter into the Kingdome of God"—Etherington claimed that there was a two-fold spiritual baptism, and he further told his readers that

> Outward baptisme it cannot be . . . because one may be saved that is never baptized therwith. . . . [Rather] there is no principle of Christ so speciall and necessary called by the name of Baptisme, and signified by owtward Baptisme, that is required to the first plantation of a Christian (besides the Baptisme of the Holy Ghost) but onely repentance. . . . Therefore the first part of regeneration is the Baptisme of repentance, even the same which *John the*

Jesu Christ, and in the Making-up and assaulting of the evill things then submitt yourselves alwaies to the Obedience of the Requyring of the Serviceable Woorde [that is, the Law], to your Saving from the Sinne: and beleeve and hope upon Christ in that sort, as namely upon his Coming into you, in his Glory, and in your inward Man, to become One with him, in the heavenly Being. For that cause before this Coming of Christ into you, in his Glory/yee shall not in your following of Christ; namely, in the Supper of his passeover; confesse any thing els at the first, but your Sinnes, and so publish the Death of Christ for your Sinns cause (namely, so long as the Sinne hath yet the Power of the Upperhand in your Members) and trust in that sort upon Christ, and stand fast in the hope of your saving from the Sinne, and that, in the patience, till unto his Coming, as is before said."

[8] Etherington, *Defence*, 52.

> *Baptist* a speciall Minister and patterne thereof preached in the power and spirit of *Elias*, wherewith hee made ready a people prepared for the Lord, as it was prophesyed of him *Esay* 43. And is a turning and dissolving of the heart, which naturally through sin, is hard and stony, to water as it were, to flesh, as the Scriptures speake, even to weeping and mourning and humble confession of sinnes unto God, as Christ himself expresseth it in a Parable, saying; *Wee have lamented unto you* (Mat. 11. 17), *and yee have not wept*, and is caused by the speciall power and working of the Holy Ghost, and is of the Gospell, and not of the Law.[9]

Here, like HN, Etherington was arguing that there was a first baptism of repentance, which he equated with the baptism of John the Baptist. And as with HN, this baptism of repentance was not merely a logical distinction. Etherington believed that repentance was distinct from justifying faith, coming before it and preparing the way for it in time and function. Against his London puritan opponents, he argued vehemently that "repentance . . . is and must be before justifying faith; I say not all kinde of faith, but justifying onely. We must repent, that is to say, returne from the pleasures of our vaine and evill wayes, and sinnes, to a true and deepe sorrow and mourning for the same, and in humblenesse and contrition of heart confesse them unto God."[10] Only after this period of mourning and confession did the believer receive justifying faith to the remission of sins. At this point, the believer received, as it were, a second internal baptism:

> The second part of this birth from above is that Baptisme of Christ which *John the Baptist* also spake of to his disciples, whom he had prepared by the Baptisme of repentance, saying, *I indeed Baptise you with Water to repentance; but he that commeth after me is mightier then I, hee shall Baptise you with the Holy Ghost and with fire,* as if hee had said, I indeed through the power and Spirit of God preaching unto you repentance, have prepared you ready for the Lord, I have brought you into the travell of the birth, to weepe and mourne for your sinnes, the first laver of regeneration. But Christ which cometh after me, he is mightier then I, he by a more excellent gift of the Spirit (as it were with fire) will purge and sanctifie your hearts by faith and so justifie you from all your sinnes, he will deliver you that labour and are heavy loaden and accomplish in you the new birth, comfort you that mourne, bind up your broken hearts, and speake peace to your soules: For although repentance be a part of the Gospell in a generall consideration, the first principle, and of the purchase of Christ . . . yet the Word preaching peace by Jesus Christ the glad tidings of remission of sins to the repentant is the Gospell, and so called in a speciall distinct manner from repentance, and

---

[9] Ibid., 53-54.
[10] Ibid., 10-11.

> the preaching and the enjoyment thereof by faith is a more excellent thing then the ministery and enjoyment of repentance.[11]

So then, according to Etherington, the believer was to undergo a first "baptism of repentance," whereby he repented of his sins, turned to God in sorrow, and confessed his sins; and secondly, a "baptism of Christ," whereby he was washed by the Holy Spirit unto justification and remission of sins: "So that, as, to bee Baptized with the Baptisme of Repentance, is to repent, to weepe and mourne for our sinnes, washing them as it were in this first laver: So, *to be Baptized with the Holy Ghost and with fire*, is to bee justified and purged from our sinnes by faith in him."[12] Only those who had undergone both these baptisms could wear the title Christian.

Now it should be quite evident that Etherington's doctrine in its broad outlines was manifestly similar to that of HN. Etherington was, of course, somewhat more reticent than HN in discussing the details of this doctrinal formulation. As one might expect from a man jailed for Familism and Anabaptism, he was very careful not to discuss the status of believers who had experienced the washing of the Holy Spirit (there is no duplication of HN's frank claim that those so washed shared the self-same spirit or mind of Christ, for instance). But there can be little question that this is not workaday puritan divinity in action.

Here, we need to make a few comments on the character of more conventional godly discussions of baptism, which were themselves somewhat imprecise. Most often, godly authors and preachers liked to talk of the sacraments as "seals" of the New Covenant. Just as circumcision had been the seal of the first Covenant of Works, so baptism was the seal of the second, new Covenant of promise. Just how efficacious this so-called "seal" was in conferring the grace of the New Covenant was a matter of debate and occasional cloudiness on the part of godly commentators. Where they all agreed, however, was in their claim that the mere sacrament of baptism did not confer saving grace to (adult) sinners. Unlike dreaded Papists, and their English stepchildren, the Arminians, godly preachers claimed that (at least in those who reached a mature age of understanding) baptism was saving only insofar as it represented and sealed the true inner baptism of the Holy Spirit, which ordinarily came through the word of God read, expounded, and preached. Much like Etherington (or for that matter HN) what really mattered for the godly, then, was not the actual, outward act of dipping, but the more dramatic inner transformation wrought by the Holy Spirit in the notional moment of conversion, in which divine grace invaded the believer's heart in an act of unmerited mercy, bringing justifying faith and all its fruits. Crucially, however, this act was seen

---

[11] Ibid., 54-55.

[12] Ibid., 56.

by the godly as being unitary and singular. Although puritans might make conceptual distinctions between the various functions of this spiritual baptism (that is, claiming that it killed sin, on the one hand, or raised a new, sanctified man, on the other) they never, so far as I am aware, broke this process into two separate baptisms.[13] If and when they discussed the so-called "baptism of repentance" of Mark 1, it was considered as part of the single inner spiritual baptism that came with justifying faith.

In HN's and Etherington's doctrine of double baptism, we see something quite different and distinct. Repentance is its own work, prior to justifying faith, with its own, distinct baptism. Justifying faith, which follows the preparatory period of repentance, brings a second, distinct inner baptism of the spirit. For all his vehement disavowals of the Family of Love, then, Etherington appears to have carried with him into his later years at least the outer shell of HN's doctrine of baptism. Here, we see the vestigial influence of HN, carried forward into the Caroline period by the boxmaker cum sect-master John Etherington.[14]

Traske

But Etherington was not the only eccentric on the early Stuart scene to claim that repentance preceded justifying faith, and that each was associated with its own distinct baptism. John Traske, the prophetic religious renegade most famous for his brief, but spectacular, career as an evangelical "judaizer," had made very similar claims in the 1610s, when he first appeared in his role as a self-made prophet. Traske had claimed that there was a preparatory stage of repentance, a period of self-denial in which the would-be believer subjected

---

[13] See, for instance, Thomas Taylor, *The King's Bath: Affording Many Sweet and Comfortable Observations from the Baptisme of Christ* (1620), 29 and passim. Taylor claimed that the Baptism of Christ could be seen as signifying two different parts of regeneration: "The dipping, sprinkling, or his abode under the water, signified his death and buriall, by whose power and vertue our old man is dead and buried, that is, our corruption of nature is slaughtered and consumed" and secondly, "His ascending out of the water, betokeneth his resurrection for our justification, by the power of which we are regenerated to life eternall." It is crucial, however, to note first of all that Taylor saw these as two separate aspects or significations of a *single* baptism, and secondly that these aspects are not divided according to their respective associations with "repentance" and "faith."

[14] In fact, although Etherington was very certainly directly exposed to the ideas of HN, his theology of baptism may have been mediated through the nameless English prophet T.L., who likewise borrowed HN's schema of double baptism. See [T.L.], *The Key of David, that Openeth the Gates to the Citie of God* (1610), 30-45, which was itself a translation of *De Fide* (1592). For a more complete comparison of the ideas of Etherington and HN, see Lake, *Boxmaker's Revenge*.

him—or her—self to extreme rigors in order to mortify the flesh. This period of waiting—which included apparently herculean bouts of fasting, the wearing of sackcloth, as well as other penitential forms of self-crucifixion—was merely a prelude to the onset of faith. Faith, Traske argued, brought with it a profound and awe-inspiring transformation, which translated the believer into the kingdom of heaven, and obliterated the miseries of the period of repentance. In this half-earthly, half-heavenly estate, the transformed believer was freed from sorrow and all doubts about his or her own salvation; Traske went so far as to argue that those so transformed no longer committed sin, that they shared the "mind of Christ" (here readers are advised to consider the above-mentioned claims of HN) and that they could recognize one another with infallible precision.

This very peculiar soteriology—which showed strong hints of the enthusiastic antinomianism that would characterize Traske's later divinity—has been overshadowed by his dramatic "judaizing" activities, which earned him a harsh and exemplary sentence in the Court of Star Chamber in 1618; earlier in this book, I attempted to reconstruct the place of this "judaizing" within the wider spectrum of his thought, suggesting that some of the stranger aspects of Traske's divinity might have emerged from an intellectual engagement with Familist doctrine, and that his ideas in fact represent the fusion of Familist strains of thought with those of militant, separatistic puritanism. Although this argument must in the end remain speculative, it receives tangible and concrete support from an examination of Traske's doctrine of baptism, as expressed in a passing comment from his pamphlet *Heavens Joy* :

> [The Apostle Paul] drawes us to consider of *Gods* proceeding, in bringing us to *Christ*: that is, *As many of us as are now in* Christ, *were first baptized into his death*. That is, were slaine or kild by the Power of Repentance; For here is a twofold baptisme spoken of: one *A* Baptisme *into the death of* Christ, *Another, a* Baptisme *into* Christ [Rom. 6. 3., Heb. 6. 2. Mat. 3. 11. Jo. 1. 33.] The first, giving *Sinne* his deadly wound, or killing us to *Sinne*; the other quickning us, or making us *alive* to *Righteousnesse*. After this it is added, that we are not onely dead, but buried by the first Baptisme into death: that is by *Repentance*, all the glory and beauty of our flesh is taken away [Is. 40. 6 7, 1. Pet. 1. 24], that being raised by *Faith* in *Christs* blood, wee should walke in newnesse of life. Now this *Newnes* of *Life*, notes to us this *Freedome* from our olde course of *sinning*. As it is a little after, *He that is dead is freed from Sinne*.[15]

This brief description of baptism is easily passed over; at first glance, it resembles the puritan habit, mentioned above, of discussing the various different functions of baptism side by side. But when compared closely against what we

[15] [John Traske], *Heavens Joy, or Heaven Begun on Earth* (1616), 54-55.

know of Traske's divinity, his description of a "twofold" baptism takes on a very different significance. Like Etherington, Traske claimed that repentance preceded and ended with faith. Although he does not explicitly use the phrase "baptism of repentance," Traske does speak of a "first Baptism"; this first baptism, which is associated with death to sin, is accomplished "by Repentance" in order that the believer may receive the benefits of justifying faith. Since we know that Traske (much like Etherington) claimed that repentance was entirely prior to and distinct from justifying faith, we may justly infer that Traske believed that this "first Baptisme" was temporally as well as conceptually distinct from a second baptism—the "Baptisme into Christ"—which Traske mentions but does not discuss at length. It is reasonably safe to assume, however, that he associated this second baptism into Christ with the joyful influx of justifying faith, which freed believers from their preparatory period of repentance, translating them into the kingdom of heaven.

Once again, we see the peculiar twofold typology of baptism, here expressed in a muted and guarded form, but nevertheless describing what appears to be a religious experience very similar to those mentioned above: a period of heartfelt repentance and sorrow, followed by an overwhelming experience of divine grace, which eclipsed the preparations of repentance, delivering the lucky recipient into a mystical state of bliss. In Traske's case, as in the case of HN, very exalted claims were made for those in this state of grace, including hints that believers were one with Christ, even as they walked on earth. Etherington, at least in his later years, appears to have been a good deal more circumspect about such matters, but there can be no question that he, too, had borrowed his basic typology of the process of salvation from Hendrik Niclaes.

Neither Etherington nor Traske were members of the Family of Love as described by Christopher Marsh. Indeed, although both men appear to have borrowed the basic structure of HN's typology, each also seemed to have rejected other aspects of his writing or thought. If we compare HN's words to Etherington's, we see that although the Englishman duplicated the pattern of double baptism faithfully, and retained hints of Niclaes's language, he had ejected almost all of the allegorical and elliptical excesses that were so central to HN's rhetorical and prophetic style. In Traske's case, the excision of HN's voice is even more complete: all that remains is the structure of Niclaes's thought, now recast entirely in the language of English puritanism. It would thus be utterly unwarranted to describe either man in an unqualified way as a "Familist." As Peter Lake has demonstrated, Etherington's own mature opinions may be roughly described as a blend of Familist *topoi* with the priorities and obsessions of English puritanism, all understood against what appears to have been a backdrop of intense eschatological expectation. Traske likewise appears to have adopted and adjusted the principles of Familism to the milieu of militant and separatist puritanism, in a process that often led him directly away from both traditions. Nevertheless, both men appear to have imbibed and been influenced in different ways by the cryptic ideas of HN. And it is perhaps not surprising that both men, having manipulated and merged these ideas with their own, appeared in the 1620s as vehement critics of the orthodox puritan establishment in London. Each would denounce mainstream puritan divinity as a "legalistic" sham designed to tyrannize and destroy the souls of seduced laypeople, and each participated in the upsurge of debate and argument over emerging problems concerning the use of Law in the lives of Christians. In this roundabout way, HN's thought, manipulated and remolded to suit new settings, survived across the decades, and fed into the development of the mode of religiosity that would come to be known as antinomianism.

Collier

The manuscript works of Josiah Collier provide a fitting end point to this discussion. If Roger Brearley may be considered the patriarch of the Grindletonian movement, Collier was its loyal son and heir. Scribe, steward, and apostle, Collier not only dutifully preserved and published Brearley's writings, but also defended and expounded his master's teachings in a series of theological treatises and poems now surviving at Chetham's Library and Lambeth Palace. These texts, which were probably written beginning in the 1640s and 1650s, can be read as something like a compendium, or summa, of Grindletonian theology. Remarkably, Collier's works duplicate faithfully the formula of double baptism, providing remarkable evidence as to the tenacious staying power of the motif, as well as the broader influence of Hendrik Niclaes.

It will be recalled that Brearley prescribed for would-be believers a period of blind, mournful waiting. Having recognized their own utter inability in themselves, they were to prostrate themselves to God, waiting in nakedness and obedience for the birth of Christ within them. Collier replicated this formula, arguing that through this process "every house and tabernacle that he hath builded to himselfe is made to him a desolation and he in sylence set upon the ground weeping in the bitternes of his soule."[16] In this state of total self-abnegation, believers gave themselves over to God's glory and judgment: "all things that hath beene seemingly good to him comes to an end and dying to them he stands nakedly in his spirit before the liveing god seperated from the world and the lusting thereunto: in which condition he is willing to justifie god in his righteous judgment, that if he do perish god is righteous in his condemnation. and if he will shew mercie his mercye shall apeare to the glorie of his owne right hand."[17]

---

[16] Chetham's Library MS. A. 2. 24, fol. 79r.

[17] Ibid., fol. 79v-80r.

Yet this period of silent misery was a prelude to a much more dramatic intervention of God's spirit:

> Thus doth god prepare him for the receaving of his promise, that in this condition he truly knowing his weakenes and inabilyty in all the worke of his owne hand might stand still becoming truly simple and in beleeving behould the salvation of god:
>
> For in this Condition he is or stands baptized with the baptisme of repentance for the remission of sins: wherin the voyce of the true baptizer cryes prepare the Lord his way or make streight steps. whose voyce haveing it[s] effectuall power in the spirit of man whereby it is so prepared in that Jordan of teares, and in those effectuall cryes of the soule, that nothing can now give it contentment nor in reason perswade him that his state is good, untill he come who is to come after, whose baptisme is with the holy ghost and with fyer.[18]

Like HN, Etherington, and Traske, then, Collier postulated an internal double baptism, entirely separate from the external watery baptism of infants. These two baptisms were distinct both in time and function. The first baptism of repentance was a period of misery and blind waiting, during which the aspiring saint denied the self, crucified his or her flesh, and patiently submitted to God's will. Having died with Christ on the cross, the true believer was now ready for the seal of the spirit:

> That as sin thus in him hath reigned unto death so also might grace by Jesus Christ reigne in him unto eternall life: And thus out of death god raiseth the spirit of man unto life. For thus it became powerfull over Christ Jesus through the patient suffering of which, he overcame and entred into life, by the mightye working of the eternall spirit and glorye of the father which raised him from the dead. through the which it being to us Imputed, and thereby being planted together in his like death, by the selfe same power of the same spirit may we be raised up together with him into the same life, in the power of which we shall live forever.
>
> And this is the baptiseing of him who baptiseth with the holy ghost and with fyer. whereby the flower is purged and the wheat gathered into his garner. For herein Iniquitie is forgiven, guilt is taken away. death and gods justice is removed, and life is renewed by the same life that was in Christ Jesus. and mans spirit thereby is quickened together with him, and raised up together with him to sit in heavenly places in true dominion above Iniquitye, and to be one in Christ Jesus in one spirit that in him he may be one in the father and no more in lust which is sinfull to be drawen away from him. and in this happynes and peace that passeth understanding.[19]

---

[18] Ibid., fol. 79v.

[19] Ibid., fol. 80r-80v.

As argued in Chapter Eight, the Grindletonians likened this state of unsurpassed happiness to that of Adam in paradise, arguing that believers were perfected insofar as they were joined to Christ in simple, unmixed unity.

In its rough outlines, Collier's doctrine would appear to be identical to the positions of Etherington and Traske.[20] Like them, he appears to have abstracted the doctrine from its original Familist context, rendering the concept not in tones drawn from the garish, almost lurid, palette of HN, but rather in the more prosaic puritan script of "imputation" and "free grace." Nevertheless, the lineage of the motif seems indisputable.

We cannot of course know whether Collier was here articulating a secret doctrine that had been taught privately by Brearley (whose surviving writings are decidedly unforthcoming with respect to the subject of baptism). In many ways, this is not relevant. The argument here is not that Collier was a Familist. Indeed, Collier need never have read HN to have embraced and reproduced the formula of double baptism.[21] As the examples of Etherington and Traske reveal, the doctrine—and the complex of assumptions and associations that went along with it—had long since seeped into the broader currents of radical puritan thought. Disassociated from direct connection to the cursed names of HN and the Family of Love, the motif lived on, surviving as a mode of awakening, describing and shaping religious experience.

---

[20] The one point at which Collier does not exactly follow the other two is in their strict identification of the first baptism with repentance and the second baptism with justifying faith. These questions, along with the issue of whether repentance was taken to be finished after the second baptism, are not explicitly addressed in Collier's works.

[21] This is possible, but not likely, especially given that HN's newly republished works saw a resurgence during the revolutionary era.

APPENDIX B

Familist Extracts from the Diary of Edward Howes (British Library, Sloane MS. 979)

[fol. 18v] Col: 3. Love which is the bond of perfection.
Heb: 6. Let us goe forth unto the perfection.
Deut: 18. e thou shalt be perfect.
Joshuah 24. e serve him in perfectnes.
Math. 5 be perfect as your heavenly father
19. e if thou wilt be perfect
Luk 1. 8. to make ready a perfect people[22]
6. and every man shalbe perfect
I Cor 2. 6 among them that are perfect.
14. d in will be perfect
2 Cor 13. be perfect.
Eph. 6. c stand perfect in all things.
Phil: 3. c.
Coll. 1. d.
2 Tim 3. d.

[19r] A loving Admonition sent from a Lover of the Truth, unto all goodwilling harts to God and his righteousnes: for them to beware of some that are Deceived and would deceive (by seditious Libells and false doctrine) perswading men that it is not possible to attaine unto the perfection, or yet be delivered from the subjection to Sinne, in this life, while men walke on Earth.

Thus saith Christ, whoe soe confesseth me before men, him will I alsoe confesse before my heavenly father and the Angells of God, and whoe soe denyeth me before men, him will I alsoe denye before the Angells of God. Luk. 12.

ffirst note these 2 principall poynts, wheresoever thou readest in holie scriptures of this word PERFECTION then consider [19v] the same is only to be understood of CHRIST JESUS./

2. And wheresoever thou readest of repentance, forsakinge, mortifienge, or subduing of sinne, that cometh to passe by the grace of God the father (which hath

---

[22] Note that this and some of the other scriptural verses appear to have been miscited.

called us thereunto in the obedience of his word) and the free pardoning and taking away of our Sinns that is only wrought (through Christ the perfection) in those that have attained to the said PERFECTION./

And sith it hath pleased the father that in him should all fulnes dwell Col: 1. Therefore let us first submitt to his holy lawe, to the mortifieng of our sinfull lusts and desires, wayting for the Coming of the Lord Jesus Christ, whoe (being once fashioned and obtayninge a livinge shape or [20r] forme in us in the spirit soe that we may dwell in him and he in us) is at that tyme our PERFECTION, our righteousnes our Ellection, our Redemption; our justification and salvation, which after all our beleife Hope and longinge remaineth and standeth sure./2 Cor: 13. a. Joh: 15. 6. 1. Cor: 3 Col: 3. c. 1 Tim: 1. 6. 2 Pet: 2. d. Joh: 2. a. 2 Cor: 1. d. 5.d. gal: 2. d. phil: 3. b: c: d/for God that bringeth salvation to all men hath appeared to us (in the service of his Christ) and teacheth us that we should denye ungodlynes and worldly lusts, and live soberly, righteously, and godly in this present world, looking for the blessed hope and appearinge of the glorie of the great God, and of our Saviour Jesus Christ. wch gave himselfe for us, to redeeme us from all sinne and unrighteousnes and to purge us, for a peculiar people unto himself, being fervently inclyned unto good works./

[20v] Therefore let us continue in the wholesome doctrine which we have learned, and presse forth unto the perfection, or marke appoynted, which hath bin alsoe taught us out of the holy scripture by all godlie learned.

And this perfection (in whomesoever it dwelleth) is Christ Jesus, as is afforesaid. And soe many then as are without him, or his spirit, those are none of his, and are but cast awayes, and a heape of misbelievers or uncircumcised heathen.

But over all those that are of the household of God, all good willing obedient and faithful ones (in whome Christ, the perfection of all the worke of God dwelleth and liveth) the remission and cleane taking away of sinns standeth fast promised for ever: if they doe hartilie repent of theire former sinfull life [21r] and doe exercise themselves in that which is right and reasonable, taking up alsoe theire Crosse daylie on them, and soe imitate Christ (theire righteousnes and perfection) in death and life, to the renewing of theire spirits and minds in him, which taketh away theire sinnes, and the sinnes of all that beleive, and fastneth all that is against them in the Lawe unto his crosse. For they have noe pleasure in sinne, and therfore are not theire infirmities (wherewith they are often tymes over taken), accompted any more for sinne unto them, but are cleane put out of remembrance, (and pardoned in Christ) and shall never more be thought upon e[t]c for love covereth them all. And for that cause they are alwayes enemies to sinne, as strive daylie (in a firme beleife) to the subdueing of sinne. Rom: 6.

[21v] And that sinne is the only thinge which God hateth, and hath alwayes forbidden, and is it which hath separated man from his God, as also the cause of

Curse, death and Condemnation ov[e]r all those that take pleasure therein./Rom: 5. 6/Jam: 4. 6./1 Joh: 2. e./1 John: 1. d.

ffinally this is according to the gospell of Jesus Christ, that we in true repentance through his grace, and in the obedience of his comand, should be nourtured to the resisting and mortifyeng of the sinfull lusts and desires, untill Christ come and dwell in us by faith with out whome there is noe remission of sinnes./

But such as desire not to walke in this narrow waye, and in whome this perfection is not, nor that have any desire thereunto. They are such as deny Christ to be come in the flesh 1. Joh: 4. and therefore very ANTICHRISTS, HERETICKS, ATHEISTS, LIBERTINES, and (if they continue therein) not better then castawayes. 2. Cor: 13. d.

[22r] Cantica prima
To Complaine over the evill and to pray unto God.

1 O Lord my God awake to me
Unstop thyne holie eares
my humble harte I turne to the
harke to my plaint and teares

2 The burthen of my wicked deeds
doth make my harte fall out of ease
I must declare the greife it breeds
O Lord, if that it may thee please.

3 But turne to me thy gracious eye
behold my sore and grevous case
let not the sinne lead me awrye
enlarge 'ore me thy heavenly grace,

4 O Lord behold my sorrow and paine
together with my heavienes
thy comfort let me now obtaine
in this my greife and great distresse.

5. The evill hath my harts lusts caught
and brought me into miserie sore,
[22v] O lord for thy deliverance
I longe deferre it not noe more,

6. O Purge and purifie my harte
thy holy spirit of life give me
for evill bringeth me great smarte
And hath not wherewith to releive me

7. In lastinge good would I could live
then should my soule have present rest

but sinne doth cleave to me soe fast
to crave thyne aide o lord, I am prest.

8. O let me not goe to decaye
nor perish with the wicked wight
Thy love let me enjoye then may
I stand before the in thy sight

9 To walke in thy free paths and wayes
O lord in earnest I desire.
nought then should harme me any wayes
but all would to my gaine conspire.

[23r] 10 Good God, thy mercie shew on me
and alwayes in thy paths me guide
Embrace me in thyne armes lamely [?]
or I shall never be satisfied./

21 Cantica:
Gods light will hidd noe longer be,
but riseth bright most cleare to see
and; from within; doth lighten such
whose harts Gods love doe favor much
for god in us hath soe expressed
the livers in Love are surely blessed,

Apparently now doth Gods light
stand; livingly, soe firme and bright
in that most blessed house of Love
whence none shall it from thence remove
for God in us hath soe expressed
the livers in love are surely blessed.

[23v] Come all ye people high and lowe
and to the house of love lets goe
for therein may we have true light
Elsewhere the day is darke as night
for God in us hath soe expressed
the livers in love are only blessed.

Consider in tyme whoe is your head
you that would live but are yet dead
What is it that true life imparts
but Gods love livinge in your harts./

For God in us etc.

For without Love tis a plaine case Darknes over all doth take the place

All sorts of evill deeds and words Consider now who are your lords
For God etc.

In Darknes the Divell is head, they more and more in error love
they which despise the Love of God, shall dyeing taste the deadly rodd
For God in us etc.

God only is the lovinge love, which liveth in us that Lovely prove
let us agree to advance him high whose love is greatest majestie
For God in us. etc.

Where envie malice wrath and rage
and lust not love shall be theire page,
which thousands prove in every age.
Now leave your follies and outrage.[23]

[23] Compare against the very different translation from HN, *Cantica. Certen of the Songes of HN* (n. p., 1574?), sigs. A2r-v, A4r-v.

APPENDIX C

Truth and Fiction in the Archives: Sources, Source-Skepticism, and the Sport of Heresy-Hunting

Sources for the study of religious heterodoxy in the early modern period leave much to be desired. Church court records, often at the heart of any investigation into the subject, generally record testimony furnished by hostile witnesses, a class of observers whose motives and reliability are often in serious doubt. Even where the court records allow accused persons to speak for themselves, they provide fleeting glimpses of anxious or self-conscious defendants struggling under the shadow of dangerous, even lethal, accusations—once again not a situation conducive to ingenuousness or candor. Moreover, court documents inevitably reflect the preoccupations, fears, and habits of thought of the officials who administer them, adding a second layer of uncertainty to already problematic pieces of evidence. Our second main source of information concerning religious heterodoxy, hostile polemical literature, remains open to similar criticism. Such accounts, whether in manuscript or print, were very often guilty of exaggeration, distortion, and misunderstanding, if not outright duplicity. Indeed, these methodological and evidentiary problems have led certain scholars to dismiss such sources as virtually useless. In the annals of recent English historiography, this strain of source-skepticism perhaps reached its apogee in J. C. Davis's *Fear, Myth and History* (Cambridge, 1986), wherein it was proposed that the Ranters were largely a polemical illusion invented by overzealous civil-war heresiographers. On Davis' account scholars such as Christopher Hill had been far too credulous in accepting the testimony of hostile observers such as Thomas Edwards and his informants. In embracing the often preposterous claims of presbyterians and Royalists, historians had managed to reproduce the paranoid polemical structures of these seventeenth century observers, creating a fictional Ranter "movement" where no such entity existed.

Davis's doubts were by no means misplaced. Given the inherent limitations of hostile sources, there can be little question that skepticism is and should be the appropriate methodological posture. Used with the requisite care, however, both church court records and polemical literature can prove surprisingly enlightening. The following brief account seeks to address these methodological difficulties through an examination of the case of John Everarde.

By close comparison of Everarde's own words (as recorded and published by his followers) against those attributed to him by hostile official sources, the reader can begin to see the degree to which the courts distorted or otherwise misrepresented Everarde's admittedly curious opinions. Such a case-study offers fascinating insight into the limits (and the virtues) of such hostile sources, providing a useful index as to where truth ends and fiction begins.

Our first fragment of evidence derives from an unnamed listener who recorded details from Everarde's recantation sermon at St. Martin-in-the-Fields in December 1627. Readers will recall that Everarde had been charged with denying the validity of prayer for temporal blessings. According to the informant, on the appointed day, Everarde had defended himself by arguing "That howsoever it might be lawfull for them that were children and Infants in Christ and such as were not yet perfect to pray for temporall blessing, as health, and wealth. . . . Yet that it was not necessary, no nor convenient for them so to doe, as being an allaying and an Embasement of their Prayers. for which case they that are perfect and sublime us'd it not."[24] The informant went on to claim that in answering the objections against his position, Everarde had set forth a series of highly controversial propositions. Thus, against the claim that by virtue of his argument "the old fathers and patriarchs were condemned, who sought and prayed for temporall blessings," Everarde had allegedly responded "true it was, but they were children, elementary Jeues, ab[e]cedary olde men, and elementary boyes in respect of us, who have now cleerer light, and a more perfect way to walke by, therfore they to be now of our patterne."[25] Perhaps most outrageous was his answer to the objection "That by this doctrine he opposed the Liturgie of our Church in which there be many prayers for temporall things"; to this, Everarde was said to have retorted "That the Church had wisely provided for all sorts of men, spirituall things for the perfect men, and temporall thinges for the weake. If men be in love with Gew-Gawes, and trifles and bawbles there they are for them."[26]

These are precisely the kinds of accusations that should provoke doubts in the scrupulous researcher. The arguments here ascribed to Everarde were so extreme, so insolent in their calculated challenge to convention and authority, that we might reasonably dismiss them as the imaginative eruptions of an ingeniously hostile witness. Fortunately, this was not the only occasion on which Everarde tackled the problem of prayer for temporal blessings.[27] After assuming his lectureship at Kensington, Everarde delivered at least two sermons on the topic, each of which was later published by Everarde's admirer

---

[24] PRO, SPD 16/41/73, fol. 109r.

[25] Ibid., fols. 109v-110r.

[26] Ibid., fol. 110v.

[27] John Everard, *Some Gospel-Treasures Opened: Or, The Holiest of all Unvailing* (1653), 238-50, 571-81.

Rapha Harford. Here was a "friendly" rendition of Everarde's opinion on the subject, one that at least purported to correspond exactly to the doctor's own words. By comparing the hostile account with its nonhostile counterpart, we can assess the usefulness and probable accuracy of the informant's report.

As at St. Martin's, Everarde's position on the matter seems to have provoked a certain amount of discomfort among his listeners at Kensington. His initial sermon on the subject appears to have caused something of a stir, and once again, Everarde felt compelled to offer a lengthy explanation. As at St. Martin's, he claimed at Kensington that "I never denied prayer for temporal blessings."[28] Nevertheless, he did exhort his audience to "*put away childish things*, and be ashamed to be *crying*, and *whining*, and *begging* for Bables and Rattles, for riches, and honor and beauty."[29] Although he did not go so far as to imply that the liturgy of the Church amounted to a host of "Gew-Gawes, and trifles and bawbles," he made the suspiciously similar argument that "I never denied *children* to do *as children*, they may and must do so, because they are *weak* and cannot go, let them have *Go-carts*, and *Hold-bies*, we hope they will come to be *men* in time."[30] These statements, with their playful yet stinging evocation of images of children's "trifles," are strikingly similar to those recorded by the informant at St. Martin's. So likewise, the alleged claim at St. Martin's that the Old Testament patriarchs were mere "children, elementary Jewes, abecedary olde men" was matched by the parallel argument at Kensington that the Jews had misunderstood "those *promises* made to the *children* of *Israel*" by wrongly taking them to apply to temporal goods: "because they were *children*, they took them *litterally*," and thus missed the hidden, spiritual significance of the promises.[31]

All of this suggests that in broad outline, and indeed in many specifics, the hostile observer at St. Martin's gave a faithful and accurate version of Everarde's altogether unrepentant "recantation" sermon. Nevertheless, it is also worth noting that in certain respects, the informant may have flattened out or embellished Everarde's argument, perhaps exaggerating some details for effect. Thus, although Everarde was not above resorting to a language of perfection in some of his private lectures, there is no indication in the Kensington sermon that he defended his position by crudely referring to the "perfect and sublime" ones, who had utterly transcended the need for temporal prayer. This may well have been an interpretative flourish offered by someone who was all too familiar with the general tenor of Everarde's preaching. So, too, one wonders whether Everarde had really been so forthright as to claim that

---

28 Ibid., 576.

29 Ibid., 572.

30 Ibid., 577.

31 Ibid., 576.

the Jewish patriarchs were "abecedary olde men"; to judge from his later performance at Kensington it is perhaps more likely that he had dismissed "the Jews" in a general manner, without specifically impugning central figures such as Abraham and Moses. In the same vein, we should probably retain a healthy if reluctant skepticism regarding Everarde's alleged attack on the "Gew-Gawes, trifles and bawbles" of the liturgy. This riotously provocative statement may indeed have been something of a creative interpretation of Everarde's words, a logically sound extrapolation that conveniently highlighted Everarde's combative and puritanical disposition.

This tendency to distort, reshape, and decontextualize statements may be observed more clearly in the High Commission articles lodged against the doctor in the late 1630s. Here, again, Everarde's sermons provide a wonderful counterpoint to the official charges. In Chapter Seven, Everarde's own words were adduced to demonstrate that he had indeed maintained something very similar to the alleged error that "God almighty was not only a bare permitting or forsakeing Cause but an actuall and working Cause of all things and consequently of Synne and so was in the fall of Adam."[32] Somewhat less fair was the accusation "That God is everye thinge and all els is but accidents and so take away the accidents and the substance is God, I instanceing the same in a bedpost, stickes, stones, and trees, adding that the Creature is nothing but God clothed with accidents and take away the accidents and you have God uncloathed."[33] In Chapter Seven, it was demonstrated that Everarde's actual position was that "God is *in* everything"—including lowly insects, vegetables, and blocks of wood—although he was not coextensive with creation. The High Commission, however, charged him with the rather more extreme claim that "God *is* everything," implying outright pantheism. This oversight, whether deliberate or not, tells us a great deal about the ways in which courts and hostile observers tended to reshape the words and opinions of those suspected of heterodoxy. Through this simple maneuver, Everarde's own position was stripped of all nuance and context, making him appear even more outrageous and unorthodox than he was in actuality.

A similar propensity for creative misinterpretation is evident in the High Commission charge that "in the presence of two credible wittnesses without excepcion I [Everarde] sayde That I had bin foure yeares Lecturer at Kensington yett never exhorted the people to any good dutye."[34] This accusation suggested a crude libertinism: Everarde not only failed to exhort his listeners to good works, but he even boasted about the fact in public. This article was almost certainly derived from statements Everarde had made in the pulpit,

---

[32] From Bodleian Library, Tanner MS. 67, fol. 143r-v. See above, Chapter Seven.
[33] Ibid., fol. 143v.
[34] Ibid., fol. 144v.

which match almost exactly both the form and content of the High Commission charge. At a sermon preached at Kensington shortly before he was removed from his lectureship, Everarde had delivered the following words, which were duly recorded by an admirer and subsequently published by Harford:

> though I have preached to you these three years, yet ye never knew me to hazzard a Sermon at the cutting off any one of these particular sins. I never set my self to preach against any one individual vice, as *swearing* and *drunkenness*, or *whoredome*, or the like, as many do, inveighing against some one particular external gross sin, many months together. Perhaps I might have forced and perswaded you to leave them, and so may they: but what reall good have they done? but I knew if I left the *root* behind, they would grow again, if not the same way, yet another way as *bad* or worse.[35]

Once again, we see a striking convergence between the High Commission version and the more reliable text published by Everarde's friends fifteen years after the fact. Yet clearly, the passage in question had been radically decontextualized in a manner that quite subverted its meaning. It is true that Everarde was here poking fun at "literal" divines who harped in a futile chorus against this or that sin; yet to suggest, as the High Commission and its informants did, that this passage savored of libertinism was to offer a transparently flawed reading of Everarde's words. Such misreadings need not have been intentional; indeed, it is more likely that the witnesses who tattled on Everarde were, Rashomon-like, recalling his words precisely as they had heard them. Those accustomed to more conventional sermonizing would rightly have interpreted Everarde's statements as a mocking rebuke to "literal" and childish divines who busied themselves with formalities such as the preaching of the Law and obedience to God's commandments. It is not difficult to see how hostile ears might recast the doctor's words into a more general attack on the Law and good works. Having thus ripped his words from their context, and having conveniently forgotten Everarde's more general point about weeding out the ever-tenacious "root" of sin, such "credible witnesses" produced a very slightly garbled (but nonetheless highly damning) piece of testimony for the High Commission.

In all of this, we see a pattern of misinterpretation and misreading that should serve as both a warning and a guide for those who would attempt to hunt down heretics through the reports of their enemies. Three main points need to be underlined: first, it seems that hostile observers very rarely reported opinions, statements, or events that had no basis in reality. In each of the cases cited above, there was an underlying substrate of fact—in this instance, Ever-

---

[35] Everard, *Gospel-Treasures*, 168.

arde's words as actually delivered—with which each of the hostile observers worked.

Secondly, however, it is crucial to understand that those basic and stubborn facts were often misrepresented, manipulated, or rewrought in sometimes subtle ways, thereby distorting the opinions and intentions of the presumed heretic. In general, it is best to assume that the more outrageous the charge, the more likely it was to have undergone some sort of manipulation. Similarly, in certain cases, it is wise to be wary of accusations that conform very closely to widely acknowledged stereotypical categories of heretical opinion, for as argued with respect to Peter Shaw, such preconceived heresiographical categories were easily and sloppily imposed on men and women who could not be readily categorized.[36]

As a third and final caveat, however, it should be remembered that despite this undeniable tendency toward misinterpretation, in some cases even the most hostile witnesses told the truth. A single example shall suffice. One of the more improbably outrageous stories recorded in the church court records involves Joan Lane, wife of Richard Lane, the antinomian tailor's apprentice.[37] When confronted with the accusation that she and Richard had engaged in premarital intercourse, Jane offered the jaw-dropping response that "Shee the said Joane being demaunded by the Court why shee suffered the said Richard Lane to have the use of her body before marriage, answered, I could not resist the power of God."[38] This fabulously self-defeating response—which is inscribed in the official manuscript Act Book of the High Commission—at first appears to have the distinct ring of falsehood to it. Surely, one asks, Lane must have said something else? The reader immediately wonders whether her words had been retouched or torn from their context by heresy-hounds engaged in an enthusiastic search for faint hints of lasciviousness and blasphemy.

Fortunately, we again have a second account of the same event, as recorded in the final edition of Ephraim Pagitt's *Heresiography: or A Description of the Hereticks and Sectaries of these latter times* (1662). The account may have been authored by Pagitt, but it is equally likely that it was provided by that assiduous, indeed prurient, sect-watcher "T.S.," who had furnished Pagitt with extensive material on John and Dorothy Traske for the same edition.[39] Whoever the author was, it is exceedingly unlikely that he had seen the Act Book of the High Commission, not only because such documents were presumably unavailable to the public, but also because his account furnishes de-

[36] For Shaw, see above, Chapter Nine.

[37] For Richard and Joan, see above, Chapter Nine.

[38] CUL MS. Dd. ii. 21, fol., 107v.

[39] For T.S., see above, Chapter Five.

tails that are absent from the Commission's own relatively laconic records. For this reason, we may safely consider the two sources to have been independently generated. The author of the account in Pagitt's book had thus either observed the hearing himself, or received a very detailed account of it from an eyewitness (and here the reader should take note of the fact that High Commission sessions were open to members of the public). After retelling the story of Richard's errors and incarceration, the author introduced Lane's lover and co-religionist:

> at last one *Joan Wilkinson*, otherwise called perfect *Joan*, comming often to visit him [in jail], he got her with Child, and she growing somewhat bigge, and he at last obtaining liberty, to go now and then out of Prison, he married her in *Southwark*, but these things being known, she was apprehended, and both of them carried to Doctors Commons, and there examined by the same, where they joyntly made affidavit, that each did not know the other carnally before marriage, but after conviction they gave privately their reasons of the lawfulness of this oath to them, for that they were spiritual and not carnal, and therefore they could not know each other carnally . . . but these two were again brought to a Commission court to know whether they would justifie their false oath, and there *Richard* being called, the Bishop asked him whether it was lawfull for him to know her carnally before marriage, and to take a false oath to the contrary? Richard answered with a loud voyce, to the pure all things were pure . . . then *Joan* was called and asked why she lay with him before marriage, and took a false oath to the contrary? her answer was, that she could not resist the power of God; at which some of the Bishops shook their heads, but she having the late born child in her armes crying, the Bishop of *Canterbury* turned her away, but bid the Keeper take *Richard* back to prison.[40]

This account perfectly matches all the details of the High Commission Act Book, adding a few additional facts that actually clarify the records of the court.[41] Astonishing as it may seem, we can thus conclude with near certainty

---

[40] E. Pagitt, *Heresiography: or A Description of the Hereticks and Sectaries of these latter times*, 6th ed. (1662), 216-17.

[41] The High Commission account, for instance, provides the following description of the events leading up to their appearance: "both of them being further charged that they had in an Ecclesiasticall Court and before an Ecclesiasticall Judge committed wilfull perjurie in delivereing and affirming by vertue of their oathes that he [sic] had not at any time before their intermarriage had the carnall use and knowledge of each others bodyes Whereas it hath since appeared as well by theire owne Confession as by Records extant that they had the Carnall use of each others bodyes before their intermarriage; For that being marryed the three and twentieth day of February . . . 1631 . . . in the parish Church of St George in Southwarke, the said Joane was delivered of a man child the Eighth day of Auguest next fol-

that Joan did in fact offer up precisely this scandalous answer, and that it was recorded by the High Commission accurately and without manipulation.[42] In certain cases, then, even the most outrageously lurid or dubious sources can lead us to that ever elusive commodity, historical truth.

lowing the which child was baptized in St. Olaves Church in Soutwarkc the 24th day of the said moneth of August which appeared by sevrall Certificates made thereof unto this Court." CUL MS. Dd. ii. 21, fol. 107v.

42 What Joan meant when she gave this answer is another question. For the suggestion that there may have been a fairly sophisticated theological context underlying her response, see the speculations in Pagitt, *Heresiography*, 217, wherein the author explained that "these two stood very much upon that opinion of an absolute reprobation, that God had decreed a certain number to be damned, and the other a far less number to be saved, and that Christ dyed not for the greater number no more than he did dye for the Devills, but for the lesser number, for which he only dyed, he upon the cross cancelled all their sins, both past, present, and to come, and according to this decree his power brought both the Elect and the Reprobate to their severall ends; and this was it which *Joan* harped upon when she answered the Bishop that she could not resist the power of God."

APPENDIX D

Schedule of Errors Alleged Against Roger Brearley, 1616/17

Bodleian Library, Rawlinson MS. d. 399, fols. 196-197:

[196r] Certaine erronious opinions gathered from the mouth of Bryerley and his hearers.

1. A motion riseing from the spiritt is more to be rested in, then the word it selfe; neither Dare they take their ground from the woord, because the devil may wrest it to his purpose.

2. It is a sinne to beleeve the word, as it is the word, without a motion of the spiritt.

3. The child of God in the power of grace doth performe every duety so well, that to aske pardonne for faileing in matter or maner is a sinne.

4. The lord manifesteth himselfe in every ordinance to the child of god to his contentment more or lesse

5. That after a man hath assurance, of the forgivenes of his sinnes, he can never doubte againe.

6. That faith and feeleing are things inseperable.

7. The christian assured can never committ a grosse sinne.

8. That in conference if the childe of god be willed to speake low for giveing offence it is a sinne to doe it, for gods spiritt will not be ashamed.

9. The childe of god in his comfortable estate cannot but prayse god.

10. That every convert hath grace wrought in his heart, and affections before his understanding be inlightened.

11. Grace being wrought in the heart the spiritt abolisheth all former knowledge, and they bidd away all scripture knowledge.

12. One haveing attained to the power of grace can more confirme a weake sainct then a preacher with 20tie sermons.

13. It is a sinne to remember presentlie anie thing that the preacher hath spoken or to meditate thereof, for the spiritt will bring it to their remembrance when they neede it.

14. A soule sanctified must soe aime at gods glorie, as he must never thinke of salvation.

15. They hould it unlawfull to pray for forgivenes of sinne after conversion.

16. They confidentlie affirme that whatsoever sinne they lye in, when they heare it reprooved in the ordinance they never committ againe.

17. A minister unsanctified cannot either convert or confirme.

18. They say they are soe filled with the spiritt that they cannot reade a chapter trulie, yet can expound it, and in prayer they are soe ravished that they cannot speake a woord.

19. If temptation be offered, it lighteth upon them as uppon a wall, and re-boundeth backe againe, but if att anie time they fall they can by the power of grace carrie theire sinne to the lord, and say heere I had it and heere I leave it.

[196v] 20. It is not necessarie to take notice of their sinnes to humble them, for that will god doe by his spiritt when it is needefull.

21. They hould it a sinne to chatechise the ignorant for knowledge is an hinderance to grace.

22. If anie one doe not yeald to their opinions, instantlie they say they see the devill in him.

23. If they hear a sanctified minister preach, they know when he speakes by the spiritt and when not.

24. They care not for falling into a sinne, for god turnes that to the best.

25. It is an error (say they) to hould that where there is most grace, there is most humiliation.

26. That a minister sanctified can preach no errors.

27. That it is not fitt to pray for an excellent minister which is like to be silenced, for they say they will not be more pittifull then god.

28. They hould it a great sinne to read any booke but the bible, and they hould it to be a horrible sinne to reade it either in publique or privat without exposition.

29. If they heare a man talke, they can tell immediately how farr he is gone in christianitie, and whether he be an hypocrite or noe.

30. That everie man should pray without meditation.

31. A man humbled in his soule for sinne ought not to putt upp any prayer to god in the name of christ, till by faith he is assured that christ dwelles in him.

32. That god hath not revealed enough of himself to mans salvacion in his woord, but that wee must search further by spirituall revelation.

33. That a man haveing the spiritt may read, pray, or preach without any calling whatsoever.

34. That the efficacie of woord and sacrament dependes uppon the worthines of the minister.

35. As when the wedge of gould and the Babilonian garment weare hid in Achams tent, god would not be present with the Israelites; soe looke what church or chappell hath within it a surplisse, Crosse or such like, there will the lord never reveale himself either to preacher or people.

36. That the Arke of the covenant is shutt up and pinned within the walls of Grindleton chappell.

37. A christian is of noe parish, neither hath he any pastor, but him by whom he was converted. and to him must he resort every sabboth day, though he be never soe farr of.

38. Neither the preacher nor they pray for the king, and reason is because they know not whether he be elected or noe.

39. He is a devill that ever studieth before he preacheth.

40. He is no christian unlesse he dare say in every prayer, lord now take me to thee, for I am fitt for thee.

[197r] 41. That they have received such abundance of grace, that now they canne stand without the use of the meanes; and soe will doe when Mr Bryerley goes, whom they terme the Angell of England and the onelie one of a thousand.

42. That the Bishop of Yorke is a second Felix, for when he was about to pronounce sentence of silencinge against Mr Bryerley there fell uppon him such a trembeling that he durst not doe it.

43. That Mr Shute vickar of Gigleswicke and mr Brooke minister of Garg[r]a[ve] are both either ignorant or malicious persecutors of sincerity.

44. If Mr Bryerley may stand but a while longer 3 or 4 of the best christians in every parish of England will be assembled thither.

45. That they are behouldinge to god for nothinge, for whatsoever god hath bestowed uppon them, he did it for himself. they yealding it freelie againe to him in obedience.

46. That they cannot have more joy in heaven, then they have in this life by the spiritt.

47. That a christian may have more then faith, and more then assurance, for he may have god himselfe.

48. They hould it not fitteing in the pulpit to bring Quotations, for they say the devill alleadge scripture.

49. That the Apostles did convert noe soules before christ his ascention. and that the prophecie of Joell (your young men shall see visions, and your ould men shall dreame dreames, and your daughters shall prophecie) is now fulfilled att Grindleton.

50. That there is as much difference betwixt Mr Bryerley's preaching and other mens, as betwixt salvation and damnation, and that a wicked man may doe as much as most men preach, nay may obey all the written woordes, and be damned.

APPENDIX E

Letter of John Eachard, 1631

Letter of John Eachard, vicar of Darsham, Suffolk, concerning the London minister Samuel Prettie. Transcribed from PRO, SPD 16/520/80, fols. 119r-121r. According to Eachard's sentence before the High Commission, the letter was written around St. James Day (July 25) 1631, for which see CUL MS. Dd. ii. 21, fol. 76v.

[119r] To all you faithfull in Christ Jesus Saints by calling, justified by his blood and righteousnes, and sanctified by faith in him, that take the L. Jesus to be your wisdome, righteousnes, sanctification and redemption, Grace, mercy and peace to you from God our Father and from the L. Jesus Christ. When the Apostle Paul foresaw that hee was ready to be offered up, and the time of departure at hand, said, I have fought a good fight and have finished my course, I have kept the faith, henceforth is laid up for mee a Crowne of righteousnes, gave many exhortations to his son Timothy, and others to remember him when hee was dissolved and gon to Christ. So likewise the faithfull servant of Jesus Christ Mr John Eaton[43] that Planter with Paul and Father of many Children (for to your knowledge he begat many in the faith and the L. blessed his labours from heaven more then any mans in our time) Hee having run well and obtained the crowne of righteousnes; Least any should waver, stagger and fall back from the faith wherein wee have begun, let us consider what the Apostle writeth to Timothy.1. 6. And let us all fight the good fight of faith. Lay hold of eternall life whereunto thou art called, and hast professed a good profession before many wittnesses. I chardge thee in the sight of god; who quickeneth all things, and before Jesus Christ, who under Pontius Pilate wittnessed a good confession keep this Comaundement without spott and unblamable untill the appearing of our L. Jesus Christ. For thou hast fully knowne my doctrine (as Timo: did Pauls) manner of liveing, purpose, faith long suffering, love, patient persecutions and afflictions which came to mee at London, Norwich and Wickham which persecutions I suffered but from them all the Lord deliverd mee, yea and all that will live godly in Christ Jesus, shall suffer persecutions. 2. Timo: 3: 12. Be not thou therfore ashamed of the Testimony of the Lord, neither

[43] Eaton's name is underlined in another hand, referring the reader to a marginal note: "John Eaton was divers years questioned and censured by the high commission for mainteining that God cannot see sinne in the justifyed."

of mee his prisoner, but be partakers of the afflictions of the gospell according to the power of god 2 Timo: 1. 8. And as you have seene him suffer afflictions, so you, as good souldiers of Jesus Christ suffer Afflictions. 2. Timo: 3. 8. For if wee suffer with Christ, wee shall also reigne togither with him, if wee deny him, he also will deny us, if wee beleeve not, yet abideth hee faithfull, he cannot deny himself. And haveing showed Timo: that hee should fight a good fight, and left him to warne some that they teach no other doctrine, but even such as might bring love out of a pure heart, and a good conscience and faith unfained, from which things some have erred, and have turned back to vaine janglings. 1. Timo: 1:6. Also hee seeing many to fall back in his lief time, might justly suspect Timo: after his departure, And dothe therefore tell of divers backsliders that hee might the more take heed to stand fast shewing that some had made shipwrack of faith as Hymineus and Alexander: therfore beware. 1. Timo: 1. 19. for certaine are turned back after Satan Cap: 5:15. And this thou knowest that all they which are [119v] in Asia be turned from mee of which sort are Phigellus and Hermogines therfore beware thou 2. Timo. 1. 15 and make speed to come to mee at once for Demas hath forsaken mee, and embraced this present world Chap. 4. 10 a fearefull Condition and therfore to beware to stand fast. Therfore it is no new thing for men to fall back from the true faith which they have professed. Now forasmuch as the Apostle Paul sheweth that after his departure, should grievous woolfs enter in, not spareing the flock. Acts. 20. 29. which no question now the faithfull Pastor Jo: Eaton is departed, you shall finde some which shall cause the stonny Professors to fall quite off and others to waver and stagger. As a brother desireing to be faithfull unto you, haveing heard that Mr Pritty begins a little to waver and stagger in that hee hath professed, and in that hee hath encouraged mee and others I am the bolder to requite his love with this Counsell at this time desireing him and all you to stand fast in the liberty wherein Christ hath made us free and be not entangled with the yoak of bondage. Galat. 15. 1. O watch ye, stand fast in the faith, quitt you like men, be strong. 1 Cor: 16. 13. and waver not.

Reason 1. For hee that wavereth is like a wave of the Sea tost of the winde and carryed away; neither lett that man think that hee shall receave any thing of the Lord, a dubble mynded man is unstable in all his wayes. Ja: 1. 6. 7. Therfore let us draw neare to god with a true heart, with assurance of faith, our hearts being pure from an evill conscience, and washed in our bodies in pure water let us keep true profession of our hope without wavering, for hee is faithfull that hath promised, and lett us consider one another to provoke unto love and to good works, nor forsaking the fellowship as the manner of some is How the just shall live by faith, but if any withdraw himself, my soule shall have no pleasure in him; but wee are not they which withdraw our selves to perdition, but of them that follow faith to the conservacion of the soul. Heb. 10: 22, 23, 24, 35, 38, 39.

Re. 2. Secondly: Remember the councell of our Saviour Christ to beware of backsliding, saying, What man is hee that doth begin to build a Tower, and doth not sett downe first and count the Chardge whether he hath Wherewith to finish, least haveing began and leaveing off, all men that pass by laugh and say, This man began to build a Tower, but had not wherewith to finish; so will it be with all you that profess free justificacion by the blood and righteousnes of Jesus Christ that hath made the Church without spott or wrinkle in his sight, and now in the midway to leave off you shalbe made a laughing stock to all for both good and bad will scoff at such.

Re. 3. Thirdly. Fall not back for you have the example of Moses, for hee chose rather to suffer affliction with the children of God then to enjoy the pleasures of sin for a season, for hee had an ey to the recompence of the reward for the momentary afflictions of this lief, are not worthy of the glory to be revealed. None do know that the people are the children of God for [120r] they have bin truely converted by the preaching of the word, they have bin cast downe in the sence of their miserable condicion by sin and built upon Christ and his love is in them, therefore for you to forsake the Comunion of the Saints which you say you beleeve and know are Saints, is to forsake the Lord and his people. They went out from us, but they were not of us, if they had bin of us, they would have continued with us, but this cometh to pass that it might appeare that they are not all of us 1 Joh: 2.19.

Re. 4. Fourthly consider what a scandall tis to your owne self, and Professors of the righteousnes of Christ, and a greif to all your faithfull freinds that shall heare of it, if you waver to fall back first to your self, the salt that hath lost its savour is good for nothing but to bee troden on under foot of men, the Lord will bring such as have put their hands to the plough and look back into contempt and derision of all good men. Eleazer had a care of this, that hee would rather dy then any should say that hee was fallen from the truth 2 Macab: 6.24. And concerning the faithfull you shall cause them to be reproached, and hereby the adversaries to say, you will all do as such did when the triall comes. Thus you shall make sad the hearts of the Saints which you should comfort, which will hardly ever receave you againe, without Jealousy, and as for the opposites they will condemn you also.

Re. 5. Fifthly. Consider that hee that seeketh his lief shall loose it and hee that seeketh honours and riches by denying the trueth that hee professed shall loose them all, for it may be Satan hath scared some of you, with the prison, or suspencion, or promised some a great Liveing to forsake that, that once you professed, as to choak you with a Benefice or the like; We are not ignorant of his devices. I answear, what should it profitt you to win the world and loose your owne soule, to win temporall riches, and to loose spirituall faith and a good conscience; tis like a man that forsaketh a great many old freinds and choseth false acquaintance, which will labour what they can to make you forsake your true freinds, which when they have don they will forsake you too. Like the Spaniard that haveing perswaded by money or bribed any man to betray his Countrey, Citty, or Ship, when they have obtained their purpose will comonly kill him, and say if he will not be true to his owne Countrey, hee will never be true to us. So you that shall forsake your old faithfull freinds to get new, your new ones, shall never truely love you for they will allwayes suspect you, and suspicion brings the bane of love if the love take the bane at first, it will be feined at last. Do not think that I go about to perswade you to hold any phrases but those in scripture, for I [120v] intend it not, but to hold the substance of that you have professed to your faithfull freinds that you know are in Christ Jesus, but you shall come to clip the Lords righteousnes that god sees all our enemies, therfore our sinns, and that the spirit sees sin, and mortifies sin it will prove leven at the least. It seems these have forgotten the two grounds: First that God doth not behold in children under the law, but under grace, therfore their enemies sins are all drowned in the red sea of Christs blood, like the Egiptians in the botome of the red sea. Secondly that God doth behold men in Adam or in Christ for once darknes, but now light in the Lord, once the children of wrath, now sons and heires risen with Christ, and sit with him in heavenly places, once in your sins, now a glorious Church by Christ, except you will make mungrell Christians betweene Adam and Christ that should stand before god sometimes in Christ, and sometimes out of Christ, sometime in Adam or half Adam, and half Christ, half darkness, and half light, half a new creature, and half an old, which the scripture will not allow. So for any to say that God sees all our enemies, therefore all our sins, is to deny the first and second part of free justificacion, and to say namely that Christ hath not loved us, nor washed us from our sins before his heavenly Father, by that his righteousnes hath not covered us, and made us kings and Preists unto his Father. Revelat. 5. And to deny the perfect remission of sins and to bring them under the law before god, and then who shall not lay any thing to the Chardge of gods Chosen, contrary to the scriptures. Rom. 8. 33, 34. And to say that the spirit sees sin because wee by the spirit do mortify the deeds of the flesh is to affirme that the spirit sees us of Christ in darknes, or sees not how Christ preserves his whole Church without spott or wrinkle, or any such thing, or that the spirit doth not see the blood of Christ and the wedding garment upon us. For though wee by th[a]t spirit do mortify our members on earth Col. 3. 5. that is to be understood to manward, therfore called members upon earth not in heaven for wee are dead to sin already before our Father in heaven, and buried too, as the Apostle saith, ye are dead, and your lief is hid with Christ in God, and how shall wee that are dead to sin live therein i.e. before god. Rom: 8. 6. Count your selves dead i.e. beleeve your selves to be dead to sin before, for thus hee would have you beleeve, and that you are so, and alive to God through Jesus Christ our Lord, For hee would not have you Count that which is not, therefore you beleevers are dead to sin before god and buryed also, for you are buryed with him in baptisme. And as men do not use to mortify him that is dead and buried already, so beleevers do not take away their sinns out of gods sight by mortificacion because they are dead and buryed unto sin before god in Christ, already by god in baptisme. [121r] So that though you by virtue of the spirit do mortify our members upon earth yet the spirit of god doth know that their sin is pardoned, washed away and putt out of gods sight, covered and not imputed, which all signify the same thing the perfect remission of sins. And though sin do now ly upon thy conscience and thou art mortifying of it the spirit knows it is forgiven us for his names sake 1. John 2. 12. And that wee have redemption through his blood the forgivenes of our sins. Col. 1. 14. And the spirit writeth that Jesus hath made us. et. Revelat. 15. therefore wee are to beleeve, that the spirit seeth us such as hee would have us to beleeve that wee are made before god by the blood of Christ, so that is one thing wee see and feele, when as by the virtue of the spirit of god wee do mortify our members on earth. i.e. before our selves and the world, and tis another thing that wee are to beleeve wee are before god in Christ. Therfore I beleeve the spirit of god seeth every beleever in the wedding garment at all times. Heb: 10. 14. Thus hopeing that the Lord shall reveale his will unto my loveing brother Mr Pritty I desire you my faithfull fellow labourers. Mr Towne. Mr Thrask. Mr Hodges. Mr Emmerson, and all others the faithfull in London to reade this to him with the spirit of meeknes, considering thou maist be tempted. Now unto him that hath loved us, and washed us in his owne bloode, and made us Kings and Preists to his heavenly Father be praised for evermore. Amen.

Your brother in the faith once
delivered to the Saints
John Echard.

Bibliography

Manuscripts

American Antiquarian Society, Worcester, Massachusetts

MS. Sermon Notes, Denison (1637–39).

Bodleian Library, Oxford

Bodleian MS. 154. Dionys Fitzherbert's recollections.

Rawlinson MS. c. 554. Translation of six chapters of HN's "Glass of Righteousness."

Rawlinson MS. d. 106. Life of Mary Carleton, daughter of Tobias Crispe.

Rawlinson MS. d. 398. William Strode's poem, "The Townes new Teacher."

Rawlinson MS. d. 399. Copy of High Commission allegations against Roger Brearley.

Rawlinson MS. d. 1350. "That the whole law of Moses is wholy abolished."

Tanner MS. 67. High Commission form of submission for John Everarde, 1639.

Tanner MS. 70. Copy of the confession of Giles Creech.

Tanner MS. 71. Letters and ecclesiastical materials.

Tanner MS. 72. Letters and ecclesiastical materials.

Borthwick Institute, York

HC AB 16, 17. High Commission Act Books.

Inst. AB 3, 5, 6. Institution Act Books.

Original Wills. Chancery, Prerogative and Exchequer wills.

Vis 1615 CB. Visitation call-book.

Vis 1619 CB. Visitation call-book.

British Library, London

Additional MS. 4933B. Sermon notes of Elkanah Wales.

Additional MS. 11045. Letter of E[dward?] R[ossingham?] to Viscount Scudamore. Eyewitness account of the trial of John Everarde.

Cotton MS. Jul. C. iii. Letters of John Everarde to Sir Robert Cotton.

Egerton MS. 2877. "Consolations for all troubled Consciences" by W.P.

Harleian MS. 339. Simonds D'ewes, "the summe of the Law."

Harleian MS. 374. Letter of Simonds D'ewes to Edmund Cartwright, 1625.

Harleian MS. 837. Theological Letter of John Goodwin, c. 1632-1640.

Harleian MS. 1198. Sermons of Obadiah Sedgwick, 1630.

Harleian MS. 1219. Satirical anti-puritan manuscript pamphlet.

Sloane MS. 979. The diary of Edward Howes.

Sloane MS. 2538. Manuscript translation of the *Theologia Germanica*.

Stowe MS. 549. Warrant for search of John Everarde's house.

Cambridge University Library

Additional MS. 3117. Sermon notebook of Robert Saxby.

Ely Diocesan Records B/2/35. Consistory Court Act Book.

MS. Dd. ii. 21. High Commission Act Book (missing volume from State Papers series).

MS. Dd. iii. 83 (19). Pastoral letter of Thomas Gataker.

MS. Dd. vi. 47. Sermon notes of Sarah Wilson, 1635.

MS. Dd. vi. 70. Sermon notes of Sarah Wilson, 1634.

MS. Dd. xii. 42. "God's government of his Church under the Law; and the government of his Church now under the Gospel."

MS. Dd. xii. 68. John Everarde, translation of the *Theologia Germanica* and other works.

Chetham's Library, Manchester

MS. A. 2. 24. Grindletonian Manuscripts.

MS. A. 2. 132. Religious poetry of Robert Heywood, Roger Brearley and others.

Congregational Church Library, London

MS. I. f. 2. Diary of Ellis Crispe.

MS. I. h. 48. Warwickshire sermons, 1638–39.

Folger Shakespeare Library, Washington, D.C.

MS. V. a. 222. John Everarde, translation of the *Theologia Germanica*.

Guildhall Library, London

MS. 204. Diary of Nehemiah Wallington.

MS. 1176/1. St. Margaret New Fish Street, Vestry Minutes.

MS. 4457/2. Churchwardens Accounts of St. Stephens Coleman Street.

MS. 4449/2. Registers of St. Stephens Coleman Street, 1636-1689.

MS. 6536. Baptismal Register of St. Bride's Fleet Street.

MS. 9537/13-14. Visitation records, diocese of London.

MS. 9539A/1. Subscription book, 1627-42.

MS. 10091/6, 13. Allegations for marriage licenses, diocese of London.

Lambeth Palace Library

MS. 942, items 14, 16. Laud's lists of London lecturers.

MS. 3391. Papers of John Bramston relating to Enoch Grey.

MS. 3461. Grindletonian Manuscripts.

Lancashire Record Office, Preston

WCW. Original Lancashire wills, proved at Chester.

Library of the Society of Friends, London

Swarthmore MSS. 351, 356. Letters of Thomas Barcroft and Richard Farnsworth.

London Metropolitan Archives

DL/C/341, 343. Vicar-General's Books, diocese of London.

National Library of Scotland, Edinburgh

Advocates MS. 33.1.6, vol. 20 (Denmilne State Papers). Examination of John Pecke.

Public Record Office, London

E334/16, 19. First Fruits Composition Books.

E334/19. First Fruits Composition Book.

PROB 11/139, 11/158. Prerogative Court of Canterbury. Probate Registers.

SPD 14. State Papers Domestic, James I.

SPD 16. State Papers Domestic, Charles I.

STAC 8/61/27. Star chamber suit (James I), Best v. Traske.

Queens College, Oxford

MS. 390. Diary of Thomas Crosfield.

Somerset Record Office

D/D/CA 140, 189, 379. Consistory Court Act Book.

DD/SOG/1208, 1211, 1214. Transcripts of the parish registers of Frome.

Trinity College, Dublin

Trinity College, Dublin MS. 293. High Commission articles and answers in the case of Henry Roborough, 1634.

West Yorkshire Archive Service, Bradford

5D94/4/1. Bingley All Saints, Churchwardens Accounts, 1651-1686.

Busfield-Ferrand MS. D. Legal and business papers of Benjamin Ferrand.

West Yorkshire Archives Service, Leeds

BDP/29/1/1/4. Parish Registers of Guiseley St Oswald, 1585-1720.

Modern Editions of Primary Sources

Armitage, G. L. and Chester, J. L., eds. *Allegations for Marriage Licenses Issued by the Bishop of London, 1611 to 1828*, Publications of the Harleian Society, 26. London: Harleian Society, 1887.

Bacon, Francis. *The Letters and the Life of Sir Francis Bacon*, edited by J. Spedding. London: Longman, Green, Longman, and Roberts, 1861-74.

Birch, T., ed. *The Court and Times of James the First*. London: H. Colburn, 1849; reprint, New York: AMS, 1973.

Calvin, John. *Treatises Against the Anabaptists and Against the Libertines*, edited and translated by B. W. Farley. Grand Rapids: Baker Book House, 1982.

Collections of the Massachusetts Historical Society, 3rd series, 9 (1846). Letters from Edward Howes to John Winthrop, Jr.

Collections of the Massachusetts Historical Society, 4th series, 6 (1863). Letters from Edward Howes to John Winthrop, Jr.

Freshfield, Edwin, ed. *The Vestry Minute Books of the Parish of St. Bartholomew Exchange in the City of London: 1567-1676*. London: Rixon and Arnold, 1890.

Gardiner, S. R., ed. *Reports of Cases in the Courts of Star Chamber and High Commission*. Camden Society, N.S., 39 (1886).

Hall, David. D., ed. *The Antinomian Controversy, 1636-1638: A Documentary History*. Durham and London: Duke University Press, 1990.

The Hartlib Papers: A Complete Text and Image Database of the Papers of Samuel Hartlib (c.1600-1662) Held in Sheffield University Library. 2d edition. CD-ROM. Sheffield: Humanities Research Online, 2002.

Heywood, Oliver. *The Reverend Oliver Heywood, B.A., 1630-1702: His Autobiography, Diaries, Anecdote and Event Books*, edited by J. Horsfall Turner. 4 vols. Brighouse and Bingley: A. B. Bayes, T. Harrison, 1881-1885.

Kiffin, William. *Remarkable Passages in the Life of William Kiffin*, edited by William Orme. London: Burton and Smith, 1823.

Laud, William. *The Works of the Most Reverend Father in God, William Laud, D.D.*, edited by W. Scott and J. Bliss. Oxford: John Henry Parker, 1847-1860.

Le Hardy, William, ed. *Calendar to the Sessions Records*, Middlesex Sessions Records, New Series, Volume 3, 1615-1616. London: Sir Ernest Hart, 1935.

McGiffert, Michael, ed. *God's Plot: Puritan Spirituality in Thomas Shephard's Cambridge*. Rev. ed. Amherst: University of Massachusetts Press, 1993.

"Trask in the Star-Chamber, 1619" in *Transactions of the Baptist Historical Society*, 5, (1916-7).

Primary Books and Pamphlets

Anonymous. *A Curb for Sectaries and Bold Propheciers* (1641).

Anonymous. *A Discovery of the Abominable Delusions of those, who call themselves the Family of Love* (1622).

Anonymous. *Gospel Grounds; or, Christ Declared to be the onely Treasury of all Good* (1644).

Anonymous. *New Preacher, New* (1641).

A., J. *A Manifest and Breife Discovery of some of the Errours contained in a Dialogue called the Marrow of Moderne Divinity* (1646).

A[insworth], H[enry]. *An Epistle Sent unto two daughters of Warwick from H.N.* (Amsterdam, 1608).

Ashmole, Elias. *The Way to Blisse* (1658).

Baillie, Robert. *A Dissuasive from the Errours of the Times* (1646).

[Bakewell, Thomas]. *A Faithfull Messenger Sent after the Antinomians* (1644).

________. *The Antinomians Christ Confounded and the Lords Christ Exalted* (1644).

Bentham, Joseph. *The Societie of the Saints: Or, a Treatise of Good-fellows* (1630).

B[oye], R[ice]. *The Importunate Begger, for Things Necessary, or Necessity, Without Denial* (n.p., 1635).

_______. *A Just defence of the importunate beggars importunity* (n.p., 1636).

Boulton, Samuel. *Medicina Magica Tamen Physica: Magical, but Natural Physick* (1656).

Brierley (or Brearley), Roger. *A Bundle of Soul-convincing, Directing and Comforting Truths* (1677).

B[urton], H[enry]. *A Plea to an Appeale: Traversed Dialogue Wise* (1626).

_______. *The Law and the Gospell reconciled. Or, The Evangelicall Fayth, and the Morall Law How they Stand Together in the State of Grace* (1631).

Church, Henry. *Divine and Christian Letters* (1636).

Clapham, Henoch. *Errour on the Right Hand, Through a Preposterous Zeale* (1608).

Clarke, Samuel. *The Lives of Thirty-two English Divines* (1677).

Claxton, Lawrence. *The Lost Sheep Found: Or, The Prodigal Returned to his Fathers House, After Many a Sad and Weary Journey Through Many Religious Countreys* (1660).

Coore, Richard. *The practical expositor of the most difficult texts throughout the holy Bible* (1683).

Cowling, N. *The Saints Perfect in this Life, or Never* (1647).

Crandon, John. *Mr. Baxters Aphorisms Exorized and Anthorized* (1654).

Crispe, T. *Christ Alone Exalted in the Perfection and Encouragement of the Saints* (1646).

Culverwell, Ezekiel. *A Treatise of Faith: Wherein is declared how a man may live by Faith, and find releefe in all his necessaries. Applied especially unto the use of the weakest Christians* (1623).

Denison, Stephen. *The White Wolfe, or A Sermon Preached at Pauls Crosse* (1627).

Dent, Arthur. *The Plaine Mans Path-Way to Heaven* (1603).

Dow, Christopher. *Innovations Unjustly Charged upon the Present Church and State* (1637).

Eachard, John. *Good Newes for all Christian Souldiers* (1645).

_______. *The Great Day at the Dore* (1648).

Eaton, John. *The Honey-Combe of Free Justification by Christ Alone* (1642).

_______. *The Discovery of the Most Dangerous Dead Faith* (1642).

Emersone, John. *The Worlds Prospect: Or, A Commentarie upon the 33 of Isaiah* (1646).

Etherington, John. *The Defence of John Etherington against Stephen Denison* (1641).

_______. *A Brief Discovery of the Blasphemous Doctrine of Familisme* (1645).

Everard, John, transl. *The Divine Pymander of Hermes Mercurius Trismegistus.* (1650).

_______. *Some Gospel-Treasures Opened: Or, The Holiest of all Unvailing* (1653).

_______. *The Gospel Treasury Opened, or, The Holiest of all Unvailing* (1657).

Falconer, John. *A Briefe Refutation of John Traskes Judaical and Novel Fancyes.* (St. Omer, 1618).

Firmin, Giles. *A Brief Review of Mr. Davis's Vindication: Giving no Satisfaction* (1693).

F[isher], E[dward]. *The Marrow of Modern Divinity: Touching both the Covenant of Works, and the Covenant of Grace* (1645).

_______. *The Marrow of Modern Divinity: Touching Both the Covenant of Works, and the Covenant of Grace*, 2d ed. (1646).

_______. *The Marrow of Moderne Divinity. The second part. Touching the Most Plaine, Pithy and Spirituall Exposition of the Ten Commandments* (1648).

Fuller, Thomas. *The Church-History of Britain* (London, 1655).

Gataker, Thomas. *Gods Eye on His Israel* (1645).

Geree, Stephen. *The Doctrine of Antinomianisme Confuted* (1644).

Gifford, George. *A Sermon on the Parable of the Sower, Taken out of the 13. of Matthew* (1582).

_______. *Certaine Sermons, Upon Divers Textes of Holie Scripture* (1597).

_______. *Foure Sermons upon Several Partes of Scripture* (1598).

Greville, Robert. *A Discourse Opening the Nature of that Episcopacie, which is Exercised in England* (1641).

Gunter, Peter. *A Sermon Preached in the Countie of Suffolk, before the Clergie and Laytie, for the Discoverie and Confutation of Certaine Strange, Pernicious, and Hereticall Positions, Publickely Delivered, Held, and Maintayned, Touching Justification, by a Certaine Factious Preacher of Wickam Market* (1615).

Harford, R. *A Gospel-Engine, or Streams of Love and Pity* (1649).

Hebdon, Returne. *A Guide to the Godly* (1648).

Hildersam, Arthur. *The Doctrine of Fasting and Praier, and Humiliation for Sinne* (1633).

Hinde, William. *The Office and Use of the Morall Law of God* (1622).

_______.*The Office and Use of the Moral Law*, 2d ed. (1623).

Howes, Edward. *Short Arithmetick: or The Old and Tedious way of Numbering, Reduced to a New and Briefe Method* (1650).

Huit, Ephraim. *The Anatomie of Conscience* (1626).

Lancaster, Robert. *Vindiciae Evangelii: Or, A Vindication of the Gospel with the Establishment of the Law* (1694).

[L.,T.]. *The Key of David, That Openeth the Gates to the City of God* (1610).

Muggleton, Ludowick. *The Acts of the Witnesses of the Spirit, in Five Parts* (1699; reprinted, 1764).

N[iclaes], H[endrik]. *Cantica. Certen of the Songes of HN* (n.p., 1574?).

_______. *Evangelium Regni* (n.p., 1575?).

_______. *Exhortatio. I. The First Exhortation of H.N. to his Children* (n.p., 1574).

_______. *Introductio to the Holy Glass of Righteousness* (n.p., 1575?).

_______. *Revelatio Dei*, 2d ed. (1649).

_______. *Terra Pacis. A True Testification of the Spirituall Lande of Peace: which is the Spiritual Lande of Promyse* (n.p., 1575?).

Norice, Edward. *The New Gospel, Not the True Gospel* (1638).

Pagitt, Ephraim. *Heresiography: or A Description of the Hereticks and Sectaries of these Latter Times*, Sixth ed. (1662).

Perkins, William. *A Commentarie or Exposition, upon the five first Chapters of the Epistle to the Galatians* (1604).

_______. *A Treatise Tending unto a Declaration Whether a Man be in the Estate of Damnation or in the Estate of Grace* (1590?).

Preston, John. *Foure Godly and Learned Treatises* (1636).

Prynne, William. *Hidden Works of Darknes brought to Publike Light* (1645).

Reynolds, Edward. *Three Treatises of The Vanity of the Creature. The Sinfulnesse of Sinne. The Life of Christ* (1631).

Rogers, Richard. *Seaven Treatises Containing such Direction as is Gathered out of the Holie Scriptures* (1604).

Rogers, Richard, et al. *A Garden of Spirituall Flowers* (1609).

Sclater, William. *A Sermon Preached at the Last Generall Assise Holden for the County of Sommerset at Taunton* (1616).

_______. *An Exposition with Notes upon the first Epistle to the Thessalonians* (1619).

Sedgwick, John. *Antinomianisme Anatomized. Or, A Glasse for the Lawlesse: Who deny the Ruling use of the Morall Law unto Christians under the Gospel* (London, 1643).

Shepard, Thomas. *Subjection to Christ in all his Ordinances and Appointments* (1652).

_______. *The Parable of the Ten Virgins Opened & Applied: Being the Substance of Divers Sermons on Math. 25.1–13.* (1660; reprint edition, 1695).

Sibbes, Richard. *The Returning Backslider, or, a Commentary upon the whole XIIII. Chapter of the Prophecy of the Prophet Hosea* (1639).

Simpson, John. *The Perfection of Justification maintained against the Pharise: The Purity of Sanctification against the Stainers of it: The Unquestionableness of a future glorification against the Sadduce: In several Sermons* (1648).

Taylor, John. *A Swarme of Sectaries, and Schismatiques* (1641).

Taylor, Thomas. *Regula Vitae, The Rule of the Law Under the Gospel* (1631).

Torshel, Samuel. *The Three Questions of Free Justification. Christian Liberty. The Use of the Law* (1632).

Torshel, Samuel. *The Three Questions of Free Justification* (1632).

Towne, Robert. *The Assertion of Grace* (1645).

_______. *A Re-assertion of Grace. Or Vindiciae Evangelii* (1654).

Trapnel, Anna. *A Legacy for Saints; Being Several Experiences of the dealings of God with Anna Trapnel* (1654).

Traske, John. *A Pearl for a Prince, or a Princely Pearl. As it was delivered in two sermons* (1615).

_______. *Christs Kingdom Discovered. Or, That the true Church of God is in England, clearely made manifest against all sectaries whatever* (1615).

[Traske, John]. *Heavens Joy, or Heaven Begun on Earth* (1616).

Traske, John. *A Treatise of Libertie From Judaisme* (1620).

_______. *The True Gospel Vindicated, from the Reproach of a New Gospel.* (n.p., 1636).

Turner, Jane. *Choice Experiences of the Kind Dealings of God* (1653).

Underhill, Thomas. *Hell Broke Loose: Or an History of the Quakers Both Old and New* (1660).
Walwyn, William. *The Power of Love* (1643).
_______. *Walwyn's Just Defence* (1649).
_______. *A Word More to Mr. Thomas Edwards Minister* (1646).
Wastfield, Robert. *Christ coming in the Clouds; or, The dawning of the Day* (1647).
Ward, Samuel. *Woe to Drunkards* (1622).
Webster, John. *The Saints Guide, or Christ the Rule, and Ruler of Saints* (1653).
Widdowes, Giles. *The Schysmatical Puritan* (1630).
Wilkinson, Robert. *The Saints Travel to the Land of Canaan* (1648).
Wilson, Thomas. *A Dialogue About Justification by Faith: Wherein the nature and office, the property and power of Faith is Plainely taught, against such as deny the certainety or particularity and powerfulnesse of Faith* (1610).

Modern Secondary Books

Ball, Bryan W. *The Seventh-Day Men, Sabbatarians and Sabbatarianism in England and Wales, 1600-1800*. Oxford: Clarendon Press, 1994.
Black, Robert C. *The Younger John Winthrop*. New York: Columbia University Press, 1966.
Boyarin, Daniel. *A Radical Jew: Paul and the Politics of Identity*. Berkeley: University of California Press, 1994.
Bozeman, T. D. *To Live Ancient Lives: The Primitivist Dimension in Puritanism*. Chapel Hill: University of North Carolina Press, 1988.
Burns, Norman. *Christian Mortalism from Tyndale to Milton*. Cambridge, MA: Harvard University Press, 1972.
Burrage, Champlin. *The Early English Dissenters in the Light of Recent Research (1550-1641)*. 2 vols. Cambridge: Cambridge University Press, 1912.
Clark, G. *A History of the Royal College of Physicians of London*. Oxford: Clarendon Press, 1964.
Collinson, Patrick. *The Religion of Protestants*. Oxford: Clarendon Press, 1982.
_______. *Godly People: Essays on English Protestantism and Puritanism*. London: The Hambledon Press, 1983.
Coolidge, J. S. *The Pauline Renaissance in England: Puritanism and the Bible*. Oxford: Clarendon Press, 1970.
Cooper, T. *Fear and Polemic in Seventeenth-Century England: Richard Baxter and Antinomianism*. Aldershot: Ashgate, 2001.
Davis, J. C. *Fear, Myth and History: The Ranters and the Historians*. Cambridge: Cambridge University Press, 1986.
Dietz Moss, Joan. *"Godded with God": Hendrik Niclaes and his Family of Love*. Transactions of the American Philosophical Society, 71, Part 8. Philadephia: American Philosophical Society, 1981.

Edwards, M. U. *Luther and the False Brethren.* Stanford: Stanford University Press, 1975.

Evans, B. *The Early English Baptists.* London: John Heaton & Son, 1862.

Faulkner, T. *History and Antiquities of Kensington.* London: T. Egerton, 1820.

Fincham, Kenneth. *Prelate as Pastor: The Episcopate of James I.* Oxford: Clarendon Press, 1990.

Foster, Stephen. *Notes from the Caroline Underground: Alexander Leighton, the Puritan Triumvirate and the Laudian Reaction to Nonconformity.* Hamden, CT: Archon Books, 1978.

Gager, John. *The Origins of Anti-Semitism: Attitudes Toward Judaism in Pagan and Christian Antiquity.* New York and Oxford: Oxford University Press, 1983.

Haller, William. *The Rise of Puritanism.* New York: Columbia University Press, 1938; Paperback edition, New York: Harper Torchbook, 1957.

Hambrick-Stowe, Charles E. *The Practice of Piety: Puritan Devotional Disciplines in Seventeenth-Century New England.* Chapel Hill: University of North Carolina Press, 1982.

Hamilton, Alastair. *The Family of Love.* Cambridge: James Clarke & Co. Ltd., 1981.

Hill, Christopher, *Society and Puritanism in Pre-Revolutionary England.* 2d ed. New York: Schocken Books, 1967

________. *The World Turned Upside Down: Radical Ideas During the English Revolution.* Paperback edition. London: Penguin, 1991.

Huehns, Gertrude. *Antinomianism in English History: With Special Reference to the Period 1640-1660.* London: The Cresset Press, 1951.

Jones, Rufus M. *Spiritual Reformers in the 16th and 17th Centuries.* London: Macmillan and Co., 1914. Reprint, Gloucester, MA: Peter Smith, 1971.

________. *Mysticism and Democracy in the English Commonwealth.* Cambridge, MA: Harvard University Press, 1932. Reprint, New York: Octagon, 1965.

Kaplan, B. J. *Calvinists and Libertines: Confession and Community in Utrecht, 1578-1620.* Oxford: Clarendon Press, 1995.

Katz, D. S. *Philo-Semitism and the Re-admission of the Jews to London, 1603-1655.* Oxford: Clarendon Press, 1982.

Kendall, R. T. *Calvin and English Calvinism to 1649.* Oxford: Oxford University Press, 1979.

Kevan, E. F. *The Grace of the Law: A Study in Puritan Theology.* London: The Carey Kingsgate Press Limited, 1964.

Knight, Janice. *Orthodoxies in Massachusetts: Rereading American Puritanism.* Cambridge, MA: Harvard University Press, 1994.

Lachman, D. C. *The Marrow Controversy.* Edinburgh: Rutherford House, 1988.

Lake, Peter. *Moderate Puritans and the Elizabethan Church.* Cambridge: Cambridge University Press, 1982.

________. *The Boxmaker's Revenge: 'Orthodoxy,' 'Heterodoxy,' and the Politics of the Parish in Early Stuart London.* Stanford: Stanford University Press, 2001.

Mack, Phyllis. *Visionary Women: Ecstatic Prophecy in Seventeenth-Century England*. Berkeley: University of Calfornia Press, 1992.

Marchant, R. A. *The Puritans and the Church Courts in the Diocese of York, 1560-1642*. London: Longmans, 1960.

Marsh, C. *The Family of Love in English Society, 1550-1630*. Cambridge: Cambridge University Press, 1994.

McGrath, Alister. *Iustitia Dei: A History of the Christian Doctrine of Justification From 1500 to the Present Day*. Cambridge: Cambridge University Press, 1986.

McGregor, J. F. and B. Reay, eds. *Radical Religion in the English Revolution*. Oxford: Oxford University Press, 1984.

Miller, Perry, *The New England Mind: The Seventeenth Century*. Cambridge, MA: Harvard University Press, 1939. Reissue, Cambridge, MA: Harvard University Press, 1967.

Morton, A. L. *The World of the Ranters: Religious Radicalism in the English Revolution*. London: Lawrence and Wishart, 1970.

Newman, W. R. *Gehennical Fire: The Lives of George Starkey, an American Alchemist in the Scientific Revolution*. Cambridge, MA: Harvard University Press, 1994.

Nuttall, G. F. *The Holy Spirit in Puritan Faith and Experience*. Oxford: Blackwell, 1946. 2d ed., Oxford: Blackwell, 1947. Paperback reprint, Chicago: University of Chicago Press, 1992.

Ozment, Stephen E. *Mysticism and Dissent: Religious Ideology and Social Protest in the Sixteenth Century*. New Haven and London: Yale University Press, 1973.

Pearse, M. T. *Between Known Men and Visible Saints: A Study in Sixteenth-Century English Dissent*. Madison and Teaneck, NJ: Fairleigh Dickinson University Press, 1994.

Pettit, Norman. *The Heart Prepared: Grace and Conversion in Puritan Spiritual Life*. New Haven: Yale University Press, 1965.

Richardson, R.C. *Puritanism in North-West England: A Regional Study of the Diocese of Chester to 1642*. Manchester: Manchester University Press, 1972.

Seaver, Paul S. *The Puritan Lectureships: The Politics of Religious Dissent, 1560-1662*. Stanford: Stanford University Press, 1970.

________. *Wallington's World: A Puritan Artisan in Seventeenth-Century New England*. Stanford: Stanford University Press, 1985.

Shaw, W. A. *A History of the English Church During the Civil Wars and Under the Commonwealth, 1640-1660*. London: Longmans, Green, and Co., 1900. 2 vols.

Sippell, Theodor. *Zur Vorgeschichte des Quaekertüms*. Giessen, Ger.: Alfred Töpelmann, 1920.

Smith, Nigel. *Perfection Proclaimed: Language and Literature in English Radical Religion*. Oxford: Clarendon Press, 1989.

Spufford, Margaret, ed. *The World of the Rural Dissenters, 1520-1725*. Cambridge: Cambridge University Press, 1995.

Stachniewski, John. *The Persecutory Imagination: English Puritanism and the Literature of Religious Despair*. Oxford: Clarendon Press, 1991.

Stoever, William. *"A Faire and Easie Way to Heaven": Covenant Theology and Antinomianism in Early Massachusetts*. Middletown, CT: Wesleyan University Press, 1978.

Swain, J. T. *Industry Before the Industrial Revolution: North-East Lancashire, c. 1500-1640*. Chetham Society, Third Series, 32. Manchester: Chetham Society, 1986.

Thomas, Keith. *Religion and the Decline of Magic*. New York: Charles Scribner's Sons, 1971.

Tolmie, Murray. *The Triumph of the Saints*. Cambridge: Cambridge University Press, 1977.

Trevor-Roper, H. R. *Catholics, Anglicans and Puritans: Seventeenth-Century Essays*. Chicago: University of Chicago Press, 1988.

Turner, J. Horsfall. *Ancient Bingley: Or, Bingley, its History and Scenery*. Bingley: Thomas Harrison for the author, 1897.

Tyacke, N. R. N. *Anti-Calvinists: the Rise of English Arminianism, c. 1590-1640*. Oxford: Oxford University Press, 1987. Revised paperback edition, Oxford: Oxford University Press, 1990.

________. *The Fortunes of English Puritanism 1603-1640*. London: Dr. Williams Trust, 1990.

Webster, Tom. *Godly Clergy in Early Stuart England: The Caroline Puritan Movement, c. 1620-1643*. Cambridge: Cambridge University Press, 1997.

Weeks, William Self. *Clitheroe in the Seventeenth Century*. Clitheroe: Advertiser & Times Co., [1927].

Williams, G. H. *The Radical Reformation*. Philadelphia: The Westminster Press, 1962.

Winship, Michael. *Making Heretics: Militant Protestantism and Free Grace in Massachusetts, 1636-1641*. Princeton: Princeton University Press, 2002.

Wodderspoon, John. *Memorials of the Ancient Town of Ipswich, In the County of Suffolk*. Ipswich and London: Pawsey; Longman, Brown, Green and Longmans, 1850.

Yates, Frances A., *The Rosicrucian Enlightenment*. London and Boston: Routledge and Kegan Paul, 1972. Paperback edition, Boulder, CO: Shambhala Publications, 1978.

Articles

Bozeman, T. D. "The Glory of the 'Third Time': John Eaton as Contra-Puritan," *Journal of Ecclesiastical History*, 47 (1996).

Brigg, Mary. "The Forest of Pendle in the Seventeenth Century," in *Transactions of the Historic Society of Lancashire and Cheshire*, 113 (1961).

Collinson, P. "Elizabethan and Jacobean Puritanism as Forms of Popular Religious Culture." In *The Culture of English Puritanism, 1560-1700*, ed. C. Durston and J. Eales. New York: St. Martin's Press, 1996.

Como, D. "Women, Prophecy and Authority in Early Stuart Puritanism," *Huntington Library Quarterly*, 61 (1998).

_______. "Puritans, Predestination and the Construction of 'Orthodoxy' in Early Seventeenth Century England." In *Conformity and Orthodoxy in the English Church, c. 1560-1642*, ed. P. Lake and M. Questier (Woodbridge: Boydell and Brewer, 2000).

Como, D., and P. Lake. "Puritans, Antinomians and Laudians in Caroline London: The Strange Case of Peter Shaw in its Contexts," *Journal of Ecclesiastical History*, 50 (1999).

Davis, J. C. "Cromwell's Religion." In *Oliver Cromwell and the English Revolution*, ed. J. Morrill. London: Longman, 1990.

_______. "Against Formality: One Aspect of the English Revolution," *Transactions of the Royal Historical Society*, 6th series, 3 (1993).

_______. "The Levellers and Christianity." In *Politics, Religion and the English Civil War*, ed. B. Manning. London: Edward Arnold, 1973.

Foss, D. B. "Grindletonianism," *Yorkshire Archaeological Journal*, 67 (1995).

Foster, Stephen. "New England and the Challenge of Heresy, 1630 to 1660: the Puritan Crisis in Transatlantic Perspective," *William and Mary Quarterly*, 38 (1981).

Hayes, T. Wilson. "A Seventeenth-century Translation of Nicholas of Cusa's *Idiota*," *Notes and Queries*, 28 (1981).

_______. "A Seventeenth-century Translation of Nicholas of Cusa's *De Dato Patris Luminem*," *Journal of Medieval and Renaissance Studies*, 11 (1981).

_______. "John Everard and the Familist Tradition." In *The Origins of Anglo-American Radicalism*, ed. M. C. Jacob and J. R. Jacob. London and Boston: Allen and Unwin, 1984. Paperback edition, Atlantic Highlands, NJ; and London: Humanities Press, 1991.

Hill, Christopher. "From Lollards to Levellers." In *Rebels and Their Causes: Essays in Honour of A. L. Morton*, ed. M. Cornforth. London: Lawrence and Wishart, 1978.

_______. "Dr. Tobias Crispe, 1600-1643," in *Balliol Studies*, ed. J. Prest. London: Leopard's Head Press, 1982.

_______. "Antinomianism." In C. Hill, *Liberty Against the Law: Some Seventeenth-Century Controversies*. London: Allen Lane, The Penguin Press, 1996.

Lake, P. "Defining Puritanism—Again?" In *Puritanism: Transatlantic Perspectives on a Seventeenth-century Anglo-American Faith*, ed. F. J. Bremer. Boston: Massachusetts Historical Society, 1993.

_______. "'A Charitable Christian Hatred': The Godly and their Enemies in the 1630s." In *The Culture of English Puritanism, 1560-1700*, ed. C. Durston and J. Eales. New York: St. Martin's Press, 1996.

_______. "The Laudian Style: Order, Uniformity and the Pursuit of the Beauty of Holiness in the 1630s." In *The Early Stuart Church, 1603-1642*, ed. K. Fincham. Basingstoke: Macmillan, 1993.

Lake, P. and D. Como. "'Orthodoxy' and Its Discontents: Dispute Settlement and the Production of 'Consensus' in the London (Puritan) 'Underground,'" *Journal of British Studies*, 39 (2000).

Loomie, A. J. "Bacon and Gondomar: An Unknown Link in 1618," in Loomie, A. J., *Spain and the Early Stuarts*. Aldershot: Variorum, 1996.

Maclear, James. "'The Heart of New England Rent': The Mystical Element in Early Puritan History," *Mississippi Valley Historical Review*, 42 (1956).

________. "Anne Hutchinson and the Mortalist Heresy," *New England Quarterly*, 54 (1981).

McIntyre, D. M. "First Strictures on the 'The Marrow of Modern Divinity.'" *The Evangelical Quarterly*, 10 (1938).

Ozment, S. "Luther and the Late Middle Ages: The Formation of Reformation Thought." In *Transition and Revolution: Problems and Issues of European Renaissance and Reformation History*, ed. R. M. Kingdon. Minneapolis, MN: Burgess Publishing Company, 1974.

Segal, A. "The Risen Christ and the Angelic Mediator Figures in the Light of Qumran." In *Jesus and the Dead Sea Scrolls: The Controversy Resolved*, ed. J. H. Charlesworth. New York: Doubleday, 1992.

Smith, R. M. "Christian Judaizers in Early Stuart England," *Historical Magazine of the Protestant Episcopal Church*, 52 (1983).

Tyacke, N. R. N. "Popular Puritan Mentality in Late Elizabethan England." In *The English Commonwealth, 1547-1640: Essays in Politics and Society*, ed. P. Clark, A. G. R. Smith, and N. Tyacke. Totowa, NJ: Barnes and Noble Books, 1979.

White, B. R. "John Traske (1585-1636) and London Puritanism," *Transactions of the Congregational Historical Society*, 20 (1968).

________. "Samuel Eaton (d. 1639) Particular Baptist Pioneer," *Baptist Quarterly*, 24 (1971).

Wootton, D. "Reginald Scot / Abraham Fleming / The Family of Love." In *Languages of Witchcraft: Narrative Ideology and Meaning in Early Modern Culture*, ed S. Clark. Basingstoke: Macmillan, 2001.

Unpublished Theses

Cassidy, Irene. "The Episcopate of William Cotton, Bishop of Exeter, 1598-1621: with special reference to the State of the Clergy and the Administration of the Ecclesiastical Courts." B. Litt. thesis, Oxford University, 1964.

Darling, Justine. "The Grindletonians: Roger Brierley, John Webster, Robert Towne." Ph.D. diss., Columbia University, 1988.

Graebner, Norman Brooks. "Protestants and Dissenters: An Examination of the Seventeenth Century Eatonist and New England Antinomian Controversies in Reformation Perspective." Ph.D. diss., Duke University, 1984.

Hessayon, Ariel. "'Gold Tried in the Fire': The Prophet Theauraujohn Tany and the Puritan Revolution." Ph.D. diss., Cambridge University, 1996.

Hunt, Paul R. "John Everard: A Study of His Life, Thought, and Preaching." Ph.D. diss., UCLA, 1977.

Index